THE POLITICAL KINGDOM IN UGANDA

THE POLITICAL KINGDOM IN UGANDA

*A Study in
Bureaucratic Nationalism*

•

BY DAVID E. APTER

PRINCETON, NEW JERSEY
PRINCETON UNIVERSITY PRESS

TO ANDREW

PREFACE TO THE FIRST EDITION

In 1955, when the first of these studies was written on the development of modern nationhood in Ghana, the model for African political development was found in the institutions and practices of government in the West. Today, Ghana is herself a model for other countries. Leaders of nationalist movements elsewhere in Africa have turned to Ghana as the exemplar, hoping to learn from her successes how best to develop the new nations of Africa, and hoping to learn from her mistakes some of the more likely pitfalls of independence. Ghana's independence was thus a landmark in the political emancipation of Africa. It is unlikely that without her independence neighboring territories, particularly in former French West Africa, would be proceeding to self-government.

Just as Ghana is now a model for other countries, so has Ghana helped African leaders elsewhere to turn their attention inward to the continent itself. They are anxious to create new African communities. The Pan-African Freedom Movement of East and Central Africa is one such effort to unify the diverse peoples of those areas into wider, more effective political communities. Symbolic of this turning inward for inspiration are the concepts of African personality and *negritude*. Both are efforts to comprehend the unifying genius of a whole people in both its particularities and its universal contributions to man's cultural heritage.

Uganda shows a very different pattern of development from the one which occurred in Ghana. Not only does it represent a fundamentally different system of traditional authority, but, when the political leaders of Africa contemplate Africa's future, Uganda will be one of the more puzzling and difficult countries to understand. In Ghana, for example, the forces of tradition and ethnicity arrayed themselves unsuccessfully against the more secular growth of a modern nationalism devoted to sweeping change. In Uganda, and most particularly in Buganda, there has been, in sharp contrast, a traditionalization of change itself. Indeed, it is this latter phenomenon which lies at the root of Uganda's political troubles today. Nationalism has been aggressive but ethnically parochial. Not anxious for wider and more sweeping political amalgamations, the people of Buganda represent a problem for secular nationalists both in Uganda and elsewhere in East Africa.

Thus the problems of Uganda are interesting not simply from a theoretical point of view. They represent too a phenomenon in Africa which has been much overlooked as the successes of secular nationalism have naturally focused our attention upon anticolonialism. Uganda raises the question of what shall remain when colonialism departs. What are the stubborn and persistent forces of an accommodated traditionalism which will remain in the new Africa, to be absorbed or not as time and wisdom decree?

Both Ghana and Uganda are part of a restless continent. Strenuous efforts are being made to create new political units released from the boundaries imposed during the colonial period. New nations are being born and with their birth there is an anticipatory spirit of renascence which has brought a search for cultural meanings intrinsic to the African scene, yet universal in their message for modern man.

What Ghana and Uganda have in common and indeed share with other African countries is their desire for freedom. All colonial territories regard the political kingdom as the passport to other kingdoms: those which harbor racial dignity and stature and by means of which the hunger to be free of social discrimination and invidious slurs on culture and history can be satisfied. Behind the struggle to end colonialism is not only the Africans' demand for political power, but the beginning of a new freedom from the stigma of race.

In this respect all African nationalism reflects the wider significance of the changes undertaken in Africa today. The problem of our generation is the elimination of race as significant in evaluating men. The eighteenth century was a battle for political freedom and individualism. The nineteenth emphasized economic equality and opportunity. The present century is a struggle for racial equality. Because racial discrimination has restricted both economic equality and personal liberty, the struggle for racial equality inevitably involves the other two. Events in Africa thus have a moral dimension which is fundamental to our age, and which brings the struggle for political freedom in Africa close to the social problems which engulf our own nation.

Bearing in mind these wider concerns of African nationalism, we can now turn to Uganda. The present study focuses primarily on the most important political group in Uganda, the people of Buganda. By their special relationship with British authorities as well as their devotion to their own institutions, these people have successfully · prevented a wholesale assault on their ethnic autonomy. Neither colonial officials nor nationalists have been successful in whittling away the autonomous position of Buganda within Uganda or within a larger context of East African nationalism.

In doing this study I have sought help in many quarters. In all cases it has been freely given. The year 1955-1956 which I spent in Uganda included some of the more dramatic episodes in the recent history of Uganda. It was the year in which the Kabaka of Buganda returned from exile to become a constitutional monarch. Although it was a difficult time in the relationships between British and Africans, nevertheless the cooperation necessary to complete my research was unfailingly offered with great courtesy and hospitality. My first acknowledgment is to the former Governor of Uganda, Sir Andrew Cohen, whose wisdom and talents cannot be dimmed by the unfortunate crisis in Uganda which marred an otherwise brilliant administration. He provided me with access to the materials and men necessary for me to carry on my work; and insofar as it was in his power to do so, he turned over to me the intellectual keys to the kingdom.

His chief antagonist during my stay in Uganda, His Highness, the Kabaka of Buganda, also gave me support in this work. Officers of both governments, Protectorate and Buganda, gave every assistance. More specifically, I am indebted to Mr. Don Marshall, Mr. G. B. Cartland, and Mr. J. V. Wild in the Secretariat, Mr. C. A. L. Richards, Resident, Buganda, and members of their respective staffs. Several assistant residents and district commissioners gave me the opportunity of touring with them and I enjoyed their hospitality on many occasions. Two in particular, Mr. Tommy Gee and Mr. Nigel Oram, became good friends as well. Their detailed comments on a first draft of this manuscript were invaluable.

Although he disagrees with many of my conclusions, I am

heavily indebted to Mr. A. Kalule Sempa, now the Omuwanika in His Highness' government. The Katikiro, Mr. Michael Kintu, made possible extensive interviews among officials and assistants in the Buganda government. His assistant, Mr. E. Kigundu, was particularly helpful in this respect, allowing me to share his office for prolonged periods of time. The saza chief Sekibobo and his wife granted me hospitality in their home as well as allowing me to go on safari with them in Kyagwe.

My gratitude to the staff of the East African Institute of Social Research must be recorded. Indeed, it was at the original invitation of Dr. Audrey Richards, then Director, that this study was undertaken, although the final product is in a form very different from that which we both contemplated. Dr. Richards served as a real source of inspiration. The Institute was indeed a center of intellectual life in Uganda and reflected her own enquiring and restless personality.

The Institute was also a creature of Makerere College and there I made many real friendships among staff who were anxious and willing to share their more expert knowledge and wisdom of things African. In particular, R. C. Pratt and Anthony Low, the former a political scientist of McGill University on leave to Makerere and the latter a lecturer in history at Makerere, were unfailingly generous with their ideas and knowledge. Their own study of Buganda, *Buganda and British Overrule*, is a most useful one and many of my ideas about Uganda were shaped by theirs.

Many others helped make this volume possible. In England, Miss Margery Perham made her files on Uganda available to me and I enjoyed the hospitality of Nuffield College while doing my preparatory research before going to Uganda.

The research itself was made possible through the generosity of the Ford Foundation. An Area Research Training fellowship enabled me to spend a year in England and Africa. I must also record my debt to my former colleagues of the African Studies Program of Northwestern University and its director, Professor M. J. Herskovits. They made a substantial contribution toward the costs of this research and gave me good guidance and stimulation.

The main burden of writing was accomplished during my year

as a Fellow at the Center for Advanced Studies in the Behavioral Sciences at Stanford, 1958-1959. To the Director and Fellows of the Center I am deeply grateful. The intellectual vitality of that year cannot be shown in these pages, for such enrichment can only reveal itself in more reflective efforts.

There are many others who in the course of the years since I first became interested in Uganda have given assistance. In the Legislative Council Mr. J. T. Simpson, leader of the Representative Members Organization, and his associate, Mrs. Barbara Saben, were both extremely helpful. In government I must record my gratitude to Sir Amar Maini, the Minister of Corporations and Regional Communications. He and his wife helped make our stay in Uganda a pleasant as well as an interesting one.

To the leaders of various political parties I must record gratitude. Mr. I. K. Musazi was most helpful, as were some of the younger and more up-and-coming new political leaders. Mr. E. M. K. Mulira gave me access to his personal files and to his extensive knowledge of Buganda. Both leaders have since fallen on more difficult political times, but their zeal and devotion to the cause of nationalism cannot help but be rewarded.

Friends who worked with the various responsible political groups in one capacity or another, such as Mr. Senteza Kajubi and Mr. Erisa Kironde, both former masters of King's College Budo and now of Makerere, also proved extremely helpful. Without Mr. Kironde's help, I would not have been able to administer questionnaire materials to the branch chairmen of the Uganda National Congress.

Space does not allow me to record the names of the many others who helped in this endeavor and who extended to us the hospitality for which Uganda is justly famous. However, I must record my indebtedness to the work of Mr. Neil Ascherson. I was able to make use of his notes on the Uganda National Congress which he prepared for the East African Institute for Social Research. During the year at the Center, Mr. Simon Musoke, formerly of the Institute and currently with His Highness' government, provided me with valuable material to fill the gaps which inevitably appear during the writing-up stage of work. Joshua L. Zake, a leading political personality in Uganda who figures in these pages, gave detailed comments on an earlier draft of the manuscript.

Acknowledgment is due to Professor Carl G. Rosberg, of the University of California, Berkeley. The three models of authority which underlie the present analysis were developed with his collaboration and first presented in a joint paper, "Some Models of Political Change in Contemporary Africa," at the African Studies Association meetings in Boston, 1959.

I must make a special acknowledgment to my friend and colleague, Professor Lloyd A. Fallers of the University of Chicago. It was he who first turned my attention to Uganda when we were both at Princeton University in 1953-1954. Later, Professor Fallers succeeded Dr. Richards as Director of the East African Institute of Social Research and I was able to profit from his field knowledge and advice. Finally, we were Fellows together at the Center. In the course of these years of association my intellectual debts to him are so great that this volume is in a real sense a joint work. I can no longer trace the pedigree of ideas or separate his from my own. Both he and my wife, who shared with me the research and preparation of this volume, helped read the proofs. Finally, a special debt of gratitude is due my wife for preparing the index. Miss Judy Walton of the Princeton University Press provided good editorial counsel and careful editing.

In spite of all the best efforts of these and other people, the errors contained herein are my own responsibility. I hope that the intrinsic qualities of Uganda and its people will shine through the obfuscations of scholarly enterprise. To these people I record my greatest gratitude.

D. E. A.

Winter 1960
The University of Chicago

PREFACE TO THE SECOND EDITION

RECENT events in Uganda have been exciting and disturbing—a king expelled, a constitution suspended, a political opposition obliterated. These events are familiar enough both in Africa and elsewhere in the developing world. In Uganda, however, concern over such occurrences was uppermost in everyone's mind right from the first days of the independence movement. Yet it was not until the late summer of 1965 (during my last visit to Uganda) that the crisis which began so long ago with the formation of the Protectorate government re-emerged, to be directed this time against the government of Prime Minister Milton Obote.

One felt the tension during the last weeks of the summer. A political denouement could not be far away. Plans for action were being laid. All the signs were present—the evasiveness of old friends now occupying senior political posts, the discontent in the atrophied constituency parties of the Uganda People's Congress, and a general malaise. The U.P.C. hardly gave the appearance of a powerful nationalist party which had successfully challenged its rival, the Democratic Party, and brought the country to independence in October 1962. Above all, within the atmosphere of watchful patience, one heard the steady rumble of Buganda discontent. After a surprisingly long and at times spirited period of national political growth, politics was slowly and reluctantly returning to its provincial center, to the classic conflict between Buganda and the government of Uganda. At stake was the future of the political kingdom.

Although the showdown was inevitable, it seemed for a time that it might be avoided. Prior to independence, a series of concessions had been made, giving Buganda federal status and thereby securing the autonomy laid down in the 1900 Agreement, and granting similar status to the other kingdom states. As a national party, the Uganda People's Congress clearly appealed to a widely diverse electorate—to Bantu as well as to Nilotic, Catholic, Protestant, and Muslim—and represented some sort of unity. Its chief opponent seemed divisive; the Democratic Party had never shaken off its Catholic origins, and in Buganda it had become a real threat to an already shaky Protestant control in the Lukiko. The Baganda, pressed by the D.P., organized the Kabaka Yekka, a "king's own" party which not only formed a coalition with the

U.P.C., but succeeded in drawing the support of many Catholic Baganda who feared to stand against the Kabaka. Under these circumstances the prospects for a stable government after independence were quite good, and the U.P.C., a successful national party under the direction of Obote, took the center of the political stage. For the first time, effective political participation included the people of the districts. The constituency parties of the U.P.C. were a growing force, offsetting the religious, clan, ethnic, and constitutional rivalries which had for so long been the basis of Uganda's political life.

This was reflected clearly in the elections held prior to independence, which ended in the downfall of the D.P. government. The results were as follows:

Uganda People's Congress	37
Democratic Party	24
Kabaka Yekka (indirectly elected by the Lukiko)	21
	—
Total Elected Seats	82
Specially Elected Members (selected by the National Assembly)	
Uganda People's Congress	6
Kabaka Yekka	3
	—
Total Specially Elected Seats	9
	—
Total National Assembly	91

For the moment, at any rate, Buganda, although not pushed aside, had to play a secondary role. Kabaka Yekka, to a very large extent a reaction against the strength of the Democratic Party in Buganda, joined forces with Obote's U.P.C. Together they dominated the Parliament and provided a coalition government. After independence, His Highness, the Kabaka of Buganda, was made first president of Uganda—a point on which the Baganda themselves insisted.

It appeared that Buganda would work with the rest of the country to create a stable society. The coalition, however, could not last. The main reason that the Kabaka Yekka had been willing to form a coalition with the U.P.C. was to prevent the Catholics from gaining power in Buganda. The main reason the U.P.C. was willing to form a coalition with the Kabaka Yekka was to prevent an obstreperous Buganda government from disrupting politics at the center. Before long, the Kabaka Yekka members of Parliament began causing difficulties over Obote's solution to the "lost counties" issue, as well as other matters. Several members of the Kabaka Yekka in the Cabinet crossed the floor. The coalition was destroyed. Having accomplished its purpose of eliminating the Democratic Party as an opposition from Parliament, the Kabake Yekka then broke apart.

With politics in Uganda once again centered on the relationship between the national government and Buganda, which coincided with the decline of the U.P.C. constituency parties in the district, it was clear by the summer of 1965 that Mr. Obote was in serious difficulty. Either he had to act with considerable dispatch against Buganda, or face a revolt in his own party, brought about by the disintegration of party discipline and the emergence of rival leaders. The situation was ominous, and in the next months Obote took two drastic steps. First, in February 1966, he imprisoned five U.P.C. members of the Cabinet—including Grace Ibingira, the Secretary-General of the party—and suspended the constitution of 1962. Second, in April he announced a new provisional constitution with himself in the role of executive president. Members of parliament were required to take a new oath of allegiance. The Baganda were infuriated. On May 20 the Buganda Lukiko passed a motion requesting the central government to remove its offices from Kampala, claiming that the Uganda government was now illegal and unconstitutional. This resolution was interpreted by Obote as an act of rebellion. The army immediately attacked the Kabaka's palace, and the Kabaka was forced to return to exile in London.

At present, the political and constitutional situation is being transformed radically. The National Assembly has been charged with the responsibility of designating a constituent assembly for drafting a new constitution. The federal and semi-federal relationships of Buganda, Ankole, Bunyoro, Toro, and Busoga have been terminated. The civil service has been centralized. The Buganda High Court, which in effect represented a parallel judicial system

to that of Uganda, has been abolished. Chiefs have lost the *mailo*
lands associated with their offices as well as their voting rights in
Lukiko. Uganda has become a unitary system in which the electoral and constitutional privileges formerly reserved for Buganda
and the other kingdom states have at last been abolished. With
their abolition the special economic and political positions which
the chiefs had been able to maintain for so long, especially in
Buganda, have disappeared. The administrative framework in
Buganda has been to that extent weakened, and the powerful
structure of civil service chieftaincy—which was the effective
means whereby Buganda could continue to act as a political party
with the Kabaka as its head—has more or less come to an end.
Today there is no effective government of Buganda. With the
Kabaka in exile, it is constitutionally impossible for his government to act. And the Baganda, while not reacting as overtly as
under the administration of Sir Andrew Cohen, have made it almost impossible for the four administrators assigned to the Kingdom of Buganda to carry out their duties.

The last chapter of this book suggested three alternative solutions to the problem of Buganda. First was the possibility of closer
union between Kenya, Uganda, and Tanganyika. Although some
efforts were made to use the East African Common Services Organization as a nucleus for such a union, all attempts failed. A
second and opposite solution was for Buganda to go it alone. However, this was never a serious possibility, largely because of the
economic and political vulnerability of an independent Buganda.
The third alternative made it an obligation of the central government to see to it that Buganda would remain inside a self-
governing Uganda within the context of effective parliamentary
government. For a while it appeared as if the U.P.C. would serve
to unite the diverse groupings, religious and ethnic, which divided
the country. Obote maneuvered carefully and shrewdly. But when
the U.P.C. was weakened internally and the U.P.C.-K.Y. alliance
was broken, the third solution was no longer viable. It was then
that the conflict became inevitable.

The struggle of Buganda to preserve autonomy against the
growth of modern national politics has been one of the most interesting of the so-called tribal disputes to be found anywhere in
Africa. Whether or not one agrees with the position of Buganda,

one must nevertheless admire the tenacity and skill with which the Baganda have fought to preserve their separate identity. If they had been successful, Buganda would have run Uganda as a national state and as an empire. To that extent, the struggle was not between Obote and the Kabaka, or between the Central Government and the Buganda government but rather Buganda against the rest of the country.

D.E.A.

Autumn 1966
The University of California, Berkeley

CONTENTS

xix

CONTENTS

ILLUSTRATIONS

MAPS

(The maps on pp. 33, 51, and 52 are from *The Economy of East Africa: A Study of Trends* [London: Economist Intelligence Unit, 1955]. Reprinted with permission.)

PHOTOGRAPHS

Plates follow page 178

1. The Kabaka of Buganda, Uganda *(British Information Services)*

2. Opening of Uganda's new Parliament building, showing the Governor, Sir Frederick Crawford, and the Colonial Secretary, Mr. Iain Macleod *(British Information Services)*

3. Sir Andrew Cohen, former Governor of Uganda, speaks at the opening of Buganda's *Bulange*, or Parliament building. Beside him, under the umbrella, is the Kabaka, Mutesa II, ruler of Buganda *(British Information Services)*

4. Sir Frederick Crawford, Governor of Uganda, speaks at the opening of Uganda's Parliament building. On his left is the Colonial Secretary, Iain Macleod *(British Information Services)*

5. In the central lobby of the Uganda Parliament, from left to right, Bishop Leslie Brown of Namirembe (Kampala), the Mukama of Toro, the Mugabe of Ankole (with stick and not robed), the Mukama of Bunyoro, and Bishop Kiwanuka of Masaka *(British Information Services)*

6. The Kabaka of Buganda

7. Drummers at the enclosure of the saza chief of Buddu

8. The king's flutist

*All photographs not credited
to the British Information Services
were taken by the author*

THE POLITICAL KINGDOM IN UGANDA

CHAPTER 1

THE POLITICAL KINGDOM AND THE
POLITICS OF PROVINCIALISM

TODAY in Ghana, Nigeria, Sierra Leone, Guinea, Mali, Senegal, and elsewhere, European administrators are packing their bags. They are having a last look around the compounds with the whitewashed stones and the tropical flowers, the orderly district offices, the cool and old-fashioned bungalows. The magazines left in the rest houses of country stations are increasingly out-of-date and the service and crockery become a bit more chipped and run-down. Africans, dressed not in khaki drill shorts but in trousers and jackets, begin to move in. Their servants grow beans where the district officer's wife had her English garden. Chickens and children obliterate the careful paths and remove the atmosphere of casual exclusiveness. History, having irrevocably left its mark on a changing African scene, has now taken a new turn—perhaps to leave as indelible a stamp upon the West.

Profound though contact with the West has been, Africa can no longer be viewed as a consequence of European institutions planted in exotic soil. In the history of Africa the colonial period is but a short moment in time. The changes presently under way represent a process which has a much longer history than European intervention and which, indeed, was interrupted by the colonial experience. African institutional life has a vitality which transcends the specific structural innovations of European origin.

If this perspective is accepted, the colonial experience should no longer be viewed as the institutional watershed for contemporary events. We need a different point of vantage from which to contemplate processes of change in Africa. However, if we are not to follow after events with *post hoc* explanations which change with every variation in political arrangements, we need a set of abstractions which will help us find our way through the exciting multiplicity and complexity of change. In our first study, *The Gold Coast in Transition*,[1] we tried to examine the role of a par-

[1] David E. Apter, *The Gold Coast in Transition* (Princeton: Princeton University Press, 1955).

3

ticular kind of authority system, based on charisma, yet expressed through roles and institutions embodied in British practice. We examined the prospects of parliamentary democracy as a unifying medium in Ghana. We turn now to a very different set of authority relationships in Uganda. Our central concern is with a type of authority called a *modernizing autocracy*.

We shall first indicate briefly how the modernizing autocracy differs from other types of authority systems. Second, we shall explore the general social and economic complex within which it operates. Our third task will be to show in some detail the characteristics of Buganda as a modernizing autocracy—indicating some of the cleavages and ambiguities of the system—and the dualism running through that society. Fourth, we shall try to show how the traditional characteristics of Buganda helped to shape the direction of more contemporary problems in which the autocracy itself fought to maintain its autonomy while demanding drastic innovation and change. Finally, we shall describe characteristic patterns of conflict which, culminating in the deportation of the King of Buganda, have now reached the point where Uganda as a nation must make the following choice: either the modernizing autocracy will accede to the needs of a modern state with an all-embracing representative government, or else the prognosis for the future will be one of increasing ethnic and parochial strife, impeding progress toward independence itself.

This analysis will conclude with a discussion of the efforts to create a modern representative government in Uganda.

A Perspective of African Political Development

The changeover from European colonial officialdom to African administration is taking place against a much wider backdrop of political change in Africa. African political leaders rather than administrators are representatives of the new Africa. They must do their best to transform the societies which they have now inherited. They need to find the most useful political machinery which will enable them to achieve their objectives. Some, as in the case of Guinea and Ghana, have sought to *mobilize* the total energies, resources, and skills of the country for a grand assault on the problems of poverty, ignorance, and backwardness. Others, such as Nigeria or, for a time, Mali Federation, have tended toward some union of important constituent parts—a kind of *consociation* which seeks in political unity a common denominator to unite all of the groups within the country for purposes of common action.

The third type, exemplified in Buganda, is more rare. In this situation, change is filtered through the medium of *traditional* institutions; examples of this may be found in Morocco and Ethiopia. But in such cases, modernization and change have become traditionalized, and innovation is regarded as a characteristic of the traditional system. Each of these three types—the *mobilization system*, the *consociational system*, and the *modernizing autocracy*—represents a dynamic political arrangement which approaches change in a different way.

Such types are interesting to examine in a theoretical sense. The analysis of change is always precarious and, for that reason, one of the most taxing of man's urgent tasks. To dissect living history challenges man's capacity to absent himself from the immediacy of his own world in order to compare it with others. Such an effort is never entirely successful. We are a product of lives lived before us and part of a chain of cultural and social continuity which carries the past into the future. Yet is precisely because the present is always the transmitting medium, transmitting, moreover, through ourselves, that we try to seize upon those changes which we hope will provide a perspective of the future.

If each of these three types of political tendencies is a consequence of political arrangements which sort themselves out in the politics of contemporary Africa, they leave unanswered a larger and prime question. Will they have the capacity not only to absorb change but also to generate a new civilization?

Each of the three types has developed as a result of the great challenge which has emerged with lightning speed: the extension of political democracy and freedom to Asia and Africa. This has ended the Western world's political hegemony and affirmed instead the road to both spiritual and material achievement in Asia and Africa. However, what remains to be accomplished in Africa is the creation of new civilizations. The question is whether those different changes which are occurring will simply raise the level of material life in Africa or whether they will lead to fundamentally new systems of belief and culture which will have as profound an impact on the world as have the great civilizations and religions of Islam, Christianity, Buddhism, and Marxism. In their separate ways, these systems have defined the purposes and achievements of the material cultures which represent them. For in the largest sense, a civilization requires a religion or cosmology as well as a defined system of political and social organization. It is the latter which is now emerging in Africa on African terms. The former is still to be created.

Each of the three types of systems represents a type of political and social organization rather than a civilization. Each has certain affinities with ideologies and religions, but it remains impossible to predict what combinations will occur. Certainly, contemporary nationalism which is characteristic of all three is political in its materialism and its concern for rapid development. In the case of the mobilization system, Marxism as a secular religion gives a spiritual dimension to this materiality. The modernizing autocracy, on the other hand, characteristically retains more traditional religious ties, absorbing and filtering modifications in social structure and life through the screen of Islam or Christianity. But so far there have been only tentative tendencies toward the combinations of religious and social organization which could impel the new African states toward a fundamentally new civilization. Some of the factors inhibiting this process have been the result of the rapidity and success of anticolonialism and nationalism. There has been no time to develop an ideology much less a religion, since so far both have been unnecessary. Another reason may be that, born in the West, nationalism is still essentially a product of Western secularism. Having subordinated the political arm of the West, the nationalists can take a tolerant view of its religions. Indeed, perhaps the saving grace of the West is that its religious arm, born in political subordination, can gracefully reassume that position by individualizing its faith and removing it from political prominence.

The latest form of nationalism, namely pan-Africanism, is, as yet, neither religion nor a fully developed ideology. It does not represent a transcendental system of belief compelling man's allegiance to a system of moral imperatives, nor does it advance a particular code of ethics. Conforming to its political function, it argues for political independence and it relies on the similarities of the tasks of political leaders in developing their countries; it relies, too, on similar sympathies born of a common colonial heritage. All these, united by a bond of color, produce new unities in a free Africa. But pan-Africanism is not a new civilization; it is therefore at the mercy of traditional factors in African society and is vulnerable to the immediate politics of parochial nationalism. For example, pan-Africanism has been virtually without success in Uganda where traditionalism of the Buganda kind has held at bay not only pan-Africanism but also efforts to build a larger national unity. Pan-Africanism asks only that people of color be free to make their own choices, to be psychologically free through the achievement of independence and socially free by using political means to material development.

It is the heavy reliance on the political form which is the vulnerability of pan-Africanism. It is bred out of the needs of nationalism and it can also be victimized by those needs. Where traditional religion, belief, and practice are thoroughly intertwined in contemporary social institutions, pan-Africanism feels itself gravely threatened, for it cannot substitute one belief for another; rather, it offers emancipation from belief itself. Hence there is an increasing reliance on the state as more than just a political form. The state acquires a special meaning and a mystical relevance when pan-Africanism is the ideology of nationalism.

To varying degrees the mobilization systems have the greatest affinity with the new pan-African state. The consociational systems cut across pan-Africanism by substituting for its ideology some loose political framework or alliance which allows for cooperation between African states and territories. But what of traditional systems? Essentially theocratic, they result in powerful sentiments for local and parochial institutions. The nationalism of a theocratic state is no less compelling than that of a pan-African state. Occasionally we can find strange combinations within the same territorial setting. For example, in Nigeria in the north a theocratic state collaborates with a mobilization system in the Eastern Region and all are within a consociational framework.

An interesting variant of the modernizing autocracy will be our primary concern in this study. Such a system is a secular but traditional political and social organization. It is not a theocracy but rather a political kingdom. The theocratic elements have been stripped away and do not serve as obstacles to internal change and development. Such occurrences are rare and this is one of the reasons for studying them. For they raise a form of secular traditionalism which, while maintaining its separatist character, can keep pace with the new emphasis on development. Such a system includes the pan-Africanist emphasis on modernization while offering to maintain the stability of cherished institutions. The essence of secular traditionalism is that it demonstrates a resoluteness of culture and continuity which does not falter in the face of change. Its special characteristics are not unlike those of the early European monarchies which, emerging with the separation between church and state, were the forerunners of modern nationalism. It is for this reason that we will call Buganda a modernizing autocracy, to emphasize both its secular traditionalism and its easy response to innovation.

The modernizing autocracies of the Western world gave way to representative government. If one threat to pan-Africanism, albeit a local one, is to be found in a modernizing autocracy, so representative government is a threat to the modernizing autocracy. For its most distinguishing characteristic is a hierarchical principle of authority which admits a two-way chain of communications but bases its legitimacy upon the right of a monarch to rule. In this respect, the civilization normally expressed in religious or cosmological principles in a theocratic state is expressed directly in the principle of authority in the secular traditional system. The effect is to personalize the solidarity of the members of the state by unilateral agreement on allegiance to the king. To preserve this allegiance is a first priority. The success of such a system cannot fail to exact curiosity from Western observers. If one considers that almost all elaborate political systems are by their very nature frangible, at least Buganda arouses our curiosity by its amazing durability. History is strewn with political societies and the pace of discard has if anything quickened in the political tempo of today's world. This is particularly so with tribal systems in Africa. Culture does not die easily. It shows amazing persistence and stubbornness. To a smaller extent, social institutions can show great resilience, but political institutions, dependent for support and legitimacy on the entire network of social and cultural institutions, are notoriously fragile.

One answer to the puzzle of Buganda is that its political forms and social institutions are virtually identical. Politics is the arrangement not only of the state but of the society. That is why we can call it a political kingdom. Yet, as we have observed above, it depends upon the legitimized notion of pure power. In this it differs from theocracies. Even the seventeenth-century monarchies could not claim autonomous power without employing a religious support—witness the need to proclaim the "divine right of kings." But the king of Buganda is not a divine king, nor does he make any claim to be. Equally, when Christianity swept over Buganda it did not weaken the system. On the contrary, it strengthened it. Hence we find in Buganda a secular monarchy geared for adaptation and innovation and built around a central hierarchical system of authority. It is this pattern of authority and its survival that we shall examine, for it now faces its greatest challenge: the twin pressures of pan-Africanism and representative democracy.

Uganda and Buganda[2]

In its formal institutions of government, legislature, ministerial system, conciliar pattern of local government, and the like, the Uganda Protectorate shows a devolution of authority somewhat similar to that which occurred in British West Africa. There is an African majority in the Legislative Council. Direct elections have been held in several parts of the country. Constitutional reform continues rapidly. All signs point to the development of self-government leading to independence. There have been repeated assurances that independence within the British Commonwealth is the goal of the political administration and the British government.

[2] Uganda, the Swahili term, has been applied to the entire country which is composed of four provinces, only one of which is the Kingdom of Buganda. It is Buganda which is "the political kingdom" and is the basis of this analysis. Historically, Buganda has been the most important political entity and has always had special treatment. Her relationship with the British government stems from the Uganda Agreement of 1900 and its subsequent modifications. At present, in the effort to build a Uganda nation, the remaining provinces of Uganda are assuming greater prominence than ever before. (For a discussion of the administrative and ethnic groups in Uganda, see Chapter 2.)

The advent of self-government in Tanganyika and the independence of the Belgian Congo make it clear, moreover, that there is no possibility that independence for Uganda will be compromised. Indeed, it is possible to say at present that progress is being impeded less by the reluctance of the Protectorate government than by the ethnic fastidiousness of some of its people. The most important political unit in Uganda is more concerned with safeguarding ethnic autonomy than securing self-government for Uganda in the shortest possible time. Indeed, the quixotic situation has occurred where the Uganda Protectorate represents a system which remains alien to its members, so long as Africans refuse to participate in it.

Inside the Protectorate of Uganda is Buganda, the Kingdom of His Highness the *Kabaka*. The Protectorate government seeks to build a national secular state. The Kabaka's government is a modernizing autocracy. It rightly foresees that in such a secular national state its own institutions can only be diminished and eroded.

Some Patterns of Political Behavior in Buganda

Before launching into the main body of our analysis we can sketch in some of the more general behavioral characteristics which have long prevailed in Buganda. Buganda is central to our analysis. A semiautonomous province, its capital, where the king or Kabaka resides and where his government is located, is called Mengo. It is Mengo which claims, and receives, the larger loyalties of the Baganda. As a result, little higher loyalty to Uganda as a nation can be found, for Mengo has a universal appeal throughout Buganda.

Nor was the nationalism of this modernizing autocracy dissuaded by the appearance of motor cars, typewriters, electricity, and other accoutrements of modern life. The central focus of the society remained inward, enriching itself by nurturing its grievances, feeding on its internal conflicts, and remaining ethnically puritanical. The Baganda have always been puritans, if not always in a religious sense, then at least in observing the proprieties of national pride which itself became a religion.

The insularity of the Baganda may appear provincial to the outsider, but life does not lack sparkle and grace to those inside.

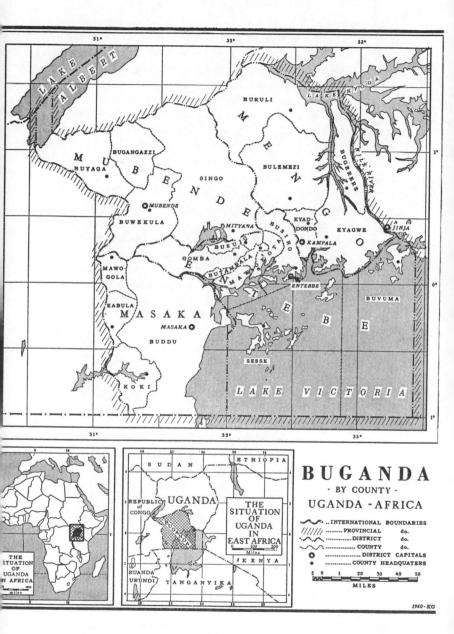

BUGANDA
- BY COUNTY -
UGANDA - AFRICA

〜〜〜 ..INTERNATIONAL BOUNDARIES
/////// .... PROVINCIAL do.
〜〜〜 ....DISTRICT do.
〜〜〜 ....COUNTY do.
◎ .... DISTRICT CAPITALS
● .... COUNTY HEADQUATERS

1960 - KG

11

Like "suburbia," it is relatively sophisticated. Several factors have contributed to this unique Kiganda quality. For example, in traditional Buganda there was no fixed capital. The court buildings were made of elaborately woven reeds and it was a relatively simple matter to set up a new capital. Labor obligations assured a willing and available labor force to work on a new capital and it was regarded as very desirable to have one's area chosen as the site. Moreover, since fire frequently destroyed the buildings, there was incentive to move to new ground. Kabaka Suna moved his capital three times, Kabaka Mutesa fourteen times, mostly within a narrow radius.

Another reason for the suburban quality of Buganda is the constant mobility produced by frequent mobilization. Buganda is a system admirably adapted for war, and was in an expansionist phase when intervention occurred. Chiefs marshaled their followers to military encampments and the forces were relatively mobile, dispatched over the excellent road network which the Baganda constantly maintained. Yet because of the high quality of traditional agricultural capacities, a stable and dense population provided the foundation on which the military and political superstructure was built. Stability and physical mobility, military expansion and internal security, were characteristic. The pivotal center was a person, the Kabaka, rather than a place. In addition to moving his capital, he went on frequent safari. With him went large masses of followers and retainers who were joined by those on the spot who immediately took temporary place in his entourage.

The metropole was wherever the Kabaka held his court. Subsequently, after British intervention, when it became centered permanently at Mengo, there was little estrangement from the rest of the country. Life in Mengo, where the *Lukiko* or parliament sat and where the courts heard appeal cases, was open and casual, formal and graceful. If the Lukiko was in session, large numbers of people from every county could be found in the courtyards. Adjacent, separated by a reed fence, was the Kabaka's palace, to which the Buganda government offices seemed as outbuildings and appendages to the main center of power. The mere physical presence of the Kabaka's palace was in its own way overpowering and there was a sense in which even the most arrogant minister was intimidated by that pervasive sense of presence.

Provincialism was very important in Buganda because, unless a traditional counterpart could be found, it exerted a drag upon the efforts of political leaders to create new and important political groupings. Temporary political groups and alliances formed only for limited purposes. Only the limited purpose organization was possible, not the durable and well-organized party. What formed instead were political associations rather than political movements or parties, a pattern which has continued until today. Nationalism was of such a nature that if a movement were to develop, it would be an all-Buganda movement, parochial in nature and directed against an external threat. Outside interference caused people habitually to rally around their official leaders, no matter how much they disliked these leaders on other grounds: no other important intermediate groupings held powerful attachments for the people.[3]

Through their modernized political instrumentalities, the Baganda accepted the view that as a people they were enlightened and advanced. In the face of criticism their response was not a psychological defense but a political one. They drew their institutions around them like a cloak of dignity. They considered themselves envied by Europeans—in particular they thought of England as a cold island, overpopulated and imperialistic, anxious to send its people to a place with greater potentialities and easier living. Europeans were regarded as greedy, whose exploitations had been kept to a minimum by the artful work of the Baganda themselves. Economic conflicts helped to underscore this view. Thus if the Baganda felt themselves aggrieved, they did not feel degraded.

What is the nature of this warm and prepossessing provincialism? Bound up with it are the notions of kingship, propriety, and modernity. At the center of this system is the Kabaka, himself a figure of interesting contrasts, paradoxes neatly blended into a pattern which characterizes all Buganda social life. As a figure of dignity he receives much reverence—a reverence usually reserved for the mature and elderly. However, when the Kabaka is young, his youth does not remain independent of his dignity but is made to serve it.

The Kabaka is the symbol of the past and the continuity of an

[3] The sole exception to this was the clan.

historical tradition. If more than a hint of scandal periodically surrounds the court, the court nonetheless has about it an atmosphere of primness. An assault upon moral virtue becomes, in its own way, an expression of moral virtue itself. The departure from the norm, in the case of the Kabaka, appears simply to reassert the norm. This is a direct contrast to the Oriental or Middle Eastern potentate, where the chase and pleasant pornography give hint of more subtle immoralities. Hence in the court in Buganda there is no atmosphere of debauchery, but, rather, a slightly varnished uprightness, in which a lapse in grace, no matter how common, is regarded as an isolated act and no departure from moral norm.

This atmosphere is pervasive. It spreads to the more isolated sazas, the county headquarters where the offices and houses of the county chiefs are usually clean, spacious, and sparsely furnished—the atmosphere of the court pervades only in the sense that one can expect the Kabaka to visit here, and if he comes he will find a workmanlike office and a house worthy of a senior civil servant and a representative of the Kabaka. Everywhere, on a smaller scale, are the same intimate formality and social graces as in the Lukiko and around the court. The murmurings of long elaborate greetings float on the air. There is hubbub in the courts where cases are being heard, and everywhere, familiar and contemptuous, are chickens scratching in the dust for meal, finding no entrance barred to them. Children wander, wide-eyed and in varying states of dress, through the gates and to the functions to which the adults attach importance.

In the enclosures, before the new Buganda government offices were built, there could be found small groups of men and women discussing matters of importance or passing the time of day. Women in their bustle-bottomed dresses gracefully and sedately floated through the courtyards and woven reed enclosures, and sank gently to the ground to murmur extended greetings to important chiefs and people of distinction. The windows of the old Lukiko building were big enough and low so that people could sit quite comfortably on the window frames (no window glass being required) and listen to Lukiko proceedings. Others leaned casually against the whitewashed and rustic walls.

Often there was a shout, a blowing of horns, and the beating of royal drums to announce that the Kabaka was leaving his enclosure, and a thrill would run like a current through the crowds. No matter how often he appeared, there were few who remained emotionally casual at his appearance.

There was hierarchy in this system, but a great fraternalism as well. Chiefs in long white kanzus and tweed jackets would walk in quiet self-importance from one meeting to another. Gossip was a constant murmur, stilled only when the last business of the day was done and people, walking in long lines, flowed out of the grounds enclosed by the reed fence, filling motor cars with friends or riding sedately on bicycles back to their farms and families. Quiet descended when the only people left were the Kabaka's policemen outside the palace and the Lukiko grounds. Visitors who had no place else to go huddled with the guards around small fires, brewing tea, preparing to sleep outside the gates.

For the Baganda this was the metropole, not London, or Nairobi, or elsewhere. Mengo was where the rules of propriety and modernity were laid down. For fashion, for the important news, for the renewal of social acquaintanceships, for the conduct of political and other business, Mengo was the center of the universe. Its influence was so great that it incorporated the entire country within its immediate embrace. This is why Buganda today seems like a vast suburb. For if all roads lead to Mengo, the roads from Mengo go everywhere.

In addition to being a provincial society, Buganda is also a polite one.[4] There it is not contempt which is bred from familiarity, but rather manners and courtesy.

This politeness, while it facilitates social relationships, has its negative side. The Baganda can withhold few secrets from one another. It disguises a social life which tends to be relatively atomistic, at least by comparison with other African societies. Politeness covers up the ambitions of men. In the effort to disguise motives or actions from one another, a deep-rooted pattern of mutual suspicion and quiet distrust is also characteristic of the political life of the Baganda. Because he is on such intimate terms with the others, each person imputes motives to his enemies

[4] Sir Harry Johnston described the Baganda as "the Japanese of the Dark Continent, the most naturally civilized, charming, kindly, tactful and courteous of black peoples." (Quoted in Roland Oliver, *Sir Harry Johnston*, London: Chatto & Windus, 1957, p. 331.)

that he feels sure are real. And since actions are always open to informal scrutiny, there is a passion for secrecy. Rarely, as we have indicated, is secrecy successful, but there is a never-ending attempt to engage in public acts with some degree of privacy. This leads to intrigue and a political life which feasts on the disclosures made by certain individuals about the acts and motives of others.[5]

One result is that anyone who enters into political life or becomes socially prominent needs to defend himself against the intrigues of others. Such protection is afforded by building up a following—a group of intimates who can be relied upon for support and loyalty. In its own way, this duplicates the old chieftaincy pattern, at least to the extent that some measure of a man's importance is judged by the number of followers upon whom he can call.

There is, then, a passion for faction. Faction is based upon the need to find stable support whereby an ambitious fellow can get ahead with the help of his supporters, and who will in turn reward those supporters when the time comes. Such hydra-headed factionalism has two consequences. First, it propels the most successful intriguers to the top, where they collide with other successful intriguers (or intrigue with them); second, in this civil service state, it introduces the element of petty graft. Graft is dependent upon family loyalties and nepotism far less than in most societies in Africa, although some of this does of course go on. More usually, the pattern of special favors is reward to followers. Tax relief, special employment, favored positions at the market place, special knowledge about land and crop speculation—all these are characteristic rewards for followers.

Given the competitive and volatile character of politics in Buganda, the successful intriguer can be on top one day and despised and rejected another. A dramatic disclosure of some intrigue on the part of some high official can even cause him to be denied Kiganda origins. A common practice is to denounce someone, when it appears safe to do so, by claiming he had a Munyoro father or is not a rightful member of a proper Kiganda clan.

---

[5] This is a characteristic of bureaucratic politics, where overt norms of unity and rationality prevail, and where a hierarchical principle of rule is supposed to minimize conflict about authority.

Denying his proper antecedents is one way to cast doubts upon an opponent's credentials.

And precisely because these factions are relatively fleeting and do not congeal into major power blocs for very long, the presence of faction and competition among faction leaders prevents widespread ruptures in the social body. Few people dare to stand against the system. There are no rebels in that sense. Quite the contrary, each person sees accomplishment in participating in the system, and except for problems raised by election and representation in the Lukiko, personalized factionalism has led to a basic unity in Buganda. If under politeness there is intrigue, under intrigue is general agreement on the nature of society.

Intense interest in Buganda and the Buganda government, widespread acceptance of the system, and competitive intrigue which accepts the rules of the game and plays the game to the fullest is the norm. Disclosures, resulting from the passion for secrecy, give an atmosphere of crisis without in fact producing crisis or destroying the pattern of courtesy by which members deal with one another. Disclosure is personalized, directed against individuals, and the individual who does not take his downfall when it is expected of him gets into serious trouble, because the factions will unite against him.

These then are general characteristics of Kiganda politics. Provincialism leads to intimacy. Intimacy leads to intrigue. Intrigue leads to an emphasis on loyalty. Loyalty requires followers. Their own intimacy involves further intrigue. The pattern of Kiganda political life consists of these swirling patterns of intimacy and hostility and the chipping and bending of factions, while the civil service chieftaincy system serves as a bland and integrative set of roles in effective relationship with one another, disguising the more personal and bitter activities of individuals.

Buganda possesses remarkable adaptive propensities. Nevertheless, her people have shown reluctance to develop central political structures. Fear that central government will become powerful at the expense of the Lukiko of Buganda has inhibited popular support not only of central conciliar bodies but even of a system of direct elections to the national legislature.

There are reasons for this suspicion. Uneasiness persists widely that a non-African dominated legislature might vote for federation with the other two East African territories, similar to what occurred in Central Africa, despite the objections of Africans themselves. There is fear, too, that important local concerns will be submerged in a sea of national politics. There is mistrust of those who might achieve political power.

Because of the efforts to retain autonomy by the Baganda, there is in Uganda today a situation of political stalemate. The Protectorate government is checked by the political antagonism of the Kabaka's government. But other potential coalitions arise within the general body politic. Below the level of central government other localized groupings form real and potential coalitions against central government and in turn are themselves divided and checked. These are religious and ethnic groupings.

Several conditions perpetuate such a situation. One factor which prevents latent conflict from coming to a head is a surprising degree of satisfaction with things as they are. Partly this can be accounted for by relatively high social mobility and expectations of continued economic growth. Partly, as well, with multiple and shifting group alliances, governments and political groups remain cautious. Caution produces responsiveness to public demands. Yet clearly, Uganda is in a stage of latent reorganization. This means that the ground is being prepared for a re-crystallization of forces which need only the "right" combination of events to act as a catalyst.

What are some of the conflicts that have checked the growth of large-scale political movements? We shall list some of these for Uganda as a whole:

(1) *There are reasonably good sources of income and wealth to Africans.* Poverty is not regarded as the fault of the system but as due to discrimination practiced by foreign groups engaged in economic enterprise, that is, Asians and Europeans. The obvious solution, for these groups are viewed as obstacles to African advancement, is to work for their removal and thereby provide opportunities for Africans. Antagonism is thereby expressed against foreigners and the economic agencies they control, such as the marketing boards which are the link between the producers of coffee and cotton and the world market.

(2) *There is considerable tribal parochialism.* This means that

membership in a particular tribe is a significant factor. It also means that the wealth and independence of the tribe itself produces personal satisfaction. This is increased as tribal prosperity and power increase. To a large extent, tribal affiliation still takes precedence over other affiliations. The result is that commitment to a viable central authority is at best lukewarm lest central government be put in a position that would weaken or strengthen one tribal group against another. District councils have become the repositories of local power in defense against central power. Jealous regard for local interest promotes coalitions of smaller tribal groups against larger ones, against Buganda, for example. Indeed, one result has been a fear on the part of Buganda that if it participated fully in central government institutions, it could be consistently outvoted by a determined opposition based on other tribes forming parliamentary associations or coalitions against Buganda.

(3) *There is generalized ethnic conflict between Nilotic groups and Bantu groups.* This helps to make possible tribal coalitions based upon wide linguistic and ethnic identification. Northern Nilotic peoples, for example, are, in varying degree, fearful of aggressive domination by southern Bantu. It was only a short while ago that a northern representative in the Legislative Council reminded the other members of the revolt that followed independence in the Sudan among the southern Nilotic Sudanese, to whom the northern Nilotic tribal groups in Uganda are related.

(4) *There is religious competition between Catholics, Protestants and Muslims.* These conflicts have historic roots, especially in Buganda where the first important consequence of missionary activity was the outbreak of religious warfare which led to British hegemony and the resultant drastic revision of the Buganda government. Such conflicts have inhibited the growth of political parties (as has *tribal parochialism*) and parties have become identified as characteristically Protestant or Catholic in their membership.

(5) *There is conflict between representatives of older, traditional forms of political organization and representatives of more accommodated forms.* In Buganda, for example, rapid change in traditional organization had already been underway at the time of European intervention. A system of client-chieftaincy had for

many years been displacing a more decentralized clan-kinship system. Europeans elected to amalgamate the monarchical system into a ramified colonial administration and made little provision for the more traditionally-based clan elements.

A variety of groups are the carriers of these and other sources of antagonism. The wide range of issues causing differential division allows diverse coalitions. Catholics can combine against Protestants on some issues and for the moment religious membership can assume highest priority. Ethnic and tribal groups may bury the hatchet and resist the Protectorate government in the face of some greater threat, such as amalgamation of Uganda with Tanganyika and Kenya, a widely-held fear.

As Gluckman has pointed out, conflicts not only divide but unite.[6] Hence conflict and division also produce solidarity and provide permanence to the social groupings in the societies of Uganda. What may divide on one level may unite on another. It is precisely because there is such a wide range of possible coalitions, each member of which is supported by a relatively firm institutional base, that some singular and overwhelmingly dominant group has been unable to make its appearance. And it is because the coalitions are themselves frangible that their potential range is very great.

Out of the wide and diverse patterns of change in Africa, Uganda represents the case of nationalism without mass political parties. The nationalism of Uganda is separatist and in some ways xenophobic. Yet there is throughout the country a growing sense of common identity and a sense of the need for cooperation. Government, parties, and local territorial governments each seek to maintain different points of view with respect to the conditions under which nationhood is tolerable. A formula is being sought. Some common denominator needs to be found.

The Theoretical Framework: Models of Political Change in Africa

Three types of authority patterns appear in contemporary Africa. Ghana represents the first, the mobilization type. There the emphasis is on social mobilization. A second is found in

---

[6] See Max Gluckman, *Custom and Conflict in Africa* (Glencoe, Illinois: The Free Press, 1955). In these six lectures, first presented on the Third Program of the B.B.C., Gluckman shows some of the integrative consequences of conflict.

Nigeria. It is called the consociational type. The third, essential to our study, is the modernizing autocracy.

The types themselves are based upon five variables: (1) patterns of legitimacy, (2) loyalty, (3) decisional autonomy, (4) distribution of authority, and (5) ideological expression. The descriptive categories which compose each type show how specific regimes respond to both internal and external stimuli.[7]

Buganda, the political kingdom, is a modernizing autocracy. One of the characteristics of the modernizing autocracy is that authority emanates from the position of a king whose role is based upon the ideas and practices of power itself. Such ideas are enshrined in the past, validated by an elaborate history which shades off into obscure, mythical tradition but is nonetheless pertinent. It is the role rather than the individual to whom the characteristics of power are attached.

Our key hypothesis is that *the modernizing autocracy can adapt and adjust institutions without great difficulty until the point is reached where the principle of kingship is itself challenged. At that point, either modernization and change are halted, or the entire system shifts to a different principle of authority, conforming to either a consociational or mobilization type.*

These three models, by no means limited to Africa, are held to be universally valid systems of authority. Let us examine their characteristics more closely.[8]

[7] These categories were derived with the assistance of my students in a seminar on comparative method at the University of Chicago. I am indebted to the perceptive comments of Roger Masters, Aristede Zolberg, Leo Snowiss, and Louis Cantori.

[8] A model, as we are using the term, is a way of expressing a theory in simplified form. Each of the models established here makes some presumptions about the way people behave. The expectation is that a certain pattern of behavior will follow with one model which will vary with the second. The type of authority system which each describes makes different demands upon people. Those whose behavior conforms to one model type will, characteristically, deal with problems in somewhat different fashion from those of another.

The models themselves are *developmental* types. They represent typical clusterings of variables which are observable in the contemporary scene. The range of variables from which these developmental syndromes have been established is shown in a three-dimensional comparative scheme. All dimensions—social stratification, political group, and government—have been linked together, while the variables of which they are composed form a conceptual scheme. Here, the effort has been made to link structural and developmental analysis together, something which has not been done in the past. For the structural scheme see D. E. Apter, "A Comparative Method for the Study of Politics," in the *American Journal of Sociology*, November 1958. Application of the developmental types to African

The Mobilization System

A mobilization system is one in which a party or regime engages in drastic and thorough reorganization of the society. The concept has been borrowed from Selznick, who refers to the organizational weapon as follows: "We shall speak of organizations and organizational practices as weapons when they are used by a power-seeking elite *in a manner unrestrained by the constitutional order of the arena within which the contest takes place*." It is crucial that "organizational weapons exploit a source of power that is latent in every group enterprise. This is the capacity of almost any routine activity to be manipulated for personal or political advantage."[9] The organizational weapon is the crucial characteristic of the mobilization system.

Parties and states of this type in Africa tend toward the view that in order to produce the new Africa, the structural precedents of African society have to be altered and a new system of loyalties and ideas in a specifically African secular society created. A main problem of the mobilization system is to give perspective and meaning to processes of change. For example, the Accra form of the mobilization type seeks to do this by giving substance to the idea of African personality.

Leaders of a mobilization system have a perspective approaching revolution and, government being exclusivist, they live in a world of friends and enemies. Moreover, they find themselves uneasy when negotiating on other than their own terms.

The mobilization approach involves efforts to combine the skills and talents of a community and utilize them for a wholesale assault on the problems that lie ahead. The need for such "organizational weapons" is evident in every country facing rapid change and having a fairly clear idea of the kind of society envisaged.

The characteristics of the mobilization model in Africa may be summarized as follows:

---

politics is in D. E. Apter and Carl A. Rosberg, "Nationalism and Models of Political Change in Africa," in *The Political Economy of Contemporary Africa*, Symposia Studies No. 1, D. P. Ray. ed. (Washington, The National Institute of Social and Behavioral Sciences, 1959).

9 P. Selznick, *The Organizational Weapon: A Study of Bolshevik Strategy and Tactics* (New York: McGraw-Hill Book Co., 1952), p. 2.

(1) *Hierarchical authority.* Power resides at the top of the organization, generally in a single leader who also monopolizes legitimacy. National conferences, delegates' conferences, and others give formal validity to the leaders' decisions. Adjacent agencies, such as trade unions and student associations, act as the auxiliaries, mobilizing consensus in the public.

(2) *Total allegiance.* The party demands a fundamental commitment and involvement on the part of the individual. The party defines membership, and an individual is either in or out, friend or enemy. It can make claims on the energies, time, and money of the individual.

(3) *Tactical flexibility.* The party can make quick changes in its alliances and alter its goals and targets. It is tactical- rather than policy-oriented, and has a remarkable freedom of action with a minimum of accountability.

(4) *Unitarism.* The organization is devoted to the establishment of new political units which are essentially new subordinate, solidarity groups. Hence other alternative solidarity groupings, political or ethnic, which oppose the aspirations of the organization are attacked.

(5) *Ideological Specialization.* Although it tends to have very pronounced ideological views on the main issues of development, a mobilization system is in a peculiar sense less ideological than utopian.[10] Fundamentally, the party or the state will most often act on grounds of expediency and necessity, using ideology to give perspective and justification for what already appears necessary. Thus the immediate tasks of the day, whether to build a dam, change the tax structure, or modify the political arrangements in government, are put in the context of ideological slogans as a form of communication. A moral component is brought in by our assuming some future new society which the acts of government and party are supposed to induce. Nevertheless, except where political leaders feel called upon to justify their decisions and actions, opportunism remains more compelling than ideology. The political "culture" of the members is based on their common organizational affiliation. Men of diverse views will have as their overwhelming "ideological" commitment devotion to the organization itself. "The party (or the state) is everything."

[10] See Karl Mannheim, *Ideology and Utopia* (New York: Harcourt Brace & Co., 1946), pp. 49-93.

Consociational

This model is harder to define than the first. Its outstanding characteristic is that it places a high value on compromise among groups which may demonstrate a wide range of ideas and ambitions. Willing to accommodate a variety of groups of divergent ideas in order to achieve a goal of unity, the consociational approach sacrifices precision in organization and militancy in outlook in order to allow diverse interests to congregate. This is why it is subject to a greater concern with unity than the mobilization model. It seeks the best unity it can get rather than some ideal of it. *Technically, consociation is a joining together of constituent units which do not lose their identity when merging in some form of union.* Consociational forms may range from a relatively loose confederation of groups and states to federal arrangements with a recognized structure.

A characteristic feature of the consociational system is that its consensus derives from an acceptance of a common denominator or a shared set of interests by which groups are willing to interrelate. It is essentially a system of compromise and accommodation. Flexible in internal policies because it does not require a total commitment on the part of its members (whereas the mobilization type does), it is nevertheless subject to *immobilisme* because of the need to find agreement on common action before action is itself possible. Hence it is given to crisis, fission, and recombination as part of its natural history. The pace of change is tied to the wishes of recurrent pluralities. It is characterized by continued arguments over values, goals, and tactics.

A summary of the main elements of the consociational type includes:

(1) *Pyramidal authority.* Power is dispersed and shared between the constituent units and a central agency. Legitimacy inheres in a representative principle and is shared by the whole collectivity. Collective or corporate leadership is characteristic.

(2) *Multiple loyalties.* There tends to be a system of loyalties functioning on various levels. The individual may belong to several solidarity groupings in society. Political groups and parties do not demand the sole allegiance of individuals to a leader or to

the aims of the organization. Moreover, the party does not serve as the chief disciplinary weapon of the society.

(3) *Necessity for compromise.* This fact is based on the voluntary nature of the consociation and a policy which almost inevitably is a minimal program acceptable to all.

(4) *Pluralism.* There are diverse and competing social and political subgroups.

(5) *Ideological Diffuseness.* The consociational type tends to place high emphasis on an ideology in order to develop a set of shared symbols and beliefs by which to cement in a more substantial fashion what would otherwise remain simply a set of mutual alliances. Ideology becomes extremely important, providing meaning and coherence both to political roles and structural alliances among constituent parts, and making political marriages deeper than mere convenience. One example of this in French West Africa has been the emphasis on *negritude.* Involved in the concept is a philosophical dimension stressing the unique but shared esthetic and moral features of African life. Both in its search for spiritual values distinctive to Africans and in supplying a universal dimension to the cultural values of people other than Africans, negritude seeks to add something to universal man from the genius of Africa, while emphasizing the commonality of that genius.

At the minimum, loose alliances stressing common ideological and political and economic benefits are sought. At the maximum, a federal principle is adopted to achieve greater organization and consensus.

Modernizing Autocracy

Hierarchical in authority and buttressed by traditional concepts of legitimacy, the modernizing autocracy represents those systems in which change can be adopted and absorbed so long as the system of authority itself is not threatened. It is adept at employing skills and establishing the accoutrements of modernity in schools, social welfare activities, and bureaucracy. As well, it shows facility for economic development.

By its very nature, however, the modernizing autocracy requires a profound solidary core with an ethnic or religious basis, which maintains support for the political leaders or king who makes claims over the members of the system and controls them.

Such systems can normally tolerate wide changes in social and economic life and adapt quickly to the establishment and employment of a bureaucracy. They cannot easily cope with new social and political groups which demand a change in the political system and principles of legitimacy. For example, modernizing autocracies have great difficulty in becoming transformed into representative governments. Indeed, if the price of economic change is political democracy, the modernizing autocracy is normally prepared to resist economic advance. One striking exception to this rule was nineteenth-century England.

Areas which show modernizing autocracies either in their government or in political groups are no longer exempt from pressure from representatives of the other types. How durable they will be remains to be seen, but they are becoming the last strongholds of a significant parochialism.

Characteristics of the modernizing autocracy are as follows:

(1) *Hierarchical authority.* Power resides at the top, as in the case of the mobilization type, but there is a substantial difference. Whereas in the mobilization type the top leadership serves to underwrite its own legitimacy, authority in the modernizing autocracy is the institutionalized property of the leadership role. Occupants are transitory, they can come and go, but the role continues. Whoever occupies it exercises power and delegates that power to members as he sees fit. Thus discretionary authority is traditionally enshrined and the limitations on action are set by the role, that is, by institutionalized limits beyond which the leader is not empowered to act.

(2) *Exclusivism.* Membership is the most fundamental and significant social fact to the individuals concerned. In most cases membership is tantamount to citizenship. To belong means not to belong to another social grouping of a similar nature and not to divide one's fundamental allegiance. Within this allegiance, however, persons can belong to a range of voluntary associations and political groups. When called upon by leaders to act in terms of traditionalist norms, however, the individual, by virtue of his membership, is obligated to conform.

(3) *Strategic flexibility.* Such systems are able to plan long-term strategies, particularly for the advancement and aggrandizement of their group, but they cannot normally make tactical adjustments, particularly if these jeopardize the authority principle. Less able to be opportunist, they must be constantly aware of the implications of change which they are anxious to produce and control. Their traditionalism, however, tends to limit the range of tactical alternatives which might be considered readily available by, for example, the mobilization type.

(4) *Unitarism.* Like the mobilization type, the structure of the organization tends to be unitary. Power cannot be shared or distributed except with provision for recall, and structural modification is not easily accepted unless it is clearly nonpolitical.

(5) *Neo-traditionalism.* Normally neo-traditionalist or revivalist, the ideology needs to embody the moral prescriptions of the past and apply them to modern conditions. Hence the ideology is normally highly symbolic and, in a manner of speaking, "epic," yet sufficiently adaptable to allow innovation to be traditionalized and thereby sanctified.

The modernizing autocracy is adaptable, retaining the shell of society while changing its contents. It prevents fragmentation and allows new solidary groupings to form which, often fulfilling new needs in society, remain essentially supporting rather than destructive forces. Japan was perhaps the most clear-cut modernizing autocracy. Ethiopia and Morocco are other examples. Tsarist Russia was developing such a system.

We shall indicate some of the characteristics of the modernizing autocracy as a system, but first we need to mention two important preconditions of it. The first is a hierarchical pattern of authority without intermediate and relatively autonomous sources of power. The second is a set of roles and institutions which can be summarized as being essentially instrumental in their orientations. Such a system must be able to use authority pragmatically, with adaptiveness regarded as a desirable attribute of the social system.

It is the contention of this book that the Buganda Kingdom has both of these preconditions: the hierarchical system of authority and the complex of values called instrumental. In this it represents a nice contrast to the traditional system examined in our previous monograph, that is, the Ashanti, whose authority system was pyramidal and whose values were consummatory. We shall explore the implications of the pattern of authority and the complex of values as they appear in the development of Uganda.

CHAPTER 2

THE SOCIAL AND ECONOMIC ENVIRONMENT

IN DESCRIBING the first visit of Lugard to Buganda, Margery Perham wrote that as he (Lugard) entered the Kingdom, "he was amazed, after all he had seen of emptiness and of primitive humanity on his march, at the degree of civilization in this remote place. He marked the roads, the tall regular fences, the people's long garments of russet barkcloth or spotless imported cotton, and their dignity and respectful manners. He marched westwards parallel with the lake, through Buganda's alternation of low, grassy, flat-topped hills and its forested lowlands, descending at intervals into swamps of black mud matted with beautiful plumed papyrus and water lilies. Round each hut were the dark cloisters of the banana groves which supplied the staple food of the people."[1]

Travelers to Uganda are no longer forced to make the long and uneasy safari inland from the coast. Nevertheless, no matter how they travel, few can help remarking on the loveliness of the countryside, the fertile, well-watered valleys, the farms, the well-built houses, and attractive dress of the Baganda. Kampala, the capital, is equally prepossessing, built as it is upon seven hills and crowded with prosperous new commercial establishments, offices, banks, and retail stores. It exudes prosperity. And it has no "African quarter" like so many East and Central African towns. There are slums outside, such as Kisenyi or Mulago, sometimes quite fearful ones, but by and large African immigrants live there. Baganda tend to live on their estates or rented *bibanja*, or small holdings, and have many of the characteristics of dwellers in suburbia. Every morning large numbers of Africans commute by bicycle and bus to work in Kampala and return at night to their gardens and farms.[2]

[1] See M. Perham, *Lugard* (London: Collins, 1956), p. 209.
[2] The same pattern is repeated in other towns, such as Jinja, site of the Owen Falls dam and a new center of economic activity at the source of the Nile in Busoga.

Population and Administration

The country is divided up into districts which in many cases conform to tribal groupings. Buganda, a province, is ruled under an Agreement which provides a status of considerable political autonomy. Some districts, such as West Nile, are made up of several ethnic groups, such as the Lugbara, the Alur, and the Jonam. Others, as Acholi or Lango, are based essentially upon a single ethnic group. Outside Buganda there are twelve districts, one subdistrict (Madi), and one township (Mbale). Within Buganda are three districts (although they are no longer significant political entities): Masaka, Mubende, and Mengo.[3] The latter contains the palace of the Kabaka of Buganda and the seat of his government. Between Mengo and Kampala lies the Kibuga, a *gombolola* or subcounty, containing the main offices of the nationalist politicians. (Many of Uganda's contemporary political problems arise precisely because Buganda represents only one province out of the four in Uganda, and one ethnic population out of many. The remainder of the country is extremely varied in terrain, peoples, and culture.)

The three largest towns are Kampala, with approximately 60,000 inhabitants, Jinja with 25,000, and Mbale with 13,000. Economic centers, the three towns are primarily Indian.

Kampala was founded by Lugard when, arriving in Uganda for the first time as the employee of the British Imperial East Africa Company, he visited Mengo, the capital of the Kabaka of Buganda. Building his fort adjacent to Mengo, which occupied one hill, he could look out to Namirembe hill where stood the Protestant mission, and Rubaga hill where stood the Catholic mission. Kampala was thus almost symbolically situated between the three groups which became major contenders for political power in the days before the establishment of the Protectorate.[4]

---

[3] Mengo is divided in two for administrative purposes.

[4] For a useful study of African towns in Uganda, see A. W. Southall and P. C. W. Gutkind, *Townsmen in the Making*, East African Studies No. 9 (Kampala: East African Institute of Social Research, 1956). See also C. and R. Sofer, *Jinja Transformed*, East African Studies No. 4 (Kampala: East African Institute of Social Research, 1955); see also their "Social Survey of Jinja," in *Social Implications of Industrialization and Urbanization in Africa South of the Sahara* (Paris: UNESCO, 1956). In the same volume see also Southall, "Determinants of the Social Structure of African Urban Populations with Special Reference to Kampala (Uganda)."

DIAGRAM OF PROVINCIAL BOUNDARIES

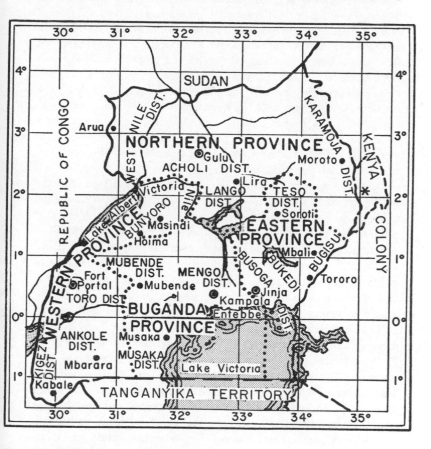

BOUNDARIES:

━━━━━━━━━━━ INTERNATIONAL

━━━ ━━ ━━ INTERCOLONIAL

• • • • • • • • • • PROVINCIAL

✱ ADMINISTERED BY UGANDA

31

The entire country is approximately 94,000 square miles. The headwaters of the Nile originate at Jinja. Lying south of the Sudan, the northern province of Uganda has a large number of Nilotic Sudanese inhabitants. To the west is Ruanda Urundi, a Belgian mandate which is heavily overpopulated. Thousands of immigrants have poured into Buganda and other parts of Uganda from Ruanda Urundi and the north. These immigrants have become an important part of the population, in some parts of the country forming over half the population of parishes or subcounties.[5] Not yet a major political problem, the immigrants are a potential source of political friction. So far they have made strenuous efforts to be absorbed as members of the political community in Buganda.

Uganda shares her southern border with Tanganyika. For the most part that country had been considered the most backward of the three East African territories and it was not expected that political advance would proceed there as rapidly as elsewhere, particularly in Uganda. However, immobilities in the political situation in Uganda and a high degree of political astuteness and political cooperation in Tanganyika have now produced a situation startling to African political leaders in Uganda. Tanganyika will become politically independent before Uganda.[6]

The most important outside neighbor of Uganda is Kenya. Fear of Kenya and domination by white settlers has colored much of the relationship between Buganda and the Protectorate government. The Kabaka of Buganda and other African political leaders have sought assurances that the eastern border between Kenya and Uganda would be an impenetrable political barrier and that any effort to integrate the two territories would fail.

Within Uganda itself there is considerable ethnic variation. In the west and northwest are three "kingdom states," Toro,[7]

5 For an analysis of the immigrant problem see the excellent study by A. I. Richards and her associates in the East African Institute of Social Research, *Economic Development and Tribal Change* (Cambridge: Heffer, 1955).

6 One of the consequences of the modernizing autocracy in Buganda has been an inhibited growth of mass parties.

7 Having been reconquered by Kabarega, king of Bunyoro after an interval of 50 years, Toro was freed and made into an autonomous unit by Lugard. Lugard said, "I here established Kasagama, the son of the late King Nyika, whom I brought to reinstate in his father's country of Toru, when I should have expelled Kabrega (the Omukama or King of Bunyoro against whom Lugard

BRITISH EAST AFRICA
(COMMUNICATIONS)

LEGEND:

→ Railways

═══ Main Roads (==== under construction)

—·— East African Airways Services (principal routes)

—·— Principal Road, River and Lake Transport Services

⚓ Airports and Landing Strips

Miles

0   100   200   300

33

Ankole, and Bunyoro, whose political relations with the Protectorate government are watered-down versions of the Agreement between the Buganda and Protectorate governments.

Toro looks outward to the west upon the Ruwenzori mountain ranges, the "alps of Africa." South is the Kingdom of Ankole, also established by Lugard, where in more open green hill country (lion country) there is an elaborate kingdom and government with a dominant ethnic group devoted to the care of cattle.[8] Southwest is Kigezi district with volcanic hills and mountains, representing the southernmost extension of Uganda. Exceptionally beautiful, Kigezi is the only part of the Protectorate which suffers from problems of overpopulation. Every inch of cultivable land is cultivated. Terraced gardens circle to the very tops of mountains. The population of this cold, damp district suffers badly from respiratory diseases, and the death rate among children is high.

To the north the country has links with Islam and the Sudan. Bunyoro, having been reduced from its former proud position by Sudanese forces under British command and assisted by Baganda levies, is the poorest of the kingdom states. In sadly reduced circumstances with her lands diminished and much of her population living in Buganda, she remains only a vestige of the great kingdom that was Bunyoro-Kitara and which fought so bitterly with Buganda for the hegemony of the lake area. Today a territory of 4,735 square miles, only 2,350 are inhabited by Africans. The Murchison Falls Game Park which occupies a large part of Bunyoro is a lively political matter. So is the complaint that

---

fought). They built a village here, and their people began to flock to acknowledge their King. They undertook to feed my garrison. The Treaty made with Kasagama I have already had the honour to forward with my last report.

"I told Kasagama that at present I would confine his authority to Toru proper, in which district the Salt Lake is. Kitagwenda, and Bikuku, which had in old times been under his father, should for the present remain directly under the Company's control, and he would have nothing to do with them. If he acquitted himself well in ruling Toru and reintroducing law and order, I would add these countries to his Kingdom."

The report of Lugard recaptures something of the flavor of the times. "Toro Reports from Captain Lugard, No. 3," in *Africa, Further Papers Relating to Uganda, No. 2 (1893)* (London: H.M.S.O., 1893).

[8] Ankole is badly divided on religious grounds. Conflict between Protestants and Catholics is so intense that Ankole was prevented from participating in direct elections to the Legislative Council in 1959.

Buganda and other areas were granted the right to freehold land tenure while Bunyoro was refused that right.[9] Still another issue has been the Banyoro claims to lost land given to Buganda.[10]

In the hot, dry savannah country of the north are the districts of West Nile, Madi subdistrict, Acholi, and Lango. Concerned over potential political domination by Buganda, the northern peoples have nevertheless been inspired by the strong and intransigent political stand taken by the Baganda against the Protectorate government in recent years.

To the east, rising out of the plain, is Mount Elgon. In this area of the Bagisu and related peoples there is a flourishing coffee industry.[11] Local politics in these two districts tends toward exceptional viciousness.

Busoga, adjacent to Buganda, once served as an outpost of the Kabaka's kingdom. Around the turn of the century the population was decimated due to a sleeping sickness epidemic. Only recently have large areas of forest land, hitherto closed for tsetse fly control, been opened. One of the many grievances expressed

[9] See *Report of the Land Commission Appointed by H. E. the Governor* (Bunyoro: Church Missionary Society Press, 1931).

[10] As the Omukama wrote, "I am well aware that Government divided the districts in this Protectorate according to tribes, customs, languages, and regime; but this policy has not been followed at all in this nation of Bunyoro-Kitara. Bunyoro-Kitara has been divided into many parts and has thus lost her major portions which originally belonged to her and which have been transferred to foreign countries to which they did not belong before. Moreover, the people within these territories are compelled to speak a foreign language and to give up using their mother tongue—the Lunyoro language."

We cite this not only because it remains an important political issue, but because it expresses the attitudes of ethnic parochialism which still prevail. The foreigners referred to are the Baganda, and the language which they must now learn is Luganda. See *The Bunyoro's Claim of their Lost Lands* (Nairobi: East African Standard Press, n.d.), p. 15.

[11] Indeed, Bugisu, under the Bugisu Coffee Cooperative, is one of the most important coffee districts in Uganda, producing exceptionally high-grade coffee. A coffee scheme established in the 1930's had introduced the crop, and the benefits were widely distributed throughout Bugisu, aided in part by the highly egalitarian social structure of the Bagisu. Coffee production was under the control of African producers who were organized in a politically active union, called the Bugisu Coffee Union, which, with its affiliated societies, was very often troublesome to those responsible for the Coffee Scheme itself. In 1955 a Bugisu Coffee Ordinance abolished the old Bugisu Coffee Scheme and a Bugisu Coffee Board came into being with general legal powers over most of the crop and with charge of the field staff and general control over accumulated funds. Marketing was handed over to the Bugisu Coffee Union. See *Annual Reports for the year ending December 21, 1955* (Entebbe: Government Printer, 1957), pp. 23-24.

by the Basoga has been that land was denied them because of the sleeping sickness epidemic brought by Europeans.

One cannot conclude a brief overview of Uganda without some mention of the Karamojong and the Suk. In a closed district in the northeast, as if sealed against time and change, are the "clusters" of tall, graceful, and shy peoples who, caring for their livestock as for life itself, are left over from another age. There are still cattle wars in Karamoja among the Karamojong, Suk, and neighboring peoples in Teso. In the administrative center of Moroto, where the district commissioner's bungalow nestles beneath the Moroto hills, a sign at a swimming pool found in a small glade warns the casual visitor to beware of the leopard. The signs of progress are found even here. Karamoja has a district council. Karamojong who served in the war have returned with new perspectives on life. Health and sanitation are gradually penetrating to the small, thorny thickets which are the kraals and houses of the Karamojong. The Uganda National Congress for a time had a small branch in the district.[12]

Population

Relative strengths of ethnic populations are as follows: Buganda is the largest group with approximately 17.0 per cent of the total. Iteso, Basoga, and Banyankole are, respectively, 9.4 per cent, 8.7 per cent, 7.9 per cent. Banyaruanda immigrants make up 5.9 per cent of the population, mainly in Buganda. There are 21 major ethnic groupings in Uganda.[13]

A relatively high proportion of the total African income accrues to the Baganda. Not only have they been blessed with fertile lands and relatively good transport and ginning facilities, but they have a steady supply of labor in immigrants from Ruanda Urundi and elsewhere in Uganda. Large numbers of immigrants make their way each year into Buganda from West Nile, Acholi, and Toro. While 34 per cent of the total 1948 population of Uganda were immigrants, in some areas within Buganda the

---

[12] The branch was not very strong, however, and disappeared when the local chairman, an employee of the district council, was sent to jail for taking district council funds.

[13] See *East African Population Census, Geographical and Tribal Studies* (Nairobi: E.A.S.D., rev. 1953), p. 4.

immigrant population ranged up to 65 per cent.[14] These immigrants represent a virtually untapped but politically potent force if they are ever organized. Buganda could well have its own "race" problem.

Analysis of the age grouping of the African population shows that 40 per cent are age 15 or under. This puts a very heavy pressure upon the contemporary African family system to feed, clothe, and educate such a population. While population problems do not yet seem very dangerous, they are important enough to warrant further research.

A more active source of racial tension, manifested most recently in a prolonged and costly boycott of Asians, is represented by the growth of the European and Asian populations. With foreigners still occupying most of the choice economic and administrative posts in the country, African concern is not limited to envy but extends to the future political role of immigrant communities in the political life of the country.

Few Africans have much to say on the most important and critical development decisions that are made. The presence of Africans on various development boards and commissions is still novel enough so that opportunities for African participation are not used to the fullest.[15]

The increase in European and Asian population can be seen as follows:

NON-AFRICAN POPULATION IN UGANDA[a]

Race	1948	1959
Europeans	3,448	10,866
Indians/Pakistani	33,767	69,103
Goans	1,448	2,830
Arabs	1,475	1,946
Others	827	2,313
Total	40,965	87,058

a See *Report on the Census of the Non-Native Population in Uganda Protectorate* (Nairobi: 1953), and *Report of the Census of Population, 1959,* printed in *Report of the Constitutional Committee, op.cit.,* p. 51.

14 See Richards, *op.cit.,* pp. 95-96.

15 The present constitutional proposals do not, however, envisage special legislative seats for minorities. See *Report of the Constitutional Committee* (Entebbe: Government Printer, 1959), p. 13.

TABLE 1*

Population of Uganda by District

PROVINCE AND DISTRICT	Area in sq. miles excluding swamp and open water	1948 African	1948 Non-African	1948 Total	1959 African	1959 Non-African	1959 Total	Percentage increase in total	Density per sq. mile
West Mengo	4,618	487,203	18,897 }	913,716 }	688,146	37,070	726,216 }	46.4 }	157
East Mengo	5,102	407,616			606,598	5,946	612,544 }		120
Mubende	2,668	84,878	348	85,226	99,066	308	99,374	16.6	37
Masaka	3,837	317,688	2,220	319,908	439,934	3,697	443,631	38.7	116
TOTAL BUGANDA	16,225	1,302,162	21,465	1,323,627	1,833,744	47,021	1,880,765	42.1	116
Busoga	3,443	505,988	8,318	514,316	660,320	16,903	677,223	31.7	197
Bukedi	1,575	332,870 }	3,889 }	602,910 }	397,766	2,782	400,548	27.3 }	254
Bugisu	1,636	262,447			352,966	526	353,492		216
Mbale Town	9	3,704 }			8,433	5,136	13,569		1,508
Teso	4,306	402,654	2,625	405,279	453,474	4,401	457,875	13.0	106
TOTAL EASTERN PROVINCE	10,969	1,508,512	14,832	1,523,344	1,872,959	29,748	1,902,707	24.9	173
Karamoja	12,116	125,567	53	125,620	(159,244)	452	(159,696)	(27.1)	(13)
Lango	4,569	265,890	767	266,657	352,943	1,368	354,311	32.9	78
Acholi	10,783	215,655	478	216,133	284,664	1,316	285,880	32.3	27
Madi	1,717	37,756	435 }	336,498 }	50,627	110	50,737	29.4 }	30
West Nile	4,147	298,307 }			383,589	1,093	384,682		93
TOTAL NORTHERN PROVINCE	33,332	948,175	1,738	944,908	(1,230,967)	4,339	(1,235,306)	(30.7)	(37)
Bunyoro	4,752	108,380	926	109,306	126,875	1,323	128,198	17.3	27
Toro	4,745	288,873	501	259,374	347,451	1,875	349,326	34.7	74
Kigezi	1,901	395,529	1,014	396,543	493,444	1,044	494,488	24.7	260
Ankole	5,928	400,924	494	401,418	529,715	1,623	531,338	32.4	90
TOTAL WESTERN PROVINCE	17,326	1,163,706	2,935	1,166,641	1,497,485	5,865	1,503,350	28.9	87
TOTAL UGANDA	77,852	4,917,555	40,965	4,958,520	(6,435,155)	86,973	(6,522,128)	(31.5)	(84)

Excluding persons in transit

* Reprinted from *Report of the Constitutional Committee*, p. 52. (Figures in braces are estimates.)

The greatest concern is over the position of Asians, not of the British. In the latter's case, only 10 per cent of the British population in Uganda was locally born. A high proportion of these were the children of civil servants who would return to England with their parents. On the other hand, 44 per cent of the Indians were locally born, and the figure continues to rise.[16] In the past, Asians were not shy about asserting that birth in Uganda was a claim to citizenship and equal rights to participate in the political life of the country. Indeed, at one time, along with some members of the European community, they asked for safeguards for minority rights in the new constitution.[17]

The problem of racial pluralism is relatively mild in Uganda, compared with multiracial territories elsewhere in Africa. Yet there still prevails a climate of racial exclusiveness. In spite of the small degree of discrimination in buses, restaurants, and other public facilities, Africans do not mingle on equal terms with Europeans and Asians. As a result, considerable racial antagonism and misunderstanding is generated. Today the tenure of alien races in Uganda is very insecure.

In a recent debate in the Legislative Council the matter was put quite clearly by one of the African members: ". . . I think that we have enough immigrant races to be another trouble. (Laughter) I wish to mention in this connection that, for instance, in Busoga we are hardly united. Even in other districts people are hardly united. All Uganda is advocating parochial institutions. Where you have such troubles within a country, I think the fewer the immigrants, the better for that country."[18]

Meanwhile, the Indian and European populations continue to grow—and in growing they become more and more visible. Since the war, European dwellings in Kampala have swarmed over hills and terraces which were once barren of housing. Everywhere, in the small as well as large townships, Asian and sometimes Arab shops are to be found.

[16] See *Non-Native Census, op.cit.*

[17] More recently their position has changed. Calling for a central legislature of 60 elected representative members, the Central Council of Indian Associations advocated a common roll without reserved seats for minorities. See *Uganda Argus*, September 2, 1959.

[18] Proceedings of the Legislative Council, 34th Session, 6th Meeting, 17 February 1955, p. 131.

Relatively few Africans have come to live in urban areas. In marked contrast to the West African pattern, the people of Uganda live neither in villages nor towns, which are largely European or Asian. Nor are Africans engaged in full-time wage labor; according to the 1948 Census, the proportion was only 10 per cent in 1949, rising to 12 per cent in 1952.[19] An enumeration of African employees in 1957 showed an estimated 330,000 Africans in wage-earning employment.[20]

Administration

The districts are governed by district councils with a secretary general, or, as in the case of Bunyoro, Toro, and Ankole, the three "kingdom-states" somewhat similar to Buganda, by a king and a prime minister. In addition, all the district governments have a minister of finance, or treasurer, and a chief justice. Under the District Councils Ordinance of 1955, the councils received both executive and legislative authority.[21]

In the case of Toro, demands for status equivalent to that of Buganda have prevented the district from coming under the 1955 Ordinance. In Busoga internal conflict has had the same effect. In Bunyoro skillful negotiation between the *Omukama* (king), the younger elements (led by a medical practitioner), and the District Commissioner resulted in a new Agreement signed in 1955 which restricted the powers of the Omukama and made him a constitutional monarch.[22] Each district demonstrates somewhat different problems. In Toro the palace traditionalists remain

[19] See *Reports on the Enumeration of African Employees in Uganda*, 1949, 1952, East African Statistical Department. Cited in A. Southall, "Determinants of the Social Structure," p. 558. See also *Classified Trades and Professions of Uganda* (Entebbe, G. P., 1958).

[20] In *Uganda: Colonial Reports*, 1957 (Entebbe: G. P., 1958), p. 20. See also *The Patterns of Income, Expenditure, and Consumption of African Unskilled Workers in Mbale, February, 1958* (Entebbe: E.A.S.D., Uganda Unit, July, 1958).

[21] The district governments remain under the African Local Government Ordinance of 1949 unless they opt for coming under the District Administration (District Councils) Ordinance of 1955. For the constitutional regulations applying in the earlier ordinance, see Proclamations, Establishment of District Councils, Cap. 74, African Local Governments, in *Laws of Uganda*, 1951 (London: Waterlow & Sons, Ltd., 1951); and *The District Administration (District Councils) Ordinance*, 1955 (Entebbe: G. P., 1955). See also *Special Supplement to the Uganda Gazette*, Vol. LI, No. 7, 10 April 1958.

[22] See the Bunyoro Agreement, 1955, *Supplement to the Uganda Gazette*, Vol. XLIX, No. 5, 26 January 1956, p. 50.

strong. In Ankole, in spite of bitter religious conflicts, relatively moderate groups around the palace and among the chiefs have ensured a balance between those representing tradition and custom and those coming up and seeking a place in the socio-political hierarchy.[23]

Outside Buganda, the district is the main unit of government. It is most effective in those areas where traditional and contemporary politics have succeeded one another within the intimate environment of a single ethnic group, as is the case in Teso, Toro, Ankole, Bunyoro, Lango, Acholi, and Busoga.

In addition to being the main units of local and ethnic government, the districts are the crucial centers of Protectorate government administration in the field. The administration, headed by a district commissioner, his assistant district commissioners, and other staff—including forestry, medical, and veterinary officers, community development, educational, and other officers—represents the policies of the various ministries of the government. A rather effective blending of policy and participation has been worked out in Uganda at the district level. The various technical officers, the district commissioner, and several officers of the district government together make up a district team. This team represents an "entrepreneurial committee" concerned with local development and social welfare. The district team has served the purpose of identifying the most publicly sought projects and schemes and finding local means for going ahead with them. At the same time, they have helped to keep the district and lower councils informed of developments in public policy at the center.[24]

If the district councils and their administrative staffs are the crucial units of government, they are also the most politically alert. District governments in many cases have been the spearheads of local parochialism. As well, the districts in the past have been the constituencies for the representative members of the Legislative Council. District councils once served as electoral colleges electing their representatives.[25]

[23] Provincial councils, established in the African Local Government Ordinance of 1949, functioned only briefly. They failed because as entirely artificial bodies they had too few functions to perform.

[24] It must be noted that the excellence of the district team is often at the expense of the district council, which is technically responsible for many of the matters for which the district team determines policy.

[25] See Chapter 16.

Both below and above the district there are other units of government. At the more senior administrative level there is a provincial commissioner responsible for the affairs of the province. Provincial commissioners are intermediate between the minister of local government and the district commissioner and between the chief secretary and the district commissioner. A good provincial commissioner can exert a great deal of influence over the direction and form of administration in the districts and can generally lay down a hard or soft administrative line in his province. There is, nevertheless, an anomalous quality about the post. In spite of its many important duties it has no conciliar counterpart and is in danger of getting into political difficulties with the elected district councils on the one hand, and the representative legislature on the other. Relatively untouched by the contemporary pattern of political development, the provincial offices are conveniences of government. Sooner or later, however, if they do not become administratively trivial, they will become objects of a renewed political attention.[26]

The provincial administration has its own departmental representatives, including health and medical officers, educational officers, and the like. As well, there is a provincial team which deals with those services cutting across several districts. These are useful devices for coordinating departmental efforts in the field.

Lower councils are modeled after those established in Buganda. These are the county, subcounty, and parish councils. Most of these councils have unofficial majorities, that is, representatives of the people who are neither chiefs nor employees of the local authorities. The best organized single bloc in most of the councils remains the chiefs. Serving as localized representative bodies, the tendency is for the *parish* to be the most crucial body for the ventilation of local grievance. The *subcounty* tends to be the most crucial body for achieving inter-parish cooperation on such matters, for example, as local public works. The *county* tends to be the most politically complex body mustering considerable political tension and competition.

Although the tiered local council system was developed in Buganda, in most of the districts the lower councils work more effi-

[26] See D. E. Apter, "Some Problems of Local Government in Uganda," in *Journal of African Administration*, January 1959.

ciently than in Buganda. There, local government reform is long overdue. The politics of chieftaincy and the lack of effective supervision by Protectorate government officials have caused a good deal of malpractice at the lower levels of local government.

The entire system of African local government was for years quite separate from the administration of European and Asian affairs. The legislative council system, which did not develop until after the First World War, was primarily to represent the commercial interests of the European and Asian communities. The African councils, at first advisory, and slowly evolving to greater local responsibility, were considered to be appropriately divorced from the affairs of the central conciliar institutions. Thus a political dualism grew up in which a local focus was maintained for Africans, their pipeline into central government being held by the district and provincial commissioners.

Such a dualism allowed very little political exchange between Europeans and Asians on the one hand, and Europeans and Africans on the other. Nor was there much exchange between districts. The district boundaries were ethnically and politically separate. Prewar administrators had considered their work to be a slow and evolutionary gradualism. With "unlimited time" to develop the institutions of the country, they had sought those "natural" boundaries which had meaning for the people themselves.[27] Thus ethnic and political boundaries were made to coincide where the ethnic groups were large enough to appear economically viable. This was not born out of a desire to produce political separatism or to hold back political advance. Neither of these ideas would have occurred to district and provincial officers to whom political advance simply meant local improvement. Rather, the common view among administrators was that African ethnic groups were, in their "natural state," constantly at war with one another. By compartmentalizing the local units of government it was thought that peace could be more easily maintained, the rule of law established, and ethnic antagonisms more or less eliminated.[28]

[27] When the British arrived, many of the ethnic groups were composed of warring and hostile clans. In concentrating on building up cohesive units they overlooked the danger of tribal separatism.

[28] Early accounts of Uganda by missionaries and explorers gave administrators reason to believe that the establishment of law and order and peaceful and stable political administration was itself a civilizing mission. The accepted view was that

Buganda, differently conceived from the districts, remains a government with certain quasi-autonomous powers. The relationship between the Buganda government and the Protectorate government is such that for the future only a federal solution seems politically feasible. The Buganda government has its king, the *Kabaka;* a prime minister, the *Katikiro;* and five other ministers: the *Omuwanika* or Minister of Finance, the *Omulamuzi* or Minister of Justice, and the Ministers of Health, Education, and Natural Resources.

Buganda is officially a province. Instead of a provincial commissioner there is a resident, with an office at Kampala. Assistant residents are maintained in Mubende and Masaka, as well as in Mengo districts. Largely restricted to providing advice and technical help, the Residency is an important link in the chain of information between the Buganda and the Protectorate governments, it being necessary for the Katikiro to channel his ordinary communications to the Protectorate government through the resident.[29]

There are twenty counties, or *sazas*, which are the main units of local government in Buganda. The counties are divided into subcounties, or *gombololas*, and parishes, or *mirukas*. At each level there is a chief and a *Lukiko*, or council. The chiefs are responsible to the Katikiro for all matters under the control of the ministers of the Kabaka's government. All the county chiefs sit on the Great Lukiko as do three representative members from each county. The lower councils have a somewhat similar structure. Gombolola councils contain the miruka chiefs and unofficial members selected from each of the mirukas. Selection of representatives from lower councils to higher ones is by election.[30] Rep-

---

Africa prior to European intervention was a great hive of local warfare, poisonings, murder, and slavery.

[29] Technically, the resident is the governor's representative in his relations with the Kabaka's government, with functions to advise the Kabaka's government in the discharge of its functions, to keep the Kabaka's government informed of the policy of the Protectorate government, and to keep the Protectorate government informed of the views of the Kabaka's government and of important developments in Buganda. See *The Buganda Agreement, Supplement to the Uganda Gazette,* Vol. xlviii, No. 60, 20 October 1955, p. 25.

[30] For representation on the Great Lukiko see The Law for Selecting Unofficial Representatives to the Councils, 1945, L. N. 241 of 1945 in *Laws of Uganda,* Vol. vii, p. 1264; and *Supplement to the Uganda Gazette,* Vol. xlvi, No. 86, 8 October 1953, p. 359.

resentatives of the lower councils in Buganda, as in the districts, are chosen by popular election with all taxpayers voting. The chief at each level is the chairman of the council.[31]

For both the Great Lukiko and the district councils the committee system has been in operation for many years. In the districts these normally include a finance committee, an appointments committee, and a general purpose committee.[32] As well, the district council is the local education authority, conducting its day-to-day business through the medium of an education committee which contains, by statute, representatives of the voluntary agencies.[33]

In Buganda there are the following standing committees: Finance, Public Works, Education, Health, Natural Resources, Local Government, and Community Development. There is also a separate Appointments Board. *Ad hoc* committees can be established for any purpose.[34]

The country as a whole under the responsibility of the governor is governed by an Executive Council and a Legislative Council. The latter has had African representation since 1945 and now has an African majority. The pattern of central government is similar to that of other British African territories which have moved from Protectorate or Crown Colony status toward independence via devolution of authority to local inhabitants through the establishment of responsible and representative self-government.

Uganda also participates in the East Africa Central Legislative Assembly. This has been a major bone of contention, with African public opinion universally condemning the participation of Uganda on the Central Legislative Assembly.

There are a host of councils at the senior government level. These are usually chaired by Europeans. There are, for example,

[31] For a survey of local government in Uganda, see Lord Hailey, *Native Administration in the British African Territories* (London: H.M.S.O., 1950), Part I.

[32] These are the minimum number of committees. Other committees vary with the constitutional regulations which, under the local government ordinance, lay down the exact structure of local government for a particular district. For example, the Acholi District Council has three committees, while Kigezi District Council has six.

[33] For the role of the education committee and its composition, see *Annual Report of the Education Department*, 1955, p. 9.

[34] See the Buganda Agreement, 1955, *Supplement to the Uganda Gazette*, Vol. XLVIII, No. 60, 20 October 1955, L. N. No. 190 of 1955, pp. 20-21.

the Advisory Council on African Education, the Uganda Civil Service Consultative Council, the Makerere College Council, the Uganda Cooperative Development Council, the Uganda Development Corporation Ltd., the Consultative Council, and the Royal Technical College Governing Council. Among the boards and para-statal bodies are the Town and Country Planning Board, the Uganda Electricity Board, the Uganda Development Corporation, the Languages Board, the Lint Marketing Board, the Coffee Industry Board, and the African Trade Development Advisory Board.

Although there are African members on almost all of the councils and boards, they rarely take a leading part. Hence a high proportion of the work associated with government is undertaken by Europeans and Asians.

In addition to boards and councils, there are a large number of committees appointed for special purposes, such as the Scientific Committee on Human Nutrition in Uganda, or committees of the Legislative Council.[35]

For most Africans the important units of government remain the Buganda government or the district governments, although the central importance of the Protectorate government as a desirable political structure is slowly being recognized.

Uganda, then, is a country where the rural way of life has sustained separatism and localism. There are no real African towns where people rub shoulders with one another, share a common fate, or see one another's destiny as common "life chances." There are few class differences. Meaningful discriminations are made between cultural and ethnic groups, between those who are educated and those who are not, and those who work for government, central or local, and those who are not in official capacities. Only recently have political efforts been made to create overarching political associations throughout the country, but these efforts have by no means been very successful.

The Social and Economic Environment

What were the objects of British intervention in Uganda? According to Sir Harry Johnston, Her Majesty's Special Com-

[35] For complete listings of councils, boards, and committees, as well as their composition, see *Staff List* (Entebbe: G. P., 1958), pp. 115-125.

missioner, there were four. First, there were two political reasons: whoever controlled Uganda controlled the Nile; and Uganda was an important stage on the way to British India. Second, the Protectorate was necessary for a philanthropic reason. The social and religious uplift of the natives was a moral obligation. Then, since philanthropy as a practical solution required capital, Johnston wished to bring in European settlement and economic growth in those areas deemed suitable. Fourth, Uganda would provide an outlet for Indian enterprise. "On account of our Indian Empire we are compelled to reserve to British control a large portion of East Africa. Indian trade, enterprize, and emigration require a suitable outlet. *East Africa is, and should be, from every point of view, the America of the Hindu.*"[36]

Johnston's more casual views did not prevail in Uganda. European farming was restricted to Toro and a few small grants of land in Buganda. The Great Depression wiped out most of those settlers who had survived earlier fluctuations in world prices. As a result, an African peasant agriculture developed. Asians confined themselves to commerce. Europeans were found in government or in commercial activity. Despite this compartmentalization of social life into ethnic-economic sectors, the situation in Uganda never hardened; social mobility was never entirely restricted to within the racial communities. This is in very sharp contrast to Kenya. In a plural society such as Kenya, where cultural, ethnic, and economic boundaries coincide, ethnic and social relationships which cut across them were at best heavily ritualized in roles which have narrowly prescribed limits, such as those of masters and servants. Social relations beyond these limits created difficulties and strong sanctions against offending individuals were applied.

The situation was otherwise in Uganda. By 1920 many officers of the government were opposed to further alienation of land to Europeans and, more important, fought against the plantation system. African growers, first in cotton and subsequently in coffee, eventually came to participate in the fringes of commercial activity. The expansion of welfare and health measures was directed into local channels requiring an effective framework of African local governments, and Africans entered quickly into

[36] Parliamentary Papers: Africa. No. 7 (1901), Sir Harry Johnston, *Report by His Majesty's Special Commissioner on the Protectorate of Uganda* (London: H.M.S.O., 1901), Command 671. (My italics.)

official tasks. The emphasis was upon development and the criteria of participation were "never made subject to racial affiliation. Thus while in general Africans were growers, Asians were merchants, and Europeans were in administration or large-scale crop marketing, the barriers to African entry into the latter two activities were never those of principle. African entry was slowed down by the depression and by World War II. But both Africans and Europeans recognized that in the postwar period a renewed emphasis on development would be the major task of government. The original Worthington plan for Uganda[37] was published in 1946. Development, inhibited by the War, came to the fore as a major policy of the Protectorate government. It was the logical consequence of social welfare colonialism which had as its major object the raising of living, educational, and social standards for all.[38]

Development efforts have continued to be a strong point of the Protectorate government. The first blueprint for this was a joint report on postwar development issued in 1944 by the Standing Finance Committee of the Legislative Council. Two years later the Worthington report was published. A year later the development commissioner revised the development plan which was to spend £34¼ million in ten years. By 1954 the plan was to spend £30 million between 1955 and 1960,[39] in a plan now completed. Already preparations are underway on a new expenditure forecast.

In the case of per capita real income, the African population of Uganda does not compare unfavorably with other poor countries, but per capita real income is low. The total net money product per head of total African population from commercialized activities in indigenous economies and from wages earned outside them was approximately £12 in 1952. This was considerably higher than Northern Rhodesia, Kenya, and the Belgian Congo. Imputed money value per head of subsistence activities, which is always

[37] E. B. Worthington, *A Development Plan for Uganda* (Entebbe: G. P., 1946).

[38] "The greatest service which could be rendered to the colonies would be to make them capable of maintaining a steadily increasing standard of living and expanding public services without need to call for outside assistance. Since the standard of living cannot rise unless the income of the individual family rises, and public services cannot expand unless revenue is buoyant, the first aim of development must be to cause production in all its forms to increase at a greater rate than the population." *Ibid.*, p. 7.

[39] See *A Five Year Capital Development Plan*, 1955-1960 (Entebbe: G. P., 1954).

difficult to calculate realistically, was approximately £5. Money income per capita in the African sector of the population thus amounted to approximately £17. This income level would seem to leave only a modest sum for investment saving and for disposing upon imported goods.

The main sources of African income are coffee and cotton. Uganda is the biggest producer of coffee in the Commonwealth and the biggest producer of cotton in all the colonial territories. These two crops account for 85 per cent of the total value of exports and 35 per cent of the value of the exports of the whole of East Africa. All the cotton and 90 per cent of the coffee are grown by peasant farmers; only about 10 per cent of the coffee is estate produced.[40]

Future development of the country is likely to be heavily contingent on world prices for coffee and cotton, and the internal market and development is of course heavily dependent on those two export commodities.

Coffee and cotton are handled almost entirely through the facilities of marketing boards.[41] Large sums of money have been

[40] See W. Padley, "Uganda's Wealth—and its Problems," in *The Manchester Guardian*, East Africa Survey, April 24, 1956. It can also be noted in this regard that the development of mechanized farming was thought to be a great potentiality. A variety of mechanized farming schemes has been under experimentation and there was some dislike of the "family farm" or family cultivation system on grounds, since proved erroneous, that mechanized farming was superior. See *White Paper on Mechanization of African Farming in Uganda* (Entebbe: G. P., 1954), pp. 1-4.

[41] Control of coffee and cotton marketing has a long history. It begins with control of the cotton industry after the First World War. In common with the experience of other primary producing British territories, efforts were made to establish standards, increase the efficiency of marketing, and expand the territorial share of the world market sales. Government normally worked closely with the major firms engaged in the enterprise.

Wartime experience and postwar fears that depression would return helped to develop the marketing board system for coffee and cotton. The main idea is as follows: throughout the buying season, growers are assured guaranteed prices for their crops. A reserve was built up to serve as a cushion or insurance scheme for growers against the vagaries of world market price. As well, in the immediate postwar period, the marketing boards served to prevent inflation. Indeed, it is not too much to say that fiscal policy manipulations made possible through the marketing boards have been one of the most flexible features of the economy.

In Uganda after 1945, fears of inflation resulted in a Protectorate government policy of holding back considerable funds from the grower. This was one of the underlying grievances of the 1949 riots in Uganda and the origin of the political demand by farmers to market their produce directly on the world market. Since 1953, however, the government has paid world prices to growers. As prices need

made available for investment through the Lint and Coffee Marketing Board reserves. This represents an important part of African investment.[42]

The Marketing Board arrangements act as an insurance scheme and a price stabilization fund. Ever since a ceiling on necessary reserves in the Price Assistance Fund was set at £20,000,000, any excess can be paid over into an African Development Fund which has been established for approved projects, mainly those involving capital development to be used for the benefit of Africans. This constitutes a very important part of African investment. The Coffee Price Assistance Fund also allocates sums to the African Development Fund. Purposes of the Fund have been to finance both recurrent expenditures and capital development. For example, £10 million has been allocated from the African Development Fund to meet both capital and recurrent costs of the expansion in African education, including technical education.[43]

With respect to Africans in professional and administrative posts, almost all professional work is carried out by Europeans. Commercial positions are "parcelled out" by Asian business proprietors to their relatives. Government and private posts as arti-

---

to be guaranteed before the crops are sold, a Price Assistance Fund has to be maintained. When in 1955, for example, world prices for cotton suddenly dropped, approximately £4½ million was withdrawn from the Price Assistance Fund and paid to growers.

Wrigley comments that "by the end of 1953 the farmers of Uganda had involuntarily contributed nearly £30 million to price assistance funds and about £22 million to development projects of various kinds, in addition to about £30 million paid in export duties which contributed to ordinary revenue. Rarely during this period did they receive as much as three-quarters of the price which would have been warranted by the state of the export in market. In 1950 they obtained only 50 per cent of the actual value of their cotton and a mere 27 per cent of the value of their coffee. In 1951 the figures were 39 and 31 per cent; in 1952 they were 45 and 43 per cent. Since then the levies have been greatly reduced and there actually have been some disbursements from the price assistance funds. But for more than a decade the growers, *qua* growers, were consistent losers, and losers on a very substantial scale." See C. C. Wrigley, *Crops and Wealth in Uganda*, East African Studies No. 12 (Kampala: E.A.I.S.R., 1959), p. 70.

[42] Marketing board practices were the object of heavy attack in the Royal Commission Report which took the view that the producer should receive his own funds without marketing board intervention or price stabilization, so as to increase substantially African entrepreneurship. In Uganda, however, the practice of giving the grower his full return has now been established. See *Royal Commission on Land and Population in East Africa* (London: H.M.S.O., Cmd. 9475, 1955), pp. 82-93.

[43] See *A Five Year Capital Development Plan*, 1955-1960, p. 5.

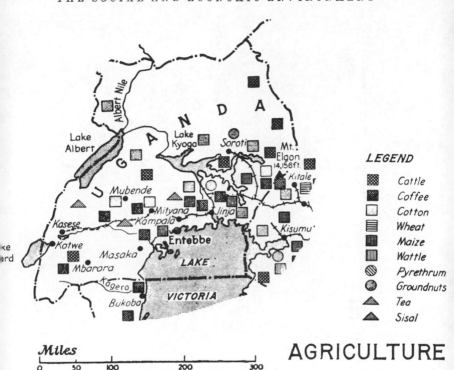

LEGEND

▨	Cattle
◪	Coffee
☐	Cotton
▤	Wheat
▦	Maize
▥	Wattle
◍	Pyrethrum
●	Groundnuts
▲	Tea
◮	Sisal

Miles

AGRICULTURE

sans are filled by Asians. Asians received some of the highest incomes, but Europeans had the highest average income. In strong contrast to African income, European incomes represent approximately £500 per capita. In his analysis of working groups in Jinja, Cyril Sofer estimated that Africans earned about an eighth as much as Asians, and a twelfth as much as Europeans. He concluded that the most important single attribute determining an individual's social status is his race membership.[44]

Capital investment in Uganda has increased dramatically since the War (see Table 2 below).

With the assistance of the Uganda Development Corporation, industrial and mining investments have increased. The export of

[44] Sofer, "The Working Groups in a Plural Society," in *Industrial and Labor Relations Review*, Vol. 8, October 1954, p. 70.

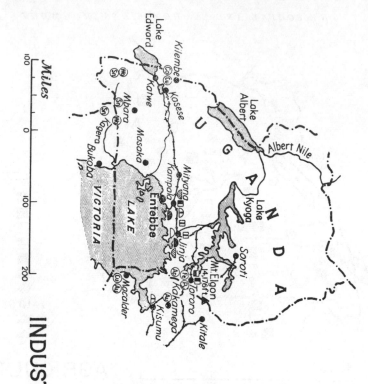

INDUSTRIES AND MINERALS

Miles

100   0   100   200

LEGEND

PRINCIPAL MINERAL DEPOSITS

- (Cu) Copper
- (Co) Cobalt
- (Au) Gold
- (Py) Pyrochlore
- (Sc) Soda Carbonate
- Diamonds
- (Fe) Iron ore
- Coal
- (Pb) Lead
- (Sn) Tin
- (Wf) Wolfram
- (D) Diatomite
- (Mi) Mica
- (Th) Thorium
- (Ap) Apatite

PRINCIPAL INDUSTRIES

- Cement
- Sugar refinery
- Containers
- Paper
- Glass
- Textiles
- Building materials
- Tobacco manufacturing
- Meat canning
- Fruit canning
- Household utensils
- Brewing
- Footwear
- Margarine
- Soap
- Fertilisers

Map labels: Lake Edward, Lake Albert, Kiembe, Katwe, Kosese, Albert Nile, Mbara, Masaka, Kagera, Bukoba, VICTORIA LAKE, Entebbe, Kampala, Mityana, Jinja, Soroti, UGANDA, Lake Kyoga, Mt. Elgon 14,176 ft., Tororo, Kakamega, Kisumu, Kitale, Macalder

copper, phosphates, and tungsten is expanding and a downturn in the economy appeared to have reversed itself by 1960.[45]

Under the auspices of the Uganda Electricity Board, the large Owen Falls dam and hydroelectric station built at Jinja, in

TABLE 2

ANNUAL NON-RECURRENT EXPENDITURE
GENERAL ECONOMIC DEVELOPMENT

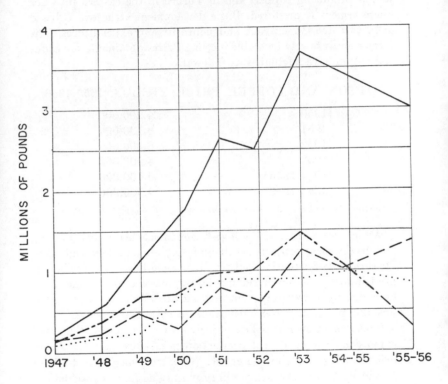

Key: Total: General Economic Development _____
     Urban Development . . . .
     Housing and Offices __ _ .__. ___ . __ .__. __
     Communications __ __ __ __ __ __ __ __ __ __

[45] The source of Table 2 is *Background to the Budget*, 1958-59 (Entebbe: Ministry of Finance, G.P., 1959).

Busoga, opened in 1955. Capable of an output of 150,000 kilo-watts, the dam has great power potentialities. The number of its consumers remains one per cent of the potential of about one million. There are three possible additional dam sites on the Nile between Jinja and Lake Kyoga, with an estimated output of 500,000 kilowatts.[46]

Elaborate development schemes under the Uganda Development Corporation have been underway in Kilembe, with the object of producing copper, and in Tororo in the eastern province where cement is produced. Basic development structure is based upon two items, recurrent and nonrecurrent expenditures. The former needs to rely on stable income. Prices obtainable for coffee and cotton have fluctuated as follows:

COTTON AND COFFEE PRICE YIELDS, 1955-1956[a]

1950	£4,200,000
1951	8,100,000
1952	8,300,000
1953	4,000,000
1954-1955	6,400,000
1955-1956	4,300,000

[a] Source: W. Padley, "Uganda's Wealth—and its Problems," in *ibid.*

A high proportion of the investment in schools, roads, welfare, and development projects results in heavy recurrent expenditures. However, the fluctuating pattern of income has cut down investment in many fields of fundamental importance to Uganda. Fear of incurring heavy recurrent expenditures is a consequence of unstable prices and overdependence on cotton and coffee.

Thus, as an overall policy objective of government, the rapid expansion of agricultural production is essential. As the *Economist* Intelligence Unit observed: "Over the long term to 1974 it is likely that the economy will grow only as fast as production: chiefly agricultural production. Investment and production are interdependent in the sense that investment will raise production and production will encourage investment. Primarily it is a ques-

[46] See "Electricity for Uganda: The Owen Falls Scheme," by W. D. D. Fenton, Chairman of the Uganda Electricity Board, in the *East Africa Survey of the Manchester Guardian*, April 24, 1956.

tion of opportunities for investment, and in East Africa it is the market created by agricultural production which makes the opportunities. In 1945, much investment was overdue; in 1955 it would appear that many opportunities for industrial and other investment remain. But by about 1960 it seems probable that there will be fewer opportunities for new industrial investment, and from 1960 onwards the rate of total investment will follow, more closely than hitherto in the postwar period, the pace of advance of agricultural production."[47] Africans remain both the primary producers and consumers.[48]

Urban life is dominated by Europeans and Asians engaged in major commercial enterprise. In Buganda, where freehold land tenure was established by the 1900 Agreement, the Lukiko distributed 8,000 square miles of freehold. Very little of this land was alienated to Europeans before 1916. After that time it became illegal and it was firmly established by 1923 that non-Africans could not acquire freehold. Customary tenancy was made secure in 1927 with the passing of the Busulu and Envuju Law, which now makes it relatively difficult for a landowner to live off the land without actually working it, because rents from customary tenants are fixed at too low a rate.[49] Most of the old estates have long since been broken up, but it remains possible for Africans to purchase or lease land. There is no landless peasantry; no compelling reason exists for farmers to migrate to the towns. The social structure remains atomistic and highly mobile.

A dual economy prevails. One section is a large and important cash crop-commercial economy. The high proportion of migrant laborers in Buganda, for example, are employed by Baganda who are engaged in cash crop agriculture, mainly coffee and cotton.

[47] *A Study of Trends, op.cit.*, p. 237.

[48] In a series of impressionistic efforts, an attempt was made to get a picture of the consumer purchase priorities in rural areas. The first item of preference was almost invariably a bicycle. The second was clothes for the women. The third was a tin roof for the house. After that a less orderly pattern of preference manifested itself. Some wanted furniture, some a wireless, etc. It is safe to conclude that both wants and expectations are expanding mightily. As income increases, the priority becomes motor cars rather than bicycles, and more elaborate housing rather than tin roofs.

[49] For excellent discussions of the effects of this law in both economic and political terms see C. C. Wrigley, *op.cit.* p. 53, and D. A. Low and R. Cranford Pratt, *Buganda and British Overrule, 1900-1955* (London: Oxford University Press, 1960), pp. 236-239.

However, there is also a large subsistence economy. Almost no African farmers are completely divorced from the subsistence sector. In that degree they are not integrated in the internal marketing system for many of their daily "groceries." This helps to insulate them from economic crises, at least with respect to the more immediate necessaries of life.

The high proportion of labor expended in the subsistence economy sector of the economy has led the Royal Commission on East Africa to emphasize how important it is to shift from a subsistence to a commercial economy. Stressing the fact that the subsistence economy is a poverty economy, while a commercial economy is a wealth economy, the Commission has held that absorption of effort and time in the subsistence sector is wasteful and inefficient. Not envisaged is the phenomenon of the "Bazaar" economy characterized by the institutionalization of exchange rather than of savings. This intermediary economic stage is important politically because from the "Bazaar" come *political entrepreneurs*. Many small traders are recruited into politics, especially those living adjacent to urban areas who have become the local political entrepreneurs. Although engaging in commercial activity, they are unable to compete on a market basis and they join political parties in order to find some other channel for their activities. To fail as a political entrepreneur carries no more stigma than to fail in the bazaar, and the attitudes of chance and gain which are characteristic of such an economy are also conducive to the development of a highly politically conscious intermediate level of political leadership, dispersed in the rural and township areas, directing considerable antagonism against Asians in particular.[50]

Thus changes in marketing structure to include cash crops have not been so drastic that the entire pattern of social organization has changed. Atomistic and resilient, the commercial economy has not displaced the older tradition of a society based on political ranks and rule.[51] Land traditionally brought both pres-

[50] We find that several important African traders have a long history of association with the various efforts to organize trading associations and political parties. For example, among the directors of the Baganda Bus Service were people with a long history of activity in politics. Among the directors of the Baganda Butchers, Ltd. were active members of the small and unsuccessful Uganda People's Party, while among the directors of the Baganda Traders and Printers, Ltd. were several prominent figures active in Mengo politics and party politics.

[51] Some have argued that the marketing boards have also inhibited the expansion

tige and political power. Success is still measured in political terms. What is valued is prestige derived from landowning, with the possibility of becoming a *mutongole* chief or being recruited into the Buganda government hierarchy.

A factor which dampens enthusiasm for economic growth is the direction and control by Europeans of almost all the major development projects and works.

African Labor and Trade

African laborers are on the whole poorly paid by the standards of Uganda. Average income for African laborers in Kampala in September 1953 was 68.40s. per month.[52] Laborers represent almost every major ethnic group in the Protectorate and elsewhere.

Heavy turnover in wage labor is common in the early stages of employment, with the highest proportion among the Baganda. Elkan indicates that "the substantial number of Ganda who come to the factory seems at first sight to disprove the contention, which is often heard, that the Ganda will not enter unskilled employment, that so many leave so soon seems on the contrary, to support it. The explanation to this apparent riddle may lie in the prospects which they find. A Ganda will stay if he sees before him a prospect of rapid increase in his earnings. Otherwise he leaves and goes from job to job."[53]

In a survey done on internal trade in Uganda in 1952, Africans were found to constitute 70 per cent of the traders of the Protectorate, with African retailers commanding one third to one half of the total retail turnover of the Protectorate. In spite of the large numbers of African traders and the high proportion of the volume, the report pointed out that "upwards of 80 per

---

of the African economy. It seems debatable whether or not the benefits of the marketing boards as a general source of investment funds in the country and as a fiscal control device in the country are less important than full returns of proceeds to the farmer from the sale of cotton and coffee. The Royal Commission argued that Uganda pays far too much attention to concerns of security and smoothness in the process of development. Nevertheless, it seems clear that Africans do have all the propensities for entrepreneurship but find it appealing to invest in land rather than in commercial activities. See *Royal Commission Report*, Chapter 5, "The Dilemma of Security."

[52] See Table 1, "The Pattern of Income Expenditure and Consumption of African Unskilled Labourers in Kampala," September 1953, E.A.S.D., January 1954.

[53] See the excellent study by W. Elkan, *An African Labour Force*, East African Studies No. 7 (E.A.I.S.R., 1956), p. 7.

cent of African shopkeepers do not make more than Shs. 1,000 per annum as net profit and cannot derive a reasonable living from their trading activities. On the other hand, it is fair to assume that probably the majority of these unsuccessful traders supplement their incomes from other sources, mainly agricultural."[54] Depending on skills and experience, African wages range from approximately £11 per month to £19, for skilled labor.

Employees whose incomes are less than £5 per month receive free housing or its equivalent.[55]

There were, in 1957, thirteen registered trade unions with a total active membership of approximately 4,800. The small size of the trade union movement reflects the overwhelming rural and agricultural character of Uganda.

Education

Deficiencies in education and training have also inhibited the rapid expansion of Africans into commercial life and into posts in the Civil Service of the Protectorate government.

There were, in 1957, approximately 290,000 African children attending grant-aided primary schools, as compared with 180,000 in 1952. There were 14,273 in secondary schools, as compared with 5,517 in 1951. In contrast, in 1957 there were 16,000 Asian children in primary schools and 3,817 in secondary schools. Expenditures on education by 1957 had risen to over four times that of 1951, that is, £4½ million.[56] The number of African children in primary schools indicates a very large, irreducible bulge at the secondary school level. A very high proportion of the children of the present African generation will have their education halted at the point of entry into secondary schools. This has made Africans conscious of the fact that Asian children, on the contrary, continue to receive better education. Many go on to higher education in India or the United Kingdom at private expense. Africans have argued that the wealth of Asians has been based on exploitation of Africans. Therefore, Africans are in effect paying Asians enough so that Asian children can go abroad and

[54] See *Annual Report of the Department of Commerce*, 1953, p. 6. The accuracy of this report is somewhat questionable and the figures are taken only in the absence of better ones. See also *Classified Trades and Professions of Uganda* (Entebbe: G. P., 1958), which lists professions and trades by company. The largest single African group is newspapers, particularly the vernacular press.

[55] *Colonial Reports*, 1957, pp. 22-24.

[56] *Ibid.*, p. 14.

receive the best education to return to Uganda and exploit Africans.

Almost 90 per cent of the schools are managed and staffed by voluntary agencies, particularly church organizations. Financial assistance is provided in the form of local government grants, which remain very small, and grants from central funds. For the most part, teachers' salaries remain low.

A major concern of the Protectorate government has been technical and commercial education. Desired is a middle range of technical education after the completion of primary school. Planned were twelve junior secondary technical schools, six managed by the Government and six by the missions.[57] At present there are four schools which provide commercial secondary education at the senior level (Secondary IV to VI): King's College, Budo; Namilyango College; St. Mary's College, Kisubi; and Tororo College.[58] Technical education is expanding rapidly. The Royal Technical College at Nairobi will provide higher technical education for the East African territories in much the same pattern as that of Makerere College in the liberal arts and physical sciences.[59]

Conclusion

This brief excursion into the land, labor, capital, and administration of Uganda is designed to put the more basic problems of Uganda in some perspective. Buganda remains the most fertile area. It leads in the production of cotton and coffee on which the economy of the country depends. In the years 1957 to 1959 there were sharp drops in the world prices of these two commodities. The economy was bolstered somewhat by the Price Assistance Funds maintained by the Lint Marketing Board and the Coffee Marketing Board, but the uncertain economic future has been brought home once again to the peoples of Uganda.

The country as a whole illustrates all the difficulties of a typical peasant economy. There is very little industrial development, nor can it be expected in the near future. Indigenous entrepreneurial

[57] See *Technical and Commercial Education in Uganda* (Entebbe: G. P., 1954).
[58] See *Report on African Commercial Education and Training in Uganda, 1953* (Entebbe: unpub. mimeo., 1953), p. 2.
[59] Present plans are to develop a University of East Africa. The Royal College of Technology has been raised to the status of a university college with a London external degree program. It is expected that a university will be built in Tanganyika in the near future.

skills are limited and easily channeled into investment in land rather than industrial or commercial enterprise. In spite of government efforts to provide fiscal facilities and to teach more efficient trading practices, these have not been used to full advantage by Africans.

For these reasons, in sharp contrast to the West Coast pattern, there has not developed an urban middle class. What middle class there is is largely composed of chiefs and old families of chiefs who, while often owning town dwellings, find their residence and social position in rural freehold estates. African teachers, traders, and churchmen are distributed widely throughout a "suburban" rural community and do not form into close-knit urban, primary, or secondary groups.

The development of the country remains largely in the hands of non-Africans. These are drawn into communities the more close-knit for being marginal. The urban communities of Uganda are mainly immigrant communities. Even the rural townships are focused primarily around Indian or Arab traders and their *dukas*. This situation has produced great bitterness among many Africans who are led to seek a solution to their problems less in their own efforts than in concern with ridding themselves of minority groups.

With all its emphasis on development, the Protectorate government has failed to stimulate the necessary diversification of the economy. Conscious of the great dependence on world coffee and cotton prices, the government has put emphasis on economic stability; but the stability has not resulted in effective economic and social priorities. There has been an over-expenditure on services (in keeping with the traditions of the modern social welfare colonial state), but it is by no means clear that planning in this regard has been effective. In spite of the high total bill for recurrent expenditures, there has been far too little investment in education. Without a large pool of secondary school and university graduates upon which to draw for administrative and technical posts, devolution of authority to Africans in the central government simply *increases* rather than decreases their dependence on Europeans or other foreigners to carry out the main business of the day. In this respect the prospects of constitutional advance urgently require greater African participation in economic life as well as in the administrative and technical services.

Demanding autonomy in the provision of services, many African political leaders complain that the Protectorate government does not do enough toward social and economic development. This may be the case. Yet Africans in their daily lives are still too rooted in the parochial concerns of a peasant society while they demand the proceeds of more advanced economies. In this regard, neither the vast majority of Africans nor their local governments do enough. They are not prepared to make the sacrifices necessary to achieve more advanced levels of economic and social gain. African taxation falls heavily on the poor. Although graduated tax was instituted in 1955, it remains purely nominal for wealthy Africans. There is no income tax (as has existed for years in Ghana, for example), except that paid by Europeans and Asians. The tradition of social welfare has allowed Africans to move almost at their own pace, content with their prejudices and comfortable in blaming colonialists for whatever conditions they do not like. Local initiative remains all too rare. Financial malpractice is common.

It is, of course, easy to overdo these generalizations and they are less true as time goes on. Increasingly Africans are participating in every form of commercial and political transaction. Those opposed to granting autonomy to Africans dwell overmuch on such considerations. Yet it is also easy to pass over them, or to regard frank discussion of these deficiencies as illiberal or intolerant. The development of Uganda needs to be dependent on African enterprise and African self-discipline. If not, European and Asian talents and money will continue to prevail, while the producers remain African.[60]

[60] The recent boycotts against Asians which gave way to sporadic outbreaks of violence and bomb-throwing in the spring of 1960 has been one means of breaking the economic superiority of Asians. The first phase of the attack was against Asian traders in the rural areas, driving them into the larger towns. Forced to close their shops because it was unsafe to live in the rural areas, the Asians left a more or less clear field for African traders, many of whom began to make money for the first time.

The second phase in the campaign was throwing bombs in the town shops of Asians which were heavily patronized by Africans. In Kampala, for example, nine shops were bombed within a fortnight. This was to prevent Africans from buying in urban Asian shops.

Although such acts were not condoned by the Buganda government, there was widespread belief that the main support for the Buganda government came from the very people engaged in the outbreaks and thus the Buganda government was not willing to take firm action to restore order. Although suffering a loss in revenues because of the effects of the boycotts, few Baganda are much out of sympathy with the aims and purposes of the boycott, even though many deplore violence.

CHAPTER 3

MISSIONARY AND MERCANTILE
IN EAST AFRICA: THE DISCOVERY AND
ENGAGEMENT OF INSTITUTIONS

In their strenuous ways, the men who make history do not begin or end it. For this reason, history itself must be called upon to provide a perspective for events linked by time if not by cause. The relevance of past experience is no less vital for inevitably being misunderstood.

In East Africa there remains a contemporary quality to the events of the last century and the beginnings of the present one. Time has covered less ground. The mark left by generations of missionaries, traders, and settlers in East Africa is reflected in the bristling cultural nationalism of contemporary politics.

Ethnic memory tends to be particularly strong in compartmentalized societies. In spite of their often close and warm collaboration with one another, the racial communities of Uganda regard one another from within the boundaries of a social existence sustained by differences in manners and morals. This type of relationship between racial and cultural communities worsens the associations between them as contact grows more intense. Events, giving rise to grievance, perpetuate prejudices that appear not dredged up to fit a stereotype, but solidly rooted in day-to-day relationships. They become contemporary sources of a reinforcing anxiety, alive in the arsenal of political conflict.

Moreover, the punctuation marks of history which might strike one community as significant—the battles, diplomatic events, or the raising and lowering of flags over some newly discovered shore—do not convey the same significance to the peoples of other ethnic and cultural background. Far more important to the African community might be the treatment received by a toothless old man in a reed hut by a Swahili servant of a British officer, or the power of surgical instruments, or the impression of external strength exhibited by a small and vulnerable band of European explorers. Indeed, in an account of the first association between Europeans and Africans, if written from an African point of view, these might loom much larger than they appear to us

In spite of many misunderstandings between British and Baganda, some close and fast relationships developed between them. These centered mainly around church activity and education. In contrast to other parts of East and Central Africa, as much liberal understanding, both humanistic and evangelical, as was possible in a colonial context characterized African and European relationships.

There grew up among the British a myth of Buganda as a knightly and feudal nation. Admired were the discipline and the bureaucracy which flourished under a monarchical system of government. The institutions of the Buganda Kingdom appeared in sharp contrast to those of other African nations. So surprised was Bishop Tucker, of the Church Missionary Society, at the complex organization of Buganda that he could not believe it had indigenous origins. Tucker regarded Buganda as the living testimony of the influence of an ancient civilization which was "roughly speaking feudal. The great territorial chiefs owe allegiance to the king as their overlord. Under these again are smaller chiefs, all holding their land on a service tenure, and all alike liable, at any moment, to be called out for military duty."[1]

Here was a system of rights and obligations, of courts and territorial organizations, of higher nobility and a *witenagemot*. There were freemen and serfs. The country was divided into territorial groupings similar to shires; the kingdom was an aggregation of shires (*sazas*). The "church" was older than the state. It had its own councils but functioned in a fashion intimately related to politics. And to make the parallels even more complete, at the time the Europeans arrived the system was changing toward a more classically "Norman" type of feudalism. The king was consolidating supreme authority. As with the Norman kings, huge estates were granted to loyal followers. The holdings were unconsolidated; a powerful chief might find his land scattered in several different areas.

One could, so it seemed, apply to Buganda the description

[1] Alfred R. Tucker (Bishop of Uganda), *Eighteen Years in Uganda and East Africa* (London: Edward Arnold, 1908), Vol. i, p. 86.

used by Stubbs in his discussion of early feudal England, after kingship emerged: "The fabric is crowned by the king: not the supreme lawgiver of Roman ideas, nor the fountain of justice, nor the irresponsible leader, nor the sole and supreme politician, nor the one primary landowner: but the head of the race, the chosen representative of its identity, the successful leader of its enterprises, the guardian of its peace, the president of its assemblies. . . ."[2]

Educated Englishmen arriving in Uganda, whether missionary or military, looked upon the Baganda as having for East Africa the pre-eminent position which England had for Europe. French missionaries, less imbued with "knightly" Victorianism, took a rather dimmer view of the Baganda and were impressed with their "savagery."

The term "feudalism" applied in fact only to a small degree. Present, as we have seen, was the principle of kingship applied in patrimonial fashion to a well-defined political hierarchy of chiefs and followers. Nevertheless, whether or not their views were correct, missionaries and administrators saw in the institutions of the Buganda Kingdom familiar instruments of government. This led to collaboration with the Baganda which, if it lacked intimacy, nevertheless gave character and strength to later administrative policy. The Baganda became a most favored nation.

Buganda was a state geared to war. But war and conquest were not the only occupations. Commerce brought in by Arab traders moved along well-demarcated routes. There were trading depots at way stations inland from the coast. Arab factors carried on a flourishing exchange in slaves, ivory, cloth, and manufactured implements. African chiefs and headmen were paid tribute in return for transit and trading privileges.[3] Trade brought not

---

[2] See W. Stubbs, *Select Charters* (Oxford: Oxford University Press, 1929, 9th ed.), Part 1, p. 13.

Sir John Gray inclines toward the view that clan groupings were independent entities which were gradually merged into a single state. See his review of A. B. Mukwaya's *Land Tenure in Uganda: Present Day Tendencies* (Kampala: East African Studies No. 1), in *Uganda Journal*, Vol. xviii, No. 2, September 1954, pp. 204–205.

[3] Mackay, one of the earliest C.M.S. missionaries, estimated that as a result of trade the Kabaka of Buganda kept a permanent force of about 6,000 men engaged in constant warfare with neighboring peoples in search for slaves. One musket was

only war, but order as well: enough stability was required to make the risk of goods and life worth taking on the part of Arab traders.

The first British explorers saw the beginning of the slave trade in Buganda. They arrived only a few years after the first Arabs had made their way inland to the court of the Kabaka of Buganda, to be met by Kabaka Suna (1832-1857). To the British and French missionaries Arab slavery represented the enemy. Slavery, it was held, was a fundamental feature of Islamic religious belief. Hence political intervention was easily attached to missionary endeavor. By the time Livingstone died in 1873, missionary heroism had almost reached the proportions of a folk culture. "A revolution was set in motion which was to bring a new kind of missionary into Africa and a new and more numerous class of subscribers on to the societies' lists. In missionary circles the talk was no longer of 'perishing heathen,' but of Africans 'suffering' and 'neglected.' Soon it was to be of 'open doors' and 'untouched millions.' "[4]

Two years later H. M. Stanley was in Rubaga, the capital of Mutesa I, Suna's successor, and a marriage between European commercial interests and the missionaries began. Commerce, Christianity, and enlightenment were to attack the religious obscurantism and traffic in human beings conducted by the Arabs. Commerce and Christianity were the epitome of enlightened and progressive thought, embodying as well a lively sympathy for Africans.

The concern with Uganda evolved in the context of extensive missionary efforts along the coast of East Africa. The collaboration of the Sultan of Zanzibar in helping end the trade had been secured. Efforts to rehabilitate freed slaves had already been made. After the famous Stanley letter to the *Daily Telegraph*

---

worth two slaves, one red cloth was worth one slave, and 100 percussion caps were worth one female slave. Kingship, or at least formal chieftaincy, was stimulated by trade and the need for political orderliness. If traders were to find secure trade and transit conditions along the routes to the coast, they needed control and protection. If wealthy tribes like Buganda or Nyamwezi found their income prejudiced because of the disorderliness of adjacent tribal groupings, punitive expeditions would result and hegemony extended over unpoliced areas.

[4] The best discussion of the part played by the missionaries is found in Roland Oliver, *The Missionary Factor in East Africa* (London: Longmans Green, 1952), pp. 34-35.

of November 15, 1875, setting forth the opportunities for Christian endeavor in Uganda, missionary effort in Buganda began in earnest. It was followed by the activities of chartered companies whose zeal and purpose in liberal directions were in the classic tradition of Benthamism and Whiggism. However, among the missionaries and their friends, the merchants, the attitude of warmth was not without condescension. Friendship was in some measure an affection by the British for an African version of themselves, cast in a mould of self-idealized benevolence.

Buganda was known along the East African coast long before excursions into the interior by the Arabs had become common. Stories of a nascent African kingdom, powerful and virile and quite without peer in East Africa, greeted the first British explorers who found their way inland from the coast.

Coastal hegemony by the Arabs of Muscat (based in part on the slave trade), which presumed to extend to the interlacustrine areas, meant little to the people of Uganda. Arabs only reached the interior around 1844. The Europeans followed some fifteen years later. His Highness the Sultan of Zanzibar, Seyyid Majid bin Said, sent a caravan to Buganda in 1869 bearing gifts for the Kabaka of Buganda. Kabaka Mutesa I, anxious to expand trade with the coast, returned the compliment with a gift of ivory.[5] At the time this exchange took place, Buganda under Kabaka Mutesa I was extending its control over neighboring tribal groups. Most of her conquests were at the expense of Bunyoro, the kingdom north of Buganda with which it shared a traditional cultural heritage. Not all of this expansion was by conquest, however. Occasionally there was voluntary affiliation of small states with Buganda for protection, or through intermarriage of princely families.[6]

The first Europeans to enter the country were Captains Speke and Grant who, attempting to trace the headwaters of the Nile, made their way inland from Zanzibar and the coast toward the lake regions of Central Africa. In 1858 Speke discovered the

5 See Sir John Gray, "Sir John Kirk and Mutesa," in *Uganda Journal*, Vol. xv, No. 1, March 1951, pp. 1-2.
6 Koki, one of the counties of Buganda, was obtained in this fashion.

lake which he called Victoria Nyanza; in 1862 he stood at Ripon Falls, the source of the Nile.[7]

The route from the coast was not the only path for entry to Buganda. Sir Samuel Baker, as representative of the Khedive of Egypt, pushed his way southward into Uganda from the Sudan; the Sudan was then under Egyptian dominion. Baker made contact with Kamurasi, the Omukama of Bunyoro. Speke met Baker at Gondokoro. Two routes had been carved into Uganda, from the north and from the east.

Baker became Governor of Equatoria Province for the Khedive and attempted to annex Uganda to Egypt. It was only the first of such attempts.[8]

It was H. M. Stanley, however, who pointed out the fertile field for missionary endeavor among the Baganda. He appealed to the sense of philanthropy and Christian spirit which so widely prevailed in England in the latter half of the nineteenth century. The Church Missionary Society responded to these appeals with an expedition whose most important member, Alexander Mackay, became a key figure in the history of Buganda. Arriving in Buganda in 1878, the Protestant missionaries were soon joined by French Catholics. Thus three groups, Arabs, Catholics, and Protestants, contended for the Kabaka's favor.

[7] See J. H. Speke, *Journal of the Discovery of the Source of the Nile* (London: Blackwood, 1863). Speke's claim to discovery was disputed by others and the controversy aroused by his announcement that the Nile headwaters were at the north end of Lake Victoria left him an embittered man. He died from a hunting accident a day before he was to debate the matter with his chief rival.

[8] Subsequently Gordon, Baker's successor in Equatoria Province, sent an American, Colonel Chaille-Long, to visit Mutesa, the King of Buganda. Mutesa had heard of the treatment received by the Banyoro at the hands of Baker and resolved to keep out of difficulty. Without intending to do so, Mutesa signed a document acknowledging Egyptian suzerainty.

What had made Mutesa nervous was the fact that although Baker had a great reputation as an administrator, especially amongst the Acholi, he had burned the enclosure of Kabarega, Kamurasi's successor as Omukama of Bunyoro-Kitara. This news upset Mutesa considerably. See Sir Samuel Baker, *The Albert Nyanza, Great Basin of the Nile* (London: Macmillan, 1866) and, more important, *Ismailia* (London: Macmillan, 1874). See also Sir John Gray, "Mutesa of Buganda," in *Uganda Journal*, Vol. I, No. 1. Baker's second visit to Bunyoro coincided with a bitter factional dispute between Kabarega, the newly incumbent king of Bunyoro, and a rival. Baker refused to intercede on behalf of Kabarega, causing the latter to entertain bitter antagonism against Europeans. When British penetration began in earnest, the Banyoro resisted and were defeated; as punishment, much of their land was given to Buganda. (See Sir Samuel Baker, *Ismailia*, Vol. 2.)

On the heels of the missionary intervention came the merchants, in the form of the Imperial British East Africa Company. The I.B.E.A.C. was a peculiar body. Identified with philanthropy and service on the one hand and commerce on the other, it was ambiguously the carrier of British overrule, although it did not engage Britain in formal undertakings of colonial acquisition. Responsible for keeping peace and order without formal hegemony, the Company was in perpetual difficulties with the Baganda, the Arabs, and the Christian factions.[9]

The Kabaka came to view the Company's intervention with increasing dismay. News of the struggle between Arabs and Europeans on the coast was particularly disturbing. The Arabs pointed out that British efforts to patrol the coast and reduce coastal slavery had reduced the Sultan of Zanzibar from the role of a powerful Imam with territories reaching along the major part of the Eastern African coast to a petty potentate under British protection.[10] Disturbing as well were the activities of the

[9] The relationship between commerce and missionary effort was quite common. It was a feature of the African Lakes Company whose moving figures, the brothers Moir, were closely identified, at times unpleasantly, with Livingstone. Sir John Kirk, who was for years the most important Foreign Office official on the east coast, the Consul at the court of the Sultan of Zanzibar, was concerned with carrying on the tradition of Livingstone through the agency of the Imperial British East Africa Company. He became one of its directors. Sir William Mackinnon was the leading director. "The Company suffered much more than the others from the divided aims of administration and commerce inherent in these institutions, while some of their directors, notably Sir Fowell Buxton, were more interested in a third aim, that of philanthropy." See M. Perham, *Lugard*, Chapter 10, for an excellent discussion of this period and the Company's activities. Lugard himself, in a passage which recaptures something of the flavor of the times, puts the matter as follows: "If our advent in Africa introduces civilization, peace, and good government, abolishes the slave trade, and effects other advantages for Africa, it must not be therefore supposed that this was our sole and only aim in going there. However greatly such objects may weigh with a large and powerful section of the nation, I do not believe that in these days our national policy is based on motives of philanthropy only. Though these may be our *duties*, it is quite possible that here . . . advantage may run parallel with duty." See Lord Lugard, *The Rise of our East African Empire* (London: Blackwood, 1893), Vol. 1, pp. 381-382.

[10] A distinguished Muganda chief, the late Hamu Mukasa, reported the following story told to Mutesa by the Arabs. "Sir, Kabaka, once upon a time in days of old, there was a Kabaka in another country as wise as you are and as rich and important as you are. A European trader bought a cow and asked the Kabaka for a place where he could peg out the hide to dry. The Kabaka agreed and gave him a place without any suspicion that there was any trap in regard to the place for drying the hide. He just thought 'Let me give him what he asks and let him dry his hide' and gave it to him. The European then killed the cow, flayed it and cut off a very narrow thong equal to ten plantations amounting to 2½ acres. He

missionaries. Gathering around them converts, lay readers, and catechists who were loyal in their support of the missionaries, the latter came to be regarded as "chiefs." Yet as "chiefs" the missionaries owed no allegiance to the Kabaka. The key to the Kiganda system of government was the control over followers by chiefs who were themselves replaceable at the pleasure of the Kabaka. Missionaries, by accumulating followers, came to represent independent sources of power. So long as they employed themselves with strictly religious pursuits and allowed their talents to be used by the king, trouble was kept to a minimum. Mackay, for example, the most talented of the C.M.S. missionaries, was an excellent craftsman and the Kabaka availed himself of his skills. But when the missionaries sought to widen the scope of their authority and to influence the behavior of the king, Mutesa immediately saw the relevance of Arab warnings.

Nor did competition between French Catholic and British Protestant missionaries simplify matters. As Thomas and Scott put it, "Mutesa had much to perplex him. He observed that there was little more cordiality between the two Christian missions than

---

encircled the area thus with this thong, which was similar to the leather thongs which bind a drum head. . . . Then they said to the Kabaka, 'Sir, the European dries his hides by cutting them into thongs and his hide has absorbed the country. Little beginnings have big ends. Sir Kabaka, they are eating up our country.' He answered, 'What are you afraid of,' so they held silent.

"Now when the European said to the Kabaka, 'Sir, my hide has dried and where it reaches, there I have placed my fence within which I will build the house which I will erect. Permit this my lord, what is a little estate of 2 acres, wonderful and august Kabaka, the owner of such a vast country?'" The story goes on to relate how the Kabaka granted this and the European asked for a deed of ownership. When he had received this he began to import horses and cannon and guns which he gave to the Kabaka (the Sultan of Zanzibar) and then the Kabaka had to build a road on which horses and carriages could go. To build roads required labor and taxes. To get taxes and take charge of construction, Europeans were required. Finally the Europeans displaced the old advisors to the Kabaka. The Kabaka gave official status to the Europeans by signing certain papers. The story concludes as follows: "Now when the time arrived all these things were written down in confirmation of what he had agreed to do. When a fish has swallowed the hook, baited with a piece of meat, there is nothing left to do except pull it in: its strength is finished. Such was the agreement whereby the Kabaka agreed to give away his power and his laws, having no authority left whereby he could oppose those to whom he had handed over his powers whereunder they did everything legally. Further, if the Kabaka tried to oppose them in any matter which was displeasing to him they would be able to depose him and install another. . . ." See Hamu Mukasa, "Some Notes on the Reign of Mutesa," *Uganda Journal*, Vol. II, No. 1, July 1934, p. 63. See also R. Coupland, *East Africa and Its Invaders* (Oxford: The Clarendon Press, 1938), *passim*.

had subsisted between the Anglicans and the Arabs, and though Egypt had abandoned direct aggressive action against his kingdom, her troops were still near his frontier. He suspected the complicity of England, Egypt, and the Anglican missionaries, and, learning that the French priests were subjects of a rival political power, deemed it prudent to maintain them as a potential check to English influence."[11] The situation was difficult enough so that the French mission had to withdraw temporarily; in a climate of deteriorating relationships, Mutesa died in 1884.

Two years later in 1886, British and Germans made their first agreement partitioning Africa.

It was in a climate of mutual fears and hostilities that Mutesa's successor, Mwanga, came to rule. Fearful of Egyptian efforts, concerned over the new role of the priests and the missionaries, and upset over the efforts of all to divest him of his power, Mwanga had a difficult task. Impossible as it was to be a responsible Kabaka in the traditions of his immediate predecessors without restoring the vitality of old social institutions, he sought to bring pressure to bear on first one group then another. The French missionaries, who had withdrawn from Buganda, were invited to return, several Protestant readers were burned, and Mwanga's Musoga "governor," Luba, was ordered to kill the newly-arriving bishop James Hannington, the first Anglican bishop to be appointed for Uganda. News of this event, along with word that the brave little band of African readers had been attacked and proscribed by Mwanga, brought a passionate public outburst in England. It was not long before the Catholics received the same treatment and between 1885 and 1887 approximately 20 Catholics and 15 Protestants were martyred.[12]

Mwanga was oppressed by an increasingly stifling pattern of controls by missionaries. In addition to giving advice, they now controlled the selection of pages to the court of the king (these pages normally having been the main group from which chiefs were selected). Control over the chiefs, one of the crucial aspects of Kiganda authority, was slipping from Mwanga's hands.

[11] See H. B. Thomas and R. Scott, *Uganda* (London: Oxford University Press, 1935), p. 19.
[12] For an interesting study of the Uganda martyrs, see J. P. Thoonen, *Black Martyrs* (London: Sheed & Ward, 1941). See also H. B. Thomas, "The Baganda Martyrs, 1885-1887," in *Uganda Journal*, Vol. xv, No. 1, March 1951.

Mwanga was angered by these strong-willed and dogmatic men whose voice was always the voice of authority and whose words were backed by the implied threat of support from beyond the seas. His own behavior had earned him condemnation (the Protestants in particular having disapproved of his personal life). Too many Baganda were learning to read under missionary auspices and had become ardent religionists. A church council had been set up by the Church Missionary Society. Hemmed in on all sides, an object of constant scrutiny and deception, Mwanga was determined to rid himself of all who were not pagans. In April 1888, he tried to destroy Arab, Catholic, and Protestant groups by leaving them on an island where they would starve to death. The readers, refusing to embark in canoes and ignoring the commands of the King, organized a revolution; entirely successful, it resulted in Mwanga fleeing the throne. His elder brother Kiwewa succeeded him, largely at the behest of the Muslims. Kiwewa, who remained a pagan, was deposed and murdered after refusing to accept Islam and become circumcised. Kalema, another son of Mutesa and a half brother to Mwanga, was put on the throne.

It was under such circumstances that in September 1888 the Imperial British East Africa Company received a royal charter from Lord Salisbury's government with instructions to preserve law and order in Buganda.

It was the beginning of the end for the Arabs. At their moment of triumph Mwanga wrote a rather plaintive letter to Mackay of the C.M.S. in June 1889. "After compliments, I, Mwanga, beg of you to help me. Do not remember bygone matters. We are now in a miserable plight, but if you, my fathers, are willing to come and help to restore me to my kingdom, you will be at liberty to do whatever you like.

"Formerly I did not know God, but now I know the religion of Jesus Christ. Consider how Kalema has killed all my brothers and sisters. He has killed my children, too, and now there remains only we two princes (Kalema and myself). Mr. Mackay, do help me. I have no strength, but if you are with me I shall be strong. Sir, do not imagine that if you restore Mwanga to Uganda he will become bad again. If you find me become bad then you may drive me from the throne, but I have given up my former ways and I only want now to follow your advice."[13]

The Christian forces, reorganized under the command of the Protestant general, Apolo Kagwa, successfully attacked Kalema. Islam was defeated by 1890. The first of the religious wars was at an end. The missionaries returned to their work. Mwanga was, once again, Kabaka of Buganda. Mackay described his restoration in the following terms: "It is 1889, and the 12th of October has again come round. On that day of the previous year, the Arabs were the victors and the Christians the vanquished. Now the order is reversed. These same Arabs have had to leave their bones on the same hill-side where many Christians had fallen in the treacherous attack of the year before. With loud and real rejoicing, Mwanga is carried shoulder high from the Lake to his former capital, and is made Kabaka once more. All the posts of authority are occupied by Christians, all the land falls into their hands; even the king himself is no more their despotic master and murderer, but a helpless instrument in their hands."[14]

It was not long before new conflict broke out between the French Catholics and the British Protestants. Mwanga, desperately playing one off against the other, became a Catholic. Pere Lourdel and M. Hirth, the two leading Catholic figures, became Mwanga's advisors during intervals of his allegiance to Catholicism. The Protestants, who had previously had a large hand in the education of Mwanga, were not only chagrined at this, but regarded the Catholics as a group of sinister Frenchmen playing a papist game and willing to go to any lengths to seduce the Baganda to the ways of Catholicism.[15] Behind this dislike for things French was the long history of Anglo-French rivalry in Africa. Anglo-European relations at the time were characterized more by sympathy with Germany than with France.

13 Quoted in Tucker, *op.cit.*, pp. 27-28.
14 See the biography by his sister, *Mackay of Uganda* (London: Hodder and Stoughton, 1890), p. 470.
15 For an account of the war between the Catholic and Protestant factions, and for a recounting of the issues and charges raised by Waddington, the French Minister, Hirth, etc., and their refutation by Lugard, see Africa No. 1 (1893), *Further Papers Relating to Uganda*, in continuation of Africa No. 8 (1892) (London: H.M.S.O., January 1893), C-7708. For maps showing the original outlines of Uganda and sites of missionary activity in 1900, see Africa No. 8 (1900), *Maps Illustrative of the Preliminary Report by Her Majesty's Special Commissioner on the Protectorate of Uganda* (London: H.M.S.O., 1900), C-361.

Catholic pleas to Mwanga for greater freedom were coupled with a demand that more chieftaincies in Buganda be allocated to their side. Since the position of both parties depended in large measure on the chiefs under their respective sectarian banners, it was natural for the Catholics to follow their demands for freedom with the important political consequence of the demand—chieftaincies. And it was precisely this issue on which the Protestants were not prepared to give way.[16]

Nor could the Protestants openly state their fears of the Catholics. They believed that if the Catholics once achieved full power there would be no freedom for the Protestants; but until the Catholics were in such a position, Protestant assertions would have to remain unproved. Hence the ambiguous position of the Protestants. To prevent their downfall at the hands of the Catholics they could rely only on beliefs easily branded as prejudice. Unlike the Catholics, whose religious position did not make a pretense of religious toleration and generosity, the Protestants *were* concerned with freedom—hence their vulnerability to the charges and the sensitivity with which they reacted to the Catholic complaints.

The French Catholic missionaries were no less determined than Mackay, Walker, and the other C.M.S. people to dominate a chastened Mwanga and to challenge the position of the other. So anguished were the French that they sought out Dr. Carl Peters, a German explorer and trading company agent, and induced Mwanga into signing a treaty recognizing the protection of Germany rather than suffering Protestant control backed up by the Company. When news of this effort became public the Protestants were outraged. The leading Protestant Muganda, Apolo Kagwa, the Katikiro, claimed that Mwanga had already accepted the protection of the Imperial British East Africa Company. Although Mwanga had signed the German treaty, he was forced to repudi-

[16] The Catholics implied as well that the British Protestants were aided by Lugard and other members of the Imperial British East Africa Company and charged that they were being used unfairly. Indeed, Lugard had to face charges of favoritism by both sides and of having played an important part in fomenting civil war. From these charges he had considerable difficulty exonerating himself. See, for example, the letter from Hirth to Sir Gerald Portal on the latter's arrival in Uganda, in Africa No. 8 (1893), *op.cit.* For an analysis of the charges and a discussion of Lugard's career see M. Perham, *op.cit.* Lugard's own defense was eloquently put in his book, *The Rise of Our East African Empire* (London: Blackwood, 1893).

ate it by Jackson for the Imperial British East Africa Company.

These and other events spurred the missionaries into ever more intense competition. Each of the two factions sought out any and all uncommitted Baganda to enlist them within one religious camp or the other. Nor were the zealots always British or French. Many effective proselytizers were Baganda.

The main effort of the missionaries was through education. By this means they probed deep into the Kiganda social structure by establishing schools and churches which introduced new foci for intellectual and community life. Mackay laid down the line. An African educational elite was to be created. "Instead of vainly struggling to perpetuate the method of feebly manned stations, each holding precarious existence, and never able at best to exert more than a local influence, let us select a few particularly healthy sites, on which we shall raise an institution for imparting a thorough education, even to only a few."[17] Here was expressed the model for the later pattern of education which resulted in Mengo High School (later King's College, Budo) and St. Mary's College, Kisubi.

Moreover, Baganda became missionaries elsewhere in Uganda. Protestant Baganda went into Ankole to proselytize.[18] The struggle between the two Christian factions was translated quickly from a doctrinal matter, which only confused the Baganda, into a struggle for power, which they well understood. The French or *Ba-Franza* and the English or *Ba-Ingleza* respectively controlled certain chiefs who carried on a struggle among themselves for domination, and the division carried quickly throughout Buganda and into neighboring areas.

This accounts in part for the relative alacrity with which the Baganda accepted one or the other religious position. To remain aloof was to become powerless. The period of Christian endeavor resulted in a revolution in which important features of the traditional Kabakaship, expression of authority, and religious beliefs were swept away. The age-old institution remained to be dis-

17 *Mackay of Uganda*, p. 462.

18 "The Baganda have a peculiar aptitude for teaching. So sanguine am I with regard to this project that I shall be greatly disappointed if within a very few years we do not have not only a large body of native lay evangelists scattered over the land, but also the foundations of a zealous native ministry." Tucker, *op.cit.*, pp. 114-115.

covered afresh by the Baganda at a later period; remodeled, it became a singularly powerful institutional structure sometimes aiding and sometimes impeding social progress and development.

It was not that the traditional ancestor cult, the pattern of pagan worship, was unsophisticated. Tucker referred to it with some admiration as a "degraded" form of Christianity which he believed to have been Egyptian in origin—a belief he held about other attributes of Kiganda culture. But traditional religion suffered from its intrinsic association with the clan system which, losing political ground to chiefs, was declining. Traditional religion also declined, it can be conjectured, providing a religious lacuna quickly filled by Christianity. In turn, Christianity emphasized the secularity of government and provided an individualistic ethic.

Mwanga succumbed to the missionaries and their followers. The missionaries succumbed to the administrators. The British sphere in East Africa was defined in the Anglo-German Agreement of 1890. Uganda, controlled by the Imperial British East Africa Company, saw the arrival of Captain Lugard in Buganda. Summing up that rather crucial year, Oliver says: "During the course of 1890 the British Company's flag became the outward symbol of Protestantism: the Catholic crucifix became the badge of royalist opposition to British power (Mwanga being at that point allied with the Catholic party) ; while northwards, in Bunyoro, the Muslim party gathered their strength for a new invasion, established communication with the Arabs on Lake Tanganyika by a new land route passing to the west of Buddu by which they received large quantities of arms and ammunition."[19]

Lugard's instructions were to deal impartially with all factions, Muslim, Catholic, and Protestant. His most compelling need was a firm treaty with Mwanga. A first effort to obtain such a treaty almost ended in violence. The chiefs of Buganda recognized the awful finality of Mwanga's signature on a document. But they were powerless to prevent the inevitable.[20] The first formal arrangements between the British and the Baganda were marred by the latter's bitterness and reluctance. Lugard himself admitted that the treaty was signed against the Kabaka's will.

[19] Oliver, *op.cit.*, pp. 138-139. See also Tucker, *op.cit.*, Book I.
[20] Mwanga, when the treaty was finally signed, attempted to blot his mark.

Lugard's position was complex. The *Mujasi*, the general of the Kabaka's armies, was a Catholic and close to the French. The Katikiro, Apolo Kagwa, was the most powerful Protestant. Lugard's own forces were small. He had only one European subordinate, regular army officer, Captain Williams. Together they mustered only 275 Swahili and Sudanese carriers and troops. In 1891 the reluctant Christian factions joined forces once again to march under Lugard against Kabarega, the King of Bunyoro, who was allied with the Muslims.

After pacification of the Bunyoro, Lugard turned his attention elsewhere. To the west was an area under Bunyoro hegemony which had at one time been regarded as an independent country. At the urging of Kasagama, the claimant to the kingship of Toro, that country was separated from Bunyoro and established as a separate kingdom. Bunyoro was drastically reduced in size. Many of her districts were occupied by the Baganda, a situation later regularized in the Uganda Agreement of 1900.

Lugard was concerned to extend the control of the Company to territories adjacent to Buganda. He had defeated the Muslims and the Banyoro before proceeding westward. He had restored Kasagama to the kingship of Toro in return for a treaty. He was now concerned with contacting the Sudanese mercenaries who, loyal to the Khedive of Egypt, had come to Equatoria from the Sudan with Emin Pasha and were left behind when Emin was rescued by Stanley. Well-armed and tough from years in the field, the Sudanese under the command of a remarkable officer, Selim Bey, agreed to join forces with Lugard. Lugard thereupon returned to Buganda in a triumph which turned quickly to despair when he was notified of the decision of the directors of the Company to withdraw from Uganda because of expense and uncertainty of the Company's future.[21]

Lugard kept that decision a secret. Meanwhile, the trouble

[21] The Company's decision to pull out of Uganda was based partly on financial considerations, the cost of administration far outweighing the paltry parliamentary grant which it annually received, and with little but a promise of trade to offer to the directors. As well, the Company could see no future in Uganda without an assumption by the British government of heavier responsibilities. Lugard, the Company's representative, was sharply abused by both French and English missionaries and charged with partisanship by both. On his return to England he found himself in even more difficult straits, missionary charges having propelled him into the midst of Liberal politics. His strong actions were under heavy criticism.

brewing for so long a time between the French and English factions finally broke out. The Catholic faction was more successful than the Protestants in evangelizing. The Company now gave effect to an alliance between Lugard and the Protestants which had, at best, been only incipient. In 1892 the Battle of Mengo broke out between the Catholics and the Protestants and the Company stepped in to save the day for the Protestants.

When in 1891 after the Bunyoro campaign Lugard had returned to Mengo to find the message from Sir William Mackinnon, the director of the Company, notifying him of the Company's decision to withdraw, he had decided to ignore the decision. Now he sought to reverse it. The result of his strenuous efforts was an agreement by the Company to maintain its agents in the field for an additional year if Bishop Tucker could find £15,000 to help cover the cost. Tucker was easily successful. He raised £16,500. The year's grace so provided, a campaign was mounted to get the British government to take over Uganda. Lugard himself stumped the country. As well, he wrote a spate of articles on the subject of Uganda. Contributing to his efforts was the Church Missionary Society, which emphasized the philanthropic role of Empire. Using the drama of the Baganda martyrs to inflame public passions, and emphasizing the devotion of the Baganda to Christianity, they found it possible to enlist wide public support for the acquisition of Uganda.

Thus the representative of the Imperial British East Africa Company, the missionaries, and those interested in considerations of imperial politics joined forces and were successful in persuading a reluctant British government that not to add Uganda to the Empire would be the violation of a moral trust. By 1892 the campaign had not only roused the ire of Methodists, trade unionists, and others in the disestablished and evangelical traditions, but by this time, competition among the major European nations for colonial possessions had become pronounced. The Little England position all but disappeared.[22]

With powerful public support and C.M.S. leadership, popular subscriptions reached £40,000. Sir William Mackinnon of the

[22] See the excellent article by Anthony Low, "British Opinion and the Uganda Question: October-December 1892," in the *Uganda Journal*, Vol. XVIII, No. 2, September 1954.

Company countermanded the evacuation order and the Company stayed.[23]

Meanwhile in England, Salisbury, long a thorn in the side of Lugard on the Uganda question, was defeated in the general election of July 1892. Now the question became more openly one of official government action. Lord Rosebery, the Foreign Secretary in the new government, thereupon sent Sir Gerald Portal, H.B.M. Counsel-General in East Africa, to investigate the situation in Uganda.

In Buganda chiefs and missionaries uneasily awaited the arrival of Sir Gerald Portal, whose mission it was to report to the British government on the desirability of setting up a British Protectorate. The C.M.S. missionaries fully expected that matters were coming to a head in their favor. They were quite right. Portal, as they had expected, understood the desirability of establishing at least interim imperial control until a final review of policy would bring the formal establishment of a Protectorate. Portal made it his first object to effect a settlement between the French and British. After accomplishing a settlement he made a firm treaty with a most reluctant Kabaka.[24] He then decided to haul down the flag of the Imperial British East Africa Company and run up the British flag.[25] It was a gesture that few but the Protestants were happy about. Despite the fact that this did not mean that the official decision to declare Uganda a Protectorate

23 For contrasting views of Lugard's activities in Buganda, especially those leading up to the Battle of Mengo, see Oliver, "Some Factors in the British Occupation of East Africa, 1884-1894," in the *Uganda Journal*, Vol. xv, No. 1, March 1951, *passim*; and Perham, *op.cit.*, Vol. i.

24 The Baganda tend to ignore the immediate context in which the Agreements of 1894 and 1900 were signed. They find it expedient to forget items such as the Provisional Agreement of May 29, 1893, which includes items such as Article 9: "I, Mwanga, fully recognize that the protection of Great Britain entails the complete recognition by myself, my Government, and my people, throughout my Kingdom of Uganda and its dependencies, of all and every international act and obligation to which Great Britain may be a party, as binding upon myself, my successors, and my said Government and people to such extent and in such manner as may be prescribed by Her Majesty's Government."

25 Although Portal set up, in Oliver's words, a "provisional" regime, it was not until June 13, 1895 that Parliament voted £50,000, the balance necessary for a £250,000 compensation to the Company for the £538,000 which it had spent in trying to administer the East African territories. The bulk of the sum turned over to the Company had been deposited with the British Treasury when the German government bought out certain East African coastal claims of Sultan Barghash of Zanzibar. See Oliver, *op.cit.*, p. 63.

had been taken (this would come later), it was with a sense of relief and of the action's ultimate irreversibility that the English missionaries heard of the decision.[26] For them the hard campaign against the Company, the French, the Catholic Baganda, the Arabs, had been rewarded. Mwanga, beset by missionary advisers on all sides and confounded by his own chiefs, wondered at the consequences of signing a treaty. Catholics, chagrined but resigned, settled down to the longer struggle for supremacy—a struggle which would involve generations.

Laconic, and in a sense foreboding, was the entry in Portal's diary for the day so fateful to the Baganda and the others. "12 o'clock—Hauled down Company's flag and hoisted Union Jack. Guards of honor and royal salute. King sent me to ask for a flag like this; told him he could not have it."[27]

Portal departed from Uganda with a sense of accomplishment. Yet in a real sense he had not dealt with the Baganda at all. He had dealt with the missionaries. The key figures in the treaty and settlement were Hirth for the French faction and Tucker for the British. After days of negotiation Tucker wrote: "At length, on April 19th, I called the chiefs together and placed before them the draft treaty which had been prepared by Sir Gerald Portal. I explained all its provisions. . . . 'This treaty,' I said, 'is between the king and chiefs of Uganda and the British Government. The French Bishop does not sign it, neither do I. . . .' With this explanation they were satisfied. We then knelt in prayer (we were assembled in my house) and asked God's blessing upon what was about to be done. . . . Then rising from our knees the treaty was signed, and henceforth the Katikiro and Bangareza (Protestant) chiefs were committed to a policy of conciliation and peace."[28]

---

[26] See Tucker, *op.cit.*, Vol. I, Chapter 20.

[27] Sir Gerald Portal, *The British Mission to Uganda* (London: Edward Arnold, 1894), p. 219. There was to be much ado about the flag on subsequent occasions. The Baganda, acutely conscious of symbolism, desired their own flag. This was refused them and they were required to fly the Union Jack. This was not viewed with very great favor among the Baganda.

[28] Something of the anomalousness of the situation struck Bishop Tucker. He wondered whether the history of diplomacy had ever known such a treaty. Well aware of its drama, for him the scene was "the heart of savage Africa, A Missionary's house; the actors, the Missionary Bishop, the gathered chiefs . . . now having been brought out of darkness. . . ." Tucker was in raptures over the occasion because only the day previous to signing the treaty, 40 of the Protestant chiefs brought him a statement signifying their intention to give up their slaves.

Portal had recommended that the Imperial government give more permanent effect to his interim arrangements in Buganda. This was now easily accomplished. A new treaty was signed with the Baganda in 1894; Colonel Colville, who obtained the settlement, was made the new commissioner and occupied himself with pacifying the rest of Uganda.

For a short time, as long as the pacification of the rest of Uganda was involved, the Baganda remained enthusiastic allies of the British. The downfall of Bunyoro was received by them with particular gratitude and the reward for the use of Baganda levies in the campaign was the assignment to Buganda of five and a half Bunyoro counties which were incorporated into the Buganda Kingdom by the 1900 British-Baganda Agreement.

But even the prospect of an enlarged Buganda Kingdom could not for long make up for the blows which the Baganda had suffered in their internal structure. Competitive proselytization proceeding rapidly brought Catholics and Protestants into continuous conflict, and the Baganda were still riven by religious conflict. Among the C.M.S. alone, for example, there were 725 African evangelists in 1896 whose efforts throughout the country had resulted in some 60,000 readers under Christian instruction.[29]

Competition between French and British missionaries for the effective control of the Kabaka and his court did not end with the establishment of the Protectorate. Increasingly, Mwanga's personal life became an object of attack; whichever faction was temporarily out of favor tried strenuously to make him politically unimportant and impotent. Politically, the Protestants were clearly ascendant. Apolo Kagwa, a devout Protestant, was the Katikiro. However, the *Mujasi* or commander-in-chief of the Kabaka's armies remained a Catholic. These powerful contemporaries

---

He felt his measure of reward and achievement was indeed full. (Tucker, *op.cit.*, p. 270.)

A fine contrast in interpretation of this act is provided by Portal's notation in his diary: "A paper given me signed by 40 Protestant chiefs saying they had determined to follow 'coast custom' and free all slaves. This seems suspicious, also rather too radical, as throwing thousands of people free at once. It would make it impossible at first to get any work done by any one, and it is perhaps only a pretext to avoid work on roads, etc., by pleading as excuse no slaves." The missionary view and the official view of the same act had very different meanings. (See Portal, *op.cit.*, p. 227.)

[29] See Tucker, Vol. II, pp. 76-77.

brought religious conflict directly into the king's household.

Visibly suffering, the Baganda nevertheless remained committed Christians, driven by the implacable exclusiveness of their respective faiths and missionary leaders. The stern, soul-searching Calvinism of such churchmen as Mackay produced a strength of will and sacrifice which made a virtue out of strife and trouble, while the more worldly but equally persistent fathers of the church militant grimly set about the task of waiting for the time that would be on their side.

Meanwhile, persistent and intermittent troubles plagued the new Protectorate government. In 1897 Sudanese soldiers revolted, and for a time missionaries and administrators alike were seriously imperiled. Behind the mutiny were the remnants of Arab and Muslim influence, and only the loyalty of Baganda levies kept the mutiny from being successful.[30]

The vulnerability of the missionaries and the small force of British administrators suddenly became apparent to both Mwanga and Kabarega, the Bunyoro king. Islam, instead of a spent force, became in the hands of the Sudanese a weapon of African unity against the British. It appeared to Mwanga that he at last had found a way out of his troubles. Mwanga revolted and fled from his palace to the county of Buddu. There, with his Mujasi and several other important chiefs, he prepared his last campaign. A medical missionary wrote at the time that "nearly all the police have deserted us. They went off with guns last night to join Mwanga." The Katikiro, remaining loyal to his Protestant mentors, observed that the people hated and detested the conquerors. "The king hates the Europeans because they stopped his gross immoralities. The chiefs hate us because a Christian is expected only to have one wife and because no slaves are allowed; and the people hate us because they say they are obligated to carry loads, and to make roads . . . and because the old heathen customs are dying away."

The struggle made it apparent that as long as the king was himself an object of control there would be conflicts. The system

---

[30] See J. V. Wild, *The Uganda Mutiny 1897* (London: Macmillan and Co., 1954). The Sudanese, it will be recalled, had been employed in the Sudan by Emin Pasha. Left behind by Emin, they remained under the leadership of Selim Bey, whom Lugard brought into Toro, and many of whose followers were recruited into the Uganda Rifles. The Sudanese constituted the only regular forces in Uganda.

of Kabakaship in Buganda would not easily admit overrule. The social autonomy and political structures of the nation were intimately bound up with the devoted service which each person gave to the Kabaka. If the system were to be maintained at all, it would be necessary that the large-scale social adjustments required after missionary and administrative intervention be carried out without bringing the Kabakaship into controversy.

We shall discuss the role of the Kabaka in the political system of Buganda in a subsequent chapter. Here it is important to note that the effect of Mwanga's rebellion strengthened rather than diminished the institution of the Kabakaship by removing it, temporarily, from politics. Gathering his chiefs around him, Mwanga first established himself in Buddu. A battle followed in which the Baganda levies loyal to the authorities were successful. Mwanga was defeated and fled into German territory. He then made common cause with Kabarega, the Omukama of Bunyoro, and the two fled to Lango. They were able to remain at large until 1899 when, due to the efforts of several of the Baganda leaders, notably Andereya, the Kimbugwe, and Semei Kakunguru, one of the most important Protestant chiefs, in collaboration with Indian troops, both Kabarega and Mwanga were caught and the remaining Sudanese mutineers defeated.

Mwanga's son, the infant Daudi Chwa, was placed upon the throne. The government of Buganda was placed in the hands of three Regents, Apolo Kagwa, the Protestant Katikiro, Zakaria Kizito Kisingiri, the Protestant Kangawo, and Stanislaus Mugwanya, the Catholic Katikiro. Twelve of Mwanga's chiefs, of whom all but one were Catholics, were proscribed. For the first time the Protestants were clearly ascendant all around. The Catholics, having been compromised by their support of Mwanga, could no longer prevent a working alliance of senior chiefs, British missionaries, and administrators. As if to demonstrate that Providence was on the side of the Protestant missionaries, Sir Harry Johnston, the newly appointed Special Commissioner, arrived in December 1899 with plans to reorganize the affairs of Uganda and establish settled administration.

In reviewing the events which led to the establishment of the Protectorate, an observer cannot help being struck by the contemporary quality of events long passed. Many of the grievances voiced today were first heard as the missionaries became troublesome features of the political landscape in Buganda. They came on the invitation of Mutesa and before long had engineered the downfall of the kingdom. The Protectorate regime was established under duress, Mwanga having been forced to acquiesce. The people were divided by alien religious and political controversies which were transported to Uganda with disastrous results. The glory of king and state was dismantled by the thundering conviction of the missionaries that theirs was a rightful course, regardless of the consequences.[31]

It was Johnston who engaged the Baganda in the Uganda Agreement of 1900, a document so fundamental to the relationship of the Buganda and Protectorate governments that it has taken on the proportions of a constitutional instrument. Of such consequence was the 1900 Agreement that, before we go on to discuss its effects, it is necessary to examine the traditional society of Buganda. How Buganda adapted, in part through the mechanism of the 1900 Agreement, is central to our analysis.[32] It marks the end of the pioneering phase and the beginning of political administration.

[31] The best account of the work of Sir Harry Johnston and the establishment of settled administration is to be found in Low and Pratt, *Buganda and British Overrule* (London: Oxford University Press, 1960), Part I.

[32] Although called the Uganda Agreement, the terms and conditions were applicable only to Buganda. It was an Agreement between Sir Harry Johnston and the Kabaka of Buganda.

CHAPTER 4

THE TRADITIONAL SETTING:
CONCEPTS AND HYPOTHESES

IN CONCLUDING his volume on social structure, the late Professor Nadel remarked that it seems impossible to speak of social structure in the singular. Analysis in terms of structure "is incapable of presenting whole societies; nor, which means the same, can any society be said to exhibit an embracing coherent structure as we understand the term. There are always cleavages, dissociations, enclaves, so that any description alleged to present a single structure will in fact present only a fragmentary or one-sided picture."[1]

Perhaps this is the reason why traditional societies are so often presented as if they were static and fragile entities bound by iron-clad custom and limited by immobilities of space, landscape, and ideas. Indeed, the term *traditional* has come to imply a stiff cultural system, imprisoned in the past.

The case of Buganda, although perhaps not typical of traditional societies, nevertheless throws considerable light on the dynamic aspects of traditionalism. Obviously some traditional ethnic groups have shown greater flexibility than others. Here we attempt to indicate some of the factors which make traditional societies differ from one another with respect to change.

The history of all African ethnic groups shows a steady pattern of innovation and adaptation; responses to stimuli differ, of course, depending on the groups' beliefs and social structures. The creation of new forms of authority suits the environment and needs of each ethnic group. In suggesting a highly general model for the analysis of traditional authority, we hope to deal in abstract with the processes of traditional change in African history—a subject still to be concretely explored. Davidson asks: "What motives inspired this forming and re-forming of tribes and tribal groups—sometimes of disparate elements, of men and women from

[1] S. F. Nadel, *The Theory of Social Structure* (Glencoe: The Free Press, 1957), p. 153.

other tribes . . . ?" He finds his answer in an exploration of African history.[2]

While it is not our purpose to delve into the mysteries of African history, we should affirm that generalized analytical statements about traditional societies must, like all general categories, be solidly rooted in particular facts. We can only show here how the "general" in the "particular" helps us understand the traditionalism of Buganda in its contemporary political role. Until we know much more about the history of Africa's cultural and structural development, such formulations as ours can remain only suggestive. We offer more than mere sets of logical categories, but we recognize the need for arduous examination and testing of our suggestions.

Bearing in mind the tentativeness of our approach, and emphasizing that our purpose is not historiography, we can distinguish two basic types of values and two types of traditional authority systems in Africa. The value distinction, common in contemporary sociology, refers to differences in the relationship of means to ends with which different societies approach their problems. We refer here to the broad distinction between those systems having *consummatory* values and those having *instrumental* values. An illustrative question might help to put these in perspective. To determine which category a system falls into, we want to know whether or not means and ends are so closely linked that modifying means will substantially alter the acceptance of ends themselves. For example, will changing from a short-handled hoe to a tractor so corrupt the ritual of the hoe makers, the tillers, the pattern of woman's as compared with man's work, as to challenge religious beliefs and social propriety; or will the introduction of the tractor simply make it easier to grow a particular crop? In the first instance the tractor is a dire threat. In the second it becomes a desirable means to attain already determined ends.

The second distinction to which we referred above relates to structure. Efforts to distinguish structural types begin with the broad classification in Fortes and Evans-Pritchard, *African Political Systems*. The authors pointed out the difference between

[2] Basil Davidson, *Old Africa Rediscovered* (London: Victor Gollancz, Ltd., 1960), p. 36. See also E. W. Bovill, *The Golden Trade of the Moors* (London: Oxford University Press, 1958), *passim*.

systems with differentiated political structures and those in which political functions are widely distributed through the kinship organizations. Those with centralized authority are called primitive states. Those without such authority are called stateless. In the first, kinship plays a more subordinate role than in the second, and the regulation of relationships is determined by administrative organization. In the second, segmentary lineage regulates political relations.[3]

Dealing with authority systems of the more politically differentiated types, Southall has recently introduced a new dichotomy. We shall make considerable use of his distinctions which rest on a dichotomy between *pyramidal* and *hierarchical* systems of authority. Southall considers the former type of structure more proximate to the segmentary to which Fortes and Evans-Pritchard refer. There is more diffuse distribution of power, although it remains vertical. "The important point about powers exercised in this way is that they are virtually of the same type at the several different levels of the pyramidal segmentary structure."[4] This is in sharp distinction to those hierarchical systems where similar powers are not articulated throughout the various levels of the system, but inhere at the top.

Hierarchical chieftaincy was typically geared for war. Found in "imperial" states, it had characteristically a system of taxation and revenue coterminous with authority. Vertical patterns of communications and deference provided a basis for giving orders with fewer impediments than in those systems with segmentary or pyramidal structures.

Under the pyramidal system, legitimacy obtained at each segmentary level. Built into the situation was considerable local autonomy. This is in sharp contrast to the hierarchical system where legitimacy inhered in a king or chief. Pyramidal systems tended to have consummatory value systems. Diffused throughout their network of roles and social activities was the close identification of means and ends. They tended to have more complex patterns of checks and balances and, as was the case of Ashanti, when threatened by war they had to alter their structure and

[3] See M. Fortes and E. E. Evans-Pritchard, *African Political Systems* (Oxford: Oxford University Press, 1940), pp. 5-6.
[4] Aidan Southall, *Alur Society* (Cambridge: Heffer, 1956), pp. 250-251.

shift over to the hierarchical type if they were to survive. Thus in Ashanti the various elements in the authority pyramid, independent and relatively autonomous on a political level, became subordinate elements in the armies of the Asantehene so that one chief became a leader of the right wing, another of the left, and so on, while the stages of the pyramid became rankings of subordinacy.[5]

In contrast, the hierarchical systems made no distinction between social and military organization. As in the case of Buganda, these had a system in which chiefs reflected delegations of authority in their favor but had none in their own right. Although political groupings were territorial, they did not become solidary associations with independent attachments to local figures. The relationship of the citizen was to his king. The relationship to the chief depended on the latter's position as king's lieutenant.

The pyramidal and consummatory combination was an extremely subtle integration of religious and social ties which, easily frangible, was less adapted to change than the hierarchical and instrumental type. The hierarchical and instrumental type, based upon a traditional bureaucracy and autocratic kingship, was more amenable to change, modernization, and social development, absorbing the consequences of such change so as to strengthen, not weaken, the system.

Thus although both systems show political specialization, in sharp contrast to the "stateless" or "segmentary" type, the *hierarchical and instrumental is capable of serving as a modernizing autocracy.*[6]

[5] See R. Rattray, *Ashanti Law and Constitution* (London: Oxford University Press, 1929), *passim*.

[6] To further clarify these distinctions we can take the example of the Ashanti in Ghana, which is of the pyramidal and consummatory type. Ashanti is in that sense the very opposite of contemporary secular societies. Means and ends are closely tied together. To gather the yams is not only an economic act in Ashanti, but a ceremony of fruition, expressing gratitude to gods and ancestors. Conduct is constantly scrutinized by ancestors. At the pinnacle of the hierarchy is the *omanhene* or divisional chief. Independent in his sphere of authority, he is nevertheless hedged in by restrictions. His is a religious role, symbolized by lineage relationships to ancestors, and only members of a founder's or royal lineage are eligible to be elected to chieftaincy. Below the *omanhene* are various village chiefs and headmen. These too are elected in like fashion from eligible lineages and are supreme in their spheres.

This society is in a broad sense consummatory. That is to say, the values associated with daily activity and the acts taken as a means to rendering those values satis-

A given type of traditional system (or combinations thereof in a territorial area) has marked affinities for adaptation to a given form of central government type.

---

fied are strongly ritualized and meaningful in and of themselves. The entire system, one could argue, is in the religious mode. In the introduction to his volume, *The Ancient City*, Fustel de Coulanges writes of Greece and Rome that their history is a witness and an example of the intimate relations which always exist between men's ideas and their social state. Examining their institutions without a knowledge of their religious notions leaves them "obscure, whimsical, and inexplicable." He goes on to say that "a comparison of beliefs and laws shows that a primitive religion constituted the Greek and Roman family, established marriage and paternal authority, fixed the order of relationship, and consecrated the right of property, and the right of inheritance. This same religion, after having enlarged and extended the family, formed a still larger association, the city, and reigned in that as it had reigned in the family. From it came all the institutions, as well as all the private laws, of the ancients. It was from this that the city received all its principles, its rules, its usages, and its magistracies." See Fustel de Coulanges, *The Ancient City* (New York: Doubleday Anchor Books, n.d., originally published in 1864), p. 13.

Most of these remarks are applicable to Ashanti. There, the emphasis on the religious mode links all social activities. There is the emphasis upon solidary and corporate groupings, the family writ large, which amalgamates increasingly larger sections of the population, emerging in the urban congeries of kinship and semi-kinship groupings of the Athenian or Roman city. There are subtle patterns of restraint on personal behavior and on rulership as well.

All of these features are in strong contrast to the hierarchical and instrumental system of Buganda, for example, which has few solidary groupings. The nuclear family plus some relatives is perhaps the most solidary unit, with a highly generalized sense of citizenship through the kingdom for all its members, united in their support of the Kabaka. There is no effort to live in towns or urban conglomerations, and indeed these are abhorred. Participation in politics is not marred by caste or aristocratic elements.

In terms of contemporary adaptation to modern institutions, the Ashanti show a great deal of resistance to political changes. Not only did they fight several campaigns against British authorities, but more important, they tried to cope, unsuccessfully, with the introduction of new ideas and new values which worked like a yeast in Ashanti. The result was that Ashanti tended to fracture along well-established lines. Conflict between urban and rural, youth and age, politicians and chiefs, all showed themselves in a generational antagonism, occupational competition, and a power conflict. The same people who took a side on one of these conflicts took the same side on all the others. This produced a deep gulf in the society between those out to "modernize" and those out to "preserve."

The religious aspect of traditional political and social structure in Ashanti was important in maintaining the network of suitable restraints on behavior. These were easily disrupted by innovation. Disruptions involved religious problems, with attitudes toward chiefs, elders, brothers, and ancestors all intertwined. To break with tradition thus meant guilt, anxiety, and erratic behavior. Those who broke away also shattered lineage eligibility as a guide to political recruitment. Wealth or occupation became increasingly important, with deep internal conflict produced as a consequence in the society. The rural Ashanti young man leaving his village had to enter into a new solidary grouping in which the old criteria and the old religious sanctions did not apply, but in which the warmth and intimacy of association with others was not destroyed. Hence the political party served as a new

Southall's dichotomy, while an improvement over that offered by Fortes and Evans-Pritchard, suffers from some of the same defects. Moreover, the truly dichotomous quality of the distinctions is less clear in Southall than in Fortes and Evans-Pritchard. For example, there is some hierarchy in the pyramidal type. Bearing these deficiencies in mind, and with the further qualifications that the expansion of typologies is itself of only limited theoretical value, we can advance the following set of authority types and value types.[7]

This scheme gives us four types. For the authority systems having instrumental values the major types are IA and IB. For those having consummatory values they are IIA and IIB.

Recognizing the limitations inherent in this approach (which even at this level needs considerable refinement), we find that for a long period of time Buganda was undergoing a transition from a pyramidal-consummatory system (IIB). The clan system was declining. In its place, over a period of about 100 years, a system of autocratic kingship and a client chieftaincy system grew up. Thus when the Europeans arrived, the system of rule in Buganda was predominantly hierarchical-instrumental (IA).

---

solidary affiliation. Indeed, some of the "toughest" of the politicians in Ghana are Ashanti who have "left home" to find their way into the Convention People's Party. The party thus became the modern answer to modifying social structure. It was the useful and successful alternative to tradition—but it could not compromise with it. The people in effect chose sides, and those who opted for participation in the party did not easily return to custom.

In very sharp contrast, the hierarchical-instrumental systems, serving as adaptive mechanisms themselves, simply meant that the sights for the kingdom be set on the new tasks that lay ahead. In this immediate sense, the traditional system in Buganda could become more modern in its objectives and its procedures, as part of its own evolving tradition, up to that point where the keystone in the arch of authority, i.e. the Kabaka, was tinkered with. Once that occurred the reactions became more complex. The system was unable to react simply as an adaptable mechanism of discipline and authority.

We shall show that almost every major crisis in Buganda is associated with an attempt to tamper with the position of the Kabaka. The conflicts which we will examine in the study are mostly involved in some effort to modify the position of the Kabaka. The nationalism of Buganda, in strong contrast to the highly secular but highly emotional mass party politics in Ashanti, remains narrow, ethnic, and xenophobic, concerned with restoring to the Kabaka his power and privileges.

[7] Typological analysis is regarded here as probably the most primitive form of scientific work. Wanted, of course, are more abstract models of political behavior of which the traditional systems become empirical cases. In the absence of models which are more than modifications of ideal types and which constitute little in the way of a theoretical advance, we shall simply expand the structural dimensions offered by Fortes and Evans-Pritchard and Southall.

TABLE 1

Typology of Traditional Systems

	Authority Type*	
VALUE TYPE	A. Hierarchical	B. Pyramidal
I. Instrumental	(IA)	(IB)
II. Consummatory	(IIA)	(IIB)

* Although it remains outside the scope of the discussion here, a third authority type, the segmentary system, suggests hypotheses. For example, in segmentary coalition types with instrumental values, we would expect to find atomistic political behavior, separatist church movements, and aggressive forms of political organization in contemporary politics. Among the tribal groups which follow this description are the Kikuyu in Kenya and the Ibo in Eastern Nigeria. On the other hand, there is some reason to suspect that some rural village communities in India are of the segmentary-consummatory type retaining a high degree of structural solidarity while furthering the development of community life. On this latter score, see McKim Marriott, ed., *Village India: Studies in the Little Community* (Chicago: University of Chicago Press, 1955), *passim*.

The reforms introduced by the missionaries and early administrators in Buganda resulted in a modification of the traditional system, but they did not need to change either the values inherent in the system or the principle of kingship, particularly after Mwanga was deposed and the infant, Daudi Chwa, put in his place. The principle of autocratic kingship, then, did not interfere with the practical affairs of Buganda. Reforms resulted not in a major type change but in the establishment of a bureaucratic system. Chiefs were still appointed in the name of the Kabaka, only now they were civil servants.

Conflict in a shift in major type is necessarily very intense. In Buganda the change from clanship to chieftaincy was a major change in the system, involving a replacement of values of the type II variety (consummatory) by type I (instrumental), and changing the system of authority from (B) pyramidal to (A) hierarchical. The theory is that any shift from one major system type to another produces great conflict because the principle of legitimacy and the structure of values embodied in each type become quite altered and are opposed to one another in principle.[8]

[8] In this scheme, Ashanti represented type (IIB), although we shall continue to refer to it under the more general rubric of a pyramidal system. One of the consequences of early nationalism in Ghana, especially in the interwar period, and the

If our theory is correct, the tentative hypothesis which emerges is this: types of systems with consummatory values (type II) will be the most difficult to integrate into a contemporary political framework without causing grave internal disruptions. Those systems having instrumental values (type I) are capable of separating means and ends. The prospects for a parliamentary form of government with a federal structure are best with IA or IB types. If the IA system is extremely powerful, it will prefer either the parliamentary unitary form as cabinet dictatorship or a frank form of autocracy or oligarchy as the mechanism for central government.[9]

We shall now proceed to a closer analysis of Uganda, considering the two major types of traditional system on the scene, the hierarchical and the pyramidal.

Pyramidal and Hierarchical Authority in Uganda

Pyramidal systems are represented by the Acholi, the Lango, the Alur. Hierarchical systems include the Baganda, although aspects of an earlier, more pyramidal system are retained in the clan structure.

A subtype can be found in Ankole, where a Hima aristocracy had buttressed its authority by ethnic exclusiveness and produced a "class" system, that is, Hima and Bairu. The myth of origin is that a Hima ruler came from "somewhere," and was associated with cattle-owning[10]. In Buganda, while there is a well-defined status hierarchy based largely on political power, there has not

---

economic development of a prosperous cash crop economy based on cocoa, was a shift from consummatory to instrumental values. However, the very grave conflict produced by this was reflected in the fights which occurred over the principles of recruitment; that is, lineage eligibility as distinct from more universalistic criteria, such as training and ability, helped to create a rupture in the society. Here the source of conflict was not system type but value type.

[9] The prospects for a unitary government under representative and parliamentary mechanisms would be greatest with the Ibo and the Kikuyu, for example. The prospects for a parliamentary-federal system would be greatest with the Baganda. The Ashanti, having a consummatory value system, have helped to produce their own opposition in the larger setting of Ghana, which, in its attacks on chieftaincy and traditional systems, has become increasingly autocratic.

[10] Traditionally, the *Omugabe* or king of Ankole was said to have owned all the cattle in the country while the chiefs tended them. The rank of the chief depended upon the number of cattle for which he was responsible, as well as upon territoriality. This system did not prevail in Buganda. The cattle have some symbolic value and the king's herds produce prestige as well as milk.

been a "class" system whose boundaries, difficult to cross, might have inhibited social mobility by political means.

We can diagram these two types of authority, pyramidal and hierarchical. Then, in order to examine the kinds of conflicts and political groupings which emerged, we can indicate the way in which the pyramidal hierarchy integrates with the larger social system.

The simplest form of pyramidal system is as follows:

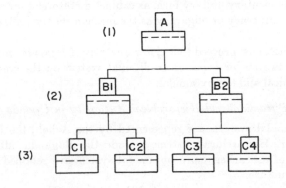

Diagram A

Each of the levels represents particular segmental groupings organized on kinship lines. Segments may conflict with one another, join in alliances with one another, and share in common activity, depending upon the rules and the task at hand. Migration of segments or absorption of one segment by another is common, as is the case among the Bagisu and others in Uganda. At each level there is a chief or some collective equivalent. In its extreme form of collective leadership the combination of functions common to chieftaincy may be dispersed throughout the clan, especially if the patterns of authority are manifested in age grading systems.

In Uganda, at any rate, some form of chieftaincy is common in all such pyramidal type systems, although in some instances the form is fairly rudimentary. At each segment the powers of the chief, or their equivalent, are more or less identical; the levels of the pyramid are based upon historical seniority which may, under certain circumstances, allow or require intervention of a senior into the affairs of a junior segment. Rules of combination of segments are relatively precise.

In a sense the "family" image prevails. The chief is linked to his clan on lineage grounds and lineage is normally based on descent from a mystical ancestor whence legitimacy is derived. Hence blood lines and eligibility to positions are fundamentally intertwined.

Such systems are normally highly consultative. While in some, such as the Ashanti, pockets of "autocracy" may be allowed to the chieftaincy role, these are relatively circumscribed and help serve to shore up the symbolic position of the chief.

In an important variant of this system, the levels of segments and chiefs assume hierarchical characteristics when organized for war. If the chiefs take their place in some prearranged military formation with patterns of subordinacy and superordinacy, then, as in the case of the Ashanti or the Yoruba, some hierarchical principle of paramountcy prevails.

The simplest form of hierarchical system can be designated as follows:

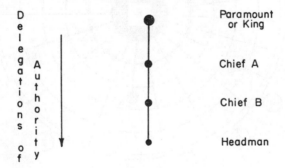

Diagram B

Here the top figure is the paramount or king. He combines in his role symbolic, integrational, ethnic, and other functions.[11]

[11] For a more detailed discussion of the functional requisites of chieftaincy, see my book, *The Gold Coast in Transition* (Princeton: Princeton University Press, 1955), *passim*.

Subordinate chiefs have power at the king's pleasure and normally they administer territorial units within the kingdom. Such systems usually have a problem in gathering information and have councils which serve such purposes, but in no sense can the councils be regarded as "legislative" bodies.

Chiefs then have delegated authority in the hierarchical systems and normally administrative titles of rank which indicate patterns of subordinacy with great clarity. The hierarchical pattern of chieftaincy in Buganda can be viewed as follows:

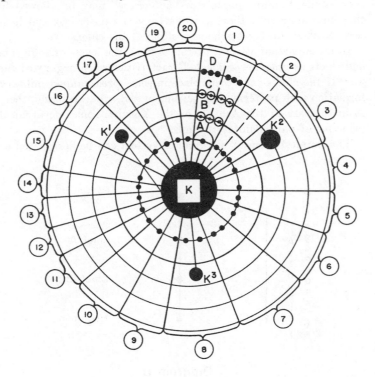

Diagram C

Hierarchical Authority in Buganda

The circle in Diagram C represents a territorial area demarcated by territorial subunits. The diagram shows 20 such units, because in Buganda there are 20 *sazas* (counties) in the country. Of varying size, each saza is composed of lower ranking units, *gombolola* (subcounty), *miruka* (parish), and even a lower level not properly part of the present-day civil service system but of major importance in the basic governing of local areas. At this bottom level, chiefs are called *Batongole*.

Each chief holds administrative responsibilities and today can be promoted, demoted, transferred, and retired, although originally nothing like such stable tenure applied to the role. At the pleasure of the Kabaka, chiefs could be removed from office and shifted around in various positions of responsibility, but the differentiation between chiefs was a good deal more vague than now. There were *Bakungu* chiefs and *Batongole* chiefs, the former being generally more important than the latter. The most important of the Bakungu chiefs were in effect the governors of those provinces which today are counties of the Kingdom of Buganda. Others were the *Katikiro* or prime minister, who at one time was also commander-in-chief of the armies; the *Mujasi*,[12] who became the general of the armies; the *Gabunga* or admiral, who was also a *mutaka* of the Lungfish clan; and the *Kimbugwe*, a household figure whose nominal responsibility was to take charge of the king's umbilical cord—an object of great religious veneration in customary practice.[13]

In the diagram, then, 20 saza chiefs are designated in the A circle, one in each saza. In saza 1, the more elaborate hierarchy of chieftaincy is indicated; this hierarchy is consistently maintained in all the sazas. There are some exceptions to the general rule of appointive chieftaincy. The saza chiefs of Busuju and Butambala were until recently hereditary chiefs. Saza Chief Mugema of

[12] The Mujasi was first established by Kabaka Mutesa I when the practice was initiated of having a standing army.

[13] When the Uganda Agreement of 1900 was signed, the number of sazas was increased from the traditional ten to double that number by the incorporation of new areas from Bunyoro and elsewhere. This increased the number of senior chiefs and gave others, like the Kimbugwe, a saza over which to rule rather than relying on estates going with a household position which in effect ended with the rule of Mutesa I. Along with the Queen and the Katikiro, the Kimbugwe was called "king" because he paid no tribute. The Kimbugwe was a favorite of the king and had ready access to him. The Kimbugwe had large estates. Like the Kago and the Sabaganzi, the Kimbugwe went out of office on the king's death, although he still held claim to the title. See John Roscoe, *The Baganda* (London: Macmillan, 1911), p. 235.

Busiro was both an hereditary chief and an hereditary clan leader, that is, the head of the Monkey clan which had special functions in Buganda, such as "crowning" the Kabaka.

Whatever his position in the hierarchy, each chief holds his mandate from the Kabaka, but subordinate chiefs serve the chief next higher in the echelon. The Batongole chiefs are most intimately associated with the affairs of village life and with the ordinary people (*Bakopi*). With the establishment of civil service chieftaincy, the Batongole were not included in the paid hierarchy. Today they remain important in the contemporary system of local government. Batongole are in the main selected because they are landowners,[14] responsible, and essentially conservative figures.

The solid circles denoted by K^1, K^2, and so on, indicate Kabaka's estates which are his private patrimony. Scattered throughout the various sazas, these estates are controlled by the deputies of the Kabaka himself. In the past, important chiefs were often given charge of these estates which served to secure the counties more closely to the king through the presence of king's men and king's land. Further, since it was customary to shift the capital of the Kabaka and there was no fixed locale for his residence, the roving quality of his authority further emphasized the fact that boundaries between sazas were simply administrative conveniences and not local solidary groupings. As a result, the allegiance which attached to the chief was an allegiance which attached to the king. Indeed, when some effective and powerful chiefs made alliances against the Kabaka and with the other members of the ruling family eligible for kingship, it became the practice to kill the potentially competing eligibles. This tended to establish the king more securely.

Senior chiefs (Bakungu) as well as the king had properties scattered through the counties. These properties were primarily attached to the office, not ascribable to the individual; in effect, they as well as the office reverted to the Kabaka when an occupant was removed or died.

The pattern of authority within this saza can be put as follows:

14 Roscoe defines Batongole as the private servants of the king. They were the staff of the king, including servants, guards, policemen. They were given estates in the counties and were directly responsible to the king. Today they are landowners who represent the lowest level of chieftaincy. (*Ibid.*, pp. 257-258.)

Saza Singo

Saza Chief-Mukwenda

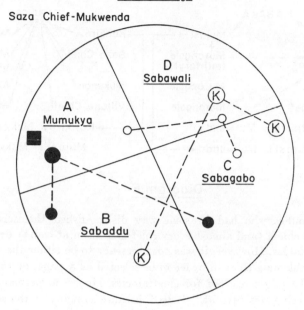

●   Estates of the Katikiro's Mukwenda

○   Estates of the Mujasi's Mukwenda

Ⓚ   The Kitongole of Kisuna under Mutongole *Musuna.*

■   Kabaka's land under Mutongole

Diagram D[1]

[1] I am indebted to Dr. Martin Southwold, of Cambridge University and formerly of the East African Institute of Social Research, for the main outlines of diagrams D and E.

Noteworthy is the system of cross-linkages which apply here, giving derived authority to each of the levels of chiefs, but always retaining for the Kabaka the ultimate power of appointment and therefore removal.

The pattern of recruitment was as follows: Pages were sent to the court of the king by clan elders and chiefs. They were selected

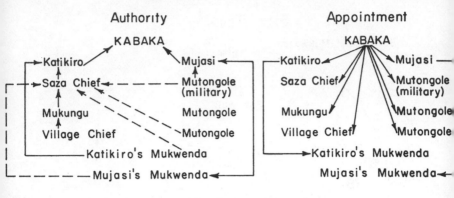

Diagram E

from families who had in some way distinguished themselves, either as chiefs (and almost every chief had a son at court) or as other notables. However, it was not necessary to be either the son of a notable or a chief in order to be selected as a page, or to be among the pages selected for chieftaincies. Hence no permanent social barring was present.[15] Indeed, because so many of the sons of chiefs had been killed either in war or intrigue, it was a common practice of the chiefs to send their slaves' sons. If a slave's son was sent he went as a chief's or elder's son and was, of course, a clan member.[16]

In effect, then, the system was basically hierarchical with the king as "patron" and chiefs and subjects as "clients." Each of the Bakungu chiefs had special duties with respect to the king. For example, *Mukwenda*, the Saza Chief of Singo, was his shield-bearer; *Sekibobo*, the Saza Chief of Kyagwe, was his governor in Busoga, a neighboring country to Buganda, part of which acknowledged the suzerainty of the king of Buganda. *Kasuju*, the Saza Chief of Busuju, was in charge of the princes and princesses,

[15] *Ibid.*, p. 244.

[16] Partly for this reason (since the child takes the father's clan except in the case of the royal family), and partly because of the expansion of Buganda, the tracing of Buganda ancestry usually uncovers some non-Muganda ancestor, giving rise to the frequent charge that some chief or powerful figure is not a Muganda but a Munyoro. This was a favorite way of initiating the downfall of a public person.

assisted in the appointment of a new king, and managed the estates of the king's family.

The same pattern was carried out, however, without the elements of royalty, with respect to the subchief-chief relationship. Subchiefs were ranked, with special titles, in order of their importance. A large number of chiefs directly responsible to the Kabaka on the one hand, and serving senior chiefs as representatives of the Kabaka, helped to keep the kingdom geared to effective control by the Kabaka, whose capriciousness served to underline his supreme power.[17]

However, the Kiganda pattern was made more complex than simple hierarchical rule. The older alternative system associated with clans also existed. This conformed closely to the pyramidal pattern over which the Kabaka presided as *Sabataka,* the head of all the clans. If in one respect every Muganda owed his allegiance to the Kabaka, so was every Muganda a *mutaka,* a clan member. The final court of appeal and the "owner" of the land (the senior Bataka elders had special rights over clan burial places) was Sabataka. Hence the peculiar ambiguity of the Bataka toward the Kabaka. On the one hand he was the most senior clan figure who in a sense provided a formal legitimacy to Bataka claims to authority; on the other, the claims to authority which the Bataka already had, derived quite independently of the Kabaka. Indeed, in certain respects he was a usurper. Thus by virtue of kinship and clan associations the Bataka could claim an orthodoxy and tradition which more latterly has come to be identified with citizenship and with being "pure Muganda."[18]

[17] Chiefs spent much of their time at court for fear of being charged with disloyalty if they were consistently absent. Roscoe put it as follows: "Life and death were treated as of little moment; the King might cause any one of his chiefs to be bound, detained, or put to death at his pleasure." (*Op.cit.,* p. 259.)

[18] "The Kabakas appear at first to have left the bataka in possession of their land, but it gradually became the custom for the Kabaka to send his own men into the country to see how things were managed by the bataka and perhaps mainly to see to the collection of taxes. These men of the Kabaka were called Batongole, and the Kabaka took from the Bataka to whom they were sent a piece of the butaka land and gave it to them to live upon. This is the origin of the batongole tenure, and it is thought also that where the batongole were especial favorites of the Kabaka and persons consequently who gradually grew to be of great importance, in certain cases they became more important persons than the bataka and ultimately developed into saza chiefs (Bakungu), and from an administrative point of view the country was then considered to be divided into sazas each government by the 'owesaza,' a glorified mutongole and an official of the

Insofar as they were both religious and customary figures, the clan leaders also watched over the graves of the clan dead. The Baganda have always attributed great significance to burial. Indeed, the idea of "ownership" in a traditional sense with ancestral dead is still widely held. One meaning of the word Bataka refers to those clan elders who had to tend the clan burial grounds at different levels of clan organization. Hence these elders were regarded as having had hereditary prescriptive rights over Bataka land.[19]

Pyramidal Authority in the Segmentary Clan System in Uganda

The exact number of clans in Buganda is by no means clear. Some of them are original Kiganda clans. Others are "accommodated"; that is, when some of the areas conquered by the Baganda were brought into the Kingdom of Buganda, some of the clans sometimes expanded to include those of the conquered people. Hence the ambiguity. Roscoe lists 36 clans and adds 6 which joined other clans. An informant lists 64, while Dr. Audrey Richards lists 32.[20]

Whatever their exact number, the pyramid is as follows: Kiika, Siga, Mutuba, Lunyiriri, and Enda.

At each level of the pyramid there is a council. There is little doubt that a close if at times contentious relationship exists between the clans and their leaders, and the chiefs as appointees of the Kabaka. Audrey Richards puts it as follows: "Political and

---

Kabaka. In one or two cases it would appear that the mutaka became a favourite of the Kabaka and was made an owesaza, which office therefore became hereditary in his family or clan, such apparently was the case with Katambala, Kasuju, and Mugema." Judge W. M. Carter, *Report on Land Tenure in the Kingdom of Uganda*, October 2, 1906.

[19] The Carter Commission which investigated land tenure put the matter as follows: "Although there is a tradition that Kintu was the ancestor of all the Baganda, the more general opinion would appear to be that when Kintu the first Kabaka came to the country he found certain persons in possession of the land, who were the predecessors of the present Bataka, whether or not they were called by that name at first. Each Mutaka was the holder of the land surrounding his village or group of villages and he administered law to and governed the persons on his land after the manner of the patriarchs of old. On his death he was buried upon his property and the butaka land is now regarded as the land where one's ancestors are buried. His successors then took his place as the head of his clan." *Ibid.*

[20] See Roscoe, *op.cit.*, pp. 139-140; see also A. I. Richards, "Ganda Clan Structure—Some Preliminary Notes" (East African Institute of Social Research paper, unpub. mimeo., n.d.).

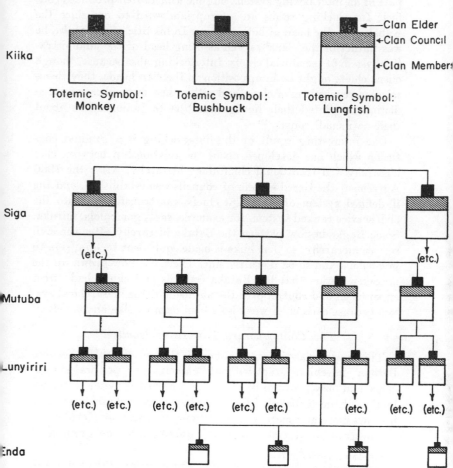

Pyramidal Authority in the Segmentary Clan System in Uganda

Diagram F

clan authorities were in fact at the end of the nineteenth century part of an interlocking system, but one which often produced conflict. Interlocking seems an appropriate word to use since the Kabaka was the head of both systems. In his title of *Sabataka*, he was 'father of the clans' as well as being head of the administrative system of territorial chiefs. Interlocking also because, though client chiefs might be in opposition to the clan heads, they themselves were members of clans, and within their own sphere of jurisdiction appointed their lineage members to junior offices about their own small courts."[21]

One interesting result of this interlocking is a gradual confusion which has developed about the relationship between clan hierarchy and traditional chieftaincy hierarchy. After the 1900 Agreement the tiered system of councils was established, and the ill-defined system of Bakungu chiefs was transformed into the civil service ranked system, for example, saza, gombolola, miruka. Some Baganda now pattern the Bataka hierarchy after the civil service hierarchy, so that kiika is made equivalent to saza, siga to gombolola, and so on down the line. There has now grown up the mistaken notion that the Bataka councils and elders had direct supervision and control over the members of the hierarchical system because each chief was also a clan member like anyone else.[22]

The Contemporary Pattern of Dualism[23]

This particular interpretation of the relationships between Bataka and chiefs is not without contemporary political significance and may prove to be at least a temporary factor in the retention of the Kabaka's effective authority as Sabataka while he becomes more and more a constitutional monarch as Kabaka.

The traditional system was well differentiated on grounds of

---

21 Richards, *op.cit.*, p. 7.

22 In point of fact, the neat comparative ranking of the two systems had no basis in custom. The systems were simply different. After the tiered system of local government was established, the Baganda tended to produce this more orderly arrangement.

23 These represent the contemporary rankings. The administrative hierarchy is by no means traditional. The clan system is. For every level of the administrative hierarchy it is commonly held today that there is a corresponding clan unit. Every Muganda is in a certain respect a *Mutaka*, insofar as he is a clan member and therefore not a foreigner. Every clan unit represents a potential organizational alternative to the administration. It has structural characteristics with its own councils, its own elders, and its own prescriptive rights.

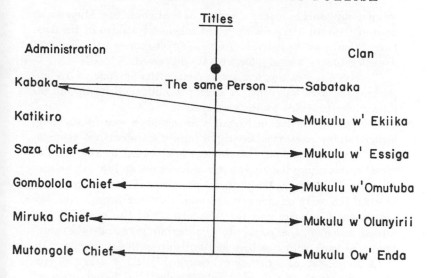

Diagram G

political hierarchy. Rank was determined by authority granted by the Kabaka and measured in the number of people under the control of a chief. Unlike the system in Toro, Ankole, or Bunyoro, no aristocratic principle prevailed. *Bakopi* or peasants could rise in the hierarchy. Princes and princesses were a relatively minor aristocracy. The selection of sons to inherit their fathers' estates was largely a clan matter, subject to election. Primogeniture did not exist. Even at the most senior levels rigid dynasty was mitigated. Recruits to the Kabakaship were numerous. Many children were eligible for the position because of the large number of wives possessed by the Kabaka. The "harem" system worked as a fairly efficient safeguard against bad kingship and was not accompanied by primogeniture.

Further, since the Kabaka inherited his mother's rather than his father's clan (in contradistinction to the more strictly patrilineal system prevailing elsewhere in Buganda), no particular individual could lay special claim to the office.

Rather shrewdly, one clan, the Monkey clan, was for various traditional reasons kept separate from the others. The Kabaka was not supposed to marry a woman of that clan. The Mugema or head of the clan had a disinterested role as "Katikiro of the dead kings," and was the individual who in effect crowned the Kabaka. Thus legitimacy was in some measure dispersed.

Clearly this was not a class system, although one of its important features was rank. A strong leveling and mediating influence was provided by the clan system.

The political system in Buganda represents a well-functioning, contemporary phenomenon—rigid, highly conservative, yet relatively open as a system. Government is attended by considerable ritual surrounding the king, but it is fraternal and in its own way populist. Indeed, it is the essential populism of this system which escaped the early missionary and administrator groups who saw mostly the hierarchy and the "despotism" of the monarch, and missed much of the relatively egalitarian give-and-take which tempered rank with courtesy and lordship with familiarity.[24]

In Buganda, no aristocracy emerged.[25] To a large degree, the hierarchical system obliterates exclusivism based upon an aristocratic principle. Although it is possible to talk about Ganda aristocrats, it is for the most part misleading. Excellence in war and undertaking administrative services was a major basis for

[24] In contrast, the kingdoms of Ankole and Kitara had elaborate overlordship systems in which the population was culturally and politically divided between Hima and Babito cattleowning rulers and Hutu or Bairu commoners, both having different ethnic origins. Today this division is strongest in Ankole and weakest in Bunyoro-Kitara. A pattern of exclusiveness was built up, based historically on conquest, reinforced by wealth and political priorities, maintained through practices pertaining to owning and tending cattle. When these distinctions declined, as in Kitara, principles of rank and government changed. Indeed, the very name of *Kitara*, the proper name for the Bunyoro-Kitara Kingdom, has largely been displaced by the term *Bunyoro*, the name meaning freed slaves, which symbolizes the gradual disappearance of an exclusive Hima aristocracy through its gradual absorption into the Bairu population.

Elsewhere, as amongst the Alur or the Acholi, both chieftaincies and clanship were operative principles in politics. This is in sharp distinction to those hierarchical systems where similar powers are not articulated throughout the various levels of the system. The Agreement states like Ankole, Toro, Bunyoro, and Buganda are clearly of the hierarchical type; in some, particularly Ankole and Bunyoro, such a system of politics was the result of control by an agency coming from outside the prevailing clans and segmentalized groups which originally prevailed. Hence the principle of hierarchy in most of the Agreement states is based upon ethnic exclusiveness.

[25] Roscoe puts it as follows: The class distinctions were marked, even though there was no blue blood among the chiefs. "Class distinctions were chiefly determined by a man's abilities and by the bravery and skill which he displayed when in the service of the King. . . ." (*Op.cit.*, p. 269.)

recruitment into the hierarchy, and the hierarchy was constantly justifying itself by the proficiency with which it served the Kabaka, that is, the state. Such a system is inherently flexible and adaptive because it does not become limited by fixed principles which are no longer operative when social and economic life are radically altered. A pyramidal type of political system is useful only as long as the clan and kinship patterns with which it is integrated are not disrupted by new means of reckoning significant social relationships. One aspect of this is to be demonstrated today in local government. The pyramidal types of traditional political systems are anomalies in modern local governments where the chiefs are civil servants. Experiments blending both customary and appointive principles have by no means been successful.

Such conflicts did not occur in Buganda, because customarily a chief's tenure was held at the Kabaka's pleasure. A hierarchical as distinct from a pyramidal system is more delicately adjusted to social considerations other than the political. Values and modes of reckoning relationships are integrated with inheritance and gift-giving. These are close to what Durkheim called *mechanical* solidarity, especially as authority at each level in the pyramidal structure is basically concerned with conflict resolution.[26]

Conclusion

This brief discussion of the traditional structures of Buganda was designed to indicate some of the characteristics which came to a new prominence following British intervention.

First, the fundamental cleavage running throughout the society which predates European intervention was described. The cleavage represents a conflict between two systems of authority and two sets of values. The clan structure was characteristically pyramidal and consummatory, the chieftaincy system hierarchical and instrumental. When the clan system began to suffer from the conflict produced by client chieftaincy, authority shifted to the hierarchical type. Traditional religion declined. Social atomism increased. The solidary institutional structure of Buganda

[26] See the highly useful discussion of necessary tension produced by conflict which helps keep the parts of a system in dynamic interaction, in M. Gluckman, *op.cit.*

changed from one having many and varied independent and decentralized centers to a highly individualistic type of allegiance of Muganda to Kabaka.

The change was accompanied by a shift to instrumental values. Competition characteristic between family members and social groups extended to favor-seeking at court for appointments to chieftaincies. Nevertheless, performance was the ultimate test of durability in a political role. The individual who made his way up the hierarchy was competing for his Kabaka's favor. But this alone was ephemeral unless he could show satisfactory performance.

The shift both to instrumental values and to hierarchical authority would have left a structural lacuna had not the role of the Kabaka emerged sharply and strongly as central in the Kiganda system. The vacuum left by the shift away from consummatory values brought about the quick demise of the traditional religious system and the pervasive spread of Christianity. These also served to perpetuate the social atomism of the system. Of the proselytizing groups, the Protestants were best able to fit the modernizing pattern which emerged with European penetration. The apotheosis of the Kabaka system and client chieftaincy coincided with European entry. With them the values of instrumentalism were buttressed by the puritanical elements of the Church Missionary Society.

But if such were the characteristics of the traditional society, then in a more stable period instrumentalism would have to turn to arts more practical than war and pursuits more peaceable than the economic activities pursuant to war. With the Kabakaship constrained, and with a settled and more stable pattern of civil rule and chieftaincy superimposed on the ordinary hierarchy of the past, the question was whether such a system could adapt itself anew. We shall try to show that it could because the process of adaptation itself was based upon the continuance of old disputes under a new guise. The transition could occur because of the instrumentalism antecedent to the modified system. The new issues of economic and political conflict appeared in the form of the old struggle between the pyramidal and the hierarchical systems of authority. Moreover, that struggle was particularly suitable for the purpose. For ultimately, the pyramidal system is "democratic." The hierarchical system is "autocratic." The problem posed in Uganda by the traditional pattern of Buganda is whether or not the instrumentalism of the hierarchical system of authority can be maintained while a democratic system of government comes to prevail. Or, can autocracy be made to give way while values based on skill and performance are maintained in a system of democracy? It is this latter issue which, at bottom, is the crucial one in Uganda.

Today, however, it is the political parties which have become the spokesmen for representative government. They inherit an old culture. For, in a practical sense, political parties are not new in Buganda. They can trace their origins in the old and stubborn conflicts between types of custom and tradition, types of institutional systems or value complexes which were inherent in the dualism of Kiganda society. Indeed, the clans were to emerge once again as a peasant party demanding that the chief's power be reduced, while chiefs stood firm as a semiaristocracy anxious to defend their private patrimony. In this fashion the more modern issues of contemporary Uganda were first put in traditional terms. We shall now attempt to describe the issues, as well as the men who represented them, more explicitly.

CHAPTER 5

FISSURES WITHOUT FRACTURE:
THE FIRST POLITICAL GROUPS IN BUGANDA

EXAMINING changes in social structure is a bit like following organized motion. It is prismatic and many-sided. When a whole people moves from autonomy to subordination, from autocracy of a patrimonial sort to a bureaucracy under a monarch, the changes are vast. The real hammer blows in culture are not easily visible. Like the upper part of an iceberg, political groups are the visible parts of a changing social structure otherwise obscure and hidden beneath the waters.

Political groups are intriguing parts of social structure. Either they want to place their members in positions of authority or they seek to put pressure on those in responsible office in order to gain something of value for the people they represent. Because political groups are always asking for something, they have a vested interest in conflict. Where they are allowed freedom to exercise that interest, limitations are normally placed upon their actions. Conflict becomes salutory and healthful, giving vitality to those parts of social structure dealing with politics and keeping alive the public interest in the society.

The typical colonial situation, however, does not allow political groups freedom to function except in a rather limited way. In free nations the limitations on political group activity are imposed through the electoral processes and regulations. The most successful political groups in a colonial situation, operating without the full paraphernalia of party government, have been those with some deep solidary basis in the society, some local core which, touched by change, springs to life when there are threats to the society.

Such political groups are an intimate part of social structure. Thus important features of them remain hidden to observers. Old issues arise through them, feeding and inflaming public passions. Old political groups serve as the rallying points for the parties to new disputes. New disputes help to give vitality to old divisions in the society.

The Period of Political Administration

In the previous chapters we attempted a brief excursion into the background and history of Buganda. We shall now analyze the period subsequent to the signing of the Uganda Agreement of 1900. The Agreement was fundamental to the evolving relations between British and Baganda. The modifications it brought about in the nature of Kiganda society are a point of departure for the examination of more contemporary matters.

Missionaries and administrators assumed that in Buganda the system was feudal. The Agreement sought to combine elements consisting of feudal rank, privilege, and property. These were rewards to loyal Christians who had become chiefs during the years of struggle and warfare.

Effective administration was to be achieved by retaining the *form* of government more or less as it was, with necessary modifications. Chieftaincy was regularized. The Great Lukiko, no longer an irregular gathering of important people and chiefs, was now turned into a formal body with regular and periodic meetings, rules and regulations. It was composed mainly of chiefs and their deputies. The ideal was a Christian, semifeudal, bureaucratic society.

The fiction of a voluntary compact was maintained by both sides in the proceedings which led to the signing of the Agreement. Johnston wanted the Agreement signed in an atmosphere of amiability and cordiality. To achieve this, negotiations were both patient and protracted. But Johnston had already worked out the main outlines of the Agreement before he even went to Buganda. He did not rely solely on his powers of persuasion; he deployed his military forces in such a fashion that it was unmistakable where lay residual power. Underlying the amiable settlement was force.

The Buganda government would continue to be responsible for most of the internal affairs of the Kingdom. For their part, the Baganda were concerned to safeguard the position of the Kabaka and chiefs. The boundaries of Buganda were confirmed and the Kingdom enlarged to 20 counties, mostly at the expense of Bun-

yoro, the defeated rival of Buganda. This provided for an expansion of stable offices. The distribution of chieftaincies on the
basis of religion, which had been reorganized by Sir Gerald Portal
in 1895, was essentially confirmed in the Agreement when land
was allocated to 1,000 chiefs and notables. Freehold land, although previously unknown, was introduced.[1] A hierarchy based
largely on political control was reinforced by economic wealth in
land which could be inherited. This introduced the potentiality of
a political-economic class system which had hitherto been alien.[2]

The Agreement created generational problems. In 1900, major
chiefs were relatively young men, steeled in war, shrewd, and
by the standard of the time the best educated. Many of them had
been closely associated with the missionaries as pupils, readers
and catechists. Young, aggressive, and capable when they came to
office, they continued in office for several decades after the Agreement and retained their preeminent positions. Few chiefs were
anxious to see power slip from their grasp. Even their older sons
were able to obtain only minor chieftaincies. The latter's prospects for promotion were rarely good. By the time the senior
chiefs were ready to retire, a third generation had already grown
up (the Makerere generation), anxious to wrest power from the
older chiefs. Members of this third generation, if they had inherited land, received only small portions of the original grants.
By this means, although the newer political aspirants were most
often related to the old dynastic families, that dynastic element
had been vitiated. Indeed, education expanded to include a much

[1] It is sometimes alleged that the *butaka*, or clan burial lands, were traditional
forms of freehold, but this is not the case. These were lands relatively sacred and
relatively immune from supervision by the Kabaka or chiefs. The conception of
freehold was introduced by Johnston.
[2] This class factor became important but never rigid or exclusive. True, the term
"noble," applied to a senior chief who was now also a big landowner, was occasionally applied to Bakungu chiefs. In this fashion a rudimentary dynastic element was introduced into Buganda. But many of the landowners sold their land
or subdivided extensively. With other forms of means available, it was not uncommon to find a retired school teacher who, having saved his money, bought some
land, farmed it successfully, expanded his holdings, and became a large landowner and prosperous farmer and a Mutongole chief.
Another reason why the dynastic element was not entirely successful was that
the sons of chiefs were rarely of the caliber of their fathers. Even though such
institutions as Mengo High School were set up to cater to the sons of chiefs,
mostly the sons were less satisfactory than the fathers and in the civil service
chieftaincy system merit was important. Hierarchy thus came to be based on
merit rather than family.

wider group than chiefs' sons. By the third generation after the Agreement, even some *Bakopi* (peasants) were clamoring for entry into the chiefly hierarchy on grounds of ability and education.[3]

Each of these modifications in the system—(1) the expansion of stable offices, (2) the establishment of freehold tenure, and (3) the stability of tenure for senior chiefs—became a source of friction and internal conflict inside Buganda. The Agreement brought a modification in traditional practices which produced enough internal tension to give meaning and vitality to the Buganda government. Rather sorry as a legal document or a constitution, the Agreement was in this latter respect a work of art as a political instrument.

What roles became important as a consequence of the Agreement? Mainly those already demarcated by political rank became more powerful. At the head of the system stood the Kabaka. He was the central symbol of the people. All acts combined to be done in his name. At the time of the Agreement, however, he was in his minority. Only later, after the attainment of Daudi Chwa's majority, did the position of the Kabaka produce conflict when interposed in the running of the Kingdom.

When the king died, it was traditional for the Katikiro, the Kimbugwe, and the Kasuju to assume responsibility for selecting a new king from among the eligible princes of the drum. The position of the Katikiro was now made immeasurably more powerful, while the latter two household officials, who had had ready access to the Kabaka and could exert considerable influence, were removed from their direct position at the court. The Katikiro's judicial and financial powers were divided between two new officers, the *Omuwanika* and the *Omulamuzi*. These formed a regency during the Kabaka's minority and, as well, a council of ministers of the Kabaka's government. *Mugema*, the last of the clan heads to be an hereditary saza chief, was deprived of some of his lands as a Mutaka, even though these were compensated for in *mailo* lands received by him in the Agreement. More junior Bataka were deprived of their lands entirely. The Agreement reduced the power and prestige positions of those primarily in the clan sector.

[3] I am indebted to Mr. E. M. K. Mulira for very fruitful discussions of these issues. Some of the ideas contained here were stimulated in these discussions.

Below the most senior officers of the government were the chiefs, ranked in order of importance by titles which showed the relative significance of the territory over which they ruled. Each chieftaincy post had an official estate, the income being enjoyed by the chief during his incumbency. New economic distinctions were added in the form of private estate-holding families. A dynastic feature was characteristic of the Kagwa, Kisosonkole, Kulubya, Mulyanti, Kasule, Mugwanya, Kisingiri, Yakuze, and Mukasa families.[4]

Perhaps the most important change was the altered relationship between chief and *Mukopi*. In the traditional system, power below the Kabaka's position was a relative thing.

The land settlement in the Agreement displaced the earlier populism of the system. Chiefs became rich. The Agreement did not succeed in transforming the "client" into a serf, but came dangerously close to it. The client was transformed into a tenant farmer.[5] The result was an important alteration in the position of the Mukopi. What was hitherto an exclusively political relationship between chief and client now became a more economic one. With the Mukopi a tenant farmer, chiefs intervened between himself and his Kabaka—chiefs who were always functionaries but had now become landlords as well.

Private land tenureship also affected the clans. As part of their immemorial rights and religious custom the clan elders possessed functions with respect to the allocation of property. The clan leader was above all concerned with nourishing the clan through compromise and adjustment of conflict. This went far beyond deciding simple rights or wrongs. The position of the Bataka was further reinforced and symbolized by their control over clan burial grounds. Their role was in part life-giving, protective of the clan and supportive of its members. The clan was thus a corporate body which gave everyone a position vis-à-vis everyone else, on kin

---

[4] Although the dynastic system does not prevail, it remains a decided advantage to have come from one of these families because between them there has been extensive intermarriage and they have supplied a large proportion of the leaders of the Buganda as chiefs and notables. Between them, too, was a sense of history, shared experience, and intimacy.

[5] The Kabaka was to receive a guaranteed income of not less than £1,500 per year, and his government would become paid officials. See K. Ingham, *The Making of Modern Uganda* (London: Allen & Unwin, 1958), p. 89.

rather than political lines. It was the clan who helped educate the young. It was the clan who buried the dead.

The clan system stood alongside the power and prestige positions directly responsible to the Kabaka in the hierarchical system of authority. The hierarchical system led to effective administration and the expansion of the state. The clan system, employing pyramidal authority, led to conservation and a nourishing of human resources.[6] The clan system now became the organizational medium whereby peasant grievance was openly expressed. For economic reasons, instead of the former political ones, the chiefs, who were now landowners, became the objects of the Bataka's antagonism. Thus the old split in the society precipitated a new conflict over economic inequality; although chiefs and Bataka were by no means discrete groups, this conflict became the most fundamental political issue in Buganda for many years, and eventually came to shape the character of Uganda as a nation.

Sir Harry Johnston regarded the 1900 Agreement as simply a treaty. For him there was nothing in the nature of a solemn undertaking about it. But Johnston had something else on his mind. He felt that he was giving the Baganda a chance to rule themselves because "the Kingdom of Uganda and its adjoining provinces in the Uganda Protectorate . . . is in justice a black man's country, a land that is to say already endowed with a fairly abundant black population which has a recognized right to a large proportion of the soil. . . ."[7] If the Baganda failed, then the Agreement would be scrapped and the British would rule by direct intervention.

Whatever the conditions of the Agreement, however, the chiefs rapidly realized that they were in fact under the control of British authorities. The power of the chiefs had been heightened by the removal of stringent rule by an autocratic Kabaka. Now the strength of the powerful chiefs derived from their immediate control over their own followers, Catholic or Protestant as the case might be. The chiefs had for the moment consolidated their power

[6] See above, Chapter 4.
[7] See Johnston's preface to J. Cathcart Wason, *East Africa and Uganda* (London: Francis Griffiths, 1904), p. 15. This volume is of additional interest since it discusses (negatively) the proposals of the British government to turn over Uganda on lease to the Jewish Colonial Trust, a hotly-debated concession to Zionism which never came to fruition.

with British support, established their strength with the people themselves, and managed to double the number of counties over which Buganda could now exercise hegemony. They were well pleased with these aspects of the Agreement. This was the end of the first or pioneering phase of the relationship between British and Baganda. It gave way to a second phase, political administration.

More nettling to the chiefs were the restrictions by which they found themselves hedged, and the admonishments and directives which were an increasing part of settled administration. Gradually, the Baganda began to look at the Agreement with a somewhat colder eye. They saw that their relationship with the British would be subject to constant review.

The result was the emergence of "official nationalism," that is, the nationalism of the chiefs. The great senior Buganda government officials like Sir Apolo, whose loyalty to the British had no peer, became concerned with protecting their own and thereby the nation's autonomy. And, as they were part of an elaborate civil service hierarchy, the official nationalism of the Buganda government and chiefs was organized through the protective abilities common to any civil service (which well knows how to draw into its shell and prevent encroachments from outsiders). In so doing, first the British officials and then the missionaries were made increasingly to feel like outsiders, rather than participants in the web of African politics and social life. The situation was thus headed for deadlock and conflict. This "official nationalism" has been a main ideological theme running throughout the Buganda Kingdom. It was to continue to plague the period of political administration, as well as subsequent periods.

Thus two main types of nationalism emerged in the political administration period. The first was popular, directed against the hierarchies of chiefs and administrators and based on (1) economic strivings, (2) status competition, and (3) personal insecurities, especially among the Protestants. The second was official. The chiefs sought to preserve their autonomy from the Protectorate government.

The Baganda took on a Janus-like quality after the Agreement. One face was turned against the Protectorate government. If the face wore a smile, it was a strained smile. The ramparts

114

stood as a perpetual reminder that the Baganda must not let down their guard or become less vigilant. To them, with all the fraternization which occurred during the day, when night came the gates shut and it was an enemy which remained outside. The other face of the Baganda was turned inward. The new strength of the chiefs was also their weakness, since many who opposed authoritarian rule by the Katikiro would have been willing to accept it from the Kabaka.

Who were the main protagonists in the internal struggles? Most important were those who represented the conflict between the two forms of authority, pyramidal and hierarchical, antique and modern, which had been going on for generations in Buganda. This conflict, represented by the chiefs and the Bataka, was an old struggle which now took a new tack. With land settlement and political power backed up by British power, the chiefs appeared to have won the day and established themselves for all times as the dominant political force in Buganda. Meanwhile, the Bataka, aggrieved and angered by the consequences of the Agreement, sought to speak in the name of the peasantry, the Bakopi, or the ordinary man. The importance of the Bataka struggle was that it identified economic grievance with social status, or the lack of it, and paved the way for the formation of the first political and economic organizations of modern Buganda.

The second main internal conflict was between two religions. Catholicism and Protestantism continued to represent differing political factions just as they had during the religious wars. Now they were more like political parties.

The chiefs and the Bataka, and the Catholics and the Protestants, represented the main internal divisions within Buganda.

Because of the vitality of these internal conflicts, Buganda became, paradoxically, more separatist and remote from the rest of the country as her economic and social institutions were more thoroughly intermeshed with the rest of the country. As the Kiganda pattern of political organization in local government was transposed to the districts of Uganda, and as commercial activity brought Buganda into closer contact with foreigners and newly-introduced cash crops, coffee and cotton, brought her into world markets and international trade, her political institutions became more formal, her political leaders more stiff, and the attitudes of her people more ethnocentric. For every success in economic and political lines brought a danger, the danger of submerging Buganda and her institutions in a sea of change.

It is easy to see in the actions of the Buganda government a retrospective wisdom and a concern for the preservation of their institutions which could easily be overemphasized. But even where Buganda government officers wanted to change and modernize, they were often held back by the internal divisions within the country. Here the conservatism of the Bataka, for example, might restrict their freedom of action. There the Protestant or Catholic faction might take up the cudgels against an impending change. Helping to muddy the waters was generational conflict. It appeared on a personal level, in the forms of ambition and jealousy, between Sir Apolo Kagwa, who ran the Buganda government with an iron hand, and the younger chiefs allied with the British administrators. As well, racial tension increased as the Kenya pattern of white settlement began to emerge more clearly next door. The implications of European settlement became clear to all. These, as well as the glorification of a mythical past, and Kiganda pride, all tended to get mixed into the relationship between the Baganda and the British. The result was three dimensions of loyalty incumbent upon each Muganda.

One loyalty, clear and unmistakable, was to the Kabaka and the Buganda government. In moments of crisis, no matter how much he did not like the prime minister or the chiefs, he was on call as a Muganda had always been. This made all Baganda like a single political party, ready for action against all other parties.

Internally, however, a Muganda might take his position with the chiefs or with the Bataka, a proponent of one group or the other, and behave accordingly. Meanwhile, as a Catholic or a Protestant he looked to different political leaders as his own. He was a follower either of Mugwanya or Sir Apolo. The curious situation arose where a man might follow the Bataka in matters affecting the allocation of land or compulsory labor, and follow Sir Apolo once again when issues threatening the autonomy of Buganda were involved.

In relation to the state itself, a Muganda could be pulled in three different directions, and since each situation had implication for the other dimensions, it was incumbent upon a Muganda to be politically aware, shrewd, and triply conscious of the consequences of his activity. This quality has served the Baganda well, for it has equipped them infinitely better than most African groups with the ability to bargain effectively with the British and to think through the consequences of an action long before it has been taken.

Thus the political postures and cleavages in the society have had far-reaching consequences for the behavior of the Baganda. They have affected outlook as well as social structure, beliefs as well as organization. Shrewdness becomes tantamount to wisdom. Deviousness becomes a form of shrewdness. Politeness becomes a form of deviousness. In the shifting forces of their relationship with one another and with the British, the Baganda themselves began to change. The expressions of warm and faithful regard that each group had for the other, and which the British and the Baganda expressed for one another, served to disguise both the sources and strengths of an antagonism made more anguished by the knowledge of deceit.

Political Groups

The Chiefs as a "Party"

When the dangers of civil war had receded and the people began to pick up and mend the pieces of their society, the chiefs were the leaders of the important religious factions. But it must not be forgotten that they had always been important political figures in the country. They were endowed with two sources of special prestige. One was customary or traditional: most of them had been pages at the Kabaka's court and were associated with the "natural" process of rulership. The other was by virtue of courage and arms: they had been readers and catechists under the missionaries, often at great personal danger.

A third source of support came from their alliance with British officers. It was the Baganda who fought with the small forces of the Protectorate against the Sudanese. For example, Kakunguru had discovered and routed Kabarega and Mwanga. And in return, the British treated the chiefs with honor and respect.[8]

[8] Each source of support also came to be a source of conflict. Because the chiefs represented continuity and legitimacy with the past, and held their office in the traditions of the past, they carried over the dispute which the chiefs had had with

In the period following the Agreement, Daudi Chwa, the Kabaka, had not yet reached his majority. Hence the hierarchical principle was not breached when the system changed to bureaucratic from patrimonial chieftaincy. For the Agreement changed somewhat the relationship between the Kabaka and the chiefs. From a client of the king, having in turn his own patrons, the chief was transformed into a civil servant—a bureaucrat of the king. Still essentially autocratic as well as hierarchical in structure, the system posed no immediate challenge because the king himself served merely as a symbol. Only later, on receiving his majority, did the Kabaka face conflict between himself and the Katikiro, Sir Apolo.

The Katikiro, who had achieved this office under Kabaka Mwanga, continued in it for 38 years. This ensured a continuity and smoothly functioning transition from the old system to the newer one. It also produced intrigue and favoritism. Sir Apolo made the position of the Katikiro more powerful than ever before. The old household offices were abolished or transformed.[9]

Of the new posts that had been created, that of the Omulamuzi was reserved for a Catholic, while the position of Omuwanika was reserved for a Protestant. The leader of the Catholic forces, Stanislaus Mugwanya, who for a time had been Catholic Katikiro, became the first Omulamuzi; the former Kangawo, Zakaria Kizito Kisingiri, became Omuwanika. Thus the three most powerful chiefs who had been the regents of Buganda after the deposition of

---

the Bataka. Because the chiefs were courageous and tenaciously religious, they continued the disputes between Catholic and Protestant (the Muslims having been effectively routed). And because their alliance with the British gave them firm support, it also opened them to influence from an outside force. Thus relations between the Buganda government officers and the Protectorate government officers grew increasingly sticky as time went on.

[9] Possible conflict in this transition was avoided quite well. A potential rival of Sir Apolo, Semei Kakunguru, was one of the major Protestant generals, and the last important occupant of the important household post of Kimbugwe. With remarkable foresight and loyalty he conveniently removed himself from Buganda by going to the east province of Uganda, settling near Mbale. There he not only engaged in successful military campaigns, but also acted as the leading Muganda agent, organizing the Kiganda system of administration in these areas. He was finally retired with honor and given estates in Mbale, in addition to land in Buganda. The position of Kimbugwe was transformed into the saza chieftaincy of Buruli. Kakunguru settled down to a quiet retirement. He appeared in the limelight once again as the leader of a branch of the Malakite movement and, refusing to allow his cattle to be inoculated, got himself into grave trouble with the Protectorate government.

Mwanga became the three officers of the Buganda government. The new posts formed a cabinet of sorts. The Lukiko, too, was dominated by senior chiefs who, having fought in the campaigns with Sir Apolo or Mugwanya, were loyal to them. They were a devoted group. Although divided by religion, they were united in their responsibility to Buganda as a whole. Quickly they absorbed the civil service ideal. Accustomed to hierarchy, they became an establishment. As the Kabaka's government they united their efforts to retain for themselves the rights as well as the responsibilities of rule. They became, in effect, a civil service party.

As a party they used their special advantages well. The patronage opportunities were enormous. Some faithful followers were notables and received land as a reward for their services. As the number of clerkships and inspectorships grew, others were given important positions in either the Buganda government or local governments. Honor, status, and land, all three closely associated with one another, were distributed by the dominant chiefs to their supporters.

Not only did the chiefs have ample patronage, but in their alliance with the British they seemed invincible. Among the senior chiefs, the Protectorate government, and the missionaries there existed a tacit agreement not to upset the new stability after the years of civil war.

As well, the chiefs justified their tenure of office on grounds of ability. They were the most capable leaders whom a generation of conflict had brought to the fore. Schooled by the missionaries, skilled at handling men, they ran a reasonably efficient system of government. Taxes were collected. Peace was maintained. The Kingdom prospered.

By means of patronage the chiefs were able to appease their followers. With support from the British their position seemed impregnable. With their ample skills, as compared with the rest of the population, they could justify their rule on grounds of ability. Thus the standard of merit, which had always applied in Buganda, became part of the civil service chieftaincy system. The carryover of old to new was relatively effective.

Nor were the chiefs simply the willing tools of the British. They rallied the public behind them on several issues. The most important of these was the autonomy of Buganda.

The chiefs fought a skillful battle in the name of the Kabaka, preserving his position as an autocratic monarch. They themselves did not lose veneration for his position. The Kabaka was to exercise "direct rule" over the Baganda. He was to be styled His Highness and be entitled to a salute of nine guns.

These and other features of the Agreement were a result of skillful bargaining. The chiefs did double the number of counties in Buganda. They reserved a large measure of autonomy for the Kabaka. As representatives of the Baganda they had served well.

On grounds of service, ability, loyalty, and shrewdness, the chiefs all felt satisfied with their work. They settled down to rule the country in peace and tranquility, content in the knowledge that they were the best men for their jobs.[10] As the leaders of the chiefs' party, they were also the Buganda government. In this they were insulated from rapid change, fickle fortunes, and popular outcries. For in the Agreement itself their offices were made fixed, secure, and salaried.[11]

The religious differences among them did not divide them greatly. Catholics supported Catholic chiefs. Protestants did the same for their chiefs. But offices were fixed allocations according to religion and not subject to controversy. This tended to be true of land, although to a smaller extent. Where there was a Protestant saza chief, the Protestants got most of the land. The same held true for the Catholics.

But it was the economic factor which helped the chiefs become an effective solidary grouping. By becoming the most prominent landowners they had added wealth to their other accomplishments. Economic status helped to weld them into a party anxious to protect its own heritage against those who would take it away from them.

A political party with economic class as its underpinning represents something deep and fundamental in a society. The chiefs,

10 It is interesting to note that of the signers of the 1900 Agreement, all but four were literate; one, Prince Mbogo, the brother of Mwanga and leader of the Muslim community, was literate in Arabic.

11 "To assist the Kabaka of Uganda in the government of his people he shall be allowed to appoint three native officers of state, with the sanction and approval of Her Majesty's representative in Uganda (without whose sanction, such appointments shall not be valid)—a Prime Minister, otherwise known as Katikiro; a Chief Justice; and a Treasurer or Controller of the Kabaka's revenues. These officials shall be paid at the rate of £300 a year." Uganda Agreement, Article 10.

while approaching that position, never quite achieved it. That they did not is extremely significant, for the essential unity of Buganda was challenged but never destroyed.

Several factors prevented the chiefs from becoming an economic class. First, the system of civil service chieftaincy maintained the separate identity of individual and office. The very tradition of service to the Kabaka prevented individuals from pre-empting as their own the roles which they had assumed. Hence the slow turnover in chieftaincy was explained by the fact that a civil service does not change its personnel quickly, rather than that individuals had become personally powerful and were using the office of the chief as an expression of personal power. Due to the nature of economic and political power, the coincidence of the two had nothing inevitable about them.

Second, the great emphasis on achievement and skill never faltered as a condition of office and as a factor in recruitment. Service to the Kabaka had been the one condition of chieftaincy. Together with education, it continued to be so. In theory, nothing prevented a skilled and educated Mukopi from becoming a Katikiro—nothing, that is, except the fact that his chance was slight and that the leading chiefs continued to occupy the important posts for a long time.

Over the long pull, however, many of those who had received large land grants sold them or parceled them out among their children. Thus few great private patrimonial estates were established. And because the missionaries were in control of education, not only the sons of chiefs but the sons of peasants also received education. Here then were two more factors working against the position of the chiefs as an economic class. They did not retain their holdings or, more important, increase them by and large. They did not have a monopoly of education. They were content with power on the basis of political office.

Thus the chiefs became a bone of contention, but not an entrenched and immutable political force. For as the emphasis on achievement persisted, not only did the sons of chiefs become chiefs, but sometimes the sons of Bakopi. No aristocracy formed on the basis of land. Indeed, when a big landowner sold land it was often a thrifty Mukopi who bought it.

Moreover, it was possible for a Mukopi to marry into a major family and thus into the chieftaincy hierarchy. Enough social mobility persisted to avoid the establishment of an economic ruling class. Nevertheless, the chiefs were exclusive enough and in office long enough to produce a profound sense of grievance in the public.

The "natural" antagonists of the chiefs were the Bataka. They represented an organized grouping throughout Buganda which, though thoroughly interwoven in all aspects of Kiganda society, could on occasion come to be considered a separate force. Thus any Muganda was a member of a clan and the clan could make certain claims upon him.

Just as the chiefs represented one strand of continuity with the past, the Bataka represented another. Theirs was a heritage of decreasing power which had not become less important for all its decline. When the chiefs began to regard the Bakopi as peasants and the term became derogatory and contemptuous, then the peasantry and the Bataka became natural allies. That is to say, some Bakopi felt they could follow those who spoke in the name of the clans. It was not unpatriotic since clanship is the essence of being a Muganda.

The Bataka as a Political "Party"

In the Agreement, many of the second-level Bataka, particularly those at the Siga level,[12] did not receive land. During the land settlement they were deprived of their Butaka estates. As we have indicated, these estates had considerable significance. Richards argues that "in spite of their gradual diminution in power clan heads still remained as potential rivals of the client chiefs who were administering provinces for the king and thus sometimes acted as centers of possible conflict. Clan heads, unlike client chiefs, lived on estates from which they could not be evicted. They were immune from arrest and they had direct access to the king and hence could slander the client chiefs whose loyalty was always in question."[13]

In administering a crushing blow to the clan heads, the chiefs went too far. The Bataka could not be obliterated without a strug-

[12] It is important to remember, however, that many Bataka were also appointed as chiefs and in this capacity did receive land.

[13] A. I. Richards, "Ganda Clan Structure—Some Preliminary Notes" (Mimeo., E.A.I.R., n.d.), p. 7.

gle. They became the spokesmen for the peasantry, for the deprived, and for all those aggrieved by the chiefs. From being a purely traditional matter, clans took on contemporary characteristics. The Bataka became a political party, attacking the chiefs.

Dissatisfaction expressed itself in several ways. There were common complaints by the Bakopi that they were dragooned by the chiefs into communal labor and forced to pay hut taxes. Though such service had always been obligatory, they recognized that the spirit of it had changed. As old habits and ties were broken up the actions of the chiefs became more distinct. Unlike the acts of the awesome representative of the monarch, the chiefs' actions did not remain unquestioned. The shortcomings and errors, disputes and jealousies which necessarily attend individual action were brought into greater prominence. Individuals became identified as unpopular, and the Bataka and Bakopi were able to concentrate their fire on the regents of Buganda as those responsible for bringing about inequity.

Land was the single most important source of grievance. Titles to land and political titles seemed almost coterminous. The Bataka and the Bakopi saw themselves at the mercy of the chiefs, and sometimes the clerk of the chief or his deputy. They saw a Lukiko dominated by chiefs. The Lukiko had distributed land. As some observed, it was impossible, without incurring popular displeasure, to parcel out the 8,000 square miles which remained available after the Kabaka, his family, and the major chiefs had themselves received the allotments laid down in the Agreement. It was also observed that the senior chiefs had all managed to do very well for themselves by the terms of the Agreement. There were murmurs that the chiefs had sold their birthright for mailo land— a charge to which they were acutely sensitive.

The chiefs, for their part, argued that in order to spread the holdings more widely, far more people received land than was originally intended. The Agreement specified that "one thousand chiefs and private landowners will receive the estates of which they are already in possession, and which are computed at an average of 8 square miles per individual. . . ."[14] But when the

[14] See N. Turton, J. B. Griffin and A. W. Lewey, *Laws of the Uganda Protectorate* (London: Rowarth, Ltd., 1936), "Native Agreements and Buganda Native Laws," Vol. vi, pp. 1380-1381.

final land distribution had been made, except for certain residual lands left over and unallocated (and except, too, those lands for whom the owners never appeared), it was discovered that some 3,700 people had received land instead of the original 1,000. "Of the allottees the three regents obtained areas of from 45 to 60 square miles each, some twenty chiefs were granted twelve square miles or over, and another 150 persons became entitled to between eight and twelve square miles. The great majority of the original allottees, however, received one to two square miles each."[15] But this did little to mollify those who had received nothing.

Nevertheless, the chiefs recognized that by their very strength they had aroused the public. Charges by the Bataka that the clan burial sites had not been awarded to the proper clan authorities eventually called in question the entire system.

The Bataka, finding themselves with potential allies among the Bakopi, now reached into both the recent and remote past for arguments which would bolster their position that they had been denied their due not only in land settlement but in the share of the political kingdom. Arguments from antiquity were carried forward cheek by jowl with events of the immediate past. It was argued that the Bataka's main political power resided in their power to select the pages who were sent to the Kabaka's court and from among whom many chiefs were selected. Thus in terms of recruitment the Bataka had had an important role to play. Recalling still an earlier time, the Bataka claimed that they also had a right to sit in Lukiko. Thus they sought to "democratize" the Lukiko and eventually came to demand both elective chieftaincy and an elective Lukiko.

Deprived of their estates, the page system abolished, and their presence in the Lukiko eliminated (unless they also happened to be chiefs, in which case they sat as chiefs), the Bataka represented the most traditional and most violated group in Buganda. They identified completely with "old Buganda." They became the keepers of custom. Just as the chiefs used land as a major issue to gain the support of the public, so did the Bataka. Moreover, what began as their demand for a return of rightful property holdings

15 The total amount allocated to African freehold was 9,003 square miles. All land classified as waste and uncultivable became Crown Land. See H. B. Thomas and A. E. Spencer, *A History of Uganda Land and Surveys* (Entebbe: Government Printer, 1938), p. 66. See also Low, *op.cit.*

evolved into a challenge to the leadership of the chiefs themselves. With their monopoly of power and prestige, the chiefs failed to see a vulnerability in the midst of their strength.

In time, several conditions came to favor the Bataka and the Bakopi. The most important of these was the fact that the Kabaka was growing up. The older he grew, the more anxious was he to assert the prerogatives of his role. To the Katikiro and leader of the chiefs' party this was extremely uncomfortable. Sir Apolo had the utmost respect for the Kabaka, in the abstract, but this boy whom he had treated almost as a son could not easily be transformed into a master. Conflict between the Kabakaship, a functionally diffuse and intensely symbolic role, and the Katikiroship, a more functionally precise and instrumental role, was inevitable.

It was the Bataka who represented the people, to whom in some measure the Kabaka turned for support. Like the Kabakas of old, he reasserted the popular support which was the basis of his authority.

The chiefs, manipulating the same public in the interests of Buganda solidarity, sought to retain the autonomy of the Baganda. By doing so they too received the support of the Kabaka, who made alliance with the chiefs against the British.

The British, some of whom were increasingly anxious to remove the older chiefs and replace them with young blood, became useful to the Kabaka as he sought allies against Sir Apolo Kagwa, while the Bakopi looked to the British to rectify the economic and political inequities they found. Indeed, missionaries and administrators soon found themselves in increasing sympathy with the Bataka and the Bakopi. Thus all the major parties were allied with one another on some issues and against one another on others.

The Religious "Parties"

That Christianity so quickly entered Buganda and became a part of the belief system is not a matter to be taken lightly. One reason for it was the growing separation between the institutions of traditional religion, allied as they were with clanship, and the growth of a secular authority surrounding the king. This had the effect of continuing the process of atomization in the society which made an individual Muganda responsible to his lord rather than to his clan group. Religion aided in a process of secularization.

But religion had another side to it. If in the old system obedience to the Kabaka was the *sine qua none* of service and the key principle of society, Christianity preached divine salvation on a more direct basis. There were now appeals other than the authority of the Kabaka. Right conduct and firm purpose were testaments of godliness. However, since the Kabaka was not a religious figure it did not require the dropping of one allegiance to pick up another. One could believe that service to the Kabaka and service to God were one and the same.

All the important chiefs were intimately acquainted with the Bible. They quoted extensively from the Scriptures. This intimacy with religious belief brought a double accolade: the first was conviction and self-righteousness; the second was knowledge. Both were useful attributes of a civil servant *cum* politician.

However, the chiefs had no monopoly of religiosity. Many of the Bataka and the Bakopi were also almost clerical in their devoutness. Where the chiefs had religious authority the Bakopi had the strength of their poverty. For was not poverty only a temporary suffering, to be alleviated by work and the goodness of God?

We have already pointed out that religion helped bind together the chiefs and the people. Protestants found in their leaders the hope that political redemption would reward the loyal. Catholics sought the strength of the corporate church. Religion brought the missionaries into close communion with all ranks of the population.

But while religion exercised a healing force in Buganda society, devoutness did not bring its own reward. Protestant and Catholic leaders had also to reward devoutness with something more tangible. To dispense the proper rewards, Protestants needed to retain their proportion of the chieftaincies and, through these, revenues and influence. Catholics, with a growing population, sought to enlarge their share. Thus the healing influence of religion was to some extent offset by religious competition.

The respective diocesan councils now became the focal point for the policies of political groups. Politics became intense when the quality of the catechists and readers began to decline and lapses in their devoutness began to appear.[16] The struggle to maintain standards was thus a struggle to retain orthodoxy. Orthodoxy could not be posed against the lack of it. But it could easily be directed against another form of orthodoxy. Thus each of the two orthodoxies, Catholic and Protestant, was essential for the other's survival. Only a few Baganda broke away to become religious separatists. In the main, the Catholic and Protestant factions divided the country effectively between them and maintained their active and aggressive hostility for one another. Moreover, since both the major churches were "Catholic," that is, Roman and Anglican, the intensity of competition was all the greater. There was one major sphere in which the missionaries could exercise influence—the schools—and Protestants and Catholics vied with one another to expand the educational system. By gaining pupils they accumulated adherents.

In each community the parish church and the parish school, along with the parish council, became the focal points of social life. Important solidary units, they had their own hierarchy, and the cathedrals surmounting the hills of Rubaga and Namirembe, Catholic and Protestant respectively, symbolized the head of each. Further, old boys' societies, such as the United Budonians, were composed of people of common educational experience as well as common religious background.

Thus religious groupings were not simply ephemeral and superimposed upon society. They came to represent solidary clusters which, alongside the Bataka, clan structure, chieftaincy, and territoriality, helped to produce a sense of community strength in Buganda.

It is interesting to summarize what did not emerge from the Agreement. There was no *noblesse de la robe*. No clerical nobility appeared even when the Church Missionary Society expanded Africanization through the Native African Church. Indeed, as

---

[16] For the most extensive treatment of the religious problem, see the excellent study by John V. Taylor, *The Growth of the Church in Buganda* (London: C.M.S. Press, 1958). Taylor points out that it was not only the African clergy who suffered lapses in their devoutness, but the chiefs as well. "Lapses of the chiefs and the falling off of catechists inevitably led to a serious decline among the ordinary adherents. For them the Christian life meant perpetually holding at bay the three constant temptations of drink, sexual laxity and magic, and the growth of material prosperity in the country enhanced the strength of these." (p. 80.)

we have indicated, the African clergy were in many respects regarded as second rate and not always held in high esteem by the public.

Nor did a secular nobility develop, although the chiefs came to consider themselves a nobility, at least in some respects. As we have indicated, the dynastic principle was defeated. There are distinguished families, but belonging to one does not guarantee one an important position.

A landed aristocracy as well almost developed, but failed to crystallize primarily because most of the estates were very small and were soon broken up and distributed among children, or bought up by ambitious school teachers and clerks who received a wage for their work and saved their money to buy land. But anyone could lease land. Eviction of a tenant from a *kibanja*, or holding on leasehold, was virtually impossible. This prevented the creation of a landless peasantry. Divided loyalties could be held, religious affiliations did not preclude others, and social class never became a fixed and self-conscious pattern.

Since many Baganda benefited from the Agreement—in the form of immediate gains, or the increase in land obtained under its terms, or the legal consolidation of areas formerly outside the area (although in fact Buganda had to give up claims over other outside areas, such as Busoga)—the general aftermath of the Agreement was satisfaction mixed with chagrin. Crosscutting allegiances to chiefs, to clan elders, religious leaders, and to British officers helped prevent fundamental cleavage in the society. More latterly, as the Protectorate government became a focal point for Buganda nationalism, both chiefs and Bataka and then younger men not identified with either sought to preserve Buganda autonomy and offer to the rest of Uganda and to the Protectorate government a united front.

There is, then, an interesting paradox in Buganda which made all this possible. Social atomization on an individual level was coupled with high social responsibility to the Kabaka and thereby to the state. What divided men were corporate and solidary groupings which, centering in the parishes and the local communities, or in tradition and family, could pose stubborn conflict. But what united men were the overriding loyalties and obligations to the state and to the Kabaka. In this respect, faction, intrigue, and politics served to make the institutional structure of Buganda unstable, lively, and riddled with anxiety and insecurity. But it also served to make the national entity, Buganda, strong and vigilant.

Influences of Education and Religion in the Post-Agreement Period

The conflict between peasant and chief as exemplified in the chief-Bataka conflict was important. So was religious factionalism. But religious divisions were not coterminous with the chief-Bataka struggle. Overlapping allegiances helped to prevent fundamental cleavage in the system. Both education and religion produced profound changes in society, but such changes were mediating and beneficial.

Religion and education were inextricably linked. The Church Missionary Society, for example, had stressed education as the moral basis of the Christian presence in Uganda.[17] The White Fathers and the Mill Hill missions also recognized how important education would be, both to the missions and to the country. Catholics and Protestants vied with one another to produce the more effective educational programs. King's College, Budo, and Gayaza High School, for boys and girls respectively, were the main Protestant secondary schools. Kisubi or St. Mary's was established by the Catholics. As well, "the Protectorate authorities welcomed students at all levels of education since it was only they who could fit into the increasingly complex pattern of modern administration. So there began to emerge a new class, an aristocracy of education which in time tended to usurp the positions of importance formerly occupied by the men who had led the religious factions in war and had won their place in a peaceful land by their strength of character, by their experience and by their powerful following."[18]

Education, then, became one important point of entry into positions of power and prestige.

A second and mediating influence despite factional disputes

---

[17] "The basis of all church life in Uganda is the school." This was a widely held view. See, for example, Herbert Gresford Jones, *Uganda in Transformation, 1876-1926* (London: C. M. S. Press, 1926), p. 61.

[18] K. Ingham, "Some Aspects of the History of Buganda," in *The Kingdom of Buganda* (Kampala: The Uganda Society, 1956), p. 11.

was religion. Missionaries had in many crucial respects become part of the hierarchy.[19] Religious factionalism did not coincide with economic class. Catholic chiefs and peasants, for example, represented a unified social group, centering in the community activities of the church.

Low describes the victory of the Christians and their gaining control of the traditional political system in battle as the Buganda revolution: "Where therefore the Christians gained control of the traditional political system, they gained control of the only structural organization within Buganda to which men yielded a firm loyalty, so that there were no longer traditional organizations or loyalties to challenge the Christians advance. . . . For the Christian element in Buganda arose out of the traditional, revolted against it, gained control of it, and so became reincorporated with it."[20] And by becoming reincorporated with it, religion became an adaptive and mediating force rather than a focal point of conflict in any fundamental sense. Instead of producing fundamental differences in the ideology of the Baganda, religion served to add to a new consensus. In this respect the religious parties appeared more like "political parties." There was competition in placing individual representatives of their "side" in the bureaucracy. But none represented an ideology hostile to the regime.

Why did this occur? Low points out that there was "nothing in the indigenous religion which was culturally essential as an expression of the tribal sentiments for solidarity. These senti-

[19] During the early days of missionary intervention, clients of the missionaries were in effect "stolen" from other chiefs. The position of the missionary developed inside and outside the hierarchy. The missionary was a "chief" who in effect vitiated the absolute authority of the Kabaka; thus this most profound principle of Kiganda political custom was shaken. Religion became then a focal point of trouble, not simply because of the factionalism which grew up between Catholics and Protestant clients of the respective missionaries, but because the struggle of factions was in effect to determine who would control the Kabaka.
When in 1890 Lugard sought to get the Kabaka to sign a treaty, he was at first unsuccessful. The danger of a war grew from his efforts. But the next day after his second attempt, "a wonder happened, for the treaty was signed by the recalcitrant Roman Catholics and the king, and the storm was stilled." Lugard was astonished. "He need not have been astonished, for the explanation of the great change is simple enough. The French fathers bade their faction sign the treaty, an order which was immediately obeyed." See R. P. Ashe, *Chronicles of Uganda* (New York: Randolph & Co., 1895), p. 155.
[20] See D. A. Low, "Religion and Society in Buganda 1875-1900." (Mimeo, E.A.I.S.R., 1956.)

ments were, rather, focused on the unique and exclusive office of the Kabaka. Similarly, reverence for, and dependence upon, ancestors does not seem to have been so strong as elsewhere, and there was certainly no firmly entrenched ancestor worship to provide a stumbling block to the new religions." The Kabaka was not a priest and had superiority over any priest.[21]

A second reason given by Low is perhaps more tentative but extremely interesting as a hypothesis. He remarks that both Anglicanism and Roman Catholicism were peculiarly acceptable to the Baganda because, as in the case of Buganda, they are hierarchical to the extreme. The "Anglican Church even established its Lukiko, the Synod, and today the Rural Deanery boundaries are commensurate with the Saza boundaries, and Rural Deans like to be thought of as ecclesiastical Saza chiefs." Thus "in Buganda the situation usual in other parts of Africa was reverse and it was the pagans, not the Christians who were 'detribalized.' "

Christianity had easy access to the system. By supporting the hierarchy, it helped to produce consensus rather than conflict. Joining together groups which might otherwise have split apart on grounds of economic grievance, it prevented the development of economic class consciousness by establishing more fragmental notions of social status. But status is a more personal affair than class membership. Moral uplift, status striving, and individualism were thus encouraged, within the larger solidarity of Buganda itself. Moral uplift and status competition were, however, translated into more concrete terms. The Christian groups acted as political parties. Those whose educational and religious training were regarded as sound were boosted by the missionaries into positions of importance in the hierarchies of both church and state. Concern with status, which was always significant in Buganda, was thus partly translated into religious terms. But by becoming the means of political and personal advancement by "party" activity, religion was itself secularized.[22]

[21] *Ibid.*

[22] Differences between Catholic and Protestant religious practices and beliefs are significant. The Protestant clergy which came from England were, including the Scottish missionaries, upper middle class. They were, as Low indicates, historically linked with the gentry and the squires. The Anglicans had identification with "Tory radicalism," i.e. social welfare traditions of benevolence for less for-

These remarks are most applicable to the individualistic self-help pattern of Protestantism. The effect of concern for status was that a respectable Muganda must, with the assistance of the church, help himself to become higher on the scale of civilization. Such higher status would derive from individual effort. By introducing social welfare measures, including rural schools, the church made it possible for individual enterprise and effort to count for much. The C.M.S. provided facilities through the church for the reward of individual effort. As a result, the Protestants came to modern nationalism more quickly than the Catholics.

Indeed, a strong argument can be made that the Protestant missionaries heightened the social tension of those Protestants who were closest to achieving the prestige and position offered through the church. This was so because the Protestant missionaries themselves had high status and because they were vastly different in social life and amenities from the Africans with whom they came into contact.[23]

The more education and the greater welfare work of the church, the greater the burden put upon the individual Protestant Muganda. With the exception of those who had achieved truly exceptional positions in the church, even the African clergy (and the church was rapidly Africanized after the establishment of the Native African Church) became markedly status-conscious. They compared themselves to the hierarchy of chiefs and officials. They complained that their pay was low. They were often not particularly well-educated. The best-educated Protestants went into government rather than the church. Thus within the Prot-

---

tunate orders. Scottish groups had traditions of personal responsibility. A pattern of Calvinistic individualism ran through the church. In the C.M.S. these two patterns in a sense combined. In the first instance it led to tremendous concern for the social well-being of the Protestant Baganda and the church hierarchy became a welfare hierarchy. In addition, this put considerable pressure upon government, whose members came from much the same religious tradition, e.g. Tory radicalism.

23 The Protestants brought their wives with them. They reconstructed, in a ruder fashion it is true, the home atmosphere and routine of English cottage life at the minor gentry level. When a Muganda brought his wife to tea in a missionary's home he often emphasized the differences between himself and the missionary. He could see the tangible evidence of those differences in the way tea was served, in the books on the walls, in the husband-wife relationships. And it emphasized how far the ordinary Muganda had to go to achieve what came to be regarded as a fundamental aspect of high prestige—English manners.

estant church itself there developed a strong sense of grievance and a leadership which persisted in feeling underprivileged.

The Catholic missionaries were of two types. There were rather aristocratic French and later Italian senior clergy. Then there were much poorer and lower class farmers. The first ran the church almost as "political" officers. The second ran agricultural training programs and the like; their work was essentially practical and useful. Aristocracy and skill joined hands in a common endeavor. The pattern of celibacy and the simplicity of the corporate life of Catholic missionaries helped to emphasize the ideal of the church spiritual. The Catholics made fewer pretenses at equalitarianism than Protestants but practiced a friendly paternalism. The Protestant missionaries, by emphasizing equality as an ideal, demonstrated its absence. Guilt, avoidance, and a Victorian sense of sin seem to characterize the Protestant Baganda more than the Catholic.[24]

Most of the effective nationalists in Uganda are Protestants (with a few "relapsed" Catholics). The Protestant's appeal is more political. The Catholic's appeal is more religious. The Catholics accept the African priest on precisely the same footing as the European priests. Their paternalism is not on an individual or ethnic basis. Hence the Catholics' mixture of dogma and authoritarianism has less sharp racial overtones than is the case with the Protestants, despite the Protestants' much greater claims to liberalism.

Religion, while it has had a powerful effect on Buganda, has served in part as a progressive and adjustive influence on the social and political hierarchy. It has provided political "parties" in the form of competing groups, Catholic and Protestant. It produced neither fundamental ideological conflict nor repudiation of tradition and custom.

[24] Commenting on this observation, a leading Catholic missionary related in interview: "The Protestants do not understand sin, they are always trying to abolish it. But we know that sin is the state of man. It is part of the human condition. That is why there is a church. No sin—no church." He was arguing that the results of the Protestant attempt to "abolish sin" had produced severe tensions amongst the Protestants. This, he pointed out, coupled with the prestige and status consciousness of the Protestants, had made them aggressive nationalists.

CHAPTER 6

THE ANATOMY OF INTERNAL CONFLICT
IN BUGANDA

IN THE PREVIOUS CHAPTER we attempted to outline the major
protagonists within Buganda who reflected the various groups—
economic, social, and political—which were firmly rooted in the
social scene. Each of them, chiefs, Bataka, Protestants, and Catholics, represented overlapping membership. There was no single
group to which a Muganda gave his generous and overriding
loyalty. That was reserved for the Kabaka. That the autonomous
power of the Kabaka was checked by the superordinacy of the Protectorate government did not lessen the former's right to rule,
although it did serve to intensify the latent conflict between the
Baganda and the Protectorate government.

In practice in the post-Agreement period of political-adminis-
tration, the three regents of the Kabaka's government composed
the government itself. The Great Lukiko became the "parliament"
of Buganda. The Katikiro was made the ex officio president of the
Lukiko, the Omulamuzi was made the vice-president. Decisions
were to be made with the advice of the Lukiko, with that body
serving in some respects as a court of appeal. The Omuwanika
was made the "Speaker" of the house, that is, its presiding officer.

The Kabaka's business with the administration was conducted
by the three ministers, while Her Majesty's chief representative
(earlier the Provincial Commissioner, more latterly the Resident)
had direct access to the Kabaka at any time.

The system of government as established provided for good
working relationships between senior chiefs and Protectorate government officials. The broad cleavages which later appeared in the
relationship were always there, but had been carefully papered
over by the mutual advantages which both British and Baganda
for so long received from the Agreement.

Sources of Instability in Buganda

After the Agreement it was the task of the three regents to
govern Buganda with the advice and consent of the British au-

thorities. The Great Lukiko was "to discuss all matters concerning the native administration of Uganda, and to forward to the Kabaka resolutions which may be voted by a majority regarding measures to be adopted by the said administration."[1] The Lukiko was an extremely important advisory body. It served as a court of appeal from the courts of first instances, held by county chiefs. Built into the Agreement, however, was a check on the Lukiko. The Kabaka was required to consult with Her Majesty's representative before promulgating into law measures and resolutions voted by the Lukiko. Left ambiguous was the degree of responsibility which the Kabaka (and his government) had to the Lukiko. Was the consent of the Lukiko necessary before the enactment of a measure by the Kabaka or was it strongly recommended? Was the Kabaka required to be accountable to the Lukiko to a very high degree or not?

It took a generation before this became an interesting point of issue. But in the immediate post-Agreement period the question was not argued.[2] The legal status of the Lukiko vis-à-vis the Kabaka was less relevant than the fact that it appeared to carry on and formalize a pre-existing pattern by which the Lukiko and the Kabaka were in more or less continuous association with one another and the Kabaka customarily took the advice of the Lukiko on most important matters. In constitutional terms, Article 6 of the Agreement stated that "Her Majesty's Government agrees to recognize the Kabaka of Uganda as the native ruler of the province of Uganda under Her Majesty's protection and over-rule. The King of Uganda shall henceforth be styled His Highness the Kabaka of Uganda. . . . *The Kabaka shall exercise direct rule over the natives of Uganda*, to whom he shall administer justice through the Lukiko, or native council, and through others of his officers in the manner approved by Her Majesty's Government."[3]

[1] See Article 11 of the Uganda Agreement.

[2] Much later, the Protectorate government chose to assert that the Kabaka was not technically responsible to the Lukiko even though he normally acted on their advice, while the Kabaka chose to argue that his accountability to the Lukiko was so great that he could not act without their consent.

[3] Uganda Agreement of 1900, Article 6 (italics mine). Indeed, British officials during the Kabaka crisis were inclined to the view that the intent of Article 6 was that if H.M.G. withdrew recognition of the Kabaka, then so far as the Protectorate government was concerned the whole Buganda government machine would disappear and there would be direct rule.

For all intents and purposes the Buganda government after the Agreement consisted of the three regents, of whom the most powerful figure was Sir Apolo Kagwa. They effectively controlled the Catholic and Protestant chiefs in the Lukiko.

With what major decisions were they concerned? External requirements, not internal demand, whether missionary or Protectorate government, are visible in a list of the earlier Buganda laws. The first, passed in 1904, dealt with the prevention of abortion; the second dealt with short-changing among peoples not familiar with British currency (the prevention of cheating law). The third forbade the carrying of large knives (the carrying of knives law). The fourth was concerned with the use of indecent language (the law of using indecent language).[4]

Not until 1908 was an important law passed and this dealt with the nature of freehold among the Baganda (limits of disposal, inheritance, and easement). This in itself is significant. The chiefs were the major landlords. The important matters of the day were those which affected them. Otherwise, the only significant measures were entertained by the Lukiko at the request of the Protectorate government. From 1908 until 1913 all laws passed by the Lukiko dealt with land. The single exception was a 1908 sleeping sickness law which the Protectorate government requested after the great sleeping sickness epidemic which decimated parts of Busoga and threatened the lake area of Buganda.

After 1913, laws were passed aimed at preventing venereal disease and smallpox.

Because the tax regulations and provisions for law and order had been laid down in the Agreement, and considering also that many of the problems of the Baganda with respect to crime, inheritance, labor, gardening, and so on, were soluble without a series of laws, the concerns of the Lukiko remain remarkably small and cramped. The real issues of the day were those significant to the chiefs. It was not long before popular grievances began to be heard. In particular the Bataka charged the chiefs with irresponsibility. The chiefs responded not only as a party of chiefs, but as members of the bureaucracy.[5]

---

 [4] A set of the early laws can be found in Turton, Griffin, and Lewey, *Laws of the Uganda Protectorate*, Vol. vi, "Native Agreements and Buganda Native Laws."

 [5] A powerful bureaucracy grew up which was an extended arm of the Protectorate government. The bureaucracy had its own canons and its own methods

It was here that the chiefs were so powerful, for, faced with competition, they had reinforced their own positions. First, they were a major political group, defending their interests against others who had not received land in the Agreement. Second, they were the government. As a government, not only did they represent themselves as a party but they heeded the wishes of the Protectorate government. Third, they were the administrators of the Kingdom. They had powers as representatives of both the Kabaka and his government and the Protectorate government. As administrators they were in a position to apply almost arbitrary power.

After the Agreement, then, tremendous power accrued to the chiefs centering in the three roles open to them in the exercise of power. To whom was the government accountable? In terms of the internal workings of the system, it was accountable to the Lukiko. But the Lukiko was almost entirely dominated by the chiefs. Hence the chiefs were largely accountable to themselves.

Equally, at each level of the chieftaincy hierarchy there was a similar pattern of accountability: councils dominated by official majorities whereby important issues were made known at a local level to the *nkiko* at the miruka, gombolola, and saza levels. If appeals from the decisions of lower councils were to be heard at a higher level, it was the chiefs in Lukiko who had to decide whether or not to forward an issue from a lower to a higher council. Hence the principles of accountability worked on a ramified local government level in much the same way they did on the Buganda government level. It was the chief who controlled the local council, thus it was the chief's political group which was dominant in local affairs. It was also the chief who in his executive authority wielded the powers of both central and Buganda government at the local level.

This meant that in addition to extensive controls provided by the tiered council system whereby information on local issues was sent upward to the Buganda government, the local councils helped to preserve the local organization of the chiefs as a politi-

of playing politics; more than anything else, with its duties of maintaining order and discipline, collecting taxes, and administering local justice, it provided a model of rational calculation. It built on traditional military and territorial notions of rule, thereby maintaining a traditional underpinning. It was associated with high church membership, propriety, and the unabashed use of power. It was headed by the most powerful figure in Buganda, Sir Apolo.

cal party. Here was no unstructured group based simply upon landholding. It was organized by the very structure of government itself. Each local council was, in effect, a local solidary unit of the chiefs' party, dominated by the chiefs. As administrators, the chiefs carried out the interests of the oligarchy which as a party controlled the government. As administrators, too, they controlled coercion and punishment, handled manumission of fees and taxes, and had magisterial duties for certain classes of cases. Hence the administrator was tax collector, judge, controller of local police forces, and determinant of entry into the power and prestige positions of the local community. He was restricted by only three groups: the Protectorate authority, with which for a long period the chiefs were in close alliance; the missionaries, who had in fact schooled and trained the senior chiefs; and the Bataka, who suffered such severe blows under the Agreement that for a long time they could not pose a serious threat to their powers.

From 1900 until 1914 there were few audible grumblings about the system. Those that were heard came from the chiefs themselves, dissatisfied as they were about certain features of land redistribution and surveying. After 1914 the system began gradually to show signs of weakness and decay and, fittingly enough, it began and appeared in controversy over the function and position of the Kabaka.

Meanwhile, the older generation of administrators and missionaries, those who had been the firm friends and allies of the chiefs, began to make ready for their departure. Younger men, more concerned to take an active part in administration, interested in active government at the center, began to replace them. The smooth working relationships between British officials and chiefs slowly became impaired. Impatience and concern began to mar their cordiality. Multiple images of the same situation began to develop, as well as a selective recall of historical events by the participants, causing a growing dissimilarity of viewpoint between British and Baganda.

The Bakopi and the Bataka began to push their grievances with greater resolve. They complained about the monopoly of power maintained by the chiefs. They complained about certain issues over which Sir Apolo exercised tight control. These complaints began to reach the governor. One petition in 1913, for example, read that "Sir Apolo is doing us very bad indeed because he does not hear us if we take our cases in the Lukiko and he talks in a big voice so as to make us stop so that his friends win the cases. He is not listen to us but only tries cases as he want for those he wants to win them. We tell you this Sir because we fear very much that Apolo will make our Kabaka a bad man also."

In November of the same year, reports with reference to the vacant saza chieftaincy of Kabula, which had a large Catholic population, said that if anyone other than a Protestant was appointed to the chieftaincy, trouble would be visited on the entire Roman Catholic community of Buganda.

Finally, a new factor began to enter. The Kabaka, no longer a child, began to hear clan cases as Sabataka. This brought him into direct contact with the clan elders.

We can discuss each of these matters in terms of three important issues. One was the investiture controversy. A second was the Bataka and the land. The third was the dismissal of Sir Apolo.

The Investiture Controversy

On August 8, 1914 the Kabaka's investiture took place. The first to occur after British control, it was a matter of central concern to the three main participants, the British administration, the missionaries, and the chiefs.[6] The missionaries were concerned that a suitable religious ceremony, on a Westminster model, should accompany the investiture. For them the coronation was in essence religious: a compact between a king and his people on the one hand, and a king and God on the other. Furthermore, since Daudi Chwa, the new Kabaka, had been brought up as a Protestant, it would be a ringing testimonial to the power of the Protestant churches, both C.M.S. and Native Anglican Church. The government, on the other hand, took the position that the coronation was an official function between Her Majesty's government and the Kabaka's government.

The chiefs, too, participated in the preparations. They took up questions of protocol and tradition. They raised certain mat-

[6] The previous investiture was that of Kabaka Mwanga, whose coronation was the last to seem in accordance with custom.

ters of custom and tradition; so did the Bataka. Sir Apolo advised on every stage of the affair. One problem became central. If the Kabaka was to be properly installed, what traditional features of his role had to be retained at the ceremony? The Mugema, at that time still hereditary saza chief of Busiro, and also head of the Monkey clan, argued that he was the one to have first order of eminence at the coronation and that his office should, as in the past, administer the oath. Furthermore, he argued, the other hereditary officeholders should come forward and take "premier" positions. Legitimacy was laid down by the traditionalists to the chiefs.

Further, just as in mythical lore Kintu was the first Kabaka and the Baganda are *Bantu* (children of Kintu), only the descendants of Kintu according to a hereditary principle can change the customs and traditions of the Baganda. Hence, although the investiture took place under the auspices of British and Baganda, did not the British view of the proceedings violate the strength of custom? Indeed, did this not make the chiefs into agents of British rule, disloyal to custom? There was little doubt that the Mugema represented both an important and popular view.

Both government and the missionaries became concerned at the controversy. To the latter, a coronation was a solemn and Christian occasion. The Mugema, although a Protestant, could not see the issues of custom as either Christian or pagan. The government, on the other hand, wished to demonstrate that the ceremony was a public and official affirmation of the Agreement itself, binding upon a new monarch about to take office. It was certainly not concerned with orders of precedent for traditional leaders. On the Mugema's claims for precedence for himself and other customary officials, the Protectorate government referred the matter to the Lukiko. The Lukiko thereby became involved in matters of custom with just the group it felt to be its greatest antagonists, the Bataka. For the Mugema was not only head of the Monkey clan with his special prerogatives as a saza chief. He was also the leading Mutaka in the country.[7]

To resolve the conflict, two ceremonies had to be held, one

[7] It was not long afterward that Mugema was stripped of his saza chieftaincy and the chieftaincy of Busiro was made appointive.

European, the other customary. A breach had been made, not so much between what was Christian and what was not, as between "true" Kiganda and "foreign." From now on, the Baganda's struggles were associated with the proper position of the Kabaka in the system. With the investiture of the Kabaka, the question of his authority and its legitimacy became important.[8]

All these issues loomed on the horizon with the investiture of His Highness, Kabaka Daudi Chwa. Conflict between the clan leaders and the chiefs, which had been going on for generations, broke out afresh, this time in the context of a growing Buganda nationalism—a nationalism focusing on the position of the Kabaka himself and thereby on the basic relationship of Buganda to the Protectorate government. This conflict, in the context of the post-Agreement period, threatened to embroil the chiefs in their three capacities, as a political group, as a government, and as administrators. It threatened as well to imperil their relationships with the missionaries and the Protectorate officials, the two outside groups with whom they had hitherto been firm allies.

The Bataka Controversy[9]

The Bataka controversy came to a head right after the close of the First World War. By May 1922, two Bataka factions in Buganda were identifiable. The first, headed by the Mugema, was particularly aggravated that the Lukiko was controlled and dominated by Sir Apolo Kagwa. The second was in effect Sir Apolo's organization, created as a counter to the first. The Bataka Association, the group headed by Mugema, had in its membership

---

[8] Of course, what occurred in the "true" Kiganda ceremony was not entirely faithful to custom. They did not, for example, adorn the king with back tendons of a son of the Nankere. Even "old custom" was purged and Christianized. I am indebted to L. A. Fallers for bringing this point to my attention.

[9] The term *Bataka* has, as we have seen, several meanings. The organized Bataka which appeared on the political scene were not coterminous with the clan system. In each case, from 1922 down to the present, the organized groupings which bore the name *Bataka* were never the clan system as an organized force. They were simply some members of it, usually not the leading members who spoke sometimes in the name of the clans generally but in most instances only for their own particular grouping within the clans. Difficulty in defining the Bataka "movement" has arisen because there are so many referents to the term. In its most generic form, it can be said that every Muganda is a Mutaka. This means that the identity of a Baganda is in terms of his clan. It is clan membership which separates the Muganda from the non-Muganda and it is the clan which in that respect is the keeper of genealogy. A basic kinship structure, it allows individuals

16 clan heads and one representative of the Sabalangira. The anti-Mugema group, "The Association of the Bataka which protects the Agreement of 1900 regarding the land of the Bataka," later changed its name to the "Association of the Bataka which disagree with the questions regarding land which Mugema brought forward in connection with the Agreement of 1900."

Two important figures, both senior Bataka, were instrumental in establishing the Bataka movement. The first was the Mugema, who regarded himself as a holder of custom and virtue, while the more ephemeral chiefs were opportunists. Wrapped up in his role were the two important issues of land rights and legitimacy.

The second was James Miti, who was to play such an important part in the rise of Kiganda nationalism and to die in custody of the police. He had been an important chief in Bunyoro, a senior Mutaka of the Genet clan. He was concerned over the alliance between chiefs and British; more particularly, after his retirement as a chief, he became interested in Bakopi affairs.

---

to expect help from other clan members even when they are strangers.

This has facilitated mobility within Buganda. For example, if a member of a given clan comes from Busiro and travels to Buddu, he can expect shelter, food, and assistance from his clan member in Buddu. In that sense a sharing of responsibility by one Muganda for another is present through the clan system. Representatives of the different clans, although clustered more heavily perhaps in one saza than another, are nevertheless widely dispersed throughout Buganda. In this widest sense, then, citizenship is a clan matter, and identity is in clan terms. Every chief, for example, upon receiving his appointment, establishes his identity by stating his clan as well as his immediate family. It must be remembered that the Kabaka as Sabataka is head of all the clans. Hence clan identity and citizenship are both social and symbolic. Actually, *chaka* means land, *Mutaka* and *Bataka* are personal derivatives, and *butaka* means homestead.

The ramified use of the word *Mutaka* to extend to every Muganda is thus simply a reference to one aspect of dual association and membership in Buganda; it emphasizes an integrative base which fundamentally relates the Baganda to one another.

Bataka also refers to the clan elders at the differing levels of kinship organization. These levels, from Kasolya on one hand, to Enda on the other, are important both as allocative mechanisms in terms of land use and property inheritance, and evaluative with respect to proper behavior. Having such sanction and support, the Bataka are the official watchdogs of personal behavior according to Kiganda standards. Hence they are keepers of custom in a very real sense.

Richards, citing a study made by Sir Apolo Kagwa, notes that there were 23 clan authorities who "avoided meeting the Kabaka because they had formerly been independent and hence did not care to see the man who had been their equal and had then 'turned them into peasants (*bakopi*).'" The situation was remedied by Kabaka Mutesta I, but the animosity persists to this day. See Audrey Richards, *East African Chiefs* (London: Faber and Faber, 1960), p. 46. See also Low and Pratt, *op.cit.*, pp. 233-236.

Their joint complaint to the Kabaka initiated a long and difficult series of events. The complaint read as follows:

"1. To start the reorganization of Butaka estates that existed before the advent to this country of His Majesty's Government of England.

"2. To give back all Butaka estates to the original proprietors in accordance with our native customs.

"3. To preserve and see that each one gets his original Butaka estate and the British Government ratifies and preserves same.

"4. To recognize all clan institutions that exist in the country and their relative duties to our Kabaka and for each clan to have a representative who airs his interests in the central legislature as we used to do in the olden times."[10]

The issues thus joined in the Bataka affair were as follows. First, there was the question of the estates themselves, involving the alleged injustice done by the Lukiko in its allocation of land.

Second, as the petition was directed to the Kabaka, the question of the Kabaka's power vis-à-vis the Lukiko was raised. Did Sir Apolo overrule the Kabaka by his control over the Lukiko? Did the Lukiko have the power to override a decision of the Kabaka?

Third, the issue of the Agreement itself came to a head. Did failure of the Bataka to agree to a position taken by the Buganda government and the Lukiko constitute disloyalty and the undermining of the Agreement? Conversely, did the Lukiko's failure to allocate land according to one interpretation of its mandate (an interpretation accepted by the Kabaka) constitute a non-sanctioned act and thus represent a violation of the Agreement?

It was the Agreement which was flaunted in the faces of the Bataka Association leaders. Sir Apolo argued that some Bataka were determined to break the 1900 Agreement which "was entered into on behalf of the Kabaka, chiefs and people of Buganda as it appears in the preamble of the Agreement; every Muganda is therefore bound to preserve and protect it." In effect the Bataka Association was charged with disloyalty. Unrepresented in the Lukiko, opposed on a political level by the much more powerful chiefs' group, and regarded as working against the interests

10 See Chapter XVI in P. M. K. Lwanga, *The Life of James Miti* (an unpublished manuscript in the E.A.I.S.R. files).

of Buganda, the Bataka seemed to be without allies and without major support. Moreover, by this means a precedent had been set. The Agreement was now to be regarded as an inviolate document, and whoever controlled the government of Buganda would be its apparent interpreter.

Sir Apolo replied that the Butaka lands as well as the whole country were always in the absolute power of the Kabaka. Going further, he said that in its allocations of land the Lukiko was not obligated to provide Butaka estates. Indeed, it revived the precivil war custom by respecting some Butaka claims.[11]

The Kabaka, his antagonism to Sir Apolo increasing, heard the case which the Bataka Association brought before him and decided in their favor. In his decision of May 13, 1922, the Kabaka found

1. That the Bataka submissions were mainly justified;

2. That as a result of the distribution of freehold over Butaka holdings the bones of the dead were exhumed and presumably moved;

3. That while the chief Butaka estates (*kasolya*) were in fact in the hands of the rightful owners under mailo distribution, the secondary Butaka or branch estates (*amasiga*) were less fortunate. These were in many cases lost to the clan. A third level of Butaka estates, subbranch, was eliminated. These estates were

[11] No one principle of allocation seemed actually to prevail over all others. All the most important and well-known Butaka lands of every clan were returned to the head of each clan *who was a chief at the time.*

The Carter Commission quoted a White Fathers' memorandum as follows: "The number of miles (8,000) having been shared out to a great number of chiefs, they then, the great chiefs beginning, chose their miles wherever it suited their good pleasure, preferring of course the 'byalo' (villages), the most densely populated and the most fertile. Many a time were the rights of the bataka or the founders or chiefs of the masiga (branches of the family) violated. The order of dignity was followed in the taking of possession of the miles, the King's miles being chosen first, followed by those of the Regents, then those of chiefs of counties, and lastly those of the smaller chiefs or batongole. It happened more than once that a village possessed by the founders or chief of such and such muziro (totem) fell into the hands and possession of a member of a totally different muziro. And it must be said that the chiefs themselves did not bother much about the bataka, and more than once a chief of clan who had villages belonging to such a totem family, was evicted from his right of tenure. Complaints were quickly stifled, the chiefs saying that this was a new order of things introduced by the Government, so that those who were the natural proprietors of the land, or at least a great number of them only kept a small part of it, or saw a great number of their villages pass into the hands of those foreign to their totem or muziro."

either individually held or belonged to deities (*Balubale*) which were "abolished by religion," that is, were abolished when Christianity became pervasive. He ruled that the Lukiko should allocate land to any Mutaka who could prove that he had lost his estate. This land would then be used by the Mutaka in exchange for Butaka estates already held by landowners. As Pratt puts it, "It was a shrewdly-conceived and very moderate solution. Unlike the British proposal of 1918, it would not have forced the present mailo owner to give up Butaka land on his estate and accept other land in compensation if he did not so desire. Rather it would be the Bataka who would be given other land in compensation. However, the heavily-biassed Lukiko rejected this proposal and offered, instead, a resolution that whenever Butaka land were offered for sale by its present owner the Bataka would be given first option on its purchase."[12]

The Kabaka's decision was a great boon to the Bataka. The Association adopted a new name, the Federation of Bataka Bamasiga. Their most powerful leader (until he was deported) was the Mugema. Then James Miti, a powerful senior Mutaka who had been a Muganda saza chief in Bunyoro until his retirement, took over. Secretaries of the Federation were Daudi Basudde and Yuda Musoke Kasa, both farmers and lower ranking Bataka.[13]

Under the strong leadership of Sir Apolo, the Lukiko rejected the Kabaka's solution and sought a compromise formula empowering the Lukiko to evaluate Butaka claims. Meanwhile, the Association rejected the Lukiko's views. "It is difficult for a person who instituted a case for the recovery of his Butaka land and won it, to be told that he would merely be thought of by the Lukiko consisting of the people who previously deprived us of our Butaka estates and whom we have defeated in our case." Rather, the Bataka suggested that an area the Kabaka proposed to give to the Bataka should be reserved for those who illegitimately occupied Butaka lands. The latter could then release their Butaka holdings which would revert to the Bataka. Indeed, the Bataka Association argued this was the only way the chiefs— who broke the Agreement, since the Agreement had said that the

[12] See Low and Pratt, *op.cit.*, p. 235.

[13] It is James Miti who provides a thread of continuity between the first Bataka disputes and the later Bataka Party; the party developed in the thirties and forties and was banned for its part in riots in 1949.

rightful owners should be confirmed in possession—could rectify matters.

Further, argued the Bataka Association, a new Lukiko was required; the Lukiko of 1922 was all on the side of those who deprived the Bataka of their estates. The Association claimed that "the present Lukiko says we shall sit in the Lukiko to settle the matters of your Butaka lands, what can you do, when you have no voice in the Lukiko, it is in our power to agree or to refuse to give you back your estates and you will have to beg."

The issue was important enough for the Protectorate government to become involved. The Bataka Association brought their charges to the Governor. They were not successful. The alliance between Sir Apolo and the Protectorate government was weakened but still held. Agreeing only partially with Sir Apolo's interpretation of the Agreement, and fearful that if the question of allocation were raised the whole matter of land would grow to monstrous proportions, the government indicated that the Lukiko had properly done its work. Nevertheless, it turned the matter over to a commission composed of the Chief Justice and the Provincial Commissioner.

Political Effects of the Bataka Controversy

The Federation became a mechanism whereby (a) clan leaders at many levels within the same clan felt themselves aggrieved and began to communicate with one another; and (b) clan leaders at the siga level in different clans (often living in the same area) began to do the same thing. Several members of the early organization, particularly Shem Spire Mukasa and Serwano Kulubya, were powerful in Mengo. They publicly proclaimed that when the Lukiko was to embark on its land allocation duties each saza chief was ordered to prepare a list of persons in possession of land, in terms of Article 13 of the Uganda Agreement. The Lukiko scrutinized these lists, examined applications, and adjudicated on many disputes and issues. They argued that many people did not recognize the meaning of freehold land tenure and therefore did not press their claims, or, if overlooked, did not take the matter up. The Lukiko had given weight only to the most senior Bataka who were also mostly chiefs. Therefore these senior Bataka acted with the chiefs and were, in clan terms, disloyal. These arguments helped to identify chieftaincy as the enemy. As well, they were well calculated to appeal to the Bakopi; for example, they identified a common poverty and abuse at the hands of the chiefs who were also the landlords. In a manner of speaking, the traditional identification of the clan system with rural life was given an additional focus. This focus was based on mutual deprivation of Bataka and Bakopi by the hierarchy. It was not long before this sense of grievance became centered on the Katikiro, Sir Apolo and his ministers.

When the Commission of Enquiry, consisting of the Provincial Commissioner of Buganda (J. C. H. Sturrock) and the Chief Justice (Charles Griffith), concluded its two-week investigations, it found itself sifting charges and countercharges which involved questions of customs and tradition as well as of fact. Sir Apolo's position was that there was no difference between Bataka land and other land; all, he argued, were in the absolute power of the Kabaka. This was quite correct. But in practice it was relatively rare for the Kabaka to deprive the clan of Butaka holdings, except in the late nineteenth century. This, the answer of the Bataka, was also correct. Charged with favoring the chiefs at the expense of the Bataka, Sir Apolo argued that Sir Harry Johnston had paid no attention to Bataka claims to land but was concerned only about the chiefs. Indeed, it was Sir Apolo and the regents who went back to precivil war custom in order to ensure the restoration of important and well-known Butaka lands to every Mutaka who was then a chief. The Federation replied that the qualification of chieftaincy, and not of Mutakaship, had been the instrumental factor in the restoration of these lands. Kagwa answered that in the old days land was distributed not for the benefit of clans but to create new chieftaincies. There was no Mutaka who ever drove out a Mutongole from his estate, but it was a recognized custom for the Batongole and principal chiefs to deprive the Bataka of their Butaka lands and estates and the Bataka were thus rendered mere tenants. In fact, argued Sir Apolo, the Bataka were attempting to get back lands lost under previous Kabakas. He charged James Miti, who he admitted was an important Mutaka, with having lost his estates in 1893 when Stanislaus Mugwanya (the leading Catholic chief, a regent and former co-Katikiro with Sir Apolo) distributed land in Mawokota among the Roman Catholics. Miti was a Protestant and therefore lost his estate. But Mugwanya gave the Butaka land of his clan to Miti's nephew, a Roman Catholic. Meanwhile, the Bataka attempted to specify two types of land, Butaka lands under the control of the Kabaka as Sabataka, the supreme Mutaka, and land under the chiefs given out by the Kabaka as Kabaka for administrative purposes. Sir Apolo admitted that the allotment of land was not subject to the native custom of the clan system of Buganda but was "mainly for the benefit of the principal chiefs." It was an argument that fell on increasingly unsympathetic ears.

The controversy itself was not resolved. Rather, it fizzled. The Bataka were of course disappointed that more positive action was not taken on their behalf. They wrote to the Governor as follows: "Your Excellency, we took our matters to H. H. Kabaka asking that our seats which were taken from us be returned to us (Bataka) in which we used to sit before all the kings of Buganda. Your Excellency these seats were taken away from us in 1900 while our Kabaka was still young, and the Batongole filled them up in order that they might keep us out of the Lukiko which deals with our nation affairs (*sic*) and in order that we may not have a voice with which to state what we see is wrong and what is ruining our nation. We wrote three letters to H. H. Kabaka asking for these seats.

"In Kabaka's reply to our first letter he stated that it is impossible for Bataka to sit in Lukiko, in his second letter he said that the Lukiko of Buganda Kingdom is for Batongole only. In his third letter . . . he stated 'the matter of having the voice of the Lukiko which you ask for cannot be agreed to by me as the 1900 Agreement put you out and the Batongole remained in Lukiko. . . .' We wrote to the P. C. Buganda putting before him the same matter but we did not receive his reply whereas we Bataka bore our children and these children are given to Kabaka and they are then called Batongole. Well it is therefore not desirable for them to discuss the nation's affairs while we who bore them are absent."[14]

The Colonial Secretary, to whom the matter was finally referred in 1926, did not propose to take any action. He informed

[14] Letter from Jalaki Musajakawa and others to His Excellency the Governor, 30 September 1925.

the public that he would not interfere in whatever settlement the Baganda made. The Lukiko did not take further action. The Bataka, although weakened by the deportation of the Mugema who had become involved in a Malakite movement, began to meet regularly, once a week, in James Miti's house, even though Miti was mostly away in Bunyoro. Though Miti himself has since died, these meetings have continued up to the present.

The Bataka won a moral victory for themselves. The lower ranking Bataka elders were identified with peasant demands. Some features of clan organization were put to the service of a loosely-knit and fluctuating political organization, an organization which identified more and more with Kiganda nationalism. A wider use of the term Bataka, to include all Baganda, a more populist but also more conservative and nationalist meaning, became widespread. Less and less a parochial and somewhat defensive group, the Bataka became more of a peasants' party— wronged, aggrieved, proud, and traditionalist. They reserved a higher and prior right, based on custom, to evaluate the actions not only of chiefs but of the Kabaka himself. We shall return to the more contemporary role of the Bataka, as they appeared in the Bataka Party, in a subsequent chapter.

The Apolo Kagwa Case

Writing about Sir Apolo's days as one of a small band of Protestant intimates which included Zakaria Kizito Kisingiri, Henry Wright Duta, Batolomayo Musoke, and Yairo Mutakyala, Tucker says that he asked Apolo what the difference was between the old days and the new. According to Tucker, Apolo replied, "Oh! it is the joy, I had no joy in life then, but now it is all joy." Tucker commented that he could well believe it and felt that a happier Christian never praised his Lord.[15]

Another view of him is offered by Lugard. "At the beginning of April, 1891, the Mohammedans having made continual raids into the country, the Christians, under the leadership of Kagwa —now Katikiro—marched against them with some four thousand seven hundred guns and twelve thousand spearmen. . . . No sooner had the burning question of who should be the general of

[15] Alfred R. Tucker, *Eighteen Years in Uganda and East Africa* (London: Edward Arnold, 1908), Vol. I, pp. 120-121.

the combined armies been settled than the Katikiro demanded a Union Jack to carry as the flag of the army."[16]

Finally, Roscoe, writing of the band of teachers and chiefs who represented progress and devotion, said of Sir Apolo that he "stands out as a leader, not only in religious matters, but also in civil and political life; he has been a wise guide and faithful leader in everything that would lead to progressive development. He has ever been ready to take an active share even in menial work that would be for the good of the country; after hours spent in court with the consideration of complicated questions of government, he would be found writing the minutes of meetings with the results of their discussions, or fashioning windows and doors. He was also able to fit his house with electric bells, he learned to ride a bicycle, and he introduced habits of progress and comfort into the small matters of daily life, while during business hours in court he was introducing enlightened measures for governing the country, under the guidance of British officers. In more recent years he has obtained a printing press, and has issued various booklets, giving the history of the country, with many valuable details concerning former kings and clans with their peculiarities, together with other useful information. In addition to these booklets he has published official pamphlets and papers for the guidance of chiefs and other persons in authority who in the heart of the country may be cut off from the help and guidance of the British officials. . . . Yet in spite of all these labours he has ever been studying new ideas for his personal improvement, has collected information about his own people and his ancestors, and has found leisure to show attentions to travellers and friends, and not least to attend to family worship, Bible study, and religious services."[17]

A Christian, a soldier, a leader of his people, an interpreter of customs, and a model of progress and endeavor in his own life— it is small wonder that not a little of the high regard of the British for the Baganda stemmed from their respect and affection for such men as Sir Apolo. Roscoe adds that while "Sir Apolo deservedly stands at the head of his nation, he is widely and ably

[16] Sir F. D. (later Lord) Lugard, *The Story of the Uganda Protectorate* (London: Marshall & Son, n.d.), pp. 111-112.

[17] John Roscoe, *Twenty-five Years in East Africa* (Cambridge: Cambridge University Press, 1921), pp. 172-173.

supported by a large number of capable men whose lives will bear the closest inspection, and who will become more illustrious the better they are known." Seldom has a corps of African leaders been so highly regarded by alien rulers, and rare have been the men of Sir Apolo's character. Much of the structure, organization, and progressive oligarchy which characterized Buganda after the Agreement was his own work.

Sir Apolo gave the British small cause for complaint. Not that he was simply their instrument: he was a toughminded man who quite understood the mechanisms of power. Gradually, however, the inner circle of his intimates, those who had fought the civil wars and been important in missionary circles, whittled down. A generation of relatively poor and despised African Anglican clergy identified with the Bakopi rather than the chiefs. A new generation of English missionaries shared their sympathies. A peasant priesthood developed.[18]

The time came when the men who had worked long and continuously with Sir Apolo—Sir Harry Johnston, Sir Frederick Jackson, Wilson, and others in the administration—had to be replaced by newcomers. One of those who took up duties as Assistant District Commissioner of Kampala was a former insurance agent who had entered the Colonial Service. He was a person whose stature (both physical and intellectual) was so small that Sir Apolo ignored him. It was he who precipitated the crisis leading to Sir Apolo's downfall. Becoming Assistant District Commissioner in Kampala at the start of his second tour in Africa in 1911, Postlethwaite recalled that with respect to Uganda he felt "rightly or wrongly, that we had no definite native policy there.

"At every corner we ran up against the Uganda Agreement and the powers of self-determination which that treaty had conferred upon the Buganda. We seemed neither to have the will to break the Agreement in the interests of the advancement of the Buganda (*sic*), nor the willingness to accept loyally the position

[18] The selection of clergy was such that they came mainly from the ranks of the Bakopi. By 1925 there was one Christian teacher to every 660 people for Uganda as a whole (including outlying districts). The high concentration of peasant priests provided a major factor in the alienation of younger educated groups and peasantry from Sir Apolo. For a discussion of these peasant priests see H. Gresford Jones, *Uganda in Transformation, 1876-1926* (London: Church Missionary Society, 1926), pp. 241-242.

as it was, and develop on slower lines. We appeared to be eternally giving orders which were obeyed or not, at the sweet will of the Buganda Native Government, the entire virtual authority of which was vested in the Katikiro Sir Apolo Kagwa. Apolo, incidentally, was already becoming frightened of losing his power owing to the approaching manhood of Daudi, the Kabaka, to whom many of the Baganda definitely looked to free them from the Katikiro's despotism."[19]

Postlethwaite was not impressed with the history of collaboration between Sir Apolo and the British. He was in the vanguard of those administrators who were concerned to administer, mete out justice, and establish orderly progress and efficiency. His was not the explorer and adventure-loving kind of administrator of an earlier generation, but the first of the bureaucratic-colonial generation. He felt that the chiefs as an oligarchy running the government and as a party representing itself had produced basic inequities in the system. He was appalled by the treatment of the Bakopi by chiefs who regarded them as serfs. In particular, he was outraged about such practices as *kasanvu*, the system of forced, paid labor, whereby the government got much of its work done. It was a system which lent itself to abuse and favoritism on the part of chiefs responsible for this form of labor.

Postlethwaite's first clash with Sir Apolo was over forced labor. He requisitioned a number of men for forced labor when his Provincial Commissioner was absent and his District Commissioner ill, and only half the number arrived at the given date. In his own words the situation looked "impossible and undignified, and with considerable trepidation I informed the Katikiro that I considered failure to meet our requirements constituted a breach of the section of the Agreement which insisted upon the loyal co-operation of the native government, and that unless the full number were forthcoming within twenty-four hours, I required the Lukiko . . . to be suspended until the matter had been referred to the Governor."[20]

For this action, Postlethwaite found himself exceedingly unpopular with everyone, administrators and missionaries, not to

[19] J. R. P. Postlethwaite, *I Look Back* (London: Boardman and Co., 1947), p. 42.
[20] *Ibid.*, p. 43.

speak of Sir Apolo, who regarded him as a very junior novice quite beneath notice. Postlethwaite had committed a monstrous breach of an etiquette which had grown up between British officers serving in Buganda and the Kabaka's government under Sir Apolo. One or the other party would have to be humiliated. Postlethwaite was transferred to another province.

Nevertheless, what was latent among younger government officers had been given voice at least for the first time. They were anxious to ensure Sir Apolo's accountability to the administration. What remained was to find a way to bring Buganda more directly into line with Protectorate policy.[21] By 1925, when Sir William F. Gowers was appointed Governor, the situation had become apparent to all. For his ally the Kabaka sought the support of the Governor, who was most sympathetic to the Kabaka's complaint.

The regular Provincial Commissioner, well aware of the state of affairs, nevertheless retained considerable affection for Sir Apolo. His staunch loyalty to the British government and his infinite capacity for hard work brought him both friends and enemies, and the Commissioner felt that most of the attacks on the Katikiro were unfair. Moreover, he was not convinced that the Kabaka, a "boy of slender experience," could successfully stand up to Kagwa. Troubled by the situation, he turned to the Chief Secretary in whom he found a sympathetic listener. Thus the Chief Secretary and the Provincial Commissioner supported Sir Apolo, while Postlethwaite, a man infinitely junior to both, received the support of the Governor. At this juncture, the Pro-

---

[21] Complicating matters for the British authorities was their obligation to support an increasingly restive Kabaka. Either the Kabaka would be unable to make decisions, with the Katikiroship responsible to him in name only, or Sir Apolo had to be curbed. The conflict between Daudi Chwa and Sir Apolo had reached critical proportions by 1922 when the Kabaka wrote to the Governor that Sir Apolo caused divisions in the Lukiko on matters under discussion so as to favor his own party, or promoted dissension so that issues could be kept undecided. He charged further that Sir Apolo caused argument over appointments of chiefs and did not want chiefs of his own age to resign. He would not reduce the number of old men who always sided with him. There was favoritism in selection of new chiefs; sometimes the new appointees were relatives by blood and marriage. Further, Sir Apolo kept decisions to himself and ignored majority decisions of the Lukiko. Because of his strategic position he was able to control the range of issues brought into Lukiko for discussion. Finally, the Kabaka noted that "from the very first day on which His Majesty the King of England confirmed me as Kabaka of Buganda we have not ceased to disagree as to our duties." See Low and Pratt, *op.cit.*, pp. 219-223.

vincial Commissioner went on leave and Postlethwaite applied to the new Governor for the post of Acting Provincial Commissioner of Buganda. "I told him that I should, if appointed, consider it my duty to join issue with the existing state of affairs, and from now on I was conscious, throughout a somewhat worrying official spell of work, that I could depend upon Sir William Gowers for the benefit of his guidance, based on the experience of many years of African administration, and for his official support when it was needed."[22] The Governor accepted this position and Postlethwaite was appointed Acting Provincial Commissioner.

The incident which precipitated major conflict related to beer permits. The Protectorate government had, in the early 1920's, asked the Buganda government to help limit beer drinking in the Kibuga, a heavily populated African area on the outskirts of Kampala. This area also includes Mengo and the seat of the Buganda government. The Kibuga is a gombolola. Although an urban area, it is run by a gombolola chief, the *Omukulu we Kibuga*. It was his responsibility to enforce the law regarding beer permits.

To assist the Omukulu we Kibuga, the Katikiro first instructed the Secretary of the Lukiko to provide the gombolola chief with lists of those who had received permits. But the Secretary failed to do this and the Omukulu we Kibuga appealed to the Kabaka for help; with typical caution, the Kabaka simply reaffirmed that drunkenness must be reduced.

The Acting Provincial Commissioner supported the Katikiro. But to his surprise, Sir Apolo was now arguing that the Secretary to the Lukiko did not need to issue lists. This left the Omukulu we Kibuga in a most difficult position. He was blamed for the drunkenness in his area but was not provided with the necessary information about licenses to do anything about it. The Katikiro now charged that the whole matter was simply an attempt by the Omukulu we Kibuga to gain the power of issuing licenses on his own authority.

Matters quickly came to a head. Said Postlethwaite, "As so often happens, the turmoil of the resumption of control, and the assertion of our right and duty to superintend the native government's machinations, commenced on quite a minor issue. . . .

[22] *Ibid.*, p. 108.

There had been a great increase of drunkenness in the Kibuga, or native capital, and the chief in charge of the Kibuga came first to the District Commissioner and then to myself, and stated his inability to exercise adequate control, owing to a curious system by which the Katikiro and the clerk to the Lukiko, incidentally, the former's son-in-law—issued permits for the introduction of beer into the Kibuga, without prior consultation with himself. I found from the office records that Mr. Sturrock had, some months previously, written to the Katikiro, ordering him to change this system and entrust the beer permits to the native official responsible for the good conduct of the town."[23]

Postlethwaite wrote to the Katikiro, requesting him to give effect to his predecessor's orders, but Kagwa replied that "he did not admit my right to interfere and that, in his opinion, no Buganda Chief had a right to approach me except through the Katikiro.[24] In addition to the offensively impertinent tone of the communication, this raised an issue of some magnitude, namely, the right of a native to approach the Provincial Commissioner, without which I failed to see how I could keep in touch with the people or adequately advise the Kabaka on the conduct of his territory."[25]

On October 22, 1925, the issue was joined publicly. In a speech to the Lukiko, Postlethwaite indicated that the period was a critical one in the evolution of the country. Buganda was small and comparatively unimportant among the countries of the British Empire. Its prosperity would depend on the efficiency of its government. The Buganda government left a great deal to be desired, especially with respect to finance. Idleness, dishonesty, injustice, and drunkenness was such that the "ruling classes should face and defeat these evils."[26] Postlethwaite then congratulated the saza chief Kangawo, an associate of Sir Apolo's, upon his retirement. He congratulated the Kabaka for having dismissed a gombolola chief for drunkenness.

Sir Apolo, furious at what he regarded as the impertinence of the Acting Provincial Commissioner, replied that "the Kabaka

[23] Postlethwaite, *op.cit.*, p. 108.

[24] This is a particularly important matter because subsequently, after the Kabaka crisis of 1953-1955, the Buganda took the same stand with respect to touring officers (Assistant Residents and Resident, Buganda).

[25] Postlethwaite, *op.cit.*, pp. 108, 109.

[26] *Ibid.*, p. 110.

will henceforth not tolerate drunkenness. . . . I will mention that it is the Government who abolish our own former policies; sometimes persons approach the British Government on any matter, which they settle for them, with the result that any person with any such matters can refer them to the British Government. It also sometimes happens that they ask if any Mukopi has anything to say, which the Government settles without any reference to us. The consequences are that when we wish to introduce any policy which we wish the people have this freedom to follow (or not to follow), it simply becomes impossible to make them do so. We must therefore ask the Government to let us know what policy is to be followed so that we may exonerate our country from the charge of laziness."[27]

Postlethwaite regarded these remarks as an offensive tirade. But Sir Apolo would not retract them. The situation rapidly grew more involved, with the Kabaka trying vainly to smooth ruffled waters and being reprimanded for his efforts, the Chief Secretary being thoroughly annoyed with Postlethwaite, and the Governor thoroughly angry with Sir Apolo. When the Omukulu we Kibuga went to complain to the Provincial Commissioner, Sir Apolo flatly asserted that he had no right to do that; going even further, he made it a principle that chiefs were not to report to officers of the provincial administration and if they should continue to do so, the Buganda government would take no action on advice received from the provincial commissioners as a result of such reports.

That this would have been clearly impossible for the Protectorate government to accept is obvious. The situation, however, was complicated by the fiction of autonomy which had been preserved and largely accepted by the Protectorate government. Not wishing to appear to dominate the Buganda government, the government indicated that it could not accept the principle because it would hamper the Protectorate government in its task of educating the Buganda government.

To give effect to the principle would result in making the provincial commissioner's office ineffective. He would have no infor-

[27] Speech by Sir Apolo Kagwa in Lukiko, October 22, 1925 (Buganda government files).

mation and thus be unable to advise chiefs and government. But there was a reason for Sir Apolo's action. He felt that help should be given by the provincial commissioner's office only after the Kabaka requested it from the Protectorate government. Otherwise there was nothing to prevent every chief with a grievance from running to the Protectorate government and playing havoc with the Buganda government itself.[28] At this point the Governor intervened in no uncertain terms. He enunciated the principle of direct access by anyone to the district and provincial officials. He implied, furthermore, that if the Kabaka persisted in his point of view, he might be faced with loss in prestige and support. This was enough for the Kabaka. He pleaded that the Baganda were still learning, hence they sometimes made big mistakes. He acknowledged that at the present time the British government stood as instructor and therefore must expect to meet with difficulties. On the Kabaka's instruction, Kagwa wrote to Postlethwaite apologizing for his earlier letter on the subject of intoxicating liquor and admitting that it was wrong of him to write to Postlethwaite prior to consultation with his Kabaka. This was magnanimously accepted.

Sir Apolo was crushed. He had been forced to his knees by an unimportant young civil servant. He had been brought to heel by the Governor. And he had to rely on the Kabaka to get him out of the situation. This the Kabaka did by causing the Katikiro to acknowledge that acts taken without consultation with the Kabaka were no longer to be tolerated. It remained only to remove Sir Apolo from office. Postlethwaite managed to get Sir Albert Cook, a doctor who was an old friend of Sir Apolo's, to indicate that Sir Apolo must resign for reasons of health. Sir Apolo believed that Sir Albert had been put up to this by Postlethwaite. He appealed in a long memorandum to the Secretary of State for Colonies, indicating his long service, his loyalty to Great Britain, and recounting the many deeds and accomplishments of his long tenure as Katikiro. It was embarrassing and pathetic. But in the end he had to resign. Less than a year later Sir Apolo Kagwa died.

[28] The view enunciated by Sir Apolo was held most devoutly by later Buganda governments. After 1955 the Residency was put in the position advocated by Sir Apolo.

When the whole matter died down, Postlethwaite found that the situation with respect to beer permits and drunkenness had not been remedied. He proposed to take no action. The Chief Secretary agreed that no action should be taken. It was the end of the affair.

Conclusion

The investiture controversy, the Bataka case, and the Apolo Kagwa affair—each indicates a type of problem emergent in the post-Agreement period. There is still major concern over the nature of the Kabaka's authority, as was exemplified in the investiture controversy. The alliance between Bataka and Bakopi continued, coming to the fore after the Second World War in riots and bloodshed. The result was eventual reform of the economic structure of Uganda as a whole. Most important, it gave rise to the most successful political party in Uganda's history, the Uganda National Congress which is the lineal descendant of the peasant grievances and Bataka organizational efforts. The Apolo Kagwa affair raised important questions about the autonomy of the Kabaka's government—most of all whether it could be free of interference from the Protectorate government. Eventually, Sir Apolo's position came to be accepted by the Protectorate government, but not until the Katikiro and his government were made responsible to a democratically controlled Lukiko. But a democratically controlled Lukiko was precisely the demand of the Bataka. In that sense an accommodation of positions occurred over the years. The Kabaka remained powerful but more constitutional. The Bataka were reduced as a political force, but not until most of the issues which gave rise to them were won for the Bakopi. The Kabaka's government received its semiautonomy, but not until the system was democratized and the power of the chiefs as a party greatly diminished.[29]

We can now shift our focus to the national scene and examine the relationship between the two governments, Buganda and Protectorate.

[29] It will be noted that the English version of the Agreement reads, "The Kabaka of Uganda shall exercise direct rule over the natives of Uganda to whom he shall administer justice through the Lukiko." But the Luganda version, in translation, has been made to read, "The Kabaka of Buganda shall rule all the Baganda *without anyone to order him,* but he shall try all cases in consultation with the Lukiko and other chiefs." The Baganda follow the vernacular version as translated here. However, the Agreement states that the English version is binding on both parties.

CHAPTER 7

THE DEVELOPMENT OF A NATIONAL GOVERNMENT

THE FIRST CONCERN of the Protectorate government, once relations with Buganda had been regularized, was the establishment of district administrations with a minimum of cost and with small staff. Watered-down versions of the Agreement were concluded with Toro and Ankole.[1] In some areas settled administration came relatively late; in West Nile, for example, it did not properly begin until 1916.

First efforts included surveying and establishing boundaries. Education and public works were left largely in the hands of missionaries and chiefs. The Kiganda system of tiered local government was established throughout the Protectorate. In most instances county chiefs were Baganda brought into the districts for the purposes of establishing local administrations and training the local population in the machinery of local government.

The boundaries of the districts were fixed more or less along ethnic lines. Kavirondo was separated from Uganda and turned over to Kenya for administration, somewhat to the chagrin of the Baganda who claimed hegemony over certain parts of the area.

One of the main tasks of commissioners from Sir Harry Johnston to Sir H. H. Bell was the building of administrative centers. Local branches of the Public Works Department were established. Rest houses were constructed. Courts and treasury buildings were built.

The Secretariat remained small. For a long time, perhaps the most important official in the Secretariat was the Chief Medical Officer. Problems of health and sanitation, the establishment of dispensaries, the inspection of homes and villages, and the development of health standards were a major preoccupation of government. The sleeping sickness epidemics which decimated Busoga and parts of Bunyoro and Buganda required extensive campaigns and preoccupied public health officials and missionaries. Large areas were evacuated to halt the spread of the disease

[1] For having resisted the British, the other kingdom state, Bunyoro, was treated punitively. Not until 1933 was an agreement concluded with Bunyoro.

and the Commissioner, Sir Hesketh Bell, used fairly drastic measures to compel compliance.

In the case of Buganda little active interference with tribal government took place between 1900 and 1919. Most of the Lukiko funds derived from court fees and these were left unsupervised by the British. By 1916 the Protectorate became independent of British Treasury grants. The growth of local revenues made it possible to step up the development of education, medical, agricultural, and other government services. Much of this was accomplished through the chiefs who were responsible for promoting cash crops, surveying mailo land in Buganda, and enforcing forestry, veterinary, agricultural, and medical rules.

From 1919 on, there was a rapid expansion of administrative personnel and new responsibilities.[2] This marks the beginnings of the bureaucratic-colonial system in which central government assumed a more positive role by taking on duties additional to those of maintaining the peace, health, and good order of the territory. For one thing, financial policy superseded health as the most important feature of government, and a Financial Secretary's post was set up concerned with planning and development. As well, government interceded in Buganda's local affairs. Local financial policy was altered to reduce financial malpractice.[3]

The Protectorate government began to take a more active part in the recruitment of senior chiefs. For long, the Provincial Commissioner had simply followed the advice of Sir Apolo, approving those names selected by the latter for chieftaincies. The Kabaka himself requested more active Protectorate government intervention in hopes of getting chiefs less subservient to Sir

[2] In 1920 chiefs were put on a salary basis instead of relying for their income on 10 per cent rebates on poll tax, as had been the rule previously. The system of salaried chiefs spread to other provinces. See K. Ingham, *The Making of Modern Uganda* (London: George Allen & Unwin, 1958), p. 171.

[3] For example, in Buganda, commutation of *luwalo* was possible by payment of 10*s.* by men employed on contracts of more than three months' duration, engaged in trade, or who owned more than one square mile. 60 per cent of such funds went into the Buganda Government Treasury and 40 per cent remained with the saza. The power of commutation became important when such large sums were involved. By 1926 luwalo tax commutation receipts had reached 1,000,000*s.* Abuses commonly occurred in the misappropriation of funds and a new official, the Provincial Luwalo Inspector, became highly influential. To prevent abuse an elaborate system of accounting was established whereby chiefs received their salaries in the form of a percentage rebate on taxes collected. Annual auditing by the Protectorate government was also established at this time. See *ibid.*, p. 167.

Apolo. The result was a Native Civil Service Board. Established in 1927 under the chairmanship of the Director of Education, it was composed of the Treasurer, the Provincial Commissioner of Buganda, and the Assistant Chief Secretary. Closer supervision over chiefs and other African civil servants resulted. By mid-1927 the watchword had become efficiency. The entire administrative structure of the Secretariat was reformed. Buganda was made to assume some of the financial burden for special services by the Protectorate government. Suddenly, Buganda was being governed in earnest.

The emphasis on economy and financial planning focused attention once again on economic matters. Close supervision of local African governments, efficiency in central government, and economic development became the chief characteristics of the Protectorate government. These three factors underlay the formation and development of the legislative council system in Uganda.

The Establishment of the Legislative Council

Deep concern with economic matters characterized government directly after the war, partly because the prosperity and expansion so confidently expected in Uganda did not occur. The war and depression imposed an impossible burden upon planters and growers whose capital requirements were high and inadequate to tide them over the bleak years of low world prices for primary commodities. Moreover, their comparative advantage was worsened by the very high cost of transport, railway, and freight charges necessary to bring crops to world markets. Finally, plantation crops, particularly cocoa and rubber, which many had thought commercially feasible, failed to develop on a commercial basis. Even tea and coffee, the latter to become as important for Uganda's economy as cotton, were attempted only on a very small scale.

The Protectorate government soon came to realize that the basic economy of the country depended on African agriculture. Capital development would require cooperation between government and private European and Asian interests.

In the first instance, along with more stringent fiscal measures in the local governments, district and provincial officers were expected to maintain a steady acreage devoted to cotton production. This was difficult to achieve because cotton prices were low after

World War I and African producers had no financial incentive to grow cotton. Instead, administrative officers applied exhortation, propaganda, and the pressure of taxation (poll tax). This was justified by the view that the financial stability of Uganda depended and would continue to depend upon cotton. Government services were contingent on African growers.[4]

The European and Asian communities could not be "administered." If the government in its emphasis on economic development was to rely on them, their voluntary cooperation was required. Uganda's legislative council system developed from the need for closer consultation between various kinds of business interests, both planter and commercial, and government. Government would then be able to move along policy lines, having as its objectives the facilitation of economic growth and development.

Uganda was relatively late in establishing such a system.[5] The Uganda Chamber of Commerce petitioned the government for a stronger voice in political affairs.[6] The request was looked upon with favor by the Governor, Sir Robert Coryndon. The time was considered ripe for setting up both Legislative and Executive Councils. Royal instructions and the Order-in-Council providing for both were issued in 1920. The Legislative Council was given the power to legislate by ordinance subject to the Governor's power of veto and disallowance.[7]

[4] Thus the tightened system of administration had an economic basis. Each African government was the responsibility of an administrative officer. The vertical pattern of administrative authority allowed consultation between an African government and the administration, but did not facilitate horizontal communications or cooperation between districts. Nor was it considered that a higher or more representative body should include Africans. See C. C. Wrigley, op.cit., p. 57.

[5] The first Legislative Council in the Gold Coast dates from 1850 and there were African members on it from the start.

[6] The Chamber of Commerce represented European firms. Membership was limited to "qualified traders of Uganda and gentlemen distinguished for public service or eminent in commerce or manufacture." The most important of the firms was the Uganda Company which was associated with the introduction of cotton in Uganda and the development of the cotton industry. The Uganda Company was founded to take over the commercial and industrial activities of the Church Missionary Society. Its influence has thus been strong on two counts: its missionary origins and its economic power.

[7] A note on the legislative council system might prove useful to those unfamiliar with the system. A legislative council is not "democratic" nor is it intended to be. It is an advisory body which is enabled to pass bills for the governor's approval. An official majority predominates until such time as responsible and representative government becomes government policy. The official majority

The Executive Council first established in Uganda was limited to ex officio and official members. No unofficial members were appointed. Its two most important figures, besides the Chief Secretary, were the Chief Medical Officer and the Financial Secretary.

The Legislative Council was to consist of four officials and three unofficials. The latter were to include one representative of the planters and ginners, one representative of the business community, and one Indian. The Indian Association was asked to nominate three names from which one would be chosen by the governor. This innocuous request to the Indian Association proved to be a major cause of controversy. For if the Asians complied, they thereby assented to a legislative council which recruited European members on grounds of the functional groups they represented, that is, planters or commercial, while Asians were to be invited on grounds of race. From the start, the problem which has since come to plague the political evolution of East Africa—the problem of racial representation—was clearly recognized in Uganda. And for the first time in Uganda, the "Asian problem" became a point of issue.[8]

---

is such that government can ensure for itself the acceptance of any measure it proposes. The chief secretary is normally the leader of government business, while the governor has both an original and casting vote. The purpose of a legislative council is to make government more responsive to public demands. Government remains oligarchical and responsible to the British Parliament. Only when an elected, unofficial majority prevails does the legislative council begin to alter its character, because by this means, representative government is introduced. Representative government is based ultimately on public consent, and the legislative council begins to take on the characteristics of a parliament. The next step is independence.

The peculiar genius of the legislative council system is that it proves infinitely flexible. Built into it is an evolutionary pattern which allows for its modification into a sovereign parliament by easy stages.

[8] An explanatory note on the Asian community in Uganda is in order here. Indians were found in coastal towns by da Gama in 1498, and Sir Harry Johnston spoke of their penetration as far inland as Toro, Bunyoro, and the Congo by the end of the nineteenth century. They were mostly traders, moneylenders, and bankers. Like the Europeans who followed them, their primary concern in Uganda was business. Unlike Europeans, they were willing to adopt permanent residence in Uganda.

Europeans have tended to regard the Indians as a single group. But they are in fact divided into several major communities. This is one reason why a controversy arose when it became known that Asians, who outnumbered Europeans, were to be given only one seat, while Europeans received two, in the Legislative Council. The Indians were divided on religious lines: Sikhs, Pakistani Muslims, and Hindus each represented divergent communities. Among the Muslims alone there were many variations. Although not strongly represented, orthodox Sunni

The problem of representation that was raised was not based only on the nature of representation, whether functional or communal; it was also racial. Involved, too, was the proportionality of numbers. The Asian population in 1921 numbered 5,000, while Europeans numbered 1,000. Ten years later the Asians had more than doubled their number.[9] What rights were due such rapidly expanding minorities with respect to legislative seats would continue to be a problem.

Meanwhile, the Indian Association rejected the Governor's request that they nominate candidates for appointment to the Legislative Council. In 1921, therefore, when the Council met for the first time, it had the following composition: the Chief Secretary, Attorney General, Treasurer, and Principal Medical Officer, with the Governor as President; all were on the ex officio side, with two European unofficials, H. H. Hunter, a lawyer from Kampala, and H. E. Lewis, the Uganda Manager of the British

---

sects were also found. There were the Ismaili Khojas (followers of the Aga Khan) and others as well.

Among the Hindus the problem of caste was important. Almost every Hindu business establishment was a family concern (with family obligation a substitute for contract). Caste considerations entered into the business as well as the social life of the Hindus. Moreover, Gujerat, where a large proportion of the Hindu community came from, is a heavily caste-ridden part of India.

The nature of Indian social organization was only dimly understood by Europeans and Africans; in addition, a folklore had grown up about them which readily lent itself to prejudice. It was widely believed, for example, that the Indians who came to Uganda were actually indentured servants brought for work on the railways. This was not the case. In an unpublished monograph, "Why Indians Came to East Africa," Nigel Oram writes that approximately 31,983 Indians were imported to East Africa, of whom 16,312 were time-expired contract laborers and dismissed (the Indian Government permitting emigration for a term of three years); 6,454 were invalided and 2,493 died. Oram indicates, "This left 6,724 who presumably stayed in East Africa unaccounted." Since the Uganda proportion of the unaccounted would remain relatively small, the myth of Indian coolies as the basis of the Indian population is easily discounted.

The Indian population has thus always had an ambiguous place in Uganda. Disliked by both British and Africans, misunderstood as to their intentions and motives, and often sharing in the prejudices of Africans and British for one another, they demanded parity if only because both the Indian Association and the Ismaili Khojas each wanted a representative on the Legislative Council.

For this discussion of the Indian communities of East Africa I have relied on discussions with various members of the Indian communities and, as well, Sir Amar Maini, Minister of Corporations and Regional Communications in Uganda. Other help was given by Mrs. Diana Noakes, Secretary of the Indian Association, and from notes by H. S. Morris, "The Structure of an Indian Community" (East African Institute of Social Research files, unpub. mimeo.).

[9] See *Report on the Census of the Non-Native Population of Uganda Protectorate* (Nairobi: W. Boyd & Co., 1953), Table VI, "Comparison of Population in Census Years," p. 15.

East Africa Company (the successor to the old Imperial British East Africa Company). The Council's most immediate task was to assist in postwar reconstruction and development. The Indian post remained vacant, being temporarily filled by Major A. L. Renton, an erstwhile M.P. who, although not resident in Uganda, held estates at Mityana.

Thus the first Legislative Council was an entirely European body composed of officials and unofficials who habitually had been in consultation with one another and whose task it now was to make laws for the good of the entire population of the Protectorate.[10]

Not anticipated was an African reaction to the establishment of Legislative Council. Yet if racial representation for Asians was admitted, then Africans could demand participation. If functional representation were admitted, then Asians did not belong on the Legislative Council *per se*. African reaction took the form of a letter from Daudi Chwa and Sir Apolo to His Excellency the Governor (dated March 21, 1921); it read as follows:

"We are naturally anxious to learn of the proposed introduction of a Legislative Council in this Protectorate, as we are not aware of the extent of its legislative powers with regard to the Native Administration of Buganda Kingdom. Hitherto, the Buganda Kingdom has enjoyed complete self-government as far as native administration is concerned, guaranteed to it under the Uganda Agreement, 1900. By Article 5 of this Agreement, laws made by the Governor for the general government of the Uganda Protectorate are applicable to the Buganda Kingdom only so far as they are not in conflict or at variance with the terms of the Agreement.

"It is feared that the introduction of the Legislative Council in the Protectorate will necessarily affect the existing position of the Native Administration of the Kingdom of Buganda, since this Council will be empowered by the British Imperial Government to legislate for the whole of the Protectorate irrespective of the various Agreements entered into by the Imperial Government with individual Native Tribes of the Protectorate; with the natural

[10] It was regarded as the job of the official members to safeguard the interests of Africans. By 1925 the issue of racial representation was resolved by the Governor's rejection of the principle of selecting suitable unofficials, regardless of race, to represent the whole country. Thus the Kenya "solution" was never established in Uganda.

result that the interests and welfare of the Baganda will be relegated to the background and will necessarily form a secondary consideration in the deliberations of the Council in view of the general interests and progress of the whole Protectorate."

The Kabaka also asked for assurances that the 1900 Agreement would not be affected, and he expressed concern over the growing power of the European and Asian communities in Uganda. It is at this point that Kiganda nationalism makes its first appearance in modern dress. This position with respect to the Legislative Council has never wavered. The Baganda have been implacable in their resolve to minimize both their participation in the Legislative Council and its potential effectiveness as a legislative body. As we shall indicate, the position of Buganda with respect to the Legislative Council has been one of the most significant political concerns throughout Uganda, and it seriously affects both present and future constitutional prospects.

Thus we see that from both Indians and the most powerful African government in Uganda opposition to the Legislative Council developed. The first was over the matter of representation and numbers of representatives. The second was over powers and scope of discretion. Implicit in each was the matter of racial differentiation and the relative position to be accorded to the different races in Uganda. Africans were excluded. Asians, as British subjects having some special protection from the government of India, were included. The Indian government took the position that eventually all British subjects, European and Asian alike, should be elected to the Legislative Council on a common electoral roll and a common franchise.[11] That view was not accepted by the government.

The Legislative Council was a special club. It was a mark of distinction to have served there. If for a considerable time it was relatively inconsequential, it nevertheless conferred a token of responsibility upon the participants. From it there radiated an ideal of good service by the *best* people in the interests of the *whole* people. Although neither functional nor racial principles were accepted in theory, both the functional and the racial re-

11 The position of the Indians was attacked by a group of Baganda in Nairobi in their newspaper, *Sekanyolya*, but their position was repudiated by the Young Baganda Association. See Ingham, *op.cit.*, p. 176. The government tried to reassure the Baganda that establishment of Legislative Council would not interfere with the terms of the Agreement.

mained, in practice, the first criteria of eligibility for unofficial seats.

From 1921 until 1945 the Legislative Council underwent few major changes. The principle of nonracial representation was maintained in theory. Africans, particularly in Buganda, remained fearful of its potentialities. The real distinction on the Council was between officials and unofficials. The latter were expected to represent the interests of the organizations, establishments, and races to which they belonged *only* as such representation did not prevent members from considering the needs of the whole country. For a long time the composition of the Council was remarkably stable. Once African representation occurred, its later evolution was sudden, consisting of expanding the official side to bring officials responsible for diverse and enlarged government concerns into contact with unofficials. And the unofficial side was enlarged to represent a wider range of interests. Although it was not until 1942 that it first became clear that Uganda would develop primarily as an African country, the issue of African representation had been raised before. By 1945, in the face of considerable opposition from the Baganda, the first African representation occurred. Henceforth the Council experienced constant modification. We can best demonstrate these remarks by the table on the following page.

What functional groups were represented? Of the permanent and temporary members of the Legislative Council during the 1921-1945 period, there were, by session, 15 lawyers, including Indian lawyers, 10 representatives of the major companies, that is, British East Africa Company, the Uganda Company (cotton) and Baumann's (coffee). Ordinary businessmen, including insurance agents and retail sellers in major business outlets, were by far the largest group: 23. Six planters or members of planters' associations and 5 ginners represented European and Asian agricultural interests. For the rest, 8 sessions had bankers and 5 had doctors, either temporarily or permanently appointed.

An analysis of early governmental development at the center shows two worlds. One is African. Governed administratively, it has a single line of authority from the governor down through the provincial commissioner and district officer and chief. These are assisted by a system of graded councils. In Buganda there is

TABLE 1

Legislative Council, 1921-1945*

(Sessions at least yearly)

DATE	OFFICIALS	Race	No.	Occupation
			Unofficials (Appointments to "permanent" seats for two years)	
1921 to 1924	Governor	Europ.		
	Attorney-General	(p)	2	lawyer; business mgr. of B.E.A. Co.[a]
	Chief Secretary	(t)[b]	3	2 planters; 1 insurance manager
	Principal Medical Officer	Asian		
		(p)	1	vacant
1925 to 1926	Governor	Europ.		
	Attorney-General	(p)	2	lawyer; business mgr. of B.E.A. Co.
	Chief Secretary	(t)	4	3 planters; Gen. Mgr. Uganda Co.
	Director of Medical and Sanitary Serv.	Asian		Hindu
		(p)	1	lawyer
	Director of Agric.	(t)	1	businessman
	Director of Educ.			
1927	Same	Europ.		
		(p)	2	lawyer; business mgr. of B.E.A. Co.
		(t)	2	Gen. Mgr. Uganda Co. banker
		Asian		
		(p)	1	lawyer Hindu
1928	Same	Europ.		
		(p)	2	lawyer; banker
		(t)	1	businessman
		Asian		
		(p)	1	lawyer Hindu
1929 to 1931	Same	Europ.		
		(p)	2	lawyer
		Asian		Hindu
		(p)	1	lawyer
		(t)	2	businessman; cotton ginner
1932 to 1933	Same	Europ.		
		(p)	2	planter; banker
		(t)	1	businessman (Uganda Co.)
		Asian		Hindu
		(p)	2	businessman; lawyer
		(t)	1	cotton ginner
1934 to 1935	Same	Europ.		
		(p)	2	2 bankers
		Asian		Hindu
		(p)	2	businessman; lawyer
		(t)	4	cotton ginner; cotton exporter; 2 doctors, 1 of them Pres. of Indian Assn.

(table concluded on following page)

DATE	OFFICIALS	Unofficials (Appointments to "permanent" seats for two years)		
		Race	*No.*	*Occupation*
1936 to 1938	Same	Europ.		
		(p)	2	2 bankers
		(t)	1	lawyer
		Asian		Hindu
		(p)	2	doctor; businessman
		(t)	1	insurance agent Muslim
1939 to 1942	Same	Europ.		
		(p)	2	cotton ginner; manager of Uganda Co.
		(t)	5	4 businessmen (1 from Uganda Co., 1 from Baumann Co.); cotton ginner
		Asians		
		(p)	2	insurance agent Muslim doctor (Pres. Indian Assn.) Hindu
		(t)	2	2 businessmen
1943 to 1944	Same	Europ.		
		(p)	2	lawyer; businessman
		(t)	3	businessman (insurance); businessman (cotton); businessman (coffee)
		Asian		Hindu
		(p)	2	lawyer-businessman (cotton); doctor (Pres. Indian Assn.) N.B. latter replaced by former businessman (insurance) Muslim
1945	Governor Attorney-General	Europ.		
		(p)	2	businessman (cotton); businessman (cotton)
	Chief Secretary	(t)	3	businessmen (cotton); (Uganda Co.); (insurance)
	Director of Medical and Sanitary Serv.	Asian	2	businessman (insurance) Muslim
	Director of Agric.	(p)		
	Director of Educ. Development Commissioner			lawyer-businessman (cotton)
		African		
		(p)	3	1 to be nominated by the Kabaka of Buganda, 1 to be Katikiro of the Kingdoms of Ankole, Toro, or Bunyoro, each to serve in turn, and 1 to be Secretary-General of either Busoga, Bugisu, Bukedi, or Teso, each to serve in turn. Their term was limited to 1 year so that turns would be frequent. The Northern Province and Kigezi were unrepresented.
	N.B. The official majority was maintained by the addition of the Development Commissioner 8 officials 7 unofficials			

* This table is based on data made available to me by the Government Archivist, Uganda.
a B.E.A. Co. is the British East Africa Company.
b (p) means *permanent*; (t) means *temporary*.

modification of this practice. There the pattern of partial autonomy is maintained, but increasingly the provincial commissioner and his staff in the districts tighten their control. Agricultural and other policy is brought into greater conformity with the rest of Uganda, while much greater autonomy in local matters is retained by the Baganda themselves.

The other world is European and Asian (the latter divided amongst themselves). There was increasing concern that Uganda, whose economic horizons had proved somewhat narrower than originally anticipated, provided more challenge than opportunity. Africans had to be cajoled into greater cotton production. Europeans were not bringing in capital or creating new capital in very striking amounts. Hence the central government's very special concern to favor those interests of Europeans and Asians through the device of the Legislative Council. Policies of government expansion in railway, roads, and other transport were thus developed in consultation with unofficial members and the interests they represented. Taxation policies were revised on the advice of the various planters and growers associations in order to stimulate plantation agriculture.

Africans were *acted upon*, with respect to economic policy. Europeans were *consulted with*. Originally an instrument of consultation with development as its focus, the Legislative Council became regarded as the headquarters of European administrative and commercial interests whose decisions were dictated by a commercial view of welfare, that is, the assumption that what benefited business enterprise and economic development was good for the country. In the post-World War I period, then, we see the establishment of a dyarchy—a dual system of administration in which there were separate systems of consultation and policies, one for Africans and another for Europeans and Asians. Efficiency, development, and social welfare were its emphases, under a doctrine known as *trusteeship*. It was a curious blend of liberal economic views and Tory traditions of rulership with responsibility. With the establishment of this period of bureaucratic-colonialism, the focus of government shifted from Mengo to become centered in Entebbe, the headquarters of the Protectorate government. The change of emphasis was bitterly resented by the Baganda. For, if Mengo was the door to Buganda, Entebbe was the passageway to the rest of the British Empire.

CHAPTER 8

THE DEFENSE OF BUGANDA INTERESTS:
THE CAMPAIGN AGAINST
TRUSTEESHIP AND CLOSER UNION

BEFORE 1918, policy applicable to the more settled older Commonwealth had seemed entirely inappropriate to Africa. After the war, the loyalty of the Commonwealth members, such as Canada, Australia, New Zealand, and to a smaller extent perhaps, South Africa, captured the imagination of many in England. The Commonwealth as a collection of free peoples in voluntary association, and having common ties of language, religion, and institutions was in keeping with British traditions of freedom. And it had a tutorial aspect. The dominion idea had seemed to work in South Africa: why was it not equally appropriate to other areas where the European population had a permanent commitment?[1]

With the defeat of Germany and the establishment of a British mandate over Tanganyika, the possibility of an East and even an East and Central African dominion seemed feasible. In an appendix written by one of the members of the Economic Commission of the East Africa Protectorate which published its report in 1919, the following position is put:

"The East Africa Protectorate is an artificially defined territory without natural frontier (except on its seaboard). It constitutes one of the group of territories under the British Crown comprising (in addition to British East Africa) Uganda, the conquered territory German East Africa, Nyasaland, and the Rhodesias. The territories of this group, which in this chapter will be referred to as Middle Africa, are to a very large extent homogeneous in character, forming together one predominantly agricultural domain of boundless richness and fertility. Middle Africa is, in fact, one of the world's great unopened storehouses. . . .

"The strategical advantages attending unification of control

[1] When administration was taken over from the British South Africa Company, Southern Rhodesia was put under the Dominions Office rather than the Colonial Office. The model in this regard was South Africa, where it was felt that dominion status had mended a nasty rupture in the European populations, Boer and British.

and administration of the various territories of Middle Africa would be of inestimable value in the event of Great Britain again being involved in warfare there. The defensive strength of such a combination should be sufficient to render any hostile designs futile.

"The advantages of federation in the sphere of finance would be of scarcely less importance. A Dominion approximately equal in area to the sister Dominion of South Africa, and certainly not inferior to it in natural resources, would be able to command support for the financing of large scale railway and other projects necessary for development, where a number of minor states, incapable of acting in concert, would be unable to find accommodation.

"Apart from such material advantages, the union of the British territories of Middle Africa would powerfully promote the spreading of the British idea, which we are convinced is what the best interests of the people of Africa demand."[2]

To others in East Africa the virtues of such a dominion were not quite so self-evident. It seemed plausible enough to those with little or no contact with East Africa. The question of dominions in East Africa suddenly brought into view the prospect of a very different place for the Baganda in the hierarchy—a place of subordination along a horizon shared with other "natives."

Closer Union

The first major effort to assess the potentialities of closer union was a commission of enquiry, the Ormsby-Gore Commission, which, in 1924, investigated the situation in East Africa. The Commission recommended periodic conferences of the governors of East and Central African territories and regular interterritorial conferences among heads of departments. The post of East African Trade Commissioner was established and a formula for economic integration with political decentralization sought.[3]

But the required formula could not easily be found.[4] The sec-

[2] Quoted in C. F. Andrews, *The Indian Question in East Africa* (Nairobi: The Swift Press, 1921), pp. 6-7.

[3] See *East African Commission Report* (Ormsby-Gore Commission, London: H.M.S.O., 1925, Cmd. 2387).

[4] One of the reasons no political formula could be found was the severity of the conflict over Asian representation on legislative councils in East Africa. Not only

ond major effort to evaluate prospects for closer union sought
inspiration in the doctrine of *trusteeship*. This doctrine seemed
both sensitive and satisfactory. It allowed the governments in
East Africa to view the general development of the territories as
a moral trust which would enhance the inheritance of Africans.
Mutuality of interest, mutuality of obligation, with government
shared between private interests and administration, characterized
the ideal. As the Hilton-Young Commission put it, trusteeship
stood: *"First*, for the moral and material development of the native inhabitants; *secondly*, for humanity as a whole (the duty here
being to develop the vast economic resources of these territories
for the benefit of the whole world—a duty the conception of which
has been made familiar by Lord Lugard in his doctrine of the
'Dual Mandate') ; *thirdly*, for the immigrant communities, whose
initiative, knowledge, and material resources are necessary instruments in the fulfillment of the first two tasks." The report went on
to emphasize that "properly interpreted, they are complementary
parts of a single obligation which cannot be fully performed if
any of those parts is neglected."[5]

In spite of these rather lofty conceptions, it remained impossible to agree on the principles of participation in the legislatures
of the East African territories.

Europeans continued to object to Asians' equal participation
on legislative bodies. "As pioneers of British civilisation, their
ideal is to create a political unit . . . modelled on British institutions and embodying British principles and standards of efficiency in its administration. They are afraid lest the admission
of the Asiatic vote on the same terms as the European might lead

in Uganda, but in Kenya as well, protracted debate went on over Indian participation in a central legislature. Whereas in Uganda the principle of Asian participation was not recognized but the fiction was preserved that the best man for the
job of representing the whole people would take his seat, in Kenya the communal
principle was accepted. This then raised the issue of proportionality. Asians took
the view that as British subjects they were entitled to equal protection from the
law and equal participation in the legislatures. They were supported in this contention by the Government of India, and were able to cite the position of the Imperial Conference of 1921 which had adopted the position that "there is an incon-
gruity between the position of India as an equal member of the British Empire
and the existence of disabilities upon British Indians lawfully domiciled in some
other parts of the Empire."
 [5] *Report of the Commission on Closer Union of the Dependencies in Eastern
and Central Africa* (Hilton-Young Commission, London: H.M.S.O., 1929, Cmd.
3234), p. 36.

in the end through superiority of numbers to the control of their interests and institutions passing into the hands of another race, and they are not satisfied that an initial limitation of the strength of the Asiatic vote is a safeguard that can be permanently maintained."[6]

The Hilton-Young Commission in their report reviewed the arguments in favor of communal versus common roll representation and concluded that the communal system was best suited for the immigrant communities of Kenya. Arguing that it was Anglo-Saxons who had an especial aptitude for the successful operation of representative institutions, the Commission felt that if European and Asian candidates were to compete against each other at the polls, racial antagonism could easily be inflamed and that such a situation would produce the lowest order of politician seeking to gratify his ambitions by profiting from racial tension.

On the other hand, the Commission felt that separateness of the communities, emphasized by communalism, must be reduced. "The determining consideration in a sound political system should be not the immediate interests of particular communities, but the ultimate good of the whole territory. The electoral system should be framed on lines which will enable all the communities to progress in harmony towards that ultimate good of the whole territory. The electoral system should be framed on lines which will enable all the communities to progress in harmony towards that ultimate good. The leadership, to which it is claimed that the European community by virtue of its greater political capacity is entitled, will never be secure until it rests on consent and not on privilege. If the European is to lead the other communities in Kenya, he must study their needs and their susceptibilities, and he must be prepared to convince them that he is the best representative of their interests in the administration of the State. Similar considerations apply to the Indian candidate. If he is to establish his claim to participate on equal terms with the European in the government of the country, he must study the European point of view and learn to cooperate with the British in their zeal for efficiency of administration."[7]

---

[6] *Ibid.*, pp. 206-207. While the argument was specifically limited to Kenya, there were many Europeans in Uganda who shared the same attitudes.

[7] *Ibid.*, pp. 208-209.

European principles and standards were thus to be accepted by Asians and, in the degree that they were prepared to accept them, they could participate in a common community.

Finally, the Commission was aware that European and Asian representation would not be permanently exclusive. "Processes have indeed already been started which cannot be stopped and which must inevitably lead to a stage when the native peoples will demand some voice in the management of their own affairs. Wise statesmanship must therefore prepare to lead the natives on a course of steady mental and moral advancement, so that when they realize their power they may be properly qualified to use it."[8]

The Hilton-Young Commission advocated not a premature scheme for a unified executive management, but closer union in the form of a "central authority" with power to settle policy on matters which affected Eastern Africa as a whole. Also advocated was the creation of a Governor-General of Eastern Africa whose duties would be:

"(a) To secure Imperial interests and the proper discharge of His Majesty's Government;

"(b) To hold the scales of justice even between the various racial communities;

"(c) To coordinate services of common interest."[9]

Amidst the claims and counterclaims and the matters of high policy, it was the Baganda who saw most clearly the implications of closer union. With such success did the Buganda government set its small voice against the movement for federation that the Protectorate government itself grew increasingly hesitant about closer union with other territories until the Great Depression put an end to the matter for a time.[10] Their attack was levied first against the Legislative Council which the Baganda rightly saw as the potential instrumentality of closer union.

The Response of Buganda to Closer Union

Point Three of the Hilton-Young Commission's terms of reference laid down as part of their enquiry an obligation "to make recommendations in regard to possible changes in the powers and

---

[8] *Ibid.*, p. 38.

[9] *Ibid.*, see *Summary of Recommendations*, Part I, pp. 288-289.

[10] For a discussion of the closer union problem see the British Government *White Paper*, "Future Policy in Eastern Africa" (London: H.M.S.O. 1927), Cmd. 2904.

composition of the various legislative councils of the several territories (a) as the result of the establishment of any Federal Council or other common authority; (b) so as to associate more closely in the responsibilities and trusteeship of Government the immigrant communities domiciled in the country; and (c) so as ultimately to secure more direct representation of native interests in accordance with (4) below."[11]

In a "Supplementary Memorandum on the Proposed Federation of the British East African Dependencies," the Kabaka took issue with point Three of the six terms of reference in the Hilton-Young Commission. Arguing against the legislative council system he stated, "It has always been my fear that as a result of the establishment of a federal council any changes in the powers and composition of the Legislative Council of the Uganda Protectorate will necessarily affect adversely the present status and constitution of the Uganda Kingdom, since it is certain that such Federal Council will of necessity be composed of a large number of Unofficial Members of the various immigrant races possessing vast interest in their deliberation in such Council. It is needless to point out that the interests of foreign and immigrant races in a country must inevitably be in conflict with the interests of the Natives of the country. It therefore follows that it would be almost impossible 'to secure more direct representations of native interests'. . . ."[12]

Further, argued the Kabaka, the special interests of Buganda as safeguarded by the 1900 Agreement would no longer be maintained. "It will not be possible for the Central or Federal Council to accord special consideration to the interests of the Baganda and the constitution of their Kingdom as has hitherto been done by the local Government of the Uganda Protectorate. The Federal Government will be confronted with divergent interests and

11 Hilton-Young, *op.cit.*, p. 5. Point Four mentioned a recommended dual policy by the conference of East African Governors, and initiated the following query: How best can the complementary development of "native" and non-native communities be progressively applied in the political as well as the economic sphere? This dualism did not include representation by Africans in the Legislative Council; in the case of Uganda, representation was explicitly regarded as applying only to local government.

12 His Highness, the Kabaka of Buganda, *Supplementary Memorandum on The Proposed Federation of the British East African Dependencies* (Mengo, Uganda: no publisher or date listed), pp. 1-2.

tribal customs of the native races composed in the Federation, while at the same time the interests of the foreign and immigrant races will be found almost always to be antagonistic to the interests of the native races for which the Imperial Government are trustees."[13]

As well, the Kabaka pointed out very politely that the Baganda would take such a federal council and the modifications in Legislative Council attendant upon it as a violation of the Agreement.

The complexities of the matter called for still further investigation. In 1930 a joint select committee of both houses of parliament held hearings on closer union. Once again the Baganda made their position abundantly clear. In testimony before the committee the Baganda delegates made it clear that they would regard the establishment of a central East African government as a violation of the 1900 Agreement because it would alter the position of Buganda.[14]

Indicating that they were quite satisfied with their present position, under the terms of which they enjoyed a large measure of consideration from the Protectorate government, the Baganda delegation implied that the vast intellectual differences between tribal groupings in East Africa gave no grounds for a uniform "native" policy. In testimony, when asked about the presence of any Africans in Legislative Council in Uganda, S. Kulubya, one of the delegates, indicated that there were none and that the Baganda did not want such representation.

What were some of the Africans' genuine concerns? They can be indicated as follows:

(1) Fear of dominance by settler populations in Kenya. The attitudes and the "frontier" spirit at large amongst European settlers primarily in Kenya were taken as a direct threat to the interests of Africans.

(2) Fear of changes in land tenure leading to alienation of

---

[13] *Ibid.*, p. 2.

[14] "In the absence of any specified guarantee and in view of the almost studied avoidance of such guarantee we cannot help but feel that there are official doubts as to the possibility of bringing Buganda into Closer Union during the existence of the Buganda Agreement as it stands today. For ourselves we cannot understand how Closer Union can be effected without seriously impairing our rights and privileges as provided for in the Agreement." Testimony of Serwano Kulubya before the Joint Select Committee on East Africa, *Minutes of Evidence* (London: H.M.S.O., 1931), Volume II, p. 550.

land. The various protective ordinances which provided in Buganda for the limited leasing of land to Europeans (and that only under careful supervision) and which eliminated sale of land to Europeans under ordinary circumstances were felt to be endangered.[15]

(3) While gratified by the doctrine of paramountcy for African interests, the Africans were concerned about its implementation. Fear grew that the main means of promoting African interests was by economic development, with economic development largely in the hands of Europeans. Thus they felt threatened by the economic arguments for closer union.

(4) The political implications of trusteeship seemed to produce, by their vagueness, a justification for paternalism for Africans and political participation in central legislatures in the territories for Asians and Europeans. A single federal legislature for East Africa would increase control by small groups of Europeans who would more and more come to dominate larger numbers of Africans. Hence the political consequences of trusteeship seemed to pose severe threats to the future of the Africans.[16]

Nor did the attitudes of Europeans in East Africa allay these

[15] "Another most important feature of the position of my country which differs from that of any other native tribes in the Uganda Protectorate is the system of the tenure of land among my people in Buganda. In no other country of any other native tribes in the East African British Dependencies will you find private ownership of land by individual natives. In Buganda, under Clause 15 of the Uganda Agreement of 1900, certain native private landowners were recognized and their claims or titles to land registered by the Protectorate Government. These natives can do exactly what they like with their land in the matter of alienation among themselves and even to foreigners under certain circumstances and with the express consent and approval of both my Native Government and His Majesty's Representative in the Protectorate. So that freehold tenure of land among my people is considered as one of the most fundamental and important provisions of the Uganda Agreement." See His Highness, the Kabaka (Daudi Chwa), *Further Proposals on the Memorandum on Closer Union* (Kampala: Uganda News Press, 1931), p. 3.

[16] Nor were Africans the only people to sense this danger. In provisions dealing with land, for example, the language of trusteeship, which had a certain nobility about it, seemed to leave genuine safeguards diminished. Several members of the Hilton-Young Commission were quick to point that out. In a letter to the Secretary of State for Colonies, L. S. Amery, three members wrote as follows:

"The alienation of substantial areas for long periods to European settlers would undoubtedly come to be regarded as a violation of their (African) rights. Possibly, a few natives immediately affected might be tempted by the prospects of rents, but this would not excuse the Government. We are impressed by a very strong conviction that if, as a result of such provisions as the leasehold clauses of this Bill, it came about that substantial areas in the native reserves passed into the occupation under long-term leases of European settlers, such a result would in the end deal a blow to the confidence of the natives in the justice of

1. The Kabaka of Buganda

2. Opening of Uganda's new Parliament building

3. Opening of Buganda's *Bulange*, or Parliament building

Sir Frederick Crawford, Governor of Uganda, speaks at the opening of Uganda's Parliament building. On his left is the Colonial Secretary, Iain Macleod

5. Three hereditary rulers wait to greet the Colonial Secretary

6. The Kabaka of Buganda

7. Drummers of the saza chief of Buddu   8. The king's flutist

9. Saza Council meeting, Kyagwe

10. A saza chief of Busoga

11. Branch members of the Uganda National Congress

12. Ruanda immigrant girls

13. Typical Muganda farmer
and his son

14. Katwe, site of main nationalist political offices

15. Typical African shop in rural area

16. An Indian commercial college for Africans at Kampala

anxieties. Arguing that British imperial policy had moved against them, settler groups in three East African territories, including members of the legislatures and representatives of planter and business interests, held unofficial conferences whose object was to influence official policy. In the East African Unofficial Conference of 1932, European settlers demanded a more direct say in the affairs of Government in the three territories. "At present," went one argument, "we are entirely under the thumb of the Secretary of State for the Colonies at home who is influenced by every faddist who happens to have a vote and who may know nothing of East Africa. There is nothing whatever to be said for that form of Government.

"At present, we are suffering from the absolute autocracy of an ignorant democracy—(Laughter)—and the sooner we wake up and realize that the better."[17]

In the end this conference resolved: "That in the opinion of this Conference, White Settlement is the dominating factor towards Trade and Civilization. Properly controlled it is a standing example to the Native Races in agriculture, sanitation, and better living. It therefore urges the adoption of a White Settlement policy to attract suitable settlers with the necessary capital, ambition and energy to East Africa. Such policy should include inducements such as freehold in lieu of leasehold grants (the conveyance to be in fee-simple) and direct alienation instead of the auction system."[18]

The Conference concluded that administrators were lacking in experience. Hence "this Conference feels convinced that it is

---

British rule from which it might never be able to recover. If the safeguards which are included in the Bill are intended to guard against such a result and to prevent the alienation of important areas, then one may well ask what is the great significance or urgency of the measure. The impression, however, which we have gained . . . is that it is indeed contemplated that substantial areas may be alienated, but it is considered that 'the conditions governing any alienation by lease are strict enough to preclude any danger that the leasing clauses may be used to take land from any native community in opposition either to its will or its interests.'

"We regret that we cannot feel the same confidence in the efficacy of the conditions. . . . The 'will' of the natives in fact means very little at the present stage, and consultation with them will neither provide a sufficient safeguard against mistakes, nor reduce in any degree the ultimate responsibility of the British Government." While the concern here was with proposed land legislation in Kenya, the general problem was of paramount interest in Uganda. See Hilton-Young, *op.cit.*, pp. 350-351.

[17] East African Unofficial Conference, *The Financial Problems of the Territories* (Nairobi: East African Standard, 1932), p. 4.
[18] *Ibid.*, p. 8.

essential, in order to overcome this defeat, that the Unofficial Community should be more closely associated with the Administration of these Territories than is the case at present."[19]

There was nationalism here, too: the nationalism of settlers who had no illusions about Africa, who had worked hard to preserve their stake during the economic crises and were now fighting for their farms in the great depression. They expressed their determination in economic and political terms, terms most frightening to the Baganda since they implied land alienation and domination by white settlers.[20]

Similar views were lacking in Uganda. The Uganda Chamber of Commerce, while willing to explore economic links with the neighboring East African territories, opposed political association. The fact that Kenya automatically pre-empted senior partnership in any federation made its prospects most unpopular among Europeans and Asians in Uganda.

The efforts of all parties in Uganda on the closer union issue were remarkably successful. The report of the joint committee, though ambiguous, made clear that closer union was not feasible, at least for the time being. In his despatch to the Governors of Kenya, Uganda, and Tanganyika, the Colonial Secretary concluded the matter as follows: "On the main issue before them the Committee advised that it is not the time for any far-reaching steps in the direction of political or constitutional union, but recommend that the machinery of the Governors' Conference should be increasingly utilized for the purpose of ensuring continuous and effective cooperation and coordination in regard to all matters of common interest to East Africa."[21] The issue was not dead but it was to remain dormant for some time to come.[22]

[19] *Ibid.*

[20] It must be pointed out that this was not settler opinion in Uganda. The President of the Uganda Planters' Association, for example, stated in 1922, "We have everything to lose and little to gain by amalgamation with Kenya. . . . It is a case of a bankrupt undertaking fusing with a firm in a sound financial position." Quoted in Ingham, *op.cit.*, p. 179.

[21] See *Correspondence (1931-1932) arising from the Report of the Joint Select Committee on Closer Union in East Africa* (London: H.M.S.O., 1932), p. 3. In 1934, the Uganda Chamber of Commerce withdrew from the Association of Chambers of Commerce of Eastern Africa.

[22] The Association of Chambers of Commerce persisted in demands for closer union. A 1935 Arusha conference composed of unofficials, and without any representatives from Uganda, proposed union between Kenya and Tanganyika, but even this was refused.

CHAPTER 9

THE GROWTH OF ECONOMIC NATIONALISM

IN THE CLOSER union controversy the Baganda found that they could organize themselves effectively for political purposes against the Protectorate government. Moreover, because they were successful in their efforts, the relationship between the Protectorate and the Buganda governments now required subtlety and tact. The Buganda system had been strengthened by the conflict. Chiefs dealt with the British in evident good faith but they stood ready to man their defenses against the Protectorate government should the occasion arise. Collaborationist or not, few Baganda genuinely identified any longer with the Protectorate government. They could have good friends among the members of that government. They could recognize the futility of putting unnecessary obstacles in its way. By their shrewdness, however, they were able to gain the day on all issues which were of fundamental importance to the preservation of Kiganda autonomy.

The Baganda thus saw much to content them. Yet by the very success of their efforts in the political sphere, the leaders of government became careless in the economic and social spheres. The old family groups, those who had received large landholdings during the 1900 Agreement, still ran the Kingdom as if they were a squirearchy. Economic issues now began to loom large, and in Buganda the three main guides to social position were land, education, and family connection. Social position was secured by a rank in the political kingdom. Peasants were now beginning to get education. As well, they wanted land and political power. So much attention had been given to economic matters in the conflicts over closer union that these took on a new political significance. The Baganda were increasingly angry at the economic control of European and Asian merchants. They were beginning to feel that unless the Buganda government paid more attention to peasant demands, it would be serving as the instrument of the Protectorate government and the European and Asian minorities. Thus economic issues came to have crucial significance for the next round of political development in Uganda.

In this chapter we shall concern ourselves with those economic issues which sharpened internal conflict. Such conflict was not simply a matter of poor against rich; the landlords did not unite against the Bakopi. But growers and producers in Uganda were making their first bid to move beyond simple cultivation and to try and control the land, labor, and capital of a people who increasingly came to regard themselves as a nation.

Moreover, economic grievance was composed of more than a demand for greater shares in the economic wealth of the country. There was resentment against European and Asian domination and anger that the old families of Buganda should retain such a proprietary hold on land and commerce. In the cycle of production as well as in the more ramified marketing distributing and consuming network, Europeans ran such major marketing agencies as the Uganda Company (cotton) and Baumann's (coffee). Asians controlled most retail outlets, including those in the villages and rural areas. These were represented on the Legislative Council and able to influence policy. The old families of Buganda virtually monopolized their Kingdom's political life. What was left for the ordinary Muganda was the role of peasant producer—part subsistence crop, part commercial crop—and if he were particularly fortunate he might have the assistance of agricultural laborers from Lango, Madi, West Nile, or Ruanda-Urundi. Thus racial and economic stratification was almost complete, while for Africans, land holding and dynastic family connections were the best insurance for a good political post.

However, as we have suggested earlier, the dynastic system did not, finally, come to prevail. Bakopi who became educated in rural mission schools or as servants in the households of African or European clergy found their way into the political hierarchy as lower ranking chiefs or clerks. Old family social exclusiveness never developed into a nobility. In the resulting fluid situation, a wide range of potential conflicts and potential coalitions existed between differing groups. Just as chiefs, peasants, and Bataka had united against the Europeans and Asians in the closer union controversy, so could they unite against their own government in Buganda when they thought it was serving interests other than their own.

Concerned as it was with economic development, the Protectorate government did not entertain very seriously the idea of African entry into the commercial and marketing sectors of the economy. As a result, in the African sector there was virtually no occupational specialization and differentiation excepting in the political administration.

The ginning and marketing of cotton was, as we have pointed out, in the hands of Asians and Europeans respectively. These were able to control cotton policy more effectively through their participation in the Legislative Council, putting their demands in the form of national economic priorities. Thus government tended to fend off as unrealistic the demands of Africans for greater participation.

Who were the leaders of the newly aggrieved farmers? Many were the children of older chiefs who themselves had had unsuccessful experiences as chiefs and had been removed. With inherited land, a sense of their own worth, and considerable education, such farmers attempted to engage in economic enterprise to restore their social situations. They formed growers' and producers' associations. They attempted retail distribution. In most cases they could not compete successfully with Asian and European business groups, or else they came up against government restrictions. Whether these were in the form of actual restrictions or only reluctance on the part of government to provide special aid for African businessmen, many of the most important chieftaincy families soon found themselves with members who were estranged from both the Buganda and the Protectorate governments.

The full force of public antagonism came to rest upon two major officials of the Buganda government. Martin Luther Nsibirwa, who came to the Katikiroship after the short and unsuccessful term of the Kisosonkole government, tried to run Buganda in the manner of Sir Apolo Kagwa. It was, after all, Sir Apolo who had produced the image of the firm, capable, progressive autocrat, anxious to innovate and at the same time close to Protectorate government authorities. And the Omuwanika, S. Kulubya, fresh from his successful testimonials against closer union, considered the time ripe for a financial cleanup and renovation. In this he was firmly supported by the Protectorate government. Chiefs, the main supporters of government, had cause to be concerned that the Omuwanika might carry his reforms too far.

The peasants, too, began to resist more openly the dynastic

system. When Sir Apolo resigned, the *Damula* (staff of Katikiroship) passed to a Kisosonkole, one of the great dynastic families. It then passed to Martin Luther Nsibirwa, who had been Omuwanika in the Kisosonkole government.[1] As it happened, Nsibirwa was a Mukopi. Although from peasant origins, he had been a servant of Sir Apolo Kagwa, was educated by missionaries, as was possible for any servant at the Katikiro's enclosure, and became a clerk in the Lukiko. Not only did he have the confidence of Sir Apolo: he became one of the latter's closest friends and a trustee of his will.

Successful at his clerical post, Nsibirwa became a gombolola chief and then saza chief of Bugerere and Singo before becoming Omuwanika in the Kisosonkole government. Thus, despite his peasant origins, his associations had been entirely with the main dynastic families. People saw in him an extension of Sir Apolo and the influence of the Protectorate government.

The proportion of chiefs and chiefs' sons who retained their influence and control in the Lukiko remained high. Kulubya was himself the son of an important gombolola chief in Singo. If we consider the 30 children of Sir Apolo, for example, we find that 5 became gombolola chiefs. One was a deputy Katikiro under Martin Luther Nsibirwa and another became Katikiro in 1945. Nsibirwa, who was in effect the real successor of Sir Apolo, was a very close friend of Sir Apolo, and the circle of intimates around him included Hamu Mukasa (Sekibobo), Amoni Bazira (Kago), Petero Sendiwanawa (Mukwenda), Ezera Kabala (Omuwanika), Susane Muinda (later Sekibobo), and Yosiya Kagwa (Canon and leader of the African priests)—all from important families.

The way to become a chief was to be the son of a chief, have a good education, and get a job in the provincial commissioner's of-

[1] The Saza Chief of Busiro, Kisosonkole (the father of the present Kabaka's father-in-law), was chosen by the Kabaka and the Provincial Commissioner as Katikiro to replace Sir Apolo. The new Katikiro was under great pressure from the British administration to bring in younger chiefs, and indeed had been friendly to the Gombolola Chiefs' Association, an organization formed in 1926 to oust Sir Apolo and many other senior chiefs who seemed to permanently bar the promotion of gombolola chiefs by their long tenure in office. The influence of the British was particularly strong with the younger chiefs, and now that Sir Apolo was no longer a force to contend with, the Kabaka preferred the older chiefs who, under attack from the administration, had come to stand for Buganda nationalism. Caught between fires, Kisosonkole had to resign.

fice or some administrative post in the Buganda government.[2] One might become an assistant educational officer, or a Luwalo (public works) inspector, or a clerk in the Omuwanika's office. There, noticed by chiefs or by British administrative officers, the man who did good work would be appointed to a gombolola and move up the chieftaincy hierarchy. Hence one important element for a prospective candidate for chieftaincy was the connections he had, so that the attractiveness of a first job depended on whether it gave the person the opportunity to bring notice upon himself for a job well done. Merit was always a strong element in selection, but in the wrong post merit could go unrewarded.

Economics and Politics

For about six years after Sir Apolo's downfall Baganda affairs were quiet enough. As we have indicated, closer union had drawn them together and a battle had been won about the Agreement. For the Baganda there was now regard for the Agreement as a constitution; as a fundamental law. For the British the Agreement was an important legal document but in no sense a constitution. Without the stand taken by the Buganda government, the British would have treated it as it was originally intended to be: a convenient mechanism for securing a relationship between British and Baganda which could not remain static.

As a constitution, however, the Agreement now had to become a basis for separatism. Separatism emphasized the need for greater flexibility and more appropriate policies on the part of the Buganda government; policies, moreover, which could stem the rising tide of peasant grievance. This the Buganda government singularly failed to do. No matter what other changes had taken place, the chiefs' party was still in control. Bataka and Bakopi claims were not heard. There remained no way in which they could effectively present their grievances.

So in the depression period economic grievances gave rise to economic groups. These groups, putting forward both economic and political grievances, gave rise to limited purpose associations with concrete objectives. Such objectives were associated both with

---

[2] In traditional Buganda, while a chief's son did not necessarily succeed to office, it was a common practice for him to take the office of his father. See John Roscoe, *Twenty-five Years in East Africa*, p. 249.

economics problems of peasant cash crop agriculture, particularly cotton, and with the removal from office in the Buganda government of certain figures who appeared to obstruct economic objectives. Due to the nonparticipant nature of the regime, these associations were individually unsuccessful; but, like waves lapping on a shore, each left its mark. Agitation increased in the rural areas until there occurred a series of political events which, seemingly unconnected but actually an almost inevitable way of expressing common grievance, produced political crisis in Buganda in the wartime and immediate postwar period.

It will be recalled that the Bataka Association and the Bakopi had made common cause against the chiefs. After 1927 these alignments changed in form if not in substance. For one thing, landlords and Bakopi began to draw closer together in the face of a common problem—cotton income. For another, many sons of chiefs who had inherited land from their fathers proved unsuccessful in succession. Disappointed and to some extent humiliated by the Buganda government, and forced into early retirement, many of these sons turned against the Buganda government and tried to create growers' and producers' organizations or to enter business. To do this they had to appeal to the farmers for support. If they failed in their enterprises, as many did, this led them to shift over from the organization of directly economic enterprises to those with an increasing political object.

In general, however, landlords and peasants did not clash. Rather, they made common cause during this period. Most of the grievances which the Bakopi had held against landlords—such as abuse, arbitrary removal from their holdings, and violations of what was regarded as leasehold by the authorities but as customary tenure by the Bakopi—were virtually eliminated by the Busulu and Envuju Law of 1927.[3]

While it ended landlord-peasant controversy, the Busulu and

[3] This legislation was itself a result of Protectorate government concern over the plight of the Bakopi. The Busulu and Envuju Law was passed at the insistence of the Protectorate government as a means of protecting Bakopi interests. This law provided the payment of a rent to landlords at the fixed rate of 10*s.* per annum. The sum was commutable by one month's labor in default of cash. This payment allowed a Mukopi to cultivate as he wished. A proportion of certain products, like beer which the Mukopi brewed, had to be turned over to the landlord, as did a scheduled sum for cotton and coffee produced by the Mukopi. But these were very nominal. No Mukopi could be evicted by the mailo owner from a kibanja save for public purposes, or under carefully regulated conditions. For a

Envuju Law resulted in certain paradoxes. The holder of a small kibanja could have security on his land but rarely did he get a large enough piece of land to make much money. The freeholder who had given much of his land over to leasehold (and under customary tenure this was the practice, although the freehold and leasehold concepts were unknown) received only small returns from cotton and coffee grown on his estates by the leaseholder; the latter retained the bulk of the income. Receiving also a very small rent from leased lands, the freeholder with larger lands under lease was just as dissatisfied as the leaseholder with small holdings. Many leasehold plots were under a quarter of an acre in size, for example. Nor could the freeholder develop his land by removing leaseholders from it, since this could only be accomplished with great difficulty, including expensive litigation.

Two consequences followed from this. Increasing security in the land did not give rise to a migration to urban areas by the Baganda, but kept them a rural people. However secure their land, while it provided subsistence and a bit more, it did not provide enough income to keep pace with rising consumer demands. Landlord and peasant united in common problems.

Originally, the object in growing cotton was solely to get money to pay taxes. There was considerable resistance among the Baganda to becoming cotton farmers. The chiefs, responsible for seeing to it that taxes were collected, forced people to grow cotton in order to obtain tax money. Ten years later the situation had altered substantially. Consumption tastes were changing. Farmers wanted bicycles, more elaborate clothes for their wives, money for school fees. Cotton growing had become popular.[4]

The main alternative means of income was common laboring. Financially this was not very rewarding. Average income at the

relatively small sum, the Mukopi had his rights to leasehold made secure. He could not easily be evicted, victimized, or threatened by landlords, and in return he had to treat the mailo owner in a respectful and traditional fashion. (See Busulu and Envuju Law, 1927, General Notice 398 of 1927, 657 of 1927, 75 of 1934, 73 of 1942, 193 of 1942, 96 of 1951.)

[4] As a 1938 report puts it: "Formerly cotton cultivation was regarded by the African cultivator as a convenient means of providing for the payment of his taxes, and also in Buganda his *mailo* rent. In the more developed districts, and particularly in Buganda and Busoga, this outlook has become very much modified of recent years. Increases in the area cultivated have led to greater gross returns, and have thus left an increasingly large surplus after taxes and other commitments have been paid, which is available for expenditure on other things. . . . Cotton cultivation is looked upon as a means of providing for many things for-

time for a laborer was from 10*s*. to 11*s*. monthly. Average income for Baganda cotton farmers during the six months of the cotton season ranged from two to four times that for holders of acreage under cotton cultivation ranging from two to three acres, that is, the average size holding in the three districts of Buganda. After the payment of taxes the cotton farmer was appreciably better off than the laborer, and he still had the rest of the year to engage in other work.

Cotton became more popular as a crop. Taxes on cotton were regarded as an anathema, particularly where bibanja holdings were so small that holders were both small-scale farmers and part-time laborers.

More wealthy growers found it possible to employ immigrants from Ruanda-Urundi or West Nile to do the necessary cultivating. This was out of the question for the Mukopi farmer. He might employ an immigrant porter or servant. But as a small holder he was increasingly disgruntled. For the larger landowner the problem was rather different. For those of his lands under leasehold he received only a nominal sum. If parts of his land were not leased, he could employ immigrants, which he did in increasing numbers.[5] However, large-scale progressive farming proved so unsuccessful that landlords did not usually derive much benefit from their lands.

Aside from the grievances of farmers, a second form of concern developed among the Baganda. After the downfall of Sir Apolo, the administration tightened up. The depression required a cut in costs and increase in administrative efficiency. The Omuwanika, Kulubya, took on the task of revamping the Buganda government system of finance which had become relatively confused and inadequate. Peculation was common. Chiefs had been indifferent

---

merly regarded as more or less unobtainable luxuries, but which are now the necessities of everyday existence. It has had the effect of raising the standard of living of the cultivator to a marked degree. A moderately high standard of dress is the rule, and there has been a notable improvement in housing conditions and much greater diversification in diet (meat eating has greatly increased and there is a growing consumption of imported foods). The large number of bicycles is another symptom of increased prosperity, and school fees are recognized as a regular item of the family budget, while there is even some tendency towards a development of thrift as shown by the increase of the deposits in the Post Office Savings Bank and tendency towards investment in insurance policies." See *Report of the Uganda Cotton Commission* (Entebbe: G.P., 1938), pp. 29-30.

[5] Because of the flow of immigrants to Buganda, in some gombololas the immigrants outnumber the Baganda. See A. I. Richards, ed., *Economic Development and Tribal Change* (Cambridge: Heffer, 1954).

in collecting taxes and a general laxness was the rule. Indeed, the chiefs had rather a good thing in general inefficiency and so did many of their supporters in the rural areas. Tightening up tax collection increased their unpopularity with their people. This increased dislike of Kulubya by certain chiefs.[6]

But if cotton was important both to the Baganda and the Protectorate governments, there was little conflict between leaseholders and freeholders. For one thing, the bulk of the freeholds were under 20 acres. Neither large rents from the land nor unregulated percentages of cash crops to be returned to the freeholders were permitted. In effect, the small landowner and the small leaseholder were in much the same boat. For the large landowner the likelihood was that most of his land had been already allocated to leaseholders, but there was not much value in it for the freeholder except power and prestige. The Baganda farmers' few sporadic attempts to do "progressive" farming, using larger holdings and more advanced methods of agriculture, were not on the whole successful.

What brought both landowners and leaseholders together were their common problems of cotton and coffee revenue. Just as they became interested in cash crop farming around 1930, world market prices began to decline, fluctuating downward until 1938 when they reached their lowest point. Prices varied as follows:

Approximate Average Price Paid to Growers, 1900-1938
(Shillings per 100 lbs. Seed Cotton)[a]

Buganda	1930	1931	1932	1933	1934	1935	1936	1937	19.
Mengo	14.80	12.50	10.45	9.53	11.46	12.01	9.98	13.84	8.
Entebbe	15.16	12.54	10.52	9.06	12.06	11.24	9.88	—	-
Musaka	14.14	12.14	10.58	8.96	11.05	12.03	9.64	13.40	7.
Mubende	13.41	11.39	8.84	7.93	9.69	11.07	9.25	13.29	8.
Average	14.61	12.31	10.37	9.16	11.33	11.71	9.80	13.74	8.

[a] Source: *Report of the Uganda Cotton Commission,* 1938 (Entebbe: Government Print 1939), Appendix ix, p. 123. N.B. Variations in prices paid between districts due to variatio in transport costs.

[6] This came to have important political significance because in the long run the Buganda government was to alienate not only the Buganda public but many important chiefs as well, and had to turn to the Protectorate government for its only source of support. The long-run effect of this was to make the fight over representation and autonomy on the part of the Baganda a fight between the Protectorate government and Buganda political groups, in which the Buganda government pressed from both sides, showed great ambivalence and finally alienated everyone. We shall discuss all these factors in greater detail.

How sharp were these variations in actual returns to the growers is illustrated by income differences for growers between 1937 and 1938. In Mengo district of Buganda, where average holdings under cotton were estimated at about three acres, average cash returns per grower in 1937 were 249.12*s*.; this dropped to 161.82 by 1938. Similarly for other districts in Buganda. In Musaka, 1937 income was 241.20*s*. and dropped to 143.82 the following year. In Mubende, with an estimated two acres under cultivation per holding, income dropped from 126.25*s*. in 1937 to 78.85 in 1938. Considering that these average returns to growers do not take into account the widespread practice among those farmers with very small holdings under cultivation to pool their cotton before taking it to the ginnery and therefore share among themselves the income received, the degree of hardship and confusion engendered by such fluctuation among farmers generally and small leaseholders particularly is rendered even more pronounced.[7]

Subjected to real hardship, the farmers nevertheless became ever more crucial to the economy of the country. With their low overhead costs and cheap imported labor, the cotton farmers of Uganda could sustain the economy through depression where European and Asian estates failed.[8]

Dependence upon world cotton price for so large a proportion of the population did not bring an understanding of the principles of international trade. Fluctuations in price brought changes in income ranging up to 50 per cent from one year to the next. Angry farmers blamed the large cotton companies, the buyers' pools, the ginners, and the Protectorate government. An atmosphere of increasing suspicion vented hatred on Indian ginners

[7] *Ibid.*, p. 30. See also A. B. Mukwaya, *Land Tenure in Buganda* (Kampala: East African Institute for Social Research, 1956). In Mukwaya's sample study of landowners in Busiro, he found that in 1950, 60.4 per cent of landowners owned estates of 20 acres or less, while another 26.4 per cent owned estates of between 20 and 100 acres—86.8 per cent owning 100 acres or less. (See p. 73.)

[8] The tax returns from cotton show what an important part it played in the economy of the country. Buganda and the eastern province are the two most important cotton growing areas of the country. In the period of which we are speaking, the Baganda produced slightly more cotton, on the average, than the eastern province and indeed received approximately 45 per cent of the total cotton revenue of the Protectorate. When one considers that during the period ranging from 1911 to 1937 cotton averaged a little bit over 77 per cent of the value of total domestic exports, in spite of the growth of coffee and other export items, it becomes clear that both the farmers and the Protectorate government were overwhelmingly dependent on cotton.

and on other Indians who owned small shops in trading townships. Real grievances did exist. With cotton purchasing competitive, buyers representing Indian or European firms came around, each vying with the other for cotton. These competing groups cheated the grower through an elaborate system of short-weights and pay calculations beneficial to the buyers and ginners.[9]

In addition to antagonism against Indian and European cotton buyers and ginners, there was fear that the Protectorate government was stealing from the farmers. The basis of this fear was taxation. With farmers increasing their proportionate expenditure for imported goods (which had heavy duties on them), the farmer was made to pay part of his cotton income in import taxes. Second, there was a cotton tax imposed by the government which was shifted to the grower as well.[10]

Hence the Baganda felt they were paying penalties both ways. In addition, they had to pay an annual poll tax of 15s. per year, license fees such as those required for bicycles and guns, market dues and other fees, luwalo or its commutation at 10s. a year, and busulu or rent payable by peasants, or land taxes payable by landlords imposed by the Buganda government.[11]

Taxes, land, and authority, the perennial concerns at this time, brought about an increase in rural solidarity. Everyone stood against the economic policies of government. This spread to annoyance at the active intervention in veterinary, health, and agricultural services of Protectorate officials who issued orders and forced people, through the chiefs, to carry out unpopular but important measures in public health and agriculture. These,

[9] Cotton weighing at the ginnery was a fast process with a bar and platform weight scale. The farmer brought in his load on a bicycle, or had it picked up by lorry. A weigher threw it on the scale. Quickly the weight was read by an employee of the ginner who wrote it down. Normally the scale did not even stop quivering before the weight was read off. Opportunities for malpractice were of course obvious, and they were obvious to the Baganda, too. If a short weight was detected, the ginner could claim it was a mistake. Errors were rarely caught because the whole process worked too fast. The weights on the scales were tampered with so that they read consistently low. A clever weigher could manipulate the bale with his knee or the scale with his foot, etc. The sellers also cheated; for example, they included stones at the bottom of their bags of cotton, soaked part of the bags of cotton with water, and so on.

[10] A cotton tax was first imposed on all lint produced in the Protectorate in 1919, and the first comprehensive cotton ordinance, enacted in 1926, provided for control of cultivation, marketing, and ginning. See H. B. Thomas and R. Scott, op.cit., pp. 132-133.

[11] Ibid., p. 229.

too, became the objects of antagonism; if not directly related to the economic complaints, they served as convenient objects against which to ventilate grievance. Thus both expatriate Protectorate officials and senior Baganda chiefs found it difficult to work with the Baganda. This was a matter of growing concern to the authorities.

Efforts at Retail Trade

We mentioned earlier that a new concern to enter the field of retail trade showed itself. Africans now set themselves up in competition with Indian shop owners who were moving into the most remote areas, establishing small *dukas*, selling bicycle tires, pans, clothes, hoes, and other implements. The Asian shopkeeper lived cheek by jowl with the Africans. His children played with theirs. Clad in his brightly colored striped pajamas, and lounging in his shop, he came to be viewed as a threat to African interests.

There were several African efforts to establish commercial enterprises. In the early thirties, for example, the Uganda Traders' Union was founded. Its purpose was specifically to gain the support of both the Buganda and the Protectorate governments for African enterprise. Unsuccessful, it stimulated others to strike out on their own. During the same period two African growers' companies were started, the Mawokota Cotton Company and the Bamuta Cotton Company. Bamuta was a son-in-law of Sir Apolo Kagwa.[12] Unsuccessful as a gombolola chief, and anxious to restore himself to a relatively untarnished position, he and others formed the Bamuta Company in 1932. Since Bamuta and his associates had considerable land holdings, they pledged their land title deeds in order to get capital and launch their undertaking. When the company failed, they lost 50 per cent of their lands. Not only did this embitter many Africans who had tried their hand in business enterprise, but it tended to underscore racial discrimination in the lending policies of the banks. Africans could only get loans if the collateral which they could provide was very extensive.

12 Bamuta's daughter is the wife of Mr. A. Kalule, the Omuwanika in the present government of the Kabaka. Bamuta, recently deceased, was on the Legislative Council in 1955 and a member of the Executive Committee of the Uganda National Congress.

There were other business ventures. A cooperative was attempted under the leadership of three Baganda businessmen. The Uganda Growers' Cooperative was started under Musa Musoke, Sulimani Gyagenda, and Erisa Kasimbe, who pioneered in the establishment of nonsponsored cooperative development. A similar organization, the Baganda Growers' and Agriculturists' Society, under the leadership of O. Neneza and E. B. N. Bungo, had economic and political purposes. Both tried, but without success, to get the support of the Protectorate and Buganda governments for financial and technical assistance to African growers. In answer to their complaints, two important members of the Lukiko, Kulubya, the Omuwanika, and D. M. Kato, the son of Joseph Kate Mugema, who had studied agriculture in the United States, became the Baganda members of an Agricultural Advisory Committee formed to advise the Protectorate government on agricultural policy. These members, ignoring the complaints of the Baganda growers and resisting their demands, came to be regarded as unquestioning supporters of the Protectorate government.

We have mentioned the unsuccessful sons of the important chiefs. These came to play an important political as well as economic role in the late thirties. Many had received considerable education and had been well up on the chieftaincy ladder as gombolola chiefs or better. For one reason or another they had been forced to resign or were suspended. In a population which today is reckoned to be only a little over 30 per cent literate, the presence of a skilled, aggressive group of ex-chiefs, still relatively young, whose pride was wounded, served as a natural leadership rallying discontent against both British officials and the Buganda government. Some, such as Bamuta, had been associated with business enterprise that had failed as well as with failure in the chieftaincy hierarchy. Others, such as D. M. Mukubira, a former President of the Baganda Merchants' Association, who was later Minister of Natural Resources in the Kabaka's government and is now a Kabaka's nominee in the Lukiko, were close to James Miti, the most important leader of the Bataka and one who had been associated right from the start with the Mugema in the Bataka Association. Hence the link was established between disappointed and unsuccessful chiefs, businessmen who had attempted to compete with

European and Asian merchants and growers, and the Bataka.[13]

Centering around a few main towns which were major agricultural outlets for African producers, and also around the Kibuga and Mengo, these groups of disappointed merchants, ex-chiefs, and agriculturists whose economic interests had not been advanced formed an increasing source of dissatisfaction. Though relatively divided in the thirties, they represented a large enough combination of groups to cause concern to the central administration—a concern manifested in the belated recognition first by Sir Philip Mitchell and then by Sir Charles Dundas—that relations between the Buganda and Protectorate governments were being impaired. This impairment was expressed in the rise of a new Kiganda orthodoxy and neo-traditionalism.

[13] A letter from Mukubira to Miti as a testimonial of his services includes the following passages: "You have done plenty for this Association (Baganda Merchants' Association) in discussions in meetings and in giving advice whether the meeting place. . . . You always gave pecuniary help to advance this Association, and what is wonderful is that you have given this Association a place in your home. In short you are the grandfather of this Association and for the uplift of Mother Buganda in all those fields which are the points of discussion among all nations and which are the sources of wealth and of development, I present to you this letter as an everlasting gift to you in your life, given in appreciation of what you have done for this Association." (Quoted in *The Life of James Miti*, an unpublished manuscript by P. M. K. Lwanga.)

Although an old man, Miti was convicted for his part in the Bataka movement as being responsible for the 1949 riots and was sentenced to a heavy fine after spending some time in jail. He was one of the most interesting of the old Muganda chiefs. He escaped martyrdom during the reign of Mwanga, and was an ardent Protestant. He was one of the first Baganda appointed as a senior chief outside Buganda and, like Kakunguru, was mixed up in religious and clan politics in Buganda, while performing his job as Saza Chief in exemplary fashion in Bunyoro. After his retirement from Bunyoro in 1930, he devoted a great deal of time to clan affairs, and the Bataka Party which developed in the late thirties was in large measure his creation. One of the few carryovers from the original Bataka group, it was he who gave the Bataka Party any authenticity they might have had in adopting the title.

CHAPTER 10

NEO-TRADITIONALISM AND
THE BEGINNINGS OF MODERN NATIONALISM

NEO-TRADITIONALISM in Buganda was a special kind of political ideology. It allowed internal division in the name of internal unity. It sought to expunge from the social record those more obvious scores and issues which, alien in their expression, threatened the survival of the society itself. At the same time it took as its own those political and economic innovations which appeared to enhance the Kingdom.

Representing an instrumentalistic quality, neo-traditionalism in Buganda could serve populist and rural forces. Not content with simply removing its enemies, it needed to persecute them in some symbolic fashion.

What could serve as the symbols? The Kabakaship could, even if severely compromised. Daudi Chwa, a sick and defeated man in the 1930's, came to have a somewhat illicit relationship with the neo-traditionalists. He was not enough of a personality, however, nor courageous enough to fulfill the potentialities of the role. Nor, indeed, was it desirable that he do so, for he above all remained the rallying ground for all Baganda no matter what else divided them.

Who were the enemies? They were those chiefs who collaborated with the British authorities and were also large landowners. Thus in both political and economic terms they were the target of the neo-traditionalists. The neo-traditionalists were political populists in the peculiar Kiganda fashion of monarchist populism. And they were anti-European and anti-Asian. As we shall see, the economic groups identified with neo-traditionalism in newly established political organizations devoted themselves to the eradication of what were now regarded as evil men in the Buganda government. In this way they were joined with some chiefs and the Bataka.

We shall discuss these events in the next chapter. First let us sum up the general issues which generated irritation between British and Baganda and gave rise to political agitation.

Segregation and the Towns

As more of them came into Uganda as administrators or merchants, Europeans were living increasingly segregated lives. A rapidly-growing urban area, Kampala became a well laid-out town with almost no African residents. It had spacious homes, gardens, and a social life that was entirely European or Asian. Observing the alien quality of town life inevitably evoked African comparisons with Kenya (especially in the aftermath of the closer union controversy), and it was feared that foreigners would win by economic and social advantage in each territory what they had hoped to accomplish by closer union, namely, the supremacy of a white settler population. In addition, the prosperity of Uganda, as compared with Kenya, attracted Europeans and Asians from Kenya who were seeking not to become farmers but locally recruited civil service staff and commercial people; it also brought occasional adventurers. Masaka, Kampala, and Jinja all saw an increase in expatriate population. This occurred even though the European planters, through bankruptcy, all but disappeared from the scene.

Overshadowing Mengo, the capital of the Kabaka, the towns became alien places, inhabited by Europeans and Asians whose houses were mushrooming up on a hitherto uncluttered landscape. There were new exclusive clubs, several banks, and a department store. Even the style of architecture began to change. The low rambling bungalows of administrators, often with thatched roofs, gave way to buildings several stories high. Ugly cement structures with the names of their Indian owners engraved on the wall began to make their appearance. It looked as if foreigners had come to stay.

Friction Between Governments

In spite of the strong leadership of Martin Luther Nsibirwa and his chief lieutenant, S. Kulubya, the estrangement between the populists in neo-traditionalist guise and the Buganda government could not help affecting relationships between the Buganda and Protectorate governments. Nsibirwa and others attempted to justify their role by denying that they were collaborators of the British, but rather were using the British to further Kiganda interests.

Collaboration, so necessary between Protectorate and Buganda government officials, became increasingly ineffective. Two indications of this may be mentioned. The first was fear of racial discrimination imposed by something the administration regarded as a liberal measure. Beginning in 1929, a system of local recruitment to the Civil Service was introduced. Jobs as agricultural assistants, clerks, medical assistants, and so on were open to Africans. Asians had more important positions in the police, immigration, and customs offices, while the Europeans of course occupied the senior government positions. Emphasized was the separation between the races in the Civil Service, not only in terms of positions open on the basis of qualification of race, but also, in differential rates of pay.

With race regarded as a relevant factor, here was a regularized system of recruitment to government which emphasized the subordinacy of the Africans. Protectorate government service, one of the main sources of jobs for educated Africans who had gone to the secondary schools such as Budo or Kisubi, and perhaps graduated from Makerere College,[1] and the presence of large numbers of Africans in positions which they regarded as inferior, served as a constant irritant among the best-educated and younger groups in the population.

Nor was irritation limited to these groups alone. School teachers and African ministers, the latter poorly paid and badly regarded, the former resentful of high-handed mission treatment, were also unsatisfied.

A second issue was African cooperatives. Such organizations as the Uganda Growers' Cooperative, an organization of African

[1] Makerere College was founded in 1922. Before it became the University College of East Africa, it was primarily used to train Africans for the public service or as teachers employed by missions. In a study of Makerere students who went to the college in the thirties, Goldthorpe found that 43 out of a sample of 55 students went into government or quasi-government employment. Goldthorpe further remarks that "the qualifications formerly obtainable at Makerere were not sufficient, however, to enable their holders to rise to full officer rank. Hitherto, moreover, there has been a rule in Government service that locally recruited staff (i.e. Africans) have been paid three-fifths of the salary appropriate to a grade and qualifications which would be paid an expatriate (i.e. a European). Although in form this is not a racial distinction, it has usually been so interpreted; the more so as, when the question has arisen over locally recruited Europeans (as sometimes in Kenya) it has generally been settled in favor of the higher rate." (See J. E. Goldthorpe, "An African Elite," *The British Journal of Sociology*, Vol. VI, March 1955, pp. 33-34.)

growers comprising about 15 societies, with about 400 members, put the claims to government which were later to become more familiar. They asked:

"(1) To sell their cotton and other crops collectively; (2) To obtain a higher price for their products; (3) To have their cotton ginned and to sell the baled cotton; (4) To eliminate the foreigner in the cotton industry; (5) To own a ginner on their own account."

The government did little to deal with these claims. The Buganda government failed to act as a representative of popular interests. The Protectorate government now met with resentment and dislike. Touring officers noted an increase in rural agitation. It was difficult for chiefs to maintain effective administration. Chiefs, themselves identified with the rural demands, were more surly. Relations worsened until all parties recognized that matters stood very poorly between the Protectorate government and the Baganda. Buganda was not alone in this. Elsewhere in the Protectorate economic grievances were setting off similar complaints. In Bugisu and Bukedi and in other cotton areas similar grumbling was heard.

The Rise of Neo-Traditionalism

Neo-traditionalism was vague enough and, as conceived, different enough from the past to underscore two main themes: respect for Kiganda culture as a moral force and an emphasis upon the individualistic yeoman ethic of a freeholding peasant society.

There was a resurgence of shared values between groups through joint adherence to traditional values. This manifested itself in a cult of "interpretation." Perhaps first begun by the missionaries who were intensely interested in the Baganda,[2] it was stimulated by conflicts over land, propriety of behavior to the Kabaka, the nature of the Lukiko, and the other factors which remained politically important. Sir Apolo Kagwa was the first African to deal extensively with Kiganda culture but the Kabaka and others quickly followed suit. A great concern with custom and

[2] Roscoe was the leading figure among the "interpretationists."

its modifications became an important factor in keeping younger educated people in tune with the rest of Buganda.

Respect for old chiefs, such as Hamu Mukasa, was evident in the deference and interest shown in them by younger intellectuals such as E. M. K. Mulira. Mulira later became a teacher, a journalist, and the leader of a political party. Everywhere there was the sense of sharing in a common cultural heritage which literate and illiterate, chiefs and people, Kabaka and schoolboys, found it interesting and exciting to explore.

A retrospective view of the past became possible in which leaders and people could find considerable satisfaction with Buganda as a state and as a state of mind. Success in combat with the Protectorate government had brought, too, a recognition that with solidarity the Baganda could now employ strategy to bring the Protectorate government to a more deferential position. The Baganda could look over recent history and find, first, those means of attack on government which would bring hope of success and, second, those issues on which the government seemed most vulnerable. Thus they could select the ground on which to fight a government—a government which, in the midst of troubled economic times, wanted above all to have peace and efficient administration.

Traditional custom thus gave a unity and an enhanced sense of identity. There was great pride in being a Muganda. It kept all groups, whether cultural societies, old boys' associations, traders' associations, or others, from getting out of context. Common ground was found between such groups and the public as a whole. And since all groups, of both educated and uneducated varieties, had their family and roots in land, whether freehold or leasehold, no one was ever far removed from the immediate and practical problems of rural life.

Social Mobility

Characteristically in rapidly changing societies, those who come into the greatest conflict with the forces of tradition are the newly educated groupings. In Ghana and in parts of Nigeria, for example, the younger educated elements often competed and conflicted with the chiefs. This pattern did not emerge in Uganda. For one thing, younger educated elements did not move to towns and cities, removing themselves from the way of life of their families and friends. Quite the contrary, it was common practice for a highly educated Muganda to be a farmer. Also, just as large numbers of educated Africans from Budo and Makerere were becoming prominent, a considerable turnover in chieftaincies and clerkships was making its appearance. A Makerere generation became a political force. But it was not alienated in manners and morals from the rest of the community.

It will be recalled that with the end of Sir Apolo Kagwa's Katikiroship, the turnover in chieftaincies became much more pronounced. Postlethwaite and others attempted to compel the retirement of older chiefs. Many chiefs realized the implicit threat in the hint that earlier rather than later retirement was the capstone of a glorious career. Many of those in clerkship and functionary positions around Mengo now came into positions in the gombolola and saza chieftaincies. True, most of them were from families of chiefs, having been recruited to clerical and functionary jobs because of their education (an education having been most available to chiefs' sons). But missionary-trained Bakopi also became minor chiefs, or fell into positions vacated by those moving into the chieftaincy hierarchy.

A curious situation arose where just as the depression struck, considerable postponed mobility was now carried forward in an upsurge of new recruitment. A summary of appointment dates of chiefs in the post-World War I period (between 1925 and 1931) shows a flurry of new appointments at the gombolola and saza levels. This was due partly to ordinary retirements and obvious incapacities of older chiefs, and partly to government pressure.

Emphasis on achievement was maintained because those in power, or concerned to share it with their friends and relatives, were on the whole those with the "best" claims to rule, that is, the best education and the most wealth. Enough positions were available to the qualified Mukopi so that the emphasis on achievement did not become meaningless. One could not say, however, that a Mukopi whose qualifications were good had the same chance of getting a chieftaincy as did someone from one of the notable families of Buganda. Nevertheless, it was possible for a Mukopi to become useful and helpful to a chief, to associate with one of the notable families, and to become looked upon as a likely candidate. The notables were neither nobles nor an aristocracy. Thus there was an oligarchy but not a system of blood privilege.

It was not enough to claim descent from an important family. Family prestige gradually became separated from power as an element in social distinction. Prestige came to be based as much upon participation in church, old boys' association activities, lecture and literary societies, as upon family itself. Although they predominated, descendants of chiefs' families were not the only members of these groups. Belonging to an old family made it easier to participate in such groups and thereby in such prestige. But lack of family connection did not mean absolute disbarment. Many of the new chiefs and many who came into clerical and functional positions around Mengo, the Provincial Commissioner's office, and the county and district offices, were drawn from these new and important associations, such as the United Budonian Club, or were Makerere College graduates. And through a variety of mission schools and an African teaching-clergy of Bakopi origin, Bakopi were absorbed into the "clubs." Thus no strict pattern of self-segregation of chiefs' sons or grandsons and Bakopi occurred. It was well known whether or not an individual had land, but only at the most important levels of government was this important.

As well, the rediscovery of the traditional elements of Buganda had great importance. Much of the interest in cultural and literary societies brought school teachers, clerks, chiefs, clergymen, and others into association with one another on common ground. They did not have to come from the same "class" because class did not exist in a clear-cut manner. And because many of the Batongole (landowners) and chiefs lived adjacent to one another and in close connection with these other occupational groups, all in a rural setting, there developed an interesting kind of pride in being a prestige-bearing Muganda. Such pride remained in keeping with traditional patterns of hierarchy, that is, those based upon rank plus performance. Only now rank extended beyond chieftaincy itself and performance included skills derivable from education.

What then were the consequences? First, the usual urban-rural split was avoided. In its place a pattern of "suburbanization" or semiurbanization occurred. Second, with the re-identification of Batongole and Bakopi, the mutual antagonism of leaseholders and landholders, so common in agricultural societies, was avoided. Third, the increase in the number of various kinds of clubs and associations widened the basis of associations which carried prestige; simultaneously, there was a great increase in the number of clerical positions which a refined administrative organization brought into being. The clerks and minor functionaries thus gained the prestige of association with Mengo, that is, Kabaka and chiefs (and the hope of recruitment to chieftaincy) and, as well, the prestige of affiliations with educational and cultural associations. Such prestige helped reinforce the norm of performance on the job as a major criterion for successful continuance in office. The result was that there did not grow up a mutinous, rebellious educational group of clerical employees and functionaries representing dangers to the regime.

Fourth, the increased opportunity for recruitment to chieftaincies helped to eliminate a potential generational conflict. The fifth factor is one we have not mentioned, but one which is nonetheless important. Many of the large estates were broken up, with bits and pieces of property being sold. Hence for many of those who did not inherit property but had achieved positions of schoolmaster, treasury clerk, assistant agricultural officer, and so on, it became possible to buy land and become a landowner.

Origins of Contemporary Nationalism

Contemporary nationalism began in Buganda when the factions in Mengo became sufficiently differentiated so that those who surrounded the Bataka now mounted a personal campaign which exceeded the normal limits of intrigue against senior officials and ended in permanent nationalist organizations. The normal pattern of intrigue was not successful in changing the Nsibirwa ministry. More persistent efforts were required. Certain "populist" or Bakopi chiefs joined with certain pro-Bataka elements. Economic grievance was one basis of organization; political factionalism was the other. The personal campaign became intense. But now the chiefs and others collaborated to activate the public at the miruka level.

If the ideology was neo-traditionalist, the attack was a campaign against senior Buganda government officers. Political separatism provided propriety to the campaign. The rigidity and unresponsiveness of the Buganda government had thus readied the ground. Economic complaints had alerted the rural peasantry. Even Daudi Chwa, the Kabaka, had complained as far back as 1932 that the appointment of ministers was for life, unless there was a political crisis and he dismissed one of them.

A characteristic "syndrome" of politics in Buganda began to emerge. Intrigue and faction, if unsuccessful in removing opponents, turned to more organized means. Crisis would build up, the peasantry would be activated in the miruka, and an explosion would occur. Afterwards the civil service system would continue as it had before. Politics was a series of boils and carbuncles on the smoother texture of the civil service state, occasionally growing into something more contagious.

This pattern, an old one in Buganda, takes a different tack with the organization of political parties. These eventually must either change the nature of the civil service state and transform it into a representative one, or be doomed as limited-purpose organizations, ephemeral, coming into existence as a part of some intrigue and disappearing when the matter is concluded.

On May 28, 1938, an organization called, variously, the Sons of Kintu, the Grandsons of Kintu, and the Descendants of Kintu, was established.[3] The organization had two main objects: to direct the complaints of the farmers and merchants into channels where they would be heard, and to get rid of the Nsibirwa government.

The chief organizer and first Secretary of the organization was Ignatius K. Musazi. The leading members were Samwiri Mukasa, a 1900 saza chief in Bulemezi, and his son, Shem Seppuya (Spire) Mukasa. Both were extremely active in the Bataka movement, the latter having had some of his land appropriated by the government in order to expand Mulago Hospital. Closely associated with Musazi was James Kivu, who, with Musazi's assistance, founded the Uganda Motor Drivers' Association later in the same year.

Support for both these organizations was widespread. Mu-

[3] Kintu was of course the semimythical progenitor of Buganda and the first Kabaka of the present line.

sazi was helped by two saza chiefs (S. Bazongere, Kago, and S. K. Njuki, Mukwenda); a Deputy Katikiro (A. Sanya); a Kabaka's nominee to the Lukiko (S. Kitaka Kisingiri); an important clan leader and subsequent Mugema (J. Kamulegeya); and important landowners and traders such as Bamuta (himself a dismissed chief whose struggles to form a trading association and cotton company had been as heroic as they were unsuccessful). For the first time the younger elements around Kampala, particularly motor drivers, were brought into close liaison with those whose economic grievances were strong and whose antipathy to the Buganda government leaders had reached a new high. Many of these followers or associates, such as Shem Spire Mukasa and his brother, Paulo Robert Mukasa, were identified with the Bataka. Others, such as Bamuta who had married a daughter of Sir Apolo Kagwa, or S. Bazongere, were influential members of old families and were also the sons of chiefs, giving both a stature and authority to the organizations themselves. Other groups attached themselves to both the Bataka and the Sons of Kintu, such as Baganda Merchants' Associates under its President, D. M. Mukubira, a close friend of James Miti.

The Sons of Kintu marks the beginning of regular political organizations in Uganda. The Uganda Motor Drivers' Association launched at the same time was the first political trade union. The first propelled I. K. Musazi directly into a political career which has continued until the present. It helped to give a direct political expression to the wide range of economic and social grievances which increasingly had plagued Buganda, and it directed these grievances against the two most unpopular leaders in the Buganda government. By its explicit attempt to organize a diverse membership rather than a following along "natural" social cleavages, it brought together the demands of the farmers, large and small, the African traders, the growing group of chiefs who were dissatisfied with the high-handed rule of the Buganda government, and the traditionalists, including the Bataka.[4]

With the formation of the Sons of Kintu, we can speak of

[4] It is interesting to note in this connection that the Kabaka kept himself from coming under direct attack by his virtual retirement. He spent most of his time at his country palace and from 1935 until 1939, when he died, he participated very

modern nationalism. Although unsuccessful as a political party, it was the first attempt to form one. Musazi explicitly tried to accumulate a mass following. For this purpose he traveled with Kivu around Buganda, asking chiefs and various notables to lend support to his movement. They sought to bring pressure upon the Buganda government by activating support in the mirukas. For this purpose they circulated petitions. For affixing the names gathered for a different purpose, Musazi was convicted of forgery and sentenced to 18 months in jail.

The Sons of Kintu had two important effects. It stepped on the attack upon Nsibirwa and thus upon the Protectorate government. And it stimulated organization at the most local level, the miruka. In the first instance a firm alliance of important people was achieved, including four saza chiefs (one of whom was Samwiri Wamala who himself represented a large faction of dissatisfied chiefs) and an Assistant Omuwanika, Paulo Kavuma, who became the right-hand man of the Resident. Kavuma was particularly important because of the need to influence the Resident in the matter of appointments.[5]

Ironically enough, it was widely held that Kulubya himself expressed support for those seeking to oust the Katikiro. The pattern of intrigue reached to the highest levels. Kulubya, it has

---

little in the affairs of the country, although he was involved indirectly in several anti-Buganda government affairs.

Hailey, in a report to the Colonial Office in 1940, sheds considerable light on the actual position of Daudi Chwa. "Sir Daudi Chwa's personal record was unfortunate. Considerable attention had been paid to his education, but he had a long minority, and was subsequently away from his State for some years on War service. This circumstance tended to enhance the position of his Ministers and their authority over the administrative service of the State; they were themselves men of a character which readily secured for them the support of the officers of the Protectorate Government. The Kabaka gradually ceased to interest himself in the affairs of his State; his personal habits deteriorated, and he surrounded himself with persons of an undesirable character, who became a rallying point for intrigues against the Ministers. His attitude became one of increasing estrangement from the Protectorate Government. In 1939 the disrepute into which his conduct had brought him, and the intrigues of his favorites, produced something in the nature of a crisis in the affairs of the State; the Prime Minister and his colleagues took on this occasion a firm and independent attitude which earned the appreciation of the Government of the Protectorate. A situation of growing embarrassment was ended by his death in 1939."

[5] With the success of the campaign Wamala eventually succeeded Nsibirwa, and Kavuma was able to get an appointment as Saza Chief Kimbugwe in Buruli as a reward for his support.

been suggested, assumed that by this means he could elevate himself to the Katikiroship. When consulted by the Resident on the matter of Nsibirwa's unpopularity, he gave no support to the continuance of Nsibirwa in office. By the time it became apparent that the anti-Nsibirwa campaign would be successful, many important Lukiko members and even Prince Suna, an uncle of Kabaka Mutesa, had jumped on the bandwagon.

The second effect of Musazi's organizational efforts was the rousing of the public at the miruka level.

It was the miruka which became politically activated by the efforts of those in the Sons of Kintu and by those chiefs in the anti-Nsibirwa and anti-Kulubya factions in the hierarchy. Many of those chiefs had been members of the Gombolola Chiefs' Association in the twenties. Their links with those Baganda who had attempted to develop retail and growers' associations were strong. And, in their attempts to focus antagonism against Indian traders and ginners, they struck a responsive cord among the rural people whose most immediate political unit was the miruka.

We shall indicate that one feature of the miruka was its closeness to the public. But it was an agriculturist public which dominated in the miruka, a rural public mainly concerned with land and land issues and conservative to the core. Hence the combination of interests of greatest concern to them devolved around custom and land. Like the great mass of people everywhere, they showed ambivalence to the symbols of their country as well as to the political leaders who ruled them. On the one hand they were attached to such symbols and patriotic in the extreme. On the other they were full of specific resentment against the leaders whom they blamed for their difficulties.

The Search for a Formula

What were the small eruptions which led finally to a more organized campaign? Most of them occurred during the late thirties and early forties. They consisted of efforts on the part of the Buganda government to resist the Protectorate government's encroaching pattern of direct intervention in the affairs of Buganda. Reform was after all interference, and the Protectorate government was intent on reform. In a sense the Baganda could argue that the whole notion of the modern social welfare colonial state was invented long after the Agreement was signed, and efforts to introduce in Buganda those measures designed to carry it through inevitably resulted in a breach in the spirit if not the form of the Agreement.

Second, there were issues which had a symbolic dimension. These were part of the personal campaign against the Buganda government ministers. Perhaps the most important of these from a symbolic point of view was the Namasole Affair. This involved a breach of custom. The Queen Mother, the widow of the late Kabaka, wanted to marry a commoner. Considering himself a man of progressive views, the Katikiro, Martin Luther Nsibirwa, assented to the marriage, as did the Anglican Church which agreed to perform the ceremony.

For the neo-traditionalists this served as a useful issue. At the miruka level there was public outrage at this crime against custom. The populist chiefs attacked progressivism as a dangerous force. Nsibirwa was identified as caring little for Buganda. Thus the ideology of neo-traditionalism was employed for the first time. Even the Anglican Church came in for some bitter attacks and there were incidents against Anglicans in 1942, such as the demand for the resignation of the Rural Dean of Buddu who did not take a stand on the side of custom. Church, government, and progressivism were now arrayed against Kiganda nationalism.

In the same year there were attacks against the headmaster of King's College, Budo, with the subsequent resignation of 18 teachers, some of whom went into independent schools, such as Aggrey School. These became additional centers of nationalism aggravated by the independent schools' difficult financial circumstances and the government's failure to recognize them and vouch for their standards.

The Protectorate government was not unaware of the deterioration in the relationships between the Baganda and themselves, and between the Buganda government and the public. Indeed, they recognized that with the death of Daudi Chwa in 1939 and the appointment of a 15-year-old Kabaka, the power of regency which was vested in the three Buganda government ministers gave power to the Buganda government which had not been exercised since Sir Apolo Kagwa. That this intensified the struggle to be rid of Nsibirwa and Kulubya is without question. In the last stages of Daudi Chwa's reign, the Governor of Uganda, Sir Philip Mitchell, had seen the need for a drastic review of the entire relationship between Buganda and the Protectorate government.

Meanwhile, what of the Buganda government ministers? Why did they not see the handwriting on the wall? There were several reasons for this. They were of course concerned over their relationships with the Baganda, but this pattern of turbulence they regarded as characteristic, to be met with firmness. It did not do to compromise with the opposition.

Second, with firm British support, they expected that the opposition efforts would simply dash themselves to pieces on the rock of government.

Third, they expected to achieve for Buganda certain concessions from the Protectorate government. Hence opposition to the ministers, paradoxically enough, gave the ministers bargaining counters with the Protectorate government. It was not simply that the ministers were being dogmatic or ignoring legitimate demands of the Buganda public. Rather, in their close relationship with the Protectorate government they saw the wider aspects of government policy. For example, Sir Philip Mitchell wanted to resume capital expenditures which had all but halted due to the depression. He appointed a development committee in 1936 which was to establish development priorities and make provision for financing.[6] This was urgent because the austerity program pursued during the depression had cut into public works and public facilities and services had run down considerably. In expectation of renewed expenditures and with the prospect of greater prosperity for Buganda, the Buganda government ministers were less concerned with the pleas of Buganda farmers than they should have been. They could not foresee that the outbreak of war would temporarily halt plans for economic development. Not only were the Buganda government ministers left "holding the bag," but they had the added difficulty of organizing Buganda on a war footing. This further increased their unpopularity.

Nor was economic progress the only hope which the Protectorate government held out to the Buganda ministers. Political reform, too, had been an increasing concern of Mitchell. While the public was not informed that discussions were underway, the

6 See Ingham, *op.cit.*, p. 209.

ministers were aware that reform was in the air. The ministers thus had a nobler conception of their role. However, they misgauged the seriousness of the antagonism they aroused. Concerned that the economic demands of the Baganda (which they regarded as foolish) might prejudice the unfolding of a larger economic plan, they were aware of impending reforms which they felt would result in substantial gains for the Buganda government and for the people. What the public saw in the ministers and what the ministers saw as responsible officials produced a profound misunderstanding of both the long-term prospects of Buganda and the short-run activities of the Buganda government.

What were some of the political reforms suggested by the Protectorate government? *First*, there was an acceptance of the differences between "Protected Rule" and "Indirect Rule." The terms are not actually technical, but they refer to two somewhat dissimilar relationships to central government. The latter really involves a seamless web of political administration in which the traditional authorities are blended imperceptibly with the administering authorities under more or less autocratic administration. The first accepts a more autonomous role for the traditional group in question, and the administering officer is more of an advisor. Involved here is a dual system of government rather than a single one. Indeed, Mitchell was cognizant that the early control of administration by Protectorate officials had helped to produce a pattern of increasing suspicion, and he was determined to restore confidence by reforms.

Under Mitchell a general evaluation of policy toward Buganda was undertaken, the weak spots in the Agreement were faced squarely, and some new ideas were allowed to flourish for the first time. For one thing, imprisoned as all parties were in an Agreement—an Agreement which no one regarded as satisfactory but which safeguarded crucial rights that each side had with respect to the other—it had become almost sacrilege to speak openly of change in the Buganda-Protectorate government relationships. Much of the difficulty had arisen precisely because changes were more or less surreptitiously imposed. Mitchell proposed to modify all that. Meanwhile, secure in the knowledge of reforms to come, the Katikiro and the other ministers lost sight of the realities of their own position.

Second, it was recognized that eventual self-government was the goal of dependent territories. Once this principle was accepted, Buganda was easily regarded as a good example of an area well along the road. It had the beginnings of a parliament, the beginnings of an independent judiciary, and the Kabaka could become a constitutional monarch along lines of the English model. Indeed, there were more similarities to England. The dominance of the Anglican Church was one. On a different level, what was widely, if wrongly, regarded as a class system in which the landowning and educated elites were stable and responsible elements in the society, also appeared as highly desirable. Widely prevalent were the ideas that Buganda, under proper tutelage, was relatively quick in reproducing the underlying pattern of English history, albeit with local variations, and that the prospects for democratic government were good. By the same token, it was felt that in order to hasten the process, reform of the Lukiko was in order. In 1939 the Kabaka was persuaded to nominate a nonofficial from each county in place of the miruka chief whom he had previously nominated. This in itself began the shift away from the entirely official nature of the Lukiko to unofficial nominated members.[7]

Third, in 1938 the title of the Provincial Commissioner was changed to Resident. This, it was argued, was much more in keeping with the actual relationship of Protected Rule, following precedents established in India, Malaya, and Nigeria for the title of Resident, the immediate representative and advisor of the government. This would regularize and strengthen the position of the Resident with the Buganda government and clear out some of the ambiguity and dissension which had grown up around the Provincial Commissioner's post.

Fourth, it was held that the division of Buganda into districts, each with its District Commissioner, had itself been unfortunate because it brought district officers into direct intervention in district affairs, thereby bringing about a loss in the self-reliance and political responsibilities of the Baganda. This had carried the Protectorate government into local political conflicts. So telling was this argument that only a few years later, in 1944, the title was abolished and each was called a Protectorate Agent, dealing

7 It was not until 1945, however, that an elective principle was introduced and accepted by the Kabaka. See the Law for Selecting Unofficial Representatives, 1945.

mainly with non-African and Protectorate government affairs.

The idea behind these reforms—begun under the administration of Sir Philip Mitchell and continued by Sir Charles Dundas, who became Governor in 1940—was to strengthen both the advisory functions of the Protectorate government and the practice and independent activity of the Buganda government. With new responsibilities for the carrying on of government, the Buganda government would, in the interests of good government, necessarily rely on the Resident for advice. The latter would, in time, build up his own knowledge and expertise.[8]

[8] The Dundas reforms were very much in the spirit of indirect rule. Yet they showed a remarkable degree of confidence in Buganda. The speech which Dundas made to the Lukiko in 1944, when the reforms were ushered in, marked a new epoch in Buganda government-Protectorate government relations. The Baganda have been very much concerned to capitalize on the spirit of local autonomy which pervades the speech, while paying rather less attention to Dundas' remarks that ultimate responsibility for good and just administration is retained by the Protectorate government. On the other hand, Dundas felt that if the Buganda instance was successful, it could become a model for other African governments. With respect to the reforms themselves, Dundas said:

"I have therefore decided to institute separate administration for those affairs which are the concern of the Government of Buganda and for those outside its scope. The Resident will in future devote himself to your affairs, while those matters with which you are not concerned will be handled by two Administrative officers, who will be known as Protectorate Agents, one in Kampala, the other in Masaka. It will be quite easy to distinguish between these two sets of affairs but if at any time questions arise which affect both, they will be referred to the Resident as the Senior Administrative Officer and he will, of course, always be consulted by the Government and People as for instance, taxation and other laws applied by the Government to Buganda, but otherwise I wish him and his staff to be relieved of all business in which the Buganda Government is not concerned.

"In other parts of Uganda each Native Administration is supervised by one District Commissioner, so that each area forms a single District Administration. In Buganda, the country has been divided into three District Administrations. I consider this is wrong, because it may result in differences of practice and confuse the people, who may not know under whose authority they really live. In future the Resident and his Assistants, who will be known as Assistant Residents will be centered at Kampala only and from there will tour the whole country. . . .

"Together with this reorganization I desire to make the position and duties of the Resident more in accord with the intention of the Agreement than has been in the past (*sic*). The Agreement stipulated that 'The Kabaka should exercise direct rule subject to the King's over-rule' which, of course, is delegated to the Governor. It is for this reason that a Resident cannot have the authority nor fill the functions of a Provincial Commissioner. His duty is not to direct affairs or to control your officials but to advise your Government and advise me in the exercise of my authority. But since he cannot direct and control, he cannot assume responsibility for the actions of your Government and its servants. That responsibility lies with Your Highness acting on the advice of your Ministers and Council subject to the Governor's over-riding powers. In the past it was necessary for British Administration to go beyond these limits and to take a direct part in detailed

What appeared then as a climate of reform to the ministers of the Buganda government was widely considered by the public to be immobilism. More than the normal ambiguity in the perspectives of rulers and ruled came into being, and in the resulting confusion, compounded by the proclivities to factionalism and conflict inherent in the post-Agreement bureaucracy and by the economic changes which had produced perceived discrepancies in advantage and disadvantage for various groups in the society, each specific action carried within it a latent explosive quality.

The entire situation was complicated by the War. The War itself created a staff problem such that those administrative officers who were not called for military duty were diverted to defense tasks. "Thus in Mengo in September, 1939, one administrative officer was struggling to organize the control of petrol and the issue of coupons, while another was endeavouring to organize the sale and distribution of trade goods in the face of a steadily and rapidly deteriorating supply position."[9] As a result, administrative officers lost touch with the public and the true state of affairs in Buganda continued to deteriorate. It culminated in the riots of 1945, which came as a rude shock to all.

If the aura of reform around the administration of Sir Philip Mitchell was obvious to all but the Baganda, the serious and aggressive dislike of the Katikiro remained obvious to all the Baganda but not to the Protectorate government. Concerned as they were with the deteriorating conditions vis-à-vis the Baganda,

---

inspection of the work of your chiefs. That meant, however, that the Chiefs were under two masters and the people, particularly in the more distant parts of Buganda, looked to the District Commissioners as much as to your Government for adjustment of their affairs. In consequence there has been a dual administration within Buganda. As I say, such was perhaps necessary, but I consider that the stage has now been reached at which it should no longer be necessary for us to go beyond the scope set by the Agreement in the way of supervision of your administration, and I do not wish to perpetuate a system which I believe was not contemplated when the Agreement was concluded.

"Accordingly, I wish the Resident and his staff to confine themselves to advice and guidance, leaving inspection and control to your Government and its agents. . . ."

A version of the Dundas speech is printed in an appendix, "Address to the Lukiko of Buganda by the Governor of Uganda on 2nd October, 1944," in *The Report of the Sub-Committee of the Lukiko* (Kintu Committee) (Entebbe: White Fathers Press, 1955).

[9] *Report on Military Affairs in Buganda and the War Effort* (1939-1945), in *Annual Reports*, 1939-1946 (Entebbe: G. P., 1949), p. 1.

they were nevertheless pleased with the strong rule of the Katikiro, regarding it as an essential condition of stability and order. And as the widespread public dissatisfaction became centered around the removal of the Katikiro, his removal became a symbol of reform itself. As the marriage of the Queen Mother to a commoner had been sanctioned (a measure whic'1 many regarded as a humane and progressive step), this issue was used to step up the campaign in the miruka against the chiefs and the government. Such was public feeling that the chiefs themselves began to turn against Nsibirwa. The Sons of Kintu petitioned the government, asking for the resignation of both Nsibirwa and Kulubya. An interacting set of cross-alliances was established.[10]

They were joined by the anti-Nsibirwa chiefs, who were supporters of S. Wamala, one of the few Mukopi chiefs. He was close to the very people who were newly activated in the miruka and, though barely literate in English, he was able to combine around himself clan leaders with one set of claims, young political leaders with political ambitions, and such distinguished figures as Prince Suna. There was not complete consistency about this. Prince Mwanda, the brother of the Kabaka who had been eligible for the Kabakaship and had been strongly supported by Nsibirwa for that post, in turn did not attack Nsibirwa, but rather Kulubya. Indeed, one of the peculiarities in the situation was that the conflict on economic grounds was intensified by the need to select a new Kabaka after Daudi Chwa's death. In spite of the strong support given to Nsibirwa by the Protectorate government, the Katikiro sided with the radical populists in favoring Prince Mwanda. Mutesa, who now came to the Kabakaship in spite of the Katikiro's opposition, was regarded as a dutiful young pro-British Protectorate government-mission appointee. The pattern of intrigue was thus fairly complete, with many participants in the various factions selectively changing their allegiances and targets.

[10] Musazi, the President of the Sons of Kintu, was a member of the first registered trade union in Uganda, the Uganda Motor Drivers' Association. The President of the Association was a supporter of the Bataka; the Secretary was Fenekasi K. Musoke, who was also the Provincial President of the Buganda branch and Secretary General of the Uganda Native Association. This group originated in 1922, in the eastern province of Mbale, as the "Young Baganda Association"; it had very admirable and progressive purposes. By 1929 it began to engage in politics and in 1935 changed its name to Uganda Native Association.

As well, some chiefs came under direct attack. Two of the most progressive, S. Muinda, the Sekibobo, and B. Mulyanti, the Mugerere, were the object of bitter attacks. The situation makes sense only if one remembers that the most progressive chiefs were also fairly authoritarian and paternalistic, while the most conservative chiefs were populist, allied with the people, the Bataka, and the various existing political movements. The latter wanted democratic reforms to reduce the Buganda government's authoritarian power, but they did so in the name of traditionalism and rural democracy. The authoritarian progressives wanted higher taxes for better services; they also wanted education, so conscious were they of the backwardness of the population.

A number of Wamala's supporters were of the Lugave (pangolin) clan, which was also the clan of several saza chiefs who were in the Wamala camp.[11]

Clan and tradition in these affairs served a direct political purpose. The most progressive chiefs had also been the religious stalwarts. The tradition of religious austerity and strong character had been exemplified by Sir Apolo, and to a large extent he served as a model for Nsibirwa. The Old Bataka was composed of many people whose religious attachments to Christianity were as profound as those of Sir Apolo. However, the more radical chiefs, such as Wamala, were less devout, less educated, and in revolt against those who identified too strongly with church and government. Thus part of the attack against Nsibirwa was against a stiff-necked churchman and against the Anglican Church. This was given substance during the Namasole affair when religious stalwarts such as Hamu Mukasa, a former Sekibobo and a highly respected figure, were forced to resign from the Lukiko because of their support for Nsibirwa and their Christian view that the Queen Mother could marry anyone she wanted. This was regarded as anti-Kiganda.

The populists sought alternative features of Kiganda culture which could be used as a substitute for the "model-churchman's" role assumed by many strong political leaders in government. Hence by calling on every Muganda as a member of a clan, the

---

[11] For example, Simon Bazongere, Kago, S. Njuki, the Mukwenda, S. Muinda, the Sekibobo, Y. Kyazze, the Kitunze, were all supporters of Wamala and members of his clan.

populists revived the sense of common identity through custom, while the attack was mounted against those churchmen who were identified with the administration and who represented wealth, privilege, and political power.

The internal strains in Buganda required rather vast changes in structure but not in fundamental values. These were retained intact during the most drastic period of change which the country had known, the period from 1900 to the Second World War. Disgruntlement with internal matters was personalized. The system was not challenged, but rather the difficulties were laid at the door of evil men. Thus the utility of villains: they allow a people to disavow acts of government and features of society without disavowing society itself. We shall look at this "personal" aspect of politics in the succeeding chapters.

CHAPTER 11

CRISIS AND THE EMERGING STATE, I

IN MOST SOCIETIES the lethargy of institutions exerts a drag on the issues of the day and the intensity of the moment. Crisis is rare and does not go much below the surface of political events. Relationships between various sections of a community may be called into question, but that which becomes distorted is rectified by some modest change in rules and rewards. A more equitable and satisfactory solution is found. Peaceful change is of this nature.

In those societies where an imbalance between public demands and government decisions goes undetected or unrecognized until severe crisis looms on the horizon, tension becomes a permanent feature of life. Most often it is kept within bounds by the use of force, as in autocratic or oligarchical systems. A variant is a cycle of "ritual revolutions" in which little alteration in society results but the political leadership is changed.

The major task of those sharing in the process of building a new political society, one able to perform effectively in the modern world, is to prevent the establishment of those autocratic or oligarchical types of political systems which create rather than diminish tension. They also need to create political institutions capable of allowing periodic changes in leadership which will not endanger the stability of social institutions. A "viable" political system balances those institutions which produce severe tension on the one hand and prevents ritual revolution on the other, while allowing effective economic growth and social development.

Both nationalist and colonialist leaders have a stake in producing "viable" political institutions. But the conditions of relationship between nationalist and colonialist do not invite a joint attack on such problems.

The colonial situation today in Uganda is one of moving from oligarchy to representative government. The process of moving from one stage to the other invites crisis. The participants in such processes are always watchful of each other; each is convinced of at least the partial bad faith of the other. Few will accept the view that changes in the relationships of authority are based on other than calculations of power. Nationalists tend to assume that when the cost of empire outweighs its gains, empire will then disappear—but not before. The calculus of power is the attribution of motivation. Each political leader conceives himself in a rough sea in which the shoals and rocks are unmarked while both the elements and the sharks seem to conspire against him.

Crisis states move from one moment of heightened unreality to the other, punctuated only by those periods of emotional exhaustion which follow activity. Acts are then robbed of their vitality. The very issues which seemed worth struggling for appear in a gray light which takes away their pretentiousness. Those are the moments in which history seems to stand still and the participants in struggle seem anxious to huddle on the beach and warm themselves, grateful for being alive.

Crisis states do not know how to reckon with crisis, or to cope with it. Each one appears to be the last. Each results in momentary exhaustion. Then the build-up begins for the next one. Where parochialism, nationalism, and immobile political instruments are combined, crisis is not only acute but the process of moving from oligarchy to representative institutions is itself a poor way to build a national society.

Not able to be an independent government, nor anxious to produce a revolution, Buganda has become a crisis state within the emerging nation of Uganda. Her crises are generated partly by the immobilities in her own political system. They affect the emerging national government itself.

The Introduction of the Representative Principle

In the late 1930's the relatively smooth development of local administration in the districts and the occurrence of progressive developments, particularly in the Eastern Province, made the Baganda appear in contrast unnecessarily complex and petulant. However, the administration was soon made aware of unpleasant portents even in the districts. Not only in Buganda was there ethnic and generational conflict. Division of local political areas into counties whose borders were drawn to coincide with local ethnic groups caused difficulties in such areas as Budama. In Bugwere subdistrict there was conflict between Bagwere and

Itesot, and Bagwere and Baganda. The response was greater reliance on local government.

The development of local governments was heralded first in Teso and soon spread to other districts in the Eastern Province. In Busoga the Lukiko President's title changed from President to *Kyebazinga*, signaling a renewed significance to African authorities. But problems of maladministration soon appeared. The Busoga Central Council was dominated by chiefs. "It is unduly influenced by that element which is solely concerned with the prestige and profit of the old privileged classes."[1] Similar situations prevailed elsewhere.

In spite of the development of local councils, there was a sharpened political jostling which came more and more into the open. Voluntary organizations such as the Bugisu Welfare Association and the Young Bagwere Association became centers of political agitation. These attacked the chiefs and wealthier elements who continued to play a part in the newly developing councils. A common retort to these attacks on district officers and chiefs was that honesty and integrity in the younger groups had all but disappeared. Education, it was held, had bred irresponsibility and brashness. The educated groups did not readily adapt their activities to hard work and responsibility. Instead, they devoted their energies to agitation. In hopes of producing a more responsible public attitude and of diminishing the grievances and complaints of these younger groups, an elective and representative element was introduced into the central councils of the districts. Local government reform thus became a major policy objective.

The provincial and district officers were upset by the behavior of the chiefs. The autocratic and domineering chief refused to move with the times. There was great affection for the progressive, if somewhat stern chief, who retained an independent demeanor but who allowed a good relationship between himself and the district officer. Few such chiefs were to be found, although they remained the ideal.[2]

---

[1] See *Annual Report of the Provincial Commissioners on Native Administration* (Entebbe: G.P., 1940), p. 10.

[2] Introducing a representative principle was indeed helpful. But public complaints continued to be widespread in many districts. In some areas, such as Busoga, the perennial demand was for mailo estates in the Kiganda pattern. After a num-

It will be recalled that "indirect rule," insofar as it became a policy, was based essentially upon autocratic principles. To introduce a representative element was to depart from a whole body of governmental practice which had developed into a lore and philosophy of government. Indirect rule was itself concerned exclusively with local native authorities, utilizing as much as possible the indigenous patterns of authority. It was not intended to be a training ground for democracy, nor was it regarded as a basis on which self-government would be established. Indeed, in the midst of establishing important and far-reaching reforms in Uganda, the Governor, Sir Charles Dundas, pointed out that it is "necessary to dispel the misapprehension sometimes entertained, that the policy of Indirect Rule envisions any state of affairs in which British Rule is to be eliminated. In my view it is much more to be likened to a system of local government."[3]

Appointments were made by councils whose composition continued to be overwhelmingly official, subject to the consent of the provincial or district commissioner, as the case might be. However, once the idea of representation for district authorities was established in the Eastern Province, it spread rapidly to other areas. The Agreement states always had conciliar bodies. District government soon came to look more and more like that of the Agreement states.[4]

Meanwhile in Buganda, agitation had reached such a stage that several inconsistent lines were taken by the Protectorate government. Stiffer control over the Baganda was wanted. This resulted in strong administration support of pro-Protectorate ministers in the Buganda government, namely Nsibirwa and Ku-

---

ber of land tenure commissions inquired into it, it was decided that Busoga could not have mailo estates. This formed the basis of a general charge of discrimination. Accusations were made that Europeans would steal land.

In other areas, such as in Bugisu, the development of high-grade coffee brought increased income but exacerbated land and clan disputes, made more complex by the fact that no indigenous chieftaincy system existed, although certain headmen had been elevated to the position of chiefs when the Kiganda pattern of local administration was introduced.

[3] Sir Charles Dundas, *Native Administration in Uganda* (Entebbe: G.P., 1941), p. 1.

[4] In the north more attention was paid to clan matters. In West Nile, Acholi, and Lango, the attempt was made to underwrite the official authority of a chief on an experimental basis by selecting chiefs from eligible chieftaincy clans. On the whole these experiments proved unsuccessful.

lubya. On the other hand, it was recognized that the overwhelmingly official nature of the regime was a problem. Administrators were sympathetic to expanding the role and significance of the Lukiko. Indeed, Dundas, in a very forthright statement, argued that "Buganda is an outstanding example of a genuine yet comparatively efficient native administration. Here we have the Kabaka, the hereditary head of the tribe, under him Ministers, Chiefs and Sub-Chiefs selected purely on personal merit. The real and ultimate authority is, however, the Lukiko against whose wishes neither the Kabaka nor his Ministers and Chiefs can act; the reigning Kabaka succeeded by will of the Lukiko and the late Katikiro was dismissed, and the present Katikiro was appointed at the behest of the Lukiko, all laws are enacted by the Lukiko and finances are controlled by them to such an extent that they refused the late Kabaka an increase or stipend for which he had asked with the alleged consent of the Governor. . . . The Lukiko is composed of Ministers, Chiefs, Sub-Chiefs, advisers and representatives of the community, and I anticipate that in due course it will become even more representative, if not elective. Excepting for the titular head, it should be possible to set up a like and perhaps more representative body in most and, as I think, in all tribes. The more it is composed of those who in pre-European days represented the primitive organization, which as I have said must surely have existed, the more it will be genuine in character if it is tribally representative, a body which can speak for the tribe, a tribal Council."[5]

Dundas' statement is rather confused because the plenary position of the Lukiko is not clear from the Agreement. But it reflects exceedingly well the thinking of the late thirties and early forties. Reform was latent, thought of in terms of native authorities and their problems. It was concerned with principles of representation. Its scope was limited.

Representation at the local level was not, however, the sole concern. At the Protectorate government level as well, reform based upon the representative principle was in the air. In 1933 Sir Bernard Bourdillon, then Governor of Uganda, agreed to fill a second Asian post in the Legislative Council "in their personal

[5] *Op.cit.*, p. 2.

capacity,"⁶ thereby admitting a second Asian but not admitting the right of Indians as a community to be represented. The problem of representation was complex in East Africa; also, it was not limited to the Legislative Council, but applied to the Executive Council too.

The general principles that lay behind unofficial membership in the Executive Council were stated in a circular from the Colonial Office to His Excellency the Governor of Kenya, May 22, 1941. "The object of appointing unofficial members of Executive Council is to bring the Government into closer touch with the community as a whole. Where there are no elected members of the *Legislative Council* the same reason exists for the appointment of unofficial members of that council. Even where there are elected members, *nominated unofficial members of Legislative Council are generally required to represent minority interests which would not otherwise be represented*, or to secure the services of those who by reason of their financial or commercial knowledge and experience would be of particular value in the conduct of public business."⁷ The statement was equally applicable to Uganda.

The latter statement combined two principles. The first one emphasized legislative and executive councils composed of unofficials whose wisdom and ability made them the most suitable to advise government in the interests of the entire country. The second principle, which added representation of interests, emphasized primarily those of a minority. The question was whether Uganda should go the way of Kenya or follow its own direction.

The Secretary of State's circular did help to clarify the position of Uganda. In attempting to think through its ambiguities, Dundas found it necessary to take a firm stand about Uganda as a special case in East Africa. He recognized that a long and well established policy of consultation with representative bodies had already been developed where particular interests had been involved. What was required was not the addition of unofficials to the Executive Council, which would add little to current practice. Indeed, Dundas was afraid that tampering with the system as it then stood would be dangerous, and he felt that additional

⁶ See Hansard, House of Commons Parliamentary Question, June 1933.
⁷ Circular A from Moyne, Secretary of State, in *Kenya Official Gazette*, 3 February 1942, p. 83.

concern with special interests would have unpleasant repercussions within African opinion. He felt strongly that the future of Uganda was as a primarily African country and that the essential characteristic of the Protectorate government was its policy of maintaining essential control over the various African governments and administrations while leaving a measure of independence in internal affairs.

It was here that Dundas executed a rather clever maneuver. He accepted the representative *principle*. Recognizing, however, that in practice it would simply increase the representation of Europeans and Asians, he wisely barred further Legislative Council changes until after the War. This prevented an entrenched Asian and European minority from claiming special rights to representation and thereby consolidate their hold over the legislature. In direct contrast to Kenya, with its larger numbers of expatriate residents, Uganda accepted the representative principle without paying such penalties as conflict over communal rolls and voter qualification when the prospect of African representation emerged. Dundas transformed the Legislative Council system from that in which unofficials were in attendance for the consultative purposes to that of representation.[8]

The question may be asked why no effort was made at the time to include Africans. Aside from the generally conservative view in this regard, there were several genuine problems. What was the constitutional position with regard to Buganda? Sir Philip Mitchell, for example, considered the idea of an African representative but excluded the possibility of his coming from Buganda in view of the constitutional question which he rightly foresaw could be raised.[9]

During most of the wartime period the problem of representa-

[8] See Ingham, *op.cit.*, p. 224.

[9] The Baganda, of course, took a stand against participation in Legco. They regarded themselves as having a government ruling over their own people; consequently, none of their nationals could be part of a Protectorate organization which might have powers over the Buganda government. If they wished to make representations to government they would do so as a government. Were the Baganda to be on Legislative Council, they argued, it would not be possible for them to speak with authority as their views might be opposed to those of their own government. If on the other hand they were merely representatives of the Buganda government, they would be unnecessary in the Legislative Council, as the Buganda government could make its representations directly.

tion and reform continued to be discussed. Debate centered around the level of government at which to propose reform. Most administrators considered the most urgent and pressing problems to be those of local government and local development. They felt that the reforms instituted at the Secretariat level by Sir Philip Mitchell in 1937—those which abolished the posts of Treasurer, Deputy Treasurer, and Principal Assistant Treasurer, and transferred to the Secretariat the work hitherto performed by these officers under a policy-making Financial Secretary, Accountant-General, and Principal Assistant Accountant-General—needed time to have their full impact felt. Here was a planning and budgetary reform of great significance which had been scarcely applied for other than wartime purposes.[10]

At the local levels, too, a newly-instituted system of district teams (planning bodies composed of the technical personnel of the district, working in collaboration with the district commissioner and with what later came to be district councils) had not yet begun to function. The War had inhibited their use. There was therefore strong feeling from within the ranks of the Colonial Service in Uganda that both central and local reforms had already been made. What remained was to put them into effect as soon as the War and problems of civil reabsorption were over. The idea of planning for a nation moving toward independence remained a remote consideration. All agreed, however, that some new formula was needed to give clarity and purpose to colonial administration and a perspective within which to establish reform.

It was Lord Hailey who found the new phrase. Commenting on the irritating connotations of the term trusteeship, Hailey said, "If we need to express ourselves in a formula at all, let our relationships be those of senior and junior partners in the same enterprise, and let it be said that our contract of partnership involves the progressive increase of the share which the junior partners have in the conduct of the undertaking."[11]

That the term partnership was not clearly defined was itself a virtue. It provided a face for reform. Novelty no longer had to

[10] See Colonial Office, Miscell. No. 470, January 1937.

[11] Quoted in Rita Hinden, *Empire and After* (London: Essential Books, 1949), p. 147.

be fitted into the pattern of indirect rule. As well, partnership proved to be a face-saving device for all parties: partnerships could be dissolved and the senior partner could become a coequal and friend. In this the partnership idea became a set of principles for guidance and lay behind the step-by-step pattern of constitutional devolution of authority to Africans. Where it meant little it did not hamper practical compromises or alter power relations. Where such relations were altered, however, partnership became the comfortable way for colonial administrators to give in gracefully to new situations while taking pride that change was a product of their own craftsmanship.

The British government was concerned to translate the policy of partnership into concrete terms. Parliament had passed the Colonial Development and Welfare Act of 1940 which in effect served notice to the colonial governments that economic considerations were to have high priority. Uganda had already placed urgent priorities on economic development during the last stages of Sir Philip Mitchell's administration (although plans had to be shelved due to the outbreak of the War). Concern with development had been the object of two committees of the Legislative Council, the Standing Finance Committee and the Development and Welfare Committee. By 1944 these committees had issued a joint report on postwar development.

At the political level, Dundas, who succeeded Mitchell, had initiated action on a range of political reforms in Buganda, many of which had originated with Mitchell but which he, for various reasons, had been unable to carry forward during his term of office. According to the Agreement, the relationship between the Buganda government and the Protectorate government had to be conducted at the provincial rather than the district level, the crucial agency being the Residency. The Resident received information from the Buganda government and served as the connecting link to the Protectorate government, as well as giving guidance and advice to the Buganda government and the chiefs.

The Dundas reforms created in effect two systems of administration. One was the Residency and its continued supervision of and association with the Kabaka's government.[12] The other was

12 For a good discussion of the reforms instituted by Governors Mitchell and Dundas, see Ingham, op.cit., Chapter 7; Sir Philip Mitchell, *African Afterthoughts*

district administration in Mengo, Masaka, and Mubende districts, where district officers no longer concerned themselves with affairs of Buganda but dealt instead with purely Protectorate government matters in these districts and with non-African affairs. These officers[13] were to have nothing further to do with the chiefs and were separated from the Resident.

This situation produced of course several difficulties. First, it put an extremely heavy burden on the Buganda government for efficient rule at a time when unanticipated postwar changes were already underway. Second, it put the chiefs in a very awkward position because of their dual loyalties: to the Protectorate government, under the 1919 African Authority Ordinance in which chiefs were responsible for law and order, and to the Buganda government. Chiefs who had hitherto worked closely with the office of the Resident in both of their allegiances could now do so only through the first but not the second. As a result, the authority of the chief was undermined.[14]

Meanwhile in the districts outside Buganda, greater attention to local government at the parish, subcounty, and county levels had had the effect of developing a more efficient local government system, particularly in the Eastern Province. In Buganda, however, local government had been left to languish. Complaints were common that the local councils did not serve as a communicating device. The main agent of local government remained the chiefs. The chiefs' councils were themselves most unsatisfactory. Indeed, with the Dundas reforms in 1944 the chiefs withdrew from positive administration, restricting their activities more and more to the collection of taxes and ensuring that minimum of activity which would keep them out of trouble with both the authorities and the public. To prevent chaos at the local level, assistant residents would often take responsibilities upon themselves which infringed upon the authority of chiefs. As a result, friction between the Resident and his officers, and the Buganda government and its chiefs, became increasingly intense.

There is little doubt that the Dundas reforms were themselves

---

(London: Hutchinson, 1954); and Sir Charles Dundas, *African Crossroads* (London: Macmillan, 1955).

13 Called Protectorate Agents after the reform.

14 See African Authority Ordinance, 1919.

extremely sensible and advanced for their time. They came into being somewhat prematurely. They needed a more cooperative and administrative-minded Katikiro, who could himself bring about administrative reform in the lower councils.

The 1945 Riots and their Aftermath

Wamala was appointed Katikiro after the Namasole Affair in 1941. He had led the successful campaign against Nsibirwa who resigned. Shortly after Wamala became Katikiro, Musazi was released from jail. The Wamala faction had affiliations with a wide variety of rural and trading groups. For the first time, Buganda had a "popular government" within the framework of the Agreement.

Wamala was the first Katikiro to reckon with public opinion. This resulted in some practical difficulties. The public was not particularly well informed. Common were stories that the Europeans drank blood and were vampires (because of efforts to create a blood bank), that the mission hospitals killed children (because few maternity cases reached the hospitals until there was difficulty), that the Europeans introduced syphilis and sleeping sickness in order to rob the lands of the Africans (and in fact there was no sleeping sickness before European penetration). Missionaries and administrators, it was widely believed, were engaged in a gigantic plot against Africans. In such a climate political reform was difficult. In this environment Wamala and Musazi (the latter in a new organization called the Buganda Common People, *Bakopi Bazukulu*)[15] fought the Protectorate government.

Concern over land tenure was given particular substance when the Protectorate government tried to force legislation through the Lukiko which would enable the Kabaka to acquire land for public purposes. Musazi in particular was able to arouse great public feeling on this issue. For a time, Wamala himself came

15 The *Bakopi Bazakulu* had its specific target, the Omuwanika Kulubya. But it also proposed that the senior chiefs should no longer be appointed by the governor but should be elected. Its change of name was due partly to a change in political leadership, but also there was a concerted effort to gain the support of all Buganda. It had allied itself with elements from the old Bataka Association, particularly James Miti and Reuben Musoke, and out of this alliance grew the reformed Bataka Party in 1946.

under crossfire when he erroneously miscalculated the degree of popular displeasure over the proposed bill. He soon discovered his mistake, indicating to the Resident that such a bill would be exceedingly unpopular. He was told to proceed with the bill and present it to the Lukiko. Wamala complied but was able to prevent its passage. He then directed public antagonism toward Kulubya, the Omuwanika.

The populist position was stated in a seditious pamphlet published in 1944 which gives the general outlook on land acquisition. In a discussion of the acquisition of land at Mulago (for Mulago Hospital) and Makerere (for Makerere College), the view expressed was the widespread one that land even for beneficial purposes is forever lost to Africans. For example, *Buganda Nyaffe* pointed out that the commission set up to enquire into higher education in East Africa (the de la Warr Commission) had proposed two sites for a university, one of which had already been purchased (part of which was being used as a golf course). This, it was suggested, was the most likely area in which to build a university. The Uganda government selected the other site because it gave the government more land. This was given as an example of "the Englishman's voracity" and the reason that the Buganda government refused to part with the land.[16] This view became so widespread that almost any proposal which embodied social welfare and development was seen as containing a threat.

With Wamala becoming more and more intransigent in the face of Protectorate government pressure, relations between the Buganda and Protectorate governments rapidly reached an impasse. Eventually, with tension rising in Buganda as a result of this situation, the Protectorate government forced Wamala to resign. Wamala supporters, realizing that he would be forced out of office, feared that Kulubya would replace him as Katikiro. Just as they had previously worked to remove Martin Luther Nsibirwa, they

[16] In fact, the Makerere site was selected because the opportunities for expanding the facilities were more limited in the alternative site. At the conference held to consider the recommendations of the de la Warr Commission, the Uganda delegation included Kulubya as one of the two representatives of the Buganda Kingdom. As well, the Kabaka had approved plans for including the Makerere area within Kampala township, with the result that the Kabaka himself came under severe criticism. See Appendix B (1), "Report of the Sub-Committee on the Name Site and Plans of the Higher College," *The Higher College of East Africa*, Proceedings of the Inter-Territorial Conference, 1938.

now intensified efforts to remove Kulubya. A meeting of several saza chiefs (A. Samya, S. Bazongere, S. Njuki, S. Muinda) and Prince Suna resulted in a petition alleging misconduct on the part of Kulubya. The petition was rejected. These chiefs then enlisted the support of Kivu, F. Musoke, and others who were both traders and Bataka Organization followers, including Daudi Mukubira, the author of *Buganda Nyaffe*, and Ignatius Musazi. Organizational activity increased. The young Kabaka who supported Kulubya came under direct attack. By January 1945 violence broke out. There were strikes in hospitals and among African employees of European firms.[17] Shortly thereafter, Kulubya resigned. The riots continued for some days more, spreading throughout Buganda.

A commission of inquiry, set up to review causes of the disturbances, concluded somewhat complacently that what was needed was more touring on the part of administrative staff and chiefs. Increased intelligence work was suggested and a better information program recommended. *Buganda Nyaffe* was banned. The report held it desirable to establish a central government security police. The commission report concluded that Buganda "seems to

[17] When the riots broke out early in January 1945, the Kabaka was immediately summoned from safari. He cut short his safari and, returning to Mengo, set up a committee after first interviewing Musazi, who told him that higher prices for produce and more pay were wanted. The committee charged that the ministers were standing in their way and should be removed. The committee also interviewed Musazi, who is purported to have told them that the claims for higher prices and wages were simply a cover. Since he knew that the report of the committee would not be satisfactory to the public, he urged its rapid submission to the Lukiko. The report was submitted to the Lukiko and considerable commotion then ensued, amid threats to burn down the Lukiko. What makes the affair rather interesting is the fact that the committee was selected by Daudi Kiwanuka, who was Acting Katikiro and supporter of Wamala. He was also a member of the Lugave clan. He appointed to the committee Bazongere, Njuki, Muinda, Kyazze. These saza chiefs were all Wamala supporters and clansmen of Kiwanuka.

The Kabaka himself gave the report of the committee in the Lukiko. It was assumed that because the speech came from the throne no disrespect would be demonstrated. Musazi, who was not a member of the Lukiko, got up and announced that the Kabaka's report with respect to economic grievances was satisfactory but that the ministers were corrupt. He called for the resignations of the ministers, particularly of Kulubya. Amid threats to burn down the Lubiri, the Kabaka returned to his palace, accompanied by his ministers. D. Kiwanuka, the Acting Katikiro, drove off to discuss the matter with the Protectorate government. The attack now widened as Kiwanuka returned. Although he knew nothing about it, he was accused of having called the police. When he then told the police to return to their barracks he was beaten up. Meanwhile, Kulubya had already resigned.

be the only part of the Protectorate which is badly infected with the political virus and it may be hoped that these disturbances may prove to have been a blessing in disguise, as having in good time brought to light some of the troubles which require to be remedied. . . . The definite impression produced by the evidence as a whole is that except in Buganda there is no real anti-British feeling and that in Buganda such feeling is not generally deep-rooted or spontaneous but has been worked up and fomented during the last few years. The vast majority realize that they are wisely governed."[18]

Unfortunately, the Protectorate government failed to recognize the seriousness of the Kiganda complaints.[19] Without thoroughly reviewing the political situation, the government continued with its plans for economic development in hopes that an improved economy would rectify all other matters.

By April 1945 a proposed investigation of the economy and its development prospects was under way. Assessment was made of the resources of Uganda. The report concluded that it was doubtful if a policy of progress would be possible by example and persuasion. Some compulsion might be necessary in order to achieve development.

The main limitations on the factors of production as specified in the report were as follows: "(i) lack of fundamental information about the country; (ii) a system of agriculture inherited from the past and incompatible with the full use of natural resources; (iii) the low capacity of the African for physical and (less important for the time being) mental work, coupled with a lack of desire for economic or social advancement; (iv) power based on the most inefficient of fuels, namely wood."[20]

That the development plan did not arouse a great deal of enthusiasm in circles outside Government House is not very surprising.

[18] *Report of the Commission of Inquiry into the Disturbances which occurred in Uganda during January, 1945* (Whitley Commission) (Entebbe: G.P., 1945).

[19] A major concern during this period was the settlement and absorption of ex-servicemen. As a result of the attention given to this problem, ex-servicemen were satisfactorily returned to civilian life. Unlike their West African counterparts, they did not become part of the nationalist movement.

[20] E. B. Worthington, *A Development Plan for Uganda* (Entebbe: Government Printer, 1947), p. 9.

Reform took the following pattern: it was decided that enquiries should be made into wages and prices. As well, it was decided to reform the Lukiko to allow greater representation. This, an aspect of the partnership policy enunciated during the war, was regarded as fundamental. Meanwhile, the Protectorate government restored Martin Luther Nsibirwa as Katikiro of Buganda after the resignation of Wamala on February 22, 1945. The latter was deported, along with other political leaders including I. Musazi, S. Bazongere, F. Musoke, and D. Mukubira. The policy of firm administration began anew.[21]

The first effort of the new policy was passage of the Buganda government Law to Empower the Kabaka to Acquire Land for Purposes Beneficial to the Nation.[22] This allowed the compulsory acquisition of land for public purposes by the Kabaka. The Lukiko, under the stern guidance of Nsibirwa, passed this bill most reluctantly. Shortly thereafter, Nsibirwa was assassinated.

Before his death, however, he had swept out of office those chiefs suspected of having been loyal to Wamala. A large turnover in personnel was involved. The object was to restore the sense of loyalty and obligation of chiefs to the Protectorate government and to the Kabaka.[23] Indeed, very few prominent saza chiefs remained except the Mugerere (Mulyanti) and the Kimbugwe (Paulo Kavuma).

In searching for a replacement for the Katikiro, an angry Protectorate government took the initiative. The Buganda were, for the time being, stunned. They did not know what kind of reprisals to expect. S. Muinda, the Sekibobo, was proposed for Katikiro. He had been an associate of Wamala who subsequently confessed to engaging in plots, thereby exonerating himself and implicating others. He became disinclined to take the post when a mob protested to the Governor at Entebbe. The Governor, Sir John Hall, urged Lieutenant Kawalya Kagwa, then on duty in Ethiopia, to take the job. Following in the tradition of his father, Sir Apolo, Kawalya Kagwa proved a tough and fearless Kati-

[21] Wamala died in deportation; it was widely held that he had been badly abused by the British (although in fact he had not).

[22] See *Laws of Uganda*, 1951, Vol. vii (L.N. 219 of 1945).

[23] Chiefs were responsible to the Protectorate government for the preservation of law and order; thus they had dual loyalties. See African Authority Ordinance of 1919.

kiro. Reform measures were passed which, if they did not always look like reform in the eyes of the Baganda, were so regarded by the Protectorate government and the Katikiro. The most important was over the question of Buganda representatives in the Legislative Council (which had been a constant source of irritation between the Buganda and the Protectorate authorities). The Katikiro became the member of the Legislative Council for Buganda. New and loyal chiefs were appointed to fill the vacancies. Mulyanti and Kavuma were both promoted to important sazas, while the Kabaka, unpopular and unhappy, went off to Cambridge for further study.

The long-overdue reform of the Lukiko was now put into effect. Elected representatives were introduced into the Lukiko.[24] In practice, however, the reforms strengthened the hand of the chiefs and gave them even greater prominence in the affairs of the Kingdom. Large numbers of miruka and gombolola chiefs were now brought into the Lukiko, in hopes of gaining the support of the hierarchy down to the lowest levels of government. The Lukiko remained a chiefs' legislature. Thus thwarted, populism which had led to conflict and bitterness in the past was simply provided with fresh fuel and a new quota of grievance.

The riots which the Whitley Commission had hoped would clear the air changed very little. The actual political reforms in

[24] See the Law for Selecting Unofficial Representatives of the Councils, 1945, in *Laws of Uganda*, 1951, Vol. vII (L.N. 241 of 1945). The differences are as follows:

Pre-1945		*1945 Reform*	
Ministers	3	Ministers	3
Saza chiefs	20	Saza chiefs	20
Notables chosen by Kabaka	60	Kabaka's nominees	6
Important persons selected by K.	6	Gombolola chiefs	14
	—	Miruka chiefs	14
Total	89	Elected members	31
			—
		Total	89

The 31 representative members were elected by a very indirect electoral system. In 1947 the number of elected representatives was increased to 36 and the number of miruka chiefs reduced. By 1950, after the 1949 riots, 40 were elected and the miruka chiefs eliminated. The latter were closest to the Bataka who demanded the election of 60 representative members. After 1950 the period of membership was extended from one to three years, coinciding with the tenure of the ministers. Women could stand for election but could not vote. A Chiefs' Appointment Committee was established and unofficial members were appointed to the Committee. See W. P. Tamukedde, *Changes in the Great Lukiko* (E.A.I.S.R., unpub. mimeo., n.d.).

Buganda did little to appease public demands. The authorities came to view the riots as simply the result of agitations caused by troublesome political leaders and by the "premature" Dundas reforms. Government treated the whole affair rather lightly, settling down to its previous concern with large-scale development plans and the eventual strengthening of local councils as the long-range solution to immediate problems. At the same time, by chastising the pro-Wamala chiefs, the government made it clear that chiefs were not to take part in politics. New attention was paid to police and information services in order to prevent the emergence of new misunderstandings.

Meanwhile, the conservative chiefs, the peasantry, and those in the various organizations which had pressed for economic reform now sought a new basis for pressing their economic and political demands.[25] In the aftermath of the 1945 riots the Bataka Party was formed. James Miti, the only leader of the old Bataka Association (and indeed the only senior Mutaka to be involved) took up the flag of Buganda nationalism. The Bataka Party had virtually nothing to do with the old Bataka Association, except that Miti had been involved in both. As a political device the meaning of Mutaka was expanded to include every Muganda. "Every Muganda is a Mutaka" was the slogan, and the appeal was made in terms of the presumed identification between clanship and citizenship.

Using the clan organization where possible, although primarily organized separately, the Bataka Party grew rapidly. Its actual membership was probably never very large, but its support was general throughout Buganda (and indeed in Busoga as well). It was a rural farmers' organization. Supporting it was almost everyone who opposed the Buganda and Protectorate governments. The Bataka Party was increasingly hostile to the Kabaka who, it felt, was under the direct influence of the British. The Party protested against the Kabaka's land acquisition act. It raised the familiar arguments against participation in the Legislative Council and unleashed bitter diatribes against the Katikiro for having been lured into Legco. It received support from Uganda's oldest vernacular newspaper, *Gambuze*, which carried on an extensive

[25] Economic grievances over cotton still remained. In 1945 cotton represented 72.12 per cent of Uganda exports.

campaign against government. The fact that the new strong Katikiro was the son of Sir Apolo, against whom the first Bataka groups were organized, helped to reinforce the Bataka Party with minor Bataka adherents. And, since the issue of land was reopened by the acquisition of the Makerere site, the populist aspect of the Bataka Party was ensured. As the capstone, in 1945 the Colonial Office published Paper 191 containing proposals for the establishment of an East African High Commission and Legislative Assembly. The old fear of closer union was thereby raised once again.[26]

[26] It will be recalled that interterritorial cooperation went back as far as the Ormsby-Gore Commission of 1924. A series of proposals had been subsequently put forward supporting closer union in the East African territories, but none had found favor. In 1926 an East African Governors' Conference with a permanent Secretariat was set up. Kenya and Uganda had already established joint customs services and a unified railway and posts and telegraph service which in 1931 came to include Tanganyika.

CHAPTER 12

CRISIS AND THE EMERGING STATE, II

THE YEARS 1945 to 1950 represent a curious period in the British colonial world. Labour had come to power in England. At the beginning of its tenure many colonial administrators viewed a Labour government with considerable mistrust. Expecting some rather wild departure from the past, they anticipated that the Labour Party would be irresponsible in its colonial policy.

However, a Labour government in England was by no means prepared to be revolutionary. By giving independence to Burma, India, Pakistan, and Ceylon, the government exhausted its more dramatic gestures. Instead, two moderate aspects of policy characterized Labour activities in Africa. The first was emphasis on local government reform, with the view of making local government the training ground of democracy. The second was economic development. The latter included several types. On the one hand there were large projects such as the Gambia Egg Scheme or the Tanganyika Groundnut Scheme. On the other were efforts to stimulate private investment. As well, there were attempts to bring Africans into trade and commerce and stimulate local economic development. Finally, it was hoped that community development would further encourage local projects.

The general direction of Colonial Office policy, therefore, was toward those activities by which to prepare the groundwork for the next phase, that of political reform at the center leading toward representative and then responsible government. Some reform at the center would accompany the emphasis on local government reform and economic development. The pace-setters were the Gold Coast and Nigeria, the two areas regarded as the most advanced, and where no settler problems stood in the way of responsible African government.

The Colonial Office view of progressive reform within the formula of partnership, which Labour inherited, was far less radical at its inception than administrative officers in the field had dared hope. Most administrative officers saw in the new proposals simply an extension of the work they had been doing in the past. Moreover, the Colonial Secretary was at some pains to stress continuity. Hence it took several years before those in the field recognized that events were actually moving more rapidly than they had been prepared for. Too, the rise of nationalism after the war was more effective and more organized, particularly in West Africa, than anyone anticipated.

There were, however, members of the Parliamentary Labour Party who helped stimulate the growth of nationalism in Uganda. Members of Parliament such as Eirene White and Fenner Brockway were in active touch with Musazi and other political leaders. Organizations such as the Congress of Peoples Against Imperialism were anxious to sponsor meetings, and attempted in particular to develop the African cooperative movement in Uganda. A few political leaders from Uganda came to know liberal and socialist groups in England, as well as coming in contact with men like George Padmore and T. Ras Makonnen who had devoted their lives to pan-Africanism.

Nationalism produced a favorable response with a strong Labour Party group. In Labour circles generally, crisis in the colonies was regarded as a natural result of conservative and ill-informed policies of colonial governments. The ultimate answer could only be African freedom and African responsibility.

To administrators in the field such a view was an anathema. If they regarded Labour policy as better than expected, they could not easily accept what they regarded as Labour irresponsibility in forever coming down on the side of African nationalism, regardless of the issues. Most administrators took the view that such nationalism was little more than the agitation of malcontents who if given half a chance would become the new tyrants of Africa, exploiting their own peoples with great gusto.

Interestingly enough, colonial administrators were helped over the gulf created by these divergent views when highly respected figures such as Margery Perham, Lord Hailey, and others who were by no means prepared to feel sentimental about African nationalism pointed out the advantages of political reform.

Let us discuss the two main policy objectives of local government reform and economic development and indicate their consequences for the rise of nationalism in Buganda.

Local Government Reform

In the now famous despatch from the Secretary of State for Colonies to the colonial governors, an extensive policy of political, social, and economic advancement was laid down. The Colonial Secretary emphasized the need to develop an efficient and democratic system of local government. "I wish to emphasize the words efficient, democratic, and local. I do so, not because they import any new conception into African administration; indeed these have been the aims of our policy for many years. I use these words because they seem to me to contain the kernel of the whole matter; local because the system of government must be close to the common people and their problems, efficient because it must be capable of managing the local services in a way which will help to raise the standard of living, and democratic because it must not only find a place for the growing class of educated men, but at the same time command the respect and support of the mass of the people."[1]

The political emphasis was to be put squarely upon the development of local government institutions. The policy of partnership would be translated into increasing African participation and responsibility for local affairs. Representation of Africans was regarded as desirable, although it did not resolve the question of exactly what the Africans on the Legislative Council now represented. It is clear, for example, that when the Kabaka agreed to the appointment of Kawalya Kagwa, the Katikiro of Buganda in 1945 to Legislative Council, he assumed that the Katikiro was in effect the official representative of the Buganda government on the Legco. In other territories the principle of African representation would lead to communalism and racial representation. Would not the same problem arise with respect to Uganda? These were all troublesome questions, but the main concern was less on the central legislature than on building a strong local foundation

[1] *Despatch from the Secretary of State for the Colonies to the Governors of the African Territories,* 25 February 1947. It is of some interest that there was objection to the term "democratic" in certain quarters. Afterwards, in published official correspondence, the term "representative" was put in its place. In its review of East and Central African territories, the Colonial Office put it as the aim of policy "to secure an efficient and representative system of local government. . . ." See *The British Territories in East and Central Africa 1945-1950,* Cmd. 7987 (London: Colonial Office, 1950), p. 12.

in order to create later a more viable national polity. In his reply to the Secretary of State's memorandum, the Governor, Sir John Hall, emphasized this. He pointed out that Uganda represented in herself a great degree of diversity "within this single small territory, and that no common sentiment of unity exists among its units. The administrative boundaries have not in all cases been drawn to conform strictly with tribal divisions and have therefore the less significance in the African mind; and in some of the districts there is a miscellany of tribal units each possessing a strong tribal consciousness and each jealous of the position of the others. Moreover, the development of indigenous political institutions in the Protectorate has been uneven, with the state of Buganda taking the lead. It is therefore a matter of prime importance to devise some unifying process which, over a period of years, will tend to produce a sense of common interest and of common purpose—and later, it is hoped, of common nationality—and at the same time to encourage, and not impede, the growth and development of indigenous political institutions. . . . The Uganda Government hopes to find this unifying process in a progressive development, both in executive responsibility and in their representative character, of the system of councils, with official and elected members, at the levels of province, district, county, parish, and village (to use comparable English terms), each Council acting as an electoral 'college' for the Council above it."[2]

The progressive character of this new concern was unmistakable, even if the proposals contained features which would lead to other than the desired results.

Although mainly concerned with the district unit, the attempt to build up local authorities went both lower down the scale than district levels and higher up. It was proposed to establish provincial authorities and district authorities; the former were not similar to Buganda, to be sure, but involved provincial councils which would serve to unite the districts within the province. Thus two opposite and consistent pulls were exerted: there was the effort to breathe life into local government by new emphasis upon

[2] *Despatch No. 11*, Sir John Hathorn Hall to the Rt. Hon. A. Creech Jones, M.P., Secretary of State for the Colonies, 29 August 1947. In practice, the provincial councils, short-lived as they were, served as electoral colleges in the Legislative Council.

the councils within the districts; and there was an attempt to establish higher provincial councils.[3]

The African Local Governments Ordinance of 1949, building upon the system of African administration and native governments, was the major reform which was to realize the political aims of the Hall administration. The Buganda government had been declared a corporate body in 1939, with others being so considered in 1944 and 1946.[4] In 1949 district councils were formally established for all the districts, with regulations to be set out for each district to accord with its needs and with the ordinance. Chiefs were to be appointed or approved by the Governor, be responsible to the Governor, and administer the laws of the Protectorate which fell within their jurisdiction. Powers to appoint financial, standing, and advisory committees were left to the District Commissioner. District councils were empowered to make bylaws binding on the African of the district.

In the same ordinance the Governor was empowered to establish provincial councils (although these were not given the power to make laws or bylaws).[5] Eventually the provincial councils withered on the vine and were abandoned.

Greater economic development also received top priority. What had not been anticipated were its political side effects. In the *Development Plan for Uganda,* the government sought by economic planning to increase agricultural output by 25 per cent through improved farming methods, including mechanical cultivation. Pilot schemes which would have involved a great deal of supervision and control were also suggested (most of them showing the defects of poor judgment and inadequate knowledge of the people involved,

[3] In order for the first to be successful, the focus of social and political life had to be increasingly the district. This made the provincial level artificial and meaningless.

[4] See African Administrations (Incorporation), Cap. 73, *The Laws of the Uganda Protectorate,* Vol. VII, p. 1147.

[5] See The African Local Governments Ordinance and District Council Proclamations and Regulations, 1949. Composition of the councils varied according to the district, but nominated and official majorities prevailed. Busoga had (and still has) 7 ex officio members, 20 nominated members, and 1 elected member for each 1,000 taxpayers in the district. Bukedi has 9 ex officio members, 20 nominated members, and 1 elected for each 1,000 taxpayers, while Teso has 10 ex officio members, 29 nominated members, and 1 representative member of each 1,500 taxpayers. This system was changed under the District Councils Ordinance of 1955, but some districts, such as Busoga, still remain under the 1949 Ordinance.

of their customs, and of the practical problems of peasant agriculture). The Baganda, the Basoga, and others feared that the development plan would by-pass the direct interests of the farmers, as they conceived them to be, in order to satisfy what the government felt it ought undertake in the "interests of the nation." The Baganda were not against progressive rural development and increased agricultural productivity. They were concerned that the development plan had been developed without their participation, yet was hailed by the Governor as a main point of departure for developing Uganda. Taken in the context of Paper 191 and the renewed discussion of East African federation, the Protectorate government began to appear more than faintly sinister.

Meanwhile, for many Colonial Service officers the new programs provided an opportunity for imaginative work long postponed by depression and war. There was an atmosphere of rebuilding, a consciousness of the high calling of "social engineering." Efficiency and representation on the political level, the building up of conciliar bodies, increases in the well-being and services for the people through economic growth and planning—all helped to imbue officers with pride in their profession. Indeed, the officers who had stayed in Uganda since before the War, and were in a position to contrast the accomplishments of the prewar period of depression and retrenchment, achieved a sense of daring and excitement. They felt they were beginning the job of building a nation from the bottom up.

It was precisely the new enthusiasm and energy which the Baganda came to fear. For it now appeared that the populists were both radical and backward, and that if the administrators were to have their way the days of Kiganda autonomy would soon be over.

African Trade and African Nationalism

After the War, Uganda, like other colonial territories, entered into a period of unparalleled prosperity.[6]

[6] The original development plan of Worthington anticipated the expenditure of £44,400,000 over a 10-year period. A revision of the plan by the newly established Development Commissioner, Sir Douglas Harris, envisaged the expenditure of £62,-743,000 over the period 1947 to 1956. The plan was fulfilled earlier than anticipated, although in modified form, and a development plan approved by the Legislative Council in 1955 planned expenditures of £30 million in the 1955-1960 period.

As European and Asian commercial activities expanded, Africans began to enter trade in very large numbers. Only a few Africans were successful in establishing shops before 1944. After that date there followed a period when goods generally were in short supply. In respect to some important commodities, such as cotton piece goods, the government arranged special importations. Allocations were made to all traders, including Africans, on the basis of fixed prices and profits. Many returning soldiers used their gratuities to establish themselves in trade. By 1953 there were approximately 12,000 African traders, constituting more than 70 per cent of the total traders in the Protectorate.[7]

Almost all of this trade was very small-scale. Indeed, the bulk of the traders averaged £50 average annual profit and 18 per cent of them made no profit at all.[8] Most of the trading was in rural areas. In 1952 only 2.5 per cent of the traders in Kampala were Africans. Nevertheless, the increase in trade and the spread of African petty traders was of major importance. Far from feeling prosperous, these new African traders were concerned over their relative inefficiency compared to Asians and Europeans. A common belief was that the Asians were cheating them. Moreover, Asians were able to rely on family sources of credit, borrowing from a wealthy relative or by the pooling of family resources, as well as borrowing from banks, while the Africans had no such reserves. The few wealthy Africans did not in the main lend money but tended to buy larger estates with their funds. In spite of a 1933 Trading Centers Ordinance which was supposed to protect Africans in trade by restricting non-African trading areas, Africans felt that little had been done to assist them in the form of loans and training programs which would allow them to compete with Asians and Europeans. The greater the number of Africans in trade, the more there were with grievances. No longer were unsuccessful and partially successful traders a small group allied with the farmers. Their ranks were swelled. Each small trading stall and *duka* now became a focal point of organization. Farmers who bought their grains and implements at these dukas or came to repair their bicycles remained to discuss matters of cotton and

---

[7] See *Advancement of Africans in Trade* (Entebbe: G.P., 1955), p. 14.
[8] *Ibid.*, p. 15.

coffee prices. The result was that an increase in economic transactions also meant an increase in political organization.[9]

However, such outlets did not develop solely in rural areas. African trading outlets developed in Katwe, near Mengo, the seat of the Buganda government and the palace, and Wandegeya, adjacent to Makerere College. Large numbers of petrol sellers, beer sellers, bakers, and small printers were packed in cheek by jowl with Asians in crowded slum conditions. This urban area was not under the municipal control of Kampala, nor did it enjoy the same services as Kampala. Petty traders short of funds, competing with Asians, lived adjacent to the rapidly growing town of Kampala itself, with its street lighting, its sewage disposal, its public park, and its gracious and generally clean streets where the homes of wealthy Asians and the bungalows of European civil servants looked out from superb gardens to the Kampala hills.

If Katwe was a growing slum, under the control of the township gombolola chief, it was also a center of communications. The small traders were just those whose knowledge of rudimentary bookkeeping and organization was necessary for the political organization. Suspended chiefs, released deportees, some of whom were small-scale African businessmen, such as Fenekasi Musoke, provided the nucleus of a "secretariat." The editor of *Gambuze* had become a spokesman for the Bataka Party and a regular party organization began to develop.

Traders from Katwe used their establishments as their offices. Local beer halls served as meeting places. Trading was not a full-time occupation and each trader also had his small farm or plot of land from which he received either rent or income from produce. The line between rural and urban never became strict because the trader was almost invariably a farmer as well. No separation in outlook between farmer and businessman developed. Instead, the traders in the rural areas acted as the spokesmen of the farmers. In traveling to Kampala or other centers to sell produce or buy merchandise, both farmers and traders would see the leaders of the Bataka and other newly-established parties. One of the central meeting places was the lorry and bus park in Kampala, the major center of African transportation. The lorry drivers, themselves

[9] Indeed, the Bataka Party was led by small traders who were the best agents of political organization in the rural areas.

increasingly politically conscious, helped to stimulate the political tempo and disseminate information.

For the first time, indeed, an entirely new pattern of communications grew up which was completely outside the official hierarchy of chieftaincy. The Resident's Office and Mengo were less and less the primary sources of information and knowledge. Yet this was not because of inactivity. The operation of government under M. E. Kawalya Kagwa, the Katikiro, had never been more efficient. Luwalo had been raised from 12s to 14s. There was talk of raising it further. Bore holes were being drilled. Mechanical cultivation experiments were approaching the experimental stage. The Katikiro regarded the public, which at no time appeared very enthusiastic for his reforms, as backward and in need of firm administration.

Once again the situation was ripe for trouble. It was brewing in the Lukiko, which was still primarily a chiefs' body. The number of elected members had been increased from 31 to 36 in 1947 by reducing the number of miruka chiefs. This did not abate public antagonism against the Lukiko. Instead, by being expelled, the miruka chiefs were brought into even closer identification with the people. In many cases they became firm supporters of the Bataka Party.

Inside the Lukiko there was now an elected element anxious to have more power. This consisted largely of small businessmen and farmers. They obstructed the proceedings of the Lukiko. In an interesting paragraph in the Buganda Government Annual Report, the Resident pointed out that not only was there increasing estrangement between chiefs and people, but the elected members also were a major source of difficulty. "It would not be out of place to say here that one of the most important causes of this [gap between chiefs and people] was evidently that the newly appointed unofficial members of the Lukiko, who had a year or two previously been brought into the government of Buganda as a measure to assist in associating the ordinary people with their appointed leaders, had shown in almost every instance a lamentable lack of responsibility and had nearly all failed properly to appreciate their positions. These people, who represented but a fraction of the electorate, such was the lack of interest in the elections shown by the Ordinary Muganda, normally used their

newly-found power to criticize and attack constituted authority
and to persuade the common people that it was they, and not the
Chiefs, to whom they should turn for help and guidance. This gap
between Chiefs and people, which was complicated by the fact that
many of these unofficial representatives were men of extremely
poor calibre, was therefore one of the first of many important
problems which had to be faced. . . ."[10]

The representative members in the Lukiko were acting as politicians. Without anyone to guide them, they were reaching out
into the areas which they represented, trying to establish their
leadership and contact the local groups. Many of them had helped
organize the Bataka Party units, as well as voluntary and recreation societies and the new farmers' groups which were being organized throughout 1947 under the auspices of I. K. Musazi.

Not only were the Lukiko representative members close to these
organizations, but they were physically close to their headquarters. The main centers of the Bataka were near Wandegeya
(where there was an urban concentration of African shops) and
Namirembe.[11] The main center for the Uganda African Farmers'
Union was Katwe. Both of these urban centers were close to Mengo
and in spite of the efforts of the recently formed Special Branch
of the police to keep a close eye on their activities, the latter were
provided with very unreliable information and were not able to
keep the government informed.[12]

For the educated there were social welfare associations, such as
the Mubende Social Welfare Association founded by Simon B. K.
Musoke, then a saza chief of Buwekula and a Makerere old boy
(1929-1930). Other old Makerere and old Budonians formed
football and other athletic clubs. They sometimes joined together
to produce newspapers in Katwe.[13]

[10] *Annual Reports, Kingdom of Buganda* (Entebbe: G.P., 1950), pp. 5-6.
[11] At James Miti's house, which became the meeting center of the Bataka leaders.
[12] Indeed, it was a common practice for the African police informants to work
both sides of the street and provide information, often faulty, to both sides.
Police informants were relatively easy for the Baganda to recognize, however, and
did not prove a satisfactory means of providing government with information.
[13] The list of officers of the Old Budonians Club for 1950 reads like a Who's
Who of Buganda. Well-known figures such as Prince Badru Kakunguru and
Hamu Mukasa (along with Reverend Canon, H. M. Grace, and Lord Hemingford
of Achimota College) were Vice Presidents. The Patron was, of course, the Kabaka.
S. Kulubya and S. Kasule were Treasurers. A. K. Sempa, the present Omuwanika,
was a Tennis Captain. Committee members included E. M. K. Mulira, President

Finally, having returned from England and cooperating with the Protectorate authorities, the Kabaka received an increasing share of the public blame for events which had occurred. His chiefs had, in 1948, asked that the Bataka Party be proscribed. His actions were entirely under the guidance of the Resident and the Katikiro and throughout 1948 a constant attack was kept up against the Buganda and Protectorate governments by the Bataka Party—attacks which soon widened to include the Kabaka himself. Regarded as subservient to the missionaries and the Protectorate government, the Kabaka became controversial as soon as he took up an active interest in government. Suspect for having relied on Kulubya in the past, he had ignored the complaints of the farmers. He was identified as an unreliable young man.

It is of some significance that it was the stimulation of both local and rural political activity which made possible the Bataka as a political organization. Moreover, it was rural economic activity which paved the way for the first efforts at large-scale African cooperative organization. Before discussing both the Bataka and the African Cooperative Movement, let us first consider the miruka, which stands at the opposite end of the hierarchy from that of Mengo.

The Miruka as a Political Unit

In the miruka all men know one another as members of a community. They are the areas of immediate association with neighbors, where the local churches and their schools are located and where men pay their taxes.

Mirukas are characteristically rural areas. A few Indian or African stores at a crossroads might constitute a village. People meet at the miruka council headquarters, at the churches, or at the stores. These are the places where people had the most pervasive and intimate face-to-face contacts with one another.

Not quite a community as we would consider it, the miruka does

---

of the Progressive Party until his rustication, G. Katongole, old Makerere and Assistant General Secretary of the United Budonians, R. H. Kakembe, and J. W. Kiwanuka. Kiwanuka and Lubwama had newspapers; the former had been editor of *Matalsi* and the latter launched the *Uganda Pilot*. Later, Kiwanuka was to begin his own newspaper, in which he attacked the government bitterly and was frequently accused of libelous and seditious statements.

not receive much personal attachment as an entity in itself. But as a boundary around activity, more intense interaction goes on among the members within it than outside. It is composed of people who associate far more intimately as a community than is the case in the larger gombolola or saza units, the other two units of local government. Thus while in theory the miruka represents the lowest step in the hierarchy, it is in fact a local universe in and of itself. Although miruka chiefs are supposed to be promoted to gombolola chiefs, most gombolola chiefs are actually recruited from outside (from posts such as clerkships in the Resident's office, or in European employ). In contrast to the gombolola chief, who is generally much better educated than the miruka chief, the latter is turned inward, to his miruka, rather than outward to the civil service hierarchy itself. He is close to the people and in many respects allied to them.

The miruka chief is almost invariably a landowner appointed by the Kabaka on the recommendation of the gombolola and saza chief. Characteristically he is a powerful Mutongole influential in local affairs. Normally chosen from the area in which he is given a chieftainship, he holds a special attachment to the people in the miruka. Miruka chiefs are not transferred or promoted as readily as those of other grades, so that this attachment is further enforced.[14]

Close to the miruka chief and often serving as his deputy is a Mutongole. The Batongole are part of the populist movement. In agricultural advantages they are, for all practical purposes, no better off than the tenants.[15]

The miruka councils were supposed to start the process of send-

[14] Richards considers the term rather unsuitably translated as "parish." "The muruka was in effect a collection of villages. . . . A 'village' is a collection of houses strung along a ridge between two valleys." (A. I. Richards, ed. *East African Chiefs* [London: Faber and Faber, 1960], p. 58.) Richards also points out that 41.2 per cent of present gombolola chiefs were at one time muruka chiefs. My own estimates, based on chiefs' records in the Residency, are somewhat lower.

[15] The task of the Mutongole or his representative is to help carry out government orders at the most basic level, as well as to assist people in a variety of ways. The Mutongole, while a representative of the Kabaka, receives his directives from the miruka chief, who stands at the lowest rank of the paid Civil Service hierarchy of administrative chiefs. The miruka chiefs hold Nkiko, attended by Batongole and usually anyone else who wishes to attend. "Thus the Miruka chief had been accustomed to hold a Lukiko at which it was the duty of the Batongole to attend, in order to receive orders communicated from above and to help the chief to arbitrate in disputes. All such meetings were public, and both

ing public demands upward to the more senior councils. Eventually, important issues would find their way to the Buganda government. On the miruka council were the chief, his deputy (*Omusigire*), the clerk of the office, and the major landowners. All landowners were entitled to direct access to the miruka chief. This was because the Batongole residing on their own estates did not pay land rent to anyone and were directly responsible to no one but the miruka chief.

At the miruka level antagonism against the regime was at its height. Exhorted by the entire upper bureaucracy of chiefs and government officers to grow more cotton, introduce sanitary measures, build better houses, and so on, it remained the unit of government with the least power and the most demands upon it. It was here that taxes were collected, although no services were provided by the miruka itself. Issues raised in miruka council rarely seemed to result in appropriate action from government.

Forbidden to use the parish hall for meetings, Bataka leaders often met at the home of some prominent Mutongole. People from all over would gather, and a generally festive if sometimes angry mood prevailed. Besides giving advice about cotton and coffee prices and the need for African ginneries, they would exhort the public to place no reliance upon gombolola and saza chiefs and councils. A common charge was that the chiefs were government servants, therefore disloyal to the Baganda, and that they were all bribed by Asians.

The exhortation against Asians was particularly common among local Bataka. At the miruka the people's chief contact with Asians was of two sorts. The first was at the ginnery where the farmer brought his cotton. He was, of course, convinced that he was being cheated, as often indeed he was. His hostility was reinforced every time he brought in his cotton crop. He also saw

---

peasants and resident aliens, for example Indians, could attend, though aliens had no voice as of right in the proceedings of the Lukiko.

"The ordinary man was unlikely to go regularly, but if he was a party or a witness in a dispute, or if there was an interesting case under arbitration, he had a right to address the Lukiko or Miruka on any subject, and if he felt strongly about any matter of local concern it was in the Lukiko or the Miruka that he would voice his complaint. It was then the duty of the Miruka chief to convey the feeling of his Lukiko to his Gombolola chief." Hailey, *Native Administration in the British African Territories* (London: H.M.S.O., 1950), p. 15.

the Indian when he went to buy any manufactured item such as a wash pan, tin, or corrugated roofing for his house, a bicycle tire, or cloth for his family. In the first instance what money income he received from cotton was paid to him by an Indian at the ginnery. In the second most of that same income was turned back to an Indian trader. Thus most financial transactions involved Asians on both the giving and receiving ends. Thus, too, the effectiveness of Bataka arguments. Would a Muganda in control over his own country expect to be paid by a foreigner and see his income go not to an African trader but to the same foreigner? At the miruka level the sense of being owned body and soul by Indian traders was especially acute. What was the value of the Agreement, and what were the rights of the Baganda, when their entire financial standing was in the hands of Asians who were widely regarded as plunderers (and usurers as well, since Africans were often in debt to them)?

What the ministers and many of the saza chiefs failed to realize was that as these grievances became more widespread, their own power was gradually being called into question. The chiefs were unaccustomed to having their prestige and power as representatives of both the Kabaka and the Protectorate regarded as anything less than overwhelming. The Buganda government regarded the miruka as a more or less negligible entity at the bottom of the scale. It was left to the Sons of Kintu and the Bataka to first recognize the potentiality of the miruka itself.[16]

---

[16] Indeed, there is still today a marked difference in tone and intimacy which strikes the observer when comparing miruka council meetings with those of the gombolola or saza. There is less formality in the miruka council. People speak more freely and ventilate grievances at the local level for there is far less sense on the part of the participants that they are being observed. At the miruka council one finds "the people" who are in effect representing themselves and their families. At the other councils there is much more a sense of "politics" with participants eyeing one another for possible appointments and seeking to catch the eye of some important person close to the Kabaka. In the gombolola or saza council one is dealing with the "representatives" of the people rather than with the people themselves. The miruka council meeting has perhaps some of the characteristics of the New England town meeting, whose uniqueness is rightly recognized to derive from its high participation and its political combination of both individualism and local solidarity. Much the same can be said for the miruka council, with the added factor that the miruka, as the bottom unit of administration, is the one place where the Bakopi can truly ventilate their grievances. Hence there is something of a "class" factor to it, in which the poor and the politically unsuccessful find common ground. As well, one finds a sturdy yeoman characteristic about it, individualistic, traditionalistic, and proud.

The Bataka Party

The Bataka Party's position is perhaps best illustrated in a pamphlet which was published several years before the Party itself came into formal being. Warning of the inroads made by economic development and investment, it pointed out that Baganda should understand that whenever sums of money were invested in the country for some development scheme, the land on which it was established ultimately became the property of those responsible for the scheme. If anybody happened to raise the matter of ownership of the land in question, the large sums expended would be used to justify alien control. Citing India as the example, the pamphlet pointed out that whenever the Indians demanded freedom, the British told them that they expended large sums of money to develop India, "by which sums they appear to have bought up the country and its peoples."[17]

The Bataka Party was founded in 1946. It was able to organize branches most successfully at the miruka level. Bataka, in its new and wider meaning, included all members of clans who not only owned but leased a bit of property—virtually everyone who was a proper clan member. Many dancing and recreation societies using old Kiganda dress and decoration on festive occasions now identified themselves as Bataka Party affiliates and wore the yellow crossed ribbons of the Bataka Party as part of their costume. The members of such groups were farmers, small-scale duka owners, and especially those whose clans had some particular traditional service function for the court—whether bark cloth making or drum making, which were now part of the range of minor honorifics associated with the clan rather than with individuals.

The Bataka Party was of course not limited to recreation and building societies, but these were an important feature of their organization. In one miruka in Kyagwe, for example, local units of the Bataka Party joined together with voluntary groups to build two schools, Catholic and Protestant, and a beer hall. Members of the Bataka unit considered that in this fashion clan affiliations which united people in their identification with the Kabaka

17 *Buganda Nyaffe* (n.p., 1944; trans. by the staff of the East African Institute of Social Research), p. 15.

and Kiganda patriotism could break down conflicts based upon religious differences. In this particular instance Catholics and Protestants helped each other in building their separate, local school buildings.

From the most local units, the miruka, to the leadership of the Party, the Bataka was a populist group, conservative in attitude toward Buganda, angry at the Buganda government hierarchy and at the chiefs who had replaced those removed from office by Nsibirwa and were now acting firmly as civil servants "above politics." There were large numbers of landlords in the Party. A leading spirit was the Reverend Spartas Mukasa.[18]

The chiefs were a major bone of contention. The Bataka began to demand elected chiefs who would be popular representatives, that is, subject to public pressure. Elective chieftaincy would also serve to put their own members in the reformed Lukiko since they were confident that Bataka Party representatives would be elected to chieftaincy.

While it is true that the Bataka Party was not representative of the clans as such (any more than it was of miruka chiefs), it was nonetheless supported by clan elders at a variety of clan levels. Many did service tasks for the Bataka Party leaders. Even though it was not led by clan leaders, the Bataka Party did have clan support. For their refusal to support the Bataka Party, two senior clan leaders, Antonio Nzamba, the head of the Bushbuck clan, and Josfu Namwana, head of the Colobus Monkey clan, were attacked and their houses burned down in the 1949 riots.

As we have indicated, the Bataka Party was persuasive. Its formal membership probably never amounted to very much. As a form of social and political organization it claimed allegiance on the basis of nationalism and support of Buganda and threat-

[18] Mukasa, with I. K. Musazi, had founded the Sons of Kintu. When Musazi was released from deportation at the end of October 1946, he and Mukasa quarreled. Musazi then turned his attention to the organization of farmers which later led to the establishment of the Uganda African Farmers' Union, while Mukasa worked closely with Miti in the establishment of the Bataka Party. Mukasa was himself a member of the Alexandrian Orthodox Church and a founder of an independent school. Although not a Mutaka in the proper sense, he was able to skirt the usual affiliations which helped divide the Baganda from one another, such as church membership or the old boys' associations which played such an important part in the social life of educated Buganda. Mukasa is now a Kabaka's nominee in the Great Lukiko.

ened the framework of government and its chiefs. For the first time, the system of political organization in Buganda was under attack as having violated the traditions of Kiganda nationhood.

Outlawed after the 1949 riots, it declined and gave way to a host of small parties, such as the Uganda Nationalist Movement Party, which charged the missionaries with having deliberately reduced the population of Buganda by introducing monogamous marriage; or the Bannansi B'Omu Buganda which, under the presidency of a member of the Lukiko, Zake Muwanga, openly proclaimed aims similar to those of the Bataka.

In yet another fashion the Bataka elements remain. The older and less educated groups of peasants, the miruka chiefs who feel they have been passed over, and the old mystique of Bataka, i.e. the fundamental problem of conflict between chieftaincy and Bakopi, still represent a latent force. Meetings are still held in James Miti's house at Namirembe, the old fires are stoked, and the old issues warmed over. No longer antagonistic to the Kabaka, the Bataka are among the most devoted supporters who worked for his return. In local societies, among the traditional dancers and wrestlers, and in the rural voluntary self-help associations, the crossed bands of yellow ribbon signifying Bataka are to be seen. At meetings in the gombolola or miruka, a Bataka Party element, like part of the landscape, is ever present. Theirs is latent organization, intertwined with the social institutions of the Baganda themselves. If important issues are to be discussed they will plant their flag with its blue background and yellow decoration and the letters BU (Bataka Uganda) on it, and gather their members. A symbol of yeomanry and service, the members make up in history what they lack in power and prestige. It is the Bataka who in a real sense remain the traditionalists and the extremists in Buganda. Whichever political party serves to attract them in large numbers will have captured the popular movement in Buganda —a movement which has as its last stronghold rural populism.

The Formation of African Cooperatives

We have already discussed the more or less unsuccessful efforts by Africans to organize growers' cooperatives and associations and mercantile establishments. In the postwar period of prosperity renewed efforts were made.

The Uganda African Farmers' Union began organizing in 1947. It registered on April 2, 1948 under the leadership of I. K. Musazi. Musazi was one of the most gifted of the political leaders of this period. He was well liked and few questioned his sincerity, although many expressed concern over his sense of financial propriety.

There was considerable cooperation between the Bataka Party and the U.A.F.U. In certain areas, the Masaka district in particular, the most important organizers of the U.A.F.U. were also leading Bataka Party figures, such as Peter Sonko, who was a Vice-President of the Uganda African Farmers' Union as well as active in Bataka affairs.

While the Bataka Party focused its attack on the Buganda government, the Uganda African Farmers' Union attacked cotton prices received by farmers and protested against barriers which prevented them from obtaining their own ginnery. These, it will be recalled, were the two concerns that had plagued cotton farmers for a decade: the fear that they were being cheated by Asian ginners and antagonism against the Uganda Company, which controlled the sale of cotton in Uganda; and the fear that they were being given only a small return on their cotton, compared to world prices. The Farmers' Union demanded direct sales by their own representatives on the world market. To this end, Musazi went to London and discussed the matter with Fenner Brockway and other Labour members of Parliament who, if they were not experts in matters of cotton, were at least sympathetic to the Uganda African Farmers' Union.

The difficulty with the U.A.F.U. position was that they failed to recognize the difficulties in collecting, ginning, and selling cotton. An exporters' group had streamlined both the quality control and the export of cotton itself. To tamper with the system would no doubt have produced a less monopolistic system of cotton export and sale, but a far less efficient one (which certainly the Protectorate government was unwilling to recommend). Hence the demand for direct sales by the Baganda was not heard sympathetically by the Protectorate government.[19]

---

[19] During this period the government was preoccupied with the problem of providing for the orderly marketing of the cotton crop and the maintenance of high standards so that Uganda cotton would both command a sale and fetch the best price possible in the world markets.

Equally on the matter of African ginneries, government policy with respect to collecting, storing, and ginnery quotas put special handicaps in the way of Africans ginning their own cotton. The government did little to help African enterprise over these difficulties and, without openly opposing the establishment of African ginneries, hid behind the obstacles.[20]

Leadership, Self-Image, and Revolt

It is interesting to take a brief look at some of the personalities involved in the Farmers' Union and the Bataka Party.

Both of these groups developed out of the Sons of Kintu. Two of the most important leaders in each were former associates in the Sons of Kintu, although they had struggled among themselves for control of the old organization. These were I. K. Musazi and Spartas Mukasa. A third person who was also extremely important was Fenekasi Musoke, who had been in both the Sons of Kintu and the Motor Drivers' Union. All three were 1945 deportees. Musazi launched the U.A.F.U. in 1948, using the Bataka units as the basis of the Farmers' Union. Spartas Mukasa joined with James Miti in the Bataka Party proper, while F. Musoke, remaining out of any formal organization, helped to bring the traders into contact with the Bataka.[21]

[20] Other difficulties stemmed from ineffective organization, and there were difficulties in African cooperatives. African cooperatives were allowed under the terms of the Cooperative Societies Ordinance of 1946 and a considerable number did in fact form. As well, associations of farmers and traders formed, registering under the Companies Ordinance as limited liability companies. Few of the latter were successful, although as a commission of enquiry into the cooperative movement pointed out, there was no Department of Cooperation in government to help guide and develop these organizations. At the end of 1948 there were 11 registered farmers' societies in Mengo district, 2 in Masaka, and none in Busoga; however, there were "several thousand persons owing allegiance to the Uganda African Farmers' Union. These persons were divided into groups representing the areas in which they lived. . . . We use the words 'owing allegiance' deliberately, because members of this association were extremely loose and the mere selling or handing over for the purpose of sale of a bag of cotton to the Union was, we believe, considered by the leaders sufficient to call such a person a member." See *Commission of Inquiry into the Progress of the Cooperative Movement in Mengo, Masaka, and Busoga Districts* (Entebbe: G.P., 1952), pp. 2-3. The Uganda African Farmers' Union was an unregistered society and was proscribed after the 1949 riots.

The difficulties facing African farmers are great since, in spite of greater leniency on the part of the government since 1952, there are only 8 ginneries operated by registered African growers' cooperative societies out of a total of 131 ginneries in Uganda; of the 8 only 3 are in Buganda. See *Annual Report of the Lint Marketing Board*, 1956, p. 4.

[21] Fenekasi Musoke was a Protestant, educated at Masaka Central School and Makerere College (1935). He studied telegraphy and spent four years with the

It was Spartas Mukasa who brought his nephew, Semakula Mulumba, into the Bataka Party. Both were to play an important part in future political developments in Buganda.[22] Although less known than Mulumba, Spartas Mukasa himself represented a curious element in Kiganda life. He was a representative of the Greek Orthodox Church which, while it remained unaffiliated with any of the major denominations (although Mukasa was brought up in the employ of a Protestant clergyman and received his education from the mission school), was the only organization in East Africa associated with the Marcus Garvey movement.[23] The Uganda branch of the church is a recognized part of the Greek Orthodox Church and accepted as such by the Orthodox Patriarchate of Alexandria, Egypt.

Mukasa himself formed the Greek Orthodox Church in Uganda

Postal Department. He became editor of three vernacular newspapers, *Uganda Voice*, 1936, *Uganda Commonweal*, 1937, and *Tula Nkunuonyola*, 1939. He was President of the Uganda African Welfare Association (which was regarded as a dangerous political party by the Buganda government and particularly by the chiefs). The General President of the Association was G. Busagwa, who died in 1946, while Musoke was deported. This ended the political organization, and when Musoke (who had previously been in jail for forgery in 1942) returned from deportation, he started his own business and gave support but not membership to the Bataka Party.

[22] Mukasa brought Mulumba into the Party as the proper person to represent the Bataka in England. It was because of Mulumba's alleged connection with Communists in England that the Protectorate government made a half-hearted attempt to brand the Bataka Party as under Communist influence and tried to link Communism with the 1949 riots. This was expressly repudiated in the Kingdon Report:

"But whilst it is true that Mulumba has communist contacts and has no doubt learned much from them, and it is also true that the pre-disturbance propaganda followed a well-known communist pattern, there is no evidence that the disturbances were actually communist-inspired or were fomented or financially assisted by the communists. Whatever may be the position of Mulumba himself vis-à-vis communism in England, there is no evidence whatever of communist activities in Buganda; on the contrary, it was abundantly evident that the great majority of even the intelligentsia had no idea of the meaning of communism and had no dealings or contacts with the communists." *Report of the Commission of Inquiry into the Disturbances in Uganda during April 1949* (Kingdon Report) (Entebbe: G. P., 1950), p. 95.

[23] This is in strong contrast to West Africa where, in Liberia, Sierra Leone, Ghana, and Nigeria, associations with the Garvey movement were very strong and important political leaders, such as Kwame Nkrumah, N. Azikiwe, and others of contemporary significance were deeply affected by their associations with the Universal Negro Improvement Association when they were students in the United States. See Kwame Nkrumah, *The Autobiography of Kwame Nkrumah* (Edinburgh: Nelson, 1957); for an excellent discussion of the Garvey movement in British West Africa, see J. S. Coleman, *Nigeria, Background to Nationalism* (Berkeley, Los Angeles: University of California Press, 1958), especially pp. 187-191.

as an expression of personal and political nationalism. He had sought the origins of a true Catholic church by reaching back to the origins of Christianity, and he felt that both the Roman and Anglican forms were European affairs, artificially split. The true church was African as much as European. Many of its early Fathers came into Africa. Further, the association with the Garvey movement was extremely important: it introduced a specifically African and Negro character into the church.

Mukasa did not like being treated by missionaries in the patronizing manner which they normally (even if not consciously) assumed, and he joined forces with James Miti and Reuben Musoke, the Secretary of the Bataka Association.[24] Mukasa was well-educated, having been at King's College, Budo. He served in the King's African Rifles during the war and taught English while still in service after the war. Later he opened a school.[25] Although one of the crucial figures in the Bataka Party, he was careful not to issue instructions or manifestoes in writing and thus leave behind him a trail of incriminating evidence.[26]

Mulumba was of the same clan as Daudi Kiwanuka and the main supporters of Wamala (Lugave). He had been a Catholic and was educated at Kisubi. He came from Buddu in Masaka district, where some of the best cotton farming in Buganda is found and where rural grievances were particularly strong. Chosen by the White Fathers' Mission to attend the School of Oriental and African Languages at the University of London, he was a teaching brother (Brother Francis) at Kisubi. As the Kingdon Report points out, "He returned to Africa at the end of 1946 but did not proceed to Kampala as arranged. On the voyage he had shared a cabin with a Kikuyu named Jumo Kenyatta (*sic*) and on his arrival in East Africa he went into the Kikuyu Reserve where he stayed for some weeks."[27]

[24] It will be recalled that one of the important leaders of the old Bataka Association, Joseph Kate Mugema, was a founder of one branch of the Malakite Movement in Buganda (the other branch being under the leadership of S. Kakunguru who got into great trouble by refusing to have his cattle inoculated).

[25] The material on social background was related by Reverend Spartas Mukasa in personal interview.

[26] See *Kingdon Report, op.cit.*, p. 95. "He has been clever enough to place very little on paper and he did not sign the Bataka Party's program published in *Emembya Esaze*. But he was a regular speaker at meetings of the Party and it was he who read out the significant message from Mulumba, 'You can do nothing without overthrowing the Government by force.'"

[27] *Ibid.*, p. 85.

It was Mulumba who attempted to influence British policy by contacting members of Parliament, petitioning the United Nations (through Mr. Gromyko), and a wide variety of people, including President Truman.

Another important figure in the Bataka Party, less important because he was rusticated after the 1945 riots, was J. Kivu who had founded the Motor Drivers' Union when Musazi formed with Spartas Mukasa the Sons of Kintu. Kivu, the brother-in-law of James Miti, had been at Mengo High School and during the First World War enlisted in the army. There he got into trouble with his superior officers who wanted him to perform service functions when he wanted to fight. Something of a professional rebel, he had been very close to Wamala, who had died in deportation, as had Prince Suna. He was hard and unrelenting in his hatred of the Protectorate and Buganda governments, and hostile to the Kabaka as well. More or less unsuccessful at a large number of occupations, especially those dealing with trade and business, he felt strongly that treatment of Africans in trade was always less favorable than treatment of Asians and Europeans. He had remained in close association with Musazi and Daudi Mikibi, the head of the African Traders' Union.

Musazi, the son-in-law of Mrs. Kadumukasa (the sister-in-law of Kawalya Kagwa) came from Bulemezi, where a great deal of nationalist tension has existed for some time. He was the son of a gombolola chief and was sent to Mengo High School and then to St. Augustine's School, Canterbury, where he had planned to become ordained. He was in turn a teacher at Budo, an Inspector of Schools in the Education Department, and in 1938 helped found the Sons of Kintu with Mukasa, with whom he later fell out. There is some indication that Musazi's lack of interest in the Bataka Party was due to his dislike of Mukasa.

He was jailed in 1940 for forgery. After the 1945 riots he was deported. On his release he began organizing once again and in 1946 founded the Uganda Transport and General Workers' Trade Union; shortly thereafter he began to form the Uganda African Farmers' Union, many of whose members were identical with the units of the Bataka Party.[28]

[28] It is perhaps misleading to speak of units of the Party. On the whole there were small groups of more or less constant members, or at least convinced anti-

Between 1945 and 1949 there emerges a picture of the loyal Muganda, vigilant and truculent. He has fought against inroads by the Protectorate government and against closer union. He has engaged in constant battles against traitors from within, such as Nsibirwa and Kulubya. Despoilers lie in wait for him to take away his land, often under the pretext of good causes, such as in the Makerere affair. The government takes his money, under the guise of cotton and coffee price policies which do not return the world market price to the farmers. The banks discriminate against him and African traders and farmers cannot get credit. The calculating English are engaged in a long-run conspiracy to deprive the Africans of their land and to make them into hewers of wood and carriers of water.

It required no breakdown in the insularity of the Baganda to look over their shoulders to Kenya and see the effects of European control. Stories of the treatment of Kikuyu farmers and laborers, the theft of land from Africans, and segregation in the White Highlands began to take on a prominence in Buganda which it never had before. If much of this was in the form of political rumor and wild stories, there was enough truth in the basic facts of the situation to rightly produce concern among the Baganda. The complex of men and events, grievances and images, burst forth in rioting once again.

The 1949 Riots

In 1947 a Colonial Office memorandum on interterritorial organization in East Africa gave revised proposals for the establishment of a four-year Central Assembly and an administration for scheduled services consisting of the officers administering the governments of Kenya, Uganda, and Tanganyika and a supporting staff of interterritorial advisory and consultative bodies. Among the duties of the High Commission were listed the administration of scheduled services "exercising the usual powers of a Colonial

government people who would use whatever was the current political group as the vehicle of their sentiments and activities. Normally they were the same people who were bitter about cotton pricing policy and were anxious to form their own economic organizations. The Bataka Party did not have membership cards or any really formal structure, hence it was easier to identify those who were not in it than those who were. It certainly had widespread general support. But the term membership is meaningless when applied to the ordinary followers of the Party.

Government in respect of them," "to hold land," and to "enact legislation applying to East Africa as a whole with the advice and consent of the Central Assembly."[29]

To the Baganda in particular and more generally in Uganda, this seemed once again like closer union. They had questioned the need for a Legislative Council in Uganda and now there was to be a Central Assembly for all three territories. They could distinguish between specified services of the East African High Commission and services already performed by colonial governments. The provision in the memorandum dealing with powers to hold land seemed to confirm their worst suspicions that this was the central motive in establishing a supergovernment: the appropriation of land under the domination of a supergovernment controlled by Europeans, controlling essential services with its own Assembly. Furthermore, the earlier fears that the Legislative Council would commit the people of Uganda now appeared to be realized. A largely European body with only a token representation of Africans, and those not elected, would be able to commit Uganda to legislation for the three territories. It did not satisfy the Baganda that the proposals were for a Central Assembly limited to a period of four years after which its functions would be reviewed.[30] They argued that the proposal was the wedge in the door to closer union which they had been fighting for years. To the obvious need for efficient administration of railways, harbors, customs and other matters, the answer was that in Europe, which had more countries than three, interterritorial services seemed to be managed quite efficiently without a high commission of some sort.

In the face of these events, the Bataka Party in particular was successful in arousing wide public feeling. By 1949 their main effort was to take power away from the Protectorate government and to remove its impact upon Buganda. Buganda separatism began to emerge as a well-defined political program.

The day before the first Lukiko session of 1949, one of the leaders of the Bataka wired the Kabaka that the Lukiko would not sit unless the number of elected members was 60 and certain chiefs dismissed. The man was immediately tried and imprisoned

---

[29] See *Inter-Territorial Organization in East Africa, Revised Proposals* (Colonial Office: H.M.S.O., 1947), Colonial No. 210.

[30] *Ibid.*

for two years. On the following day crowds gathered for the opening session. The Bataka threatened to stop the proceedings if their claims went unattended. The Kabaka heard their claims (which included reforms in the number of elected members of the Lukiko) and announced his intention to look into the matter of chiefs. From March to April there were discussions and meetings. Public meetings were held by the Bataka and the Farmers' Union. Their representatives met with the Kabaka. Under scrutiny was almost every act of the Protectorate government, whether it involved setting up a regular postal service, the hydro-electric stations at Owens Falls, town planning, land acquisition, or interterritorial service.[31]

We have discussed the overlapping membership between groups such as the Bataka Party and the Farmers' Union. Both clan and lower ranks of chiefs, particularly at the miruka level, were at the part-time disposal of the Bataka Party leaders. The combination of unsatisfied demands and fears for the autonomy of Uganda, particularly of Buganda, became thoroughly mixed together. The slogan BU (Butaka Uganda, and pronounced Boo) became the Bataka battle cry. Mulumba wrote in the *Uganda Star*, "Sons of Kintu, rise up with the ghosts of our grandfathers. You are no longer children, no longer deceived by Indians—they hurt us—they cheat us—we shall also hurt them by not giving them our cotton. . . . BU is hated because it is fighting for the people."[32]

Hammering away at the cotton issue, Musazi said, "My opinion is that it would be very silly of us if we simply gave our cotton into the hands of robbers and thieves as if we did not know that it

[31] It must be pointed out that the original proposals contained in Colonial 191 contained assurances that political union was not proposed: "His Majesty's Government in the United Kingdom have accordingly come to the conclusion, after taking the advice of the East African Governors, that political federation or fusion in any of the various forms which have been discussed during the last twenty years is not practical politics under existing conditions." This did not preclude the eventual political union of the territories, and it is of interest that recent liberal opinion in Buganda among younger educated groups has moved in favor of federation worked out by African nationalists from three territories, particularly with Julius Nyerere of the Tanganyika African Union and Tom Mboya of the Nairobi Peoples' Convention Party. The principal force behind this most recent move to promote unity is the Pan-African Freedom Movement of East and Central Africa (PAFMECA), which has close links with the Secretariat of the African League and All-African People's Solidarity Movement.

[32] *Kingdon Report*, p. 83.

is our own cotton for which we have laboured so that it might get good profits to take us from the bonds of slavery of poverty. . . . Therefore every African of Uganda should avow that it is better to die than give away the wealth of the country of their heredity."[33]

The image of despoliation and deprivation, of lost opportunity as a kind of slavery, of rank without superiority, penetrated almost everywhere. Finally the focus shifted to the Kabaka. The Bataka leaders decided to petition the Kabaka directly and to make representations in person. A pamphlet was distributed telling people to come to Mengo: "God of Creation—God of Buganda" was the headline of the pamphlet; "We supplicate you in this gathering—you who have never failed us—be with us, lead us, and support us. All the people, natives of Buganda, men and women, old and young come, come. Come to the center, Mengo, when the world will present before His Highness the complaints of the people. The same complaints about which they have cried to him several times. Come so that we may inform the Kabaka the things that are undermining him and our country, Buganda. . . ."[34]

As people gathered outside the Lubiri, the Kabaka wrote that he was prepared to see representatives of the people but warned that a large meeting would produce a disturbance of the peace. Nevertheless a crowd began to gather at Mengo. Although it was illegal for an assembly of more than 500 people to gather there, the number of people quickly surpassed that figure. A delegation of eight representatives of the Bataka Party was admitted to the Kabaka. They presented five demands. They asked for democracy and the power for the people to select their own chiefs; 60 representative members in the Lukiko; abolition of the present Buganda government; the right to gin cotton; and free trade and the direct sale of produce in the outside world. They argued that often the elected representatives to the Lukiko acted as chiefs rather than popular representatives. And the chiefs did not relay popular feelings.

Police detachments arrived when the crowd began to get restive. It was decided to arrest certain leaders. An arrest party went out and resistance ensued. Violence was touched off. Buildings were burned in the Kibuga. Later, houses of chiefs were burned in the rural areas. Sporadic violence broke out in widely

[33] *Ibid.*, p. 84.   [34] *Ibid.*, p. 18.

separated areas. Lorry drivers helped the organizers of the riots to find their way to important government chiefs whose houses were burned and cattle destroyed. For several days formal government broke down and the situation was more or less out of control. Arrests totaled 1,724. To meet the emergency, Europeans and Asians were enrolled as special constables, while troops of the King's African Rifles were brought into Kampala. A state of emergency was declared, and for the second time within four years the pattern of stable government was interrupted.

The reply of the Governor to the outbreaks followed the same pattern as in 1945: "A comparatively few evil and self-seeking men have brought great trouble and disgrace upon Buganda. Acting on Communist inspiration from their so-called representatives in Britain, they are seeking to oppose by violence, intimidation, arson and murderous assault all constituted authority, the authority of H. H. the Kabaka's Government, the authority of the Protectorate Government and of the King's forces of law and order. In so doing they are following the usual pattern of Communist penetration, with which people in Europe and the Far East are already familiar. Their attempt was prefaced by a long campaign of foul lies and slander aimed at deceiving the people and shaking their confidence in His Highness' Government and the Government of the Protectorate. This too follows the usual Communist pattern.

"The great mass of the Buganda, conscious of how much has been done for their welfare by their own Government and by the Protectorate Government, were too sensible to be deceived by these lies and slanders, so failing in this part of their campaign these wicked people have had to resort to violence. In this they will surely fail, because their dupes and supporters are few and the forces of law and order are strong and will be still further strengthened until the evil doers are crushed and peace and security restored."[35]

The Protectorate government accepted the view put forth in the Kingdon Report that the disturbances were a planned rebellion against the Kabaka and his government, organized by the Bataka Party and the Farmers' Union. The government agreed that Semakula Mulumba (in England) was more responsible for the affair than anyone else, that there was no substance to the

[35] Message from the Governor, Sir J. Hathorn Hall, 27 April 1949.

grievances put forward, and that the behavior of the troops used in the disturbances was admirable.

As after the 1945 riots, it was agreed that reforms were in order. The number of representative members should be advanced in the Lukiko. More responsible and educated representative members should find their way there. The Protectorate government advised the Buganda government to consider new techniques for the handling of emergencies and pointed out the need for more efficient policing.[36]

We have considered the nature of economic and political grievances, building up over a period of many years and aided by intergenerational and other conflicts. The most important issues brought forward by the Bataka Party and the Farmers' Union were those dealing with reform of the Lukiko and the Buganda government and economic reforms. There was substance to their political complaints. The Buganda government itself was not satisfactory. Of 32 items dealt with by the Lukiko in its two sessions in 1949, none were important. The Lukiko discussed raising Luwalo tax, resolved that the father's name should be entered on birth certificates, rejected a law for the prevention of theft, and so on. Five items dealt with chiefs and their benefits. The one important proposal, that two extra unofficial representatives should be sent to saza councils from each gombolola, was withdrawn after it had been agreed that the existing arrangement was satisfactory.[37] No attention was paid to the demands of people in the mirukas.

If to the touring officer the people had great needs, they were regarded as sorely misled by agitators, suffering from the irresponsibilities of politicians, unsuccessful as traders, and the sons of chiefs.

For the Baganda, their efforts to preserve themselves from advice, which contained a hidden threat, and to avoid control by the Protectorate government began to assume proportions of an ideology and mythology. In every gesture, benevolent or not, they saw the threat of control. Reform had to be on terms worked out by themselves and compromise became simply a cloak for

[36] See Memorandum by the Uganda government on the *Report of the Commission of Inquiry into the Civil Disturbances in Uganda during April 1949* (Entebbe: G.P., 1950), *passim.*

[37] *Annual Reports*, 1949, pp. 10-13.

disguising motives and gaining covertly what could not be obtained overtly. Each side, British and Buganda, viewed the intransigence of the other as a cover for hidden motives. Each side felt it had at last discovered the real and underlying character of the other, laying bare as it were the complexity and essentially negative characteristics to which for a time they had been blind.

In relationships between the Kabaka and the Protectorate government, both conflict and collaboration were involved in almost every action. By this means the Kabaka preserved his role. By preserving his role he retained the highly instrumental structure of the society. By such preservation, that structure remained flexible in that it could adapt, while remaining rigid in its actual organization. The Buganda government and its chiefs remained the spine of the system. Conflict gave it spring and flexibility and toughness. What the system could not stand was the absolution of its grievances and the curing of its ills.

Instead of a rural and peasant form of egalitarianism or socialism arising (or even a major economic and social reform movement which challenged the values of the system and sought to replace the autocratic principle with a democratic one), grievance was expressed through traditionalism. The few shibboleths of postwar progressivism, such as democracy, representative government, elections, and the like, were used in a rather small way in Buganda. Attacks were personal and issues were specific—change the marketing arrangements for coffee and cotton, direct sales for world prices, remove the interference of the Resident, minimize the influence of the touring officer, and the like. Thus the new leaders who emerged were not like those in West Africa who were concerned with democracy and representative institutions in their widest sense.

Chiefs, Bataka, the Residency officials, nationalist leaders—all sought to speak in the name of the people. Each exhorted the people to listen. Each sought to inject a note of realism by his own "explanation" of the true situation. Pulled in several directions by leaders of the various groups, the atmosphere of unreality became increasingly intense. It was a period that can be called "hortatory realism," inasmuch as the language of the day was less a form of ordinary discourse than a restless exhortation by diverse leaders, each claiming for himself the twin virtues of wisdom and realism.

CHAPTER 13

AUTHORITY AND MEN:
A BATTLE OF ROLES AND PERSONALITIES

In a fascinating parable of the Grocer and the Chief in his volume, *The Passing of Traditional Society*, Daniel Lerner points to the difference between modernity and traditionalism. Traditionalists cannot even visualize themselves in secular modern roles. They cannot transpose themselves into a more modern and contemporary social structure.[1] The grocer, alerted to the potentialities of trade, is the role of entry into modernity. The chief, concerned with sustaining the traditional way of life, is confused and saddened by the changes in material and social life which have warped his position and vitiated his authority.

This is the more usual picture of the conflict between traditionalism and modernity. The conflict can be found in Africa among many groups. The Ashanti have shown it, and the Yoruba in West Africa. In northern Nigeria as well, buttressed by Islam, a similar concern for traditionalism sustains itself. Among the Futa Jallon chiefs in Guinea one could find the same resistance to change and the same lack of understanding and inability to "empathize" into new and more modern roles.

This is not the case in Buganda. The Baganda were quite adept at empathizing the roles of democratic political institutions. These they explicitly rejected. This is precisely what is so interesting about the whole pattern of Kiganda nationalism. It does not reject modernity, but only certain political expressions of it.

We shall now indicate that the emphasis upon modernization which began during the administration of a liberal governor was the most difficult period the Baganda ever had to face. For in liberalism the principle of representation becomes elevated to a new warrant of legitimacy in political rule. This principle, running contrary to that of autocracy, needed to be fought hard. Yet precisely because it was becoming increasingly difficult to attack "democracy," the principle of autocracy had to be main-

[1] See D. Lerner, *The Passing of Traditional Society* (Glencoe: The Free Press, 1958).

tained in the name of it. The governor had to be put in the position of violating democracy. Provincialism was the *means* whereby the preservation of local autonomy became a fight for states' rights and against colonial domination. The interesting situation arose, as it has at times in the United States, where the politics of provincialism became a fight against the encroachment of a liberal state power, and democracy consisted in adhering to cherished but antidemocratic institutions.

The Era of Good Feeling and Reform

Events in West Africa were beginning to have their effect in East Africa, which seemed to belong to another generation. To speed up the much slower pace of reform in Uganda, efforts were required to reduce the disparities in educational and cultural development between West Africa and East. Hundreds of Africans had university degrees in Ghana or Nigeria. Only a tiny handful could be found in all three territories of East Africa. The net geographical national product of Uganda was roughly half that of Ghana which was of comparable size and population.[2] The general level of consumption habits and material conditions of life were considerably lower in East Africa than in most parts of British West Africa.

The first step in creating a new atmosphere was the decision of the Labour Party Colonial Secretary, James Griffiths, to appoint Sir Andrew Cohen, then Under-Secretary for African Affairs in the Colonial Office, as Governor of Uganda. Cohen was identified with liberalism and reform. He had helped shape the generous policy of political devolution in West Africa which led to self-government for the Gold Coast and Nigeria. He was widely respected among the African political leaders who knew him and he was a favorite in Labour Party circles.

Almost the first act of the new Governor was to tour the country extensively. Standing less on ceremony than had previous governors, he sought to find out the conditions in the districts. He spoke to district officers rather than listening to what Secre-

2 In 1950-1951, the net geographical product of the Gold Coast was £152 million, while the net geographical product of Uganda in 1952 was only £81,200,000. (See Appendix IX, *East African Royal Commission Report*, Cmd. 9475, London, H.M.S.O. 1955.)

tariat staff said district officers were thinking. He spoke to large numbers of Africans, concerning himself with the points of view of African traders, farmers, and chiefs. The main emphasis which he attempted to introduce was precisely the one which had been lacking in the past: African participation. In this he was concerned not only with participation on a political level but with local and community development. As much as possible his administration was to bring the public into self-help schemes, local development projects, and political reforms so that they could begin to plan for their own future. Protectorate staff were to serve as technical and managerial guides to assist Africans in the first stages of reform. Two key features of this program of reform were community development and African local government.[3]

On a more personal level the Governor was concerned to end the excessive formality which had characterized the atmosphere of both officialdom and Government House. For one thing, the remoteness of Entebbe, the cool, secluded, and completely European Secretariat area, with its club for Europeans only and its pleasant bungalows and swimming pool for service officers, was becoming more an outpost of the country and less a capital.

The first emphases of the new administration were soon felt. The Community Development Department was expanded and a community development officer appointed in each district. These worked in conjunction with district teams and, in the case of Buganda, with the Community Development Committee. Their

[3] For Sir John Hall, local government had meant reform without politics. Behind the 1947 despatch of Creech Jones was a philosophy of government which had been specified in the Colonial Governors' Conference of 1947. This philosophy was essentially the one which emerged in the Gold Coast and Nigeria: local government reform and high political participation would be accompanied by reform at the center so that local people could be brought into Executive Council in charge of departments. A progressive increase in local representative membership would eventually require the ministerial system with a responsible and democratic elections system.

This general approach toward the devolution of authority in the colonies had been partly due to the efforts of Sir Andrew Cohen while he was in the Colonial Office. The tradition which he helped to establish was to be carried out in Uganda. In practice this meant putting an end to the forms of discrimination characteristic of an older colonialism. The theme of his administration was political evolution toward greater responsibility and participation by Africans and a relaxation of all forms of economic and political barrier from those posts of responsibility hitherto reserved for Europeans.

activities would also be carried on through the county councils (sazas in the case of Buganda and those councils just below district rank in the districts).[4]

In order to provide maximum collaboration between county councils and both the community development officers and the district officials, a new training center was established on a hill not far from Government House. Special courses for training officers of cooperative societies were instituted, as well as adult education, chiefs' courses, and so on.[5]

Shortly after the new Governor arrived in Uganda, C. A. G. Wallis arrived from the Colonial Office to inquire into local government in Uganda. He made a two-pronged attack on the local government system. Buganda was to have its system reformed and the districts would be granted greater powers, making them responsible for a wide range of services. In the case of Buganda, local government was to be regarded at the saza level and below, while in the case of the districts the district councils were in fact to be local councils.

The Wallis report was fully in accord with the change in ad-

---

[4] In a despatch to the Colonial Office after his first six months of office, Sir Andrew Cohen wrote, "From all that I have so far seen and heard in this country, I am convinced that a vigorous program of community development is needed, and urgently needed."

Remarking on the fact that there had been a great deal of economic development in such items as the hydroelectric station at Owen Falls, the Kilembe copper mine, and the cement works at Tororo, he pointed out that "the development of mining and secondary industry in Uganda is needed to broaden the basis of the country's economy and to reduce its dependence on agriculture, and at the same time to provide the foundation on which the social services may be built up and the political development both at the center and locally may go forward smoothly. But if our progress is not to be unbalanced in the opposite direction, the great economic projects which I have described must be accompanied by solid and progressive advance in the Protectorate and local government services in the rural areas: it is here that the need for a vigorous program of community development is felt. . . ." The despatch then pointed out that "an organized program of community development cannot succeed without an efficient system of local government." See Despatch No. 490/52, 22 July 1952.

[5] The Nsamizi Training Center has as its objects: "To give a fuller understanding to the people of Uganda, men and women, of the duties of good citizens, and to inculcate the idea of self-help, to train chiefs and local government staffs in their duties while at the same time increasing their understanding of some of the problems of Uganda and the world outside it, to train Community Development Assistants, men and women, in their duties, broadening their outlook and instructing them in the use of some of the techniques suitable for adult education work, to instruct government staff, who have acquired their technical knowledge at their departmental training centers, in the art of how to 'put over' that knowledge to the general public. . . ." See *The Nsamizi Training Center* (Entebbe: G.P., n.d.).

ministration. After extended hearings and investigation in the country, Wallis stated that "in modern times local government cannot be developed in a vacuum. . . . If scientific, technical and economic skill are to be exploited for the benefit of the people, there are few services in which the Central Government does not take an interest and few in which local government can do without the active help of the Central Government. A system of partnership is being developed in which central and local government work side by side in the same area. It is therefore necessary that local people, councillors and officials should be encouraged to take an active interest in the machinery and operation of central government.

"Critics who say that a politically inexperienced people should first learn the arts of local politics before they dabble in central politics miss the point that local and central Government can no longer be kept in separate compartments. You do not graduate from one to the other as from a primary to a secondary school. So one arrives at the paradox that if it is unfortunate to be compelled to grant power at the center to a people untrained in local government, it is impossible to train them in local government unless they also participate in central Government. For modern local government needs central Government to give it unity and purpose."[6]

The Legislative Council was now to become more central to the affairs of the country.[7] Under Sir John Hathorn Hall, African representation in the Legislative Council was introduced in 1945 and increased in 1950. Under his successor drastic changes were made within a few years, including the introduction of a ministerial system.

Established was the Uganda Development Corporation, whose objects were the facilitation of industrial and economic development of the Protectorate, and carrying on research into the industrial and mineral potentialities of the Protectorate. The Corporation was given the power to promote and finance any under-

[6] See C. A. G. Wallis, *Report of an Inquiry into African Local Government in the Protectorate of Uganda* (Entebbe: G.P., 1953), pp. 15-16.

[7] By 1950 the Legislative Council had grown to 32, of whom 16 were government officials and 16 unofficials (8 Africans, 4 Europeans, 4 Asians). By 1954 the Council consisted of 56 members, with 20 of them Africans. A year later the number was changed to 60 members; half of the total were Africans, most having been elected by district councils or, in the case of Buganda, an electoral college.

taking in the Protectorate, lend or advance money, engage in capital financing, and act as the financial agents and managers of business undertakings. Similar to others in the colonies, this scheme would provide for joint private and public investment and development.[8]

A Coffee Industry Ordinance was passed in 1953, providing for the control and regulation of the Coffee Industry Board based on its reorganization; the principal aims were increased participation by Africans both in primary marketing and the processing of coffee. Differences between methods of marketing coffee grown by Africans and Europeans were abolished. A Uganda Coffee Industry Board was established to supervise the industry and organize marketing and disposal of the coffee crop (a coffee industry fund acts as a reserve fund for price variations). Demands long made by Africans for the ginning of cotton were now facilitated by an Acquisition of Ginneries Ordinance of 1953 which helped African cooperative unions acquire ginneries for themselves.

Technical education was reviewed and expanded, particularly in the light of the opportunities presented by the new Royal College of Technology in Nairobi, which was to serve the East African territories.[9] Moreover, the government suggested that it would consider grants-in-aid to independent schools in spite of the low standards prevailing there and the fact that independent schools had been centers of nationalist feeling.[10]

A committee was established to examine the position and needs of Africans in trade; proposals for developing African trading helped to assuage the feelings of those shopkeepers and small African merchants who had been among the most aggrieved in Uganda and whose political activities were of major importance

[8] See Uganda Development Corporation Ordinance, No. 1 of 1952, 31 March 1952.

[9] See *Technical and Commercial Education in Uganda* (Entebbe: G.P., 1954), especially Appendix VI. The Royal College of Technology has now been raised to the status of a university college.

[10] Schools such as Aggrey Memorial School, which was founded by Dr. E. Kalibala, were formed after the teachers' strike at King's College, Budo, and were centers of nationalist feeling. Many of the teachers at Aggrey had come from Budo after the strike. Promises of a more sympathetic position on the part of the government with respect to independent schools was regarded as a very welcome step. (See *Memorandum by the Protectorate Government on the Report of the African Education Committee*, Entebbe: G.P., 1953, p. 7.)

Education had been a major target of previous administrations. See *Outline Scheme of Development of African Education, 1944-1954* (Entebbe: G.P., 1954).

in the country. Not only had African traders increased in great measure after the war, but they had led the attack against Asians, for whom they reserved their fiercest epithets (and to whom they were often in debt).[11]

The increase of the urban population, particularly in such areas as Katwe, Wandegeya, and Mulago, and adjacent to the larger towns like Masaka—where not only were housing facilities far below standard but people were packed in—became a primary concern of the new administration.[12] Other areas showed great variations in population density. The new plan instituted by the government was to establish balanced and integrated urban communities having a community center, churches, schools, and marketing facilities. The main objective was a healthy community life. As the Governor in his speech to the Legislative Council, November 20, 1952, had indicated, "The problem is to create proper communities for those who go to live and work in the urban and industrial areas; communities which offer a hope of a reasonable life and provide for the education of children, for social welfare and for sport and recreation. . . ." Some, as at Ntinda, were to be owner-occupied estates where people bought their houses.[13]

Point by point, the grievances which for so long had been characteristic of the African scene in Uganda were being considered. Each specific grievance group, whether trader, farmer, teacher, or political leader, had been given a vision of concrete reform which in practical terms was beyond what they had expected to receive. Not only did the reforms go to the heart of the difficulties facing Uganda but, as well, the government stole the initiative from the public. It became the most aggressive and positive force for change—change, moreover, whose object was to draw together the nation as a whole.

Perhaps most startling of all, following recommendations made by Wallis and others, it was decided to transfer certain services from the departments of government to the Buganda government. It was agreed that the Protectorate government would hand over to the Buganda government responsibility for running primary

[11] See the report which emerged subsequently, *The Advancement of Africans in Trade* (Entebbe: G.P., 1955).
[12] See A. W. Southall and P. C. W. Gutkind, *Townsmen in the Making*, East African Studies No. 9 (E.A.I.S.R., 1956), p. 8.
[13] See *Statement of Policy on African Urban Housing* (Entebbe: G.P., 1954).

and junior secondary schools, rural hospitals and dispensaries, subdispensaries, aid posts and rural health services, the field service for improvement of farming methods and soil conservation, animal health and livestock breeding, and so on. In order to pay for such services the principle of graduated taxation would be established by the Lukiko, but, as well, the Protectorate government would provide sources of funds. Additional ministers would be appointed to the Buganda government and in the Lukiko the number of elected representatives would be increased to 60. Even the demand that chiefs be elected representatives was considered; though rejected, this was done so delicately that few could argue against the decision. Finally, the Kabaka agreed to establish a system of local government in accordance with the principles laid down in the Wallis report.

To emphasize the essential unity of the effort he was making, the Governor established a cross-bench in the Legislature in which both government and representative members participated. The object was to indicate that the entire Legislature was a single team devoted to the purposes of developing the nation and not a situation in which a government and an embryo opposition would face one another in somewhat sterile debate.

In this wise, more reform was packed into the first years of the administration of Sir Andrew Cohen than had ever been seen in Uganda. It was possible to push through such a program partly because of the unparalleled prosperity the country had been enjoying due to high postwar prices for coffee and cotton and also because the economic policies of the previous administration had now begun to pay off. Almost everyone was caught up in the spirit of the new changes and the social engineering. The dynamism of the Governor unleashed new energy and provided new leadership to all groups. Such Baganda as Kawalya Kagwa shook their heads that it was too rapid for the public. Some old-line colonial officers agreed. But in the main, Africans, civil servants, and the Governor began working together with less of the usual frictions over race, privilege, and status than had been characteristic for many generations.

There were other advances. The Cooperative Societies Ordinance was amended to facilitate African cooperative organization. Labor conditions were investigated. The complaints about discrimination in the Civil Service were for the time being silenced by the appointment of Sir David Lidbury as chairman of a commission to examine and make recommendations about the civil services in the East African territories.[14]

Perhaps the only group upset by the new reforms were the kings of Uganda.[15] They were disturbed that events were going to leave them as anomalies. Thus their only recourse was to revive the fears of unification, that is, the loss of a "national personality." In the districts the effect of the Wallis reform would make the kings into honorific figures. In Buganda the Kabaka, although essentially agreeable to the changes which he saw coming, reckoned without the more traditionalist elements in the society who considered the reforms a danger to the principle and position of kingship in Buganda. The Abakama of Toro and Bunyoro were concerned with their own positions and, indeed, there were factions in both these areas which desired the reduction of the power of kings.[16]

Major reform of Legislative Council was also considered. In 1952 the practice was to select two African members from each province, all members being nominated by the Governor. The two nominees from Buganda were put forward by the Kabaka because in 1950 the Great Lukiko had refused to select them. In

[14] See Sir David Lidbury, *Report of the Commission on the Civil Services of the East African Territories and the East African High Commission, 1953-1954* (London: Eyre and Spottiswoode, 1954).

[15] In a 1952 kings' conference they issued six resolutions: (1) that kings be allowed to give opinion on Legislative Council laws or regulations before they are passed; (2) district teams are undermining the district councils; (3) the title of the local governments should have the term *local* removed and the name of the "country" put in its place, e.g. Bunyoro government, Toro government, etc.; (4) that the African governments be allowed to buy shares in big companies or cooperatives that invest in their territories; (5) that game reserves which are closed areas and "do not allow people to exercise liberties" be abolished; (6) that government overseas scholarships should be increased.

[16] An extremely interesting chapter in Uganda history deals with the negotiations conducted by a committee of "Young Turks" who sought, successfully, to limit the power of the Omukama of Bunyoro. The delicate bargaining and negotiations that were undertaken would properly be a book in itself. The result of the negotiations, however, was the Bunyoro Agreement of 1955 which, reducing the powers of the Omukama, put the Rukurato in much the same position as the other district councils having both executive and legislative powers. The Omukama of Toro has been successful in avoiding such a rebellion and instead has spearheaded the drive to produce a new constitution in Toro which gives greater powers to the Toro government than is acceptable to the Protectorate government. As a result, at present writing, Toro still operates under the 1949 African Local Governments Ordinance, and a deadlock on constitutional matters continues.

the western province the Katikiros of the three Agreement states took the second western seat in rotation. Cohen wrote that "the defects in the African representation from Buganda are that, as the result of the attitude of the Great Lukiko, there is no element of popular choice in the selection of the names put forward and that the two members are not associated in any way with particular areas of Buganda. Outside Buganda there is the still more serious defect that the provincial basis of representation is completely unreal. Apart from the existence of Provincial Commissioners and Provincial Technical Officers, there are no special ties between, for example, Kigezi and Bunyoro in the West, Lango and West Nile in the North, or Busoga and Teso in the East, except that each are in fact on a Protectorate rather than a provincial level."[17] The suggested reform was to have African members elected from the district by the district council, for "abler representatives would be likely to be chosen, since it is the district which is the natural unit of public life everywhere outside Buganda; here tribal loyalty and cohesion is strong and the District Councils are already much valued by the people and are the source of local pride."[18]

Finally, if community development and local government went hand in hand, the role of central government would become even more crucial. "The Protectorate is too small to grow into a series of separate governments, even if they were federated together. The different parts of the country have not the size, nor will they have the resources to develop, even in federation with each other, the administrative and political organs which modern government requires. This can only be done by a Central Government of the country as a whole, with no part of the country dominating any other part, but all working together for the good of the Protectorate."[19]

The Governor proposed that on the nongovernment side there should be fourteen African unofficial members who would be called representative members instead of unofficials. These would be drawn from each district outside Buganda with the exception of Karamoja; the remaining three would be chosen from Buganda.

[17] See *Correspondence Relating to the Composition of Legislative Council in Uganda* (Entebbe: G.P., 1953), p. 3.
[18] *Ibid.*, p. 3.
[19] *Ibid.*, p. 4.

Balancing the fourteen African members would be seven European and Asian unofficial members chosen by nomination of the Governor. The government side would then be strengthened by the addition of both more officials and of a "cross-bench" of "distinguished members of the public, who would have complete freedom to speak and vote as they wished except on an issue treated by the Government as a matter of confidence." The cross-bench would thus emphasize the highly participant nature of the new regime; although on a vote of confidence, since popular representative government had not been established, the colonial government could not be allowed to fail.[20]

Hence there was now to be unified policy. Powers were to be given the districts under terms worked out by Wallis and to be drafted in a new district government ordinance. African education, technical and academic, had been examined. Housing had been reviewed and new estates were being built. Everywhere there was an attempt to listen to public grievances and take them into account before drafting some new item of legislative business. Above all, there was to be a new focus—the Legislative Council. "It follows clearly from this that we must take every possible step to encourage the people of this country to realize that the Protectorate government and the Legislative Council are not something alien to them, but part of their national life."

The period of economic and social reform included a dramatic period of expansion in mass media. Ten vernacular newspapers were started between 1953 and 1954. Their combined circulation was 82,680. Some of these were new organs of the rising nationalist movements. The *Uganda Post*, owned by J. W. Kiwanuka, was frankly an organ of the Uganda National Congress. *Uganda Eyogera* was the organ of the Progressive Party. Interestingly enough, one of the editors, P. M. K. Lwanga, was a son of James Miti. The owner of the paper was E. M. K. Mulira, the President of the Progressive Party.

Other papers were older. *Gambuze*, the original African ver-

[20] These plans had been envisaged in the earliest stages of the new administration. One difference between the usual governor's appointment and that of Sir Andrew Cohen was that the latter had already been responsible for much of the policy which had been carried out in Uganda because of his post in the Colonial Office. Arriving in Uganda made it possible for him to put into effect plans and reforms which had been worked out or at least sketched out before.

nacular newspaper (other than those started by missionaries), was founded in 1927. It became the mouthpiece of the Bataka.

Although the press flourished, their concern with world news was minimal. They were almost entirely devoted to Mengo and local politics. We have indicated that the world, in microcosm, was seen through Buganda provincialism. And the microcosm remained just that. In the newspapers the world was divided into the protective forces of Mengo and the enemy forces of the Protectorate regime. Once again, the attention of the people was focused on their own institutions.[21]

Not only did the press expand, but there was a sudden proliferation of political parties.[22] The most important of these was

[21] *Uganda: Annual Colonial Reports, 1958*, pp. 123-124.

Twenty-four newspapers were published regularly in Uganda by 1957. Of these, 10 were African-owned and financed; 1, the *Uganda Argus*, was partly European-owned and financed, and 2 were owned and financed by the Roman Catholic mission. The remaining 11 were published with public funds; 5 of them by the Department of Information and 6 by other Government agencies, i.e. the Community Development Department and various African local government bodies.

Name of Paper	Language	Circulation Claimed	When Published
African Pilot	Luganda	12,000	Monday & Thursday
*Agafa e Buvanjuba	Luganda	10,000	Monthly
*Agari Ankole	Runyankore	5,000	Monthly
*Amut	Lango	3,000	Monthly
Dodobozi lya Buganda	Luganda	3,400	Monday
Emambya Esaze	Luganda	6,500	Tuesday & Saturday
Erwom K'Iteso	Ateso	5,000	Monthly
*Lok Mutimme	Lwo	2,000	Monthly
*Kodheyo	Luganda	5,000	Monthly
Mugambizi	Runyoro	2,000	Weekly
Munno	Luganda	7,800	Tuesday & Friday
Muwereza	Luganda	4,000	Tuesday & Friday
Mwebingwa	Runyoro	2,680	Weekly
Ndimugezi	Luganda	850	Tuesday & Friday
Obugagga Bwa Uganda	Luganda	7,000	Weekly
Uganda Argus[a]	English	8,200	Daily
Uganda Empya	Luganda	8,500	Monday & Thursday
Uganda Eyogera	Luganda	12,000	Tuesday & Friday
Uganda Post	Luganda	9,000	Wednesday & Saturday
Uganda Times	Luganda	5,000	Wednesday
*West Nile	Lugbara & Alur	2,500	Monthly

* Published with Public Funds

[a] The only daily paper and the only one to be published in English. *The East African Standard*, a well-established newspaper published in Nairobi, is also read in Uganda.

[22] Among the parties which appeared were the All-Uganda Party, the Uganda Nationalist Movement Party and the Uganda People's Party. These had very small support. There were some variations among them. The All-Uganda Party

the Uganda National Congress, the first party to consider seriously both the economic and political needs of the country. We shall discuss the Uganda National Congress at some length below. At the moment it is sufficient to say that as an organization it was the creation of Musazi, who built it on the base of his Federation of African Partnerships, the organization which replaced the Uganda African Farmers' Union after the latter was banned in 1949. The U.N.C. was in many respects the same organization as the Federation of Partnerships. The efforts to build the Federation of Partnerships and subsequently organize the party were plagued by internal difficulties and weaknesses, so that neither was ever successful. There was enough freedom so that they were swamped with their own difficulties.[23]

There were a few old Bataka Party officials who, from their more or less underground positions, cautioned the Baganda to beware of the British. There were some old Mengo hands who were fearful at the turn toward good relations and saw the very existence of Buganda threatened. But it was the Governor who was the popular figure, gathering in the wake of his own enthusiasm all those who wanted to do their share in the making of modern Uganda. Many of those in various positions in one government or another, European or African, who had glared at one

---

was essentially a party of Baganda nationalists who pushed for independence for Buganda. It had considerable support from old-line chiefs who had been supporters of Wamala. Subsequently it changed its name to the All-Buganda Party. There were also religious parties such as the *Bwavu Empologoma Union* which, claiming over 20 registered societies, was a cooperative as well as a political organization. Under the leadership of Peter Sendikwanawa, it was concerned over the secularization of schools and accused other parties of being dominated by Protestants.

The Bataka Party had of course been outlawed in 1949 for its alleged part in the riots and it remained underground. An important leader of the Bataka Party, J. Matovu, became General Secretary of the Bujjaja Party, which was widely regarded as the Bataka under a new name. Founded in 1953, its articles were above reproach: "*1*. Complete loyalty to the Crown; *2*. To fight relentlessly to achieve and maintain independence for the people of Uganda and their chiefs at the earliest possible time; *3*. To promote the Political, Social, and Economic emancipation of the people more particularly of those who depend directly upon their own exertions by hand or brain for the means of life; *4*. To establish an African Socialist State in which all men and women shall have equal opportunity; *5*. The party will carry on its activities throughout Uganda in the best British traditions."

Still others were one-man parties or short-lived, such as the Uganda Taxpayers' Party, the Uganda Reform Party, and the Uganda Nationalist Party.

[23] See George Shepherd, *They Wait in Darkness* (New York: John Day), *passim*.

another through successions of disputes or spent their time in beguiling one another, now found themselves sometimes haltingly and sometimes with a firm tread marching on a common road.

The Baganda were now up against a difficult time, for the Governor was popular. Far from being able to translate their institutions in the wider setting of Uganda and national politics, the Baganda could see the handwriting on the wall only too well. Here was the interesting phenomenon of "moderns," to use Lerner's term, anxious to preserve that which served as a modernizing agent, that is, traditionalism, by protecting the autonomy of their country and their institutions. All signs pointed to a new stage in the affairs of Uganda, when suddenly a disastrous event occurred.

On June 30, 1953, the Colonial Secretary made a speech in London in which, citing the virtues of Central African federation, he made a casual reference to the possibilities of federation in East Africa.[24] This speech unleashed the most important crisis of all in Buganda.

The Parable of the Governor and the King

The Colonial Secretary's speech was reported in the Kenya newspaper, *East African Standard*. It was immediately noticed in Uganda. Of some interest is the manner in which the issue was identified, because the very people who became concerned with doing something about the speech were later berated as having been traitors to the Kabaka or were punished in one form or another by the Baganda themselves. The news of the speech was first heard by the Katikiro at the home of C. M. S. Kisosonkole, the father-in-law of the Kabaka, at a tea party being given for a minister from a Bible Society. They were joined by E. M. K. Mulira, a man of moderate views who subsequently became a newspaper owner and political leader. When the leader of the representative members of the Lukiko visited the Katikiro several days later, a letter was drafted to the Governor by the ministers

24 It will be recalled that assurances had been given that Central African Federation would not take place unless the people of the territories involved agreed to it. The assent of the legislatures of the three territories, each dominated by an overwhelmingly preponderate European membership, was taken as the requisite approval and Central African Federation came into being over the bitter protests of the Africans. In Nyasaland in particular, over a month of rioting followed the decision of H.M.G. to promote federation.

of the Buganda government. The letter indicated misgivings by the Baganda about the validity of past assurances against federation by Her Majesty's government because of the Colonial Secretary's speech. Objection to closer union was reaffirmed.[25]

In reply, the Governor wrote to the Kabaka that the article in the newspaper had not printed the text of the Colonial Secretary's speech but an interpretation of it, and that the ministers' letter having been forwarded immediately to the Colonial Office produced assurance from that office that no change in policy regarding federation was contemplated. Questions of federation would be largely determined by public opinion in the territories in question and the High Commission was not to be regarded as a step toward political fusion.[26]

The Baganda did not consider this reply sufficient. Not only were the Lukiko representative members exercised, but all those groups who had put their faith in the development and progress of the country began suddenly to renew their concern on the issue of closer union. All parties felt that they had dropped their guard, removed their defenses, and in discarding their usual wariness been captured by the reforming zeal of the Governor. Now they began to regard themselves duped by Her Majesty's government. Pervasive was the feeling that the Colonial Secretary had accidentally lifted the curtain on a projected Colonial Office plan for East African federation—a plan which everyone "knew"

[25] The relevant passages are: "Sir, the article which has appeared on the front page of the East African Standard issue of Friday of the 3rd July, 1953, is noted with misgivings and has confused this Government and our people as to the value of the assurances given to us in the name of Her Majesty's Government, on every occasion in the past, when the question of the Federation of the three British East African Territories was proposed, and when the setting up of the East African High Commission was suspected by Africans in Uganda as a steppingstone towards the realization of political fusion in the three territories.

"Sir, the statement quoted in the article, as made by Her Majesty's Minister, the Secretary of State for the Colonies can not be taken lightly and for that reason we are compelled to state that it is bound not only to shake the foundations of trust among our people, but will also badly damage the good relations which hitherto obtains between the Baganda and the British. Representing His Highness's Government and the people of Buganda, we have to state once again that our attitude towards any such contemplated political fusion is firm, and that it should be communicated to Her Majesty's Government."

The letter was signed by P. Kavuma, the Katikiro, J. Musoke, the Acting Omulamuzi, and L. Mpagi, the Omuwanika. See Appendix B, letter of 6 July 1953 in *Withdrawal of Recognition from Kabaka Mutesa II of Buganda* (London: H.M.S.O., 1953), Cmd. 9028 (hereafter referred to as the *White Paper*).

[26] *Ibid.*, Appendix C.

had existed for a long time and against which the Baganda had so long and bitterly fought. Pointing to Central African Federation which they saw in all its enormity, not only were the Baganda frightened, but they suddenly saw the "real" meaning of contemporary politics. They attributed motives of deepest insincerity to the British. Sir Andrew Cohen they regarded as an honest man who was being used by the higher authorities.

Meanwhile, each of the political groups in the country moved into position. The Uganda National Congress, the new political party founded in 1952, took full advantage of the situation.[27] So did the more conservative groups, such as the All-Uganda Party, many of whose members were part of the Mengo hierarchy. The Bataka groups were particularly upset and brought considerable pressure on the representative members of the Lukiko. The whole history of relationships between British and Baganda, of negotiations over closer union in the twenties and thirties, was reviewed and scrutinized. The transfer of Buganda from the Foreign Office to the Colonial Office after the 1900 Agreement was viewed as part of a long-term design and a sinister step toward control of the Baganda. It was because of that transfer that the Colonial Office could hand Buganda over to the control of a foreign power, namely Kenya. It became clear to the Baganda that their opposition to closer union had been successful in the past but had done no more than deflect and divert closer union. Now the attempt was being made obliquely, as it were, through the setting up of the High Commission.

What can be called the "plot conception" of British behavior was thus quickly established and taken up throughout the country. Suddenly every official of the British government was viewed as a persistent enemy. Nor were the missionaries exempted. It was recalled that the missionaries, and particularly Bishop Stuart of the Anglican Church, had not been opposed to the Land Acquisition Act. It was remembered that Mutesa had been brought up in a missionary household to be molded in accord with the wishes of British officialdom. It was argued that the position of Buganda was subordinated to that of protected states in the hierarchy of political privilege because the Kabaka had not been accorded treatment equal to that of the Queen of Tonga during

[27] For a discussion of the Uganda National Congress, see Chapter 14.

the Coronation.[28] A change of status was supposedly demonstrated by the difference in the treatment of Sir Apolo Kagwa at
the Coronation of Edward the VII in 1902 and of Mutesa at the
Coronation of Queen Elizabeth. Sir Apolo had been treated as a
distinguished *foreign* guest, Mutesa as a *colonial* guest.

As well, many of the older pro-Bataka political leaders felt the
time for a showdown with the Kabaka was near. Either he would
symbolize the nation and stand up for Buganda nationalism, or
else he was a British agent. His personal life having made him
somewhat unpopular, and his behavior in the past having given
rise to doubts about his sympathies, popular resentment against
him was particularly great just when the Governor, Sir Andrew
Cohen, was capturing the enthusiasm of the general public. Hence
for the Kabaka more was at stake than simply a temporary concern over a political blunder by the Colonial Secretary. It was
the moment for a crusade against the plans and treachery of the
British government.

The Lukiko argument which precipitated crisis was that the
policy of trusteeship should have been retained for Uganda, not
partnership which is for colonial territories. Partnership was
exemplified by the Uganda Legislative Council which, it was argued, undermined the Agreement. Furthermore, Baganda were
now on the East African Central Assembly, an external legislative body. Even industrialization, a goal which sounded noteworthy enough, was the cause for mass immigration without the
consultation of the Great Lukiko, and immigrants "flock into the
country monthly without His Highness' Government knowing their
purpose." Arguing that "we are not a colony and we have never
been a colony," the Lukiko, referring to the fact that Nyasaland
was a protectorate which had been forced into federation with
the Rhodesias, demanded that immediate steps be taken to safeguard the future. The Lukiko therefore (1) strongly opposed
any form of a political union affecting Uganda with the neighboring territories; (2) most earnestly urged that the affairs of
the country should revert to the Foreign Office; and (3) urged
that a time limit be set for independence within the Commonwealth.[29]

[28] Indeed, the Kabaka did not have a carriage placed at his disposal but had to
walk and take taxis to the various functions.
[29] See the *White Paper*, Appendix F, Memorandum by the Great Lukiko, pp. 28-30.

Once the image of British duplicity had set in, replies could not satisfy the Buganda government. For the first time since the end of the closer union controversy in the 1930's, the Buganda government led the way for all to follow. All parties within Buganda united on the issues. And they would have tolerated no sign of weakening by the ministers.

The Secretary of State went further than ever in trying to assuage Kiganda feelings. The Buganda government was informed that "Her Majesty's Government has no intention whatsoever of raising the issue of East African federation either at the present time or while local public opinion on this issue remains as it is at the present time. Her Majesty's Government fully recognizes that public opinion in Buganda and the rest of the Protectorate would be opposed to the inclusion of the Uganda Protectorate in any such federation; Her Majesty's Government has no intention whatsoever of disregarding this opinion either now or at any time, and recognizes accordingly that the inclusion of the Uganda Protectorate in any such federation is outside the realm of practical politics at the present time or while local public opinion remains as it is at the present time."[30]

The Baganda replied that the Secretary of State did not rule out the possibility of federation in the future. Moreover, what did "public opinion" really mean? Public opinion in Nyasaland had clearly opposed Central African federation, but to no avail. The assurance was regarded as a slippery evasion of the real issue. The Colonial Office had not committed itself to an absolute assurance that under no circumstances would federation ever occur.[31]

[30] *Ibid.*, pp. 33-34.

[31] The Baganda were fearful of the position which other Africans might take on this issue. While the apparent fear was of domination by white settlers in Kenya if federation should come, another fear was perhaps more pervasive. This was of the development of modern political nationalism which was against the chiefs. If younger nationalists of East Africa organized along supraterritorial lines, federation might mean the domination of African politicians, not of Europeans. That the Buganda government and other political conservatives were very much aware of this was brought out in interviews with members of the All-Uganda Party and the Uganda National Congress; tactically the U.N.C. was in sympathy with the Kabaka and therefore forced to take up the cudgels for Buganda nationalism. Among its senior leadership, however, there was full knowledge that eventually there would be conflict not with the British, but with the Kabaka, his court, and the whole tribal-political structure. Alliance with non-Baganda was for the time being the way out of the dilemma, since it was premature to raise the larger issue

There were widespread claims that other Africans in the Protectorate would not feel as concerned about federation as the Baganda, and in any case had less to protect since they were more backward and primitive and of less political status within Uganda. The fear revived that other groups in Uganda would form a coalition at the legislative level and dominate Buganda politically at the center.

In short, the Baganda recognized that they had been heading directly for a single national state in which they would have been important but constituent members. The speech gave them the pretext to reverse the situation and remove themselves from a position they considered dangerous and compromising. They demanded independence but left vague whether they meant independence of Legislative Council, political freedom of Buganda from the rest of Uganda, or independence for Uganda as a whole. Members of the All-Uganda Party affirmed that what the Lukiko meant was independence for Buganda, which is the way the British government chose to interpret the proposal.[32]

Among the safeguards demanded were the transfer of Buganda to the Foreign Office, an absolute declaration against federation, independence within a stated space of time, and a policy of trusteeship, not partnership. These were put to the Colonial Secretary. However, it was not the Colonial Secretary who had to deal with such demands, but Sir Andrew Cohen. He did so in characteristic fashion. He did not go through the classic steps of a political ballet. He could have had the demands put through the Residency. The Resident could have then negotiated with the Baganda. If deadlock had ensued he could have set up a commission of enquiry. Sir Andrew used none of the usual steps and tactics which a colonial bureaucracy has at its disposal and which can often be extremely useful in preventing issues from coming to a head until their heat has died down. Instead, he saw the Kabaka. As had been his wont in the Colonial Office, by the use

---

with the predominant membership of the U.N.C., rural Baganda who would not be in sympathy with the position of many party leaders. But the Buganda government recognized the African threat to the autonomy of Buganda via African nationalist federation. Hence this part of their reaction to the Secretary of State's speech was a carefully calculated overreaction.

[32] Leaders of the Uganda National Congress indicated that what was meant was independence for Uganda as a whole within the British Commonwealth.

of direct methods he thought he could reason with Mutesa and bring about an agreed solution. He reckoned without the depth of feeling that the issue generated. He also failed to comprehend the "overreaction" of the Baganda. He was dealing with a Kabaka who had necessarily to take a firm stand if he did not want to be regarded as a traitor by his people. In this situation direct contact left little room for maneuver. It could only lead to deadlock.

Too, the Governor received inadequate advice. Colonial Service officers were alarmed by Mau Mau in Kenya and were fearful it would break out in Uganda.[33] They regarded firmness as essential. If the Kabaka did not accept the government's position they advised deportation. The hubbub aroused by his deportation would soon die down and a new Kabaka could be appointed.

Physically slight and delicate, a dandy of sorts and very much a gentleman, the Kabaka met with Sir Andrew Cohen, a man of great seriousness, sincerity, and strength of character. The physical presence of the Governor was the opposite of that of the Kabaka. He was tall and powerfully built, with a formidable intellect. To the Governor, the Kabaka was a person to whom one showed great courtesy and respect but who represented a kind of precious royalty which had no special virtue other than that it was a Kiganda institution. Almost entirely without guile, the Governor could dominate those with whom he chose to discuss political matters on the strength of honest argument. To the Kabaka, guile (in the Greek sense) was a necessary political attribute. It allowed compromises to be made while principles quite opposite were affirmed. In a sense the Kabaka believed he was fighting the guile of the Colonial Secretary through the honesty of the Governor. He was also counting on the Governor's well-known pro-African attitudes. The Kabaka had every reason to believe that the argument and position of his own government was, if not reasonable, at least necessary, and that intransigence was a safeguard against the British government. He felt sure that when the issue was finally drawn the Governor would relent and some machinery would be set in motion which would at least appear to grant the demands of the Baganda.

33 The concern centered around the possible violence which might have ensued had the Kabaka been allowed to address the Lukiko. With the Uganda Battalion of the King's African Rifles in Kenya, and memories of the 1945 and 1949 riots still fresh, the Kabaka crisis was viewed as extremely dangerous.

Six meetings were held at Government House. The Kabaka came with his ministers and the Governor had his advisors. The specific issue at stake was a letter of the Kabaka's[34] which, repeating the Lukiko resolutions, laid out the fears of the Baganda that federation would be forced upon them, cited the case of Nyasaland as the example of what could happen to Buganda, and refused to accept partnership as the basis of British and African cooperation in Uganda. Requests for transfer to the Foreign Office and for the granting of independence were made.

The Governor could give no guarantees that federation would be ruled out forever because the feelings of the Baganda themselves might change in this regard. He felt that a failure on the part of the Kabaka to recognize the good faith of Her Majesty's government on this issue implied a lack of trust in the British government, which, of course, was exactly the case.

All the arguments which had been used over many years of Buganda-Protectorate government relations were now wheeled into position. Fears were indicated over the decline of Buganda's position. The Kabaka and his ministers felt that the policy of developing a unified system of government on parliamentary lines must inevitably result in Buganda's becoming less important in the future. Buganda did not wish to be associated with development on parliamentary lines and could not accept the idea of non-African participation in the future government of a Uganda government protectorate which included Buganda. When it was pointed out to the Kabaka that this was rather a different attitude from the compromising and conciliatory position he had previously taken with the Governor, the Kabaka readily agreed but held that the Secretary of State's statement had changed the circumstances.

The Governor pointed out that unless the Kabaka and his government dropped their demands, the reforms which included transferred services to the Buganda government could not be implemented. The Kabaka took the attitude that the Secretary of State was being intransigent and that independence should be the substance of discussion and guarantees. He refused flatly to sign a statement which repudiated the pursuit of matters in his orig-

[34] Letter from the Kabaka to the Colonial Secretary, August 6, 1953.

inal statement and which accepted the new guarantees offered by the Secretary of State against federation.

Between the first and second meetings of the Kabaka and the Governor, pressures were stepped up in Buganda to prevent the Kabaka from being swayed and to give him support for his position. At a mass meeting, the Uganda National Congress resolved: "We do not accept to be federated with other territories which have different customs, and traditions, and mode of life and which have Agreements which are different. For that reason we are determined as Members of the Uganda National Congress, Buganda Branch and have discussed and resolved that Buganda, as a recognized Kingdom, we walk out of the Colonial Office and transfer back to the Foreign Office. . . .

"In this determination to get out of the Colonial Office to the Foreign Office, we know for certain that our brothers in the neighboring countries such as Toro, Ankole, Teso, Lango, and all others in Uganda agree with us and are also determined in the same way. . . ."[35]

Meanwhile, the Lukiko passed Resolution No. 14, The Federation of British East African Territories. The resolution categorically rejected federation. The Kabaka, having been in Zanzibar when the resolution was passed, received a letter from the Lukiko dealing with the Legislative Council. "Your Highness, the Great Lukiko asked us to bring forward to you their urgent request, having reached the conclusion that when the matter of federation shall be raised it will be decided by the Legislative Council, and furthermore since the Baganda have their own recognized Lukiko the idea of sending representatives from it to the Legislative Council undermines that Lukiko.

"The Great Lukiko therefore humbly requests Your Highness to refrain from nominating members to that Council because the nation is convinced that to nominate members to that Council simply reduces the aims for which the nation is striving in its development. . . ."

The Kabaka replied that he had "understood" the position of the Lukiko. "I shall not fail to inform His Excellency the Governor about it when it is time to nominate new members to that

[35] Congress meeting, September 19, 1953.

Council, and I shall inform you of the results of our talks on this matter. . . ."[36]

The Baganda were not the only people to be disturbed. The Abakamas of Bunyoro and Toro and the Omugabe of Ankole, the kings of the Agreement states, had written to the Governor opposing federation. Expressing their dissatisfaction with the guarantees given by the Secretary of State, they noted the "indefinite nature of the intentions . . . implied"; their fears were not allayed by the statements from the British government. They therefore felt it necessary to strongly suggest a solution to the problem, "that is to say for an entire and effective revision of the relationships which now exist between Her Majesty's Government and our respective States."[37]

Discussions between the Kabaka and the Governor continued. In subsequent meetings the Kabaka made his aim clear: separation of Buganda from the Protectorate. And he remained firm on the question of transfer to the Foreign Office. When provided with a draft answer to the Lukiko on these matters, the Kabaka refused to accept the Protectorate government's recommendations which he was to present to the Lukiko with his assent. Indeed, the Kabaka appealed to the Governor that he could not go against the wishes of the Lukiko. Putting the Governor in an uncomfortable position, he presented himself as a constitutional monarch who was being forced into the role of an autocratic king of Buganda and a puppet of the Protectorate government. The Governor was forced to explain to the Kabaka that under the terms of the Agreement the Kabaka was duty-bound to accept advice formally given. The Kabaka then argued that if he had to choose between loyalty to the Protectorate government and loyalty to his people he would choose loyalty to his people.

By this time it was clear to the Kabaka that he had to accept the advice of the Governor or face the legal consequences, that is, withdrawal of recognition. The Kabaka asked for arbitration on the questions raised. This was denied as improper. The Kabaka

[36] Letter from the High Highness, the Kabaka, to the ministers of the Buganda government, October 13, 1953.

[37] Letter from Abakama of Toro and Bunyoro, and the Omugabe of Ankole to H. E. The Governor, August 10, 1953, in Parma-Ntanda, Muska R., Deposition of H.H. the Kabaka of Buganda, (Mengo, Women's League of Buganda), Appendix III (n.d.).

asked the Governor to provide him a feasible alternative and to unbend. But by this time there were no alternatives. The positions had hardened. The Governor then went through each of the undertakings suggested by the British government to the Kabaka and the latter declined them all. Once again the Kabaka was informed that persistence in his views would be regarded as a breach of the Agreement. The Kabaka was given five weeks to consider. At the end of that time he returned to Government House still adamant. He said that the Agreement was out-of-date and should be modified, and that he would not explain the position of Her Majesty's government to the Lukiko. The Governor then handed the Kabaka a letter given on the instructions of the Secretary of State which informed him that under Article 6 of the Agreement recognition had been withdrawn.[38]

It was, of course, a momentous decision. The Kabaka had not been asked to agree with the decisions of Her Majesty's government but simply loyally to communicate them to the Lukiko. It was even suggested that he did not have to abandon his opposition but to continue in private negotiations with the Crown on the matters and concerns which he had raised. But the Kabaka now refused to take any step which was not fully discussed with the Baganda themselves. And he acted with the advice of his ministers who had been participants in most of the meetings.

The Kabaka was then put under arrest and within a few hours was on his way to London. The Buganda government ministers wept. The news was received in the country with profound shock. The keystone in the arch of Buganda society had been removed.

Constitutional Monarchy

Although the Governor wanted a new Kabaka elected immediately, this was, of course, impossible. The Buganda government ministers, forming a regency, found themselves opposed at

[38] The summary of the six meetings between the Governor and the Kabaka as well as the correspondence are published in the *White Paper*. The text of the letter dated 20 November 1953 is as follows: "I am directed by the Secretary of State for Colonies on behalf of Her Majesty's Government to inform you that Her Majesty's Government, under the provisions of Article 6 of the Uganda Agreement of 1900 now withdraws recognition from you as Native Ruler of the Province of Buganda." The letter was signed by the Governor.

every turn. Administration in Buganda practically ceased. There was moaning throughout the Lubiri. The Kabaka's sister, Nalinya Kalwange, who was allegedly eating grasshoppers when she heard the news of the deportation, died of "shock" at the home of Princess Luwede in Kibuli. All chiefs and people in the area were ordered to enter the Bulange and the Katikiro told the people to remain peaceful in the midst of their suffering.[39]

It was not only the Baganda who were shocked. Missionaries and administrators with long service in the country realized what an important step had been taken. The mystery which surrounded the Kabaka was such that he could scarcely be regarded as an ordinary man. Moreover, he had been the pivot of relationships between the Baganda and the British, either in fact or in theory, ever since the 1900 Agreement had been signed.

There was also dismay that Sir Andrew Cohen, whose reputation for liberalism and justice was so wide, could have been the person to take such a drastic step. The Kabaka had believed that if pushed to deadlock the Governor would give in. Everything he knew about the Governor and his past record led him to believe that. For his part, the Governor, recognizing the pressure on the Kabaka, felt that the latter should have trusted him more and by passing over the present crisis, the reforms and other measures which would have been put into effect would have soon brought around all but the most recalcitrant Baganda.

That the Kabaka was so firm is no doubt partly due to the pressure he was under. He had been by no means personally popular. The more conservative elements in the population were exercised not only by the Colonial Secretary's speech but by their heightened sense of betrayal: that they had let their guard down for a moment. But there was another factor at work as well. This was the sense of risk and exhilaration during a prolonged period of deadlock in which tension and excitement were themselves heady and rewarding. To have stood firm against the physical presence of a brilliant governor, and by the same token to have defied the British Colonial Secretary, was a dramatic and

[39] The Katikiro, Paulo Kavuma, had been appointed after the 1949 riots. Although he had previously been Sekibobo, he had spent the previous 23 years in the Residency. Indeed, his friendships in that office went back to Postlethwaite, whom he continued to remember with affection as a mentor and friend.

grand thing to do. There is little doubt that the sense of drama was present in these meetings.[40]

At the same time, it is clear that few civil servants understood at the time the real meaning of the Kabakaship in the social structure and customs of the Baganda. The Kabakaship had to be viewed on its own terms and not on Western ideas of kingship. As we pointed out earlier, the Kabaka was the means whereby a Muganda fundamentally made common cause with his neighbors as a citizen. Both kinship and political allegiance were tied up with his presence. Underneath the calm and dignity which the Baganda exhibited to the world after the deportation, there was, most observers agreed, genuine turmoil and a sense of overwhelming deprivation.

The federation issue which had been raised by the Colonial Secretary dropped in importance. In fact, it had been more or less settled in the negotiations with the Governor. It was the issues following in the wake of the Colonial Secretary's speech—autonomy for Buganda, a timetable for independence, transfer to the Foreign Office, refusal to participate in the Legislative Council— which the Governor had been instrumental in blocking. Anger and concern were for a time directed against him. Too, many of the missionaries, concerned that the work of years would be undone and regarding the work of the Governor as a blunder of the first magnitude, supported the Baganda and shared in their sense of shock and dismay.

The most difficult burden of all was carried by the Katikiro. There were some who had accused him of having sold the Kabaka into bondage. There were others who suggested that the Lukiko should straight away elect a new Kabaka so they would not be regarded as rebels. Others, such as an important saza chief, Lutaya, offered to resign over the deportation, and there were messages from those with the Kabaka in England telling Kavuma, the Katikiro, not to allow a new Kabaka to be elected. The Resident pressed him to establish a regency of the three ministers and eventually this was done.

The Uganda National Congress issued the following statement

---

[40] There is also some evidence that the Kabaka had been impressed by the King Farouk affair when Farouk was expelled from Egypt by Neguib and Nasser, and that he feared he would eventually meet the same fate.

over the signature of S. M. Sekabanja, the Acting General President:

"In view of the deteriorating relationship between Africans and Europeans in Uganda subsequent to the deposition and deportation of the King of Buganda, the Uganda National Congress wishes to make clear that:—

"We hold the Governor and his Government responsible for this state of affairs.

"We hold the deposition and deportation of the king does not remove the issues raised in the resolutions submitted to the British Government, nor do the so-called answers satisfy the public.

"The Congress is committed to see that Uganda is developed as/and remains an African State.

"The Congress does not and will not support the constitution in existence or the Legislative Council as constituted in its present form.

"The Congress will work for the creation of a truly representative Government, and is determined to fight by all Constitutional means for the introduction of a Constituent Assembly in place of the out-moded and undemocratic interests.

"The assurances given by the Colonial Secretary on the question of Federation and the question of developing Uganda as an African State are and will remain hollow until a new constitution, formed after consultation with African rulers and people, is introduced to bring into being a Constituent Assembly."[41]

There is considerable ambiguity in the statement. Clearly some members of the leadership of U.N.C. were less concerned with the deportation than with the larger issues which it raised. Only later did they become involved in the actual return of the Kabaka when they realized how widespread was the demand for his return.

The Bataka were of course busy. One of the Bataka leaders, Reuben Musoke, helped draft a letter from "the relatives of the Queen Mother of Buganda" to the Queen. It was "a humble petition from the relatives of the Queen Mother of Buganda to Her Majesty Queen Elizabeth II, to consider most sympathetically the reinstatement of the petitioner's son, E. F. W. D. M. W. Mutesa II, Kabaka of Buganda, Captain in the Grenadier Guards,

[41] *East Africa and Rhodesia*, 31 December 1953.

First Officer of the Order of the Shield and Spears, now exiled in England."

The petitioners wrote that "our general health has deteriorated tremendously; we don't eat, we don't drink and we don't sleep; and Christian love and charity have become but . . . meaningless words to us. We have lost confidence. . . . The arrest and deportation of our son H. H. Kabaka Mutesa II has greatly troubled and haunted us. Wherefore, Beloved Queen Elizabeth II, we humbly request that the case which our son committed be made known to us, so that we may know why Your Majesty arrested, deposed and deported him. The action which was taken against him has made (him) lose dignity among his people and the chances of enjoying the benefits of his land and heritage."[42]

The churches came under attack. Among the Kabaka's followers who gathered at the Palace to hear the news of the Kabaka's deportation a Muganda was heard to say, "The Church has betrayed us. It is a purely European thing. The Bishop has connived with the Governor. It was the Kabaka who invited the Church to this country. Now the Kabaka is gone, so the Church is no more. If you look at the Church you will see it is purely European. It has a European bishop still, and the officers are European. There are still masses of missionaries in the country— we cannot get rid of them."[43]

Not only in missionary circles in Uganda was there consternation. The C.M.S. in England and the Archbishop of Canterbury were deeply concerned. So were academic people whose knowledge of Uganda was deep and whose affection for the work of all groups was genuine.[44] Miss Margery Perham in a penetrating letter to *The Times* pointed out that "of the four main difficulties, two are internal to Buganda and two of wider import. Internal is the need to face the long evaded question of the constitution of Buganda. The circumstances of Buganda's entry into British protection

[42] The petition was sent January 23, 1954 (unpublished) with copies to the Parliament, the United Nations, the Presidents of the United States, the U.S.S.R., and Egypt, the Prime Minister of India, and to Semakula Malumba who was now called Representative of the People of Uganda.

[43] Printed in the C.M.S. News-Letter, London, No. 159, March, 1954.

[44] Among them was Roland Oliver, whose book, *The Missionary Factor in East Africa* (London: Longmans, Green & Co., 1952), is a careful and sympathetic account of missionary activity and its place in East Africa.

had a crystallizing effect. Britain has since built up the Uganda Protectorate around and above Buganda, making of it a heart that could never, without fatal results, be torn from the larger body politic and economic."

Miss Perham pointed out also that as Buganda is a proud and ancient kingdom, an acceptable constitutional compromise between the idea of Buganda as integral to Uganda and Buganda as a state in itself must be worked out. Further, the "second problem centers upon the power of the Kabaka, still the essential mediator between the Governor and the people, but at present suspended bewilderingly between the old absolutism and the new status of constitutional ruler with a rapidly awakening representative assembly." Miss Perham then proposed the setting up of a small and expert constitutional commission to discuss with the Governor and the Lukiko the measures necessary to remedy the internal defects of the constitution and allow for rational and calm consideration of the problems. After that the question of the Kabaka might be dealt with with a fresh start.[45]

Her approach was a most constructive one, and in the end it was the one followed. A delegation of Baganda to London made a very good impression everywhere. The first delegation which had gone to London in an effort to secure the Kabaka's return not only aroused considerable comment, but made an effort to mount a campaign reminiscent of the one launched by Lugard and the missionaries to get Her Majesty's government to establish the Protectorate. The memory of missionary opinion, the public speeches and talks, the work of Lugard, which had all put forward in glowing terms the high hopes and the mission of Britain in Uganda, were in the minds of many who participated.[46]

It was the Governor who took the initiative in bringing about renewed talks and consultations. Sir Keith Hancock, Director of the Institute of Commonwealth Studies, London, had agreed to

[45] *The Times,* London, February 10, 1954.
[46] The members of the first delegation were M. Mugwanya, the Omulamuzi and the leading Catholic Muganda; Apolo Kironde, a lawyer and subsequently Assistant Minister of Social Services; E. M. K. Mulira, a publisher and former lecturer at The School of Oriental and African Languages, in London; and T. Makumbi, a teacher and head of the teachers' union. The Secretary was A. K. Sempa, then Secretary to the Lukiko and subsequently Minister of Education and Omuwanika in the Kabaka's government.

consult with representatives of the Baganda and with the Protectorate government on various constitutional questions relating to Buganda.[47]

From June 24 to September 17, Hancock presided over the discussions, first alone with the Constitutional Committee appointed by the Buganda Lukiko, and later with the Committee and the Governor at Namirembe.[48] Meanwhile, in a case before the High Court in Kampala testing the validity of the deportation, the Court refused the declarations of the plaintiffs (Baganda) among which were "the purported withdrawal by H. E. The Governor of Uganda of recognition of H. H. Mutesa II as native ruler of the Province of Buganda was unlawful, *ultra vires* and void. . . ."

While the plaintiffs were unsuccessful, the Court went on to say that withdrawal of recognition had been made under the wrong article of the Uganda Agreement.[49]

The Protectorate government had withdrawn recognition under Article 6 to avoid terminating the Agreement. Abrogation of the Agreement should have been the step taken under Article 20 as an act of state.

The High Court's decision was taken as a victory by the Baganda, although indeed it was not. However, *The Times*, the church representatives, and the Baganda delegates tried to transform the decision into a "new situation" in which both the Hancock recommendations and the return of the Kabaka could be discussed.

[47] His activities came to include peripheral but important concern with certain other parts of Uganda, such as Bunyoro.

[48] See *Uganda Protectorate, Buganda*, Cmd. 9320 (London: H.M.S.O., 1954).

[49] One of the consequences of the delegation's visit to London was consultation by Apolo Kironde, one of the members of the delegation, with legal experts in London. The legality of the deportation was challenged in the following fashion. The six nominees of the Kabaka in the Lukiko were to challenge the representative members as having taken their seats in the Lukiko unlawfully, since the Kabaka had been deported and his approval not obtained. Instead, the representative members had been approved by the regents. The case was filed by Kironde and two British lawyers, Kenneth Diplock and Dingle Foot, managed the case for the plaintiffs.

When the judgment was given, the word went out that the Governor had erred and that the Kabaka would be brought back. There was great jubilation, in spite of the fact that the judgment delivered was not a verdict but simply a recording of his view in the event that the case should go to a higher court. But of course the Baganda had won a moral victory. See *The Times*, London, Editorial, 5 November 1954.

It was not an easy matter. The British Cabinet had committed itself to ending the matter of the Kabaka and the decision to deport him was called "irrevocable." Chiefs in Buganda, as well as assistant residents, had been told to declare forthright to the Baganda that the decision was final, instructing the Baganda to go on about their affairs and elect a new Kabaka. A number of senior chiefs, convinced of the finality of the decision, did as they were told. Senior government officials gave assurance that there would be no point in pressing for the return of the Kabaka.[50]

In the end, however, it was decided that the best course for Buganda was a settlement involving the return of the Kabaka, regardless of the effect on field staff and administrators. The government refused to follow an authoritative decision to the end if it lacked wisdom. Paving the way for a return of the Kabaka, the Hancock Committee had produced a new situation in which not only constitutional questions but the matter of the Kabaka's return could usefully be discussed.

With this end in view the committee examined the political claims of Buganda. The conflicts which had been darkening the relationships between the Buganda and Protectorate governments were now subjected to an intensive review.[51]

The committee representing the Lukiko at the discussions contained three major elements. There was a strong Catholic contingent, including Matayo Mugwanya, the Omulamuzi; J. Kiwanuka, the Bishop of Masaka; Father Masagazi, a leading Catholic saza chief. E. M. K. Mulira and T. A. K. Makumbi, who had been on the first delegation to London (and whose wife was the sister of Mulira), were both associated with moderate nationalist politics. A. K. Kironde and J. Luyambazi-Zake were lawyers. The former became an Assistant Minister of Social Services and the latter, having been legal advisor to Mengo

[50] As well, there were Baganda who felt that the deportation was a good thing. Their numbers were few, however. Nor were many as outspoken on the subject as Kawalya Kagwa, the ex-Katikiro whose advice on the matter was sought by senior government officials.

[51] Hancock assumed that his terms of reference were "to attempt a thorough tidying up of the constitutional system of Buganda both as regards its internal structure and the distribution of powers, and also as regards the position of the Baganda as a constituent part of the Protectorate." See *The Times,* London, 6 May 1954.

and later a legal advisor of the All-Uganda Party, became a leading figure in the Uganda National Congress.[52]

Others on the Buganda Constitutional Committee were J. Kasule; Y. K. Lule, who subsequently became Minister of Rural Development; E. B. Kalibala, who had been an employee of the United Nations Secretariat; and E. Z. Kibuka, the Secretary.

The Namirembe Conference was a most remarkable affair. Meeting under the chairmanship of Sir Keith Hancock, the four main issues discussed were as follows:

1. *Responsibility versus interference.* It was the position of the Protectorate government that it had certain responsibilities for the country as a whole. It was the position of the Baganda that they had never been conquered and therefore could, as a right, return to the pre-1900 Agreement status if they wanted. Further, they had a right to make their own mistakes without the constant surveillance and attentions of the Resident and the Protectorate government.

2. *Buganda autonomy versus the construction of a primarily African Uganda state.* The arguments for the preservation of autonomy were again raised, including the idea that Buganda should not be made to pay for the advancement of other parts of the country. The federal solution to the problem was regarded as unacceptable to the Protectorate government because federalism compartmentalized and built fences around the various groupings.[53]

3. *The role of the Kabaka as an active political leader or as a constitutional monarch.* There were efforts to safeguard the position of the Kabaka. The Baganda were concerned over his return and his prestige. The Protectorate government was anxious to provide him with a strongly symbolic but nonfunctional position, that is, as a constitutional monarch. Since the circumstances of the deportation had put the Kabaka in the position of claiming to be democratic, the Baganda could not oppose the constitutional democracy proposals, and since the government had been accused

[52] Zake split with the U.N.C. in 1956, becoming one of the founders of the United Congress Party. He has since been completing postgraduate studies in anthropology, first at the University of Chicago and then Northwestern University in the United States.

[53] It is of some note that the Protectorate government did everything in its power to promote unity in Uganda. Although the perennial cry "divide and rule" has been levied against the British in Uganda, as elsewhere, if it were to apply at all, the charge could be more appropriately directed against the Baganda.

of making the Kabaka an autocratic figure, the position had to be clarified. No one accepted the view that the Kabaka *should* have autocratic powers.[54]

4. *Participation by the Baganda in Legislative Council.* The view was expressed that the Legislative Council was primarily composed of aliens who owed their allegiances elsewhere than Uganda. Participation would require an elective legislature.[55] Gradually, through hard discussion and debate, both Baganda and British came to understand that while it would be impossible to separate Buganda from the future of the country as a whole, certainly Buganda had a right to certain defined fields of operation. These and other issues were worked out during the negotiations between the Baganda and the Governor.

In the end the agreed recommendations included the following: The conduct of the Kabaka's government should be the responsibility of the ministers acting in the name of the Kabaka. Each minister would be responsible for the affairs of his department. The 1953 reforms for enlarging the number of ministers were reaffirmed. The principle of ministerial responsibility to the Lukiko was established. The office of Speaker of the Lukiko was set up. An Appointments Board was established to be headed by a chairman who would hold office by virtue of his appointment as Permanent Secretary to the Katikiro; the board would be responsible for decisions regarding the appointment, promotion, transfer, dismissal, and disciplinary control of all public officers including saza chiefs.

It was made a requirement that a solemn engagement to be bound by the articles would be the precondition for recognition of the Kabaka as ruler of the Buganda Kingdom.

With respect to the Protectorate government, the Resident would function to advise and assist the Kabaka's government and act as an information mechanism advising both governments of the other's views. For departmental matters consultative committees, on which representatives of the Protectorate government would sit, would enable the Protectorate to advise on education,

[54] Indeed, in readily agreeing that the Kabaka should be a constitutional monarch, some leaders, notably Mulira, came to be regarded as suspect by many neo-traditionalists.

[55] Indeed, there were some Baganda who felt that until that time a "fence" should be built around Buganda to safeguard her position.

medical and health questions, natural resources, local government, and community development.

In cases of disagreement between the two governments, a consultative committee under the chairmanship of the Governor would work to resolve disagreement.

Local government reform in Buganda was stated as an objective, and local authorities for the administration of the Kibuga and other townships would be examined with the object of bringing them under the Buganda government. No review of the constitutional arrangements would be contemplated until 1961.[56]

The tone of the meetings was quiet. The Baganda awaited the results of their discussions with their customary dignity. The Uganda National Congress launched a boycott against European and Asian goods which, successful for about a month, petered out.[57]

The Court case put the status of the Namirembe recommendations in doubt. The Baganda felt that if the recommendations were to be acceptable, this had yet to be determined by a committee of the Lukiko. Under the Mukwenda's direction the Kintu Committee was set up to examine the Namirembe recommendations and give its evaluation to the Lukiko.[58]

The Kintu Committee made changes of some political significance. They recommended that local government in Buganda be untouched for the time being. They did not want to upset the balance and internal structure of a system which for the first time they could control and which they understood. They recommended that procedure over clan and succession cases remain undetermined until after the Kabaka returned. This was a con-

[56] See *Agreed Recommendations of the Namirembe Conference* (Entebbe: G.P., 1954), and *Explanatory Memorandum issued by the Namirembe Conference* (Entebbe: G.P., 1954).

[57] The Congress originally was against the Hancock Commission and preferred a Royal Commission, although they eventually accepted the Hancock mission. In late October the suggestion by the Secretary of the Labour Party, Morgan Phillips, that a Freedom Day be held by dependent peoples throughout the world, stimulated the Uganda National Congress to hold a rally. They marched through Kampala carrying banners saying "Uganda for Africans Only," "Bring our Kabaka Back," and "We demand a democratic African Central Assembly to Replace the Legislative Council." See *The Times*, London, 1 November 1954.

[58] It was feared that the Kintu Committee would repudiate the Namirembe recommendations. Indeed, there is some evidence that at first the committee had come to the conclusion that a very different formula had to be found. Under the guidance of Kenneth Diplock, their English legal advisor, a compromise was found in which relatively minor changes were made.

cession to the Bataka, who felt that any alteration in the pattern of clan affairs had to be undertaken only in consultation with Sabataka. Finally, they suggested a system of direct elections to the Lukiko.[59]

Meanwhile, sentiment grew that acceptance of the reforms must be clearly dependent on the return of the Kabaka. The Lukiko decided that since the Kabaka's banishment had not, in their view, been legal, it was not proper to decide constitutional reform until the issue of the Kabaka's return had been settled. They demanded that the Kabaka be returned *first*, and constitutional matters settled afterwards. A letter putting these views forward was sent to the Secretary of State for Colonies.

Accordingly, when the time came to discuss matters with Her Majesty's government, two delegations were sent to London from Buganda. The first delegation was concerned with implementing the reforms through discussion with the Colonial Secretary and others. On May 9, 1955, the Lukiko voted 77 to 8 (with one abstention) to accept the report of its constitutional subcommittee. The delegation then left for London to plead for an early return of the Kabaka and implement the Namirembe recommendations, representing the Lukiko drafting committee (consisting of Baganda who had been members of either the Namirembe or Kintu Committees).[60]

The second delegation representing the Lukiko was sent out to the U.K.[61] A strategy was worked out so that the solemn under-

[59] See *The Report of the Sub-Committee of the Lukiko* which was set up to examine the *Recommendations Made by the Hancock Committee* (Kintu Committee Report) (Entebbe: White Fathers Printing Press, pp. 39-43). Members of the Kintu Committee were M. Kintu, Chairman, R. K. Kasule, Y. M. Kyazze, M. K. Wamala, J. K. Masagazi, Prince Badru Kakunguru, E. B. Kalibala, A. Kalule Sempa, C. M. S. Mukasa, Secretary, S. J. L. Zake, Official Translator.

Kintu, it might be noted, became Katikiro and in that capacity rejected direct elections which he himself had originally suggested.

[60] The first delegation consisted of Kintu, Sempa, Kasule, Zake, Masagazi, and Mukasa. Assisting them was the solicitor who had participated in the court case, Kenneth Diplock. Much of their discussion in London with the Colonial Secretary and Colonial Office officials was terminological, based on the genuine confusion which remained about the exact status of the government of Buganda. For example, it was not clear whether the term cabinet, council, or ministry was appropriate for denoting the government of His Highness, the Kabaka. Issues which had been discussed previously came up again, such as the question of assistant residents at Masaka and Mubende. In addition, there were questions about how the new Agreement should be signed.

[61] The second delegation consisted of the Omuwanika, the Nalinya, the Sebwana, Kasule, Wamala, and Makumbi.

taking, or declaration, which would make the new Agreement binding would be signed by the Kabaka upon his return to Buganda. The Kabaka's representatives would sign it earlier in order to have it come into force provisionally. By the time a third delegation, representing the Uganda National Congress, had arrived in London, matters were well on their way to a conclusion.

Meanwhile, the U.N.C. added to the confusion by raising the issue of multiracial government. The party distributed a printed questionnaire to serve as a mandate for claims to immediate self-government for Uganda.[62] "Discussion is urgent in view of the questionnaire held throughout the country," read the telegram they sent to the Secretary of State.

With reform of the central government having been tied to the Namirembe recommendations, the Uganda National Congress used the crisis in Buganda to attack communalism, multiracialism, and limitations on self-government. Their concern remained, as it had begun, Uganda-wide, but they had to work closely with the Lukiko and the Buganda government in order to be effective. Indeed, it was during the last stages of negotiations that the Congress achieved its maximum support from the Buganda government and Lukiko. And it was widely regarded as safeguarding public interests with respect to the problems of reform of the central government.[63]

[62] The questionnaire items were as follows: 1. Do you want Uganda to have self-government now? 2. Do you want the report about constitutional reforms in Buganda and Uganda to which the Lukiko may agree to be implemented before the Kabaka returns? 3. Would you like to see Uganda federated with Kenya and Tanganyika? 4. Are you in favor of a Legislative Council that contains Europeans and Indians representing their communities?

[63] Appendix B of the Agreed Recommendations of the Namirembe Conference affirmed the aim of building the Protectorate into a self-governing state with the government of the country mainly in the hands of Africans when self-government should eventually come. This statement the Uganda National Congress regarded as far too vague. They wanted a timetable and guarantees that "mainly" in the hands of Africans should mean an African government.

They were fearful of other proposed reforms. The Governor had suggested the establishment of a ministerial system with seven ministries for members of the public, of which five would be reserved for Africans. These would sit on the government side of the Legislative Council. Obviously, of course, this meant multiracial government which the U.N.C. opposed. "We are demanding a federal form of government now," they stated. "We cannot accept minority safeguards . . . it is our belief to attain democracy in which there will be no discrimination whatsoever and we strongly oppose the holding of political right by aliens." *The Daily Mail*, March 14, 1955.

A Namirembe proposal of the Governor's which gave the U.N.C. its greatest opportunity was a provision that, with the agreement of the Lukiko, "Buganda should participate fully in the Legislative Council through members elected by whatever method is decided to be appropriate. . . ." With participation forthcoming, the recommendation was "that the number of representative members from Buganda should be increased from three to five." In order to make this possible, the European and Asian representative members of the Council stated their willingness each to give up one of their seats, the two members concerned transferring to the government side of the Council on what was then the cross-bench.[64] For the first time, Congress saw an opportunity to enter the Legislative Council.[65]

What were some of the consequences of the new proposals? The most important long-run consequence was that the Kabaka legally became a constitutional monarch. Second, the chiefs became directly responsible to the Buganda government.[66] Third, the control over appointments was vested in an Appointments Board. Appointments of chiefs and of permanent secretaries to ministers would be made by the Kabaka on the recommendation of the Buganda Appointments Board.[67] Fourth, the position of the Kabaka and the Agreement itself were linked to the continued participation of the Baganda in the institutions of central government.

Whatever the actual points at issue, the Protectorate government was out to preserve and maintain the principle of a national government of which Buganda would be a privileged but clearly subordinate part. The Baganda, finding no alternative, reluctantly agreed to participate in the central legislature. But they

[64] *H.E. The Governor's Statement on Constitutional Development in Uganda* (Entebbe: G.P., 1954).

[65] Furthermore, since this would increase the government side of the Council from 28 to 30 members, a corresponding increase in the representative side would be accounted for by African representation. The cross-bench would disappear.

[66] One of the bitterest demands, abolition of the assistant residents, was not accepted by Her Majesty's government, but the assistant residents were put clearly in an advisory position only.

[67] After the Kabaka returned it was a common complaint that he ran the Appointments Board. In discussion with certain members of the Board, and with others in the Buganda government, this was justified on grounds that the recommendations of the Buganda Appointments Board are not binding upon the Kabaka and that the Kabaka can, in the last analysis, select those chiefs whom he wants since that is his historic right as a Kabaka.

privately avowed that the constitutional future would remain undetermined.

Each side made concessions. The Buganda government was modernized, provided with staff, and expanded. The Buganda government's control over the chiefs and other officials was strengthened. The representative principle established for the Lukiko was now combined with the principle of a constitutional monarchy. Congress saw the results as a complete overhaul of political institutions and an immediate move toward self-government.[68]

In a climate of wild rejoicing the Kabaka returned in triumph. The whole of Buganda was decorated with victory arches. The Ismaili Khoja community, the Indian Association, and the various African groups put up commemorative arches. For the Governor of Uganda it was a personal triumph which few would recognize. The reforms which for so long had been impossible to achieve appeared now to have been accomplished. The Baganda appeared to accept the principle of constitutional monarchy; it was only later, when they came to understand its implications, that they protested bitterly. Representative government remained to be achieved. Nevertheless much had been accomplished.

[68] Several important members of the Lukiko who were involved in the issues of constitutional reform and the return of the Kabaka worked closely with the Uganda National Congress. In collaboration with Congress leaders, the Buganda government decided that the Lukiko should accept the proposed constitutional changes, ensure the Kabaka's return, and then leave the attainment of self-government to the political parties.

CHAPTER 14

POLITICAL PARTIES IN UGANDA: THE SEARCH
FOR LEADERSHIP AND SOLIDARITY

ONE OF THE MAJOR DIFFERENCES between the ordinary political
party in the West and those in new countries is that rarely do
the former challenge the legitimacy of the system as a whole. Quite
the contrary, they act so as to minimize the disaffiliation of the
members of the system. In the effort to press important issues and
accumulate votes, the sore points of conflict tend to be remedied
by political parties whose leadership is engaged in a never-ending
scrutiny of public attitudes to find those issues to which catering
is vital. Thus conflict is a source of strength in democracy. Free
and open conflict identifies those sources of grievance which most
need to be rendered sanguine.

In such systems, information is as easily available as is freedom.
Political parties are in an important sense seekers after information. If they are concerned with controlling government through
popular support, failures in their communications with the public
or their unwillingness to act on the strength of that information
can lead to loss of political office. Just as the market mechanism
tends to register consumer preferences, so the voting mechanism
reveals political preferences.[1]

In colonial territories and in those nations that are trying to
achieve goals for which the public is not immediately prepared to
sacrifice voluntarily, political parties play a somewhat different
role. They need to do more than capture power: they need to
establish with the authorities their right to supplant the colonial
oligarchy. This is the organizational phase. It is, in many respects,
a phase similar to that of trade union organizing. The party
speaks in the name of a particularly aggrieved group. The leadership requires discipline from the members. At the same time, it
cannot use violence without incurring deportation, rustication,
or jail.

---

[1] See D. E. Apter, "Nationalism, Government, and Economic Growth," in *Economic Development and Cultural Change*, January 1959.

Just as we may speak of mobilization, consociational, and modernizing autocracy types of regimes, so we may use these concepts to refer to political party structure. Thus the Democratic Party of Guinea is a mobilization type of party within a mobilization type of state, while the Tanganyika African National Union is a consociational type of party within a consociational regime.

One way to achieve organizational strength is to find a leader who speaks for all and seems to identify with the common interest, while widely regarded as a person with special powers of foresight and ability which border on the mystical. Such a leader, if he can hold in his hands the power of moral propriety over others, is indeed powerful. Then the party receives voluntary public following.[2]

If such a system is to maintain itself, however, then the party must eventually take more coercive steps to keep its support. Such highly personal leadership cannot long survive on the basis of a purely voluntary following. What follows after independence is what we have termed the *mobilization* type of regime. The party takes over the state. Valid distinctions between party and state tend to disappear. The mobilization approach uses the party as the punitive arm of the state and directs the public toward the goals established. Such a system may not necessarily be "totalitarian" but it is by no means free. The real costs are in terms of information. Party leaders lose the knowledge and strength which comes from competitive party politics, often having to rely on a more expensive approach, coercion, in order to maintain a public following. Very often such systems turn into popular autocracies in which public enthusiasm is expressed for an autocratic ruler who identifies himself with the public.

The special advantage of the *modernizing autocracy* is that as long as the public accepts the legitimacy of the system of rule, then the control problem in change is minimized. Modernization and development, for example, do not unleash a whole new variety of solidary groupings now unwilling to accept authority. Coercion

---

[2] The rather commonplace view of African politics as more "personal" than elsewhere derives from this. New leadership *roles* require considerable symbolic and personal characteristics if they are to become legitimized.

is kept at a minimum and the public well understands its system of government and is pleased with it.

It is the shift from the modernizing autocracy to something different which is exceedingly troublesome, for it means the withdrawal of the public from the traditional forms of legitimacy and political values to something new.

The third system, the *consociational* type, of which we spoke in Chapter 1, most closely approximates the Western condition of competition between political parties. If there is cant and hypocrisy among them, as is a common charge, there is also compromise and agreement that the rules of party competition will continue to prevail. Very often, political parties in Africa begin as mobilization types and in the effort to seek a wider affiliation and association are transformed to the consociational type. Their leaders form a collective leadership with others from other regions or countries, trying to produce some larger supraterritorial grouping.[3] It is not clear that the political party which is internally consociational is best able to be consociational in its external relations. For the consociational type is limited by the recurrent majorities of its members, and these may be difficult to persuade to cooperate externally.

Consociational types of political parties have begun to emerge in Uganda. None of the leaders had the personal characteristics to weld a mass following which would include not only Baganda but people from elsewhere. Indeed, the only political parties to gain a following from areas other than Buganda were the Uganda National Congress and the Democratic Party, with its predominantly Catholic membership.[4]

Just as federalism seems the more likely form of government to bring together the diverse territorial and political groupings in Uganda, so the consociational party system seems to be the only basis for bringing together a diverse membership. Ethnic parochialism has made it more difficult for those in favor of the more militant and disciplined party to become more successful. Indeed,

[3] Examples are Mali Federation and Nigeria.

[4] Today the Uganda National Congress has lost most of its following in Buganda and retains some of its strength in the north, particularly Acholi. Some of the leaders who would like to start a new party find that the northern members refuse to change the name and are reluctant to go into a new party.

federalism or a consociational national system and competitive but localized parties have affinities with one another.[5]

The consociational type of system has been successful in organizing supranational associations in some areas. Some of the former French West African political parties have been able to achieve this, most notably the Rassemblement Democratique Africainé; and there have been propensities in this direction by the Action Group in western Nigeria. Nevertheless, it is true to say that the consociational type is given to fracture unless (1) it is built on a federal polity or (2) has an unusually strong base of consensus in society.

In Uganda the curious situation prevails where the consociational type has not yet been successful and efforts to build one of the mobilization type have been met with the competition of the modernizing autocracy in the form of an African government. *Thus the nationalism of the Buganda government, with its traditionalistic leadership in modernizing guise, has challenged both the mobilization approach and the consociational type in conflicts over legitimacy.* In order for one form of leadership to supplant another, more is required than a simple shift in allegiance from one to the other. Necessary is a disaffiliation from certain beliefs and institutions to the acceptance of new ones. As long as the Baganda see little to gain from changing their own system of government, the modernizing autocracy, they will not be easily persuaded to accept the new leadership of a mobilization party. Thus the failure of the Uganda National Congress which attempted to become a mobilization party under its former Secretary General, Cambridge-educated Abu Mayanja.[6]

[5] The single mass party is best suited for the first stage of political organization, namely the organizing phase.

[6] Political parties must compete for a source of legitimacy with the Buganda government, whose claim to legitimacy is historic. The legitimacy factor and the solidary factor which in West Africa came to inhere in the new cross-cutting units of the mass political movement (the Convention People's Party) have until now been retained within Buganda. In that sense, as we have indicated earlier, Buganda and its government acted much like a nationalist political party with respect to the Protectorate government. But whereas a political party needs to capture government and use it to provide the jobs, sinecures, and benefits which membership in the party promises, Buganda as a political party could provide all these within its own framework. Thus in its dual aspect of "party" and local government, Buganda was indeed in a strong position.

Traditional solidary association was reinforced by tangible benefits allocated by the Buganda government. It did not have to capture power from the Pro-

On the other hand, increasing pressure against the Buganda government to supplant the principle of autocratic rule by the representative principle has been causing that government consternation. Rarely indeed is the transition from autocratic to constitutional monarchy a smooth one.

Hence the awkwardness about public attachments to political parties. In a system in which the system of legitimacy remains based on traditionalized hierarchy, and where the representative principle continues to be viewed as threatening, not only is it difficult to establish the mobilization type of party on a mass basis, but the consociational type, normally given to fracture and recombination, is even more prone to this weakness.[7]

Consociational parties remain hampered by the need to compromise both in their internal structure ("confederal" in type, in which the branches are not without ethnic significance) and in their relationship to the center (they must come out for a federal system of government). The consociational party urgently requires the central level of government as the major scene of its operations. It needs direct elections and political responsibility. Because of its internal organization it has propensities to federalism. It cannot offend the various ethnic groupings which it seeks to incorporate in its membership. It requires the representative warrant of legitimacy in central government, as do all nationalist organizations everywhere. However, under present circumstances it finds it impossible to capture a monopoly of nationalism, which all parties share not only with one another but with the Buganda government. In their efforts to organize, and in presenting important issues, the parties have provided the two oligarchies, the Buganda and Protectorate governments, with maximum information (one of the functions of political parties

---

tectorate government as a nationalist party would have to do—but it had to wring from the Protectorate concessions and benefits which it could allocate to loyal Baganda. This helped dissuade Baganda from entering political parties which were all-Uganda in nature, and since the Baganda were the most educated and economically successful people in Uganda, a party not relying upon them was more or less doomed from the start.

[7] The Buganda government is actually under pressure to accept the representative principle at two levels. Within Buganda there is increased demand for direct elections to the Lukiko. Outside Buganda both political parties and the Protectorate government urge support for general elections on a common roll for the Legislative Council.

in representative democracies) without reaping the full benefits of participation in or control over either government.

Indeed, it is only recently that political parties have become distinguished from other types of voluntary associations in Uganda. As we have indicated, elsewhere in Africa the earmark of a nationalist political party is the special claim to legitimacy which it makes. Such parties often find it difficult to adjust to a constitutional framework after self-government is achieved, for they must then relinquish their monopoly of legitimacy; legitimacy then becomes a property of government itself and special claims to express the rights of the public are shared with other parties. Such difficulties are common in new nations. Sometimes the exclusiveness of the mobilization type of party breaks down into a multitude of competing political factions, as was true in Indonesia.[8] Sometimes the party becomes merged with the state itself, as in the case of Guinea and Ghana.

In Uganda these problems are not yet apparent. The most powerful and well-organized grouping remains Buganda, which functions like a regional political party vis-à-vis others, its clientele based on ethnicity. Although, as we have seen, in some parts of Buganda almost half the population comes from Ruanda or Urundi and from the north, these are not, for purposes of Buganda government politics, members of the political community, although some of them are becoming absorbed and will soon be indistinguishable for political purposes from the Baganda. Nevertheless, ethnicity is a fact of political life. Politicians have stubbed their toes on the district and on Buganda government units which have retained their characteristics as the crucial solidary groupings to which people belong. Only the Catholic political groups have been able to call upon people's loyalties to lessen the effects of ethnicity, and they are in a stronger position than the other groups to build a mass party of the consociational type.

We argued that in the early days of nationalist politics in a country the parties have some of the characteristics of a trade union. There is another distinction. Political parties in colonial territories cannot be simply casual aggregates of men joined

---

[8] See Herbert Feith, *The Wilopo Cabinet, 1952-1953; a Turning Point in Post-Revolutionary Indonesia* (Cornell: Modern Indonesia Project, 1958).

together for electing candidates to political office. Parties need to be new solidary groupings which cut across the old ones if political parties are not simply to reflect the ethnic lines and cleavages in the society at large. In this they need both a cause and an ideology. Both are singularly lacking in Uganda.[9]

Handicaps for Political Leaders

Uganda is still a combination of a cash crop agricultural system and a subsistence system. There has been no effort to shift completely to a cash crop agricultural pattern, hence the unifying effects of a marketing system in cotton and coffee are offset by the basic "food-stuff" orientation of the farmer. This tends to reinforce his conservatism, his concern for the security of land, and his fear of following political leaders. His sense of grievance over marketing and cash crops is thus vitiated by his security in land. This makes recruitment difficult.

Lack of urbanization tends to perpetuate the characteristics of traditional Kiganda society, favoring serious attention to the Buganda government rather than to political parties. Parties find latent support everywhere, but support which in practice has been more or less ephemeral, waxing in periods of crisis and waning afterward. There is not the phenomenon (so common in western Europe) of a depressed rural peasantry forced off the land by rural poverty. For example, in Austria in 1848 peasants were forced into an urban environment, but because industrialization was at a low level urban employment was also scarce. This helped produce an urban revolutionary group. Such a situation is lacking in Uganda. Thus even in Katwe and some of the African slums around Kampala there is very little political ideology.

Lack of ideology means that the political forces in Uganda lack the moral fervor and conviction necessary for mobilization parties. Internal bargaining and competition for power resulting in suspicion of one another's motives is an important character-

---

[9] The more usual social cement, the rallying around those demanding self-government, has been vitiated by two factors. The first is that everyone knows self-government will come in the near future and no one gets very exercised about the need to demand it. Second, and related to the first, the more pertinent question is, self-government for whom? With the Buganda government demanding self-government for Buganda, and the parties demanding it for the country as a whole, people remain confused about the issues.

istic.[10] In this respect, the parties suffer internally from the same pattern of bureaucratic "in-fighting" that was characteristic of the Kabaka's court for many generations and is today the "style" of politics in Uganda.

The political parties in Uganda are thus caught in a dilemma— a dilemma which can be solved only if the Buganda government and the Kabaka become regarded not as the center of nationalism and the leaders of a political party of their own, but as a set of archaic and anachronistic interests. Only if it appears that the Buganda system is itself a barrier to progress (which is by no means clearly the case because of the long tradition of instrumental and adaptive traditionalism which co-opted modernity itself) can this situation alter.

Moreover, until recently there was no system of direct elections to serve as an object of nationalist activity. It remained difficult for political parties to achieve more than nominal support.

In this regard, it is important to note that the 1956 decision to put through direct elections in the country was perhaps the main punctuation mark in the development of political parties. *Since political parties in Uganda could not pre-empt the right to identify and control legitimacy, their only alternative was to become parties of representation.* In other words, unlike the movements of West Africa,[11] the parties in Uganda began to develop more like those in Western representative government. For this they needed (a) increased representation in the Legislative Council and (b) direct elections. Attacking the second of these objectives, the Buganda government boycotted elections. As in the past, they took no interest whatsoever in Legislative Council.

The condition today is a most interesting one. There is no visible decline in the monopoly over legitimacy maintained successfully by the Buganda government nationalists for many years. This was manifested in the Buganda refusal to participate in direct elections. However, there is a latent decline in the monopoly, and one which will become more manifest as Kenya and Tanganyika proceed rapidly toward self-government (and the old fears of

[10] Thus in one of the more recent splits in the Uganda National Congress, it was charged that an expelled leader appropriated the party funds.

[11] Which were mainly mobilization types, intensely ideological, seeking to monopolize legitimacy as part of the struggle for self-government.

white settlers become of less concern). As both Kenya and Tanganyika have political nationalists whose points of view are East African and indeed continental, the nationalism of the Buganda government and of the Kabaka looks more and more archaic and xenophobic to many younger Baganda.

The main points which need to be borne in mind in analyzing political parties in Uganda are as follows: Because they could not serve as symbols of legitimacy, they remained relatively unideological and unprogrammatic. They began to emerge as parties of representation before genuine representation was possible. This has been true even within Buganda, where, despite a remarkable difference between, for example, the political party composition of the 1955 and 1959 Lukikos, it is still the chiefs who prevail. It could also have been true with respect to elections to the Legislative Council, except that the Baganda refused to participate, much to the chagrin of at least one major political party, the Uganda National Congress.

In the main we can identify three major efforts at political party development.

First are such organizations as the Uganda Labour Party, the Uganda National Movement, the Uganda People's Party, the Democratic Party, the Progressive Party, and the Uganda National Congress. All of these were similar in at least one major respect—they sought to become national parties. Most remained largely limited in membership to Buganda. Only two, the Uganda National Congress and the Democratic Party, were successful in gaining sizeable numbers of adherents outside Buganda. The U.N.C. was successful in Busoga, Toro, and in Bugisu and Bukedi, that is, in non-Buganda Bantu areas, and also in certain strongly Nilotic districts, such as Acholi and Lango. Indeed, in the latter instance the U.N.C. was strong enough so that at the first sitting of the newly-elected district council meeting in Lango in 1956, a motion for self-government for Uganda was passed. The Democratic Party has been fairly successful in recruiting non-Baganda and this has been because of its overwhelmingly Catholic membership. In spite of this, however, the main membership and leadership of the Democratic Party, as in the other parties listed, remain from Buganda.

A second important group is composed of the openly Buganda

parties. The All-Buganda Party and the Bannansi B'omu Buganda are of this type. Both are Buganda nationalist parties looking toward separation of Buganda from the rest of the country.

The third group consists of the Bataka Party. In a real sense this was not a political party but came closest to being a political movement within Buganda. In addition, it pressed strong claims to legitimacy by emphasizing its links with traditional features of Kiganda society. The Bataka Party was the closest to a solidary political grouping in contemporary Buganda. Controlled by people who were poorly educated and unversed in contemporary party politics, the Party was less successful than it might have been. Considerable support from the same sources characterized the Bataka Party and (after the B.P. was banned) the new Uganda National Congress which started two years later. This was particularly the case among those who had been in the Federation of Partnerships and the Bataka Party at the same time.

Although it is not our purpose to go into the rather melancholy history of the political parties of Uganda, we shall discuss the structure and objects of several of the most important.

The Uganda National Congress[12]

The Federation

For some time the most important political party, and the first of its kind, was the Uganda National Congress. Let us consider the circumstances surrounding its establishment.

The founding of the Uganda National Congress is predated by the Uganda African Farmers' Union which, banned after the 1949 disturbances, emerged again under the name of the Federation of

[12] It is impossible to acknowledge all the help received from many quarters in trying to piece together the organization and structure of the Uganda National Congress. I am heavily in debt to Neil Ascherson who did extensive work on the Federation of Partnerships and the Uganda National Congress. I. K. Musazi was very helpful in discussing the background and organization of the Congress which at the time he headed. Others who helped to interpret the meaning of day-to-day events were Erisa Kironde, whose assistance and scholarly approach to an organization to which he himself was then committed, proved invaluable; Senteza Kajubi and J. Sengendo Zake for discussions on the foundation and activities of Congress and the United Congress Party. Information on the activities of the Federation was supplied by Joseph Sonko and Diana Noakes. None of these people are responsible for the views expressed here.

Partnerships of Uganda African Farmers (F.P.U.A.F.). The "partners" registered at the Registry of Companies and Business Names were twenty "farmers." They included I. K. Musazi, Peter Sonko, George Lwanga, Erieza Bwete, and others who were prominent in the 1949 riots, Bataka, or in the Uganda African Farmers' Union.[13]

Having obtained the interest of such important people as Fenner Brockway and the support of the Congress of Peoples Against Imperialism, Musazi felt that the good will abroad compensated for the Protectorate government's official coldness and dislike. In its early stages the Federation was assisted by European cooperators suggested by Brockway.

The Federation had been associated with politics from the start. The Uganda African Farmers' Union, which had itself begun in association with the Bantu Growers' Association, had been organized around 50 small groups with main headquarters in Mengo and Masaka. Each of these growers' groups had a president and a secretary. The same units were used in the Federation of Partnerships after the Farmers' Union was launched. For each 10 to 20 groups a headquarters was set up. The two main organizers of the Masaka district were Joseph and Peter Sonko, while Musazi and George Lwanga controlled the organization as a whole from Mengo. The Masaka group later broke with Musazi and retained its character of a true cooperative.[14]

Operations of the Federation were not very well organized. "Each cooperative group of the federation (from ten to two hundred members in a group) collected their own crops and had their own officers and set of books. These groups in turn formed what was called a 'headquarters' consisting of from twenty to thirty groups. These headquarters formed a District, also with another set of officers and books. All of these records and transactions were checked and supervised by the central office of the federation. The directors of the federation carried on the supervision in the

[13] The F.P.U.A.F. was never very successful. From 1950 until its bankruptcy in 1955, it achieved a deficiency of almost £35,000.

[14] The Masaka group was reorganized by Diana Noakes, who had been urged to go to Uganda by Fenner Brockway to assist Musazi in his efforts. Increasingly dismayed at Musazi's easy confusion between Federation purposes and political needs, especially in matters of finance, she helped found Abalimi Ltd., a new African cooperative movement in Masaka.

fields. . . ."[15] A few of those who were elected officers in the field were tribal or clan leaders.

Federation formed the backbone of the Uganda National Congress. The Congress system of branches and regions was much the same as the headquarters and districts of the Federation. And the same structure of participation—branch meetings, resolutions, delegates, conferences—was carried over from Federation. In many cases even the dates of meetings were the same.

In some areas the Congress and Federation personnel were one and the same. Out of a list of ten district directors of the Federation in 1952, five were organizers or presidents of the corresponding Congress region.

Nevertheless, many in the Federation were afraid of getting involved in politics. They did not join the Uganda National Congress when it was founded. Through Federation there was some overlap in the ranks of Bataka Party sympathizers who became Congress supporters after the Bataka Party had been banned. However, no link or even relationship existed between Bataka and Congress. The latter was regarded as essentially modern and contemporary, the former old-fashioned. Some of the top leaders who, like Musazi, were identified in one capacity or another with the Bataka or the Sons of Kintu, were hardly Bataka zealots. Only two of the top leaders (Lwanga and Sonko) had been important members of the Bataka Party. In the branches the Bataka were often regarded with suspicion or embarrassment.

The relationship between Federation and Congress remained extremely close, with Musazi as President General of the latter. When a young American, George Shepherd, was hired as Manager of the Federation, it became possible for Musazi to devote more time to the organization of Congress. Shepherd thought that the political aspect of the cooperative movement in Uganda was important because of the obstacles facing African cooperative efforts and the perpetual hostility of the Protectorate government. In a letter of October 14, addressed to Fenner Brockway, Shepherd wrote, "Right now we need to hold some kind of joint demonstration of the Congress and the Federation to show the Government our growing strength, and I think this growing strength is a de-

[15] See the interesting account of the work of the Federation in Shepherd, *They Wait in Darkness* (New York: John Day, 1955), pp. 55-56.

cisive factor in our bargaining power."[16] Hence the economic arm and the political arm were considered essential and interrelated.

There are two conflicting views about the origins of the Congress itself. Musazi claims to have thought up the basic idea of Congress while in London. Others assert that it was actually the joint product of Fenner Brockway, I. K. Musazi, George Padmore, and Abu Mayanja (at the time a student at Makerere College who, having been expelled from there, was sent to Cambridge).[17]

The Congress

The first important meeting of Congress was held on March 2, 1952. Later, I. K. Musazi and Abu Mayanja held a press conference at the African Editors' Club in Mengo. They explained the aims of Congress and pointed out that the Congress would be open to all citizens of Uganda regardless of color. At the second meeting of Congress, called on Van Riebeek's Day, April 6, invitations were sent out to the editor of the *Uganda Herald*, the Mayor of Kampala, and several other Europeans and Asians. The meeting was held at the Old Budonian Club, the organizational headquarters of the United Budonians. Only one European turned up for the meeting, Mr. Handley Bird, a long-time resident of Buganda and a member of the Legislative Council who subsequently became a member of the Executive Council.[18]

Despite the interracial beginnings of Congress, no Europeans

[16] Shepherd to Brockway, October 14, 1952 (from Federation of Uganda African Farmers' files).

[17] There is evidence that John Stonehouse, now a Labour M.P. who replaced Shepherd as an employee of the Federation, was instrumental in having convinced Musazi to begin Federation in the first instance and Congress in the second.

[18] The Uganda National Congress was founded officially on March 2, 1952. The meeting at which it was established consisted of about 20 people in Aggrey Memorial School, Mengo. The first general meeting of the Congress was timed to coincide with Van Riebeek's Day, April 6, when the nonwhite people of South Africa launched their protests against the policies of the Malan Government. At the meeting resolutions were passed calling on Malan to resign and calling upon the British government not to force federation against the express wishes of the people of Central Africa.

In its original pronouncement, Congress described itself as follows: "The Uganda National Congress is an organization which seeks to remove the economic, political, and educational stains in the Protectorate so that Uganda can become a peaceful, self governing nation. Its main objects are: (1) Unification of all tribes in Uganda, (2) Self-government in Uganda, (3) Placing the control of Uganda's economy in the hands of the people of Uganda, (4) Promotion of universal education." (The Uganda National Congress, unpub. mimeo., n.d.)

or Asians registered as members and it became a purely African movement. In a reorganization of Federation shortly thereafter, the following words were added in ink before the directors' signatures: "No shares will be allotted to any person who is not of pure African descent, or to any company or corporation of which all the members or shareholders are not of similar descent." After that, while the matter of the interracial membership of U.N.C. was never decided, attempts by several Asians and Europeans to become members were not successful, Congress taking the line that until the question of citizenship was decided, the nature of non-African membership would remain ambiguous.

Congress was from the start a part of the general ferment of nationalism which was developing in many parts of British Africa and encouraged in London by such pan-Africanists as George Padmore. Congress leaders met with African leaders in London and drifted in and out of association with those who earlier had been a part of the West African Secretariat.[19]

Contacts in England continued to be maintained. Letters were exchanged with the Prime Minister of Ghana, the Secretary General of the African National Congress in Johannesburg, the Kenya African Union, and the Tanganyika African Association.[20] A conference was sought to exchange information and coordinate activities in East Africa. Nothing came of this idea, partly because of the outbreak of Mau Mau, but the idea of an all-African Conference was much discussed. It was even suggested that it be held in Accra or the Sudan. (Such a meeting was not to be held until 1958.) As one of its first "international acts," Congress sent Musazi and E. M. K. Mulira to the Rangoon Socialist Conference where they met Africans from other parts of Africa and Asian Socialists.

Thus the origins of Congress were generally socialist in their orientation, cosmopolitan, and interracial. It was part of a larger ferment which was increasingly to engulf Africa.

Socialist ideals and fraternalism did not serve as a useful rally-

[19] For a discussion of nationalism at the London end, see G. Padmore, *Pan-Africanism or Communism?* (London: Dobson, 1956). See also J. S. Coleman, *Nigeria, Background to Nationalism* (Berkeley: University of California Press, 1958).
[20] Which subsequently became T.A.N.U.

ing ground in Buganda. Baganda in particular were not much interested in the cosmopolitan origins of Congress, nor were they happy about the interracial quality of its objectives. Congress soon found itself embroiled over local matters and local concerns.

Actual organization of Congress was relatively rapid. The first organizing committees, which included members from Teso, Toro, Lango, and the main parts of Buganda, were replaced by an Executive Committee. The two most important founders were Musazi and Mayanja. Mayanja was the more extreme of the two and on occasion indicated that if force was necessary to achieve independence then force would be used. Musazi limited himself to statements of nonviolent noncooperation. The old Congress followed Musazi's lead on this line.

The Secretary General of the Congress was Dr. E. Muwazi, a Muganda medical practitioner. He had been at King's College, Budo, then Makerere and the Royal Hospital, Wolverhampton, for his medical training. Returning, he was posted to Mulago Hospital until 1952 when he went into private practice. He was much exercised over discriminatory pay scales for African doctors in the hospital in Uganda. The Treasurer General was S. E. Lukabi, a Muganda who was also the accountant for the Federation of Uganda African Partnerships. Other officers included journalists and lawyers, one of whom, A. K. Kironde, subsequently became an Assistant Minister for Social Services in the Uganda Government and a member of the Legislative Council. The leaders' average age was about 38 years, some being extremely young at the time.

The structure of the Uganda National Congress in practice and as laid down in the constitution was by no means the same.[21]

Three major organizational features were important at the

[21] The constitution took its aims and objects almost verbatim from the Convention People's Party constitution, including self-government, the establishment of a democratic socialist society, a federal government, trade unions and similar organizations, the reconstruction of a better Uganda, the promotion of political, social, and economic emancipation of the people, establishment of equal opportunity and elimination of capitalist exploitation. As well, the Congress sought to work with other nationalist, democratic, and socialist movements in Africa and other constituents with a view to "abolishing imperialism, colonialism, racialism, and all forms of national and racial oppression and economic inequality among nations, races and peoples and to support all action for world peace." (Constitution of the Uganda National Congress, unpub. mimeo., n.d.)

national level. The plenary body was the Annual Delegates' Conference. Delegates from each constituency (county) were elected. National officers of the party were ex officio members. The Conference laid down the general program and policy of the party and considered the support of the treasurer and elected members of the National Executive Council, including youth representatives, constituency representatives, and women's organization representatives. In addition, the National Executive co-opted the General Secretary, National Treasurer, and National Propaganda Secretary who were ex officio members; members of the Central Committee (20) were also ex officio members.

The Annual Delegates' Conference, unlike the case in Ghana, was not very smoothly organized. It functioned as a genuine public forum. Different factions in the leadership attempted to pack it. Several efforts to capture control of the A.D.C. resulted in a splintering of the Uganda National Congress.

The second major grouping was the National Executive Council. This organ was in theory to carry out the directives of the Delegates' Conference. It met once every three months, and when not in session its functions were vested in the third major grouping, the Central Committee. The Central Committee varied a good deal in size and was irregular and somewhat informal in membership. It constituted the central organ of the Uganda National Congress. Central Committee meetings were weekly and took place in Katwe, close to the rival Progressive Party headquarters.[22]

The decision-making core of the Uganda National Congress was the Central Committee of the National Executive.[23] The "directorate" of the National Executive Council, as the Central Committee was referred to in the Constitution of the U.N.C., was responsible to the Annual Delegates' Conference. This was in fact the case, with the A.D.C. exercising crucial power. A major split in 1957 resulted from an effort by those in the Central Committee who followed Musazi and those who opposed him. In Musazi's

[22] For a time the U.N.C. headquarters were in the dispensary of Dr. Muwazi, then in a room above the Progressive Party headquarters, and finally in a suite of offices in Katwe not far from other party organizations. The other members of the Central Committee lived close by and Katwe itself with its close-knit and packed living and working quarters for Africans was the main center of African nationalist activity. Not far from the office of the U.N.C. are various vernacular newspapers. And Katwe is not far from Mengo and the Kabaka's court.

[23] See Clause III under Central Committee title, p. 4, Constitution of the Uganda National Congress.

effort to pack the Delegates' Conference, the anti-Musazi followers withdrew to form the United Congress Party.[24]

In addition to being the directorate of the party, the Central Committee was closely associated with the parliamentary party, serving as the main disciplinary forum and tribunal within the party. The Committee had approximately 20 members.[25] At first, the leadership was a mixture of fairly middle-aged old-line politicians, such as Musazi, Dr. Kununka, Dr. Muwazi, and J. W. Kiwanuka; there was also a small "Katwe" contingent of traders and very young, highly educated teachers, such as Senteza Kajubi and Erisa Kironde.[26] Kajubi and Kironde represented the most enlightened wing of the nationalist groups in Uganda, the former having done postgraduate work at the University of Chicago and the latter having read English literature and anthropology at Cambridge.

Over 50 per cent of the Central Committee were ex-Makerere[27] and 70 per cent were old Budonians. Of those who had spent considerable time abroad, 35 per cent had taken degrees at major universities in England or the United States or had successfully completed professional training in law or medicine.

As with the branch chairmen (and the membership), the Central Committee was overwhelmingly Protestant (75 per cent), with only 1 "relapsed" Muslim, 2 "relapsed Catholics," and 1 practicing Catholic.[28]

Only 3 of the Committee members worked full-time in politics. Of the rest, 5 were shopkeepers and traders, 2 were clerks, 2 were lawyers, 4 were journalists or newspaper editors, 2 were school masters, and 1 was a student abroad.

[24] This split drew away from Congress many of the younger U.N.C. intellectuals as well as important members of the Central Committee, such as Dr. Muwazi and Joseph Sengendo Zake. Subsequently, Muwazi lost the support of the Annual Delegates' Conference and was himself expelled from the U.N.C.

[25] Material supplied here was derived from personal interviews in an unpublished survey done for the East African Institute of Social Research by Neil Ascherson and from materials in the files of the Institute. The Central Committee is of July 1958; its composition was subsequently altered.

[26] For a time, Kironde was Acting Secretary General of the Uganda National Congress.

[27] This includes old Makerere as well as new, i.e. Makerere as postsecondary and a university college providing for the London External Degree.

[28] Unlike the case of eastern Nigeria and northern Ghana, there was no interest in the Moral Rearmament movement. Only one member of the Central Committee flirted with M.R.A. for a time.

A high proportion of the members either had land or were related by marriage or descent to important families in Buganda. Only 3 of the Committee's total membership were not from Buganda: 1 was Munyoro, 1 Musoga, and the third had a Seychellese father but a Muganda mother.

Thus the top leadership of the Uganda National Congress was overwhelmingly ethnically parochial. It was primarily Kiganda, Protestant, and not merely comparatively well educated but from the best educational institutions the country had to offer. The chief specific grievance of these people resulted from differences in treatment of Africans in the Civil Service, which included government medical officers and Europeans.[29]

Regional organization followed somewhat the same organizational pattern as the center. Regional officers were appointed, according to region, by the National Executive members; hence patronage within the party could be locally based but centrally controlled. Other field organizations, such as the constituency party organization, were to be found in the constitution as guides for the future rather than as real units of the party.

The branch was the crucial organizational unit of the party.[30]

[29] This was a very serious concern. For example, for the post of Education Officer the discrepancy between an Indian Education Officer and an African Education Officer was initially £395 per year, although African salaries rose proportionately to Asians'. Salary discrepancies existed for most grades of Civil Service. See *Report of the Commission on the Civil Services of the East African Territories and the East Africa High Commission* (London: Eyre & Spottiswoode, 1954), Vol. I.

[30] There were efforts to emulate other features of the Convention People's Party organizational structure. The inner party organization was composed of a National Secretariat consisting of the General Secretary, National Treasurer, and National Propaganda Secretary. This was the managing arm of the Central Committee and related the branch to the central organization.

There was a women's section and a party youth league (founded, it is said, on the efforts of John Stonehouse, who was subsequently attacked by the U.N.C. for dishonest activities and who served as a scapegoat for the financial deficiencies of the Federation). Neither of these organs proved successful, although for a time the dynamic leadership of the youth league appeared to have potentialities.

Although desired, the party had no publishing organs. Thus friendly editors such as J. W. Kiwanuka, although they might be regarded by some as unreliable and personally unsatisfactory, nevertheless were able to keep themselves in important party positions. Kiwanuka, for example, pre-empted the leadership of the party when Musazi was in U.K., was forced to relinquish it, resigned from the party, returned to it and the Central Committee, and has been able to move in and about almost at will. When strong opposition to him arose because of tactical errors (for example, when voting for mailo distribution which would have benefited both himself and other successful leaders in Buganda as a member of the

At this level the most peculiar problems of organization in contemporary politics demonstrated themselves. It is perhaps useful,
therefore, to indicate the structure and activities of several
branches.

The branches varied considerably in number. The proportion
of dues-paying branch members was invariably small, but the
number of sympathizers in an area was generally great. As indicated earlier, many of the branches had their origins in the
Federation of African Partnerships. When the Federation went
bankrupt it was widely held that the government had forced it
out of business and taken the money which belonged to the participating growers. Thus the stigma of financial loss was borne by the
Protectorate government, not the Federation, and did not result
in withdrawal of support from the U.N.C.

In contrast to the Bataka Party, where the basic unit of organization was the miruka, the Congress branch overlapped both
miruka and gombolola jurisdictions. A powerful branch of the
Congress might affect an entire county.[31]

The typical branch consisted of a roster of "leading members."
These were almost always subbranch leaders, that is, activists in
more remote areas. They ranged in age from young, confident,
and truculent youths to more resentful and suspicious middle-aged
traders. Almost all important branch members were farmer-
traders, that is, people with both occupations.

Several general objectives seemed to unite them. They wanted
elective chieftaincy. They were loyal to the Kabaka (at least in
theory). Strong rural membership attachment to the Kabaka
acted as a brake on the Katwe group, making the Central Committee cautious about attacking the Mengo hierarchy. Wanting
Buganda to be a constitutional monarchy, they were still quite
vague about what that meant. On the question of federalism there
was widespread confusion. Many Congress followers believed that
federalism meant simply self-government. There was considerable
sentiment for restricting citizenship to Africans when the time

---

Lukiko), he went against the policy position of the U.N.C. and had to lie low for
a time. He emerged triumphant after returning from the Annual Delegates' Conference and helping to expel Musazi from the U.N.C.

[31] Organizational work remained weak, however. Congress could not count on
working through the "natural" organizations which were devoted to purely local
affairs.

came. Aims of Congressmen interviewed rarely went beyond general agreement with those expressed on the membership card of Congress, and their understanding of these was not very explicit.[32]

What was the typical branch headquarters? The actual center of operations was often the house of a prominent farmer who was a Mutongole and served as a "patron" to the branch. Behind the "patron" there was usually a more "conniving" political person, most often a small shopkeeper with a duka adjacent to several Indian dukas. On the whole, the "conniver" was financially less successful than the Indian, devoting less time to his shop.[33] While on good terms with the Indian, he disliked him heartily. The "conniver" typically had a small plot of land in addition to his shop on which he produced his own subsistence foods, particularly banana and some small amounts of coffee and cotton. He frequently had to go to Kampala on business. There he met with top Central Committee leaders in Katwe. From such contacts he would derive much local importance and strength. He would make himself known to Musazi and others. The top leadership depended in no small way upon the "conniver" for news of what went on in the general area and in the branch. Information was not always

[32] In English the card reads, "1. Unity for Uganda under African Federal Government; 2. Universal suffrage under a Common Roll for all CITIZENS; 3. Self-government at an early date; 4. African control of economy of Uganda; 5. Education, Health and Justice for all."

[33] In one area, the "conniver's" small shop served as the official post office; there most of the people in the area received their mail. A sign of importance and petty officialdom, it brought almost anyone who was important enough to receive mail into the shop, making it a branch headquarters. It is interesting that most local post offices were in Indian dukas, not African; this created further anti-Asian feeling.

In another area the proprietor of a local beer hall served the same purpose. Because of the financial success of many of these halls and the gregariousness and pleasure associated with them, the proprietors were quite often of the conniving sort, buying their way into favor with visiting party officials by gifts of beer and cigarettes and by the information they possessed. Equally important to the "connivers" were the substantial "citizens." Sometimes these were "defrocked" catechists or relapsed Catholics who had substantial land holdings but were now barred from easy association with Catholics. Others were "progressive" farmers who, more or less unsuccessful, still retained their lands while they lost their money. Still others were gombolola chiefs (the ex-miruka chiefs tended more toward Bataka) who were perhaps demoted but were still in official capacities, angry at the saza chief and bitter against the government. Some were retired railway employees and clerks; others who were literate had plots of land and careers of minor prominence.

Whatever their backgrounds, the "connivers" played an extremely important part in party life.

forthcoming from the regional propaganda secretaries and organizing secretaries whose job was to maintain liaison between the branch and the center.

Meanwhile, the "conniver" would return to his branch with sometimes real and sometimes fictional or embroidered information from the inner party councils, which gave him an importance and prestige in the branch.

Each branch had a chairman who kept in close touch with affairs at the center. On the whole, the branch chairmen were the most crucial figures in determining the success or failure of the branches. Most of them were semiprofessional politicians. That is, politics was an extremely important preoccupation which, had it been financially possible, would have involved all their energies. The chairmen were extremely young, averaging 32 years in age. They were overwhelmingly Protestant: approximately 74 per cent were Protestant, 18 per cent Catholic, and less than 1 per cent Muslim. Approximately 70 per cent had completed all or a substantial portion of their junior secondary school work. However, only a small proportion had gone to the outstanding public schools, King's College, Budo, or Kisubi.

All Protestant branch leaders from Acholi had been to Gulu High School, which was a center of nationalist activity in Acholi (and is identified with the C.M.S.). One branch leader was a Makerere student and several had been at Makerere College before it had become a degree-granting institution.

Occupationally, about 16 per cent of the chairmen regarded themselves as professional politicians, that is, earned their livelihood as branch chairmen—a surprisingly large figure. The largest proportion were traders (34 per cent), with farmers running closely behind (29 per cent). Surprising as well, compared with West African nationalism, almost no teachers were among the branch chairmen of the Uganda National Congress.[34]

Quite a number of the branch chairmen had "slipped" in social position. For example, 30 per cent were sons of chiefs, clergymen, and teachers. Of the fathers who had been chiefs, 2 were saza chiefs and the rest gombolola chiefs. Thus some downward mobility

[34] At the time those teachers who were politically active were in the teachers' union which, under the influence of T. Makumbi, tended to favor the now defunct Progressive Party.

existed among the sons. Another group, however, was clearly up-wardly mobile. Approximately 40 per cent of the fathers were farmers, while the proportion of sons in trade was much higher.[35]

Ethnically, the backgrounds of the chairmen illustrated the overwhelming preponderance of Baganda, with 50 per cent being Baganda, 11 per cent from Lango, 9 per cent from Acholi, and 7 per cent from Busoga and Teso.[36]

Among the chairmen there was a great consciousness of learn-ing and a craving for social and economic betterment. Almost all of them indicated that their concern with their own betterment was wrapped up in a generalized desire for advancement for the country as a whole. Or, to phrase the matter a bit differently, a large proportion demonstrated that they believed their own disap-pointments and frustrated ambitions were the lot of Africans generally. They regarded themselves as examples of what should not happen in the future. Hence they demanded self-government in order to make it possible to improve their own condition and the condition of people everywhere.

What distinguished them in this respect from others in society? They were extremely status conscious, taking status liabilities as a personal affront. They were testing the legitimate limits of be-havior by acting in the role of politicians. They were acutely aware of the limitations on social mobility. Not educated or sophisticated enough to become higher functionaries of the party, they were nevertheless important in their communities through their office. They were particularly sensitive to the grievances of others through their own heightened sense of grievance.[37]

They also reflected a peculiarity in the educational structure of

[35] When queried on social position, the chairmen gave ambiguous responses. Some seemed to feel that the move from farmer to trader was actually downward mobility. This is indirectly confirmed by the great number of replies to an item asking what they hoped their next job would be. A large number of traders indi-cated that they hoped they would be farmers.

[36] The proportions of chairmen do not adequately reflect proportions of member-ship. Busoga has a very large region, but the branches are extremely loyal and it is unnecessary to give much prominence to their branch chairmen. A higher pro-portion of branch chairmen (and branches) is given to Acholi and Lango, because they represent important Nilotic potentials, hence offices are multiplied and pres-tige provided as an incentive for recruitment and expansion.

[37] As an interesting sidelight, all of the chairmen save one were ethnically "pure," i.e. both parents were of the same ethnic background, although clan back-ground proved thoroughly heterogeneous.

Uganda. A relatively high proportion of those with some junior secondary education were in the equivalent position of the Standard VI "boys" in Nigeria and Ghana. They were too well educated to be content with minor clerkships. They had either not inherited land or were unwilling to engage in farming (mostly they were too young to have accumulated money to purchase land), and they were not educated enough to become teachers and clergymen. The problem can be rephrased as follows. Raising the number of people at the junior secondary level of education produced a dissatisfied group. These were aware of the great gulf between themselves and graduates of senior secondary schools.

This group was victimized by limitations in the school system. A tendency of "cut-off" at the junior secondary level resulted from the fact that many of the mission and government schools are widely distributed and easily accessible junior secondary schools. To continue with senior secondary education often entails leaving one's area and going to another place—an expensive affair.[38] Both the costs and the more difficult curriculum tended to reinforce the cut-off point of education at the end of junior secondary school. One can expect, then, a continuous flow of political leaders at the junior level, full of grievance, conscious of their position, and just well educated enough to provide modern and efficient party organization.[39]

The branch chairmen were not only organizationally important in the Uganda National Congress. They also helped to shape its character. With such a high proportion of them in trade, they were in constant competition with Asians. This gave middle-rank party leaders a more pronounced anti-Asian bias than either the rank and file or the senior leadership. Almost all those in trade were acutely conscious of the Indians' trading abilities and almost

[38] There were about 60 junior secondary schools in 1955, excluding private secondary schools not receiving government grants, and only about 13 grant-aided senior secondary schools. About 17 per cent of those pupils who finish junior secondary I go on to senior secondary I, or 890 out of 5,339. See Susan Elkan, "Primary School Leavers in Uganda," *Comparative Education Review*, Vol. 4, No. 2, October 1960, p. 102.

[39] Material on social backgrounds was derived from a questionnaire administered to 40 branch chairmen of the Uganda National Congress, April 18-21, 1956. I wish to acknowledge my indebtedness to Mr. Erisa Kironde, formerly of King's College, Budo, and now in Makerere College, Department of Extra-Murals, for making it possible to administer this questionnaire.

universally antagonistic toward them. Several in interview singled out Asians as objects of special animosity. For them nationalism was to result in the elimination of the Asians as formidable competitors. Others, unwilling to put the matter so baldly, were preoccupied with achieving through commercial courses, loans, and special training a stronger competitive position.

If anti-Asian feeling was a negative element, more positively there was a strong desire for improvement. "I am very interested with politics and later I want to try a course of accountance," (*sic*) said one. Another, a former Director-at-large for the Federation, "would like to study political science." Still another indicated that he was "very much interested in politics, farming, and in reading books as a guide to self-government. In addition to that I am very much interested in reading the history of the neighboring and foreign countries, for example, India, how Nehru struggled for self-government, Gold Coast, how Kwame Nkrumah and his Party spread all over the country." A branch leader from Toro wrote that "for the wish of God I should like to carry on as a member of the Uganda National Congress." A Muganda whose English was not quite equal to the task indicated that he wanted "English books, commercial books and self bookkeeping, industry book, and general education book." Finally, there was the most common hope, "I want to become a farmer and I want self-government now."

The comments on the questionnaire invite several observations. There was, as we have indicated, the strong desire for self-improvement. A sense of enterprise and a desire to engage in commercial or business operations was common among many of them. These were potential entrepreneurs conscious of the fact that if they did undertake financial risks they would most likely be unsuccessful. Indeed, what was most important about them was that they envisaged themselves in the roles of successful businessmen and farmers. In both instances success would bring them not only stature but leadership. In a sense they would become the backbone of society, given half a chance. Having been barred from that, they became "political entrepreneurs," seeing their futures in terms of political activity. Not important enough to participate in the Buganda hierarchy, and unsuccessful in achieving high status in their occupations, most of them saw possibilities in political work. As two comments indicate: "I would like to have general studies as well as borrowing a lump sum of money to enlarge my business at a bigger scale"; and "Besides completing Secondary VI I did three other years of studies in Metaphysic, Logic in the Major Seminary of Kahofondo. I have not married yet because I wanted to study more, but no means of doing so—I am interested in Local Government Affairs."

In this regard, one difference between the branch leaders and the top leadership of the U.N.C. was that so few of the branch leaders were products of King's College, Budo, or Makerere, compared to the Central Committee where most of the top leaders, such as Musazi, were both old Budonians and Makerere graduates. They represented an "old Makerere" generation, in common with other political leaders and chiefs who had finished their education in the thirties. To the branch leaders the Central Committee represented an educational elite. It is not too much to say that the old school ties among the U.N.C. were, for the branch leaders, an object of envy and respect.

Outside of Buganda the branches tended to be more independently nationalist. In Mbale, for example, the branch was particularly anti-Asian. Mbale is in the main an Asian town and the sense of grievance against Asian shopkeepers was particularly intense.[40]

In Busoga the U.N.C. branches were often extensions of the earlier Bataka Party. There the Bataka represented something different from Buganda, since freehold land tenure had not been established and traditional chieftaincy in a sense remained. A hierarchy of government chiefs was superimposed upon the traditional system. Hence in many areas a dual hierarchy existed, with a traditional counterpart for every government chief. In the county of Bukoli, for example, there was a government saza chief and a traditional saza chief. The same pattern held all down the line. On some matters in Busoga it was necessary for the government saza chief to initiate a decision, have it go down the level of government chieftaincy and up the level of traditional chieftaincy

[40] Links with Buganda are strong. The famous Muganda chief Kakunguru led a branch of the Malakite movement there. Traditions of protest among the Baganda around Mbale remain. In addition, local conflicts in the Eastern Province have generally made almost any organizational excuse for venting grievance acceptable.

until finally approved by the traditional saza chief before the decision would be acted on.

Deeply concerned with matters of land, the Basoga members of Congress had connections with Congress that went back to the activities of the Federation. A considerable number of Bataka were either in Congress or regarded the younger groups within the organization itself as simply their "front men."[41] Thus the Katikiro to Wakoli, the traditional saza chief of Bukoli, was also a member of the African local government in Busoga and a member of the saza council and of a gombolola council. He also turned out to be one of the leading members of the local branch of the Uganda National Congress. The Congress officers were extremely deferential and obedient to him. Thus Congress appeared simply as the most recent of the organizations through which local claims could be put. Congress and Bataka were powerful enough to prevent Busoga from coming under the District Council Ordinance of 1955 because of their bitter opposition to the appointment of a chief who had been given a sazaship in spite of local opposition.[42]

In other areas Congress activity was even more purely local. In Bunyoro, for example, the leading Congress officer, Dr. Majugo, was the chief instigator of a "Young Turks" movement which led to a review of the constitutional position of the Omukama and resulted in a drastic reduction of his power.

In Toro, on the contrary, the local branch of the Uganda National Congress firmly allied itself with the Omukama of Toro and, forming a powerful group in the Rukurato, or district council, fought off efforts to reform Toro and make it conform to the pattern of other district governments.[43] Instead, a special subcommittee of the Rukurato was appointed, with a leading member of the Toro branch of the Uganda National Congress at its head.

[41] I am grateful to B. Taylor of the Department of Community Development who helped arrange interviews with the U.N.C. branch in Bukoli.

[42] The chief, William Mwangu, was an ex-Catholic schoolmaster who served for three years as the Secretary General of the Busoga African local government. He was defeated for re-election and the District Commissioner appointed him a county chief. He is widely regarded as a "government man."

[43] The District Councils Ordinance of 1955 was made to apply to all districts excluding Buganda. However, the African local governments had to accept the conditions laid down in the Ordinance or remain subject to the African Local Governments Ordinance of 1949. In the case of Toro, the effort to bring the Omukama into line with the 1955 Ordinance was unsuccessful. The ensuing constitutional conflicts have been prolonged and intense.

It was composed of well-known U.N.C. members, including the branch chairman, Felix K. Rwambarali. The object of the constitutional dispute was to achieve special status for Toro similar to that of Buganda. Related issues were the problem of lands allocated for game parks, which the Batoro complained provided more land for animals than for men, and shares in the various economic enterprises. The Toro government already received a share in such government operations as T.U.F.M.A.C., a fish marketing scheme, and from Kilembe, the copper mines in Toro. But Congress demanded a larger share.

In Toro, Congress was extremely successful on purely local matters. They fought for Toro autonomy on the one hand and self-government for Uganda on the other, but the latter was a less pressing concern. In return, they received the sympathy of the Omukama. They were financially well established enough to have their own vernacular newspaper, *Muzahura*.[44] Efforts of some Congress dissidents to start their own party, *Iraka Iva Toro* (The Voice of Toro party), were unsuccessful.

On the whole, the proposals of the Toro branch of Congress were relatively moderate with respect to constitutional reform for Uganda, so preoccupied were they with Toro constitutional development. Contenting themselves with a note that they were perturbed by the representation of the various sections of the community on the Legislative Council, the Toro members sought a strong majority of African unofficials.[45]

On the matter of Toro autonomy they were unmistakable. "It is our ardent wish that this matter of the relationship between Her Majesty's Government, and the Toro Government be fully settled. We feel very strongly opposed to much too much intervention of the Protectorate Government in our Internal Affairs. . . . We can never learn to govern ourselves unless we are actually governing, and making necessary mistakes in the process, and taking the consequences. . . ."[46]

This pattern of local concern was also characteristic of branches in other districts. In Acholi, for example, preoccupation with clan

---

[44] The newspaper was founded November 21, 1955.
[45] Memorandum on Constitutional Developments, and Reforms in the Government of Toro (unpub. mimeo., n.d.), p. 5.
[46] *Ibid.*, p. 2.

disputes was made even more compelling through the introduction of religious conflict. Almost every U.N.C. leader in Acholi was a Protestant who had been at Gulu, the C.M.S. High School. Acholi was also the headquarters of Catholic Action and a fairly well-run machine operated out of the Verona Fathers Mission just outside of Gulu. Religious and clan disputes as well as conflicts with the district officers made Acholi Congress politics almost purely local matters.[47]

The Uganda National Congress, itself part of the pattern of politics found in other Kiganda institutions, was more like a bureaucratic association and party of western Europe than a revolutionary or nationalist party. Its very top leadership was attuned to "bargaining" nationalism, that is, involved in games of tactic with the Protectorate government instead of in the West African pattern of "moral" nationalism in which ideologies were employed as they were suitable and grand strategy was the game. Indeed, Congress exemplified "bargaining" nationalism, a variant of the consociational type (with its chief characteristic a preoccupation with tactics and gaining concessions), in contrast to "moral" nationalism whose chief concern with strategy and preoccupation is with *legitimacy*, a characteristic of the mobilization type.

Several structural deficiencies of the Uganda National Congress can be noted. The leadership lacked a sense of role. Ambiguous about their part in leading the party, many of the Central Committee members drifted in and out more or less at will. Indeed, almost anyone who was reasonably important and lived in the vicinity of Katwe or Mengo, if he was well known to the top leadership of Musazi, Muwazi, and Kununka, could attend Central Committee meetings. For a time certain members of the Central Committee were not formally members of the Uganda National Congress.

Uncertainty about roles led to lack of conviction about the party. The leaders knew they would eventually get self-government in Uganda. They were torn by the desires to enlighten themselves in the problems they would encounter with self-government, and to actively proselytize. A great thirst for information and

47 The religious conflicts also expressed itself in Congress attacks on the member of Legislative Council from Acholi, who was a Catholic.

knowledge helped to reinforce both lack of conviction and confusion over what their right and proper roles should be.

Further, there was poor communication among branches, and from the branch to the central organization. In districts where branch solidarity was high, as in Busoga or Lango, the branch was organizationally almost autonomous.[48] Although Musazi spent considerable time touring the country, as did a few other high officials of Congress, he had neither the funds nor the transportation facilities for the organizational work necessary to link the branch with the center.

Except on the most general issues, then, the various Congress branches were neither concerned with the same problems nor aware that the views they established as Congress policy were often at variance with those of headquarters. Clearly lacking was reporting and information between branches and the center. Katwe and the Central Committee represented one organization. Each of the branches represented quite separate and local institutions. In turn, the Central Committee was composed of factions. The U.N.C. leaders, Musazi, Kiwanuka, Muwazi, and Kununka, were the inner circle, able to exclude the others on occasion and considered to have the final authority.

The biggest problem of Congress was that the leaders did not know how to treat government itself. Buganda was hostile to the central government, but central government was ultimately the only meaningful one for the U.N.C. The unpopular posts in the legislature which represented Buganda were filled by members of the Uganda National Congress. Yet this was not a way to achieve popularity so long as the Buganda government continued its official hostility to the Legislative Council. Indeed, there were those who considered that Congress, by participating in the Legislative Council, was betraying Buganda.

Privately, most Congress leaders felt they had to emancipate themselves from the political untouchability of the Kabaka and his government and to attack them both. Politically, after the Kabaka's return, such an attack was suicide. This ambivalence in Congress was reflected in the Central Committee between the more

---

[48] For example, in Busoga a primary concern was directed at forcing the government to grant a freehold land tenure system in Busoga, similar to the one that prevailed in Buganda.

traditionalist, older tradesman group, the moderate old national-ists like Musazi, and the younger, impatient, and aggressive leaders like Zake, the most traditional of the younger group, Kironde, and Mayanja.

Having played an important part in the return of the Kabaka, Congress found itself hamstrung by its inability to operate freely within the Buganda political scene. Increasingly there was estrangement between the Buganda government and the Congress leaders. As for leadership itself, Musazi was, in the words of one Congressman, "a nucleus not a leader." The same informant added, "He wants the movement to carry him, not him carry the movement." The only really permanent official of the party was the Organizing Secretary, Senkezi. The Central Committee itself was more like a discussion group. It could not take important decisions and follow them up.[49]

Congress policy controversies raged around the nature of the national government which should be established. Early in its history the U.N.C. had produced a very lengthy working docu-ment, which most members had never seen much less read; it pro-posed a constitution for Uganda which was a blend of American federalism and ministerial government. Provinces would constitute the separate states of the union. Each state would have its own constitution. It was a serious attempt by a few members of the Congress to think through the problems of constitutionalism. However, the document had no official status and was left to lan-guish in the files.[50]

Only a small proportion of the proposals agreed to at Central Committee meetings were carried out. As the Congress had neither the field staff nor the executive staff at the center, the main activities at the center were to consider finances and the planning of tactics. An action by government which aroused the ire of some

[48] For example, in Busoga a primary concern was directed at forcing the have U.N.C. fellowships. These were announced. However, no provision was made for financing them. Several letters requesting information about them had been written to the Central Committee and went unanswered. Some members of Con-gress charged the leaders with having simply initiated a "stunt" and the plan was becoming a political liability. Although in a subsequent Central Committee meeting concern over the problem was manifested, nothing was done.

[50] See Memorandum of the Uganda National Congress on Constitutional Re-forms in Uganda (unpub. mimeo., n.d.).

members of the Central Committee often gave rise to action taken in the name of Congress which was disavowed by other Congress leaders.[51]

Leadership was discontinuous. The relations of the Central Committee members to one another were part-time and heavily factionalized. The support of the branches was more or less negligible with respect to policy. The only long-range activity successfully carried out by Congress was within the framework and association of the Buganda government, during the campaign to bring about the return of the Kabaka. For the rest, Katwe was a center of intimate intrigue. Much of the decision-making took place over beer at Mengo Blue Gardens, a restaurant and dance hall in Katwe. Certain factions had their leads into the Kabaka's palace and Mengo.[52]

A growing problem for the Buganda government arose with respect to Congress representatives who had been elected to the Lukiko. In the past, party politics in the genuine sense of the term were unknown in the Lukiko. The situation began to change when one of the inner circle of the U.N.C., Joseph Kiwanuka, became elected as a representative member of the Lukiko from Busiro and it became known that other Lukiko members were supporters of the rival Progressive Party. This was a situation full of portents for the future and the Buganda government was quick to recognize it.[53] Kiwanuka's entry into the Lukiko was reported to have aroused concern because he considered the role of the representative member elected on a party ticket to be different from that of other representative members. "I am responsible to the party

[51] This pattern reflected the lack of policy agreement. In one Congress statement to the Press in 1956 attacking the Governor on the matter of direct elections, some Central Committee members were totally unaware that a policy statement had been made.

[52] For example, one of the Congressmen who was important in this respect was Bamuta. Bamuta had been involved, it will be recalled, in prewar efforts to establish Africans in trade, and had subsequently become close to the palace. As a member of the Legislative Council he was involved in government affairs. Too elderly to have much in the way of personal ambition, he was a useful senior to have in the outer councils of the U.N.C.

[53] The members of the Legislative Council from Buganda were U.N.C. leaders, and there had been a tacit understanding between Congress and the Buganda government that the former would participate in central politics while remaining aloof from Buganda politics. This was, of course, impossible for Congress to do.

because the people voted for me as a party man," said Kiwanuka, "and if there is a disagreement between me and the Busiro Saza Council, they will have to learn to accept the U.N.C. position."[54]

Although Kiwanuka actually went along with most of the measures introduced by the more orthodox supporters of the Buganda government, the irritant had been introduced. He had expressed the view, hitherto never voiced, that he was responsible to Congress and thereby to the people of Busiro because he had been elected as a member of Congress to the Great Lukiko.[55]

The most important result of the activities of the Uganda National Congress has been that party politics, though difficult to achieve on a mass scale and difficult to organize efficiently, have become a permanent feature of the landscape. If Congress was a sufficient threat to the Buganda government to make the latter hostile to party politics in general, it joined the issue between those whose activities were increasingly within the framework of party organization and those whose activities were within the government of the district or of Buganda. Katwe is the center for a new political focus which has its lines out toward the central legislature on the one hand and the Lukiko, district councils, and lower councils on the other.

The period of first Congress organization and development had its high point during the Kabaka crisis. The original pan-African focus virtually disappeared. Hampered by official antagonism, local parochialism, and conflict on the Central Committee, the old Congress under the leadership of Musazi can best be compared to the United Gold Coast Convention in Ghana or the Nigerian Democratic Party. The U.N.C. found wide support, but its actual dues-paying membership rarely went above 10,000.[56] Confused over tactics, unable to discover what line to take with the Kabaka, mainly Baganda in its following, the old Congress could never develop into a mass political movement.

[54] Personal interview with J. Kiwanuka, Masaka, May 30, 1956.

[55] In practice, the question of "responsibility to Congress" was never very strict, particularly in the case of Kiwanuka, whose actions were often unpredictable to his associates both within Congress and outside.

[56] This estimate was made by several Congress and other observers in Uganda. However, the party supporters were probably around 50,000 during the Kabaka's crisis, at which time Congress was able to raise large sums of money to help fight for the Kabaka's return.

By 1958 a new factor was to enter into politics. Just as West African political successes were instrumental in determining the future of Uganda as a primarily African state, with self-government as its object, so nationalist activity in Cairo and Accra began to have repercussions on the Central Committee. The U.N.C. attempted to become an arm of the pan-African movement, its original aspiration. This was to introduce a new factor, mobilization, into the politics of Uganda, quite different from the closer union issue and far more difficult for the Buganda government to cope with. Among certain of the leadership of the U.N.C. the limitations imposed by the tacit alliance with Buganda government could in the end only destroy Congress.

The final straw came when the Buganda Lukiko rejected direct elections. By so doing it also rejected the rationale for the Uganda National Congress. A resolution passed by the Lukiko stated that "political parties are new in this country, and they have never been officially recognized in Buganda, and as the policy to be followed is as given in the agreements, the Governor is instructed to negotiate with the Lukiko on anything which affects the Constitution of Buganda."[57] This was in effect an instruction to the Protectorate government that on any important issue the views put forward by political parties were to be ignored.

Meanwhile, other important issues had been shaping up. Dissatisfaction with top leadership among some of the younger and best-educated members, along with antagonism to Musazi, promoted one split that resulted in formation of the United Congress Party. A year later, a Congress member, having been sent down from Makerere, went to Cairo as "foreign secretary of the Uganda National Congress." A Cairo office of the U.N.C. was opened under the auspices of John Kale.[58] It produced programs in Swahili and Luganda which were broadcast by radio Cairo.

The Cairo office issue became symptomatic of the crisis in the Uganda National Congress. Either it was to remain a party of tactics or become a party of strategy, that is, a "moral" nationalist movement of the mobilization type, striking out firmly for a united Uganda and attacking the parochialism of the Lukiko and Bu-

[57] *Uganda Argus*, March 21, 1958.
[58] John Kale or Kalekezi (or Kalisa) was a Muchiga. He was later killed in an airplane crash while returning to Cairo from Moscow.

ganda. The consociational view was held by Musazi. He suspended the U.N.C.'s six most important officials who favored the Cairo office and the mobilization approach: J. W. Kiwanuka, the Chairman, B. Kununka, the Secretary General, E. Otema Alimade, the Permanent Secretary, Abu Mayanja, the London representative who with Musazi had founded Congress, John Kale, the Cairo representative, and Mr. Paulo Sengendo, the President of the Youth Organization.[59] The Central Committee group supporting the Cairo office was thus eliminated, or so it seemed.

Refusing to accept the expulsion, Kiwanuka claimed that the Cairo office was already recognized. Regarding it as essentially the same as the London office, he announced plans to open a New York office. Meanwhile, Mayanja, Kiwanuka, and Kununka were among those who attended the Pan-African People's Conference in Accra. They participated in the resolutions which said that "those African traditional institutions whether political, social, or economic which have clearly shown their reactionary character and their sordid support for colonialism be condemned."[60] Returning from Accra via Cairo, Kiwanuka defended the Cairo office and identified the issue at stake: "Uganda cannot remain an island in a sea of Pan-African and universal nationalism. . . . Our establishment of a nationalist political office in Cairo has marked a great era in our struggle.

"It has broken the chains of isolation, and focused world attention on the seriousness of the Uganda people in our unshakable upsurge to freedom."[61]

Matters came quickly to a head. On January 12, 1959, the old Congress ended. At an Annual Delegates' Conference, the President of the Uganda National Congress, I. K. Musazi, was expelled. The Conference elected a new Central Committee, with Kiwanuka

[59] In announcing their expulsion, Musazi indicated that he would never trade the imperialism of one country for that of another, especially a country that had for 2,500 years controlled the whole Nile valley, and that the group expelled had no sense of discipline. Musazi also felt that the Cairo office had Communist backing. The reply of the expelled members was that constitutionally Musazi did not have the powers to suspend members without the central executive having approved it. Technically they were correct.

[60] All African People's Conference, *Resolution on Tribalism, Religious Separatism and Traditional Institutions*, Vol. I, No. 4 (Accra: Conference Secretariat, December 1958).

[61] *Uganda Argus*, January 10, 1959.

as Chairman. It went on to approve all the resolutions taken at the Accra Conference. Congress had now entered the pan-African phase of nationalism.[62]

The question was whether or not the branches and the public would see the importance of the new Congress perspective. Taking a line clearly opposed to the Lukiko, Congress sought Buganda's participation in direct elections in 1958. At the same time they asked that the Kabaka's government be given internal autonomy and be styled a state government. This was in line with the federal principle advocated by Congress. However, it was the only concession made to Buganda.

In their election manifesto for the first direct elections in Uganda, the Congress called for 120 electoral constituencies in the country. Successful candidates would fight for all the people of Uganda, regardless of color. In a foreboding statement, the manifesto pledged the Congress to a fight against anything short of democracy. Neither autocracy nor feudalism would be tolerated. If the Buganda government had laid down the gauntlet to the political parties, it was the U.N.C. which had picked it up. In accepting the challenge, the U.N.C. and the Buganda government had elected opposite directions. Congress pressed for an all-Uganda nation.[63] It was Congress which suffered defeat. In

[62] Two notes may be of some interest here. They deal with the two founders of the Uganda National Congress, Mayanja and Musazi. Each illustrates the position they have come to occupy. Abu Mayanja charged the Buganda government with having supported statements calling for the expulsion of Baganda joining political parties; he labeled as sabotage the refusal of the Lukiko to support direct elections. He was answered in an "official" letter by the Secretary to the Buganda electoral college, the body which had refused to elect new members to the Legislative Council to replace certain of those who had resigned. The Secretary warned Mayanja and his "army" that "neither his imaginary force of 'intellectuals' nor any other earthly power or mission will drive Baganda into the present Legco blindfold—nature, history and heaven will not permit such wanton forces." (See letter from Cyprian K. Kawoya in the *Uganda Argus*, March 21, 1958.)

The second matter concerns Musazi. Attempting to hold a political meeting he was drowned out by rival party loudspeakers and greeted with a shower of eggs. Distributing leaflets which were headed "Say No! to Communism," Musazi had invited Barbara Saben, a leading European representative member of the Legislative Council, and R. Mehta, the President of the Indian Association, to speak on the same platform. The answer of the crowds were insults to Musazi and shouts of "Musazi is a traitor" and "Musazi is selling Africa to the Europeans and Asians."

Both Musazi and Mayanja neatly illustrate the predicament of party politics in Uganda.

[63] The party has since split again. Kiwanuka was expelled after allegedly receiv-

the end, Mayanja, its former Secretary General, was expelled from the U.N.C. and, with Milton Obote, merged his U.N.C. faction with the U.P.U. to form the Uganda People's Conference. The Uganda National Congress ceased to be a political force.

The United Congress Party

If Congress without Musazi became for a time an important political factor in Uganda, "Young Turks" who split off from Musazi at an earlier stage were unsuccessful from the start. The United Congress Party was unable to capture the branches of the U.N.C., and found itself in many of the same difficulties of the old Congress group. The United Congress Party split off from the Central Committee partly for ideological reasons and because of laxness in organization and use of funds in the Congress. The leaders of the United Congress Party included the most dynamic elements in the original Uganda National Congress group.[64] It is noteworthy that all the Protestant members were from King's College, Budo, at least six having gone on to higher education at Makerere and elsewhere. The United Congress Party chose to take the line of the Buganda government, not without grave misgivings. As a result they fought against the participation of Buganda in direct elections. One of their members, Dr. E. Muwazi, won a seat in the Lukiko as a representative member.[65]

By and large their own members lacked faith and purpose. They found themselves in much the same position as the old

---

ing funds for the party from Moscow, but retained for his faction the UNC name. He became Chairman of the UNC splinter group, with Dr. Kununka as Secretary General.

[64] Among the leaders of the break-away group were David Lubogo, who became President General, Joseph Zake, who owned the newspaper *Mambya Esaze* (The Dawn), Godfrey Binaisa, Secretary General, Dr. Muwazi, who was the former Secretary General of the U.N.C., Erisa Kironde, one of the most thoughtful and sophisticated of the younger group, and Senteza Kajubi, one of the most brilliant of the younger group; he subsequently became a member of the Democratic Party. Of the 14 members composing the senior leadership of U.N.C., 4 were lawyers, 3 were journalists, 2 were shopkeepers in Katwe, 1 was an accountant, 1 a medical practitioner, 2 were teachers at Budo, and 2 had been salaried employees of the Uganda National Congress, 1 of whom was also a journalist (and was included in the above number of journalists). Their average age was 35 years. All were Protestants except 4 Catholics, 2 of whom regarded themselves as relapsed.

[65] From Sesse.

Congress, except that they lacked the field organization which Congress had built up since Federation days.

The Progressive Party

The Progressive Party was formed in January 1955. Where the Congress group was more populist and egalitarian, the Progressive Party was a party of the "weightier part." It sought to make up in the influence and prestige of its membership what it lacked in popular following. Important members of the Lukiko, African businessmen of some distinction, the leader of the Uganda Teachers' Association, and others who had been on various public bodies, township authorities, school boards, and church organizations made up the founders' group. It was enlightened and conservative in the immediate political sense, with a puritanical strain running through it. Many of the leaders had come together in a constructive effort, trying to think through immediate and practical reforms for Buganda. The party of the responsible and leading citizens, it included among its founders several women, the wife of the Rural Dean of Bulemezi, two sisters of Mulira as well as his wife.

The President of the Progressive Party was a remarkable man. Quiet, dignified, and courageous, he subsequently became an important figure in Buganda politics. He was a crucial figure on the Lukiko delegation negotiating for the return of the Kabaka and a member of the Buganda Constitutional Committee, playing a key role during the Kabaka crisis. Loyal to the Kabaka but sturdily independent in putting forth his views of propriety, E. M. K. Mulira deserves more credit than he has received.

Once the Kabaka had returned, the Progressive Party and Mulira in particular became unpopular with the Buganda government and the Kintu government of Buganda turned against him. Fighting against inequitable allocation of 154 square miles (which the Lukiko was preparing to accord to those who had been important in bringing home the Kabaka), Mulira was expelled from the Lukiko and charged in court with disrespect to the Kabaka. Eventually his conviction was repealed, but he was prevented from taking his seat in the Lukiko for well over a year because of this.

His firmness and consistency had won him a steady, if small, following. Clerks and minor officials of the Buganda government and more substantial citizens tended to think very highly of him. The owner of *Uganda Empya*, Mulira would not fire the editor of his own newspaper when the latter dissented from Progressive Party views.[66]

For a long time, the Progressive Party was the only one with a sizeable representation in the Lukiko. Twelve actual members and about 20 sympathizers made up the Lukiko representation. Among the regular members was the President of the unofficial representatives organization in the Lukiko. Total membership of the party in 1956 was approximately 1,400. Its plenary body of 39 members consisted of 21 landlords and businessmen, 2 farmers, 1 newspaper proprietor, 9 teachers, 2 full-time party leaders, 2 housewives, 1 doctor, and 1 lawyer. The Central Committee of the Progressive Party included committees for rural life, education, natural resources, trade and commerce, land, legal affairs, health, women's organizations, markets, information, and organization. The plenary body contained 2 Muslims and 2 Roman Catholics; all the rest were Protestants.

Curiously enough, the Buganda government which proved to be so antagonistic to the Progressive Party failed to realize that it might have been their strongest ally. The members were those with moderate views but with a strong stake in Buganda and its government. They were not sympathetic to the chiefs, however, and the Buganda government which formed at the time of the Kabaka's return was largely a chiefs' government, that is, Buganda bureaucrats whose lives had been spent in government service. Many of them had been associated with the Wamala faction and were both populist and conservative. In the Progressive Party they saw the more modern and democratic versions of Sir Apolo, Nsibirwa, and other progressive chiefs who had been so unpopular. These prestige-bearing people, successful and independent of the Mengo hierarchy, were both envied and disliked. A substantial, propertied group, they had neither the top level of educated people among their ranks nor the poorly educated. They were a Budo and old Makerere group.

Mulira himself set the tone for the organization. Reflecting on

---

[66] Getting nowhere either in the Lukiko or with his Progressive Party, Mulira later joined with Musazi in founding the Uganda National Movement which was proscribed on grounds of support for extraconstitutional political means.

the condition of Buganda after the war, he had long felt that representative government was essential. "No nation can go forward half-free. But the peasants of Buganda are far from being ranked as free. The chiefs make the legislature for them, and the chiefs execute the laws of their own making. The peasant has no say in the whole undertaking except to bow and do the will of his landlord. It would be all right if the overlord had at heart the well-being of his peasant, but when the majority look at chieftainship as a handsome way of getting on in life and securing a livelihood, it becomes hard for the ruled, for each chief tries to seek the favour of the other chief above him as an easy way of getting promoted, rather than to promote the interests of his vassals. . . .

"A representative government, therefore, is what we want. We want all the sections of the country to be represented in the government of their country."[67] This was written before the riots made reforms necessary. It was no surprise that Mulira made the chiefs uncomfortable.

In its *Manifesto*, the Progressive Party spoke of a federal system, and emphasized the need for trade and economic development as well as individual freedom. "The new idea that the Progressive Party wishes to stress and stress hard is the idea of the value of the individual. Each individual is of value before God. . . . The Progressive Party believes that there should be potential opportunity for all. In other words it believes in the equality of all individuals in the opportunities the state has to offer. . . . In our history the individual was of no value. It was the chief who mattered. The individual existed for the chief and had to obey what the chief told him without question. In other words the individual had no freedom."[68]

The Progressive Party never achieved much of a following. Indeed, making a virtue out of necessity, Mulira regarded it as a "party of leaders." "I chose the name Progressive Party," he once said, "because I thought the people wanted progress. But

[67] E. M. K. Mulira, *My Ideal Government* (manuscript), reproduced from the files of Mr. Mulira.

[68] *Self-Government for Uganda, an African State: Manifesto*, published by the Central Committee of the Executive of the Progressive Party (Kampala: Uganda Bookshop Press, 1956), p. 17.

they think progress is what the government stands for."[69] Keeping his political virtue intact and remaining politically impotent, Mulira finally sought a mass following. He came out in favor of anti-Asian boycotts and was rusticated by the Protectorate government. His is the sad story of "progressive" politics in Uganda.

The Democratic Party

It remains to speak of one other political group. The Democratic Party, which was closest in outlook to the Progressive Party before the latter's demise, shows concern with the welfare of the country as a whole and a lack of urgency about independence. The Party was founded in 1956. At its inception it had the partial assistance of Mrs. Diana Noakes who was extremely influential in Buddu, a Catholic saza which had certain autonomous tendencies.[70] Other Europeans were consulted as well, such as an Irish Catholic lawyer, long a resident in East Africa, whose home was on Rubaga Hill.

Party aims include "proper representation to Legislative Authorities and Governments so that a solid and sound policy is ensured whereby all Sections of the community are treated with equal human and political rights which should enable them to achieve ultimate independence in Uganda." Their most crucial objective was Africanization of the civil service, while assuring the public that "the policy of the Democratic Party is based on truth and social justice, and not on vote-catching slogans."

In 1958 the Party's policy statement included the following policy objectives: The "Party feels that in order to allay the fears of our people which reign now in their minds the Uganda government should increase the number of our elected representatives to one half of the membership of the House so that the Protectorate should now have a representative government—the first major step towards autonomy. . . ."

Stressing the Africanization of the Civil Service, the statement indicated, "This must be Africanized as quickly as possible. But

---

[69] Personal interview, E. M. K. Mulira.

[70] Mrs. Noakes had broken with the Federation of Uganda African Farmers after arguing with Musazi over general policy and the mishandling of funds. Her group of growers was organized with the help of Joseph Sonko, a former associate of Musazi who had also split with him. Mrs. Noakes and Sonko formed Abalimi Ltd., a producers' cooperative in Masaka.

we will take care to see that only people of quality are given responsible positions. The idea of reserving certain positions for Europeans must be done away with. Appointment at the present moment should go by merit only. We recognize that at the moment all posts of the Civil Service can not be filled by Africans, but we say that those which can should be taken over by them at once."

Dealing with the delicate matter of minority rights, the statement assured foreigners "who have decided to spend the rest of their days in this beloved land after Independence that we of the Democratic Party are committed to provide this Country with a Government which will recognize and respect vested rights. . . . No one of us has the slightest desire to exclude all other races from Uganda, but we shall exclude all those people from participating in our government who will not have chosen to become citizens of Uganda, i.e. our Government will not include people of two passports."

Finally, on the matter of Buganda's independence, the Democratic Party forthrightly said, "The idea should be discouraged as far as possible. It is not impossible of achievement but it is short sightedness and lack of realism that has prompted it rather than foresight of any real advantages that might emanate from it when achieved. . . . As a National Party our desire is to see this Country as one independent and prosperous Uganda."[71]

Although not a Catholic party in a restrictive sense, it is nevertheless composed primarily of Catholics. Just as the leadership of the Progressive Party, the United Congress, and the Uganda National Congress remained overwhelmingly Protestant, so the leadership of the Democratic Party is overwhelmingly Catholic. Its first President, Matayo Mugwanya, a Catholic, was a former minister of the Buganda government and in 1955 came within three votes of being elected the first Catholic Katikiro.[72] Most of those who join the other political parties do so for reasons other

[71] Handbill of the Democratic Party. More recently the party has indicated a slight preference for unitary forms of government. The only party to refrain from premature judgments in favor of federalism, it shows great political courage. See *Forward to Freedom*, the D. P. Manifesto (Kampala: Patel Press, 1960), pp. 22-23.

[72] There is considerable feeling among Catholics that they would have won if the Kabaka had not replaced several of his representatives in the Lukiko who voted for a Protestant.

than their religious affiliation. This is less true for the members of the Democratic Party; they join it because it is a predominantly Catholic party.

The former Secretary General of the Party was a tutor at Kisubi (St. Mary's College). The new Secretary General, Balamu J. Mukasa, is a Protestant, a former Katikiro of Bunyoro (his mother is a Munyoro) and a graduate of Yale University. The President General, Benedicto Kiwanuka, is a well-known Kampala lawyer. The Treasurer, Stanley Bemba, also a Protestant, was an assistant clerk of the Legislative Council. He had spent a year in the United Kingdom on a parliamentary course. The leadership includes one member of the Legislative Council from Acholi and a representative member of the Great Lukiko from Buddu. The Democratic Party has made an effort to recruit people from the north, particularly since the work of the Verona Fathers in West Nile, Acholi, and Lango has produced large Catholic followings in those areas. In such areas as Kigezi, for example, where elections to the district councils are quite often a straight fight between Catholic and Protestant candidates, the Democratic Party is the only political party to have contested the elections to the Legislative Council.[73]

The aims of the Democratic Party differ little from those of the old Progressive Party. For a time there were efforts to merge the two. It is clear that the main impetus for its support in Buganda comes from the generally aggrieved views of the Catholics who find themselves restricted to an obsolete system of awarding chieftaincies on the basis of religion, while the total Catholic membership of Buganda is now larger than that of any other single group. Protestants have allied themselves with Muslims in an effort to stave off Catholic numerical supremacy in the chieftaincy hierarchy. As it stands now, the Catholic representative members of the Lukiko are slightly preponderate.[74]

[73] In that election the Democratic Party candidate, Z. R. Babukika, was defeated by the Protestant candidate, A. Bazanyamaso, by only 3,000 out of a total of 78,000 votes cast in an election in which 85 per cent of the electorate voted. See *Uganda Argus*, February 2, 1959.

[74] Muslims play an increasingly active role in politics. For example, in 1956 the Uganda Muslim Union declared itself to be a political party. Its aim was to unite Muslims to seek their "proper representation on all government bodies." The union claimed 12,000 members. Demanding an end to discrimination, they demanded three more saza chieftaincies than the two presently allotted to them,

There is a curious ambivalence about religious politics among the party leaders. On the one hand, they are not willing to recognize that religion means much when comparing Catholic and Protestant loyalty to the Kabaka, service to the country, or any other significant "traditional" political criterion. Yet religious rivalries are still intense. Partly because so many of the political leaders and the chiefs are descendants of the old chieftaincy families which developed during the religious wars, the old prejudices are kept alive. As well, there is rivalry between old Kisubi and old Budo boys. More fundamental perhaps is the importance of the church in the daily lives of the Baganda. Rubaga and Namirembe, rising on their separate hills, represent the deep commitments of many Baganda. Those Protestants who are no longer concerned with religion tend to regard Catholics with deep misgivings as agents, albeit sometimes unwitting ones, of Rome.

Religious cleavage in Uganda is not a burning issue, but it is a constant one. As a result, political parties reflect religious denominations. Since the educational and chieftaincy systems are historically linked with religion, the religious differences of associated groups such as the old Budonians tend to be reinforced by educational associations and voluntary groups.

Even if its success was fleeting, the most popular and important of the political parties was the relatively lower middle class Uganda National Congress. Based upon organizations' work which predated Congress itself, it had its roots in farmers' organizations and the Sons of Kintu as well as in the beginnings of trade unionism.

The defunct United Congress Party group was composed of the intellectuals whose educational standards were high but whose social position and economic power remained small. They were too high on the educational scale but too low on the power scale to cut deep into Uganda society. Regarded as young malcontents whose loyalty to the Kabaka was uncertain, their organization simply drifted apart. One leader went to the United States. Another joined the Democratic Party. Still another took a post

---

and an end to the public holiday in Buganda which commemorates the victory of the Christians over the Muslims (October 5). See *Uganda Argus*, September 20, 1956.

at Makerere and gave up his interest in politics. The remainder joined the Uganda National Movement.

The Progressive Party was the Namirembe group of ex-Makerere boys. Preoccupied with self-improvement, it was more concerned with propriety and property than the others. It represented the successful African businessmen, particularly those who worked their way into important jobs and political positions. These had the respect of the clerks and others who were in the main satisfied with the general structure of Buganda laws and customs but thought it needed modernizing. In this sense the Progressive Party was the logical descendant of those progressive chiefs who were concerned with self-improvement and national development. Whereas the progressive chiefs were autocratic, the Progressive Party was democratic. To some extent, the conflict of the Progressive Party with the Buganda government was a conflict with the old Wamala faction of conservative but populist chiefs in whose group were the Katikiro, Kintu, and even Sempa, the present Omuwanika and the leading spirit in the Buganda government.[75]

The Democratic Party represents moderate Catholics. It has every chance of being extremely successful. Egalitarian in the special tradition of Catholic social welfare, it is the only party successful in recruiting large numbers of Banyaruanda laborers in Buganda. It is also the only party to publicly consider issues fundamental to the political future, such as the problem of selecting the head of state, civil rights, and other important matters.

In the widest perspective possible, the Uganda National Congress was the center of pan-African activity in Uganda. By its occasional orientations toward Accra and Cairo, it introduced new factors into politics which will undoubtedly loom larger in the years to come.

Conclusion

In September 1958 a most significant event in the development of nationalism in East Africa occurred. At a three-day conference in Mwanza, Tanganyika, 21 African political leaders from five territories—Uganda, Kenya, Tanganyika, Zanzibar, and Nyasa-

[75] One of the leading figures in the former Progressive Party is now a minister in the Buganda government.

land—agreed to form a Pan-African Freedom Movement of East and Central Africa. The object of the organization was to coordinate nationalist programs to speed up "liberation" of East and Central Africa. The key figures were Tom Mboya from Kenya and Julius Nyerere from Tanganyika. Both Mboya and Nyerere are enormously successful East African politicians. The latter heads both the Tanganyika African National Union and the Pan-African Freedom Movement of East and Central Africa. Mboya, who was Chairman of the Accra Conference held in 1958, is perhaps one of the two leading pan-African figures in the English speaking parts of Africa. The only delegate from Uganda at the talks was Mulira of the Progressive Party. Declaring itself against white racialism and black chauvinism, P.A.F.M.E.C.A. also proposed to work for "true parliamentary democracy."[76]

The Mwanza movement is not antithetical to the Accra-centered pan-African movement. However, it has its own base in the various nationalist organizations in the East and Central African territories. With anti-European feeling growing stronger and with the struggle under way against Central African federation, the prospects for pan-Africanism in East and Central Africa are good.[77] In a real sense the issue will now be determined by the general support which the Baganda in particular and the other people of Uganda decide to give to one type of party or the other. The Uganda National Congress, until its demise, became increasingly radical, noncooperative, and ideologically left. But it prepared the ground for its own replacement.

Meanwhile, the Buganda government increasingly recognizes that no political party can stand for Buganda autonomy other than itself. Either the Buganda government will have to succeed in its efforts to become independent of Uganda or it must reconcile itself to representative government, a vastly different kind of political society than prevails in Buganda at present.

[76] Quoted in the *Uganda Argus*, September 20, 1958.

[77] More recently a P.A.F.M.E.C.A. conference had a much larger contingent from Uganda, and pan-Africanism was explicitly on the agenda. P.A.F.M.E.C.A. is potentially important in East Africa and the nationalist threat of "closer union" will be much more serious than the old Colonial Office threat. As well, support from Nyasaland and northern Rhodesia is growing as both the Malawi and United National Independence Parties use P.A.F.M.E.C.A. to assist in the drive to split up Central African federation.

Two other possibilities remain to be mentioned. One is the possible amalgamation of all the political parties. For a time, in November 1958, efforts at amalgamation were made by leaders of the various political parties, in the wake of the Pan-African Freedom Movement for Central and East Africa meeting. Serious consideration was given to a possible merger of the Progressive and Democratic Parties and the reuniting of the Uganda National Congress with the United Congress Party. But the existing cleavages appeared too deep and these efforts were unsuccessful.[78]

Another possibility has become very real. This is the establishment of a non-Buganda party employing Legislative Council strength as part of its bid for real power. As support for a central legislature becomes more widespread throughout the country, the entire political focus is shifting away from Buganda.

Particularly among Nilotic groups there has been a strong feeling for the establishment of a political party which would unite the country's anti-Buganda forces. On one occasion a leading northerner, citing the serious strife which occurred in the Sudan after independence, warned that it could happen in Uganda as well. In December 1958 a new political party designed to provide "strong and effective leadership" for the whole of Uganda was formed. Citing the preservation of the position, dignity, and prestige of the hereditary rulers and of other leaders of the tribes of Uganda, it condemned imperialism and colonialism. In strong contrast to the other political parties, the party contains no Baganda. Its leadership includes seven members of the Legislative Council from Bunyoro, Acholi, Busoga, Toro, and Bugisu. It is known as the Uganda People's Union. One of its leading figures resigned from the Uganda National Congress to join it.[79]

Members of the party view the Legislative Council as the important political body of the future. By developing a strong par-

[78] Several efforts were made in 1959 to produce new organizations. The Uganda National Movement helped launch an anti-Asian boycott, was banned, re-emerged once again under the name Uganda Freedom Movement, and suffered a like fate. It emerged again as the Uganda Freedom Convention and the Uganda League; it was banned each time. At present writing both Mulira and Musazi are rusticated for their share in these efforts.

[79] Three representative members of the Legislative Council chose to remain within the Uganda National Congress (A. M. Obote, Lango, B. K. Kirya, Bukedi, and P. Oola, Acholi). One chose to remain in the Democratic Party (Gaspare Oda, west Nile, a former parliamentary secretary).

liamentary organization, they have sought to wrest advantages for the non-Buganda areas of Uganda so long as Buganda preferred to act noncooperatively.[80]

The Uganda People's Union represents the first major effort at political organization outside Buganda. In its own way it represents a different form of attack on Buganda. Properly organized, the non-Baganda representatives in the legislature can dominate the Baganda, unless the representative proportions of Legislative Council members are altered to favor the Baganda. With the establishment of a more representative system, the Baganda would be in a most awkward position of having to rely on political parties and coalitions in order to achieve their ends.[81]

Most important of all, however, is the fact that of all the political parties, only one minor one, the All-Buganda Party, is in genuine support of the system of legitimacy dependent on the Kabaka's position. All others privately admit that a new system is required, based upon the consent of the governed. Neither a chief's assembly nor an indirectly-elected body is any longer sufficient in the Lukiko. What is clear is the growing popularity of the representative principle which is gradually supplanting the hierarchical principle in popular appeal.

Meanwhile, political party organization, faced with the difficulties of organization in Buganda, will require the implementation of a new constitutional framework. The Wild Committee Report was strongly in favor of nationalist politicians and supported a universal franchise. It was not fully implemented by the government. The hereditary rulers of Toro, Bunyoro, and Ankole, as well as the Kyabazinga of Busoga, have continued to meet with the Kabaka of Buganda to ensure that any future constitutional changes will take their positions into account. Meanwhile, in 1960 a further split in the Uganda National Congress resulted in the formation of a new Uganda People's Congress, led by Lango's representative member to the Legislative Council, A. M. Obote.

[80] One important impetus for the party has been the more or less open assumption of political superiority by the Baganda. This was brought home sharply when the former Omuwanika of Buganda indicated that the Kabaka should be the king of Uganda. Other groups took sharp exception to the statement.
[81] The Wild Report recommended increasing the number of elected members of Legislative Council. Representation based on approximately one member per 90,000 people as the Report suggests would give Buganda 20 seats out of the recommended 72. See *Report of the Constitutional Committee 1959*, p. 17.

With only limited support in Buganda, the U.P.C. includes leaders from Toro, Busoga, and Lango, as well as representatives from the Uganda Trade Union Congress and the African Railway Union.

A more moderate group consisting almost entirely of Baganda has also formed a political party and in June 1960 the United National Party was launched, headed by two ministers in the Protectorate government. The party leader, Apolo Kironde, is a former member of the Uganda National Congress, a Protestant, and a lawyer. The other minister, Mr. Y. K. Lule, a Muslim who converted to Protestant, had been a lecturer at Makerere and had stood for election as Katikiro of Buganda against the present incumbent. Most significant of all is the fact that the former Secretary General of the U.N.C., Abu Mayanja, who became the Minister of Education in the Kabaka's government, thus signing the death warrant of the Uganda National Congress, has become publicity secretary of the new party. It has stated its objective to merge with Obote's Uganda People's Congress. The U.N.P. is interesting because it shows the convolutions of political party leaders in the face of Buganda government opposition to political parties. The initiative for founding the new party came from two lawyers. One, Oxford trained, was J. S. Mayanja; the other was Lameka Lubowa. They were successful in arousing the interest of Abu Mayanja and Apolo Kironde, both of whom had been active in the Uganda National Congress. But behind the efforts of the two lawyers, it is alleged, is the figure of the Kabaka himself. Indeed, the party is considered royalist inspired, having the support of the Kabaka of Buganda and the Omukama of Toro.

The future of political parties now rests with how effectively direct elections, scheduled for early 1961, can be carried out in Uganda. The Wild Report recommendations of a chief minister and an executive council responsible to the legislature—which for a time were rejected by the Colonial Secretary—require immediate implementation. For if they are to carry Uganda forward into political democracy and self-government, the parties need at their disposal resources and power far greater than those which reside in the African provincial and district governments. Recognizing this, in September 1960 the Colonial Secretary accepted the principle of direct general elections to a new national assembly with an elected African majority.

CHAPTER 15

THE BUGANDA GOVERNMENT AND THE DEVELOPMENT OF CONSTITUTIONAL GOVERNMENT

WE HAVE INDICATED that Buganda as a modernizing autocracy possessing instrumental values was able to adapt herself to and invite the modernization of all her institutions except the hierarchical principle of government with legitimacy stemming from the Kabaka. Demands to make the Lukiko more representative, a constant theme as far back as 1923, did not appear to challenge the principle of legitimacy; rather, they enabled the Kabaka to become familiar with a wider range of issues than before, especially those which his subjects thought important. Representation in the Lukiko was thus regarded as a means of providing information and knowledge to the Kabaka's government and to exert leverage upon the chiefs, whose tendency to identify their own interests with the interests of Buganda grew as the "establishment" expanded. Representation was not regarded as a principle of legitimacy which might eventually replace the autocratic principle.

The situation is otherwise today. The changeover from one system of legitimacy to another is what is at stake in contemporary Buganda, with political parties promoting the change. Chiefs are resisting because it means the end of their power. The effects of a representative principle would make them subordinate to a political government in Buganda based on a majority party or coalition of parties in the Lukiko, and while they might remain the "spine" of the nation, they would not any longer be the "head" as well. The present government in Buganda is supporting constitutional monarchy as a means of preserving the autocratic principle in theory while in practice continuing to allow the chiefs themselves to act as a government.[1] Thus the way in which constitutional monarchy will be interpreted underlies the contempo-

[1] The present Buganda government is probably the last "chiefs'" government. In fact, only two of the six ministers came up through the chieftaincy hierarchy: Kintu, the Katikiro, and Musoke, the Omulamuzi. It is a chiefs' government in role rather than recruitment.

rary struggle within Buganda. Will it be the hierarchical principle of legitimacy as exercised in delegated authority by a government headed by chiefs? Or will it be based on a more pyramidal principle in which legitimacy inheres in the popular representatives of the public, that is, on the principle of representative government? On a small scale the classic battles of constitutionalism are repeating themselves in Buganda.

If the matter were a purely internal one, it might be somewhat simpler. However, just as the internal struggle over constitutionalism is occurring within Buganda, the position of Buganda as a state has come to weigh in the balance. Where previously the status of the Kabaka was a measure of the status of the Kingdom, today the representative principle can only be acceptable to the people of Buganda if the status of their country is assured. Moreover, they want ample assurance that Buganda will retain a special relationship to any future central government before representative government can become truly acceptable.

The difficulty is that with representative government displacing the colonial oligarchy at the center, special treatment for one of the constituent parts of Uganda is obviously impossible. Fear of domination by Buganda has not been alleviated by statements, made in high places in the Buganda government, to the effect that the Kabaka should be king of Uganda.

Meanwhile, from the standpoint of the Protectorate government, the need for constitutional reform has become urgent and a major effort is underway to think through the constitutional problems of the country.[2] The bureaucratic-colonialism of Uganda has almost reached the end of its tenure in Uganda in a political climate which remains overwhelmingly Benthamite.

Political reform and economic development are the climate of the day in Uganda. There are new townships with seedy-looking modern cement buildings. Filling stations abound. American phonograph records blare from the loudspeaker in the Mengo Blue Gardens "nightclub" in Katwe and in more muted tones in the lobby of the Hotel Imperial in Kampala. American tourists, somewhat disappointed that Uganda is not at all "primitive," are also a bit relieved at the large new government offices in Kampala with

[2] A Relationships Commission has been set up with this object in view.

their bright colors and their chrome and glass exteriors. Meanwhile, the new Parliament building with its elaborately scrolled facade, its offices for budding parliamentarians, and its recording equipment to catch the sounds of debate and inscribe them for immortality in the Hansard, awaits the end of constitutional deliberations so that responsible government can give life to these external symbols.

Among the European and Asian members of the community there has been a marked drawing together in a common effort to hand over the institutions of parliamentarianism, its roles and structures, to Africans. Both communities desire to make as strong as possible those European institutions which represent the best features of British democracy. Both Asians and Europeans share a common regard for the institutions of representative government. They see in their traditions a hope for themselves, respect for minority rights, and civil liberties.[3]

Moreover, the postwar economic boom has made Uganda more than ever dependent on European capital, European skills, and European enterprise. The fact is that although the number of Africans in trade has greatly increased, economic development has created jobs for Europeans and Asians as well as Africans. Thus as the transfer of political power begins to occur, it becomes imperative that Africans work out some reconciliation of their economic interests with the Europeans if they are not to find themselves in possession of political power and economic subservience. For, although the colonial establishment declines, the commercial establishment continues to develop.

A host of new tensions is thus present in society. The values of the market compete with political beliefs. It remains to be seen whether nationalist movements can themselves develop those notions of virtue and propriety which extend beyond controversies over constitutional form and political role. Unlike colonial oligar-

[3] As the *Wild Report* puts it, "The aim should be the development of a national assembly modelled on the House of Commons in the United Kingdom. . . . The substitution of what appear to be dictatorships, often military, for democratic government in some territories shortly after the achievement of independence is naturally a development which must be viewed with apprehension; nevertheless we are certain that the proper course in Uganda is to develop a fully democratic system to which the responsibility of governing can be handed over at the time of independence." *op.cit.*, p. 33.

chies in their later days, nationalists will not become obsessed with virtue as the condition of their right to rule. They present much the same problems to reformers as did the radicals in nineteenth century England who, prior to the extension of the franchise, saw the potentialities for both good and evil in self-rule and counted on the good sense of the general public to annul their fears and justify their courage.

The matters with which we have been dealing come to a head in a period which begins with the return of the Kabaka to Buganda. When deported, he was more important as a role than as a person. When he returned, a constitutional monarch, he was more important as a person than as a role. Bound up with this conflict is the whole history of contemporary politics in Uganda. How to protect the Buganda government from the growing strength of political parties was one internal problem. How to prevent the Buganda government from being submerged in the Protectorate government was another.

The Buganda Government Today

In the Kintu Committee report we find a remarkable passage. "With some nations the king generally becomes a Constitutional Monarch after there has occurred a conflict between the king and his people as regards the way the king misuses his autocratic powers, and quite often, such powers are wrested from the king by the people, by means of physical force, when the people are convinced that as long as the king retains such powers there can be no harmony between him and his people. Such a conflict usually results in reducing the social dignity of the king among his people; whereas the king is the focus upon which the glory of the nation revolves.

"In Buganda, the Baganda have never quarrelled with their King to the extent of removing his powers from him; it is because their King has never misused his powers. But, in order to avoid a future clash between him and his people, and also to avoid a recurrence of the state of affairs such as that which existed in 1953, when Her Majesty's Government was forcing the Kabaka to act against the wishes of his people, we recommend that the Kabaka should become a Constitutional Monarch. This does not mean that his dignity and his power to give counsel to his people are removed. Nor does this preclude him from being the ruler of the Kingdom of Buganda; far from it, for every administrative act must be done in his name, his signature being necessary to give finality to every law and constitutional act, there being none among his subjects ranking higher than him in the Kingdom; from no other source does any of his subjects derive power except from the Kabaka who exercises through his Ministers and his Lukiko his direct rule over his people. This is the core of the fabric of our culture and traditions to which must be adapted the new conception of constitutional monarch whereby the King is immunized from conflict with his people in matters political, but his traditional prerogative to advise his people on those matters is not impaired."[4]

This passage reflected the ideas of the Kintu Committee, the special subcommittee of the Great Lukiko appointed as guardian of Kiganda interests when reviewing the Namirembe recommendations. It was a most important constitutional statement made by important officials of the Kabaka's government and approved by the Lukiko. For on the strength of this statement the two governments were enabled to enact a new Agreement in 1955 which legally enshrined the principle enunciated by the Kintu Committee.

The new Agreement was signed on October 18, 1955. It did not replace the old 1900 Agreement, which still remains in force, but it altered in particular those sections dealing with the duties of the Kabaka, the ministers, county chiefs, and the Lukiko. In addition, it contained assurance that the British government had no intention of imposing upon Uganda federation with Kenya and Tanganyika without the consent of the people.

The Agreement stated that for a Kabaka to be recognized, the Buganda government had to affirm solemnly that it would hold to the terms of the Agreement and uphold the peace, order, and government of Uganda.[5]

The effects of the Buganda Agreement of 1955 were several. When the Kabaka was deported his position was uncertain. Upon his return, although his position as a person was extremely strong, the Kabakaship as an institution had been weakened constitutionally. The Buganda government came to assume a greater

[4] *Kintu Committee Report*, pp. 31-32.
[5] See Article 3.

official importance than ever before, although serving the Kabaka's wishes in complete loyalty and devotion.[6] It was laid down that the Kabaka and members of the royal family would continue to enjoy all their customary titles and dignities, but the Kabaka was *no longer personally and directly responsible for the governing of Buganda*. He was thus safeguarded from personal responsibility for the actions of his ministers. The council of ministers of the Kabaka's government were now the responsible agents of government. The Katikiro had to keep the Kabaka informed of all important matters concerning the Buganda government.[7]

Certain incompatibilities built into this situation were, for a time, obscured by the general postreturn climate. It was difficult for political parties to attack the Buganda government without this being widely regarded as an attack on the Kabaka and thus an act of disloyalty. Kintu's government was the Kabaka's government and worked closely with him. However, despite this, the Kintu government remained unstable and insecure.

The composition of the Lukiko remained unchanged except for the addition of three new ministers: a Minister of Health, and Minister of Education, and a Minister of Natural Resources. There were also to be a Speaker and a Deputy Speaker.

In dealing with representation by Buganda on the Legislative Council, the Agreement specified that, provided that three fifths of all the representative members of the Council are Africans and that the Africans number one half the total members on the Legislative Council (including official members), Buganda shall at all times be represented in Legco and shall have at least one quarter of the total number of African representative members. In practice the proportion was larger than one fourth, as Buganda had five members compared with thirteen from all other parts of Uganda.[8]

[6] One sign of the position of the Kabaka on his return is indicated by the display of public devotion. When he went on safari, people collected the sod on which his feet had trod, as an object of veneration.

[7] The Katikiro is selected by the Lukiko. He then chooses his ministers from names which either he himself has put forward or which have been nominated by members of the Lukiko. The Katikiro then allocates the offices to the ministers he has selected. Each minister is then responsible for the department under his control. Each minister is assisted by a permanent secretary, and the permanent secretary to the Katikiro is the head of the Buganda Civil Service.

[8] See Article 7.

The 1955 Agreement brought about other changes in the Buganda government system, and these had profound political repercussions.

One of the most important modifications occurred in the matter of appointments. Instead of appointment of chiefs and other senior Buganda government officials by the Kabaka, subject to the formal approval of the Governor, an Appointments Board was established.[9] It consists of a Chairman, appointed by the Kabaka, the Permanent Secretary to the Katikiro, who is the head of the Board, and three other members appointed by the ministers but not engaged in politics. The Chairman is chosen for several years, while the members hold office for five years. Selected as the first Chairman was Prince Badru Kakunguru, the great-uncle of the Kabaka, and a Muslim. One of the members was a Kabaka's nominee to the Lukiko and a former deportee. Two influential members of the Board were over 80; their devotion to the Kabaka did not include acceptance of constitutional monarchy. In the matter of appointments the Kabaka's influence remained strong. Prince Badru and the Kabaka were extremely close. The first Permanent Secretary, a former Treasury official in the Buganda government, a Protestant and an old Budonian, had to contend with considerable external pressure.[10]

The Kabaka's government received important grants of power in the new Agreement. It was now similar to a responsible cabinet government. Civil servants were responsible for carrying out the policy of the ministers.

Normally the ministers remain in office during the life of the Lukiko. Ministers can be dismissed by the Katikiro and the other ministers. The Lukiko can bring about the resignation of the Ministry if a motion proposed by not less than 20 members of the Lukiko is declared by the Speaker to be a motion signifying no confidence in the Ministry, and if the motion is then voted upon and supported by at least two thirds of all the members of the Lukiko. The Ministry must also resign if 40 members of the

[9] The Appointments Board was probably the most important element in the Agreement, for it handed over to Buganda effective control over patronage and thus stiffened control over chiefs by the Buganda government.

[10] In performing his duties too zealously and trying to prevent undue political influence in appointments, the first Permanent Secretary offended enough important people so that he was replaced.

Lukiko propose a motion specifically expressing no confidence and if it is voted in the Lukiko.

Protectorate government staff, which had formerly been concerned with services transferred to the Buganda government, were seconded to the Kabaka's government. Their services include primary and junior secondary schools, under the Ministry of Education, rural hospitals, dispensaries, aid posts, and rural health services, under the Minister of Health. Field services for the improvement of farming methods, soil conservation, livestock breeding, and disease control were put under the Ministry of Natural Resources.

Under the new Agreement a relatively different role was contemplated for the chief. He now acts as the representative of the Buganda government in the field, especially with respect to law and order (the Katikiro's responsibility) and with respect to the transferred services. He has also become a coordinator within his saza of all departmental work and activities. Part of his job is to act as a stimulant of social development in agriculture, health, education, and kindred matters. He is expected to report to the head of the department concerned on how individual members of the department are functioning in the field.[11]

In the transferred services, expatriate officers occupy senior posts in the ministries. However, in the senior ministries African staffing is complete. It had been the practice in the past for the Resident to exercise general supervision of the Buganda government through the Katikiro and, in the case of the administration of justice, through a legal advisor in the Resident's office. Further, through an extensive program of grants-in-aid, the Protectorate government can now exercise a general financial interest in the expenditures of the various ministries.

The Buganda government today is a relatively modern and efficient government. It has been the object of prejudice on the part of some Protectorate staff. For example, few officers come forward to volunteer for secondment to Buganda government ministries. When they do, however, the seconded officers show intense loyalty to their respective Baganda ministers. Seconded

---

[11] The reporting system remains a Civil Service matter. Thus the minister remains outside the reporting system, although he has a right to see reports.

officers, although Protectorate staff, find that many of their sympathies are with the Buganda government in the many conflicts of interest between the two governments. For example, in 1956 the Permanent Secretary of Education, a seconded officer working for the Minister of Education in the Buganda government, found himself in conflict with the educational policy of the Protectorate government.

The urge to produce an effective policy and carry it out leads irrevocably to the need for self-sufficiency and complete responsibility. Review from the Protectorate government is a constant irritant.[12]

Attacks against the Residency were only the first in a swiftly developing campaign which, for political reasons, sought eventually an end to the Agreement and independence for Buganda. Serving as a foil for such attacks was the ambiguity of certain sections in the new Agreement. The relationships of the Buganda and Protectorate governments had to be maintained so long as

[12] The situation is exacerbated because most of the assistant residents are relatively young men. To the Baganda, they no longer occupy an exalted position. Quite the contrary, from the perspective of the long service of the Buganda government officers, they are inexperienced, not knowledgeable about local affairs, and therefore unreliable. An effort to establish the Buganda government's equivalent of assistant residents to ensure review of the local governments by the Buganda government was a complete failure. Six such posts were created in 1956 but no one paid the slightest attention to them.

Although particular Residency officials might be personally well liked, both the Buganda government and the chiefs are constant in their efforts to prevent any meddling in Buganda government affairs, i.e. the affairs of a mature government controlled by sophisticated and experienced men. The attitude of some, expressed in one informant's remark that he was a chief "before that boy was born," has resulted in efforts to keep Residency officers in the dark about events in Buganda. Only the most formal efforts at communication have been made.

Interviews with the Katikiro, the Omuwanika, and the Omulamuzi indicated the following specific objections to the Protectorate government. The Omulamuzi wanted the abolition of the post of Judicial Advisor in the Residency. Appeals from Buganda Kingdom courts should be made directly to the High Court. The Omuwanika specifically indicated that Protectorate government grants-in-aid represent an unsatisfactory way of providing funds to the Kabaka's government because they can be interrupted in case of disagreement between the two governments. He felt that such funds should be given directly to the Kabaka's government as a right, with the latter allocating funds for official purposes. In addition, complaints were made that in transferring services under the new Agreement, insufficient funds for enlarged departmental establishments were endangering the quality of the transferred services. Finally, the Katikiro indicated in his criticisms of the Protectorate government that the office of the Resident was still holding Lukiko meetings in the counties as it had done long ago, and had failed to change its policy in accordance with modern times.

the Agreement was adhered to, but the most crucial characteristic of the relationship was ambiguity and conflict. This has continued as a dominant theme, pervading most aspects of the relationship.

For example, the Kibuga—a gombolola adjacent to Kampala and the center of African urban life, including Mengo, Mulago, Wandegeya, and other important dormitory areas for Africans—had long been a difficult problem. It will be recalled that the conflict between Sir Apolo and the Protectorate government in the 1920's occurred over the issue of drunkenness in the Kibuga, and the respective powers of the Omukulu we Kibuga and Sir Apolo. It was proposed in 1956 that the Kibuga area become a municipality under the Buganda government. This would establish an important precedent because all municipalities had hitherto been on Crown land under the Protectorate government. For the first time the Buganda government would have its own municipalities.

This meant that the rules of sanitation, housing construction, and local government would also apply to such municipalities. One immediate problem was that much of the housing in the Kibuga was substandard by municipal standards. (This was one reason why Africans could afford to live in the Kibuga rather than Kampala.) Another immediate problem arose over the role of the gombolola chief. A third was over the Indian and European population of the proposed municipality and the representation they might have in a municipal council, despite the smallness of their numbers.

All of these were important issues. The Lukiko committee was therefore carefully selected. It included F. Musoke, an ex-deportee who had been associated with the Bataka; the saza chief Mukwenda, James Lutaya, a devoted follower of the Kabaka;[13] Musa Parma Ntanda; and the saza chief Pokino, Mr. J. Musoke.[14] Other members included the Minister of Health, Mr. Male, as the Vice-Chairman of the committee.[15] The committee was chaired by Mr. L. Buchanan, Local Commissioner in the Protectorate government, a former Sudan civil servant, and expert on local government affairs. The Secretary was Mr. Nigel Oram who, attached to the

[13] Lutaya came to assume an extremely powerful role as a Kabaka's man. His influence has declined, however, until today he has been by-passed.
[14] Now Omulamuzi in the Buganda government and a leading Catholic.
[15] Male has since died.

Residency, was one of the best liked British officers. Unlike Buchanan, Oram spoke Luganda and was far more aware of the nuances and overtones of the proceedings than Buchanan. The latter, accustomed to working with Sudanese civil servants, assumed that since he spoke with special competence to the subject at hand, his recommendations would, after due consideration, be more or less accepted.

Quite deliberately the Baganda sought to make him ineffective. When Buchanan spoke at length of the difficulties of local government, they listened and then suggested that since it was so complex they must need a lawyer. Buchanan was forced to remonstrate that it was not that complex. Then Lutaya began speaking in Luganda to those committee members at his end of the table. The Chairman could not follow the discussion and had to have Oram translate. By this time the discussion was more or less out of control, and the temper of the Chairman rising.

The meetings followed that kind of pattern. What was accepted at one meeting was refused at another. When finally a report was drawn up by the committee, its conclusions were unacceptable to the Chairman who wrote a dissenting opinion. It was then left to the Secretary and the committee to find a further compromise because, indeed, everyone wanted a municipality to be set up.

The Buganda government remains of much greater dimension than the district governments, balanced as it is (somewhat precariously) on the political borderline between potential "viability" as a small, but independent kingdom and as an important part of Uganda as a nation. In the first instance, few in Buganda are conscious of how much the kingdom depends upon Protectorate government assistance in the form of grants-in-aid and in the provision of basic services. Instead, from "inside" as it were, the Baganda see their large governmental establishment. Recurrent expenditures in 1954-1955 were approximately £556,495. Total revenues in 1955-1956 were £1,275,591. Expenditures covered departmental establishments, a wide range of services including road maintenance, and agricultural, educational, and medical services. Expenditures in the sazas alone totalled £347,686.[16]

---

[16] See *Estimates, Buganda Kingdom, 1955-1956* (Personal Emoluments) (Kampala: Patel Press, 1956).

At the top of the Buganda government establishment is the office of the Kabaka. As with any king's establishment, there is a large number of household staff, retainers, and regular government postings. There are twelve regular appointments in the Kabaka's office. Buganda government officials, household and office retainers paid by the Buganda government but not part of its civil service, number 152. In addition, there are a great many offices whose incumbents are paid by the Kabaka himself, such as those in charge of his large estates, certain family retainers, and ceremonial dignitaries. Guards, royal drummers, royal musicians, and others on constant call at the palace are regular employees of the Kabaka paid by the Buganda government. Although the individual salaries of this group were very small, they were jealous guardians of the palace grounds and their special adjacency to the king.

In the Lubiri and Buganda government enclosures there were 9 regular postings and 82 patronage posts, also of quite low salaries. Around the Buganda government and the court swarmed a large number of poorly paid functionaries whose actual jobs were a bit vague; they served as messenger boys, drivers, special couriers, and hustlers. These produced a throng of followers who could surround any major figure in government with an officious crowd, making "processionals" rather frequent, in keeping with the dignity of higher officials.

In the Katikiro's office there were 39 posts, in the Omuwanika's there were 59, including accountants, cashiers, bookkeepers, and account examiners. The Omulamuzi's office had 110, including judges, magistrates, process servers, and others. Below the rank of judicial registrar, almost half the staff in the Omulamuzi's office had salaries of 250*s.* a month (approximately $35.00) or less.

A very small proportion of these totals consisted of regular Civil Service staff. The vast majority were more in the nature of patronage plums. If we add to these figures the new official postings for the Ministries of Education, Health, and Natural Resources, and the Buganda government departmental establishments which were transferred to the ministries (such as agriculture, education, forestry, and medical), the size of the Buganda government personnel establishment begins to loom large indeed.

In the central offices of the Buganda government there were approximately 545 regular postings.[17] Of this total, 60 were senior, that is, they had regular salaries ranging from a minimum of £336 per annum (plus increments) to £2,000 per annum or higher (plus increments).[18]

To the largest proportion of the regular postings, exclusive of the senior positions, patronage rules tended to apply. In those departments and ministries where a Catholic was in charge, more of the employees were Catholic than Protestant. The same pattern held for the other religious groups. Political patronage continued to be in great measure a religious matter. This practice has helped to keep alive religious partisanship even where doctrinal matters no longer concern anyone. By this means, religious conflict and party competition over appointments are kept alive.[19]

We have only discussed the establishment at the level of the central Buganda government. The same pattern is duplicated on a much smaller scale in the saza, gombolola, and to a very small extent the miruka levels. In a wealthy and important saza such as Kyagwe, the saza chief or *Sekibobo* is paid £1,000 per annum. He has a deputy whose salary is half his own. County employees number approximately 326, excluding the county chief and his deputy and including lower chiefs.

Thus the government establishment is not only sizeable, but it makes the chiefs extremely powerful. Both the Buganda central and local government establishments are headed by chiefs. In the rural areas in particular it is the chief who counts. Political parties can accumulate a temporary following on one matter or another, but it is not hard to see that the chiefs, particularly at the county and subcounty levels, remain the important figures in the political life of the country.

Financially and administratively, then, the chiefs remain "the establishment." They have vast patronage at their disposal in

[17] This excludes police and part-time employees, but includes Buganda government teachers. Figures derive from the Buganda *Estimates, 1955-1956.*

[18] Salaries of saza chiefs ranged from over £1,000 per annum down to £505. The salary of a saza chief is a fairly good contemporary reckoning of the importance of the saza.

[19] The patronage possibilities are an important political factor in the chiefs' retention of their strength. It is not difficult to see why they fight hard against the introduction of party politics. Any political party gaining control over patronage would substantially diminish chieftaincy.

the form of clerkships, messengerships, drivers, and minor technical posts such as auditors and small-scale accountants. Moreover,
after 1955 the Buganda government drastically expanded its
establishment in areas once reserved to the Protectorate government. It created its own administrative officers, divisional medical
and veterinary officers, and the like, drawing into the Kabaka's
government Baganda who had been posted to other districts in the
Protectorate service. Tribalism and local service appointment were
brought together as never before.

It is for these reasons that the Bataka had in an earlier day
and the political parties have today such great difficulty in dealing with the chiefs. Not only do the latter retain the sources of
power, but they are the backbone of the power of the king.[20]

In practice the Kintu government is still a chiefs' government.
The outlook of the Katikiro can be put best in his own words:
"Chieftaincy is very important in the Buganda nation as it is the
basis of national traditional ties. It is the source of this civilization, whereby the Ganda were taught obedience to their superiors.
If the system of Chieftainship deteriorates, the Ganda cannot
progress, and the country will be led into a chaotic state. The
chiefs are regarded as the leaders of the areas under their rule
and what is advantageous is the fact that when the British Administration was introduced in Buganda, it preserved the chiefs who
were then made Civil Servants. We feel anxiety as we don't want
any new measures which tend to deteriorate the dignity of chieftainship in Buganda. We want the full support of them, with
first a few modifications to fit in with modern ideas."[21]

The first Kintu government was official in its origins and firmly
allied with chiefs and other civil servants. Like its Protectorate
government counterpart, it is perhaps the last civil service regime
before party politics and popular government invade both spheres
of government. Kintu was himself the former Mukwenda and his
wife was a daughter of Sir Apolo Kagwa. Most of the other mem-

[20] The Protectorate government has regained control with respect to chiefs'
obligations to preserve law and order. See Article 34, (5): "The Governor may
give directions to the Kabaka's government as to the manner in which the Saza
Chiefs shall perform their functions in relation to the maintenance of law and
order."

[21] Prepared statement of the Katikiro of Buganda, Michael Kintu, in a
personal communication.

bers of the Buganda government had been either chiefs or officials. The most progressive and active member of the Kabaka's government, A. Kalule Sempa, had given up a civil service job as Secretary to the Lukiko in order to become the first Minister of Education. The Minister of Health, Mr. Male, had been an education officer and assistant Katikiro. Only one member of the new government, Daudi Mukubira, was a concession to rural trading and Bataka interests.[22]

The second Kintu government, which took office in 1959, was less "official." Only three chiefs were in powerful positions: Kintu himself, the former Mukwenda, and the new Omulamuzi, the former Pokino and the present Minister of Health. The Minister of Natural Resources was formerly a leading member of the Progressive Party, a major figure in the African Chamber of Commerce, and had been a representative of Uganda on the central assembly of the East African High Commission. More recently the post of Minister of Education was accepted by Abu Mayanja, formerly the Secretary General of the Uganda National Congress and of *bakopi* origins.

The Establishment

The system of government in Buganda from the Katikiro down to the miruka chief is based upon its bureaucracy. This means that authority flows downward to the miruka via the official hierarchy, sanctified by the Kabaka himself, while approval flows upward from the miruka in an increasingly elective system.

Let us consider the role of the establishment further and trace it through the levels of government. For the system of graded councils and chiefs has not produced discontinuous elements of government but a blend of elective and appointive authorities which are slowly sorting themselves out in the emerging system of authority.

We have already discussed the miruka as a local solidary unit and as a center of nationalism.[23] Bearing those comments in mind we can discuss it as the bottom unit of the official hierarchy.

[22] He was also purported author of *Buganda Nyaffe*, the pamphlet which the Protectorate government had banned as seditious.

[23] There is some indication that the gombolola is becoming more important than the miruka as the center of social and political activity.

The miruka chief is in effect the recipient of the full weight of government pressure. Yet he receives pay which is approximately equal to that of a porter or day labourer in a major town, 60*s.* per month. In addition, he receives a bicycle allowance of 15*s.* per month, and gifts from the public, usually chicken, eggs, banana, and other foodstuffs. He is able to use communal labor on his house and office and very often prisoners are found working in his garden. But the miruka chiefs are not full-fledged members of the establishment; for example, they do not enjoy pensions or gratuities on retirement.

The miruka councils are centers of local populism. Consisting of both Batongole chiefs and elected members, the councils, like the gombolola and saza councils, do not have rule-making powers. "Their traditional function was to provide a means for the expression of local views or the representation of local grievances. That is still their basic function. . . ."[24]

What are the concerns of the miruka councils and chiefs? They serve as basic units of government in which the miruka chief is responsible for the ultimate carrying out of government policy, collection of taxes, and preservation of law and order; and, though he has no official magisterial powers, he spends considerable time adjudicating minor disputes.

Meanwhile, the councils themselves are left to discuss any matters which the public or the miruka chief deems appropriate or is expected to raise. Extremely revealing are the minutes of miruka council meetings, for they indicate the subjects with which the miruka is to deal.[25] Over the years 1951-1955, three sample mirukas held 42, 35, and 39 meetings respectively. The subjects ranged widely. Of the total number of meetings, 38 dealt with local agricultural and commercial matters, 6 with law, 6 with education, 24 with public works, 11 with taxes and finance, 8 with health, 6 with politics (including resolutions to the Great Lukiko), and 11 with topics such as presents to the Kabaka, Coronation activities, and the like.

[24] See Hailey, *Native Administration in the British African Territories* (London: H.M.S.O., 1950), Part I, p. 16.
[25] I am indebted to Mr. Tommy Gee, formerly Assistant Resident, Buganda, for providing me with summaries of the council books and their translation from Luganda.

The big dividing line in the establishment is between miruka and gombolola chiefs. Of a total of 20 saza chiefs in office in 1956, only 1 had previously been a miruka chief. Of a total of 133 gombolola chiefs in office in 1956, only 37 had previously been miruka chiefs, and those tended to come from more remote areas.[26]

Salaries for gombolola chiefs are graded from I to V, with a range of salaries in 1956 between a maximum of £400 and a minimum of £100, depending upon the grade and the number of taxpayers in the gombolola.[27]

A sample of 25 gombolola chiefs showed the following characteristics: 15 had been born between 1890 and 1910, 7 between 1911 and 1920, and 3 after 1921. They were mainly in their middle 50's. The average number of promotions within the grade of gombolola chief was 2.5. Of those listing previous occupations, 12 had been clerks employed by the Buganda government or the Residency, 2 had been employed by the Protectorate government (1 as an accountant and 1 as a medical dresser), 2 had been teachers, and 1 had been a policeman. One listed his previous occupation as a mutongole chief. None had previously been miruka chiefs.

Education of the gombolola chiefs was predominantly junior secondary, with a high proportion having attended either St. Mary's or King's College, Budo.

The gombolola is the beginning of the hierarchy of bureaucratic politics. Gombolola chiefs make it a point to keep in favor with the saza chief and with Mengo. The gombolola chief has considerable leverage to apply. In his council are all the miruka chiefs in the gombolola. If they support him, he can ensure the success or failure of the work of the saza chief under whose jurisdiction he is. Moreover, the gombolola chief is most often the person empowered to assess taxes. Graduated income tax in Buganda ranges from 30 to 120*s*. Disputes over how much tax an individual

[26] These figures were compiled with the cooperation of the Resident of Buganda, and particularly Peter Gibson, formerly Assistant Resident, Buganda. They were compiled just after the appointment of a number of chiefs following the return of the Kabaka, and the proportion of gombolola chiefs who had not been miruka chiefs is probably a bit higher than usual. For a more detailed analysis of chiefs and their histories, see A. Richards, ed. *East African Chiefs* (London: Faber and Faber, 1960), especially Chapter II.

[27] *Estimates, 1955-1956* (Personal Emoluments).

should pay are common in the case of the aged or enfeebled, for example. The chief can, at his discretion, lower the required tax. Thus the aged, the disabled, and the unemployed are in some measure at his mercy. So important has the tax function become that the gombolola grades are now based upon the number of graduated taxpayers.[28]

Saza chiefs are of course the most illustrious group in the establishment. In charge of the affairs of the saza and responsible for carrying out Buganda government policy, they are generally skilled civil servants with a flare for leadership. They know how to maneuver and yet remain out of difficulty. Because they have achieved the highest level posting, however, they can afford to be a bit independent, especially if they are in charge of one of the important sazas, such as Kyandondo, Singo, Kyagwe, Bulemezi, or Buddu.[29]

Both gombolola and saza chiefs go on frequent safari throughout their areas. They visit various gombolola and miruka nkiko, explaining government policy, actions of the Lukiko, and ministerial policy. The particular advantage of the saza chief is that he is an official member of the Lukiko, sits on Lukiko committee, and thus plays an important part in determining the general lines of policy which the Buganda government follows. And as a part of government, he is in a position to report on public reactions in his county. Items of common concern, gossip, or petty grievance are the most frequent. Common questions on safari include the following. In a miruka council meeting attended by a touring saza chief, the question was asked whether or not a fine of 40s. levied by the gombolola chief for failure to have a sign stenciled on a lavatory indicating the purpose of the building was not too high. Others wanted to know what the people of Uganda get out of the profits on coffee, cotton, and maize grown in Uganda. There were complaints that taxes had been gathered in some areas in the early hours of the morning, the chief routing the people from their beds and making them pay.[30]

[28] Graduated tax was instituted in the year 1954-1955. Income for the Buganda government was by this means almost doubled, as compared with the old Luwalo system. For example, income in 1954-1955 from graduated tax was £425,327, compared with the previous Luwalo yield of £236,000. See *Annual Reports, op.cit.*, p. 195.

[29] See Richards, *op.cit., passim.*

[30] Tax evasion was common and very often a miruka chief coming to collect tax

Chiefs in turn explain government policy on community development, African trade, and so on. Notice is given of booklets, such as *The Grocer, The Hardware Merchant,* and *Using Accounts,* which are made available by the Protectorate government to advance Africans in trade. People are told of available saza courses on retail trading and accounting, the syllabus for which is made available through the Nsamizi Training College and the Community Development Department. Health, education, welfare work are all topics of discussion by the saza chief, and he and his gombolola chiefs remain responsible for ensuring the carrying out of Buganda government regulations and activities in these regards.[31]

After the 1955 Agreement was signed, the saza chiefs were, as we have indicated, brought into closer contact with the Buganda government and into less contact with the Residency. Touring by assistant residents was clearly discouraged. Many of those who in the mirukas and gombololas had looked to the assistant residents as impartial figures, and could appeal to them because they were outside the framework of Buganda politics, now had to deal directly with the chiefs. It has now become harder to appeal outside the "establishment" except to the political party representatives and unofficial Lukiko members.

The Lukiko

As we have indicated, the Lukiko, like other councils, has been until recently a chief's body. After 1953, however, an unofficial majority prevailed which today consists of a Speaker, a Deputy Speaker, 6 nominees of the Kabaka, 20 saza chiefs, and 60 elected

could not find the taxpayer. Chiefs resorted to early morning collections before the taxpayers could disappear for the day.

[31] In one saza, the county chief, C. M. S. Kisosonkole, the father-in-law of the Kabaka, had previously been a community development officer. He was from one of the old families of Buganda, related to the Mugema. His father had been Katikiro of Buganda after Sir Apolo Kagwa's resignation. Kisosonkole's wife was a community development officer and one of the two women on the Legislative Council. She was, moreover, the President of the Women's League of Buganda, and was most active in behalf of the Kabaka's return. Interestingly enough, she was not a Muganda by birth, but came from South Africa. In this saza, both the Sekibobo and his wife would often go on safari together, he explaining government affairs, and his wife emphasizing community development and women's welfare. I would like to acknowledge the assistance of the Sekibobo and Mrs. Kisosonkole for their hospitality and for allowing me to observe their work in the saza and on safari.

representatives, 3 from each saza. In the elections, which were initiated at the miruka level, the vernacular newspapers, local politicians, and retired chiefs play an important role. Few people understand the complex and indirect system of elections.[32] It is a system open to considerable abuse. In Catholic areas, for example, Catholics were told about elections through the organization *Bulungi wa Catholic*, while Protestants were left uninformed about impending elections. The Protestants did the same to the Catholics in Protestant areas.

The Lukiko which sat between 1953 and 1958 saw momentous events pass into history in Buganda. For one thing, the representative members themselves were no longer there on sufferance of the chiefs. Imperceptibly during this period the representative members began to dominate the proceedings of the Lukiko. The chiefs were, of course, still omnipresent. However, like the officials in the Legislative Council, there was a general impression that their heyday was over. No longer was it simply sufficient to be a senior chief in order to be respected and heard. A special warrant of loyalty, a special shrewdness, or some other capability was the basis of significance in the Lukiko. As a group the chiefs were important insofar as they followed the lead of the Kintu government. In other respects much of the dynamics in the Lukiko came from important representative members.

Who were the representative members? Not yet party politicians in the main, they still regarded themselves as people from the local areas. The largest proportion of them were Batongole, 32 being the sons of chiefs; but 20 were sons of Bakopi. Seven were the children of teachers. The largest single group was Roman Catholic, having an absolute majority among the representative members.

We can compare the composition of representative members and saza chiefs in the Lukikos of 1951-1953 and 1953-1958.

The chiefs were the best educated group in the Lukiko in both periods. Indeed, the proportion of Makerere-educated chiefs rose in the second period. Older than the representative members, in the first period fewer of them came from old land-owning families. There has been a remarkable increase in the proportion of chiefs

[32] See The Law of the Great Lukiko for Selecting Unofficial Representatives, 1953, *op.cit.*

TABLE 1

Comparison of Official and Unofficial Members of the Lukiko

	Unofficial Members		Saza Chiefs	
	1951-53	*1953-58*	*1951-53*	*1953-58*
Education				
Literate	05.0	01.7	10.0	00.0
Primary I-VI	40.0	38.9	10.0	11.1
Junior secondary I-III	15.0	25.4	—	05.5
Senior secondary IV-VI	30.0	22.0	65.0	61.1
Makerere College and				
overseas	10.0	11.9	15.0	22.2
Age				
21-40	32.5	36.0	10.0	05.5
41-50	37.5	39.0	30.0	44.4
51-60	27.5	20.0	55.0	50.0
61-	02.5	05.0	05.0	00.0
Religion				
Roman Catholic	45.0	53.0	40.0	40.0
Protestant	42.5	37.0	50.0	50.0
Muslim	05.0	05.0	10.0	10.0
Other	07.5	00.0	—	—
Land Ownership				
Inheritance	47.5	37.4	55.0	83.3
Purchase	27.5	23.7	45.0	16.7
No land	25.0	20.3	—	—
Previous Occupations[a]				
Buganda government	27.5	30.5	25.0	77.8
Protectorate government	10.0	25.4	45.0	44.4
Army or police	07.5	08.5	10.0	16.7
Teaching	22.5	32.2	—	11.1
Private firms	10.0	01.7	05.0	11.1
Own business	12.5	18.6	15.0	—
Present Occupations[a]				
Cultivators	67.5	57.6		
Traders	22.5	44.1		
Teachers	07.5	22.0		
Private firms	02.5	08.5		

Sources: 1951-53 figures adapted from W. P. Tamukedde, *Changes in the Great Lukiko* (East African Institute of Social Research: unpub. mimeo., n.d.) and from questionnaires distributed by the E.A.I.S.R. to the 1953-58 representative members and saza chiefs in the Great Lukiko.

[a] Note that in the two categories of previous and present occupations, many Lukiko members listed more than one occupation.

who are, in effect, the "blue bloods" of official Buganda. The figure of 83 per cent of the chiefs holding inherited land is correlated with high educational attainment. Only one chief who had reached the senior secondary educational level had purchased, not inherited, his land. And only one chief with inherited land did not gain a higher level of education than the primary level and he was a Muslim, with no school of his own in which to get secondary schooling.

Thus the "establishment" has continued to maintain itself. Indeed, it has become more exclusive in spite of the fact that the elected representatives have come to numerically dominate the Lukiko. The chiefs retain skills and knowledge about the way government works which are so far denied the representative members. In the second period in particular, the chiefs were appointed from previous employment with the Buganda government; and in both periods the overwhelming majority of chiefs had served with the Buganda or Protectorate governments prior to their appointments.

The representative members by and large represented traders and cultivators. These two groups, whose representation had been barred during the thirties and forties, and who had been most active in the campaign against the domination of Nsibirwa and Kulubya on economic grounds, were now effectively represented. Most of those elected were members of growers' or traders' cooperatives.

Incipient conflict between the representative members and the chiefs has been avoided by the Kabaka crisis in which divisions in the Lukiko did not conform to official or unofficial membership. The factions clustered around those members of the Lukiko in and out of government who could best plan and execute successful negotiations and strategy for the return of the Kabaka. Others, demonstrating loyalty to the exclusion of all other attributes, made their mark. J. Lutaya, for example, who had been saza chief of Sesse, was fanatic in his devotion to the Kabaka, offering to resign his chieftaincy after the deportation and going to England to help the Kabaka during his period of crisis. Kintu, who was the Mukwenda, took a firm anti-Protectorate government line and became chairman of a Lukiko subcommittee to look over the Namirembe recommendations. He was successful in becoming

Katikiro in the Lukiko's 1955 elections. Representative members such as E. M. K. Mulira were best able to handle negotiations with Hancock and Sir Andrew Cohen—too successfully, some argued, for Mulira's downfall was sought by others. Although related to the royal family of Koki, he did not come from a chieftaincy background.

What is the nature of popular representation on the Lukiko itself? It is hard to say. In the main, interest groups rather than territorial units tend to be represented. Baganda tend to identify their own system in terms of Bakopi, traders, landowners, clerks, chiefs, and so on, and in terms of various voluntary associations. In this respect, Old Budonians, the Gayaza Club, other old boys' associations, the various church groups and the Y.M.C.A., the African Women's Association, Toc H, music, dance and wrestling associations, and classes held by the Extra-Murals Department of Makerere College are all identifiable groups within the context of representation. The territorial unit like the saza tends to become significant in matters of appointment and religious conflict, with identifiable Catholic and Protestant sazas serving as territorial bases for religious group competition.

The preponderance of the Catholic membership of the Lukiko poses growing political problems. The proportion of Catholics in the Lukiko rose during the 1953-1958 period and, considering that this is a trend, pressure for a revision of the appointments of chiefs on a ratio of 50 per cent Protestants and 40 per cent Roman Catholics is inevitably an important issue. The official establishment which remains predominantly Protestant (and has allied itself with the Muslims) has fought bitterly to maintain political control over the Lukiko, as we shall see. If there shall ever come a time when the Katikiro will be popularly elected (which seems highly unlikely) or when the political parties determine electoral strength in the Lukiko (the Lukiko members elect the Katikiro) and the allocation of office on the basis of religion continues to be important, then a Catholic Katikiro seems almost inevitable in the future.

The functions of the Lukiko are to discuss matters concerning the Kabaka's government. It may pass resolutions recommending that measures be adopted by government, subject to the approval of the Governor. Standing and *ad hoc* committees of the Lukiko are provided for, and the following committees function regularly: Finance, Public Works, Education, Health, Natural Resources, and Local Government and Community Development. Chairmen of the committees are relevant ministers. The Lukiko is empowered to co-opt additional nonvoting members to assist the committees in their work.

The Finance and Education Committees are extremely important. The Finance Committee, for example, consists of the Omuwanika as President, 2 other senior ministers, 4 officials, and 6 unofficial representatives or nominated unofficials of the Lukiko.[33]

The Ministry of Education and the Education Committee have charge of a rather elaborate establishment in and of itself. In 1954 there were 470 schools receiving grants-in-aid, and 62,890 children in attendance. The bulk of teacher salaries and building grants is paid by the Protectorate government to the Buganda government. There were in 1955 approximately 2,500 men teachers and 1,000 women of whom close to 2,000 taught in the vernacular grades.[34] The Buganda government ran 9 schools, while the Native Anglican Church ran 211, the Catholic Church 272, and the Muslims 46. An additional 105 unaided schools of varied quality were also found in Buganda. The total number of schools aided by the Protectorate and Buganda governments was 539, with a total enrollment of 74,617; slightly more than half of these were girls.[35]

Once again, religious politics enters with respect to education. Protestants have charged that the senior Catholic schools are of a lower caliber than their own. The Catholic reply is that a higher proportion of Catholic than Protestant candidates for Makerere enter from Buganda. On the whole, the quality of education remains low and Buganda government policy has been much concerned with raising standards.

The Pattern of Contemporary Politics

After the Kabaka's return, two contradictory influences were at work. The first was competition among all groups to demonstrate their loyalty to the Kabaka. This had a unifying effect

[33] See *Financial Regulations, Buganda Kingdom, 1956* (Kampala: Patel Press).
[34] *Annual Reports, op.cit.,* p. 200.
[35] *Ibid.,* p. 199.

within Buganda. Ex-Bataka were anxious to demonstrate their loyalty and urged harsh dealings against gombolola and other chiefs who had weakened under the urging of the assistant residents. Chiefs sought to stand as the very backbone of the Kabaka's government. Representative members stood for elections as well-known Kabaka's men during the time of travail.

Each group expressed its loyalty in different form. The Kintu government expressed it in resistance to the Resident. The chiefs expressed it in making it difficult for touring officers to gain access to their areas. For example, a saza chief would make an assistant resident wait for several weeks for permission to enter his saza, and often at the last minute would plead an inability to meet him due to the pressure of urgent business. The chiefs raised the whole question of need for retention of the Residency. Collaboration with the Protectorate government on any issue became tantamount to sabotage and an offense against the Kabaka.[36]

However, within this great outburst of loyalty and its expressions of solidarity was another divisive pattern. True, each group competed for the Kabaka's favor. Each group represented itself as king's men. But hidden behind the purposeful obeisance now displayed in Lukiko was malice and political enmity. In the very act of reporting to the Lukiko on the success of his delegation's mission to the United Kingdom dealing with constitutional matters, Mulira was interpreted by a jealous Lukiko as having divested himself of any further task. Become too prominent, he was, six months later, expelled from the Lukiko he had served so well.

Religious conflict also became more intense. Protestants and, more particularly, Old Budonians, still dominate in both Lukiko and Buganda government. From 1900 on, the allocation of chieftaincy had been based on religion, with the division among the 20 saza chieftaincies as follows: 10 for Protestants, 8 for the Catholics, and 2 for the Muslims. In the 1955 Lukiko the total number of Protestants was 36 (2 ministers, 10 saza chiefs, 4 Kabaka's nominees, and 20 unofficial representatives), while the Catholics had a total of 42 (1 minister, 8 saza chiefs, 33 unofficial represent-

[36] It even took such forms as studied bad manners. For example, in the second Lukiko to be held after the Kabaka's return, the members of the Lukiko failed to rise at the entry of the Resident. The Baganda, who regard ceremony highly, meant this as a reproof.

atives) ; in fact, the Muslims held the balance of power with a total of 8 seats (2 saza chiefs and 6 unofficial representatives).

Religious politics have been brought to the Buganda government. Protestant-Catholic factionalism has become significant in a way in which it has not been since the religious wars. The Protestants have realized that if the Democratic Party is effective in the Lukiko, a Catholic Katikiro is not at all unlikely.[37]

Religion is not based on matters of doctrine. Why, then, should anyone care which religious group might hold office? Several hypotheses have been offered by local observers. First, there are a large enough proportion of devout believers among the Catholics to make the Protestants fearful that Rome is the "new imperialism." Unlike the Church Missionary Society, which assisted the development of the Native Anglican Church with its own clergy and educational work, the Catholics have Africanized within the collective hierarchy of the church. Hence European and African clergy, with a vast preponderance of the former, work side by side. But the discipline and authority of the church stems not from Africans but from Europeans.

Another hypothesis is that the aftermath of the religious wars is still not ended, and each party still competes for the upper hand.

An alternative to both these positions has also been expressed. The Protestants appear as both the most traditionalistic and nationalistic. They are at both extremist poles of the ideological spectrum. In contrast, the Catholics are moderate and progressive. They have consistently supported welfare measures and reform. But they have rarely challenged the authority of the Kabaka or the Buganda government. In that respect they are a steady, growing group, more or less united in their ideas and with stronger attachments to propriety than their Protestant compatriots. The latter, more concerned with social striving and competitive nationalism, are less reliable colleagues for one another. Protestants splinter into a host of smaller competing groups and become more prone to competitive self-assertion. The Catholics, suspect in the eyes of the Protestants, appear irresistible in their political ad-

[37] According to one source, the Katikiro approached the Secretary of State and the Archbishop of Canterbury and asked that the office of Katikiro be permanently reserved for a Protestant.

vance. To discredit them, the arguments of Romanism and alien control have been used.

How tense the religious situation has become was illustrated in the 1955 election of the Katikiro. On the Kabaka's return from exile new elections for the Katikiroship were held. The Catholic Omuwanika, M. Mugwanya, the grandson of Stanislaus Mugwanya (who was the Catholic Katikiro in the early Agreement days, sharing this position with the Protestant Sir Apolo), decided to run for the Katikiroship. In that year the Catholics had a solid bloc of 34 votes in the Lukiko. Divided among themselves and offering several candidates, the Protestants had to secure unity in voting in order to defeat Mugwanya, the Catholic candidate. In pre-election estimates the Protestants discovered that they would lose. Only through extensive work, which included changing the Kabaka's nominees, did Kintu, the Mukwenda, defeat Mugwanya, his Catholic opponent. He received 42 votes to Mugwanya's 41.

A forged document was circulating purporting to come from the Katikiro warning the Protestants against Catholics. The Catholics charged favoritism in appointments. Incompetency was charged against the Catholics. Protestant members of the Buganda government claimed that the reason there were not more Catholics was due to lack of talent and education and that Catholic education was stultifying.

Meanwhile, Mugwanya, after losing the election, became President of the newly-formed Democratic Party. At a by-election in Mawokota he was elected a representative member. On a technicality the Kintu government refused to seat him and the matter went to the High Court. This was widely interpreted as an example of vengeful Protestantism, out to protect the church "establishment."

Meanwhile, the Katikiro was careful to select a Muslim as one of the new ministers in his council of ministers, and Muslims were wooed as never before.

On the matters we have discussed, the Buganda Lukiko has increasingly become the focal point of political interest. In the 1955 Lukiko there were four leadership centers for member alignment. The most important of these devolved, of course, around Kintu. He could, as whip for the government side, marshal the votes of the saza chiefs on any matter, regardless of their religious affiliation.[38]

But there were other potential candidates of prominence. One of the most dynamic members of the Kintu government, A. K. Sempa, then Minister of Education (now Omuwanika), attracted a considerable number of members. Sempa had been a civil servant but not a chief. Part of his education he received at Achimota, in the Gold Coast, as well as in Budo and Makerere. He is able, ambitious, loyal to the Kabaka, and remains an astute politician. Kintu relied a great deal on the guidance of Sempa who sought to make the Buganda government into a creative political instrumentality; he was limited in this effort by the weight of officialdom upon him.[39]

A group in the Lukiko stood increasingly against the Buganda government. E. M. K. Mulira had attacked the educational and land policies of the Buganda government and achieved considerable popular support. As President of the Progressive Party he could count on a large number of prominent representative members of the Lukiko to support him. He was expelled from the Lukiko in 1956. Mugwanya, the leading Catholic Muganda, was, as we have indicated, not allowed to take his seat. Finally, posing the question of party politics in the Lukiko was J. W. Kiwanuka, who became a member of the Lukiko in 1956 from Busiro and made it clear that the alliance between the U.N.C. and the ministers had been only temporary.

In order to illustrate the processes of politics in Buganda, we can cite some of the more prominent issues current during the tenure of the first Kintu government.

An issue which best identifies the effective groups and at the same time gives a clue to the pattern of politics is that of land distribution. Involved in this matter were representatives of the two major political parties of the time, the Uganda National Congress and the Progressive Party, and the Kintu government. The allocation of 154 square miles of land—which remained un-

[38] It is interesting to note that during this period Kintu was a U.N.C. sympathizer himself, as was Sempa.

[39] Sempa was the leading spirit in both Kintu ministries. Handicapped by those in office around him, he was nevertheless instrumental in providing sound proposals for an expanded educational and scholarship program, local housing, and financial reform.

allocated after the land distribution following the 1900 Agreement—represented an important measure of largesse for the Kabaka's government.

Several efforts to dispose of the land had been made in the past but no principle of distribution proved satisfactory. Now, an occasion seemed to have arisen. The land was to be distributed among those who had best served Buganda in helping to bring back the Kabaka. Such an award, the Kintu government felt, presented to those who had given loyal service to the king, could not fail to be popular. The Kintu government was thus distributing an inheritance of the past in the tradition and spirit of the original allocation.

The measure was introduced in the Lukiko by A. Kalule Sempa, then Minister of Education and the originator of the motion. Reading the relevant passages of the 1900 Agreement, Sempa first indicated that the original distribution of 8,000 square miles was to worthy notables in the Kingdom. The 154 square miles now to be distributed "originate from the same Agreement. It is understood that according to the Agreement, the remainder of the distributed mailo land would be given to deserving people." Ten square miles were distributed to ex-servicemen. 144 square miles remained to distribute. "Remembering our position as Bakungu," said Sempa, "we can discuss this matter wisely. We are fortunate to live in a country ruled by a king, together with all the positions included in it (*sic*) unlike the rest of the country which is without kings as their rulers.

"All people are not alike nor equal. . . . My proposal is this. The whole land belongs to the Kabaka. Let us ask him how much land should be possessed by the Nabagereka (Queen) and himself. (Cheers)"

For the rest, Sempa specified land as follows: The ministers and Speaker, 7 square miles; regents, 3; saza chiefs, 10; 60 representative members, 30; Kabaka's representatives, 3; representative members to Legislative Council, 3.

To receive smaller bits of land were the Clerk of Council, the Namasole, the Kabaka's mother and sisters, the princes and princesses of the drum, the royal clan leaders, officers in Mengo, and gombolola chiefs, with a small bit left over for the Bataka.

Six and one half square miles were to be divided up among 44 heads of clans.

Other individuals and groups considered by Sempa to deserve a land award included the Hancock and Kintu Committee members, the political parties of 1953 to 1955, women's associations and others. No person was to get more than one square mile.[40]

In response to the motion, Mulira, the President of the Progressive Party, pointed out to the Minister that "the Mailo belongs to the whole tribe. It is not for special people. It should go to all people. (Cheers)"[41] He was joined by D. Lubowa, a newspaper editor and member of the Uganda National Congress. Lubowa said, "I am not in favor of giving out land. I would request that an amendment be made whereby the Great Lukiko should discuss the best use of the said mailo land. (Loud cheers)."[42]

In the end, after much bitter discussion, a committee was established composed of Mr. Sempa, who as chairman had originally proposed the motion, Spartas Mukasa, now a Kabaka's nominee on the Great Lukiko and a former leader of the Bataka Party, one saza chief, one representative member who was also a political party leader from the Uganda National Congress, a Protestant, J. W. Kiwanuka, and one Catholic representative member who was also a leading member of the Progressive Party, L. Bassude.

The Lukiko voted in favor of Sempa's motion and the committee was left to work out the details of distribution.

Meanwhile a storm broke in the country as a whole. Another matter had also intruded.

Only a few days before the debate on land distribution, *Uganda Empya*, Mulira's newspaper, had published an article accusing the Kintu government of accepting bribes. Under a dramatic headline, "Excessive Bribes at Mengo," the newspaper implied that it could name those who had received bribes.[43]

Challenged by the Katikiro to publish the names of those who had received bribes, the editor of *Uganda Empya*, F. W. Kakembo, replied that the names were in the hands of Mulira, the President of the Progressive Party. The reply also noted that the

---

[40] Minutes No. 16, Proceedings of the Great Lukiko, June 1956.
[41] *Ibid.*
[42] *Ibid.*
[43] *Uganda Empya*, June 6, 1956.

editor was a member of neither the Executive Committee of the Progressive Party nor of a party.

The Secretary General of the Progressive Party, L. Bassude, then wrote to the Katikiro pointing out that when a political party attacks the government on a wrong policy this does not put the political party on trial. The party does not feel compelled to list the names of those taking bribes; moreover, the Katikiro does not have any right to demand the names. Rather, Bassude indicated, the Progressive Party wanted the Buganda government to take cognizance of this malpractice "which has undermined the whole system of government as a malignant disease."[44]

The Kintu government was indignant at the charges and particularly incensed that Mulira would not back them up with more convincing evidence.[45] It was in this context that Mulira, in speaking against the land distribution motion, began to take on the proportions of a minor hero. He had accused the Kintu regime of bribery and of wanting to distribute land to notables rather than to the public.

As is so often the case in Buganda, dubious and noteworthy issues coincided. Mulira was in a weak position on the bribery issue unless he was willing to make more specific charges. But the public was not concerned about that. The Buganda government was in a weak position on the matter of land distribution and Mulira momentarily expressed what was a widely held sentiment. In the mirukas there were charges that the Kintu government was simply allocating land as a political payoff to the followers of Kintu. Others charged that it was a continuation of the efforts of chiefs to prevent the Bataka from getting their land, and they pointed to the small amount of land proposed for the clan heads. Charges of undemocratic procedure were levied against the Buganda government.

Misled by the voting in the Lukiko in favor of land distribution (73 for, 10 against, 2 abstentions), the Kintu government wanted to avoid a public outcry and debate. It did not yet know or under-

---

44 Letter from L. Bassude to the Katikiro, June 18, 1956.

45 It is interesting to note in this connection that Bassude was subsequently appointed a minister of the Buganda government. A similar circumstance surrounds the offer of ministerial appointment to Mr. Abu Mayanja, the latter having attacked the Buganda government with considerable success.

stand how to cope with popular government. A large number of individuals were to be given small grants of land. By this means, it was hoped, representatives of the vocal and organized factions would be rewarded. People such as Fenekasi Musoke, J. W. Kiwanuka, P. Muwanga and others were associated with traders, newspapers, or the Uganda National Congress were to receive land for their personal benefit.[46] While this may have satisfied the various factions, it aroused the ire of the general public. They did not see why the *Uganda Post*, *Uganda Empya*, *Munno*, *Dobozi*, *Gambuze*, and *Uganda Eyogera* (all vernacular newspapers) should be awarded 100 acres each. Indeed, it was discovered that Kiwanuka, who had first been opposed to the land distribution, was now to receive land as a politician active during the campaign to bring the Kabaka back; as the editor and owner of the *Uganda Post* and thus entitled to benefit land given to newspapers; and as a beneficiary through his wife, who would also receive land.[47] In contrast, Mulira, who, as a member of a Lukiko delegation concerned with the Kabaka's return and as owner of *Uganda Eyogera*, stood to gain, was steadfast against the land distribution.

Meanwhile, public feeling ran high enough on the land distribution matter so that the Kabaka himself had to quash the proceedings. It was decided that the time for land distribution was not auspicious.

Neither the Kintu government nor the Uganda National Congress, of which Mr. Kiwanuka was a member, was pleased with Mulira. However, the Catholics were pleased. Many of them were firmly convinced that Kintu was taking bribes and keeping Catholics out of government posts.[48] Hence the religious issue, the Bataka, the parties, and the chiefs all got mixed up in the land dispute in which tempers flared and internal division became intense. Required was an issue to remove Mulira from his position of prominence as a member of the Great Lukiko.

The chance came fairly soon. Under the terms of the 1955

46 In interviews in several mirukas, the view expressed at miruka council meetings was that the land should be used for schools or other public purposes rather than personal use.

47 See *Olupapula Olulaga Olukiiki Nga Bwerugerese Mailo 154 Ne Acres Ezijjulirize Mailo 8,000 Akawebwa Abantu be Buganda mu Ndagane ya 1900* (Buganda Government mimeo., n.d.).

48 There were efforts at this time to amalgamate the Progressive and Democratic Parties.

agreement, the Lukiko was obligated to concern itself with elections to the Legislative Council. The system of elections was to be direct, and the Buganda government had set up a committee under the chairmanship of A. K. Sempa to look into the matter. However, Mulira, in a motion on direct election of Lukiko members, argued that "we are approaching the time of Self Rule. There are two ways of elections—direct or indirect. The present election system is crooked. I desire direct elections for all men. For example, Kyaddonde could be divided up into three groups. People in those groups could on the appointed day of elections come together and each and everyone of them could elect any he wishes from a list of candidates standing for election. . . . This method of election is found in the countries where Self Rule is anticipated. . . ."[49]

A representative member from Bulemezi, agreeing with Mulira, proposed that the matter be studied. Mulira added that the matter should be adopted in principle and a new ordinance prepared.

The Katikiro argued that "there is a committee at present preparing a method of direct election to Legislative Council. While that method is being prepared I hope this one, too, will be revised. We should therefore adopt the proposal or choose a committee to deal with the matter." But he made it clear that it was more or less a superfluous measure. In the voting which followed only 21 members were in favor of Mulira's proposal, with 55 opposed. The matter was dropped.

In anger, Mulira and another representative member, Lubowa, walked out of the Lukiko meeting. Sheikh A. Kulumba, a Kabaka's nominee, charged that in walking out of the Lukiko meeting the two representative members had shown disrespect to the Lukiko and to the throne. Charges were prepared against Mulira, Lubowa, and J. W. Kiwanuka, the latter having walked out earlier in the session on another matter. After a display of irateness, Lubowa paid a fine and the matter was dropped in his case. Kiwanuka was able to show that his absence was due to business matters. Mulira, refusing to pay the fine, appealed on grounds that no disrespect was shown and that the Speaker did not have

[49] Motion on Direct Election of Lukiko Members, Proceedings of the Great Lukiko, June 1956.

the power to exert such authority.[50] Refusing to acknowledge guilt under a rule which he felt no longer applied, Mulira steadfastly refused to pay the fine and, meanwhile, was expelled from the Lukiko. He remained out of the Lukiko for well over a year and also served a short time in jail for his refusal to pay the fine. Although in the long run he won his case, he was for the time being effectively eliminated as a political leader.[51]

The controversies between the various groups in Buganda, the firm loyalty of each to the Kabaka, and the looming presence of the Protectorate government have thus, in turn, intervened in the processes of government. On his return, the Kabaka had great influence in the affairs of both the Lukiko and the Buganda government. The Kabaka justified his close association with the Katikiro in political affairs on grounds of precedent. He indicated that Agreement or no Agreement, in the past it was the custom for the Katikiro and the Kabaka to make blood brotherhood together. Mutual confidence between them was essential in both the traditional system of government and today. Hence the Kabaka felt that it was still his role to give advice to the Uganda government and to the Appointments Board. He thus remains an active participant in politics. Today he does not bear responsibility for giving advice, but he is nevertheless involved.[52]

While questions of authority, substantive and technical, remain to be solved, conflict has meanwhile arisen over the circumstances surrounding the signing of the 1955 Agreement.

As interpreted by various parties, the Agreement has come to have villainous implications. Increasingly the argument is heard that to make the Kabaka a constitutional monarch is a violation of the deepest customs of the Baganda, and that the Agreement

[50] The Speaker system was instituted under the new Agreement. In the previous system the Katikiro had been the ex officio President of the Lukiko. In the rules of the Lukiko, the Katikiro had the power to judge whether a violation of custom had been incurred by some action of a member. The new Lukiko rules had not yet been adopted and the old ones still prevailed, but the Speaker system had been adopted and the old practice in the Lukiko had been abrogated. Since Mulira was fined on the basis of a violation of custom, the old rule, there was some question about the applicability of the rule itself.

[51] Ironically enough, when J. W. Kiwanuka became obstreperous and began to take a line in favor of popular government, he was accused of plotting to assassinate the Kabaka. The case was quashed for lack of evidence.

[52] These comments are based upon an interview with His Highness, the Kabaka, August 8, 1956.

itself was put over on the people when the Kabaka was in exile and forced down their throats.

Those like Mulira who had been associated with the Namirembe reforms have been held up as dupes, although for some reason the Kintu Committee[53] which approved the reforms is still regarded as acceptable.

It would not be fair to assume that the Buganda government has consistently opposed political parties. Rather than being opposed to the party system as such, it continues to express concern over the programs supported by political leaders, particularly vis-à-vis Legislative Council. As a result, Buganda government leaders are ambivalent about parties.

The concern about political parties is intensified because there are two fundamental issues in the air. One is direct elections to the Lukiko. The second is direct elections to the Legislative Council. Later we shall discuss these matters in greater detail. Briefly, however, the Lukiko decided in November 1957 not to introduce direct elections to the Lukiko until after the Legislative Council elections.[54] Direct elections to the Lukiko require altering the indirect system whereby miruka and saza councils are electoral bodies. This would tend to favor the political parties as nominating and organizing bodies. The Lukiko can work up no enthusiasm for direct elections to the Lukiko, although it has not taken a stand against them.[55]

However, while clearly not opposing the principle of direct elections to the Lukiko, the Lukiko postponed the matter of direct elections to the Legislative Council the following year. This

[53] The Kintu Committee, elected by the Lukiko on December 20, 1954, consisted of M. Kintu, Chairman, who became Katikiro; R. K. Kasule, who became Speaker of the Lukiko; Y. M. Kyazze (deceased); M. K. Wamala, who became Permanent Secretary to the Omuwanika; A. Kalule Sempa, who first became Minister of Education, then Minister of Health, and subsequently Omuwanika. Other members of the Kintu Committee remained on relatively good terms with the new government, which represented orthodoxy rather than reform.

[54] Representative members are elected as follows: Each election year elections are held in the miruka for one representative from each miruka. The miruka representatives then elect two persons to be selected by the Kabaka as saza representatives. As well, saza council representatives are elected to the Lukiko by the saza councils. For details, see *Supplement to the Uganda Gazette*, Vol. XLVI, No. 86, 8 October 1953, p. 359.

[55] There are many people who are appalled at the idea, of course. As one saza chief put it, "We can't let the people of the market place make decisions in the Lukiko." But this is not an official view of the Buganda government.

appears to be in violation of the 1955 Agreement. In reply to the charge, the Kabaka's government held that the Legislative Council was not the same one to which reference was made in the 1955 Agreement, under the terms of which the Baganda were obligated to participate in it. If it was not, then the Baganda would be absolved of their obligation under the Agreement.

Fear of the parties has helped to propel the Buganda government to autonomy. This has reinforced the intensity and pace of Buganda separatism. The Buganda government, as we have shown, is a competitor of the political parties, vying with them in its nationalism. The target is not simply the Protectorate government, but the regular political parties as well. Thus any potential shift of strength to the political parties is fought. The Lukiko passed a resolution, for example, complaining that political parties "proposed to terminate Mengo."[56] The Omuwanika stated publicly that Uganda should have independence under the Kabaka. A Lukiko committee under Sempa outlined a plan for independence for Buganda with the Kabaka as king and with the title of His Majesty (instead of His Highness).

Meanwhile, sentiment grew for a national assembly and for a constitutional committee to represent the whole country and to resolve differences. As one writer put it, "Outstanding against the Kabaka's government and the Lukiko is the grave charge that they are fanatic separatists hell-bent on dividing Uganda and thus deter independence. Against the Protectorate government is the equally grave charge levelled against them even in the British Parliament that they failed to unite Uganda and were in fact conniving at the reactionary tribal forces, if not fanning tribal differences. It is therefore incumbent on these two Governments to nullify these charges."[57]

The issues had been made much sharper when, earlier, a Muganda member of the Legislative Council had resigned and the Buganda Electoral College had refused to elect a replacement. Resisting the idea that the Agreement obligated them to carry out their electoral functions, the College affirmed that they were not so obligated. The Lukiko decided by a vote of 79 to 0 that it would refuse to participate in direct elections until demands for

[56] *Uganda Argus,* September 29, 1958.
[57] Letter to the *Uganda Argus* from Kiwanuka-Mabira, September 17, 1958.

increased African representation were met. A case was then brought by the Katikiro against the Attorney General of Uganda seeking three declarations: a) that the present Legislative Council was not the same Legislative Council referred to in the 1955 Agreement; b) that he (the Katikiro) was not bound to take steps to elect Buganda representatives to the Council; and c) that until the Council was reconstituted to be the same as that referred to in the Buganda Agreement, no procedure existed for electing representative members to it.[58] The United Congress Party, whose members in the Legislative Council had precipitated the crisis in order to demonstrate the need for a national assembly of Africans to discuss constitutional matters, supported the Buganda government. The Uganda National Congress did not.

Meanwhile, new Lukiko elections, which had become due, raised again the issues of religion. As well, a new spirit was abroad. The Kabaka's sister was standing for election—an unheard-of event. Almost every major politician in Buganda, each representing his political party, was standing for election.

In the face of impending elections, Kintu stepped up the pace of attacks against the Protectorate government. The Lukiko passed three resolutions. It endorsed the decision to appeal against the High Court's decision against the Katikiro. It reaffirmed that the electoral law for selecting Buganda representatives to the Legislative Council was inapplicable. It announced that it was time to inform the Queen that the Agreements were to be terminated and that the powers surrendered to Her Majesty's government must now be returned. In a memorandum to the Queen, the Lukiko charged that the original Agreement of 1900 had been forced on the chiefs of Buganda, whose signatures had been "purchased." They argued that Buganda is consistently ranked with other provinces of Uganda, but the other provinces have no governments and this is to keep Buganda at a standstill. They objected to the Protectorate government's aim of building a unitary state in Uganda, and therefore asked what the position of hereditary rulers would be in a self-governing Uganda. They argued further that the 1955 Agreement had been signed under duress. The memorandum concluded by suggesting that the rela-

[58] The case was dismissed by the High Court and the three declarations were refused. See *Uganda Argus*, November 26, 1958.

tionship between Buganda and the other parts of Uganda would be worked out among themselves and that future relations between the British and the Baganda would depend upon mutual interests within the British Commonwealth.[59] The memorandum was signed by all the members of the Lukiko. It was the last major act of that Lukiko before the elections of a new one. The Kintu government had pulled out all the stops. To vote against it would be a vote against Buganda. And in his last statement to the Lukiko, Mr. Kintu affirmed that Buganda had no wish to secede from Uganda, but that Buganda and her neighbors should come together in a federal state. In return, the Resident offered congratulations to the Katikiro for the good work the Lukiko had done.[60] On a conciliatory note the first Kintu ministry came to an end, to be resoundingly reelected by a new Lukiko which contained leaders of the major political parties.[61] The first major act of the new Lukiko was to endorse the decision of the previous one to press for the termination of Buganda's agreements with Britain.[62]

The combination of religious and party conflict in Buganda had made the Kintu government extremely controversial. In the 1958 elections the political parties made their bid for participation in the Buganda government. There was still no system of direct elections, and there existed much criticism of the electoral methods of political leaders. Three representative members to the Lukiko were elected, two by the saza electoral colleges and a third by the saza councils.[63]

A record number of candidates registered for the election, from 30 in Sesse, a very small saza, to more than 200 in Mawokota. For the first time a member of the Buganda royal family contested an

59 "A Memorandum from the Buganda Lukiko for submission to Her Majesty the Queen, being the Baganda desire to bring the Buganda treaty of 1894 to an end." (Buganda Kingdom Information Office, 1958.)

60 *Uganda Argus*, January 1, 1959.

61 The new Kintu government included A. K. Sempa as Omuwanika; J. Musoke, the former Pokino, as Omulamuzi; A. Lubwama was appointed Minister of Health and Works and was a former saza chief. L. N. Bassude was appointed Minister of Natural Resources and was a former representative member from Buddu, a former member of the Progressive Party executive committee, and an important businessman. On his appointment, Bassude pointed out that the tradition of appointing important officials from among chiefs was now broken. (Both Catholic appointments were from Buddu, it will be noted.)

62 *Uganda Argus*, January 26, 1959.

63 *Uganda Argus*, November 29, 1958.

election, the Princess Irene Nalinya Ndagire, a sister of the Kabaka. Among the contestants were the President of the Democratic Party, B. Kiwanuka; the President of the Progressive Party, E. M. K. Mulira; E. Muwazi and Paulo Muwango from the United Congress Party; and the President of the Uganda National Congress, I. K. Musazi, who stood in Bulemezi.

In the elections the parties played a significant role for the first time. Their relative strengths were as follows: United Congress Party, 2 seats; All-Buganda Party, 4; Progressive Party, 2; the Uganda National Congress, 3; and the Democratic Party, 19 seats.[64]

In an effort to head off the gains made by the Democratic Party, the reelected Kintu government gave Catholics two important posts. The saza chief of Buddu, a leading Catholic saza, was made Omulamuzi, and L. Bassude, a successful farmer and a former nominated member of the Progressive Party Central Committee, was made the Minister of Natural Resources.

Whereas party politics had not been characteristic of the previous Lukiko, it was now an established fact. It is only a matter of time before the chiefs' government gives way before a "peoples government" in Buganda.

Let us briefly sum up the activities of the Buganda government after 1955. It sought on the one hand to be an effective government and provide the necessary services to the public. It was not a popular government in the usual sense of that term, but it was immensely successful, both in carrying out its tasks and in retaining popularity by successful prosecution of the interests of the Kabaka. That it did not carry out the spirit of the Agreement but rather used it as a screen to further its own autonomy was reinforced by two factors. First, the Buganda government no longer accepted the more humble status accorded to African governments. In this it was groping toward an acceptance of equal stature which, it became clear, could occur only with political equality. Thus social equality and political equality were confused with degrees of autonomy in local government—a special problem where racial, cultural, and political relationships are part of the same network of relationships. In that sense, separatism

64 *Ibid.*

and parochialism represented protest against political and social subordinacy.

Second, in competing with political parties for support, the Buganda government sought to make political parties alien bodies while stealing most of their thunder. Thus the ordinary expressions of nationalism which were undertaken by the parties were pre-empted by the Buganda government.

The 1955 Agreement helped the Buganda government to increase its patronage, to become a more important focal point of political interests, and to mount attacks against the Protectorate government and political parties. The refusal to participate in direct elections and the push to autonomy embodied in the memorandum to the Queen were the actions of a government facing the choice of becoming independent or accepting subordination. It was not going to do the latter without a struggle.

But other conclusions can also be drawn from the analysis of Buganda government actions following the new Agreement. Because the government identified itself so closely with the Kabaka, yet remained a chiefs' government, chiefs themselves were strengthened in the system. Unpopular chiefs, or those tainted with past association with the Residency, were removed. It was therefore the civil service system (and those associated with it) which was reinforced. Those who were not associated with the system but intended, nevertheless, to find new paths to power and prestige could not yet buck the civil service establishment. In joining political parties they posed a long-term threat to the system itself, as the Buganda government itself acknowledged. Those who were neither in political parties nor involved in denominational disputes, and had originally been so important in the development of nationalism in Buganda—that is, the rural Bataka sympathizers— were conspicuously absent in the Lukiko and in the Buganda government. Having been outlawed in 1949 and having shared their outburst of grievance with all groups during the Kabaka crisis, they were left deflated.[65] Since the most intense Bataka

[65] In the appointments that followed the return of the Kabaka, 4 Bataka supporters, including 1 Minister, were selected. Three saza chiefs had been Bataka supporters, as well as 3 representative members of the Lukiko, excluding the Speaker and the Deputy Speaker, both of whom had at one time been associated with the Bataka.

support remained at the miruka level, and the miruka councils were not able to present to higher councils anything but a token of local demands, the fundamental rift in Buganda which had originally appeared as an antichieftaincy movement in the post-1900 Agreement days, remained. But it was dormant. It was conservative and did not encourage people to join political parties. The effort toward autonomy by the Buganda government has in effect papered over the more fundamental cracks in the society of Buganda. When the issue of local government reform is taken up in Buganda in earnest and the issues at the miruka and gombolola levels of administration are faced squarely, the sensitive core of Kiganda society will at last be touched.[66]

Three major political trends are discernible in Buganda. The first is toward popular government. It is more than likely that the next election to the Great Lukiko will be direct rather than indirect, with the focus less on the Kabaka as an active participant in government and more upon the Kabaka's government as a responsible agency of the public.

The second trend is toward local government reform. The local system, as it stands, produces increasing criticism of the Buganda government. The concern with establishing municipalities under the Buganda government is only one feature of this trend. The second is long-overdue reform of the lower councils, miruka and gombolola.

The third trend is toward a revival of religious conflict, unless a larger concern with central government preoccupies the Baganda very soon. With a Catholic majority in the Great Lukiko, the "establishment," that is, the Protestants, will require an alliance with the political parties in the Lukiko which are predominantly Protestant, as well as with the chiefs and nonparty people, if they expect to retain power. A predominantly Catholic party with such a powerful proportion of the seats, and able to make its own alliances with other Catholics, chiefs, and representative members, means the rapid development of party politics under a religious impetus.

[66] There are several officials in the Buganda government who recognize this and give this as one reason why no one is anxious to do anything about local government reform.

CHAPTER 16

THE CONSTITUTIONAL APPROACH
TO NATION BUILDING:
IDEAS WITHOUT IDEALS

SPEAKING of the "literature of ideas," Balzac says that as a literary school it recommends itself by its abundance of facts, by the sobriety of its imagery, by conciseness, clarity, and above all a profound sense of comedy in the midst of seriousness. Comedy is kept in reserve. "It is the spark in the flint."[1] The same remarks apply to the pattern of constitutional nation building which, both in the Colonial Office and the colonial territories, has taken on a style of its own, a precision, a sense of social as well as legal propriety, and above all a well-disguised reserve of comedy. It is its own literary school, and the products, with greater or lesser durability, are scattered all over Asia and Africa. South Africa, India, Ceylon, Burma, Pakistan, the Sudan, Ghana, Nigeria—all are products of the tradition of constitutional nation building, not to speak of the special and distinctive designs embodied in West Indies federation and in Malaya where the realities of disperse geography and multiracialism have been bridged or rendered harmless by the constitution makers, assisted of course by the good will of the local inhabitants.

Uganda has now entered the stage of serious constitution making. A new national perspective is being projected over the heads of the various political communities. Political parties were until recently very shy about raising in sharp form the issue of an all-Uganda nation. And they are increasingly resentful of the negative consequences of parochialism, which, indeed, is less strong in the districts and continues to diminish even though it serves as the basis for local political strategy.

Moreover, representatives of the public have now been brought directly into the matter of constitution making. No longer do political leaders or intellectuals need to feel that their concern for

[1] Honoré de Balzac, "A Study of M. Beyle," in the introduction to Stendhal's *The Charter House of Parma* (New York: Liveright, 1944), p. ix.

the political future of their country, their utterances and manifestoes, constitutional proposals and political plans are so many
blank cartridges fired into the air. Africans have for a long time
been seriously and passionately concerned with the constitutional
future of their country. "We are still afraid to do something,"
wrote E. M. K. Mulira during the War, "and many things have
taken place which show us that we have not done what we should
have for our beloved country in this generation. Buganda invites
us to make glow the flame of civilization that was ignited by
Mutesa I and which Kagwa and his brave comrades threw to us.
That flame is now very low and it behooves us to feed it so that it
may glow with the same splendor as the electric lamps of our
neighbors."[2] Mulira was not content with mere rhetoric. With a
sometimes prophetic pen he tried to write out the conditions of
representative government in a constitutional structure applicable
to Uganda.

Mulira has by no means been alone in such efforts. We have
indicated the elaborate proposals for constitutional reform leading
to representative government worked out by the Uganda National
Congress. There has also been a large vernacular literature devoted
to the subject. District governments, private individuals, including
journalists, lawyers, shopkeepers, and cultivators, have tried to
deal with the problems of nation building in Uganda by proposing
constitutional reforms.

Most of these efforts show a seriousness of purpose. Often they
are painful and clumsy efforts to become aware of available
constitutional alternatives and devices which are manifest in the
experience of other countries. The points of view vary considerably. For example, in a mood quite contrary to that expressed by
the other political parties, the Democratic Party has argued that
while autocratic administration has outlived its usefulness and the
number of Africans in the legislature should be increased, there
is no need to establish an African national assembly, something
demanded by representatives of the Uganda National Congress.
Fearful of the consequences of such an assembly because of
controversy over who would control it, the Democratic Party has
argued that "Legislative Council is the stepping stone to self

[2] E. M. K. Mulira, *The Government of the People* (n.p., n.d.).

government and democracy. It is here that the people of Uganda must learn the art of democratic government."[3]

To these remarks, Protectorate government officials give ready assent. In the main, efforts to develop a national focus as constitutional policy emanating from the Protectorate government are, at least for tactical reasons, opposed and automatically suspect. This attitude is not simply the result of Africans' ignorance or prejudice. The difficulty with the constitutional approach to nation building is that no matter how much the impetus comes from below, in political pressures upon the governed, the initiative finally comes from above, that is, through the auspices of government. There the legal and constitutional experts seem to have that special knowledge and wisdom which, Platonic in its implications, contains both the humor and the authority of contemporary tutelary democracy.

Yet in actual practice, despite the varied experiences of the constitution makers, the actual precedents and guides to practice are crude ones. They are institutional prescriptions based upon rule of thumb formulae and experience elsewhere. Imbued with a sense of form and balance, with shrewd judgments about how power is to be shared and blended in an institutional matrix, the constitution makers try mainly to produce legal clarity; resolution of practical difficulties is left to the drafting committees which work out compromises acceptable to the various constituent parties. In that sense, when the more heady phrases are eliminated a constitutional document serves as a common denominator on the basis of which a flow of government business and a set of political roles will be directed and established.

What are some of the general conditions that need to be met in order to achieve successful nation building via constitution making?

First, political leaders in their own political commitments need to restrict their objectives mainly to those changes in society which do not require massive alteration in beliefs and customs. Second, the willingness to restrict objectives requires some belief in the practical and immediate dignity of contemporary social life and the organizational basis of the life of the people—they cannot

[3] See Benedicto Kiwanuka, *Democratic Party Policy Statement* (unpub. mimeo., 1958), p. 1.

view the way of life of their people as debased or requiring redemption.

Third, there cannot be established a set of political roles, such
as those embodied in a cabinet, a parliament, or a civil service,
without a whole range of congruent secondary roles whereby the
mechanisms and values of representative government at the top
are supported by intermediary institutions, such as state or local
councils, decentralized operations of the ministries, and a civil
service system well-padded in all ranks with Africans familiar with
their tasks. If these are developed, political parties are, perforce,
able to work within the framework and, by their own competitive
activities, to reinforce rather than disrupt the structure. Barring
this, the parties will either fragment and become virtually powerless to operate an effective government (thereby fragmenting the
public itself), or the mobilization approach will be necessary, using
political leadership as an entrepreneurial basis for changing the
structure of society, that is, forcing the people to be free. As Nadel
indicates, the coherence of role system is fundamentally involved
and this cannot be done merely by constitutional fiat.[4] Important,
then, is the establishment of mutually compatible roles which form
a ramified institutional structure that includes government roles
providing leadership and accountability roles allowing checks on
the leadership and providing information. The whole is bound together by congruency in work, that is, a great turnover in transactions, not in personnel, and a proximate acquiescence in values
associated with the roles.

A final concomitant is, surprisingly, a condition of public political apathy rather than anxiousness to participate. The bulk of the
people need to be politically apathetic at least to the extent that
they do not promote great competition for recruitment to political
positions available (putting an impossible burden on institutions
of choice, such as voting institutions, or on individuals in a position
to select or co-opt people, such as members of appointment

4 See S. F. Nadel, *The Theory of Social Structure*, p. 63. In "primitive societies,"
role linkages tend to be firm and predictable, prescriptions for behavior being
narrowly embodied in the role. Contemporary societies build into political roles
the rules for choice making and discretion, i.e. authority which, widely distributed,
requires a delicate balance of role propriety on the part of the occupant and effective use of the role potentiality in effective decision making. Leadership roles
in particular are by definition less narrowly limited than other roles in the system.

boards). In new nations there is a regrettable tendency for government to become the main mechanism of social mobility. In other words, the public needs to see social and economic opportunities in terms of roles other than political ones. It is absolutely necessary that the main bulk of social striving and role expansion take place in the economic and social spheres, rather than the political, for when politics becomes the common road to individual success, government becomes a substitute for society and the propensities are to produce, once again, one extreme or the other. Either the system fragments, as in the case of Indonesia, or a strong system of party-state discipline needs to be imposed, as has occurred in Pakistan, the Sudan, and possibly in Ghana, although the picture there remains mixed.

Thus the prognosis for nation building by constitutional means is not on the whole a very healthy one. However, the situation in Uganda has some special advantages, particularly within a federal form in which it is possible, as in Nigeria, that the mutual hostility of the parts may give life to the center and the multiplication of local structures of government may provide that range of secondary and supporting political roles necessary to make democracy a genuine possibility. Uganda will need to face these problems squarely as the bureaucratic phase of colonialism gives way to the period of responsible self-government leading to independence.

Some Characteristics and Consequences of a Bureaucratic-Colonial State

The present Protectorate government is the last before the phase of responsible and representative government comes to prevail. There is a ministerial system, set up under the administration of Sir Andrew Cohen in August 1955. The senior officer is still the Chief Secretary. He is also the head of the civil service, the general coordinator of the work of the various ministries, and the leader for the government side of the Legislative Council.

The objective of the Protectorate government is a united Uganda with an evolving pattern of devolution of authority along the general lines of Ceylon and Ghana. The 1959 constitutional proposals recommend substantial reform and responsible African government.[5]

---

[5] See *Report of the Constitutional Committee, 1959* (Wild Report) (Entebbe: G. P., 1959), *passim*.

It will be recalled that the original concern behind the Legislative Council was with European and Asian interests. Africans, it was presumed, had their own institutions. Since 1945, however, when Africans first came to participate in Legislative Council, and increasingly afterward, Legislative Council has become a more prominent feature of life in Uganda. Many fear and dislike it. Nevertheless, it is clear to everyone concerned with politics that the composition and powers of the Legislative Council will be the crucial political concern in the years immediately ahead.

Despite the efforts the Baganda have made to cut Buganda loose from the rest of the country, everyone knows that such a solution is not acceptable either to the Colonial Office or to the Protectorate regime. Although a crucial feature of contemporary relationships between the Buganda and the Protectorate governments is conflict, this still does not obscure the fact that day-to-day association remains close. Buganda is increasingly, for better or for ill, tied in with the rest of the country. Even though political demands for separation have grown, economically Buganda is more than ever dependent on the Protectorate government.

As well, the political parties are aware that it is the Protectorate or central government which in the last analysis will distribute benefits, patronage, and control finance and development. Thus power will ultimately inhere in the center. And, as we have pointed out, there is a growing urge by politicians to dominate the center. Indeed, this is the main hope for political party growth.

Most parties agree too that a program of Africanization in the political sphere is not enough in the way of reform. Africans who merely replace Europeans and take a similar seat on the Legislative Council are in the business of becoming adept at European political roles. The nub of the problem—and it is implicit in the attitudes of political leaders toward Legislative Council—is not simply how Africans can learn to become parliamentarians, but how parliamentary practices can become Africanized so that after independence they do not lose their essential proportions.[6]

Indeed, this problem fortifies Buganda separatism. For many

[6] This appears more easily said than done. In practice, after self-government it is exceedingly difficult to develop a political style that has its own integrity and meaning. It is clear that new political forms will emerge in Africa, but it will take time. See H. Spiro, "New Constitutional Forms in Africa," *World Politics*, Vol. XIII, No. 1, October 1960.

leading Baganda, the legislative world in Uganda can only be regarded as a teacher-student world. But they no longer wish to remain in that position. They see Africans placed in the latter category and the European members, both official and unofficial, in the former. Leading Europeans who regard themselves as quite pro-African, and often argue bitterly with colonial officials with respect to proper policy, still regard themselves as showing African representatives in the Legislative Council the ropes. Some African political leaders have explicitly recognized this and are coming to reject the role. Even those who are not particularly anxious to achieve immediate self-government now look forward to that stage of political development when Africans dominate both the legislature and, equally important, the tempo of society in the capital. "I have not learned quite enough yet," said an African member of the Legislative Council in the debate on election to the Legislative Council, "but I have learned much from my colleagues the non-Africans who serve on this side of the House and will try to continue to . . . learn a little bit more from those non-Africans who remain here! But still it is a national problem and indeed our people have got to start to understand their own face and Government and that is why I believe that, while I accept that non-Africans should remain nominated members, they should be regarded mostly as advisors. . . ."[7]

Several outstanding members of the European community entertained, for a time perhaps, the political possibilities of a role in interracial political parties, as has become the case in Tanganyika where the Tanganyika African National Congress is anxious to recruit non-African members. Regarding their expertise and lack of racial prejudice as the guarantors of success, they have become particularly effective with Africans in the Legislative Council. For those African representative members of the Legislative Council who were not Baganda (and even increasingly for the Baganda members), two Europeans in particular worked closely with the African members and were helpful to them. Both were the leaders of the Representative Members' Association, J. T. Simpson, the Director of the Industrial Development Corporation and one of the most responsi-

[7] Proceedings of the Legislative Council, 37th Session, 4th Meeting, 7-8 August 1957, p. 38.

ble and reflective members of the European community, and Mrs. Barbara Saben, whose political shrewdness and constructive but critical role in the Legislative Council have helped make it a useful political body when in substance it was little more than a debating society.

Nevertheless, many people are suspicious of the motives of these and other helpful groups of Europeans. Fear that they are trying simply to safeguard their own position in the country and are basically insincere remains fairly pervasive. Thus, despite the fact that Africans can now attend the most important club in Uganda[8] where members of all races mix socially and politically, there remains an almost unbridgeable gap between the various racial communities in Uganda. Africans have been brought into the Legislative and Executive Councils, but they have not been integrated socially and politically into what remains an almost purely European society where European influences and manners prevail. Both Africans and Asians have had to conform to those influences. Thus in spite of an African majority, the Legislative and Executive Councils reflect a last stage of social welfare colonial conciliarism, that is, the phase of bureaucratic colonialism. Africanizing the Legislative Council has given Africans the largest proportion of seats, but this includes "co-opted" figures as well as representative ones. Indeed, the representative contingent remained until recently headed by Europeans.[9]

The anomalous situation exists, then, in which a European-dominated legislature with an African majority sits for the entire country while remaining primarily geared to the economic life and activity of Europeans and Asians. In its districts and in Buganda, however, the African governments are geared to local African life. The world of Legislative Council and the world of Lukiko remain entirely separate in spirit as well as form.[10]

This is of some importance since European patterns of life are increasingly irritants to Africans. The psychological compart-

[8] The Uganda Club.

[9] At present the representative members are split into two groups, the Representative Members' Organization and the Elected Members' Organization. Both are headed by Africans.

[10] The next stage is now being prepared. A Relationships Commission is working on plans for fundamental reform to lead to an elected representative majority and a cabinet system.

mentalization of life persists, indeed in the most acute form long after social barriers have been lifted a bit. Much of the current attitudes of Baganda today can be attributed to the psychological discrimination which in effect says that the king, Buganda government, and Lukiko are all very well and good in their somewhat garish and shoddy way, but the real business of government, which Africans must still learn, will take place on the floor of the Legislative Council.[11]

For Africans the relative accessibility of officers of the Buganda government, the graceful and ceremonial informality of the *Lubiri*, or Court, and the sense of control and contact in one's own institutions remain in sharp contrast to the more curt, restrained atmosphere of the Legislative Council. There the air in the visitors' galleries is of novelty and display. It is not uncommon for Europeans to remark that Africans who go there to hear a debate are "growing up" and "understanding" parliamentary affairs. Their attitude has been amply rewarded by a genuine lack of interest by Africans. Thus the curious other-worldliness about the legislature—it has the atmosphere of a club in which an experiment in race relations is being somewhat self-consciously tried.

Legislative Council has become far more representative as time has passed. Insofar as colonialism assumed social welfare obligations, the importance of economic and social development has until relatively recently overshadowed all other aspects of the legislature's work. But ordinary political conflicts have not been worked out in the Legislative Council. The elaborate bargaining and compromise normal in party government have been present in only a relatively mild degree—and that predominantly between European and Asian commercial and agricultural groups and civil servants. It has remained a system in which Europeans essentially do things for Africans. Even the bitterest debates in which repre-

11 In the relationships between races it is difficult not to contrast the difference in outlook resulting from the West African pattern and the Uganda pattern. While it would be unwise to make the Europeans in West Africa appear terribly virtuous in this matter, they were more dependent on the social relations they had with Africans than in East Africa, and were thrown into more heterogeneous social transactions with Africans.

sentative members got themselves very exercised have a hothouse quality about them and an air of unreality.[12]

The club-like atmosphere is sustained by the fact that many of the official members of the Legislative Council work and live in Entebbe, which remains a relatively prim and secluded preserve of officialdom. Some African cabinet ministers, such as Y. K. Lule, the Minister of Rural Development (a former Makerere tutor), anticipating awkwardness, have preferred not to live there. The facilities and amenities are more or less exclusively European.[13] The Asian minister, Sir Amar Maini, found himself treated with a certain amount of tolerance. There was respect for his brilliance, but he was made to feel an Asian among Europeans, regardless of his urbanity, poise, and University of London background.[14]

In both Kampala and Entebbe, relationships among colonial service wives, whose social graces often included courage in inter-racial relationships but rarely complete naturalness in lowering racial barriers, are also important.[15]

The official world is still relatively small and important. It retains the characteristics of an oligarchy which only slowly and reluctantly is emerging from its shell. In 1958 the senior staff,

[12] This air of unreality is reflected in the relative calm with which flurries from the representative side are met on the government side of the house. Work with the Legislative Council is regarded as an important but hardly overwhelming part of the work of Secretariat officials. Legislative affairs are considered important but not crucial determinants of policy. Increasingly, however, African concerns and issues have come to be the overwhelming concern of the Legislative Council in recent years. Much of the behind-scenes bargaining and compromise is based on growing deference to African wishes.

[13] The character of Entebbe is beginning to alter because of the airport, the Lake Victoria Hotel, and increased commercial activities ancillary to these operations.

[14] At least one of the African ministers lived in Entebbe. One of the more attractive features of Entebbe for African ministers was that a very good multi-racial primary school was available to their children.

[15] It is widely felt among the civil service wives that under Sir Andrew Cohen, Government House became far too liberal socially, especially in the degree to which Africans were admitted to social functions. However, one of the valuable functions performed by senior service wives is the way in which they help to break down differences in social strata within the hierarchy of the Service itself, and facilitate in-service solidarity. The work of European women in the Uganda Council of Women, the Girl Guides, and St. John's Ambulance Brigade, is indeed noteworthy. As well, European civil service wives help to smooth the way for the wives of new African civil servants. In-service solidarity certainly includes African civil servants, at least in the political administration.

that is, officers in the political administration, including Secretariat and field staff, numbered approximately 154. Of that number, only approximately 15 were Africans.[16]

The predominantly European and, more pertinently, official nature of the Legislative and Executive Councils have helped to retard more genuine interest and participation in their functions. It is on the official side that "real" government is to be found. Tolerance has been extended to the representative side of the house. Irritation with officialdom is common on the part of the representative European members. There remains some of the dislike of colonial government by the commercial man.

The civil service stresses technical knowledge and administrative sagacity as a justification of its continued leadership. This has intimidated African political moderates who cannot help being concerned with the small number of educated Africans skilled and proficient in the ways of a senior civil service. In contrast with other countries such as Ghana or the Sudan, where a B.A. degree among Africans is by no means unusual, Uganda has very few Africans with higher degrees.[17]

Thus officialdom in Uganda has great prestige, education, and considerable insularity. From the point of view of *residence* (in Entebbe or Kampala), *university background,* and *social position,* the senior civil servant has been part of a ruling oligarchy with considerable exclusiveness. Capable of great effort and hard work when it comes to the social welfare of his charges and to developing the economic and social propensities of the country, the civil servant has a remarkable degree of fair mindedness and selfless service. Moreover, pure racial bias by itself is rare.

16 Actually, this represented great progress. Since then the Protectorate government has instituted a "crash" program in Africanization. (These figures were obtained from the *Staff List,* July 1, 1958.) For example, while there was one African in a "scale A" post in 1954, by 1959 there were 62. The program of Africanization is discussed in greater detail in a later section of this chapter.

17 In the political administration senior European staff numbered approximately 154, including 41 B.A. degrees from Cambridge, 29 from Oxford, and 27 from all other universities, including London, provincial, and overseas. By any standards the Europeans in the senior Service are a highly educated group, having been to the two major university "clubs" of England, Cambridge and Oxford. Among the African recruits and civil servants in confirmed or probationary posts, two had degrees from London and one from Wales.

Africans coming up against this remarkable group of men have in the past turned their aspirations inward, to the local service. Although today university graduates with a degree look forward to careers in the Protectorate civil service, graduates from Budo, Kisubi, and "old" Makerere preferred posts in the Buganda government. There in 1956, for example, not a single university degree was to be found among African civil servants in the Buganda government, although a high proportion were "old" Makerere, Budo, and Kisubi. Although several members of the 1959 Lukiko have professional training in law or medicine or have read courses in England on various subjects, such as journalism or local government, there are no higher degrees among the members.

Uganda thus remains in the last stages of a colonial service state. Good government is carried out increasingly with the advice of elected representatives, but still mainly under the auspices of a small and relatively intimate group of superior civil servants. Conscious of the need for development, for stability, and for orderly progress, the civil servants are impatient with the pettiness of ambitious politicians and the disruptive influence of irresponsibility. But they are thwarted in their efforts to extend good government because of the deteriorating political climate. As a result, their basic rationale, efficiency, has been undermined, and they are increasingly disgruntled and frustrated.

The same kinds of compromises worked out elsewhere in democratization of colonial systems are of course operating in Uganda. It is simply a matter of a few years before Africans will be in full charge.

What are African political responses to the decline of the power and prestige of the expatriate staff? Political courage becomes one characteristic. When a nationalist figure becomes rusticated or imprisoned for political activities he becomes more highly regarded by the public. Another of these is bargaining with the governor, or the secretary of state for colonies, or members of Parliament, thereby passing over the heads of even the most senior service. The authority of the civil service is hard to challenge while the conception prevails that government is a job for administrators. Those who seek to alter it by simply accepting the job of representative member in the Legislative Council look comparatively unprofessional and sometimes foolish, for reasons we have mentioned. But when they attack the right of the professional administrator to rule, they become more serious. They then begin to carry political momentum of their own and become men of consequence.

Quite another factor has helped to break down the tradition of rulership which prevailed among the senior service. Many of those in the senior service, including several on the superscale level acting as ministers of the Protectorate government, represented a prewar tradition in the service. In prewar days the Colonial Service had few qualms about asserting the right to rule, and it had an obligation to specify the general lines along which progress was to occur. In this respect, although the Colonial Service was never aristocratic and thus never injected personal claims to leadership, it was in its own way Platonic. It did not make much out of service to a utopian goal; nevertheless, the ideals of moral uplift and propriety were given great priority in its scheme of things.

Many of the best prewar colonial administrators who were trained in this tradition were carried over into the postwar period. The result under the press of political change was, for many administrative officers, genuine irritation and confusion over the tempo of events, a loss of purpose, and a cynicism about the political future of Africans. Such attitudes were quickly recognized by African political leaders and helped to intensify the subtle estrangement which characterized their relationships.

Small wonder, then, that almost all African groups, whether heads of African governments or political party leaders, wanted to create a national constituent assembly before a new constitution was created for them. They did not want to simply pass from an official to representative and responsible system of government through unilateral bargaining with the Protectorate government and the Colonial Office. But, as was the demand in Ghana and Nigeria in an earlier period, they wanted a public assembly of Africans from all over the country to draw up the terms of a new constitution which can be African in its inspiration.[18]

18 In Ghana, for example, the all-African Coussey Commission performed this role. The Convention People's Party called its own Gold Coast People's Representative Assembly at the New Era Club in Accra, November 20, 1949.

In the face of deteriorating relationships between the expatriate civil service and African political leaders, and the Baganda's stiffening resistance to his rule, Sir Frederick Crawford, the Governor who succeeded Sir Andrew Cohen, agreed to the setting up of a Relationships Commission with the following terms of reference.

"To consider the future form of government best suited to Uganda and the question of the relationship between the Central Government and the other authorities in Uganda, bearing in mind:

"(a) Her Majesty's Government's known resolve to lead Uganda by appropriate stages to independence and to this end to develop stable institutions of government which will properly reflect the particular circumstances and meet the needs of Uganda; and

"(b) the desire of the peoples of Uganda to preserve their existing institutions and customs and the status and dignity of their rulers and leaders; and

"(c) the special relationship that already exists between Her Majesty's Government and His Highness the Kabaka's Government and the Native Governments of Bunyoro, Ankole and Toro as set down in the various Agreements that have been made with the Traditional Rulers and peoples of Buganda, Bunyoro, Ankole and Toro; and to make recommendations."[19]

Until the Relationships Commission can bring forward a satisfactory set of proposals for constitutional reform, and until Uganda properly enters the final phase of responsible self-government, the position of the Protectorate government will remain obscure. The danger is that the African governments, and more particularly the Buganda government, will continue to attract much of the best available talent in Uganda. Education will be one channel through which Africans can be poured into the senior ranks of the civil service, modifying the racial and intellectual exclusiveness of this group and bringing it directly into the social life of African elites. As well, reform of the legislature will bring

[19] See Appendix I, *Despatch No. 1261 of 14th September 1960, from the Secretary of State for the Colonies in Connection with the Report of the Constitutional Committee, 1959* (Entebbe: G.P., 1960).

politicians into responsible government positions. Both of these objectives are already settled policy in Uganda.

Legislative Council, 1955-1958

Uganda has under her present constitution an African majority in the Legislative Council. Composition of the house is as follows:

Government Side (30 Total)

11 Ministers (including one Assistant Minister)

2 Parliamentary Secretaries

4 Official Members

13 Backbenchers

Representative Side (30 Total)

5 Africans from Buganda

2 Africans from Ankole

2 Africans from Busoga

3 Africans from the rest of the western province (one each Kigezi, Toro, and Bunyoro)

3 Africans from the rest of the eastern province (one each Bukedi, Bugisu, and Teso)

3 Africans from the northern province (Lango, Acholi, and Western Nile)

6 European Representative Members

6 Asian Representative Members

The racial composition of the legislature includes on the government side 3 African ministers, 1 Asian minister, and 6 European ministers. Of the latter, 1 member, the Minister of Commerce and Works, was recruited from the unofficial side. The rest were officers of Her Majesty's Overseas Civil Service. Until 1958 2 Parliamentary under-secretaries were Africans, as were 7 backbenchers. Hence there were 12 Africans on the official side and 18 on the representative side of the house. The racial totals in the legislature were 30 Africans, 21 Europeans (10 of whom were officials), and 9 Asians. The Governor, as President of the Council, had an original and casting vote. In January 1958 a Speaker was appointed and 2 additional African backbench members were added to replace the Governor's original and casting vote. The official members in the last resort have a majority on matters of confidence. The government can therefore not be voted out of office.

In the 1955 Legislature the 5 members from Buganda were affiliated with the Uganda National Congress, as was the Assistant Minister of Social Services. For the rest there were varying degrees of party association and affiliation, but few were regular members of any political party.[20]

The most important bloc in the legislature was, of course, composed of the members of the Executive Council seated in the Legislative Council. These were the people whose responsibility it was to govern.

The nominated unofficial backbenchers, who also sat on the government side, were given a Queen's appointment to the Council because of the divergent views and interests they represented.[21] They were not chosen simply arbitrarily; they received their appointments only after lengthy discussion with representative private groups and associations throughout the country.[22] Among them were the former Katikiro of Buganda, Michael Kawalya-Kagwa, the son of Sir Apolo Kagwa; Erinayo Okuilo, a treasurer of the Lango District Council and a district council member for 18 years; and T. B. Bazarrabusa from Toro, a teacher and district council member. All 3 were Protestants.

There were 3 doctors in the Legislative Council, all Africans. On the government side was Sebastiane Kyewalyanga, a medical practitioner from Buddu with a long record of service on his saza council and on the Masaka township authority.

There were 2 women in the Legislative Council, both outstanding. On the backbench side was Mrs. P. Kisosonkole. A South African married to the saza chief Sekibobo (the father-in-law of the Kabaka), she has a Bachelor of Arts degree from Fort Hare. She is a leading community development officer in Uganda, President of the Uganda African Women's League, and Vice-President of the Uganda Council of Women.

[20] This situation has changed drastically since the recent general election in Uganda. We shall discuss the implications of this below.

[21] See Secretary of State's Despatch No. 692 of July 1955.

[22] There is no formal provision for such consultation. This pattern of consultation is at the Governor's discretion.

Other government backbench members included S. W. Kulubya, the former Omuwanika of Buganda; Kenneth Ingham, an historian from Makerere College; and H. K. Jaffer, the son of a civil servant, an insurance broker, and leading member of the Muslim community. His record of service went back to 1936.

Potentially, the most important group was composed of elected African representative members. In 1955 these were elected from the district councils, which in almost all cases were themselves composed of a majority of elected representatives. The Buganda members were elected by an electoral college. Thus in Buganda and the districts a system of indirect representation prevailed.

In Buganda the selection of representative members to the Legislative Council was left to an electoral college. Among the members of the electoral college in 1955 were people of influence, substance, or political significance in Buganda. A roster of the names reads like a Who's Who. They included Mr. and Mrs. John Kale; Mr. Kale later became an object of controversy when he opened a Cairo office of the Uganda National Congress. Also Dr. E. N. Muwazi, at the time a leading figure in the Uganda National Congress and subsequently in the United Congress Party; Saule Lutete, who had been an important member in the Federation of Uganda African Partnerships; Paulo Mwanga, the former head of the youth league of the Uganda National Congress and subsequently a leader of the United Congress Party; and Mr. and Mrs. Apolo K. Kironde. Kironde was Assistant Minister of Social Services in the Protectorate government and a member of the Uganda National Congress. J. W. Kiwanuka of the Uganda National Congress was also in the college, as well as Y. S. Bamuta, long a figure in Bataka and trading affairs and then a member of the Uganda National Congress; A. Lukabi, also connected with the efforts to produce farming cooperatives; and even the aide-de camp of the Kabaka, George N. Malo.

It was an interesting group that the public selected for the electoral college. Representatives of the nationalist parties were very strongly represented, as were old Bataka and other conservative interests. A sprinkling of clerics from the major denominations and a few Muslims gave representation to the religious groups, but for the most part the political party leaders were offset by Baganda neo-traditionalists whose prestige was high enough so that the politicians had to reckon with their influence. Thus the political party leaders in the Uganda National Congress were able to convince the others in the electoral college in 1955, as part of a negotiated bargain over the allocation of offices in the Buganda and Protectorate governments, that Congressmen should get the seats reserved for Baganda in the Legislative Council. But on a subsequent occasion, the neo-traditionalists refused to supply members to the Legislative Council at all.

The African Representative Members

In the Legislative Council itself, all the African representative members (totaling 18) were born in Uganda, 4 of them in Buganda. Over 60 per cent were between the ages of 35 and 44. All had been to secondary school or higher, with 9 having attended King's College, Budo, and 2 St. Mary's. Eight were Makerere graduates; 2 had had university work in the United Kingdom, 2 had professional degrees, and 3 had had special courses in the U.K.

Occupationally they were as follows: 1 farmer, 6 African local government officials, 1 businessman, 3 teachers, 1 cooperative union employee, 1 barrister, 1 politician, 2 doctors, and 1 priest.[23] Of those whose fathers' occupations are known, 6 were the sons of chiefs, 1 the son of a businessman, and 1 the son of a farmer.

Seventeen listed their religion as follows: 12 Protestants and 5 Catholics. There were 6 who were affiliated with the Uganda National Congress; at the time of the survey, 1956, this was the only political party represented in the Legislative Council.

The representative members were almost all newcomers to the legislature. Only 2 had seen service before 1955, but all had had a prominent record in some respect. All were affiliated with a large number of voluntary associations by which they increased their influence. These included sports associations, Catholic Action, parents' associations, and educational organizations, the Fabian Colonial Bureau, scouting, United Budonians, and the Uganda African Teachers' Association. Most of the members belonged to the Uganda Club, the country's leading interracial club.

Voluntary associations play a much more important part in the

---

[23] Occupational data is incomplete on one man.

political life of Uganda than in those countries where political parties are the more established vehicles for political expression. The measure of a man in Uganda, and particularly in Buganda, is determined not by birth or origin but by substance and organization. Not only are landowning and wealth important, but the old boys' associations, church, and other associations to which he belongs measure his social personality, influence, and support. Hence the voluntary associations represent a major informal consultative channel which a man as well as his wife depend upon for position in society and power and influence. All of the African representative members of Legislative Council in 1956 were men with overlapping memberships in a widely-diverse set of voluntary associations, ranging from school associations to advisory committees of government.

They were not provincial. Fifteen had traveled extensively in Europe, especially in the United Kingdom. Three had been to Cairo, 3 to India, 2 to West Africa, and 2 to South Africa. Two had seen service in the Uganda Defense Force.

As a group they read, in addition to vernacular newspapers, the *Uganda Argus*, the *East African Standard*, and the *Times*. A sprinkling read the *New Statesman and Nation*, *Venture*, and *The Socialist*. Only one member read *Drum*.

Two of the members had at one time been imprisoned, 1 for political activity and 1 for forgery.

When given the opportunity to state their choices, 6 members opted for immediate self-government, 3 wanted to wait 10 years, 1 considered 20 years the proper time, and 1 thought 5 years would be sufficient. Others declined to specify.[24]

Three major groups could be specified in the Legislative Council. The first was the political party bloc centering around Dr. Kununka.[25] The second group centered around B. K. Magezi (who in turn was frequently assisted by Mrs. Barbara Saben, a European representative member). It included most of the members

[24] The material contained here is derived from questionnaires distributed to the members of the Legislative Council, June 18, 1956. I must record my gratitude to the staff of the East African Institute of Social Research for helping me develop the questionnaire and for secretarial assistance.

[25] Interestingly enough, the members affiliated with the Uganda National Congress regarded Kununka, rather than Musazi, as their parliamentary leader, although Musazi was President of the U.N.C.

from the north and some from the eastern province. In the subsequent Legislative Council, elected in 1958, Magezi emerged as one of the founders of a new party, the Uganda People's Union.

The third group was Asian, but so internally divided that no single leader emerged. Two Asians had been born in East Africa. Of the representative members replying to the questionnaire, 2 were Hindu, 1 was Muslim, 1 was Ismaili Khoja (Muslim). Occupationally, 1 was a lawyer and the rest were businessmen and landlords.

The Representative Members' Organization

The nominated unofficial representative members were led by J. T. Simpson, the Chairman of the Representative Members' Organization. Simpson, originally associated with the Uganda Company, became Chairman and General Manager of the Uganda Development Corporation, was a past President of the Uganda Chamber of Commerce, and a leader in the European community. Of liberal persuasion, he had spent 30 years in East Africa, 18 of which were in residence in Uganda. The Deputy Chairman of the R.M.O. was Mrs. Barbara Saben, the wife of a leading Kampala businessman and most active in civic affairs in Uganda.

Eighteen Africans were elected indirectly. The rest were nominated as representative of particular interests, or because they were outstanding individuals. A few, such as Kawalya Kagwa and Kulubya, were men who had staunchly supported the Protectorate government and had been rewarded for their service. Although generally disliked in Buganda, they did have admirers. The Asians were in an awkward position. No great enthusiasm was demonstrated by anyone for their presence, either among the Europeans or the Africans. They could not be excluded from political participation, however, without the charge of discrimination being raised, at least as long as Europeans continued to sit.

A wide range of views and associations was represented, but as a legislature it was not very exciting. It was its potentiality that remained interesting. For all its lawmaking powers, the Legislative Council in 1956 was basically an advisory body.

What was the virtue of the Legislative Council? It was an important transitional vehicle. In the issues which were put, there was often good criticism and effective modification of policy. More than that, however, although the political concerns which lay behind the attitudes of most Africans toward Legislative Council related to the power the Legislative Council would have, and how quickly it would achieve an African representative majority, the Council performed another function. It was a forum where the divisions taken on political issues were usually on grounds other than racial. This differs from the Legislative Council of Kenya, for example, where African and other members have drawn political lines on grounds of race. In Uganda the major division has been with respect to government and government backbencher on one side and representative member, whether elected or nominated, on the other. In the absence of party discipline and real party alignment in the Legislative Council (and the Uganda National Congress group was too small for this in 1956, although in 1958 the Council saw a parliamentary party being formed), the Representative Members' Organization was the closest thing to a parliamentary party, even though it had limited political significance. It remained an instrument of collaboration among different representative members and helped to provide a channel of communication to government about the opinions of the 30 representative members. As well as formal meetings of the organization prior to sessions of Legislative Council, European, Asian, and African members met frequently and informally. The Chairman, J. T. Simpson, and the Deputy Chairman, Barbara Saben, were skilled in debate and had a deep appreciation of the processes of parliamentary government.[26]

There were several important issues on which the government was made to give way in the face of strong opposition from the representative members. On one issue, the Land Forces Bill, the government desired to put the East African land forces under the control of the East African High Commission. All 30 members worked together and the government conceded. Another such issue was the Police Bill, whereby government wished to control public meetings with the end view of controlling election meetings. Claiming that such a proposal was premature and, more important,

[26] The Representative Members' Organization had its own meeting room, a small library, and a secretary's office. It received a grant of £2,000 per year for reference subscriptions, typewriters, duplicating machines, etc. The organization was able to provide information for its members and facilitated the work of the members.

detrimental to the growth of political responsibility, the members' argument for liberty of the subject won the day.

The biggest difficulty with the R.M.O. was that in the last analysis its powers were advisory. Therefore, the Legislative Council had an unreal quality to it. But, in a more revolutionary sense, it provided the way for government to more easily accept political parties. The introduction of even a few representatives of a political party into the Legislative Council cast a cloak of respectability around them which hitherto had been completely lacking. Before 1955 parties were regarded as dangerous to law and order and essentially irresponsible.

The purposes of the Legislative Council can be summarized as these: to make the laws of Uganda, to vote the finances of government, and to discuss matters of interest to the whole country.[27] The place and role of the legislature as an integrative institution, helping to build a single and cemented society, has already assumed major proportions.

The Legislative Council elected in October 1958 was very different from the old one. Direct elections had been held only after Buganda and several of the districts had refused to participate. The African representative members so elected formed their own Elected Members' Organization, breaking away from the R.M.O. The principle was thus established that election is the only proper warrant for participation in the Legislative Council, and since only Africans have been elected, this excludes all non-Africans from the new organization. Urgency to reform the Legislative Council takes on a new dimension.

The Executive Council

The ministerial system was established in September 1955. The chief change from the previous system of secretaries or officials as departmental heads was, first, that the ministers were collectively responsible for the business of government and, second, that the posts were made essentially political appointments. This meant a sharing of power, devolved from the Secretariat, and the acceptance by all of the responsibilities of high office. The groundwork

[27] All members except ministers, parliamentary secretaries, and civil servants receive an allowance of £300 a year plus travel and general costs.

was laid for a cabinet system of government when an elected and representative majority appeared in the Legislative Council.[28]

There is no need to discuss in detail either the structure or the purposes of the Executive Council. The ministerial system is a breach in the official oligarchy. Few uphold the virtues of colonial executive councils except as an interim framework of government, preparing the ground for a cabinet that is responsible to the legislature. The great virtue of the executive council system is that the official and ex officio members, that is, the civil servants holding departmental portfolios, can when the time comes easily be transposed to the normal relationship of permanent secretary to a minister, thus subordinating the role of the civil servant to a popular government. A difficulty of the system is that some of the civil servants in ministerial posts are not always of the highest caliber. In part recruited on a basis of seniority, a few of the most senior officers have protective and paternal attitudes toward Africans, while profoundly disapproving of what is inevitably considered a premature devolution of authority into political hands. Indeed, the most ardent proponents of paternalism are sometimes the most devoted and principled civil servants who, regarding their years of colonial service as the carrying out of a moral trust, find it difficult to abide what they regard as opportunistic politicians. Once in a while, too, there are less principled civil servants in ministerial posts who give lip service to the idea of rapid devolution yet basically oppose the repudiation of their tenure which is implied in demands for self-government. Such civil servants are regarded with suspicion by Africans with whom they come into contact, and while a superficial gloss of liberalism suffices to satisfy the language of the day, few Africans accept either such men or their position.

The position of the Chief Secretary becomes a most difficult one. His position is not yet anomalous, but almost so. He combines what will later become a role like that of a minister of interior with a semipolitical task as leader of the government side of the legislature. He is thus "the government" personified, and great diplomacy and charm are required to make an uncomfortable job

---

[28] Letter on establishment of the ministerial system, Hopkinson to Cohen, dated 28 July 1955, *Uganda Gazette*, 29 September 1955, p. 464.

politically useful. Rarely, however, is there a chief secretary who can combine these qualities. Hence he is often an object of political antagonism which, although seldom expressed in public, emphasizes as a living reproof to nationalism the fact that the government is run by the civil service.[29]

The function of the present leadership is to prepare the groundwork as rapidly as possible for devolution of authority to a responsible cabinet. It is in the important but unenviable position of promoting unpopular but necessary measures for ensuring a smooth transition of power.

Just as the role of the Executive Council is most difficult just before a responsible and representative system of government becomes established, so are difficult tasks imposed on district officers and chiefs. The administrators in the field in particular bear the brunt of political party abuse.

Changes in the Role of the Field Administrator

In the beginning stages of such a shift, the position of the district officer is ambiguous. Not only is his rule in the districts challenged but, more important, there arise many different groups each claiming to speak for Africans; if ignored, they attack the district officer as an oppressor. This produces difficulties for everyone concerned with administration. For example, chiefs who have been loyal to the district commissioner now find themselves caught in the same ambiguities and cross-fires.

[29] At the inception of the ministerial system in Uganda in 1955 there were some extremely able people both on the civil service side and among the nominated unofficial members. For example, one of the most sophisticated among the civil servants was J. V. Wild, the Administrative Secretary, whose father had been a civil servant before him. A product of King's College, Cambridge, he is the author of several valuable historical studies on Uganda.

Of exceptional ability is Sir Amar Maini, a lawyer and prominent member of the Asian community, who was formerly Mayor of Kampala and then Minister of Corporations and Regional Communications. One of the ablest men in the country, Sir Amar has been involved in major economic planning in Uganda. He was a storm center for a time because of African opposition to an Asian minister. He represents an excellent example of the talents and skills which Africans are in danger of losing if they persist in discriminatory attitudes toward Asians who, if employed by Africans of good will, could help immeasurably to alleviate the immediate shortages of education and experience which prevail among the African communities.

Exceptional as well, Y. K. Lule, the Minister of Rural Development, was a former lecturer in Education at Makerere College. He was originally elected to Legislative Council as a representative member from Buganda; he is a Catholic.

The district commissioner is responsible for the law, order, and well-being of the district in his charge. He is the field representative of the central government. Whereas once he had extensive authority and was more or less responsible to himself in the normal affairs of running a district, today he is increasingly under public scrutiny.

The District Councils Ordinance of 1955 provided important grants of authority for those councils that wanted to come under its provisions.[30] By this means it was hoped that district and lower councils would improve their performance and increase Africans' interest and participation in the efficient provision of local services. To this end direct responsibility for local governments has been largely shifted to the staff and members of district councils, although residual responsibilities remain with district commissioners. The Ordinance, which followed the lines laid down in the Wallis report on local government,[31] gave the district councils executive and legislative functions over a wide range of responsibilities. Thus the main instrument of local government policy has shifted away from the district commissioner to the district council. Increasingly his is an advisory role, yet the district commissioner is responsible for seeing that the district councils and the council's committees are adequate to the jobs.

To relieve the pressure on the chiefs there are now employees of the district councils, responsible to an independent appointments board,[32] with loyalties to the council for carrying out council policy and to the governor for law and order. Comparatively less well educated as new, younger, elected members come on the district councils, the chiefs find themselves attacked as conservatives. As well, younger elected members are anxious to exclude the district commissioner from the affairs of the district. Thus in the districts there is now a situation somewhat similar in nature to the case of Buganda and the Residency.[33]

[30] Those districts which were not prepared to compose some of their internal difficulties and come under the provisions of the 1955 Ordinance, such as Toro and Busoga, remained under the much more restricted provisions of the African Local Governments Ordinance of 1949.

[31] See C. A. G. Wallis, *Report of an Inquiry into African Local Government in the Protectorate of Uganda* (Entebbe: G.P., 1953).

[32] See amendment to the African Authority Ordinance, *Special Supplement to the Uganda Gazette*, Vol. LI, No. 7, 10 April 1958.

[33] For a discussion of the district officer's role and the position of the chief, see

Considerable uncertainty has crept into the role of the district commissioner and the position has become more limited. However, instead of being more resourceful and depending on persuasion and innovation, many commissioners have taken an opposite tack, becoming more cautious and looking more to the rules for guidance and to avoiding tackling difficult cases, that is, cases which might produce trouble where the rules are no longer clear.

There is increased fear of being found out. For example, if funds are short and an African clerk has misappropriated a sum or made a financial error, the district commissioner begins to wonder when he last checked the books. Often, in order to forestall possible embarrassing enquiries which would look bad, especially in the eyes of superiors and local politicians, he becomes highly moral, gives the clerk a small sentence, and pays the necessary sum back into the accounts himself in order to let the incident pass. Fear of incidents in which he might in some way be caught short has been a consequence of "muddying the role" and making the necessary changes in the position of district commissioner. Enough continuity is required in order not to interrupt a flow of authority. Enough change is involved so that no one knows precisely where that authority remains. If the district commissioner once had great power and little responsibility, the reverse is now the case. His responsibilities are far greater than the power he has.

Just as there is a reliance on increasing bureaucratization, few strong personalities remain as compared with an earlier day. The more complex the situation, the less chance for the district commissioner to take independent action. His personal qualities are subordinated to routine. The emphasis is on security and safety which can be found only in authorized action. The old district officer had a calling. Many of the younger ones regard it as a job whose definition is obscure.[34]

my article, "Some Problems of the Local Government in Uganda," *Journal of African Administration*, Vol. xi, No. 1, January 1959. See also L. A. Fallers, "Predicament of the Modern African Chief: an Instance from Uganda," *American Anthropologist*, Vol. 57, No. 2, April 1955.

[34] The comments above are compiled from notes of discussions on the role of the district officer held with a large number of younger district commissioners and assistant district commissioners. Particularly the latter were most outspoken in this regard. My view is not accepted in the Secretariat and the former Governor, Sir Andrew Cohen, and several senior civil servants with whom I discussed

Thus the political administration is in a delicate spot. Still concerned with the good government of the country, preparing the way for its own political curtailment, assisting the nationalists while being damned by them, acting as advisors in political situations which grow complex as old feuds, tribalism, private disputes, and party conflicts all seem to interfere with effective administration, the government officers find it difficult to draw a perspective within the framework of the country itself. Nationalists, with their attention on Ghana and Nigeria or even Tanganyika, evaluate the sober considerations of civil servants with a jaundiced eye.

All this increases the urgency for self-government. What have been the preparations? The most important in view of our comments on the civil service, not to mention political pressure, has been increased concern with Africanization of the civil service. In a government statement on the subject the emphasis was laid upon recruiting local staff. An estimate of the available potential staff was made and the outlook did not look too hopeful. Much would depend on education. In 1955, out of a total of 562 students at Makerere, 189 were from Uganda. In the United Kingdom there were 140.[35] By 1958 there were 279 students from Uganda at Makerere and the Royal Technical College in Nairobi. And there were 262 in the United Kingdom. With a greatly expanded secondary school program under way as well, a larger flow into the universities could be expected. The official statement on Africanization indicated that "the determination of Government to build up a civil service staffed by local officers has frequently been stressed, and it is Government's intention to press on with that policy to the maximum extent of the resources available.[36] At the same time no lowering of standards was contemplated.

these matters regard the picture as overdrawn. However, after observing the frustration and concern with their work which was visible among district officers during the year I spent in Uganda, I am forced to conclude that the view expressed here is essentially sound. Some of the differences can perhaps be laid to the usual variation in perspective which exists between the field officer and the Secretariat officer. Indeed, more recently, these matters have become more open and of public concern.

[35] See *Uganda: Colonial Reports*, p. 61.

[36] See the *Uganda Gazette*, "Statement on the Appointment of Local People to Responsible Posts in the Public Service," General Notice No. 480 of 1958, p. 236. It is of some note that in the statement, students in training in India and the United States are questionable, the suitability of their appointments depending upon whether their qualifications are recognized in the United Kingdom.

Efforts to Africanize the civil service resulted in the setting up of a Standing Committee on the Recruitment, Training, and Promotion of Africans for admission to the higher civil service. The committee, under the direction of J. V. Wild, proposed that a single salary schedule for all personnel with confirmed posts should be established, irrespective of race. This proposal was accepted and three years later, in 1955, the establishment of a Public Service Commission was proposed in the committee's final report. This too was accepted and the emphasis upon the recruitment of Africans into the civil service was given further attention by the establishment, in 1957, of a Standing Selection Board in Great Britain which receives and examines applications from African students who have ended postsecondary studies. Scholarships have been awarded to promising students to enable them to continue their schooling, with the expectation that they would take up administrative posts on completion of their studies.[37]

In fact, the rates of Africanization have been very low. For senior posts, Bustin gives the following figures:[38]

	Scale A	Scale B	Scale C
Africans	15	31	41
Europeans	393	488	508
Asians	15	18	21
Total	423	537	570

The Republic of the Congo and Indonesia are examples of countries where virtually no development of the civil service occurred before independence. Both instances have shown political disaster as a result. The old concept of the administration as the "steel frame" of a territory is certainly valid in new nations where the needs of orderly government are most demanding in the period

[37] Several students have refused to go into the civil service on completion of their studies, a matter of no small concern to the authorities. See E. Bustin, "L'africanisation des cadres administratifs de l'Ouganda," *Civilisations*, Vol. IX, No. 2, 1959.

[38] *Ibid.*, p. 145, adapted. By the end of 1959 the breakdown for the entire civil service was as follows:

	1956	1957	1958	Total
Africans	62	68	464	1,840
Europeans	506	657	677	566
Asians	24	104	438	594
Total	592	829	1,579	3,000

Source: *Uganda Argus*, April 5, 1960.

of transition to independence and in the immediate post independence period. For the civil service represents the continuation of the bureaucracy during the period of representative self-government and independence. Without the bureaucracy the bonds of national sentiment are rarely sufficient to supply loyalty to new governments if the latter cannot translate political decisions into administration. The Uganda government has been fully aware of this situation since Sir Andrew Cohen's tenure, but in spite of great efforts it has so far been unable to achieve sufficiently rapid Africanization.[39]

Experience in India, Ghana, Nigeria, and elsewhere shows that

[39] See *Report of the Public Service Commission* (Entebbe: G.P., 1956, 1957, 1958). It has been estimated conservatively that by 1962, 25 per cent of the A and B scale posts, the former comprising administrative and professional grades, the latter superior and executive grades, will be filled by local officers, roughly 300 in number. A higher proportion is estimated for the C scale posts or technician and executive grades. To insure departmental achievement of these objectives, targets have been set for each cadre of staff. Heads of departments have been asked to state their plans for achieving the targets in the stipulated period. Continuous review and inquiry by the establishment branch ensures that the effort is maintained. And the awarding of overseas scholarships has now been related to the needs of the civil service and teaching service.

The basic factor in the Africanization program is the output of school-leavers who have a school certificate, because from this source the people who go on to higher education are obtained to fill administrative and professional posts. There are 21 grant-aided senior secondary schools in Uganda, with another due to open in 1961. The total numbers of successful candidates in the school certificate examination entered from schools since 1952 have been:

1952	187			1955	296
1953	181			1956	356
1954	227			1957	491
		1958	557		

Higher school certificate courses of two years' duration were started at two schools in January 1959 and at a third in January 1960. The annual output for each school will be 30 students.

For the time being, the output of school certificate-holders has been insufficient for present needs. The best go on to higher education. The problem is even greater with respect to supervisory technical posts. Six government schools and six grant-aided mission schools have developed a three year course in trade subjects, followed by a two year apprenticeship in industry, but the academic standard of entering students is very low. The Kampala Technical Institute is being developed to the point where it will be concerned solely with top quality technical education. In addition, a new training course was opened in 1960 for potential assistant administrative officers. The course, designed to produce assistant administrative officers only as district officers are obtainable from the increasing output of Makerere graduates, is modeled after the northern Nigerian course at Zaria. A complete review of the entire Africanization program is presently contemplated.

I am indebted to the Chief Secretary, Mr. G. B. Cartland, and to the Establishment Secretary, for furnishing me with this material.

perhaps the crucial determinant of success or failure in self-government is the training of an efficient and disinterested public service that is imbued with a sense of service ideals. In the field and in the Secretariat, the program of Africanization is urgent—more urgent perhaps than almost any reform program.

Another important emphasis in official policy has continued to be economic viability. The two largest items in the budget in 1955 to 1956, for example, were £6,812,668 spent on social services and £5,357,510 spent on general economic development.

Thus the last stage of the colonial state is social welfare government. Under a government concerned to create the maximum conditions for political and economic viability, Uganda's geographical income has increased from £71.6 million in 1950 to £122.7 million in 1957. Making allowance for inflationary prices, it is probable that the average rate of increase in real income has been about five per cent per year.[40]

The real paradox in the situation is that the civil service oligarchy is called upon to exercise its maximum ingenuity as its tenure comes to a close. Community development officers, local government officers, and the hydra-headed district teams are working hard to produce economic development and social change in the all-consuming effort to establish a national society with the requisite skills and economic stability. Europeans and Asians are called upon as never before to exert their maximum social responsibility in service. They serve on the legislature, on public boards, financial commissions, and so on. Urged to take part, the unofficial European and Asian communities play an extremely important private role in development as well. The more skill and talent displayed by Europeans and Asians, however, the more they proliferate their activities and the more they are viewed with suspicion and fear by Africans. The very demands made upon the alien communities produce widespread fears that they will not only continue to dominate the society but that they are producing a system which only they themselves can operate. A common charge is that they are seeking to make themselves indispensable.

Government runs into the same difficulty. Stressing standards in the civil service and making the service perform more difficult

40 Ministry of Finance, *Background to the Budget,* 1958-1959 (Entebbe: G.P., April 1958), p. 1.

tasks has made the Africans anxious to retreat to their local governments until they can take over government on their own terms and with less concern for standards. To ready the state for self-government it has become a self-imposed task of the Protectorate government to create as many of the conditions of Western society as they can in the time they have remaining to them. Yet each step in this direction widens the gap between the numbers of trained Africans needed in government and those available.

The relatively high educational level in Legislative Council and the parliamentary adeptness of Europeans skilled in the mechanics of the parliamentary system serve to emphasize that parliament is a foreign and alien institution run by Europeans in which Africans need to "learn" to behave. Now the gulf is further emphasized. Not an institution which has settled into the general pattern of life, the Legislative Council remains unaccepted by the Baganda in fact although not in law. For others, as well, Legislative Council is a foreign body containing Africans.

Self-government has thus become a demand aimed at releasing Africans from standards set by those other than themselves. It is not simply a question of whether or not efficiency in government (the warrant of colonial government) will suffer. Rather, it is that African participation in institutions intimate to the concerns of the day have successfully taken place in the various local governments where the ebb and flow of local politics, internal conflicts, and clan and chieftaincy disputes are still the real issues. Only when there is an African responsible government in Uganda can parliamentary activity become linked to power and its consequences. The difficulty is that by the time that usually comes to prevail, the demand for immediate independence becomes overwhelming. The timetable of independence is too closely linked with constitutional stages rather than with necessities growing out out of the mutual collaboration between nationalist and colonialist in the long-run building of society.[41]

[41] Only in parts of French West Africa has there been a sophisticated appraisal of *petit bourgeoise* nationalism, with most of the French territories favoring autonomy in association with France—a most beneficial arrangement so long as discretionary termination lies with the African countries.

The Racial Factor

The above situation is worse in Uganda than it was in West Africa where a far longer time enabled a more thorough preparation of the groundwork for independence. The accomplished fact of self-government in the West African areas has speeded up the tempo elsewhere. In the West African territories, however, there had been no racial compartmentalization to speak of. In Uganda, as one observer has put it, "It is possible to spend a whole lifetime as a member of the European community without having much of an idea of African society at all." Considering the fact that commercial activity mushroomed during the War, with Europeans and Asians, their houses, children, manners, and morals everywhere coming to dominate the landscape, the East African complex (and Uganda does not avoid its consequences) remains vastly different from West Africa. It reinforces a pattern of mutual suspicion which drives men further apart just as they are pushed closer together.

There is a remarkable degree of querulousness in the relations between the racial groups. In spite of bland words in the legislature, it is as racial groups that the society is structured. It is the nationalist demand to obliterate those criteria of ranking by making the society purely African. The problem is particularly acute for the Asians, many of whom have been born in Uganda and really have no place to return to anymore.[42]

Underlying the politics of parochialism, then, in a fashion which is absent in West Africa, is the politics of race. This element affects the working of government because of the relatively discontinuous pattern of cultural transmission which it reflects. It is not simply that managerial roles are filled by Europeans, but that those roles are themselves tainted with social inappropriateness deriving (in sharp contrast to Nigeria and Ghana or to French areas) from racial compartmentalization. The Europeans' earlier judgment

[42] It perhaps came as a shock to the leading members of the European community when, in a meeting held with the Governor, June 11, 1956, they came to discuss the safeguards for the minority groups and were told that there were no safeguards save their own behavior. For a long time afterwards, the issue of direct elections was clouded over with the question of a common roll with safeguards for minorities. That issue has now been resolved and it appears that no special minority safeguards are contemplated.

of Africans on the basis of race has adversely affected the potentialities for cultural integration.

These factors make the last stages of the social welfare colonial state controversial. The accompanying benevolence lavished on Africans is not appreciated by most Africans. The standards used to justify it and thereby European contributions become a rebuke to nationalists. Dominated by Europeans and Asians, whether civil servants or private citizens, the government's very acts of devotion to the country lead it blindfold to the firing line of African public opinion.

Issues and Patterns in National Politics

All the above discussion can be illustrated in graphic form in the conflict over direct elections.

In approving certain modifications in the Executive and Legislative Councils, the Colonial Secretary, in a despatch to the Governor dated 1955, pointed out that time was needed to absorb the effects of these and other changes. Therefore, "in order to secure a period of stability for the country no major changes in the constitution should be introduced for a period of six years from 1955, after which time the position should be reviewed."[43]

Direct Elections and Democracy

Less than a year later, perhaps the most decisive step in the constitutional development of Uganda was taken. On April 24, 1956, the Governor, Sir Andrew Cohen, made a policy speech on direct elections. His last major act as Governor, this was his testament to the people of Uganda. It provided a major step toward the building of an independent, primarily African Uganda. The significance of the speech was missed in Uganda in many quarters. The Governor said: "There will, I believe, be general agreement in the House that the objective of our policy must be to introduce direct elections on a common roll for the Representative Members of Legislative Council from all parts of the Protectorate."[44]

[43] Despatch No. 692, Lennox Boyd to Sir Andrew Cohen, 20 July 1955.
[44] His Excellency the Governor's Speech to Legislative Council on 24 April 1956. ("Statement on Elections," Entebbe: G.P., 1956.)

Taken in an East African context that statement alone is significant. In its own way it sealed the future for Tanganyika and Kenya as well. With Uganda pointed in the direction of representative government based on a common roll system of elections, it was unthinkable that nationalists in the other territories in East Africa would settle for less. The Governor's remarks bear repeating: "Self government cannot be a reality in any country unless it has men and women who can effectively run its political institutions, its civil service, its local government bodies, its professions and its economic life; the last is particularly important, as on its economic progress the whole development of a country depends. To a considerable extent a self governing country can hope to obtain technical, professional, economic and administrative help from outside; but not beyond a certain limit. Beyond that limit it must rely on its own men and women. Can those who have been pressing for early self government put their hands on their hearts and say that this country already has, or will have in the near future, enough trained and experienced men and women?"[45]

In effect, Cohen served notice that it was incumbent upon Africans to make their own pace, but that they would be judged by the Protectorate government. The introduction of direct elections opened the way for debates over the shape of the future. The Baganda were caught off balance by the Protectorate government's obvious desire to move more rapidly in a direction which they themselves were not prepared for. The political parties, the Buganda government, the district governments—all had to cast a fresh eye to the future, a future in which they would have to participate.

The proposals made in London at an earlier period and approved by the Buganda government were for direct elections in 1961. It was anticipated that several years would be required to work out a suitable electoral formula. First, however, it was proposed to hold direct elections in Buganda for the Baganda representative members to the Legislative Council. The method evolved there would, if satisfactory, serve as a prototype for the rest of the country at the subsequent date.

[45] *Ibid.*, p. 4.

It had been accepted by the Kintu Committee and the Lukiko that the Buganda representative members to the Legislative Council should be directly elected.[46]

Accordingly, a joint committee was set up, composed of the Kabaka's government and its representatives and the Protectorate government and its representatives. Its objects included determining the qualifications and eligibility of voters in the proposed direct elections in 1957 in Buganda, which would then serve as the model for direct elections in the country as a whole in 1961.[47] It was at this point that the entire matter become involved in a fundamental struggle over the principles of government which would come to prevail after the change. The political parties would have a new and formidable *raison d'être* in the day-to-day politics of a competitive political system based upon representative government and democratic practices.

Moreover, events from elsewhere in Africa helped to put the issue even more sharply. Independence and self-government in West Africa were moving closer to reality. Nkrumah had come out on record in the 1956 Gold Coast elections against chieftaincy and tribalism. Political parties had laid special claims to representative supremacy and the warrant of legitimacy.

There were many neo-traditionalists who felt considerable uneasiness over this development. They saw it as a necessary concomitant of party politics. Meanwhile, forcing the issue, the Uganda National Congress demanded that elections be extended to all of Uganda at the same time that they were held in Buganda, that is, in 1957. Their demands were stepped up when in March 1957 Ghana received independence. In a congratulatory motion on the independence of Ghana in the Legislative Council, Dr. B. N. Kununka of the Uganda National Congress commented on his impressions of developments there. "When I visited Ghana last year I went through the colony area, the Ashanti area, and I had a peep at the Northern Territories themselves. I saw the people, how they were developing in various ways. I saw their local governments . . . I saw the educated class, I saw

[46] See *Kintu Committee Report*, p. 41.

[47] See *Report by Representatives of the Protectorate and Kabaka's Government on Discussions on the Introduction of Direct Elections to the Legislative Council in Buganda, 1957* (Entebbe: G.P., 1956).

the people in responsible posts. They have made tremendous progress. I agree; but I will assure this House that Uganda in many respects is just the same as the Gold Coast.[48]

Putting the matter more sharply, Musazi added that "it only remains for us here in this part of Africa to watch and see the activities of this new African State, since, as some of the honorable Members have said, we here shall have many lessons to learn from this State of Ghana and so will many territories in Africa, who will be encouraged to take the same road as our friends in West Africa have done.[49]

It is perhaps useful to consider African attitudes toward impending change. In April 1957 a motion for self-government for Uganda was tabled amid a great deal of pious talk. In the debate one member said, "We have certainly arrived at a stage when we have to run; walking is not good enough. Sir, at the stage we are at now I know we shall tumble and fall, like a toddler, but of course that is inevitable. I know we shall try and get up again after tumbling and falling and it is no good anyone telling us to walk slowly anymore."[50]

An African minister pointed out that ". . . a modern political democracy is not so easy to make work as some of the people on the other side would lead one to suppose. . . . We know that our political parties in this country are a part of the growth of this country and I believe that they will be the first to agree that they have a lot to learn and to do in the way of improving their organization and formulating sound policies for their parties. True and responsible leadership must first be established."[51]

Another member made reference to the effects of ethnic parochialism. "I might say that the Africans are worse off in this respect, as between ourselves, than the non-Africans. Certainly today every district regards self government as if it is going to come to the particular district, quite independent of the other districts. We have heard of the political parties in this country. There are three now, on paper I might say. I must be honest, I

[48] Proceedings of the Legislative Council, 37th Session, 3rd Meeting, 6 June 1957, p. 21.
[49] *Ibid.*, p. 23.
[50] Proceedings of the Legislative Council, 37th Session, 2nd Meeting, 29 April 1957, p. 25.
[51] *Ibid.*, p. 26.

said I would be frank and speak my mind, and I am going to say it, that we have no political party yet in this country which is well represented throughout the country. All I can say is that every party is 'bending its head' to Mengo. What have we heard a number of times, and in a number of papers, but that the Kabaka should be made the emperor of Uganda. Who is going to accept that outside Buganda? . . . All I can say is that whilst tribalism is still acute in this country, it would be very wrong to throw these people on the mercy of God and let civil wars start raging. . . . We cannot try and please the masses on the streets and then satisfy the intelligent people by saying one thing here and another thing there. . . . I have always maintained that what is wanted here is the acceleration of education, higher education, professional education and technical education."[52]

In strong contrast was the view of another member: "If we still say that, after fifty years of their [British] training us, we are still unable to attain self government, then we are proving that they have been doing nothing for the country. . . . A second point brought forward was that we lack the proper experience, the proper education and the proper character to run the Civil Services. Well, I do not agree with this point. For self-government the highest possible education you can have is the Primary Standard. A young man who is willing to lead his fellow Africans and who has reached Primary VI will certainly do very well in leading his people when self-government is granted."[53]

The independence motion gave all groups some pause. Uganda, with its characteristic regard for education, for specialized political institutions at the local government level, and more particularly for modernity and development, now began to appear less developed when faced with impending independence. Some argued that to dwell only on deficiencies was to perpetuate European rule for a long time. Others recognized that while overlooking shortcomings could make fine rhetoric, nevertheless, how would government be run?

In July 1957, the Lukiko confirmed the recommendations of the second joint committee on direct elections and requested in-

[52] *Ibid.*, pp. 29-30.
[53] *Ibid.*, p. 39.

creased African representation on the Legislative Council.[54] Constitutional advice was sought by the Baganda on constitutional matters and the Buganda constitutional committee showed concern over the relationship being established with the Protectorate government and with the problems of party politics. Meanwhile, the Omuwanika was reported to have declared in a rash moment that the suitable political system for Uganda was a federal government with the Kabaka at the head. The statement, although denied, produced profound repercussions throughout Uganda.

Events were moving rapidly now. A motion on direct election of representative members on a common roll was introduced in the Legislative Council. In the debate members of the Legislative Council from outside Buganda demanded direct elections to the Legislative Council simultaneously with Buganda. The issue of whether or not there would remain reserved seats for Asians and Europeans in 1961 was raised. Urging Europeans and Asians to withdraw, one speaker said, "I would implore the non-indigenous elements in this country and beg of them that their time is running out fast to build up this goodwill with the indigenous element of the community. The non-indigenous element; Sir have often declared their devotion and loyalty to this country. Now they must show their devotion and loyalty not by words, not by talk, but by conduct and convince the indigenous people that they mean what they say."[55] Recognizing that the motion had unpleasant implications of racism or "black chauvinism," Musazi pointed out soothingly that the Asians had nothing to worry about. He even suggested the withdrawal of the motion on the grounds that it might unleash race hatred. Dr. Kununka pointed out that the government had made it a condition of direct elections that safeguards for Europeans and Asians be accepted, and this he rejected. Citing the example of Ceylon, he pointed out the impossibility of legislating good race relations.

It was left to the Minister of Commerce and Works to put the issue squarely. "Now why is it that for this interim temporary period, while we are hammering out the eventual constitution, are we asking that there should be adequate and effective representa-

[54] Lukiko Resolution No. 4 of 1957.
[55] Proceedings of the Legislative Council, 27th Session, 5th Meeting, 2 October 1957.

tion of the other two races? I think most it is a matter of arithmetic. If we are going to have the Common Roll it is quite obvious that as European votes among the Africans will not number one in a hundred of the total voting roll, every European candidate is going to be rejected. I do not care what the honourable Mr. Ofwono says. He talks about the wonderful ideal in Heaven. He says that a European can stand, and, of course, if he is popular enough he will be elected. What value would he place on his African electors in Bukedi if they went and voted for a Mugisu?"[56]

The plea for integrated communities was argued by Mrs. Barbara Saben. "It is vital for the non-African communities to be allowed to play their part. They have got a part to play which is going to be of benefit to the people of this country and they must not be denied that part."[57]

It was left to Mrs. P. Kisosonkole to sum up most succinctly the fears of many Africans. Pointing out that there was no special representation in the British Parliament for those in the community who contributed most to its economy, she argued that "the right to vote in any country is granted to the citizens of that country. In Uganda the only people of whose citizenship I have no doubt at all are Africans. Surely we are not expected to force down other peoples' throats the citizenship of Uganda! If other people want to become citizens they must declare themselves ready to abide by the laws and regulations of this country. We are certainly not expected to give the right to become a citizen to every European and Asian just because they happen to be in this country. . . .

"To me, therefore, it is very clear that this motion should have come much later, after the passing of the law of citizenship." Continuing, she remarked that "we do not grudge our non-African friends for having done well for themselves in the past while the Africans were living in ignorance. But there is no need for them to be self-righteous and pretend that everything they have ever done was for the good of the Africans. If we accept them for the future we are doing so in the hope that they now realize the value of the partnership into which we would welcome them. In the future their 'know how' which was mentioned by the honorable

[56] *Ibid.*, p. 143. [57] *Ibid.*, p. 148.

friend on this side must not be allowed to gallop so far ahead of the African as to make it impossible for us to catch up with it as has been the case in the past. If they want to work for us they must work with us."[58]

In October 1957, the Secretary of State visited Uganda and announced his agreement with extending direct elections outside Buganda. This made it all the more urgent for the Buganda government to push for a reopening of the question of the composition of Legislative Council. In the same month the Legislative Council (Elections) Ordinance was passed.[59] The Ordinance left it to the governor to specify the electoral districts. A voter had to be 21 years of age or over, and be a resident in the electoral district. Further he had to be an owner of freehold or occupied land on his own account for agricultural or pastoral purposes in the electoral district; or be able to read and write his own language; or to have been employed in the public service of the Protectorate for seven years, or possess cash income of 2,000s. a year or property worth 8,000s. or more. Non-Africans were disbarred from voting.[60]

Candidates for election had to be, among other things, 27 years of age or more, capable of writing and reading English, and in possession of property worth 14,000s. or an income of not less than 4,000s.[61]

The conditions of direct elections having been specified, a new set of problems appeared. Political parties found their activities curtailed in a proposed Police (Amendment) Bill which would have made political meetings difficult. The bill was finally dropped. Next, opposition to the common roll caused the resignation of two United Congress Party representatives from Buganda. Then the Lukiko demanded a reconstituted Legislative Council. Put in the form of a motion in the Legislative Council, the proposal was for a majority of African representatives of the people, that is, 63 African elected members out of 84, leaving 21 places for senior British ex officio and nominated members. Meanwhile, the government averred that there would be no major changes before 1961.[62]

[58] *Ibid.*, pp. 155-156.

[59] Legislative Council (Elections) Ordinance, No. 20 of 1957, 16 October 1957.

[60] *Ibid.*, p. 80. This was in contrast to Ghana where all British subjects could vote in the interim period between 1950 and independence.

[61] *Ibid.*, p. 87.

[62] Proceedings of the Legislative Council, 27th Session, 6th Meeting, 20 November 1957, p. 58.

Musazi, in his retort to the government, said, "Today, Sir, when political awareness has grown and a genuine demand for African representation increased, we have now a Legislature composed of people of all races, mainly nominated and indirectly elected, but, and a big but, the British Civil Service Membership still retains its majority. (*sic*). Hence the African's fear of its deliberations and decisions. There is a well founded resentment on the part of Africans as to the genuineness of what would be the future African parliament."[63]

The Buganda electoral college, when called upon to fill the vacancies left by the resignation of the two representative members from Buganda, refused and objected to direct elections on a common roll and to the appointment of a Speaker of Legislative Council.[64]

Two months later the Lukiko passed a resolution temporarily postponing elections pending negotiations on three points: the position of the Kabaka, increased African representation on Legislative Council, and the common roll.[65] Subsequently at a special session of the Lukiko, a resolution was passed insisting on the rejection of direct elections. The Protectorate government then announced the suspension of direct elections in Buganda.

Thus direct elections took place in Uganda without the participation of the Baganda who, at the onset, were to have been the sole participants. The election was a somewhat dispirited affair since, for various reasons, Buganda, Bugisu, Ankole, and Karamoja did not participate. One correspondent described the pre-election campaign as follows: "To find out that there is an election in Uganda, go to Katwe in the heart of the Buganda Kingdom, where there are no elections. Here are the offices of the main political parties, and although it is rare to find a political leader in his own office, one can usually find him in somebody else's."[66] Balloting was completed on October 24, 1958.

The results showed that 85 per cent of the eligible electorate voted. Of 10 members returned, 6 were members of the previous Legislative Council. Five of the seats were won by supporters of

[63] *Ibid.*, p. 43.   [64] Resolution No. 6 of 1957.
[65] Resolution No. 8 of 1957.
[66] See the amusing article in the *Uganda Argus*, October 24, 1956, "In Search of an Election," by Raja Neegy.

the Uganda National Congress; 4 were won by independents, and 1 by a Democratic Party candidate.[67] Only 1 woman was a candidate and she lost her 500/ deposit—as did 19 other candidates who polled less than one eighth of the votes in their constituencies. In Acholi the Uganda National Congress candidate defeated the former member of Legislative Council by a margin of only 320 votes. The Progressive Party and the United Congress Party were both completely unsuccessful.

In his speech to the new Legislative Council the Governor pointed out that constitutional change would be an important item on the agenda leading to alteration in the Legislative Council after 1961. He reassured the hereditary rulers that the Protectorate government would make strong efforts to maintain their prestige and dignity.[68] He then appointed a constitutional committee to prepare for the next constitutional stage after 1961.[69]

What would probably be the last two "civil service" governments at Mengo and at Kampala watched the somewhat unglamorous entry of party politics into the Lukiko and in the Legislative Council.

While it has not resulted in a mass nationalism of the West African variety, the long period of conflict within Buganda and between the Baganda and the Protectorate government has induced many separate nationalisms. Africans are united in their fears on larger issues, such as the nature of participation in the Legislative Council, closer union, and the position of the Asians and Europeans in a future Uganda nation. These can be reduced to a single overwhelming concern: fear that for one reason or

[67] An interesting contrast to Buganda where in Lukiko elections the Democratic Party emerged strongest.

[68] His Excellency the Governor's Speech to Legislative Council on 17 November 1958. (Entebbe: G.P., 1958.)

[69] The committee was composed of 13 members of Legislative Council and 2 other members. Of the 13 from Legco, 10 were representative members (1 being a European and 1 an Asian) and 3 were government backbenchers: 1 African, 1 Asian, and 1 European. The co-opted members were Erisa Kironde, an Extra-Murals lecturer at Makerere, and Balamu Mukasa, an advisor to the Government Information Services. J. V. Wild was made chairman. The committee was bitterly attacked by E. M. K. Mulira, President of the Progressive Party, for its failure to adequately represent the population of the country: 10 Africans represented the total population of over 5 million, and 5 non-Africans represented about 60,000 Europeans and Asians. (See *Uganda Argus*, November 21, 1958.)

another Africans will not be in full control over their country. Such fears have reinforced the position of both neo-traditionalists and "progressives" who have sought to use the framework of the Buganda government and, in the case of the districts, the district governments to ensure local autonomy. Local government was the last stronghold left. Only a federal solution now appears acceptable.

The second concern which runs throughout the history of Buganda-Protectorate government relations is over the privileged position of Buganda. Almost by rote every Buganda schoolboy will point out that the Baganda had invited the British, no one else. The Baganda established an alliance with the British. The Baganda had a special agreement with the Crown. Thus it was unthinkable that the Baganda should submit to being outnumbered in a legislature in which other African peoples would participate.

The complex pattern of contemporary politics has unfortunately helped disguise the fact that there are important opportunities for effective participation by Africans in the present pattern of declining colonialism. Indeed, the fullest participation in government is essential if a better understanding of modern government is to develop.

The fact that so much parochialism persists in Uganda results in part from failure to understand the nature of modern colonialism. In a short space of time, social welfare colonialism has taken on a relatively liberal dimension in those areas where minority issues are not all-consuming and the representative principle becomes the ultimate legitimacy for governing. For this very condition of liberal colonialism to come about, it was necessary to have people challenge colonialism itself. Symbols of suffering had to be created. The right of colonial officials to rule had to be successfully challenged. But a grave imbalance in perspective has developed out of the real conflicts between Europeans and Africans, and between governors and governed. This imbalance is expressed in differing views of reality, or multiple images of what constitutes reality and leads to political fantasy. It has reached its fullest expression just as the concrete situation has altered fundamentally. Participation in government looks like seduction. In fact, it would provide real powers to Africans. Learning the positive aspects of government looks like collaboration. In fact, it would provide cadres of politicians skilled in leadership and experience of governing.

Not recognized by most Africans is the fact that in defeat colonialism can be of use to Africans about to take over the reins of government. This is particularly true in Uganda. Local paro-chialism in government is not simply for reasons of tribal or traditional prejudice. It is based also on a weak understanding of the kinds of activities and participation already open to Africans in Legislative Council and Executive Council. Relatively little aware-ness exists of the power already inherent in the system of African representation. Even demands for federalism remain unconvincing because few appreciate the actual workings of federalism itself and are fearful that the system which they espouse will turn out to have some hidden menace.

Hence the power and comfort manifested in neo-traditionalist ideology. One is struck in Uganda by the lack of attachment to Western ideologies. In strong contrast to the pattern in West Africa, where socialism as an alternative to both missionary and colonial influence is the doctrine of modernity, attachment to socialism or any similar "programmatic ideology" has been mark-edly absent in Uganda. As a result, there is no clear image of "capturing power" and utilizing it for particular ends. An im-portant incentive to participate in central government or to take it over is manifestly lacking.

An article in a vernacular newspaper demonstrates the confu-sion that prevails. Asking "What should the Baganda do in order to achieve self government?" the article specifies (1) to learn the meaning of truth, (2) to be trustworthy, (3) to know God, (4) to love one another, (5) to be educated in the true sense of the word, (6) to work diligently, and (7) to give up drunkenness.[70] Such a reply would be unthinkable in West Africa.

There remains in Uganda a dual urge. One is to retreat into a strengthened local government system, intimate, secure, and un-complicated. The other is to advance to a national government in spite of vast uncertainty about its potentialities. Whether the people cling to precedent and privilege or are anxious to eliminate

[70] *Dobozi*, February 27, 1956.

them, there is nevertheless a larger battle shaping up in Uganda. This may indeed bypass conflicts over the place of natural rulers and ignore limits imposed by a modernizing autocracy imprisoned in a hierarchical principle of authority. The new struggle is between those in political parties who move in the direction of the mobilization approach and seek to capture power at the center in order to drastically overhaul the institutions of traditional Uganda, and those who, favoring the principles of federalism, would restrict the pace of change in accordance with the limitations imposed by recurrent majorities. In Uganda the differences and divergences in points of view and ethnic competition would seem to make it clear that the representative government expressed in a unitary form would be self-defeating. Out of regard for the instrumental traditionalism of Buganda and the competing claims of a diverse population, federalism may in contrast produce a political compromise proximate to the needs of the public, so that change and development in both the economic and political spheres can be achieved with prudence and freedom.

CHAPTER 17

TOWARD DEMOCRACY AND INDEPENDENCE

THE CONCERN with new nations is one which challenges the institutional flexibility of Western political practice. In our efforts to chart those treacherous shoals of human action and organization which show themselves in politics, we raise questions of values appropriate to modern societies and the mechanisms which might best ensure their survival.

What are the appropriate means for resolving the political needs of new nations? Such a question lies at the heart of our traditional concerns in political science. To answer it requires renewed emphasis upon conditions of stable government, citizenship, and democracy, problems which have come down to us as the inheritance of political theory. Old issues and earlier thinkers are dusted off and admired. Historical sociology has a fresh relevance as we look for those periods in history which can bring perspective to the events of the contemporary world of new nations. Maine, Austin, Vinogradoff, Durkheim, Michels, Weber, and a host of others have taken on renewed prominence. Their speculations were centered around the development of modern societies. Their enquiries ranged over such issues as the formation of political ideas, the instrumentality of political socialization, and the organizational forms of complex systems.

Such problems are more difficult to analyze in new nations than in older ones because there the change of pace is more rapid than in the earlier transitions to industrialization and modern government which occurred in the West. As well, the establishment of political forms in new nations takes place within a framework of institutional transformation whereby new societies are being created by political means, while their substructures and underpinnings lag behind. It is this problem which Buganda illustrates above all. It has expressed itself elsewhere in Africa in tribalism, regionalism, and ethnic separatism.

Colonialism is itself an institutional matrix in which undigested portions of modernism and traditionalism are laid side by side. This situation is reflected in political actions resulting in modification of political forms brought under colonialism. Hence the study of new nations centers around propensities for institutional variability which are yet to be added to the fund of human experience in governing.

Institutional variability is itself an interesting problem. It derives from the distribution and allocation of the decisional workloads which form the substantive concerns of government. Such work loads are determined by ambitions of leaders, their sense of reality about the capabilities of new societies, and the degree of effective use they can make of prevailing structures of government and advice.[1]

If the problem of institutional variability and the appropriateness of democratic forms is central to our inquiry, to what concepts have we turned to examine the problem? In this study of Uganda we have tried to trace the stages of colonialism through which Uganda has passed. And we have tried to identify those crucial characteristics of Kiganda social life and politics which, carrying forward their own dynamic, now present a practical question, namely, what constitutional solutions are possible in Uganda which can give a measure of freedom and of stable government? We pointed to the nature of conflicts internal to Buganda and between Buganda and the Protectorate government. Indicating the institutional requirements of a modernizing autocracy, we found that its very flexibility in innovation served as a basis for separatism and political exclusiveness. Four different types of material were brought together to illustrate these processes, and it is well to review them here.

The first derived from the stages of development in colonial government. These are: (1) the pioneering stage; (2) the politi-

[1] This includes the use of semitraditional organizations such as voluntary organizations which, partly functional and partly tribal, proliferate at interstices of new societies.

In nations such as Nigeria, Ghana, and Mali, political structures geared into voluntary associations overlap government. These take the form of developed advisory commissions, regional councils, parastatal bodies, and the like. In addition to providing posts for followers, they provide a network of "informal government" which identifies less with voters as such than with the semitraditional organizations (such as tribal unions and guilds) and special interest groups such as teachers' unions, old boy associations, ex-servicemen's organizations, and the like. One result is that political parties become the mediators and integrators of such role complexes and there is a tendency for party councils to usurp the functions of the legislatures as the repositories of national power.

cal-administrative stage; (3) the bureaucratic-colonial stage; and (4) the representative self-government stage. Uganda's problems now center in this final stage.

Second, in each phase there is interaction between colonial rulers and a public organized into social organizations mainly along tribal lines. We attempted to point out some possible types of tribal systems in terms of two main variables, values and authority types. Buganda was defined as a system of hierarchical authority with instrumental values, in short, a modernizing autocracy. These two concrete structures—colonial government in its different phases and the modernizing autocracy in its ability to traditionalize innovation—formed the twin foci of examination.

The interaction of men and institutions revealed a cycle of political perceptions generated in each phase of the colonial cycle and carrying over from one to the other. These cycles of political perception show how our third dimension of analysis, social tension generated by increasing conflict between Buganda and the Protectorate government, affected men's estimates of the history of their relationship with one another and how this in turn applied to the service of national or local interests. The cycles of political perception embedded in the analysis can now be articulated. They are: (a) multiple images; (b) selective recall; (c) relative threshold; (d) hortatory realism; (e) political fantasy; (f) practical realism. We shall recapitulate our material to show how images of history and social relationship became constrained, appearing in ideological forms which created quite different retrospective views of the events shared by Baganda and British.

Fourth, the discussion of stages of colonialism, characteristics of the modernizing autocracy, and the cycles of political perceptions are seen in a larger setting of wide-scale social changes. Included in these were such institutional factors as the development of an educational system, the introduction of Christianity, the increase in wealth and social mobility, and the like. It is within the institutional limits of such major factors of economic and social life that the processes of colonial political development, the modification of traditional forms, and the changes in political perceptions occurred. These four dimensions, phases of colonial perception, and the nature of institutional change have thus formed the pattern of our discussion.

How these four dimensions operate in a new nation determines which one of the major types of systems outlined in Chapter 1— mobilization, modernizing autocracy, or consociational—will emerge in the postcolonial phase. Our major assumption is that in order to create national systems where major subsystems are either of the modernizing autocracy types, as in Uganda, or are combinations of a modernizing autocracy and mobilization systems, as in Nigeria with its different regions, the best political solution for the formation of a national society is that of a federation. Our hypothesis is that a consociational system becomes the basic solution to the problem.

To summarize thus far, the variables used in the analysis were as follows:

A. Institutional Factors
1. Religion
2. Education
3. Economic Development
4. Urbanization

B. Types of Traditional Authority
1. Hierarchical
2. Pyramidal
3. Segmentary

C. Stages of Colonialism
1. Pioneering
2. Political-Administrative
3. Bureaucratic-Colonial
4. Representative Self-
     Government

D. Cycles of Perception
1. Multiple Images
2. Selective Recall
3. Relative Threshold
4. Hortatory Realism
5. Political Fantasy
6. Practical Realism

E. Types of National Society (after independence)
1. Mobilization
2. Modernizing Autocracy
3. Consociational

Institutional Factors and the Modernizing Autocracy

In our analysis, four main institutional factors set the general limits within which change occurred in Uganda. These factors were religion, education, economic development, and urbanization. We have discussed the quick adaptation of Buganda to Christianity, its acceptance of education as an important qualification for political posts in the chieftaincy hierarchy, and the processes by which freehold land tenure and the introduction of cash crops were adopted. Such changes could occur without altering the basic social system of Kiganda society and helped to retain the pattern of hierarchical authority. In contrast, urbanization was rejected. No large urban groupings of Baganda emerged. The townships continued to be Asian and alien.[2] By the same token, those who went into trade did not give up their land, and even merchants and school teachers were purchasing land as the final token of their power and prestige if they were not already liberally endowed with acreage. Land, politics, power, and prestige were indissolubly linked and service to the Kabaka in no way detracted from the significance of these factors. Meanwhile, religion and education came to serve the ends of state.

However, as colonialism went through its several stages, how did the modernizing autocracy respond? We have seen that it was possible for the Baganda to appreciate their land holdings both in quantity and value through their initial association with the British. Chieftaincy, transformed into a civil service system, retained the support of the public. The most cherished institutions of kingship thereby continued to be honored. The transformation of the civil service resulted in a shift from what was essentially a patrimonial system into one more closely approximating a secular bureaucracy. Nevertheless, elements of patrimony remain to this day, expressed in the spreading of government largesse in posts and jobs throughout the various levels of the Buganda government. The result has been continuing stability in institutions although a duality of patrimony and bureaucracy is retained.[3]

The chiefs undertook responsibility for the collection of taxes, the allocation of freehold land, the development of reserve granaries, the establishment of markets, and promotion and transfer among their members. When cotton was introduced on orders of the Protectorate government, it was the chiefs who acted as the major agents. And it was bureaucratic chiefs such as Wamala who sought to strengthen the patrimonial aspect when to assert it was to identify the bureaucracy with the Kabaka and with tradition rather than with the Protectorate government. By this means it

[2] The result was a "homestead" rather than a village pattern of ecology.

[3] When certain key household offices, such as the post of *Kimbugwe*, were changed from the personal patrimony of the Kabaka to appointive offices in the hierarchy of government, the elements of patrimony were not lost in the bureaucracy. But the bureaucratic element itself established a relatively effective form of governmental system for modern needs.

became possible for the chiefs to act not merely as a party in their own interest but as nationalists defending Buganda as a whole. The populist chiefs downgraded the tendency toward separation between chiefs and public which had resulted from the successful development of progressive bureaucracy under Sir Apolo and his immediate successors. Economic grievance during the thirties helped to give the populist emphasis new force, and thereby assisted in the political unity of Buganda as a political party.

In spite of the growing emphasis on separatism, there was no significant resurgence of traditional religious beliefs. Kiganda nationalists remained deeply religious Christians.

Indeed, can one find any more dramatic instance of the whole-hearted acceptance of Christianity? It can be argued that this merely showed the practical good sense of the Baganda who, having observed the superior qualities of these religions, absorbed them into the scheme of things. But we know that otherwise practical people will cling tenaciously to all sorts of beliefs and practices which seem outmoded or inadequate. What prevented this occurrence among the Baganda? The decline of the Bataka was one reason. The employment of nontraditional religion was an added factor in the struggle for supremacy between chieftaincy and clanship. Yet surely it was not simply as a weapon of the chiefs that Christianity emerged successful. Quite the contrary, among the clan leaders were some of the most devout Christians of all. Our hypothesis is that the older religious forms did not include requisite prophetic and inspirational qualities. Both chieftaincy and kingship required the additional support of some essential element of revealed truth. It was the concept of truth itself which provided a new center of gravity for carrying on the traditionalism of Buganda through innovation. Hence the power of Christianity, able to enshrine those in political power with both modernity and orthodoxy, gave them also a burden of responsibility to principles of abstract justice which served as an additional link between rulers and ruled. More modern notions of Christianity could not have served the same purpose. It was muscular Christians with their emphasis upon self-improvement who gave to the Muganda yeoman a sense of his own worth and, to ensure the point, land in freehold as well.[4]

[4] Yet behind the firm façade of Victorianism in Buganda is a salty paganism which allows primness in the observances and piety in the breach. Seduction be-

The result was a practical unity of church and state, and a firmer alliance between rulers and ruled. That religion gave effect to internal conflicts we have seen demonstrated both at the inception of Christianity in Buganda with the religious wars, and subsequently in the conflict between factions. However, these were quarrels which gave meaning to political life in Buganda rather than destroying it, much as disputes within a family give vitality and strength to the institution itself.

Religion then had both its inspirational and practical strengths. Its most practical virtues lay in the establishment of an educational system which, providing the means of self-improvement to the Baganda, undertook the extension of the principle of merit as the basis for reward.[5]

Because it was not limited to the chiefs and their sons, however, education became an additional means of unity by opening the way to social mobility. No critical group of the population found itself set off from the others either in triumph or derision. Education was as much a rural phenomenon as religion itself and, thus neutralized, was readily employable by all. The net effect was an effective relationship between the bureaucracy and the public characterized by a high degree of shared knowledge and understanding.

By a curious blend of structural propensities in the system of Buganda, the institutions of change themselves were hammered into neo-traditional shape by the participants.[6]

Effects of the Modernizing Autocracy

The modernizing autocracy retains the solidary affiliations of its members by making change palatable. It also requires the bending and shaping of novelty into forms which fit into prevailing views

---

hind the cloisters is not a novelty in Buganda, any more than it was in Victorian England.

[5] In the nature of the missionary effort, it was essential to train only a few people at a time if the missionaries were themselves not to draw the wrath of the king and jeopardize their own positions. They thereby created early an elite which, forming the basis of chieftaincy in subsequent years, gave it the added warrant of having been recruited from the most educated and, in that sense, most meritorious of men.

[6] Such processes are not to be viewed as the product of a structural determinism. In the case of Buganda, change was also accompanied by a benevolent fortune. Innovation in the social spheres created a viable local system in Buganda. Even so, the dynamism of the system consistently led Buganda to a kind of political "brinkmanship" from which it emerged victorious each time.

of politics and social life. In contrast to systems which have pyramidal authority and consummatory values—and which respond to reality by withdrawing from it—are those where conflict and passion create the need for new attachments and where traditionalism effectively lays the groundwork for what becomes its alternative, that is, nationalism. In the case of the modernizing autocracy, nationalism and traditionalism come to mean the same thing. The normal consequence of passionate nationalism is a mobilization system which sees traditional political forms and social organization as feudal. Mobilization is equated with modernity. The normal consequence of a modernizing autocracy is the ritualization of hierarchical authority by making its symbolic value more relevant than its decision-making value. The classic example is, of course, Great Britain. Comparing the modernizing autocracy with other forms of traditional systems, however, we find interesting contrasts to those having consummatory values and pyramidal authority such as the Ashanti in Ghana.[7]

Among the Ashanti, for example, responses to innovation were relatively complicated. Thus chieftaincy, with its tiers of relatively autonomous powers with respect to differing units of government, was hemmed in by restrictions. It faced inward to the people with whom, by lineage and totem, the chief or headman was related. Instead of the individual atomism of Buganda which was held together by regard for the Kabaka and the external force of hierarchical authority, the Ashanti chief was linked with an elaborate system of religiously sanctioned self-restraints on behavior. When land alienation began to occur in undue measure, for example, chieftaincy was affected and the stable confines of a social system were undermined. When Christianity was introduced it helped to weaken the traditions of chieftaincy and remove the control over the living by the dead ancestors. The result was excesses by chiefs who turned to British authorities for support. When education was introduced, chiefs had to be ordered to send their children to school. While they could not disobey the orders of district officers, they often sent the children of their slave lineages rather than the children of royal blood. Thus succeeding generations of chiefs were

[7] For a discussion of the traditional system of Ashanti, see my book, *The Gold Coast in Transition* (Princeton: Princeton University Press, 1955).

by no means the best educated in the population of the Gold Coast. Outside support, required to maintain the authority of the chiefs, violated customary restraints on behavior. Excesses of the chiefs soon came to be regarded as perversions of traditional authority from which younger and better-educated elements began to disaffiliate themselves. Christianity helped intensify the process of disaffiliation. There developed, along with an increase in urbanization and the growth of villages, profound cleavage between the urban village Christian and the rural village pagan. A series of wars between the British and the Ashanti was a token of the inability of Ashanti to absorb those innovating effects of a system of colonial rule which was basically common to both Buganda and Ashanti. In the end, the *Asantehene*, or king of the Ashanti, had to be exiled. Indeed, from 1901 to 1935 the Ashanti Confederacy as such did not exist.

In Ashanti modernism clashed directly with traditionalism. The religious aspect of traditional political and social structure was an important part of a network of restraints on behavior. When these were disrupted by innovations in commercial enterprises and colonialism, traditional authority was quickly undermined. Yet, because traditional authority was so much a part of daily life and customs, those who broke with tradition found themselves in drastic need of new and powerful social affiliations. For to break with tradition was to break with family, lineage, and ancestral fidelity.

In contrast to Ashanti, Buganda remained the most powerful solidary association. Social satisfactions continued to be achieved within Buganda and its government for all those who belonged to the kingdom. This was not the case in Ashanti where the formation of a mass political party, the Convention People's Party, was accompanied by the adoption of new and powerful symbolic attachments. The Ashanti member of the C.P.P. became fiercely devoted to the organization. The messianicism of the leader was based on the development of a new morality which supplanted the old. The result in Ghana was that the deep cleavages in society were expressed in social fissures which, remaining after self-government, posed the problem of nation-building after rather than before independence.

We can summarize some of the more salient points of contrast between Ashanti and Buganda as follows:

(1) *Absorption of Innovation.* Ashanti, with its consummatory system, was unable to control the effects of innovation. Early missionaries were imprisoned. The Ashanti wars were efforts to expel the British, as a foreign body, from the body politic. The effects of contact loosened the hold of traditionalism, although it remained a powerful force. Buganda was able to control innovation. The European presence was absorbed and rendered useful. By careful planning and the use of modernizing agencies, the Buganda government increased its autonomy and control as time went on, rather than suffering partial decay.

(2) *Internal Divisions and Discontinuities.* What had hitherto been reinforcing social institutions of the consummatory system of Ashanti rapidly broke down into competing power groups and sources of internal antagonism and weakness. Thus conflicts of youth and age, royals against nonroyals, and slaves against nonslaves all represented conflict over the continuing strength of particularistic criteria which could be reconciled only so long as older religious and institutional checks were distributed. As soon as the continuity of past and present was disrupted, the various groupings rapidly came to compete. In Buganda the internal conflict continued as it had been prior to contact, between clanship and chieftaincy—all, however, under the umbrella of the king as both *Sabataka,* head of all the clans, and Kabaka, or king. The advantage of appointive chieftaincy has long been apparent in the military undertakings of the Kingdom and a secular tendency inherent in the system was simply reinforced by contact with the British. The old conflicts continued and the system was able to modify itself to restrain them sufficiently so that the principle of hierarchic kingship did not require substantial alteration. Allegiance did not become confused.

(3) *Competition for Affiliation.* Internal conflict in Ashanti produced widespread attitudes of guilt. Cleavages spread into the extended and nuclear families. Social breaks which meant modifying one's religious practices and breaking the ties with the past (and ancestors) led to migration of individuals who, building urban areas, supported very different patterns of social life. These created more fundamental differences in outlook between urban and rural groups which had grown apart within one generation but were still not socially distant. The Ashanti were able to retain

affiliations among those who represented orthodoxy. Breaking such affiliations, however, could not be resolved by a simple acceptance of heterodoxy. Rather, a new orthodoxy had to be posed against the old. Thus the new affiliation of the political party assumed the proportions of a militant religious movement.

In Buganda there was a relatively easy adaptation of internal cleavages to serve the larger purposes of the state. As a result, no Muganda repudiated his chief or the Kabaka. No unresolvable incompatibility between modernism and traditionalism resulted in an enforced disaffiliation of discontented groups. There were no discontented urban groups, anxiety-ridden and seeking drastic change.

(4) *Legitimacy Conflicts.* Just as innovation could not be controlled in Ashanti, so the secular authority of the colonial government was posed against the traditional authority of the chiefs. Immemorial prescriptive rights clashed with concepts of efficiency and performance as a basis of authority. In Buganda the autocratic principle prevailed and two oligarchies, British and Baganda, worked alongside one another. They were in constant competition but they did not challenge each other's legitimacy. Both were oriented to efficiency and performance. In Ashanti almost any outside activity, by being resisted, posed an ultimate legitimacy problem. So closely interrelated were the elements of social life and belief in Ashanti that they conformed nicely to Durkheim's concepts of fragile or mechanical societies. Ultimately all threats were threats against legitimacy, but nationalism was the most serious. The conflict between lineage and ancestral sanction (immemoriality) for current acts and secular forces was introduced by colonialism; and this conflict helped to produce the nationalism which then had to break the power of traditionalism and its residual hold upon the public. Thus modern nationalism in Ghana has resulted in an effort to create a wider legitimacy which introduces some of the same instrumental characteristics which Buganda had traditionally. *The result is a growth of an autocratic principle of leadership in Ghana*—the mobilization system serving as its own justification.

In contrast, the conflict over legitimacy never emerged in sharp form in the colonial-Buganda government relationship. Indeed, even when the Kabaka was exiled, or more recently when the present Kabaka was deported, the principle of Kabakaship was not questioned by the Protectorate government authorities.

However, now that the Protectorate government has tackled the problem of building wider affiliations, political parties are challenging the principle of hierarchical authority. *They are seeking to supplant hierarchical authority with representative authority* as the means of building a modern nation. They do not, however, need to create attitudes of universalism and performance as the basis of political recruitment since these are already widespread and traditional.

Where the consummatory system prevailed, there developed fierce competition between traditional and secular leaders to monopolize allegiance. This was expressed by the latter in efforts to build overarching and autocratic institutions which by autocratic means fostered egalitarianism in political recruitment and the exercise of authority. The problem was to prevent social atomism while mobilizing those resources of the society which could capitalize on change itself. This put exceedingly heavy burdens on political nationalists whose need for organizational control and support becomes all important. This led to the development of the mobilization system in Ghana.

Within the context of the term "traditional," both the Ashanti and the Buganda were traditional systems. Both required validation of current behavior by appeal to immemoriality. Both had myths of origin involving a powerful figure associated with the formation of the society and with whom the king has claims of ancestry. In the case of Ashanti, the powers of origin descended to the Golden Stool rather than to a person. In Buganda, descent was reckoned through the line of kings or Kabakas. That the preservation of power and continuity should reside in an object, in the case of the Ashanti, rather than in a person, as in Buganda, is not without significance. For in the first instance, those in power serve the present by serving the past. It is a symbol of ancestral concern which is the visible repository of authority. In Buganda, we observe a system which recoils from change while selecting those aspects of it which it can absorb. We find, too, that the issues which make it recoil most are those which threaten the system of hierarchical authority and kingship. Since the real estate of

Buganda is an essential part of the aggrandizing quality of the rule of the Kabaka, dangers to the sacred soil of Buganda arouse profound reactions.[8]

Stages of Colonialism and the Introduction of Representative Government

Through its organizational and ideological flexibility, the modernizing autocracy was, as we have seen, able to retain its identity. The efforts to do so were expressed in the various crises which periodically inflamed the political scene, now to die down, now rising again in a new context.

While varying in their specifics, issues such as the Investiture Controversy, the Sir Apolo Kagwa case, the Bataka-chieftaincy conflict, and those centering around economic grievance and political rights all had a common thread. This was conflict over the role of the Protectorate government in relation to Buganda, particularly the proprieties of political rule inherent in the principle of hierarchical authority as expressed through the Kabakaship.

Such issues had two effects. First, they were points of historical importance, prefacing changes in the colonial system by means of which Buganda was governed. Second, they formed the perceptual punctuation marks for succeeding generations of Baganda. The cycle of political perceptions helped produce crisis. And the memory of crisis became the living heritage of history. Indeed, contemporary observers remark on the freshness with which some selected issues, appearing minor to the administrators during the period when they arose and already forgotten by Europeans, remained real to succeeding generations of Baganda. The principle of selective recall, as we have called it, was basic to the formation of political myths which themselves had their effect in the future relations among participants.

Both the phases of colonialism and the images and roles they created as a source of perception were filtered through the screen of the modernizing autocracy that transformed the ideas and

[8] Hence the tension produced by such issues as the Makerere land affair, in which the genuine desire for education among the Baganda helped to propel them in the direction of support for Makerere, while the East African clientele of the College, as well as the actual alienation of the land for the purpose, reinforced a basic Baganda fear—that of association with other territories in East Africa.

stereotypes by which men dealt with one another. Both the general phases of colonialism and the cycle of political perception describe a pattern found elsewhere in British Africa, but the effects of the modernizing autocracy in Buganda and its institutional adaptation gave it a very different twist. Before we go on to discuss this pattern of political perceptions, some brief description of the cycle of colonialism is in order.

1. The Pioneering Stage

Although the pioneering stage was a short one in African history, it established an important set of roles, heroic in their proportions, and a mythology of uplift which became the first legitimizing basis for colonial rule. It is implied in a superb passage by Margery Perham. What she wrote of the first explorers in Africa is also appropriate to missionaries like Mackay or Ashe, or to administrators like Colville, Jackson, and Sir Harry Johnston. "These discoverers seem to be almost like a separate species of man, or men set apart by some strange mental condition. They illustrate human purposefulness in such extreme and naked fashion as to take on a symbolic meaning. This reaches, perhaps, its highest expression in Mungo Park and David Livingstone, and in the latter it is welded with a spiritual passion that has set him among the very great."[9]

By their will and determination, their firmness of purpose, and by the spiritual tone and sublime self-confidence in the rightness of their missions, the early missionaries, soldiers, and administrators established their moral claims to political hegemony. Their devotion to service was unmistakable and Africans such as Sir Apolo came not only to bask in their greatness, but to consider themselves as coworkers in the tasks of spiritual uplift and effective government. Indeed, so harmonious was this relationship between British and Baganda Christian leaders that, in subsequent periods, the initial establishment of Christian society was regarded as the ideal to which all parties sought to return.

The pioneering stage established the ethical rightness of colonialism for its participants in the succeeding phase. In the next

[9] See Margery Perham and J. S. Simmons, *African Discovery* (London: Faber and Faber, 1942), p. 14.

stage, however, while there were many men of great virtue and quality, more had feet of clay. Who could succeed the Mackays, the Lugards, and the Johnstons?

2. The Political-Administrative Stage

Settled administration occurred during this period. District government was organized and a field apparatus established. There was a first emphasis on local government and the more formal identification of chiefs with government. The rule of law was introduced into the villages and rural areas. Treasuries were set up and more active administration occurred. Field officers regarded themselves as following in the footsteps of those who had sought to bring peace and enlightenment to the continent. They spent a high proportion of their time on tour and in their spare time wrote amateur ethnographies. The touring reports of early administrators show their great attention to the customs and traditions of the people. Disquisitions ranged from courtship and clanship to festivals and religion. They needed such knowledge to carry out their duties. And they had a natural curiosity about the people they found themselves among.

In this second stage, major chiefs worked closely with administrators. The Baganda, in particular, helped to expand the Kiganda pattern of local government elsewhere in Uganda. Although friction began to arise over questions of authority, it was clearly a tutelary situation which was, in the main, accepted by Africans.

Introduced alongside the mechanisms of colonial government were expanded political opportunities for qualified Africans in local administration. Education developed too. This was the extension of the promise of benefits which inhered in the Africans' acceptance of the British connection. However, in those parts of Uganda, particularly Buganda, where the history of association was complex even before the establishment of the Protectorate, there were efforts to erase those aspects of the relationship which were shameful and to restore a proper pride in the past. Hence the significance of the writings of Sir Apolo, Hamu Mukasa, and others. Among the great chiefs were prolific wielders of the pen. However, in the formalization of administration during this second phase of colonialism, there developed multiple images of the same situation which led to differing interpretations of meaning both in government and in social relationships between chiefs and their public and chiefs and the British. This formed a basis for friction. The ending of the political administrative phase was foreshadowed in the investiture controversy and most clearly marked in the enforced resignation of Sir Apolo Kagwa. After that, a more positive notion of colonial government and social welfare colonialism begins to emerge bringing a host of attendant problems in its wake.

3. The Bureaucratic-Colonial Stage

This period was the crucible both for nationalism and for self-government. It grew in part out of the need for specialization of function and division of labor that was imposed by the more ambitious tasks which social welfare colonialism set for itself, especially in the economic and social spheres—ambitions which were in part frustrated by the onset of depression and war. In addition to these important requirements of post-World War I colonialism, however, other factors were germane to the development of a bureaucratic pattern. Bureaucracy does not derive solely from internal processes of organization. Rationalization and efficiency result also from a search for stable formulae of administrative practices and rules. Bureaucracy is thus the result of the effort to assimilate lore and accumulate inherited experience and, by organizational means, to put it at the disposal of civil servants in different areas or pass it on to newer generations. Colonial bureaucracies, no less than bureaucracies elsewhere, result from the effort to make information and experience transmittable by organizational means.

Such lore becomes part of the system of bureaucratic roles. Not only is it displayed in the following of precedent in making decisions, but, in addition, certain rules of behavior begin to emerge. In the bureaucratic stage of colonialism the traditions of a moral elect, coupled with the division of labor within the civil service, created a new emphasis on social distance both within the ranks of the hierarchy and between Africans and European civil servants. Social distance helped to create separate communities dividing Africans from officialdom. The process was aided by the increased number of Europeans who came to Africa and were in commerce. It was also facilitated by the development of the legislative council system for Europeans and Asians which excluded Africans until 1945.

Organizational goals developed in the bureaucracy in consultation with other Europeans and to a smaller extent Asians. These became the goals for Uganda as a whole. A subtle shift occurred in the system of legitimate rule which served as the basis for colonialism. Instead of a continuation of the moral hegemony which was implied in the preceding two periods, such hegemony was now expressed as the need for efficiency and technical proficiency in keeping with the new emphasis on economic growth and activity. Perhaps such a principle could have, in the end, gained wider currency. However, it was forestalled by economic depression. Neither the ambitious plans and goals of the Protectorate government nor the warrant for legitimacy which they implied could be sustained for long. Instead, the African local governments and, in particular, the Buganda government, caught in the crossfire of bureaucratic colonial objectives and administration and public grievance, found themselves increasingly forced to take sides. In the case of Buganda, these problems were particularly acute as we have seen, and a protracted struggle between the British and Baganda now came to include conflict between chiefs and bakopi which itself created strange alliances between members of the Protectorate government and staff and the Baganda.

Although the gap between officialdom and Africans widened, the period of bureaucratic colonialism also produced an increase in African posts in the expanded system of African local government. In Uganda this made the districts more vital centers of political life, although they remained quite divorced from one another. In Buganda it made provincial government more significant. Thus the Dundas reforms in effect acknowledged that if separate communities of Africans, divided from one another and from the growing body of European officers, were to work at all, much depended on the effectiveness of the African governments themselves. In Buganda, however, such reforms provided fresh fuel for the fires of Kiganda nationalism.[10]

[10] Once this pattern of separatism and social distance occurs, colonial government increasingly operates in an atmosphere of hostility. Among Africans there

This situation had been the concern of administrators from Sir Philip Mitchell on. The association of co-opted and appointed African members with Europeans and Asians in the Legislative Council in 1945 was a first step toward breaking down these patterns of separatism which had developed. But Buganda showed little desire to participate in the Legislative Council.[11]

The system of co-optation and appointment did not work very well in other African territories after the War. In the Gold Coast and Nigeria neither of the constitutions which retained these principles after the War had a very long life. Moreover, events in the West African territories helped to persuade the Protectorate government of the need for a shift from the bureaucratic-colonial phase to representative self-government which would end eventually in independence. Hence in 1956 the Governor's speech advocating direct elections paved the way for the establishment of the final stage of colonialism—its representative phase.

4. The Representative Self-Government Stage

This final stage of self-government is characterized by the participation of local leadership in central government. Normally in Africa, representative institutions have been the scene of political invasions of nationalists who transform the legislature from a debating society to an effective decision-making body.

The representative self-government stage is also the last during which government can be shaped and formulated by outside means. The difficulty is that the last stage of colonialism gives way rapidly to the first stage of independence in which a very different set of dynamics is set in motion. In that period the hothouse

---

is a demand for participation, as occurred in the West Coast, or further separatism, as occurred in Buganda. Both produce somewhat different patterns of nationalism. The first takes a wider view of society as a whole while the latter emphasizes the immediate ethnic or regional group.

[11] The reluctance of the Baganda in this regard came to be regarded by the British as an expression of antipathy to representative government toward which the system was now headed. However, it must be remembered that putting Africans on the Legislative Council was not, initially, an effort to produce representative government but, rather, to associate Africans more effectively with the decisions of the colonial bureaucracy and to break down the compartmentalization which had developed. Essentially, through cooperation and appointment it was hoped to identify responsible African leadership with government as in the earlier idealized period of the pioneers.

quality of representative institutions becomes tested in the winters of bitter internal conflict, pan-Africanism, and the cautious entry into international relations which generates its own pressures. Moreover, the preceding colonial phases which left their mark both in the institutional structure and the perceptual structure begin to recede, and antiquity and heroics go hand-in-hand in efforts to reconstruct the past in a more meaningful manner.

In Uganda the efforts to introduce representative self-government have run head-on into the efforts of the Baganda to resist participation in central government. The modernizing autocracy has been successful so far in breaking the organizational back of most of the political parties except the Democratic Party.[12] The boycotting of direct elections was a dramatic instance of the steadfastness of the Buganda government in this regard. It is the Buganda government which is entering into representative self-government for itself, with a bureaucratic phase of chieftaincy government giving way to representative institutions internally, while rejecting the principle as a basis for Buganda's relations with the remainder of the country.

This conflict is best expressed in two documents, one published by the Buganda government and the other by the Protectorate government.

One, *Buganda's Position*, reflects the continued and unchanging perspective of the Buganda government in which the meaning of history and the significance of events have now formed a pattern most difficult to alter. The Katikiro of Buganda wrote in the foreword, "When the Baganda asked for British protection, they accepted the democratic system of government, in so far as that system fitted into their traditional political institutions. The result has been that the democratic system has developed peacefully, and has grown from strength to strength without any violent political revolutions. This peaceful growth of Western democracy in Buganda has only been possible because the Baganda's customs and traditions are adaptable to new ideas which do not seek to uproot their fundamental political conceptions. The Baganda will continue to democratize their institutions according to the wishes

---

[12] This situation is underlined by the fact that one of Uganda's most important young nationalist leaders and Secretary General of the Uganda National Congress recently accepted the post of Minister of Education in the Kabaka's government.

of the majority of the people without throwing away their good and tried customs and traditions."[13]

In order to make the position unalterably clear, the pamphlet points out that "any constitution which envisages placing any other ruler, or any foreign monarch in the position of the Kabaka of Buganda, has no other intention but to cause the Baganda to cease to be a nation. From time immemorial the Baganda have known no other ruler above the Kabaka in his Kingdom, and still they do not recognize any other person whose authority does not derive from the Kabaka and is exercised on his behalf. The Kabaka's Ministers and Chiefs govern in the name of the Kabaka. This is the recognized Kiganda custom. That is why any Muganda, be he a cultivator of the soil, a hunter, or a person engaged in any other occupation, carries out his work in the name of the Kabaka."[14]

The Kabaka's government called for Buganda autonomy, for their own army, the expansion of ministries, and the basic means to develop their own country in their own way. The pamphlet was signed by all the members of the Lukiko including those who had been prominent in political parties. Efforts to control the Buganda government by effecting reductions in the grants-in-aid given by the Protectorate government only demonstrated to the Baganda the need for greater autonomy.

Meanwhile, at the Protectorate government level, a report was issued by the Constitutional Committee of Uganda. Addressing itself to the problem of developing representative government on an all-Uganda basis, the report states, "In dealing with the question of the composition of the Government and of the composition of the Legislative Council following the next elections, it seems to us essential to be clear about the ultimate aim. Our view about this is quite clear, namely, that the aim should be the development of a national assembly modeled on the House of Commons in the United Kingdom, that is to say a fully-elected legislature with a cabinet responsible to the legislature. This is in accordance with the wishes of the majority of the people of the country as we understand them through the evidence we have received. We are

[13] See *Buganda's Position*, published by the Kabaka's government (Kampala: Uganda Printing and Publishing Company, 1959), p. 1.
[14] *Ibid.*, pp. 1-2.

well aware that events in certain other countries which have achieved independence have led many to wonder whether it is right to continue to model our institutions on those of the United Kingdom. The substitution of what appear to be dictatorships, often military, for democratic governments in some territories shortly after the achievement of independence is naturally a development which must be viewed with apprehension; nevertheless, we are certain that the proper course in Uganda is to develop a fully democratic system to which the responsibility of governing can be handed over at the time of independence. The people must have the opportunity of understanding the system of democratic government before they are given the responsibility of governing themselves and subsequently making their own decisions about the form of government most suited to them."[15]

The report then goes on to urge political parties to develop along rational lines. Party government, cabinet government with collective responsibility, and a legislature with a majority of elected members were advocated so that the British authority could begin to devolve to constitutional representatives of the people. The very gains fought for by nationalists elsewhere and the reasons which formed the latter's *raison d'être* were supported mainly by the Constitutional Committee of the Protectorate government.[16]

Thus the crystallization of political perceptions, which is the inheritance of the Baganda, has helped create a situation in which room for maneuver is small. Instead of compromise and mediation, the pattern is one of recoil and repulsion between Buganda and the rest of the Protectorate. This has produced a situation of political stalemate in which paradoxically to defeat Buganda parochialism it is necessary for the Protectorate government to be defeated by Buganda. In principle the Baganda have in the past agreed to accept a relationship with the Protectorate on a federal basis, a basis on which until now the Protectorate government has not been willing to negotiate. More recently it appears that a

[15] *Report of the Constitutional Committee* (Entebbe: G.P., 1959), p. 33.
[16] It must be pointed out that the Protectorate government failed to give full endorsement to the Committee report. But there is little doubt that the Protectorate government was in accord with the general principles laid down in the report.

federal basis will be the only way to proceed along constitutional lines. Buganda will have preserved her autonomy.

Or will she? For once Buganda agrees to participate in national government, with its emphasis on national elections, budgets, posts, and so on, the political center of gravity will shift from local and provincial government to national institutions. When this occurs political parties, having had years of organizational experience, albeit with small success, will have a natural outlet as well as a more meaningful basis. In that sense, once Buganda safeguards her autonomy in federal government, the issue of Buganda separatism can no longer prevent constitutional advance, and the initiative for government will shift to the center. The phase of practical realism will begin to develop in the context of representative self-government leading to independence.[17]

It will be recalled that none of the phases of colonialism through which Uganda has passed have resulted in the formation of mass parties. We have suggested that the basic reason for this is rooted in the instrumental values and hierarchical principle of authority which, expressed in the modernizing autocracy of Buganda, allowed it to serve as a relatively autonomous political substructure in itself with many of the properties of a political party. It was the Buganda party versus the rest.

Inherent in this situation was the ability of the Kabaka's government to handle internal problems within the modified political structure of Buganda itself. By this means the modernizing autocracy was able to gain the benefits of representative government without accepting the representative principle of legitimacy. Internally Buganda embarked on a process not dissimilar to that

---

[17] The ministers of the Kabaka's government fully realize this fact. During recent interviews (April 1960) I was shown a draft of a proposed federal constitution which provided for four states—northern, eastern, western, and Buganda. Power would reside in the "national councils" of each state. An upper house would consist of elders elected from the national councils and the upper house would initiate legislation. There would be a federal supreme court consisting of the four kings of the states and the elders of federating units. Ministers would be responsible to a national federal assembly which would be popularly elected, and would be able to give assent to bills from the upper house, declare war, grant honors, and appoint judges to the federal supreme court on advice of the upper house. Such a proposed constitution indicates the viewpoint of those in the Kabaka's government who are willing to negotiate with the Protectorate government, the secretaries general of the district councils and others, for the formation of a national federal constitution. I am grateful to the Kabaka's government for putting this unofficial working draft at my disposal.

of England after the time of the Reform Act of 1832. There the principle of autocracy did not give way but became ritualized and increasingly devoid of practical political content. In the case of Buganda, the popularization of the Lukiko made it possible for the role of Kabaka to be maintained. The principle of autocracy still served as the basis for association between a Muganda and his society. Meanwhile, the Lukiko was changed into a more representative body.

To examine these processes we have traced at some length the not inconsiderable fortunes of the Baganda in Uganda. We discovered that characteristically the behavior of the Baganda has been reflected in a continuous rhythm in political affairs. There was extraordinary devotion to the king whose hierarchical authority represents what Weber calls hereditary charisma. Devotion went far beyond mere acquiescence. There was also the innovating ability of the social system as a whole which, in contrast to most African systems, showed the institutionalization of instrumentalism.

Beyond these factors one cannot help but observe the flexibility of social life, spreading political grace like a net over what is essentially an aggressive and relatively atomistic social structure. This provided the king with the basis of manipulation essential to the maintenance of a hierarchical principle of authority so that competition between individuals was able to confound competition between groups. The social structure, by remaining atomistic, channeled competition into an appointive hierarchy where the ambitions of men allowed the easy formation of coalitions; coming together for a special purpose, these did not remain durable associations. Such a pattern persisted during the period of colonial administration, although the effects of property and education did help to create more stable social groupings. Yet no classes have formed in the strict sense of the term. Even chiefs and landowners are not necessarily united. Protestant and Catholic, farmer and merchant, landowner and Mukopi, chief and follower—all are relationships of potential conflict, though cleavage in the society does not follow stable lines.

Under such circumstances the neverending pattern of crisis is productive of homogeneity and interest in the subsystem of Buganda. A Muganda faced with an issue will belong to a more or less *ad hoc* group which exists to persuade others of a point of view or to win a position. Indeed, where issues produce differential cleavages which vary from crisis to crisis, today's enemies are tomorrow's allies and the system retains vitality in spite of the everpresent shadow of colonial rule.

Hence we see in the political sociology of Buganda much more than a political system. We find a structure fed by social atomism which prevents consistent group cleavage.[18]

Despite the early emergence of commercial groupings and the formation of political groups, faction never grew into party precisely because the patterns of shifting cleavages in the society at large gave a coherence to traditional groupings which never allowed major differences to destroy the state of Buganda itself. Thus the Bataka-chieftaincy conflict, rather than challenging the principle of hierarchical authority, reinforced it by forcing modifications in the Lukiko which allowed more efficient government.

The point is that such a system helped to create within Buganda that climate of practical realism which was necessary to carry on effective government within the limits imposed by its responsibilities, while the Protectorate government retained the responsibility of caring for really fundamental problems such as depression, disaster, and the like. It was the Protectorate government, not the Kabaka's government, which bore the brunt of new problems, and in the act of resolving those problems generated conflicts over jurisdiction and role which gave to Buganda the best of both possible worlds. The most crucial national problems were handled by the Protectorate government. As these were resolved, particularly in the economic sphere, the Buganda government was able to wrest increasing warrants of power and responsibility from the Protectorate government. Internal problems in Buganda were essentially those of *allocations*, that is, of reward and office, and *distribution*, that is, benefits rather than emphasis on innovation

---

[18] The nearest approach to cleavage occurred in the conflict between chieftaincy and the Bataka, but that, too, had been part of the traditional system and served to handle new issues in such a manner as to make new social clusters superfluous. The Bataka-chieftaincy conflict was sufficient to cater to the newer demands in the system by virtue of its similarity to political party conflict and, like political parties, helped through strife to force the government to heed public grievance. By the same token, it helped to make regular political parties unnecessary.

in social welfare and development. The latter were left to the Protectorate government or to private means, particularly Asian and European.

Phases of Political Perception

Representative government is proving difficult to achieve in Uganda. Its establishment is, in Western eyes, the crucial issue of independence. Self-government is justified by the ability of Africans and expatriate officials to make those political arrangements which, balancing individual liberty with social progress, can be achieved by a constitutional government possessing a liberal elite. The search is for a mechanism which can balance social goals and social costs in a prudent relationship which implies compromise if not harmony. Thus the four phases of colonialism are seen to end in democracy, as the Wild Report clearly indicates.

Each phase of government through which African territories have passed is associated with a certain style of political life or, to phrase it differently, a certain expression of political validity which gives to the members of the community a sense of awareness of the important issues of the day, fitting these into a perspective of rights, duties, and obligations. Expressions of political validity differ in varied sectors of society. What constitutes rights, duties, and obligations are matters on which there is little fundamental consensus although there may be general compliance. This helps to create a climate of latent conflict which can burst forth in unexpected guise and in unanticipated ways.

What are some of the different sectors of the community? The ethnic and tribal sectors we are familiar with. In our discussion we pointed to others, particularly those of class and status resulting from changes of wealth and income, alterations of residence, education and occupation. We showed, too, how in Buganda there was relatively easy access to land ownership or rental and, by this means, upward mobility through the political structure to an expanding system of government.

These factors, when analyzed in relation to the system of authority and the phases of colonial government, go a long way toward answering the question of why one phase is transformed into another.

Yet there is still another dimension in which it is useful to view the patterns of political change. They are particularly relevant for an analysis of the prospects of democratic government, for at bedrock they represent the people's commitment to democratic government, without which no democracy can long survive. This dimension refers to political perceptions and, as was suggested earlier, there is a characteristic pattern in which political perceptions emerge from the various phases of colonial government.

What are political perceptions? Participants of every society, colonial or independent, cloak reality in different meanings. Indeed, those concerned with the sociology of knowledge have been struck with the importance of this fact and have devoted their efforts to articulating relationships between material and ideal factors in the establishment of any individual's perceptive universe.[19]

Such perceptive factors are crucially important to an understanding of political change. It is unfortunate that in an age of secularism, Western observers have difficulty in grasping the proportions of pure belief. For belief, rooted in the ways men see their institutions, is a stubborn quality. Leading to attachments and associations, it measures the tensility of the latter's strength. As de Tocqueville put it, "There is hardly any human action, however particular it may be, that does not originate in some general idea men have conceived of the Deity, of his relation to mankind, of the nature of their own souls, and of their duties to their fellow creatures. Nor can anything prevent these ideas from being the common spring from which all the rest emanates."[20]

The relationship of ideas to individual action and the relationship of action to the roles and institutions of a society represent a system in dynamic interplay. Human motives, ways of perceiving, choices open to individuals, and the institutional structure are intertwined.

In his able discussions of social conflict, legitimacy, and democracy, Lipset has argued that "inherent in all democratic systems

---

[19] Mannheim puts the matter as follows: "To extract out of the manysided reality its slowly changing pattern and the structure of its inner balance, is the aim and at the same time the anticipated final vision of a fully developed historicism." See Karl Mannheim, *Essays on the Sociology of Knowledge* (London: Routledge & Kegan Paul Ltd., 1952), p. 87.

[20] Alexis de Tocqueville, *Democracy in America* (New York: Alfred Knopf), Vol. II, p. 20.

is the constant threat that the group conflicts that are democracy's life blood may solidify to the point where they threaten to disintegrate the society. Hence conditions which serve to moderate the intensity of partisan battle are among the key requisites of democratic government."[21] Implicit in this statement is the assertion that in order to moderate the intensity of "battle" the participants must be genuinely committed to values of moderation and compromise as essential to the maintenance of a democratic polity.

In new nations the value of the democratic polity is by no means clear. Group conflicts between ethnic and regional groups help to maintain the vitality of institutions geared to a different social order than the national society, which is itself inchoate. Indeed, the problem of political leaders with national rather than parochial points of view is how to build those larger loyalties without which a national society is meaningless.

There are reasons why people do not accept those values requisite to a democracy and why a democratic polity is not always the most acceptable political solution to their problems. These reasons are often rooted in the dimension of pure belief, such as expressed in the legitimate authority of autocratic kingship, or in the legitimate aspects of religion, *viz.* the case of pyramidal authority with consummatory values. In the former instance it is useful to describe the cycle of political perceptions as they develop from agreement about the nature of reality among all of the participants, regardless of what sector of society they come from, to the growth of multiple images, the selective recall of some aspects of these images to reconstruct history and give validity to the present, and the growth of political fantasy and myth.

Before launching into a discussion of these stages of perception, let us first be clear as to who are the participants in the process and what the process itself describes. Those with whose perceptions we are concerned are, first of all, individuals occupying important political positions. They constitute a power and prestige group equivalent to what Weber called a *Stand*. In no small measure they are equivalent to the role of the Brahmins in India, the Mandarins in China, and the Priests in ancient Israel.[22]

[21] See Seymour M. Lipset, *Political Man* (New York: Doubleday, 1960), p. 83.
[22] See M. Weber, *The Religion of India* (Glencoe: The Free Press, 1958, trans. Hans Gerth and Don Martindale); *The Religion of China* (Glencoe: The Free

In contrast to Weber's groups, power and prestige groups in Uganda do not conform to a single community. They are composed, characteristically, of great chiefs who fit into roles that are recognizably traditional, though modified by missionary and administrator, and into the colonial administration in which case they consist of expatriates. By virtue of their superior positions both groups share their own perceptions with a wider public, the one through its traditional hierarchy, the other through the civil administration.

In each case, what perceptions are shared by the public are elite interpretations of reality. These become important to the people at large and are vital in the formation of their perceptions.[23] The process in general follows a period of compromise and reluctant mediation of conflicting views between chiefs and British, which leads to increased bitterness of relations during the phases of colonialism. This pattern of increasing bitterness is central to the discussion because in nurturing grievance, both private and public, *multiple images* of the same situation gradually develop. These multiple images, often hidden from public scrutiny, include personal affronts, fears for the political future, and ambivalences produced by conflicting claims upon loyalty. In the case of the chiefs, this is between the Kabaka and the Protectorate government. For the senior expatriate officials it is between changing government policy and the people among whom they go. For the missionaries it is between their congregations and the government; and so on.

Once differing images of the same event begin to crystallize and, more particularly, give rise to the irritations and conflict in the relations between participants, the participants are called upon to justify themselves by appealing to their relevant publics. By doing so they recite the history of the grievance, often casting it into the larger framework of national concerns. Such a recitation

Press, 1951, trans. H. Gerth); *Ancient Judaism* (Glencoe: The Free Press, 1952, trans. Hans Gerth and Don Martindale). See also Reinhard Bendix, *Max Weber, An Intellectual Portrait* (Garden City, New York: Doubleday and Company, 1960).

[23] We do not mean to imply that the public receives its perceptions only from on high, as it were. Indeed, much of the process of perception among the major chiefs, for example, is affected by what they regard as public belief and receptivity to new ideas. In that sense public views already extant shape and limit valid perceptions of leaders.

invariably includes a history of betrayals which the Buganda and Protectorate governments are alleged to have mutually perpetrated. Thus in early pamphlets and political speeches the great chiefs wrote their interpretations of Kiganda history in part to justify the way in which the Lukiko allocated freehold land in the 1900 Agreement. Protectorate officials such as Postlethwaite exhorted the public to a more realistic view of the nature of the political bond between Britain and Buganda. Indeed, much of the effort expended in communicating government policy through district and provincial officers was an effort to clarify the cloudy constitutionality of Buganda-Protectorate arrangements. In the Kabaka Daudi Chwa's pamphlets, for example, there is always a citation of the wrongs done to his government. In the British case, the more neutral style used in government reports and documents disguised the same purposes and had the same effect.

In public statements, written documents, and in the practice of ordinary political relationships, these multiple images continued to develop, proliferating as new generations of administrators and chiefs entered into the relationships. The punctuation marks of such image formation were the various crises, whether over land, authority, closer union, economic representation, or political forms. In each succeeding crisis there was also a process of selection going on. Those relevant facts of which perceptions were at base composed were filtered through the sieves of time and generations. The reality of past events became necessarily oversimplified and garnished with grievance. Thus a principle of *selective recall* was at work. This principle explains the remarkable phenomenon in Africa whereby events occurring 50 years ago can sometimes have the freshness of the contemporary and can continue to be borne as current suffering and grievance in the accumulated heritage of misinformation. The conditions under which Kabaka Mutesa I was alleged to have accepted British overrule is one such event. There are many others. Some are of a personal nature, harbored in the collective memories of a prominent family and no less politically relevant for being hidden and obscure.

At some point the growth of multiple images and the effects of selective recall result in an ideology, firm and unshakable, which becomes part of the approved mythology of men and governments and from which only the historian and the analyst are allowed to depart. When such a situation occurs and there is a hardening of the perceptual arteries, then a *relative threshold* has been crossed and a given piece of immediate history "periodized." It now has a consistency in which motives, actions, and relationships are viewed in a more integrated manner. Such a period is, in most African countries, associated with the growth of nationalism and the nationalist interpretation of events. In Uganda and more particularly Buganda it came into being with the assassination of Martin Luther Nsibirwa and the periods of riot in 1945 and 1949. By that time the approved history of Buganda was that of betrayal by the Protectorate government. The political leaders who had dealt with the British had formed part of that betrayal. So widespread had such views become and so politically important that they culminated in the Kabaka crisis and in the end reversed the usual colonial pattern. The Protectorate government had become more liberal in its views than the Buganda government.

Following such a crystallization of views which occurs when the relative threshold is passed is a period of *hortatory realism*. Political leaders of all kinds, British and African, come to exhort the public to a different perspective. In the period of bureaucratic colonialism, the voices of politicians and trade unionists are added to those of government and chieftaincy. During the period of hortatory realism the more blanket political ideologies now become sharpened and divided. In the effort to set themselves apart from one another the political parties introduce variations in ideas which they think will find a corresponding appeal in the latent perceptions of the public. Most are wrong, at least for the time being. In the competitive efforts of hortatory realism the concern with reality itself becomes even smaller. Out of the oratory and the confusion of belief so engendered there develops a period of *political fantasy*. It is characteristic that in the last part of the bureaucratic-administrative phase, just before the establishment of representative self-government, the possibilities for political fantasy reach their peak. This phenomenon is demonstrated in exaggerated fears among different political groupings. For example, one political leader who was instrumental in winning the return of the Kabaka now found himself under attack by the Kabaka and his government. Political leaders making trips to Cairo and elsewhere distributed funds whose sources were obscure, and caused political party splits. There were charges and countercharges of raids on party treasuries by important officials. The Buganda government proclaimed that membership in political parties was tantamount to disloyalty, while in the Protectorate government the Wild Report on constitutional reform was lukewarmly received by a governor whose command over the local scene was as warped as that of any of the other participants.

Nor does political fantasy limit itself to public officials and politicians. Penetrating to the public it has led to bomb throwing against Asian shops in an effort to drive Indians from the rural areas and the boycott of Asian businesses. The old economic grievances appear once again in a growing period of lawlessness and disquiet.

Political fantasy need not always have the consequences it is having in Uganda. Where effective instruments of popular government and effectively organized political parties exist, they can help to create new political views and myths which are more coherent and acceptable. Political fantasy can be creative when it centers around the development of a new nation's political and economic institutions. In Uganda, on the other hand, it has produced a climate where all actions are suspect and where all the centers of government, Protectorate, Buganda, district and local, are unsteady in their purpose and tenure.[24]

What is needed is a new working basis for *practical realism*, that is, a new state of consensus based upon the free expression of ideas. It is our assertion that the condition of democracy is that of practical realism, a situation in which people can assert varieties of points of view but share in a working consensus about the nature of daily events as well as the basis of society.

Events are moving toward a climax in Uganda. The Protectorate government is determined to hold direct elections in 1961. The Kabaka has been less willing to support his ministers in their intransigence. Political party activity has been stepped up. Everyone seeks a way out of the impasse that has been created in the

[24] Nor is the situation limited to the African governments. The morale of expatriate officers in the Civil Service is low enough at present writing to warrant talk of a strike. Moreover, serving officers in Uganda have sought to discourage young recruits from entering the service.

past few years. Even the Democratic Party, which could not be accused of overbearing radicalism, has taken a strong stand in favor of registration for the elections in Buganda, opposing the chiefs who have advised the people to remain aloof from direct elections. Increasingly, the chiefs are being warned that as civil servants they need to remove themselves from politics. Party politics is entering the Lukiko and the new National Assembly, and Uganda sees—albeit grudgingly—that modernizing autocracy is giving way to representative government. In both Kenya and Tanganyika progress to self-government is swift. In such organizations as the Pan-African Freedom Movement of East and Central Africa, the Baganda will meet with far tougher opponents than they had previously encountered in the British. At least in the earlier objections to closer union the Baganda could with justice point to the domination of Europeans over Africans that was implicit in the proposals. African nationalism has changed all that. Now it is clearly not the case that in joining with other African territories in East Africa the Baganda need to fear European domination. As they recognize clearly, Buganda will lose her ascendancy in the East African complex. The Kabaka's government is insistent that it shall have its way in preserving Kiganda institutions and political security. It is specifically opposed to the nationalism of the West African variety.

It is not only African nationalists who are increasingly concerned over Buganda's separatism. British authorities as well are in haste to create a more effective national government in Uganda before their tenure is ended. Nationalism in Buganda has been called a "backward-looking" assertion of tribalism. "Where that happens the colonial power has the depressing choice of either staying on in an atmosphere of growing hostility or leaving before there are the national leaders and national loyalties capable of holding the territory together. This is nearly the choice that Britain now faces in Uganda."[25]

The logic of the events we have portrayed has now worked its way out into two clearly opposite and final points of view. Against the advice of the political parties, leading religious spokesmen,

[25] Cranford Pratt, "A Paradox in Africa," in *The Listener*, Vol. LXIII, April 28, 1960. See also *Democratic Party Weekly News Bulletin*, No. 17, September 17, 1960 (Kampala).

and many party politicians, the Lukiko late in 1960 overwhelmingly endorsed a resolution submitted by the Kintu government declaring that the Agreement was to be terminated, and that Buganda would become an independent country on December 31, 1960. Opposed to party nationalism, fearful of the rising tide of African nationalism elsewhere in East Africa, opposed to pan-Africanism, and anxious to safeguard its position, the Kabaka's government became convinced that the Protectorate government would in the end accede to its demand for a federal system. In that victory the Baganda saw defeat. Once established, such a federal system would leave the Baganda no choice but to participate in the affairs of the country and subordinate themselves to a representative national assembly. Their steady move toward autonomy would in the end be compromised. The resolution represented an inevitable step—the demanding of complete independence.

Meanwhile, the Colonial Office, alarmed at growing violence in Buganda and anxious to prevent a further worsening of prospects for constitutional reform, accepted the main recommendations of the Wild Report. It was decided that the next elections would in all cases be direct, on the basis of a common roll. Voters of all races would be qualified to vote, subject to residency and other qualifications. While this did not provide universal suffrage, the bulk of the population was enfranchised.

Representation was to be primarily on a population basis, with seats allocated on the basis of one member for approximately 90,000 people, except in those areas where population density was less than 50 to the square mile, in which case the proportion would be one member for approximately 70,000 people. A total of 76 rural constituencies and six urban constituencies was recommended. Seats were authorized for six additional, specially elected members, to be elected by the whole council with a carefully hedged continuance of the Governor's prerogative to nominate additional members so long as these did not upset the unofficial majority nor frustrate the result of the elections.

It was also accepted that party government would prevail. An elected Speaker might be introduced later, assuming an acceptable person was available for the post, and a majority parliamentary party or suitable coalition would help constitute a government from directly and specially elected members. An unspecified number of portfolios was reserved for civil servants, so long as the majority in the Cabinet were unofficials. There would be a government side and an opposition in the legislature, with the posts established of Leader of the Opposition and Opposition Whip. The new title of the Legislative Council was to be National Assembly. The Executive Council would now become a council of ministers. Although a post of Chief Minister with a council responsible to the assembly was rejected, it was made clear that this would be an interim arrangement. Direct elections throughout Uganda were to be held by March 1961 at the latest.[26]

While these terms fell short of universal suffrage and a fully responsible government, it is clear that the way is now open for African self-government. In view of the separatism of the Baganda, it remains for the Relationships Committee to work out the basic constitutional structure of the country before final self-government can be granted. The Colonial Office has left itself room to grant those concessions leading to independence if, on the African side, solutions can be found to the most pressing constitutional problems. The way is now paved for Uganda's final steps toward independence and it is up to the Baganda to choose whether or not, by their continued intransigence, they will continue to retard the pace or, further, promote internal difficulty. Perhaps the greatest danger is that the Buganda government will retreat from its ultimatum in favor of temporarily joining with the other people of Uganda in constitutional negotiations that will lead the entire country to independence. Biding her time until the last link is severed and the Agreement dissolved by the official ending of the tie with Britain, Buganda can then either attempt to dominate the entire country, putting the Kabaka forward as king of Uganda, or, failing that, declare her independence from Uganda at some future time, even at the risk of civil war. It would appear then that before the independence of Uganda is considered, several courses of action ought to be seriously weighed to prevent this likely political difficulty.

The first and foremost is the reopening of the question of closer union at a time when African governments are in control in Kenya as well as in Tanganyika. Further, the East African High Commission might be re-examined, with a view to the establishment of

26 Secretary of State's Despatch, *op.cit.*

an African executive, an interterritorial civil service, and the closer integration of the East African forces. The initiative for such a course ought to come from those in Uganda who support pan-Africanism and amalgamation. If such a pattern of constitutional development were worked out, it would place at the disposal of an African central government in Uganda those economic resources and political facilities of East Africa which might then be brought to bear against Buganda separatism, and also make the economic prospects of Buganda much more desirable than separatism.

Second, if the Baganda are convinced of the desirability of complete autonomy, a possible solution might be to amalgamate the rest of Uganda with Kenya or, less likely, Tanganyika. Much will depend upon the foresight and willingness to cooperate of other East African political leaders. This approach envisages the state of Buganda as an independent country blocked off from the sea, a small enclave in a very large African independency.

Third, if closer union solutions are unacceptable to the political leaders of Uganda, or to the other East African countries, and if the threat of closer union does not bring the Baganda around to the view that their fortunes and safety lie in Uganda independence, then it would appear that the chance for the success of democracy and stable government is indeed slender in Uganda. This means that barring one of the two forms of closer union solution suggested above, the Protectorate government has an obligation to see to it that the Baganda are forced to remain within a self-governing Uganda, at least until political parties establish themselves and until the ebb and flow of parliamentary business become so established that it will be difficult for the Baganda to cut loose without disastrous consequences in their economic and social condition. Too, the British should remain until an effective working relationship is established between an African civil service in Uganda and African ministers responsible to the National Assembly. Tribal separatism is one of the strongest and most stubborn problems for African politicians to deal with. It is far better to establish a system whereby the costs of withdrawal by some parochial ethnic group that is politically integral to the country are great enough to discourage fanatic efforts of separatism. Only a strong political party system, now entirely lacking in

Uganda, can begin to offset such parochialism. Thus the situation in Uganda is serious. A system of responsible party government will need to develop, cutting across tribal lines, capturing the loyalties of the youth, and of the deprived as well as the educated. It will need to inculcate those attitudes of civic loyalty and pride which are the ordinary inheritance of mass nationalist movements —only in Uganda it will have to come through the top, through party government. In order to ensure that the Baganda will accept, at least minimally, that form of party government—unless the Protectorate regime is prepared either to use force or abdicate responsibility for what will follow on its departure—a federal system is essential. There is clearly no sensible alternative constitutional solution if the way is to be cleared for an independent Uganda with some prospects of political viability.

If federalism is a system badly calculated to promote political ideals, at least it allows for the gradual working out of old scores in a climate of realism. It is a bargaining system above all, with rules depriving any special group of a veto power at the price of restricting the authority of the center. It tends to parochialize demagogues and political adventurers. Federalism may not be a "best" form of government under more ideal sociological conditions, but it is often a "best" solution in an otherwise impossible political circumstance. It may hold back unity and a common consciousness, as compared to a system such as prevails in Guinea, but it also holds back the capricious exercise of political power. And that is an important condition for practical political realism and wisdom.

Of the three alternatives suggested here, the last is the most likely course of action. It is to be hoped that neither Africans nor the Protectorate government will mistake the realities of political power which lie behind the forms of representative government.

The real paradox in Uganda is that nationalists of the contemporary variety and the British authorities are increasingly concerned with Buganda as the major obstacle to political advance in East Africa. In an atmosphere of violence and boycott Buganda prepares its final defenses against the inevitable compromise which it must make with history. In terms of our analysis, the problem in Uganda is to transform political fantasy into practical realism and to change from the bureaucratic phase of colonialism to representative government leading rapidly to independence. In terms of these needs, what kinds of conclusions can be drawn about the three types of authority systems, the mobilization type, the modernizing autocracy type, and the consociational type? We shall conclude our analysis with some comments on the propensities of these three types of system.

Potentialities for Constitutional Government

In the normal course of events nationalism unites people for the common purposes of winning self-government. More particularly, it is popular nationalism which, bringing together diverse elements of a colonial country, clothes its territorial bones with the flesh of nationhood.

In the transformation of Empire into a Commonwealth of freely associated and independent countries, the pattern which has been followed by the British in Africa has not been dissimilar to the one which created the older Commonwealth. The steady devolution of authority through legislative institutions making them responsible agencies of rule reaches its end when parliamentary sovereignty is proclaimed and a new country simultaneously achieves democracy and independence.[27] Democracy springs from the principle of representation enshrined in parliamentary supremacy. Representation and legislative decision-making are the means in which those principles of legitimacy are incorporated in political practice. In Western usage we consider parliamentary or legislative supremacy as the ability of a legislature to make or unmake any law whatever.[28] Such a view is based on the notion that within parliament resides the spirit and power of the whole people.

In Africa such views are not always dominant. In systems where the shared intimacy of custom and traditional institutions are living parts of daily conduct, parliamentary institutions are often regarded as forums for discussion, as places to air issues, ventilate grievances, and serve as outlets for public emotions rather than as crucial centers of political decision-making. Or, the symbolic

[27] See Sir George Cornewall Lewis, *An Essay on the Government of Dependencies* (Oxford: The Clarendon Press, 1891, Lucas ed.); and Arthur Berriedale Keith, *Responsible Government in the Dominions* (Oxford: The Clarendon Press, 1912), 3 vols.

[28] See A. V. Dicey, *The Law of the Constitution* (London: Macmillan, 1959, 10th ed.), p. 40.

attributes of a legislature as a place where people gather in council might well be observed but the legal sovereignty of parliament takes a form more fictional than real.

This is not to say that any of the new governments have done away with constitutionalism. More to the point, they have restored "caucus" to a place it once held in the West in the earlier days of parties and parliaments.[29] Hence, although in the period of representative self-government, or what Coleman calls terminal colonialism, the flow of government business, the performance of cabinet government, and the concept of parliamentary control may all be installed with a pomp and ceremony extending to maces, bewigged speakers of national assemblies, minute papers, and instructions prepared in a most careful manner, after independence the centers of political gravity turn to those sensitive areas of social organization where allegiances and alliances are best preserved. A quick look at the new governments in French-speaking and English-speaking Africa shows that while in no case have parliamentary institutions been destroyed, in several countries they have been profoundly altered.[30]

Other forms of democracy may continue to assert themselves strongly in Africa. In the extended family, in open forms of tribal and local governments, in public "palavers" which include party branches and tribal elders, different forms of democracy are practiced. In most of Africa these provide an easy intimacy of kinship, lineage, and local association which provide alternate sources of debate and knowledge about public wants. Democracy is then dependent upon the willingness of political leaders to consult freely with a public which makes claims upon them by a variety of means. Parliaments appear less crucial for they are among a number of several possible forums.

Such alternative forms of democracy depend, however, on the

[29] For an interesting comparison see Norman Gash, *Politics in the Age of Peel* (London: Longmans Green and Co., 1953).

[30] In the Ivory Coast, for example, there is virtually no debate on major issues. Even the budget, for long the central issue of debate even under the classic period of French colonialism, does not arouse more than cursory comment. It is characteristic of legislators to register unanimity in a division, while debate and discussion occurs behind the scenes in party caucuses. See *Journal Officiel de la Republique de Cote d'Ivoire*, Debats de l'Assemblee Legislative, Nos. 14–15, March 8, 1960 and March 28, 1960. I am indebted to my student Aristide Zolberg for bringing these examples to my attention.

willingness of political leaders to shape their policies in accord with public will as expressed through these agencies. The difficulty is that political organizations have their own dynamics, and in the immediate concerns of practical politics few political leaders can serve their own and national interests by patient consultation with the public. Traditional forms might continue to exert pressures upon them for some time to come. But in the long-run independence requires coherence in the political structure.

If this is the case, what are the various opportunities of democracy with each of the types of systems we have discussed? Where political leaders at the heads of mass political organizations have been successful in winning independence there is pressure from within the party and from the public upon the nationalist leadership to bring about the advantages of independence as quickly as possible, particularly in the economic sphere. The political fantasy of nationalism during the periods preceding independence gives way to political fantasy in building for the future. Meanwhile, the system is mobilized so that by organized discipline and sacrifice major improvements can be made. Mobilization prevents cleavage by attacking it, ensures social responsibility by ostracizing or otherwise restricting contentious people and, while not necessarily eliminating the parliamentary form, sees the advantages of cabinet dictatorship within the context of a unitary system. The leaders' commitment to democratic values may not falter, but they do emphasize the puritanism of work and the discipline of mobilization. They must create by means of mobilization the conditions whereby a more fullbodied political democracy can be created for future generations. It is a course full of dangers for democracy.

The modernizing autocracy as a national system shows certain similarities to the mobilization system except that its leaders operate through more traditional roles and the structural forms by which decisions are made are not new. In few cases, however, where the modernizing autocracies have been successful in achieving rapid modernization, have they long survived. Indeed, it will be difficult for the next generation of kings in Iran, Morocco, or Ethiopia to retain the prerogatives of political power held by those now in power. Yet there is stability in such a pattern of development. There is selective mobilization so that the burdens put upon those responsible for organizing development are relatively smaller than in the mobilization system. There is a steadier march toward effective parliamentary government which is itself an ideal or objective of general development. The difficulty faced by modernizing autocracies is the point of transition from autocratic to representative rule.[31]

The mobilization system and the modernizing autocracy are better prepared for rapid economic development, particularly by governmental means, than political development. It is the consociational type of system which holds out the greatest prospects for immediate democracy in most instances. Mobilization systems require a very high degree of public restraint and political propriety if they are not to become managerial autocracies under a parliamentary facade. Consociational systems, on the other hand, are based upon the assumption that conflict is itself a generating force for political vitality. Suitably devised, they render conflict into effective government by distributing power among relevant political groups. Mediation and compromise are inherent in such a situation while conflict between the different elements of the state gives vitality to central organs of government.

In one form of consociational system, the federal, the legislature becomes the repository of national power less through the ideal of representation of the public than of places, that is, states or regions. The states or regions bear the primary responsibility for the welfare of their constituents while the central government retains principal responsibility for the nation as a whole, particularly in defense, law, public works, and the like. This division of primary responsibilities does not occur in more unitary mobilization systems. Inherent in the consociational type of system is a concern for parliamentary institutions because of their mediating qualities. Concepts of democratic representation and social responsibility to the nation may emerge less rapidly. Indeed, it is not likely that larger loyalties to a national polity will quickly develop. The pace of change is slower than in the other two types because of the need to produce stable coalitions and recurrent majorities. But the disadvantages of localism are precisely its advantages. It allows individuals to work out their differences in circumstances which do not force people into beliefs which they are not ready to accept or

---

[31] It was not easily accomplished by Japan but helped lead to a major war and defeat.

principles which they do not fully understand. Under a consociational system the functional value of representative institutions develops first. Only later do these become related to the moral imperatives of democracy itself.

Behind the propensities of these three forms of political system, however, lies a relationship to the forms of authority which we have been discussing in terms of traditional systems. We can relate political values, forms of authority, and political types as follows: *The modernizing autocracy is similar to a mobilization system insofar as both have hierarchical authority and instrumental values, the one in more traditional terms, the other in nontraditional terms.*[32] In Ghana the development of the national system depended in no small measure upon the degree to which pyramidal authority in the traditional sectors and consummatory values were transformed into hierarchical authority and instrumental values for the national society by means of the mobilization system.

In sharp contrast to both the mobilization system and a modernizing autocracy is the consociational system. *In essence it is based on pyramidal authority with instrumental values.* The task in Uganda is thus quite different from that of Ghana. Instrumental values already obtain and the difficult task of changing from one value system to another is not involved. What does remain is the task of fitting a subordinate modernizing autocracy into a national system of pyramidal authority. Until Buganda in fact becomes a local democracy accepting a representative principle of government, the future of democratic government will be disappointing in Uganda. Once this is accomplished in Buganda, and the latter accepts a consociational relationship with the rest of Uganda, then the prospects of democracy in a system of representative self-government will indeed be bright.

The Baganda are not estranged from their past, but are anxious about their future. Fortified by those institutions she considers appropriate and necessary for continuing her adjustment to the modern world, Buganda has been successful in manipulating external forces which elsewhere have played havoc with age-old institutions. Against both colonialism and pan-Africanism, she has

[32] In the case of a mobilization system like that of Ghana or Guinea, one might say *antitraditional terms.*

raised her porcupine quills in the face of political forms and economic patterns which seem to her injudicious and out of keeping
with her resolve to bite off those pieces of innovation which she can
digest, and which can nourish her. Against the turmoil and distress
of a mighty continent in motion, Buganda is a tiny figure of continuity and tradition.

In concluding this long narrative of the prismatic qualities of
political development, what general points, useful for wider application elsewhere can we find? They are mainly two. First, if
we compare the new countries of Africa, we find that the degree of
autocracy which emerges after independence is in virtual proportion to the degree of antagonism the government shows to tradition. When countries look upon the system of government, the
forms of social structure, and the patterns of decision-making
which belong to the past as feudal, reactionary, and obstacles to
the future, they take it upon themselves to substitute by political
means those functions hitherto dispersed throughout the older
institutions in the society. They multiply difficulties, rendering
more complex the pattern of change itself, blunting or destroying
the mediating social forms that might help to deflect the onrush of
modernity. In the process they develop a momentum of change, a
speed which increases the uncertainties of life so that there can be
no looking back, no regrouping of traditional forces, and no
moments of longing for a form of society now rendered impossible.
Not that it is always a matter of decision. Few political leaders
can consciously decide on the uses they will make of tradition.
Some traditional forms brook no compromises or ready adaptation
and, as we have seen, produce chaos in the face of innovation.
Others, like the Baganda, are able to adjust. Traditional forms
thus help to determine what kind of state is possible once independence is attained.

Where tradition becomes an obstacle, the party and its auxiliaries, the voluntary associations and the individuals to which
they cater, the government and its civil servants—all need as
much as possible to be welded into a single system, each a part of
the other, with the whole representing the state and the society
simultaneously. The managerial burdens are great. There is only
a small area of private life open to individuals. Utopianism and

novelty, discipline and development become aspects of the daily scene.

But where traditionalism and modernity are aspects of a continuous process, the prevailing structure of society itself facilitates a natural form of growth, with fewer ruptures and greater compromises both in its government and among its members. This being the case, then those systems that make use of tradition and render it meaningful and pervasive while not adhering slavishly to old forms and formulas have the greatest prospects of immediate democracy. This is particularly so if the political setting allows a resolution of those problems which themselves represent a constant process of decision-making and adjustment of the old in the new, which is the essence of all democracies.

If our point is valid, and autocracy grows in new nations in proportion to its attack upon tradition, then does it follow that democracy grows in proportion to its acceptance of tradition? Here it is clear that while respect for the past and cultivation of tradition is a necessary condition of democracy, it is by no means a sufficient one. The history of Buganda shows that. What is also necessary is a political framework which is itself a source of innovation, which stimulates public talents throughout the country without sucking the rural and local areas dry of thoughtful men, or threatening those who ply old trades and ways. Consociational systems, particularly of the federal form, are suitable for that. Their safeguards are designed to meet those needs. Those systems with political forms which respect the attachments and wishes of discrete portions of the public may postpone quick transformations. But they do not penalize those who have lived lives in the best way they know how, nor do they betray the natural wisdom of their peoples.

In Uganda the condition most appropriate for the establishment of a national polity is some form of consociational political system. The peculiar difficulty of subordinating a modernizing autocracy within the larger framework of representative government would appear to make that solution imperative. For behind the question of parliamentary forms and constitutional arrangements lies the need to create a genuine basis of association of all groups, whether ethnic, racial, or class. By consociational means, hierarchical authority and political fantasy can be transformed into representative democracy and practical realism. The prevailing system of instrumental values facilitates the process. The problem which confronts those men of affairs responsible for the future of Uganda is how to establish an effective decentralized system of government. It now remains to resolve quickly those political differences and difficulties that prejudice her future, so that Uganda as a new nation can make her contribution to democracy in renascent Africa.

TERMINATION OF BRITISH PROTECTION

A MEMORANDUM TO HER MAJESTY QUEEN ELIZABETH II SUBMITTED BY MEMBERS OF THE LUKIIKO OF THE KINGDOM OF BUGANDA

Here below is the resolution passed by the Lukiiko which has called into being this Memorandum:—

"The Buganda Lukiiko sitting from the 21st to the 24th September, 1960, has heard the report of the Katikkiro in respect of the talks held in London between His Highness the Kabaka, the Lukiiko Constitutional Committee and the Secretary of State concerning the Buganda Constitutional matters.

"In that report the Lukiiko was told that the talks ended in deadlock. In view of this deadlock the Lukiiko has resolved that Buganda is determined to be a separate autonomous State and consequent upon that Buganda will not be represented in the future Legislative Council.

"As Buganda has always stated that while dealing with her constitutional matters it is not her desire to stand in the way of the development of the other parts of Uganda, she would in this connection like it to be clearly understood that other parts of Uganda are absolutely free to seek the attainment of their autonomy through whatever means they think fit.

"The Lukiiko's Memorandum which explains in detail the constitutional plan for an independent Buganda is being prepared and will shortly be forwarded to Her Majesty the Queen of the United Kingdom."

We intend to divide this Memorandum into three main parts:—
(a) Geographical and Historical background of Buganda;
(b) Buganda's reasons for going it alone; and
(c) the Constitutional Plan.

The boundaries of Buganda are defined in Article 1 of the Agreement of 1900. Within those boundaries, Buganda has an area of 25,390 square miles which is well over a quarter of the size of Uganda whose neighbours are: the Republic of Sudan in the North, Kenya Colony in the East, the Republic of Congo in the West, and Tanganyika in the South. Buganda has a population of approximately two million, which is about a third of Uganda's six and a quarter million peoples. Buganda is the wealthiest of the four Provinces into which Uganda is divided, with cotton and coffee as the main cash crops. Buganda contributes nearly sixty per cent to the total revenue of the Uganda Protectorate, which total amounted to more than £26 million in 1957/58. Of this contribution from Buganda, which on that figure amounted to nearly £16 million, Buganda received back only £1½ million by way of grants from the Central Government.

Buganda is an ancient kingdom with a long history and her dynasty exceeds thirty-seven kings in an unbroken line. The history of Buganda begins with a king and continues throughout the centuries with kingship right up to the present day. There is not a single period in our history when the Baganda had no king ruling over them. The Baganda have a system of clans, and by means of royal marriages among women of various clans, and since by custom members of the royal family belong to the clan on their mother's side, a situation has arisen during the passage of time, whereby most clans have had a ruling monarch or an outstanding prince as a member of their clan. This custom has had a profound effect on the Kiganda society. Buganda kings are unique in that they play two big roles in the tenure of their office as monarchs, namely that they are rulers as well as being superheads of all heads of clans in the kingdom. As a result, the King of Buganda bears a personal relationship to every single Kiganda family in the kingdom. In other words it is inconceivable for a Kiganda society to exist without a king.

For time immemorial the Baganda have had a system of an organised form of government consisting of the King, the Parliament, and a Prime Minister. They also had an army and a navy. When the British first came to the country they found this system of government in operation, whose fundamental concepts they have preserved, enriching it as far as possible with their own democratic principles.

There is a wealth of evidence to be found in the writings of the early travellers and discoverers of what was then known as the "Dark Continent," and H. M. Stanley's remarks on Buganda are eloquent enough. Stanley was one of the great explorers of Africa in the nineteenth century and he speaks of Mutesa I, who was ruling Buganda at that time, as ". . . a powerful emperor, with great influence over his neighbours." He goes on to say: "I saw about 3,000 soldiers of Mutesa nearly civilised . . . I saw about a hundred chiefs who might be classed in the same scale as the men in Zanzibar and Omman, clad in rich robes, and armed in the same fashion; and have witnessed with astonishment much order and law as is obtainable in semi-civilised countries."

Stanley thought Mutesa would "do more for central Africa than fifty years of gospel teaching, unaided by such authority could do. I think I saw in him the light that shall lighten the darkness of this benighted region, a prince well worthy of the most sympathies that Europe can give him."

It was Mutesa I who requested Stanley to write to the British people in Great Britain that he and his people were like blind men groping in the dark and that he was anxious to invite the British to come and give him the light. This request shall ever stand to all future generations as a sign of greatness of this far-sighted King Mutesa I. As a result of this request the British Missionaries arrived in Buganda in 1877, to be followed by the French Catholic Missionaries in 1879.

This was the period of the "Scramble for Africa," and in Buganda there appeared on the scene the British, the French, the Germans, and the Arabs, each group scrambling for power over the country. The confusion into which the mind of King Mwanga was thrown by this scramble can best be imagined than stated. The Baganda eventually chose the British as their protectors, and a Treaty of Protection was signed between the Queen's Representative on behalf of the Queen, and the King of Buganda, in 1894.

In 1897, the British army in Uganda consisted mainly of Nubians under a British Commander. The Nubians mutinied, and the British were proposing to ask for troops from India when the Baganda, under the able leadership of Sir Apolo Kagwa, then Prime Minister of Buganda, volunteered to fight the Nubians whom he defeated in the battle of Bukaleba in Busoga, thus redeeming the British prestige in Uganda.

Two significant articles stand out in the 1894 Treaty between the Queen and the King of Buganda: the first is Article 2, which reads,

"And whereas Her Britannic Majesty has been graciously pleased to bestow on the said Mwanga, King of Uganda, the Protection which he requested in that Agreement. . . ."

This article clearly shows that the Kingdom of Buganda was not conquered or ceded by the British, and that British Protection was requested and so graciously bestowed. The second important article in that Treaty is Article 14 which says:—

"The foreign relations of Uganda and its dependances are hereby placed unreservedly in the hands of Her Majesty's Representative."

This article indicates that Buganda was a real sovereign state before and at the time the British bestowed their protection.

The Agreement of 1900 which followed the 1894 Treaty has no connection with, and bears no relationship to, the Treaty of 1894, and yet its conclusion was the first move by the British in an attempt to reduce the sovereignty of the Lukiiko, as may be gathered from the official documents between Her Majesty's Representative in Uganda and the Foreign Office in London.

In 1902 an Order-in-Council was passed in the United Kingdom, which self-justified the British to rule over Uganda as "a Colony, and as if it was one of our possessions." The propriety of this Order-in-Council which changed the status of Buganda without the knowledge or consent of the Baganda will ever be regarded by them as the first classic example of the first major causes of Buganda's misfortune, and from the time it was launched to the present day, the British have been following a policy designed to whittle down Buganda's powers.

The annals of history should never brush aside the important part which the Baganda have played in both administrative and social developments of the Uganda Protectorate. Let it be remembered that it is upon the Kiganda system of government that all tribal governments in the Protectorate have been based, that system having been exported to the other tribes by the Baganda themselves, on request. The same is true in the sphere of education and evangelism.

Since the advent of Pax Britannica at the end of the last century, Buganda has stood in a special relationship as regards Her Majesty's Government and the rest of Uganda. This relationship is exemplified by the provisions of the Treaty of 1894 and the subsequent Constitutional Agreements 1900-1955. As an illustration, Article 14 of the 1894 Treaty, already referred to above, could only be enacted in relation to a people who had a well-organised government run on systematic principles as recognised by Sir Gerald Portal, "Her Britannic Majesty's Commissioner" in 1894.

By the Treaty of 1894, British protection was subsequently conferred upon the rest of Uganda.

A further illustration of this special relationship is provided by Article 5 of 1900 Agreement which reads:—

"The Laws made for the general governance of Uganda Protectorate by Her Majesty's Government will be equally applicable to the Kingdom of Buganda, except in so far as they may in any particular way conflict with the terms of this Agreement will constitute a special exception in regard to the Kingdom of Buganda."

Buganda's Treaty and constitutional Agreements have been made between the Kabaka, Chiefs and people of Buganda on the one hand, and Her Majesty the Queen on the other. Whereas in the other parts of Uganda similar Agreements have been concluded as between the Protectorate Government on the one hand and any Native Government on the other. The Protectorate Government is subordinate to Her Majesty's Government.

The 1955 Agreement has once again stressed Buganda's position by the fact that part of this Agreement is embodied in an Order-in-Council and forms part of the Laws of Uganda. No such provision obtains in any other Agreements found in the rest of Uganda.

Our ancient institutions of the Kabakaship and the Lukiiko have adapted themselves to change in order to fit themselves into the modern world. Since the 1900 Agreement the tendency of the Lukiiko has been to democratise itself. Today, of the ninety-two members of the Lukiiko, sixty are elected by the people, through electoral colleges, a method which has so far proved itself as democratic as any other.

By the 1955 Agreement, the Kabaka is a constitutional monarch, who rules the country on the advice of his Ministers. The Lukiiko, the Parliament of Buganda, and the Kabaka's Government, consisting of six Ministers, operate on a Provincial basis whereas in the rest of Uganda all Native Governments operate on a District level and they are local Government units.

It is that special position which Buganda enjoys now that she wants to maintain even after Uganda's independence. The Baganda believe that they can safeguard their prestige only through the survival in a living and functioning form of the Kabakaship and the Lukiiko. The Kabaka is the spirit and motivating power of political, economic, and social activities and the Lukiiko is the legislative forum of the Baganda. That is why anything, either extrinsic or intrinsic, that tends to weaken our institutions is bound to be resisted in Buganda. One of the extrinsic forces that have tried to weaken our institutions is the Legislative Council, which was introduced in Uganda in 1921. This body, which was introduced mainly as a forum for the European planters and traders at that time, has never gained popularity in Buganda since its inception because it was regarded as foreign both in origin and composition. Secondly, and more significantly, this Council has been viewed with suspicion as a possible agent to sap the strength of the Lukiiko and to lower the Baganda's prestige. Part of the 1953 crisis, whereby the Kabaka was exiled by the British Government for two years, revolved round the controversy of Buganda's representation on the Legislative Council. This Council has failed to win the Baganda's confidence.

That is the crucial point. Her Majesty's Government have declared that Buganda shall be represented on the Legislative Council as the only means of Uganda's unity. The Lukiiko and the Kabaka's Government on the other hand have said that before Buganda reconsiders her attitude to the Legislative Council, her Treaty and constitutional Agreements must be terminated first and Her Majesty's Government should declare now that at least Buganda will be in a federal relationship vis-à-vis the future Central Government of Uganda. The Lukiiko's Memorandum of 1958 expressing their wish to terminate the Agreements resulted in constitutional talks held between the Lukiiko Constitutional Committee and Her Majesty's Representative since September, 1959, until they ended in deadlock in London this September. The sole purpose of these talks had been for Buganda to receive back the powers exercised by Her Majesty's Representative under the Agreements before Uganda attained independence. The Treaty relationship between Buganda and Britain demanded that Her Majesty's Government could not surrender their powers under the Agreements to a new Government with which Buganda never concluded an Agreement. Satisfactory conclusion of the constitutional talks would further determine Buganda's federal relationship with the future Central Government.

While these talks were going on, Her Majesty's Government formulated a Constitutional plan for the whole of Uganda. This was:

(a) Registration of voters throughout Uganda;

(b) Before the General elections there would be appointed a Relationships Commission by the Secretary of State for the Colonies to make recommendations as to the form of government most suitable to Uganda;

(c) General elections early next year for the Legislative Council, 1961;

(d) After the General elections there would be a constitutional conference, to be held in London in the summer of 1961, representative of all parts of Uganda, including Buganda, to consider the recommendations of the Commission. This conference would be attended by the elected members of the New Legislative Council.

Although this plan affects Buganda's constitutional position fundamentally, Buganda's proposals as to how it should apply to their kingdom have been brushed aside. For example, during the recent London talks, the Kabaka's delegation suggested that the Relationships Commission should submit its report before these fundamental changes took place. The Secretary of State rejected this suggestion out of hand, but yet declined to answer the relevant question as to what Her Majesty's Government would do should the Relationships Commission recommend a form of government that was contrary to Buganda's desires.

The Secretary of State has declared that he cannot deviate from that plan, whatever Buganda's representations for some modifications, hence the deadlock in the London talks.

Buganda has found it extremely difficult to co-operate in these unnegotiated orders emanating from Whitehall, which orders completely disregard the Kabaka's Government's and the Lukiiko's representations. There cannot be any other body of opinion more representative of public opinion in Buganda other than the Kabaka, his Government, and the Lukiiko. This disregard on the part of Her Majesty's Government comes as a great shock to the Lukiiko and the people of Buganda.

The Secretary of State has indicated that public opinion in Buganda and Uganda is that expressed by political leaders in this country. Nothing could be more erroneous and misleading. In Buganda there has been a move to form political parties since the early twenties, but Her Majesty's Government's policy has been to suppress them by either proscribing them or deporting and putting political leaders into prison. The result of this repressive policy has been that the political parties have failed to establish themselves firmly and win the confidence of the Baganda, whose loyalty has always been towards their Kabaka and the Lukiiko.

It will be remembered that during the 1953-1955 crisis, when political party leaders tried to see the Secretary of State concerning the return of the Kabaka from exile, the Secretary of State said that he could only negotiate with members of the Lukiiko. He did not recognise political party leaders as the right persons to treat with in constitutional matters affecting Buganda.

In those circumstances, it would be asking too much of the Baganda to trust the destiny of their country to the hands of political party leaders whose experience has not been proved by this time. This could be extremely risky in the light of recent history, which has shown clearly that politicians in emergent countries use parliamentary democracy as a springboard to virtual dictatorship. Buganda has asked Her Majesty's Government to hand back her powers to the Kabaka who under the Treaty and Constitutional Agreements entrusted them to that Government. Her Majesty's Government's refusal to do this, preferring instead political party leaders, is not only discourteous in the extreme, but also a complete oversight of the facts.

When the Secretary of State recently said at the opening of the new Legislative Council Building that he had firm intentions to act vigorously under the law in order to carry out his plan, he sounded a warning note that he would use all means to impose the British type of parliamentary democracy which he said the people of Buganda demanded. It is difficult to know what is meant by the "people of Buganda" in this context. The "Special Power Ordinance" hurried through the Legislative Council immediately after the Secretary of State's visit, which Ordinance gives the Police unlimited powers to arrest and detain anyone on suspicion that he may intimidate people who want to register or vote, shows that Her Majesty's Government is determined to introduce the British type of parliamentary democracy even by decree.

If Buganda's legitimate constitutional demands have caused all these most unlikely reactions while the Treaty relations are even still existing between Buganda and Her Majesty's Government, the Lukiiko's apprehensions as to the future Uganda Government's attitude towards Buganda are greatly intensified. We cannot expect that Government to do much better than Her Majesty's Government, as they are going to inherit this form of disguised dictatorship. Public pronouncements made on various occasions by peoples likely to be leaders of future Uganda are not conducive to unity as Her Majesty's Government envisages it. In order to avoid another "Katanga" in this country immediately after Uganda's independence, Buganda has decided and is determined to go it alone.

As a result of this decision, Buganda proposes to establish cordial relationship between Her Majesty's Government and herself for a number of reasons: mainly because the British are monarchists like the Baganda, and the special relationship that has existed between the two countries has been a paternalistic one which has been found to be unsatisfactory in the present circumstances. Since neither Britain nor Buganda desires that this superior-inferior relationship should continue beyond what is absolutely necessary, there ought to be a new Anglo-Baganda Cordial Relationship. That proposed relationship should be finalised and put into effect by 31st December, 1960, after which date Buganda will be independent. In the meantime, negotiations will be held between representatives of the Lukiiko and Her Majesty's Government with a view to formulating a scheme wherein that Anglo-Baganda Cordial Relationship will operate.

PLAN FOR AN INDEPENDENT BUGANDA

1. *Relationship with Great Britain*

There shall be established a friendly relationship between an independent Buganda and Her Majesty's Government on the following lines:

A. DEFENCE. In this connection, Buganda will have her own Army, but she will form a military alliance with Britain for a specified period of time which may be revised from time to time.

B. FOREIGN AFFAIRS. Buganda will establish Foreign Relations by herself where possible, otherwise, in conjunction with Great Britain for a specified period of time.

C. ECONOMIC AID. Buganda will seek economic aid from Britain in her economic and technical development.

A Five-Year Development Plan will be drawn up by Buganda following the attainment of her Independence, so as to give the kingdom an orderly economic development.

In her economic development, Buganda will encourage free enterprise and make conditions favourable for foreign investment. The Kabaka's Government's Policy as to State Ownership is that such ownership should be restricted to those essential services which cannot be beneficially run by Private Enterprise.

2. *Relationship with Neighbouring Countries in East Africa*

A. CUSTOMS. Buganda will join the Common Customs of East Africa.

B. COMMUNICATIONS. (This includes Road, Rail, Water and Air services.) There shall be joint negotiations as to the membership of Buganda on the bodies controlling those services.

C. HIGHER EDUCATION.

(*i*) All existing institutions of learning will automatically fall under the jurisdiction of Buganda.

(*ii*) This position will, however, not alter the present status of Makerere University College, nor will it change its legal and administrative position as an inter-State institution.

(*iii*) Buganda will have her full share in the management of Makerere, and shall be fully represented on those bodies which control and administer its activities.

D. JUDICIAL. Buganda shall have her own High Court and District Courts. Appeals from the High Court shall lie to the East Africa Court of Appeal and finally to the Privy Council.

E. INTER-STATE TRADE IN EAST AFRICA.

(*i*) Any manufacturing and/or secondary industries operating in Buganda will have to be licensed in Buganda, and all Excise Duty will go to the Buganda Kingdom Treasury.

(*ii*) There will be free movement of trade between Buganda and the States of East Africa.

F. MONETARY SYSTEM. Buganda will remain in the Sterling Area.

G. IMMIGRATION. Immigration will be controlled by the Kabaka's Government. This will apply to non-Africans as defined by the existing Uganda Protectorate Ordinance. Movement of Persons, however, between Buganda and other neighbouring countries in East Africa will be free and unrestricted.

3. INTERNATIONAL RELATIONSHIPS.

A. The fundamental rights of man, and the Rule of Law as understood in the free world, will be strictly observed. Thus there will be freedom of worship, freedom of speech, and freedom of assembly in Buganda, regardless of race, colour, or creed.

B. On her attainment of independence, Buganda will be associated with that Great Family of Nations, the Commonwealth, and like any other independent nation in the Commonwealth, Buganda will seek admission to the United Nations General Assembly.

C. Posts and Telecommunications, being services conducted on international level, such services will continue to be run as at present in Buganda. The control of those services in Buganda, will, however, fall under the Kabaka's Government, and as such Buganda will make her own Postal stamps.

4. INTERNAL RE-ARRANGEMENT OF SERVICES.

A. The Lukiiko will continue to be the Legislative and deliberative body for Buganda.

B. All powers now exercised by Her Majesty's Representative under the Treaty and Constitutional Agreements of Buganda shall vest in the Kabaka and his Government, e.g., all laws and Buganda's Budget shall be effective after the approval of the Kabaka, who is the Supreme Head of Buganda.

C. Buganda will have an army of which the Kabaka will be the Commander-in-Chief.

D. Buganda will have her own Police Force for the purposes of maintaining law and order. In this connection, the present Uganda Police Force responsible for the Buganda Province should immediately come under the Kabaka's Government's jurisdiction.

E. There will be a High Court and District Courts for Buganda with a Bench of trained, qualified and experienced lawyers. Parties will be legally represented therein.

F. Kampala, Entebbe, Masaka, Mubende, and all townships and trading centres, as well as Entebbe Airport, without prejudice to its international status, will immediately be brought under the jurisdiction of the Kakaba's Government.

G. All lands vested in Her Majesty under the provisions of all Buganda Agreements shall revert to the Kabaka of Buganda for the use and benefit of all.

The Lukiiko is fully conscious of the important fact that in order to realize the scheme as outlined above, Buganda will need technicians, doctors, lawyers and many people trained in various professions and trades. She will need a strong Civil Service. Buganda therefore intends to award as many scholarships as possible for long and short courses here and abroad to candidates who are most likely to make the maximum use of the facilities for the benefit of their country in the long run. In the meantime, Buganda will meet the shortage in personnel by employing expatriates on contract.

As to the financing of the whole scheme as outlined above, Buganda intends to use the existing resources, which will be greatly increased by the change over from British control; to raise local as well as overseas loans; and to invite outside capital.

In conclusion, this Lukiiko's decision has been made imperative by Her Majesty's Government's failure to recognise the fact that any possible parliamentary democracy ought to be built on the existing institutions in Buganda, that is to say, the Kabakaship and the Lukiiko. Her Majesty's Government's oversight of the Kabaka's, his Government's, and the Lukiiko's representations to that effect can only result in hard feelings unnecessarily. The only possible way out of these difficulties is for Buganda to go it alone and establish the Anglo-Buganda Cordial Relationship, as outlined above.

The Lukiiko would like to stress the fact that it is not opposed to parliamentary democracy as such, but it views with apprehension any induced democracy which is only strengthened by the desire for independence. To the Lukiiko, parliamentary democracy ought to suit the local conditions, because there cannot be such a thing as international parliamentary democracy. Independence should be a means to an end and not an end in itself. Buganda cannot sell all her heritage for the purchase of Uganda's independence. That heritage is much more precious in the long run. Nor is Buganda willing to sacrifice everything at the altar of Uganda's unity.

The foregoing does not mean, in the least, that we are not appreciative and actively conscious of the benefits Buganda has derived from Her Majesty's protection for the last seventy years. There cannot be a better way of expressing that gratitude than the proposed Anglo-Buganda Cordial Relationship.

(In each case, page references are to footnotes.)

constitutional monarchy, in Buganda, 349-50, 352-54, 382
constitutional reform, implications of, 390-94
consumatory values, 85-91; in Buganda, 105-07
cooperatives, 193, 197-98, 235, 244, 250-52, 252n, 311
Cooperative Societies, Ordinance of 1946, 252n
Coryndon, Sir Robert, 162
cotton industry, 49-51, 54, 59, 183, 186-92, 232n; and Uganda African Farmers' Union, 251-52; as issue in 1949 riots, 258-59
Crawford, Sir Frederick, 403
Creech-Jones, A., 237n

Daudi Chwa (Kabaka), 82, 111, 118, 165, 195, 203, 204-05n, 207; regency for, 134-39; investiture of, 139-41; and Bataka Association controversy, 144-49; and Apolo Kagwa case, 153-58; opposition to closer union, 176-78
de la Warr Commission, 227
delegations, Baganda, in Kabaka crisis, 291, 297-98
Democratic Party, 309, 344, 346, 387, 391
developmental types, 21n
Diplock, Kenneth, 292n, 296n, 297n
direct elections (1956), Baganda boycott, 308
direct elections (1958), controversy over, 422-431; voting qualifications for, 429; Buganda abstention from, 430; minority safeguards issue, 427-29
direct elections, Uganda National Congress position on, 335-36; Lukiiko position on, 381-86; basis of, 467-68
district administration, 32-36, 41, 159
district commissioner, 41-42, 413-15
district councils, 40, 238, 272, 414
District Councils, Ordinance of 1955, 40, 238n, 414
district teams, 41, 223
Dundas, Sir Charles, 194, 211-12, 219-22; reforms, 211-12n, 224-26, 232
Duta, Henry W., 149

East Africa Central Legislative Assembly, 45
East Africa, federation proposals, 17-18, 171-80; issue in Kabaka crisis, 276-79, 283-85, 288, 353

East African High Commission, 233, 256-57, 258n
Eastern Province, local administration in, 217-19
economic development, 47-61, 419; as concern of legislative council, 161-62; and closer union, 172-73; policy, 208, 224, 229, 234, 238-39, 239n
economic factors in political development, 181-94
education, 58-59, 268, 372, 418n; and missionaries, 74; influence in post-Agreement period, 129-33; and social mobility, 199-202, 441
electoral college of 1955, composition, 406-07
Entebbe, 170, 265, 399
ethnic conflict, 19
ethnic groups, in Uganda, 30, 32-36; population table, 38
Europeans, population, 37-39; role in economy, 47, 48, 51, 57; attitudes in East Africa, 63-64, 178-80; role in legislative council, 396-98
exclusivism, in modernizing autocracy, 26
Executive Council, 45, 162-63, 221, 411-13
exploration, of Uganda, 64-67
ex-servicemen, 229n

factionalism, in Buganda political life, 15-17, 20, 202-06, 213-15
family, affiliation and social status, 112, 181-82, 184, 199-202
federal principle, in consociational systems, 25
federal system, as goal for Uganda, 44, 294, 434, 467, 470
Federation of Bataka Bamasiga, 145, 146
Federation of Partnerships of Uganda African Farmers, 275, 310-13
feudalism, parallels in Buganda, 63-64
Financial Secretary, 160
Foot, Dingle, 292n

Gambuze, 232, 241, 273-74
Gayaza High School, 129
Ghana, *v-vi*, 4, 20, 199, 264
gombolola, unit of government, 30, 44, 95, 245, 365-66
Gombolola Chiefs' Association, 184n, 206
Gowers, Sir William F., 153, 154
Grant, Captain, 66

INDEX

Padmore, George, 235, 313
Pan-African Freedom Movement of East and Central Africa (PAF-MECA), v, 258n, 344-45, 466
Pan-Africanism, 6-8; and Uganda National Congress, 332-35
Pan-African People's Conference, Accra, 334
parliamentary democracy, in contemporary Africa, 471-73
parochialism, consequences of, 431-34
partnership, as administrative philosophy, 223-24, 279
party government, expectation of, 467-68, 470
patronage, and political power, 119, 360-62
peasants (bakopi), 183, 186-87, 200-02. See also bataka, land ownership
Perham, Margery, 235, 290-91
Peters, Carl, 73
pioneering phase of colonialism, 114, 448-49
pluralism, in consociational systems, 25
political-administrative phase of colonialism, 109-17, 449-50
political change, models of, 20-28, 216-17
political development, in Africa, 3-9
political groups, origin of, in Buganda, 108-33
political movements, checks upon, 18-20
political parties, 301-10; alternative roles for 344-48; obstacles to, 307-09; in 1958 Lukiko elections, 386-87; proliferation of, in Buganda, 274-75; religion and, 19; role in new nations, 301-07
political perceptions, 447-48; cycles of, 437, 459-65
political roles, conditions for, 393
political trends, post-1955 in Buganda, 387-89
population, of Uganda, 30, 36-40
Portal, Sir Gerald, 110; mission to Uganda, 78-80
Postlethwaite, J. R. P., 151-58, 200
Price Assistance Funds, 50, 59
Progressive Party, 309, 337-340, 344, 346, 387
Protectorate, establishment of, 75-83
Protectorate Government, administrative policy, 220-26; concerns of, 159-61, 167, 170; friction with Buganda government, 134-37, 196-97, 219-20,

458, 464; proposed reforms for Buganda, 206-212; role after 1955 Agreement, 356-58. See also Nsibirwa and Kulubya ministries
provincial councils, 41n, 42, 237-38
provincialism, in Buganda, 10-17
pyramidal authority, characteristics, 85-91, 105; diagram, 92; in consociational systems, 24, 475; in Ashanti, 442-46; in Buganda clan system, 99, 100-02, 105; in Uganda, 91-94

racial communities, relations between 62-63, 396-401, 419, 421-22; political attitudes of, 351
racial representation, in East African legislatures, 172-75; in legislative council, 163-67, 427-29
racial stratification, 182-83; in civil service, 197
Rangoon Socialist Conference, 314
recruitment, to chieftaincy, 184-85, 200; to civil service, 197
Relationships Commission, 403, 468
religion, and types of political system, 6-7; as solidary basis for political faction, 115, 125-27; influence in post-1900 Agreement period, 129-33; traditional Buganda, 106, 130-31. See also Missionaries
religious factionalism, in contemporary politics, 19, 34n, 342-43, 373-75, 389; in Lukiko, 371; origin of, 67-83; and patronage, 361
religious wars, 71-72
Renton, Major A. L., 165
representation, in Buganda government, 44-46
representative government, advent of, 8, 467-68
Representative Members Organization, Legislative Council, 1955, 409-11
representative principle, introduction of, 218-26; effects in Buganda, 349-50
representative self-government, stage of colonialism, 452-53
Residency, Buganda, 44, 210, 211-12n; 224-25, 242; Baganda resistance to, 356-57, 373
riots of 1945, 226-33
riots of 1949, 256-61
Royal Commission on East Africa, 56
Ruanda Urundi, 32, 182
Rubaga, 30
ruralism, 46, 59-61
Rwambarali, Felix K., 327